The Discovery of Chance

The Discovery of Chance

The Life and Thought of Alexander Herzen

Aileen M. Kelly

Harvard University Press

CAMBRIDGE, MASSACHUSETTS · LONDON, ENGLAND

2016

First printing

Library of Congress Cataloging-in-Publication Data
Names: Kelly, Aileen, author.
Title: The discovery of chance : the life and thought of Alexander Herzen /
Aileen M. Kelly.
Description: Cambridge, Massachusetts : Harvard University Press, 2016. |
Includes bibliographical references and index.
Identifiers: LCCN 2015038959 | ISBN 9780674737112 (alk. paper)
Subjects: LCSH: Herzen, Aleksandr, 1812–1870. |
Intellectuals—Russia—Biography. | Russia—Intellectual life—1801–1917.
Classification: LCC DK209.6.H4 K445 2016 | DDC 947/.07092—dc23 LC record
available at http://lccn.loc.gov/2015038959

To the memory of Isaiah Berlin

О сколько нам открытий чудных
готовят просвещенья дух
И опыт, сын ошибок трудных,
И гений, парадоксов друг
И случай, бог изобретатель.

O, how many and marvelous are the discoveries
prepared for us by the spirit of enlightenment,
by Experiment, the child of painful error,
by Genius, the friend of paradox,
and by the divine inventor, Chance.

Pushkin

Contents

Acknowledgments

I am greatly indebted to the Leverhulme Foundation for the award of a Major Research Fellowship, which gave me the necessary freedom to study fully the scientific background to Herzen's thought while I was reconsidering and reorganizing the contents and intellectual structure of the whole project. Without this support, the book could never have taken its present form.

The initial inspiration for this book and its early evolution would have been impossible without the example and influence of Isaiah Berlin, whose unique empathy and generosity of spirit were always extended with equal prodigality to past thinkers who resisted simple labeling and to the students, even those like me with no claim on his time, who were fortunate enough to cross his path.

My work has benefited hugely from Professor John Campbell's cultural horizons—seemingly boundless—which embrace equally the sciences and the arts, and from his encyclopedic memory in all the languages of the project and others around its edges, together with his permanent skepticism about the virtues of grand historical theories. He has added unexpected insights in many places, and his ordered mind has had restraining and generally constructive effects on any of my tendencies toward disorder. His sometimes indelicate but never inappropriate humor has also been invaluable. Finally, I believe the book has gained from one repeated piece of his advice, which I have always tried to follow: "However serious the work is, don't forget to have fun."

Tracing my interest in Herzen back through a prior interest in Russian to the origins of both interests, I should acknowledge the earliest help I received: from the various nuns in my convent boarding school who never thought to inspect what the students brought with them to the numerous services they were required to attend. This made it possible for me to write lists of Russian vocabulary on sheets of light airmail paper, insert them between the pages of my prayer book, and then study the book intensively—one might almost say religiously—during the services. It would have been a new kind of challenge to my undergraduate teachers a few years later, to handle a student who had arrived with an excellent Russian vocabulary but almost no grammar.

Although I was literally immersed in the Russian milieu during my two years as a research student in Leningrad, my true immersion in the best of Russian culture of all periods came from two individuals who became firm friends with me there at that time: Valentina Dmitrievna and Anatolii Lvovich Guterman. I owe more than I can say to them both, and regret that this book came far too late for me to show them the ultimate result of their educational effects and their friendship.

The last months of my efforts in the production of the book have been made much easier by the professional efficiency of my editor, Ian Malcolm, and his enthusiasm for the project. "Service well beyond the call of duty" comes to mind.

Some of the detailed arguments made in Chapters 16, 18, and 19 of this book were first presented in two books I had the privilege to publish with Yale University Press. *Toward Another Shore: Russian Thinkers between Necessity and Chance* was released in 1998 and *Views from the Other Shore: Essays on Herzen, Chekhov, and Bakhtin* appeared in 1999.

All translations in the present book are mine unless otherwise indicated.

The Discovery of Chance

CHAPTER ONE

Who Was Herzen?

Herzen awaits his readers in the future. Far above the heads of the present crowd, he transmits his thoughts to those who will be able to comprehend them.

L. N. TOLSTOY,
DIARY ENTRY OF 12 OCTOBER 1905

HE has been described more than once as a Russian Voltaire. Nietzsche wrote of his readiness to credit "such a noble-spirited and tenacious soul" with "every gift of distinction"; Tolstoy declared that he had never met anyone with "so rare a combination of scintillating brilliance and depth."[1] On his death the historian Jules Michelet wrote that the voice of millions had been silenced.[2]

Philosopher, novelist, essayist, publicist, and political agitator, Alexander Ivanovich Herzen was one of the most talented and complex figures of his time. The first socialist in Russian history, he played a crucial role in the assimilation of Western ideas into Russian thought. As a political émigré in Europe, he is acknowledged as having single-handedly created Russian public opinion by providing his native country with its first uncensored news organ, smuggled into Russia from his Free Russian Press in London: the celebrated periodical *The Bell*. In the West, his fame rivaled that of the great Russian novelists who were his contemporaries. An engaged observer of the 1848 revolution in France, he was admired by some of the most eminent members of Europe's progressive elite. His friends and collaborators included Garibaldi, Mazzini, Michelet, Louis Blanc, Proudhon, Victor Hugo, and Thomas Carlyle. His political writings, infused with moral passion and a fiery imagination, have all the vitality of the spoken word. His monumental memoirs, the work of an uncommonly perceptive social observer, with their vivid insights into personalities, ideas, and events at turning points in the history of Russia and Europe, are recognized as a literary classic, while as a philosopher he gave early expression to values that became prominent only a century later.

But he left no body of doctrine, and anyone inquiring into the nature of his intellectual legacy is faced with a bewildering variety of interpretations. The outlook and aims of this extraordinarily multifaceted figure continue to be a matter of contention. In his own country Slavophiles and Westernizers, Romantics and realists, moderates and extremists, communists, anarchists, and liberals, have on occasion claimed him as their own, or reviled him as an implacable opponent. Comparisons have been made with Stirner, Nietzsche, Kierkegaard, and Camus, to name only a few.[3] He won tributes from Dostoevsky and Solzhenitsyn, who acknowledged his formative influence on their work in both content and style. But he was also accorded the dubious honor of elevation to the Soviet pantheon, thanks to Lenin's much-quoted essay "In Memory of Herzen," lauding Herzen for his "selfless devotion" to the cause of revolution—a phrase that determined (and strictly limited) the approach of generations of Soviet scholars to his work.[4]

The official Russian interpretation of Herzen disappeared from circulation after 1991. The three speakers at a very modest conference held in 2010 in the Institute of Philosophy of the Russian Academy of Sciences to mark the 140th anniversary of his death stressed the "nontypicality" (nestandartnost) of his thought as a critic both of Western liberalism and Russian Slavophilism, and his misfortune to have been cited repeatedly for pragmatic purposes by Lenin and his successors as part of the prologue to bolshevism (defining him in this way had made it possible to assert the distinctiveness of Russian communism as no mere offshoot of Marxism.)[5] A very much larger conference with a light sprinkling of foreign delegates was held in 2012, again in Moscow, to discuss Herzen's heritage on the bicentenary of his birth. The opening speaker acknowledged that in the two previous post-Soviet decades, "we were silent about Herzen. . . . [He] was neither refuted nor rejected, not even intentionally forgotten; he simply disappeared from sight. It was as if he had fallen into a black hole."[6] Or rather as if he had fallen between two stools (popal pod razdachu slonov), pigeonholed either as the ideological ally of bolshevism or the ideological foe of the tsarist regime it destroyed. Two speakers give the main credit for the recent sudden growth of interest in his life and ideas (a phenomenon described by one as "a genuine landmark in the history of Russian social and political thought") to Isaiah Berlin, who, by approaching his personality and ideas in their historical context, had rescued Herzen from oblivion to become a significant figure in the cultural life of both Russia and the English-speaking world. They note that Berlin's writings on Herzen were the inspiration for *The Coast of Utopia*, the English dramatist Tom Stoppard's set of plays devoted to Herzen's life, which had themselves become a minor cultural phenomenon, with an extended run in Moscow.[7]

Even though the papers at that conference ranged widely (few in original directions) over Herzen's multifaceted talents as writer, philosopher, and political activist, none addressed his own frequently repeated explanation for the unpopularity of his view of history: the fear of freedom.[8] In an essay published five years after the end of Russian communism, the historian A. I. Volodin had pointed out that for all his enormous erudition and the vividness of his style, Herzen produced no system, no body of doctrine categorizable as "Herzenism." Revolutionaries and reformers, materialists and idealists alike were alarmed and repelled by his refusal to recognize any absolutes, his rejection of the logic of "either / or," and above all his contention that history follows no path of progress to a final goal, contrary to all the theories of progress that had sustained European optimism over two millennia. Volodin cites a letter to Herzen from Tolstoy in the early 1860s— "There are many people, and 99 out of a hundred Russians, who will be too frightened to give credence to your thoughts. . . . (You appear to be addressing only the intelligent and the brave.) Those who are neither intelligent nor brave will say that it is better to be silent when one has reached such conclusions"—and contends that Tolstoy's prediction was correct: the principal reason few commentators on Herzen have been prepared to consider objectively his views on socialism, religion, Russia's relation to the West, the nature of history and progress, and the goals of revolution is that "taken as a whole, his heritage is acceptable to no one."[9]

Only two Western scholars have given detailed attention to the view of history and freedom that inspired Herzen's work, and they reached opposing conclusions. In essays first published in the 1950s, Isaiah Berlin contended that the boldness and originality of Herzen's thought had been overlooked because of the tendency to classify it as yet another variety of early socialism. Focusing on Herzen's campaign for individual liberty against the great utopian visions of his time, Berlin stressed the farsightedness of his perception of the destructive power of ideological abstractions over human lives: "Herzen's sense of reality, in particular of the need for, and the price of, revolution, is unique in his own, and perhaps in any age."[10] The first major study of Herzen in English was Martin Malia's 1961 biography; although it is incomplete, it has strongly influenced the interpretation of Herzen accepted in the West, painting a picture that is the antithesis of Berlin's: Herzen as a utopian thinker motivated by "an almost unique existential egoism."[11]

Edward Acton's study of Herzen's activities in western Europe convincingly challenges this view, but presents him as increasingly behind his time in his failure to influence a new generation of Russian revolutionaries.[12] Neither Malia's interpretation nor Acton's does proper justice to Herzen's own image of himself as the herald of truths that were too alien to received ideas to be acceptable or even comprehensible to the majority. He would express ironic amusement at his contemporaries' efforts to locate him on their political spectrum—liberal, radical, gradualist, extremist. Most irritating of all, he maintained, they would accuse him of inconsistency, whereas for most of his life he had been preaching the same "two or three ideas"; but these had proved too contrary to long-cherished beliefs to be given sanctuary in the brain.

My own interest in Herzen was sparked by an exception to this rule: Isaiah Berlin's essays. These still seem to me to have best captured the distinctiveness of Herzen's thought by identifying him as a precursor, spelling out truths too novel for most of his contemporaries to understand and far too frightening for them to accept. The present study will approach his ideas in the context of the revolution in European thinking on man's place in nature that would culminate in Darwin's treatise on the origin of species.

Few commentators on Herzen's thought have given significance to his early training in the natural sciences as a student at Moscow University. The subject is not even mentioned in the chapter on Herzen in a history of Russian philosophy published in 2010, while the texts selected for translation into English in *A Herzen Reader*, published two years later, include no extracts from his most original essays, on the natural sciences and the theme of evolution: no surprise, perhaps, as the critical commentary that follows the translations dates his adoption of evolutionary theories no farther back than his "English period."[13] But I shall show that the evolutionary science he imbibed at Moscow University twenty years earlier shaped his subsequent approach to history and philosophy: he would be unique among his contemporaries in the depth and extent of his knowledge in these three disparate disciplines. This combination of perspectives lay behind his demythologizing approach to history and society, allowing him to discern (two decades before Nietzsche announced the "death of God") the erosion of that faith in a purposive universe in which the great nineteenth-century optimistic systems were grounded. In the same year as Marx's pronouncement that communism was "the solution of the riddle of history," Herzen declared that there were "no solutions": history, like nature, was an improvisation, subject to the play of chance.

We shall see that Herzen was both keenly interested in the developments in evolutionary theory that were leading to Darwin's discoveries and deeply aware of the threat they posed to cherished beliefs about the nature of history and the meaning and purpose of human life. This book will chart both Herzen's intellectual journey and his struggle to exemplify what he called "the courage of consistency" in his personal life and his political life.

His "Russian socialism," habitually portrayed as a messianic construct, was built on this pragmatic philosophy: anticipating many "third world" economists of the next century, he insisted that instead of following a notionally universal path of progress—that of the West— Russia should seek to develop the potential immanent in its own culture. As Darwin was to do in *On the Origin of Species,* Herzen incorporated the development of human societies into the domain of natural laws. *From the Other Shore*—Herzen's *confession de foi* composed in the light of the failed revolutions of 1848—urges his contemporaries to cease their pursuit of unattainable goals and address themselves to the "physiology" of history, adapting their ideals and their personal hopes to the contingencies of time and place. This precept he consistently applied to the personal and political defeats and tragedies in his own life. The account of his life that follows will give particular attention to his letters (which occupy ten untranslated volumes in the

Soviet edition of his works) as reflections of his stubborn resistance to what Nietzsche was to call the "craving for metaphysical comfort."

His early intellectual development took place under the combined influence of the two movements of ideas that began in the eighteenth century to transform humans' vision of the nature and purpose of our lives and the world in which we live: the Romantic movement and the growth of the natural sciences. The influence of the former has received due attention from Herzen's biographers;[14] this study aims to do the same for the latter. It will emphasize his role as a pioneer in addressing the theme of contingency that would be central to Darwin's theory of evolution, situating Herzen within a demythologizing tradition in European humanism that stretches back to Francis Bacon and includes Friedrich Schiller's and John Stuart Mill's assaults on the universalist assumptions of rationalist ethical systems. These all informed Herzen's attacks on the philosophies of progress that inspired so much political thought and practice in the last two centuries; he would also expose the logical and empirical defects of pessimistic antirationalism as preached by Schopenhauer (and subsequently Nietzsche).

Central emphasis will be given here to a hitherto unexplored aspect of his thought: his lifelong interest in scientific modes of inquiry and their relevance to the study of history. These were essential to his vision of the openness of time and the power and the limitations of reason. He was among the first to welcome Darwin's discovery of the primary role of chance in evolution as a momentous step toward dismantling teleological systems that misrepresent the world and humans' place in it; his own ideas were singular anticipations of the subsequent cross-fertilizations between scientific and historical thought.

In the preface to his study of science in Russian culture, published in 1963, Alexander Vucinich remarks: "Political history, social and religious thought, the arts, and most of the other dimensions of Russian life have been dealt with rather extensively in Western historical literature, but science as a component of Russian culture has been almost completely ignored. . . . Historians have often concluded that science, at least until the twentieth century, was a rationalist aberration operating on the fringes of Russian life."[15] It would seem that this

preconception has distracted attention from Herzen's most significant contributions to the history of ideas. He was not only the first
Russian socialist: he was also, in the words of Isaiah Berlin, "the forerunner of much twentieth-century thought . . . a man with a quality
akin to philosophical genius."[16]

CHAPTER TWO

Russia and the Romantic Revolution

Our civilization has made its entire journey under two banners:
Romanticism for the heart and Idealism for the head.

HERZEN

"AN extraordinary period of external constraint and inner freedom":
thus Alexander Herzen described the experience of Russia's cultured
elite in the reign of the tyrant Nicolas I.[1] Herzen's attempt to define
inner freedom and to express it in both his personal and his political
life is at the center of this study.

The principal factor determining the direction of his thought was
the coincidence of Russia's emergence as a major player on the European stage with the rise of the Romantic movement and German idealist philosophy. Their influence in Russia reached its height during
the years of stagnation and repression that followed the failure of the
Decembrist revolt of 1825. The aim of the schematic account in this
chapter is to sketch out those features of Romantic philosophy that
would shape early nineteenth-century Russian thinking on the nature
of the self, society, and history.

The overwhelming fascination Romantic thought exercised over
Russian intellectuals at that time can be explained partly by the parallels between the predicament of the Russian intellectual elite
under Nicolas I and that of the early German Romantics in the last
years of the eighteenth century. Economically backward and politically fragmented into a number of absolutist princedoms, Germany
offered few outlets for the talents of its writers and thinkers, who
channeled their energies into metaphysical inquiry on the nature of
subjectivity and its relation to the world. Their ideas would provide
inspiration for the protests of similarly frustrated intellectuals farther
to the east.

Romanticism challenged a major assumption of Western thought: that there existed eternal truths, the source of universal standards and rules for how to live, and that these truths were in principle discoverable, whether through reason, religious revelation, individual conscience, or dogmatic faith. As expressed by the mainstream of the European Enlightenment, this belief was based on Kant's ground-breaking vision of moral autonomy, according to which the principles of morality are not derived from some larger external order on which we are dependent, but follow from the structure of human thought; we draw them from our own rational will. Enlightenment rationalism perceived the world of nature and human societies as a single entity, governed by a single set of laws that are built into human nature and form a harmonious whole, providing the blueprint for happiness and virtue. The discovery of these laws through reason and science and their organization into systems would ensure the proper management of human affairs.

In the second half of the eighteenth century this set of beliefs came under increasing assault. Rousseau struck the first mighty blow at the Enlightenment, at its high point, with his assertion that calculating reason had severed mankind from nature and stifled the inner voice of feeling, our primary mode of access to the deepest cosmic truths. "Je sentis avant de penser; c'est le sort commun de l'humanité [I feel before I think; it's the common fate of humanity]," he declares at the beginning of his *Confessions*. The claim of reason to determine the limits and conditions of knowledge and establish principles of conduct was seen increasingly as problematic, particularly in Germany. The German *Aufklärung* (Enlightenment) was influenced by the Pietist movement, which held that truth is encountered through the spontaneous promptings of the individual heart rather than the dogmas of organized religion or the desiccated reason of philosophy. The most potent threat to the authority of reason was posed by the rise of historicism, as pioneered in Johann Gottlieb von Herder's philosophy of history. In a radical departure from the traditional notion of a timeless and universal ideal of virtue, he asserted that the potentialities of human nature are ever changing and developing, and are fulfilled in different ways depending on circumstance. Societies and cultures are organic wholes, their values, institutions, and language inseparable from each other: they can be understood not by the analytical methods of the natural sciences nor from some external standpoint, but only by entering into their way of life through the kind of imaginative insight characteristic of artistic genius. Breaking with the traditional canons of art, Herder's revolutionary aesthetics gave supreme significance to the artist's personal vision, as the expression of the beliefs and values that constitute the distinctiveness of his people and culture. He argued that all historical periods, societies, and cultures are ends in themselves and must be judged in terms of their own purposes. But he also maintained that in their different ways they are all striving to fulfill a common purpose: the achievement of *Humanität*—a vague term denoting an ideal of individual perfection as the full development of an individual's powers and their integration in a harmonious whole.

Herder and his mentor J. G. Hamann had a seminal influence on the artistic movement known as *Sturm und Drang* (storm and stress), whose rebellious young writers, such as the youthful Goethe and Schiller and the dramatists J. M. R. Lenz and F. M. Klinger, transformed German culture in the 1770s. They anticipated a central strand of Romanticism in their defiance of established laws, conventions, and decorum in the name of the supreme value of spontaneous feeling and direct experience, and the absolute rights of genius. Rejecting the goals of traditional morality, like Goethe's Faust they sought, not happiness, but the maximum fullness and intensity of life, which they proclaimed to be the supreme good. The *Stürmers* (*Stürmer und Dränger*) were among the first harbingers of a new humanism, a way of thinking and feeling based on a new concept of humans' relation to themselves and the world. In place of the Cartesian view of nature as a mechanism operating according to preordained, immutable laws, they advanced the vitalistic concept of a unifying force coursing through nature and man—a notion supported by contemporary developments in the human and natural sciences, such as Erasmus Darwin's theories on the mutability of species, Lavoisier's discoveries in the chemistry of combustion, and the work of Luigi Galvani and Alexander von Humboldt on the application of physics and chemistry to animals. Goethe's provocative scientific-philosophical essay of 1790, *On the Metamorphosis of Plants*, reflected the belief, central to the Romantic credo, that the organic and unitary nature of reality could be grasped not through dispassionate analysis of objects in nature but through the intuitive sense of the hidden harmony and the flow of life we associate with artistic genius. The Stürmers gave supreme importance to artistic creation as the highest manifestation of human autonomy, the expression of a quasi-divine freedom from external influences and causal laws. Their ideal was the "beautiful soul" who lives for his own self-development alone, creating his own moral principles by cultivating his receptivity to beauty in the form of noble feelings and ideals.

This pursuit of unqualified individual autonomy represented a radically new attitude to the self that has been termed "expressivism": a theory that gives central significance to feeling, intuition, and individual inner experience, not as a means to the understanding of God or of a natural or moral order external to man, but as the expression of the powers and potential unique to each person, whose development in the fullest and most harmonious way possible is held to be the self-sufficient end of all human life. As Charles Taylor maintains, this notion of self-realization is not to be confused with the age-old view of individuality as a range of variations on a common human nature. It was something wholly new, "one of the major idées-forces which has shaped the contemporary world."[2] According to the Stürmers, humans develop, not by following some formula established independently of them, but through a process of self-unfolding and self-defining that reveals to them the inner powers that are the authentic expression of their unique potential and purposes. Humans have no fixed nature: they constantly transform themselves by acting out their values in ways that cannot be predicted in advance. Values are not discovered but created. Therefore they cannot be systematized by a science of ethics, nor can there be an a priori guarantee that the values of differing civilizations, nations, or individuals will harmonize.

The Stürmers' attack on all established norms in morality, religion, and art has been seen as the protest of an emerging middle class excluded from power and privilege by the economic and dynastic interests of a semifeudal ruling caste. But although they displayed all the arrogance and incoherence of youthful radicalism, their concerns were not directly political: they were too obsessed with their inner lives to pay serious attention to the question of political reform. Their protest was inspired not by specific social evils but by a general sense that modern societies could not satisfy the spiritual demands of human beings or fulfill their potential. The new cult of feeling in German literature was linked explicitly with political radicalism only after the Sturm und Drang movement had run its course. A landmark instance is Schiller's play of 1781 *Die Räuber* (The Robbers), whose hero, Karl Moor, revolts against a corrupt absolutist system in the name of a Rousseauian vision of a society based on the principles of fraternity and justice.

The "angry young men" trapped in the stagnant backwater of the German princedoms greeted the French Revolution ecstatically as a liberating dawn, but they were profoundly disillusioned by the Terror and the subsequent dictatorship, which the French radicals justified by appealing to the authority of reason. Reflecting on the role of reason as a divisive and fragmenting force in modern societies, German intellectuals became preoccupied with an aspiration as fundamental in humans as the urge for individual autonomy: the need to belong. German idealist philosophy, from Fichte and Schelling to Hegel, grew out of the search to reconcile these two equally imperative but contrary needs: a search that still continues—and not only in Germany.

The German Background

"Französen und Russen gehört das Land, / Das Meer gehört den Briten, / Wir aber besitzen im Luftreich des Traums / Die Herrschaft unbestritten"[3] (or, at a somewhat lower poetic level, "The French and Russians own the land, / The British hold the sea, / But rulers of the realm of dreams / can only Germans be"). Heine's lines are often cited to support the view that German Romanticism was a retreat from oppressive social and political realities into the ideal world of art and metaphysics. However, as Frederick Beiser has observed, German thought from the late eighteenth century was "not so much apolitical as cryptopolitical."[4] Like the *philosophes* of the Enlightenment, the early German Romantics saw themselves as educators, articulating the moral insights that would form the basis of the ideal society of the future. They began by dismantling their predecessors' rationalist model of the self. While adopting Kant's belief that we are the authors of our own values, they accused Kant of presenting a distorted view of the true nature of man by perpetuating the dichotomy between soul and body, reason and feeling, which was a legacy of Cartesian dualism. Kant argued that the moral life is an unending struggle between moral rules whose source is pure reason (and which must therefore be binding on all rational beings) and the drives issuing from man as a creature dependent on nature. The Romantics believed that individuals would achieve harmony with their society only when they ceased to be in conflict with themselves. Their efforts to define wholeness of character were much influenced by the great art historian J. J. Winckelmann's research on Greek art, which presented them with a model of *Humanität* in the culture of the classical Greek polis. There, it seemed, humans had been at one with themselves, their society, and the natural world.

This historicist approach to the problem of self-realization was the central concern of a circle of writers who came together between 1797 and 1802 in Jena and Berlin, and whose discussions were the seedbed of German Romantic philosophy. They included the brothers August Wilhelm and Friedrich Schlegel, Friedrich von Hardenberg (known by his pen name Novalis), the philosopher Friedrich Schelling, and the theologian Ernst Schleiermacher. They feared the social atomization created by the French Revolution, the extremes of liberal individualism, and the competitive free-for-all of the emerging new Europe, and they emphasized the values of tradition and community. But despite their nostalgia for the corporate societies of medieval Europe, these early Romantics were not conservatives: while attacking the destructive consequences of rationalism, they championed the modern values of rational autonomy, free inquiry, tolerance, and individual liberty, and hoped that humans could regain their sense of unity with the social and natural worlds without forfeiting these values. Their motivating spirit was a quest for harmony. They aimed to integrate all fields of human activity—religion, philosophy, art, science, and politics—in an organicist vision of the self, society, history, and the cosmos that, by demonstrating the fundamental unity of all existence, would cure humanity of the "homesickness" *(Heimweh)* they saw as the curse of the modern age.

This vision of the historical process (a secular version of the biblical myth of primal innocence, fall, and redemption) was given an ontological foundation by German idealist philosophy. The way was led by Johann Gottlieb Fichte, the first outline of whose system, the *Wissenschaftslehre*, appeared in 1794. While acknowledging the fundamental importance of Kant's formulation of human autonomy, he rejected Kant's distinction between appearances—the phenomena of our experience—and the ultimate nature of reality and the self, which Kant held to be beyond the reach of reason. Kant's dualism seemed to condemn humanity to permanent separation from the natural world and its own nature; Fichte's monistic solution to this problem maintained that the world was wholly permeable to the human mind because it was the creation of mind. His new "science" replaced the God of revealed religion by a single cosmic spirit or absolute ego of which all humans were emanations. In order to manifest itself as moral will, the ego has posited a non-ego (the world of objects) to struggle against and to overcome. The finite self's vocation is to actualize its infinite essence and assert its freedom by transforming the natural and historical world in accordance with its freely chosen goals.

Fichte's recommendation in the opening lines of his *Wissenschaftslehre*—"Avert your gaze from all about you in order to look only into yourself"—fostered what has been described as a "collective megalomania" among his generation. The "subjective idealism" that he promoted encouraged Romantics to believe that the universe was dependent on their vision of it and could be transformed at will by the power of the imagination. His moral activism also had a strong appeal to young Romantics: he was a prominent radical publicist in the 1790s, passionately insisting on the right of revolution and claiming a just society to be the highest good on earth. As a professor of philosophy in Jena he would close his lectures with the call "Act! Act!" But the logic of his philosophy precluded millenarian hopes: If we realize ourselves as moral beings only through struggle, the goal for which we strive—complete independence from all that is not the self—can never be achieved. Moreover, Fichte's view of the external world as mere material for human self-realization was incompatible with the communion with nature for which the Romantics yearned.

They found what they needed in the thought of Schelling, whose *Naturphilosophie* (which appeared in 1797 and was developed in succeeding years) and *System of Transcendental Idealism* (1800) are the key texts of Romantic philosophy.

Schelling was strongly influenced by the holistic approach of the late eighteenth-century life sciences, which saw natural phenomena as interacting forces rather than irreducible substances. He drew on contemporary research into the phenomena of magnetism, light, electricity, oxidation, and combustion to construct a dynamic, evolutionary model of the universe that removed Kant's obstacle to the integration of the mind with the world by positing the identity of spirit within us and nature without. In Schelling's monistic vision of the universe, matter and mind, spirit and nature, are not distinct kinds of entities, but simply differing degrees of organization and development of an evolving organic whole, a single primal force or absolute, striving upward in a process of self-discovery, whose highest manifestation is achieved in human consciousness. The Cartesian model of the world gave primacy to reason as the tool for apprehending reality; in Schelling's organicist vision, imagination and intuition (as expressed in art and religion) are the primary instruments for penetrating the mysterious underlying unity of the universe. At the summit of being is the artist, whose creativity represents the fusion of consciousness and the unconscious, expressing their foreordained identity.

The Romantics often referred to the artist as a seer or high priest, whose special spiritual powers give him access to the hidden meaning of life and allow him to mediate between the visible and invisible world, transmitting his perceptions of ultimate harmony to others: all great acts of creative self-expression—friendship, love, feats of heroism—are forms of communion with the hidden harmony of the universe, which we sense intuitively but which is concealed from us by our dissecting reason. Schleiermacher declared imagination to be "the supreme and prime quality [*das Höchste und Ursprünglichste*]" in man; Wackenroder speaks of "the divinity of art [*die Göttlichkeit der Kunst*]," which allows us to commune with the fountainhead of all being.

The early Romantics commonly expressed their notion of the unity of being in mystical and pantheistic terms, as the immanence and omnipresence of the Absolute in nature and in man—who communed not with a transcendent deity but with the divine essence of his own nature and was thereby elevated to a status denied him by traditional religion. Their longing for wholeness, combined with suspicion of analytical reason as an obstacle to its achievement, led many to make the transition from pantheism to theism. In 1799 Schleiermacher, Friedrich Schlegel, and Novalis announced the need for a new "church": a brotherhood of the spirit without the idolatry, superstition, and prejudice of past religions. The final destination of all three turned out to be Catholicism, while Schelling became a Christian.

As Germany entered the nineteenth century, self-surrender to an absolute in the world of the spirit eventually seemed poor compensation for the stifling of talent by authoritarian petty princedoms and national humiliation at the hands of Napoleon's army. German Romantics yearned for self-affirmation in the arena of history. How could this aspiration be reconciled with the equally profound need to belong? An answer was provided by political messianism.

As the French Revolution's promise of universal liberation was transformed into Napoleonic imperialism, young Germans found consolation in a Romantic nationalism inspired by Herder's rejection of the Enlightenment view that there is one right life for all and his belief that each people has its own "soul," its distinctive values. They became fervently patriotic, glorifying the Middle Ages as a time when the people had been an organic community, untouched by the destructive forces of modern civilization. Pursuing the study of the Teutonic past in literature and art through folk songs and legends, they sought their roots in the simple people who expressed the authentic *Volksseele*. In his *Lectures to the German Nation* of 1807–1808, delivered to an eager audience in a Berlin under French occupation, Fichte affirmed that the freshness and purity of the German spirit, uncorrupted by alien influences, equipped them for their historical mission—the spiritual regeneration of mankind. This foundational text of German nationalism resonated with the *Heimweh* of talented young men who longed to identify with some larger whole that would give their lives a universal meaning and purpose. As Martin Malia observes, for men who were not only alienated as individuals but also frustrated as classes and nations, messianic nationalism was a liberating ideology of compensation, presenting the defects of backwardness as the virtues of boundless potential. In this historicist version of idealist metaphysics, the Absolute became "a kind of historical Providence . . . which would accomplish for them what they could not accomplish themselves."[5]

The Consequences in Russia

The great perturbations that rocked the European intellectual landscape were slow to reach Russia, but the aftershocks there were deeper and ultimately more destructive than at the epicenter in the West.

The mid-eighteenth century saw the beginnings of the "Russian Enlightenment," when, with the encouragement of Empress Catherine II, the discourse of the intellectual elite was driven by the ideals and aims of the Age of Reason and the faith of the philosophes in the perfectibility of society through the eradication of prejudice and uncritically accepted tradition. Catherine's flirtation with the Enlightenment did not survive the outbreak of the French Revolution, and those of her subjects who dared bring aspects of her rule before the tribunal of reason were severely punished. The most significant figure of the Russian Enlightenment, Aleksandr Radishchev, received a death sentence (subsequently commuted to lifelong exile) for his critique of serfdom and autocracy.

The philosophes' ideal of the enlightened ruler as the source of progress seemed realized at last with the accession in 1801 of Alexander I, who appeared as the champion of a new Western-style openness. Mikhail Speransky, entrusted by the tsar with the preparation of proposals for constitutional reform, expressed the dominant mood of the Russian educated public in the preamble to his project for a constitution: "No government can resist the mighty spirit of the age and survive." But the early nineteenth century also saw a growth in national consciousness and patriotic pride among the intellectual elite, stimulated by the experience of war against Napoleon in 1812–1813 and the influence of European Romantic nationalism. Admiration for the common people's feat in repelling the invader led to a deepening interest in the history and distinctive characteristics of the Russians as a people. The value of Russian native traditions had already been stressed by eighteenth-century aristocratic critics of absolutism such as Prince

Mikhail Shcherbatov, who had criticized Peter the Great's reforms as corrupting Russian morals. But the new interest in national distinctiveness (*narodnost*, as it came to be called) drew its main inspiration from the ideology of the Romantic movement.

From its beginnings in the 1730s, modern Russian literature had developed by closely following trends in the West. The later years of Catherine's reign saw the flowering of a pre-Romantic style and sensibility in poetry, the development in prose of a sentimentalist movement strongly influenced by Rousseau, and the beginnings of experimentation with Sturm und Drang, fantasy, and the Gothic. Russian Romanticism is generally agreed to have reached its maturity in the early 1820s with the rise of the influence of Byron, but its origins have been traced to the poet Vasilii Zhukovsky's translation in 1802 of Gray's *Elegy in a Country Churchyard*. In the first two decades of the nineteenth century the theories of the European Romantics were propagated and their works translated by Russian writers and poets.

The teachings of German idealist philosophy were slower to make an impact on the Russian educated public. The ideas of Herder and Kant were known in Russia in the late eighteenth century, and in the first decade of the nineteenth century idealist philosophy was spread through Russian seminaries and universities. Schelling's thought, in particular, disseminated by three professors in Moscow, came to dominate the teaching of the natural sciences and the aesthetics of Russian Romanticism. In 1823 a group of young poets and critics, followers of Schelling, founded a society known as the *Lyubomudry* (Lovers of Wisdom), and published the first Russian philosophical periodical, *Mnemosyne*. Only four issues appeared, and the group was dissolved after the uprising of 1825, but it was of pathbreaking importance in the development of idealism in Russia. Among its members were Prince Vladimir Odoevsky, whose writings in the 1830s played a key role in transplanting Romantic conservatism onto Russian soil, the brilliant young critic Dmitrii Venevitinov, and the future Slavophiles Aleksandr Koshelev and the brothers Ivan and Petr Kireevsky.

Despite these developments, in the first two decades of the nineteenth century the discussion of Russia's present state, future prospects, and relation to the West continued to be framed in the discourse of Enlightenment universalism. The campaigns following the victory of 1812 had given many Russians their first direct contact with European institutions and culture, and a small but significant number returned to Russia determined to end the shame and horror of serfdom and set their country on the path of economic and political progress on a Western model. After Alexander's reforming projects were abandoned in the second half of his reign, when he came under the influence of reactionary advisors, an organization of aristocrats and officers from elite regiments formed a conspiracy with the goal of introducing constitutional rule through a coup d'état. There were strong elements of Romantic nationalism in the Decembrist movement, among whose leaders were two of the most prominent representatives of Russian Romanticism, Aleksandr Bestuzhev and Kondratii Ryleev. The Decembrists reproached Peter the Great for not respecting national traditions, and idealized the ancient republican city-states of Novgorod and Pskov. But they nevertheless saw themselves as a Westernized elite. Some were liberal constitutionalists, others radical republicans, but all believed firmly in Enlightenment ideals and their applicability to Russia.

The failure of the uprising of 14 December 1825 led to the alienation of the aristocratic elite from the government. Few of Russia's leading families were unaffected by the reprisals against the conspirators. Five (including Ryleev) were hanged, and hundreds were exiled for life to Siberia. In the police state set up by the new tsar, Nicolas I, it was dangerous to discuss political matters even in private gatherings.

December 1825 marked the defeat not only of a political movement but of a vision of the world. Confidence in humans' power to determine their fate and impose a rational structure on external reality was replaced by an agonizing sense of separation from a world that seemed fundamentally at odds with the noblest human aspirations. This new sense of alienation was epitomized in the form that the Romantic movement assumed in Russia in the decade after 1825. All the elements of that movement are to be found in European Romanticism, especially the German variety, but the heroism and futile sacrifice of the Decembrists gave the Russian version of Romantic revolt a special tragic resonance and intensity of philosophical reflectiveness. These characteristics are succinctly summarized in L. G. Leighton's description of full-blown Russian Romanticism as expressed in the work of poets such as Bestuzhev, Lermontov, and Tiutchev:

> The revolt against reason became not only a battle cry, but also a profound emphasis on emotion and feeling that paved the way into the realm of fantasy, irrationality, subjectivism, idealism. Individualism became escapism or rebellion, and both led into nationalism, the exotic and the alien. . . . Heroes became personal, rather than epic, and literary characters became obsessed with their relation to "crass" society and the personal experiences that led to bitter disillusionment. The replacement of a conception of the world as static, mechanical, "knowable," and rational with one that contemplated chaos, hidden essences, "other-worldness," and dynamism, as well as the new view of man as estranged from nature by his own civilization, yet ultimately reconcilable with his God and with nature, led to an organic conception of the world. This estrangement and bewilderment led not only to disillusionment, but also to isolation, elitism, proud individualism, and a total reevaluation of the place of man in the order of things. . . . The new reflective view of the universe as infinite, rather than finite and closed, led to a concern for essences, the mysterious ways of God, and a new symbolism and connotative imagery, a love of nature, a celebration of the poet as a member of a chosen elite—as a seer or a maker.[6]

In their revaluation of the world and the self, the Russian intellectual elite drew heavily on Schelling's aesthetic idealism. Odoevsky affirmed that for nineteenth-century Russians reared on the philosophy of the Enlightenment, the discovery of Schelling was no less momentous than Columbus's discovery of America had been more than three centuries before: "He revealed to man an unknown part of his own being, his soul."[7]

As Malia has argued, the defeat of the Decembrists produced in Russia a reaction similar to the effect in Europe of dismay at the outcome of the French Revolution: "The generation of the aftermath in Russia, like that of a few years earlier in the West, was driven to seek the explanation of a reality no longer clear and simple in the sinuosities of metaphysics rather than on the straight highway of empiricism. . . . They turned inevitably to the school of frustration, Germany, just as their predecessors had turned to the school of action, France."[8]

The high point of the Romantic movement in Russian literature coincided with the beginnings of an intense fascination among the young generation with the metaphysics of German idealism, which they embraced with the fervor of religious converts seeking refuge from baseness of the everyday world in the realm of eternal truth. Odoevsky characterizes a young Lover of Wisdom: "The petty worries that weigh down weak humanity are alien to him; he does not notice them from the heights to which his spirit has soared; even the destructive rule of time is nothing to him, for his spirit does not age." In 1826 Yevgenii Boratynsky wrote to his fellow poet Pushkin: "All the Moscow youth dream only of speculative philosophy."[9]

The question of Russia's relation to the West remained a central concern of the cultured elite, but, as Nicolas Riasanovsky has observed, with a change in the terms of intellectual discourse after 1825: "What used to be a pedagogical problem of learning and progressing according to the universal postulates of the Age of Reason became a metaphysical issue of establishing and asserting the true principles of the unique Russian national organism, of ensuring its historical mission."[10] The former Decembrist Bestuzhev wrote from his Siberian exile in 1833: "We . . . live in an age of history, moreover in an age of history par excellence . . . now history is not simply in fact, but in the memory, the mind, the hearts of the people."[11] The historical mission so close to the heart of the new generation was conceived in terms of the expressivism the young Russians had absorbed from German thought. In a widely read essay of 1827, "On the State of Enlightenment in Russia," Venevitinov explained that all the historical and moral efforts and achievements of a people as a collective personality issue from the drive to self-knowledge and are the expression of a particular spiritual essence. He believed that Russia's version of this drive was severely impeded by the foreign influences that dominated its culture, but some of his contemporaries were more optimistic. In a long essay published in 1852, Ivan Kireevsky affirmed that progress in Europe, held back by the destructive influence of rationalism, had exhausted its potential. The way was open for Russia—the traditions of whose people (as reflected in the structure of the commune) were infused with Orthodox spirituality—to assimilate the best elements of European enlightenment and revitalize the dying culture of the West.[12]

Such hopes drew copiously on the anti-Enlightenment philosophy of the later Schelling, the Schlegel brothers, and Franz von Baader, with their critique of the rationalism, materialism, and social atomization of bourgeois liberal systems. The German Romantic conservatives' praise of the pristine purity of their young nation had a special resonance for their Russian readers. As Isaiah Berlin has remarked: "They rightly judged that if youth, barbarism, and lack of education were criteria of a glorious future, they had an even more powerful hope of it than the Germans."[13]

At the end of the 1830s the Slavophiles would begin to develop these views into full-blown doctrines of Russian messianism, but in the dark decade that followed the Decembrist revolt most young intellectuals found consolation in personal rather than national expressivism, compensating for the grimness of external reality by cultivating their egos in accordance with the precepts of aesthetic idealism. Public service, whether in the army or the bureaucracy, lost all attraction for young members of the gentry, who flocked instead to the universities of Moscow and Saint Petersburg, where the teaching was controlled rigidly by the authorities but where like-minded intellectuals began to set up small informal circles for private study and discussion—the famous *kruzhki* that were to be the seedbed of Russia's radical intelligentsia. The critic Vissarion Belinsky, a member of the most important of these circles, which took shape at Moscow University in the 1830s, describes its members' sense of alienation: "Our education deprived us of religion; the circumstances of our lives (due to the state of society) gave us no solid education and deprived us of any chance of mastering knowledge [contemporary Western thought]; we are at odds with [Russian] reality and are justified in hating and despising it, just as it is justified in hating and despising us. Where then was our refuge? In the desert island which was our *kruzhok*."[14]

The desert soil of introspective idealism proved too sterile to sustain healthy intellectual and psychic growth, and the first post-Decembrist generation soon sought some form of reintegration with their surrounding reality. Many found it, as Western Romantics had done, through identification with some collective abstraction, whether messianic nationalism or liberal and radical versions of Hegel's March of History. But Alexander Herzen took a far more challenging path, seeking to combine rational self-determination with the pursuit of expressive unity, the insights of the Enlightenment with those of the Romantic reaction against it, philosophical speculation with the empirical methods of the natural sciences. Such was the lifelong project whose path will now be traced.

CHAPTER THREE

A Romantic Youth

What did the idealist Schiller give us? Noble aspirations.

NICOLAS OGAREV,
AUTOBIOGRAPHICAL FRAGMENT

ALEXANDER Ivanovich Herzen was the illegitimate son of Ivan Alekseevich Yakovlev, a wealthy and cultivated aristocrat, owner of more than a thousand serfs, whose family could trace its origins back to the pre-Petrine nobility. Born in 1766, Ivan was one of four brothers who, like most of the young men of their class, followed a brief career in military service (in his case, the elite Izmailovsky regiment) with a life of relative idleness subsidized by the income from their estates. After ten years of traveling in Europe, he returned to Russia in 1811, bringing back with him a girl of fifteen, Henriette Wilhelmine Luise Haag, the daughter of a minor German official, whom he installed in his Moscow house where she gave birth to Alexander on 25 March 1812.[1] The couple remained together until his death, but he never married Luise, possibly because of her plebeian birth, although the surname he bestowed on his son could be interpreted as a sign of his affection for her.[2]

When Herzen was five months old, the family was trapped in the burning city as drunken French troops killed and looted around them. Ivan Yakovlev was sent by Napoleon to Saint Petersburg with a message to the tsar while Alexander with his mother and the ten-year-old Yegor, his father's son by a serf,[3] set out on a journey to Ivan's country estate, about 200 miles south of Moscow. An elderly uncle accompanying them died on the way. In his memoirs Alexander imagines the ordeal of his sixteen-year-old mother, who spoke no Russian, among *"half-savage* men with beards, dressed in bare sheepskins, speaking in a wholly unknown language, in a little smoke-blackened peasant hut, and all this in the month of November of the terrible winter of 1812."[4] The epic struggle that ended with the Russian army's triumphant entry

Luise Haag, Herzen's mother. 1820s painting by I. Z. Letunov.

into Paris was imprinted on the child's awakening consciousness. "Tales of the fire of Moscow, of the battle of Borodino, of the Berezina, of the taking of Paris, were my cradle-songs, my nursery stories, my *Iliad* and my *Odyssey*."[5]

The family returned to the ruined city a year later, to a household shared with one of Ivan's brothers. Herzen's memoirs begin with a description of his childhood in that vast, gloomy domain, dominated by his father's misanthropic temperament: as portrayed by his

Ivan Alekseevich Yakovlev, Herzen's father. 1820s painting by I. Z. Letunov.

son, Ivan Yakovlev was an early example of the "superfluous man" who was to become a stock character in nineteenth-century Russian literature:

> My father was hardly ever in a good humor; he was perpetually dissatisfied with everything. A man of great intelligence and great powers of observation, he had seen, heard, and remembered an im-

mense amount; an accomplished man of the world, he could be extremely amiable and interesting, but he did not care to be so and sank more and more into wayward unsociability.

It is hard to say exactly what it was that put so much bitterness and spleen into his blood. Periods of great unhappiness, of mistakes and losses, were completely absent from his life. I could never fully understand what was the origin of the spiteful mockery that filled his soul, the mistrustful unsociability and the vexation that consumed him. Did he bear with him to the grave some memory that he confided to no one, or was this simply the result of the combination of two elements so absolutely opposed to each other as the eighteenth century and Russian life, with the intervention of a third, terribly conducive to the development of capricious humor: the idleness of the serf-owning landed gentleman?[6]

Herzen presents his father as the archetype of the cultured Russian of his age, exposed to the influence of the Enlightenment but lacking any useful outlet for his intellectual energies. "Foreigners at home, foreigners abroad, spoilt for Russia by Western prejudices and for the West by Russian habits, they were a sort of intellectual superfluity, and were lost in artificial life, in sensual pleasure and in unbearable egoism."[7]

Mordant irony was Ivan Yakovlev's habitual weapon against his family, servants, relatives, and visitors. In his more irascible moods he would remind Herzen's mother of her ambivalent position in his household, although he seems to have loved her in his way: they remained together for thirty-five years and together with his sons she inherited his fortune. But she led an isolated life in a separate apartment within the Yakovlev brothers' vast house, her social position a barrier to forming acquaintances. Her life was spent in minor domestic occupations, reading German books and caring for Alexander and his cantankerous father. But she seems to have been cheerful and good-natured. Herzen recalls her charm and kindheartedness; he was to remain close to her all her life. Although timid by nature, she was not wholly submissive, persuading the reluctant Ivan to treat his unloved elder son on the same footing in the household as her own child.

Ivan Yakovlev's favored son was spared the full force of his irony, but the oppressiveness and stultifying boredom of Herzen's surroundings was increased by his hypochondriac father's unfounded anxieties about his physical health, which kept him indoors for weeks at a time in winter. Herzen was to be almost totally isolated from the outside world until the age of seventeen, his only contacts with it being his tutors. He compensated for the lack of companionship by frequent visits to the servants' hall to play with the house-serfs' children. His country cousin Tatiana Kuchina (later Passek), who befriended him on her visits to Moscow, depicts him in her memoirs as a lively, noisy, self-willed child, cosseted and overprotected as the sole object of his father's affections, spoilt by the uncle who lived with the family and by the servants: "Sasha grew up in isolation, did not understand a refusal or how to make a compromise, did not like other children and did not know how to play with them; the slightest contradiction drove him into a rage."[8] He was still very young when stray remarks by servants made him sense that there was something exceptional about his and his mother's position in the household. At about the age of thirteen he finally learned the facts about his parents' relationship on overhearing two family friends referring to his "false" social position and advising his father to establish him in a military career, which would give him an entry into aristocratic society. His cousin recalls how he tearfully reported the conversation to her, concluding defiantly, "If that's so, then I don't depend either on my father or on society—that means I'm free."[9] From that time his relations with his father became more strained, as he began to sense himself alien in the circle of relatives and family friends to which he no longer felt he belonged by right. His wounded self-esteem expressed itself in a growing rebelliousness against his father's capricious authority; one can discern in it the seeds of his later identification with the humiliated and oppressed. He developed a sense of outraged dignity on which he would brood in the isolation of political exile, writing later to his fiancée that he had felt "completely alien in my parents' house, insulted at every step—and what insults they were!" The "benevolent charity" of his father's family had been worse than the humiliations inflicted on him by the tsarist authorities. To another friend he would recall in the 1840s: "I knew nothing of family relationships: in my childish mind they were surrounded by some sort of stain, which I had to overcome, to blot out."[10]

When Herzen reached adolescence, the contents of his father's extensive library became his means of escape from the dreary confines of the paternal house. It consisted entirely of eighteenth-century French works (according to Herzen, his father never in his life read a single Russian book). Herzen had acquired French from his tutors, as well as German from his mother. He rummaged unsystematically among his father's books, indiscriminately devouring novels in the sentimentalist tradition inspired by Rousseau, and plays (of which *The Marriage of Figaro* was his favorite). Attending Sunday services with his mother, a Lutheran, he acquired a thorough knowledge of and love for the Gospels, which schooled him in morality rather than in religious faith.

At the same time he became a fierce patriot, his imagination stirred by his parents' and their servants' constant reminiscences about the terrible and glorious year of 1812. His father's old comrades from the Izmailovsky regiment, heroes of a bloody war, were often at their house, describing the battles and reveling in the great victory. The young Herzen was particularly enchanted by the stories he heard from Count Miloradovich, one of the generals of the 1812 campaign.

His rebelliousness found a political focus when he was nearly fourteen, in the aftermath of the failed Decembrist uprising. Moscow was swept by rumors of arrests; parents trembled for their children. Some relatives of the family were among those arrested, and the Moscow aristocracy was in a state of consternation for months. In his memoirs Herzen dates his political awakening from that time. The accounts of the uprising and the subsequent trial and executions made a deep impression on him. "A new world was revealed to me that became more and more the center of my moral being; I don't know how this happened, but although I had no understanding, or only a very dim one, of what it all meant, I felt that I was not on the same side as the grapeshot and victory, prisons and chains."[11] A new tutor, an ardent follower of the Romantic movement, encouraged his interest in Schiller's dramas and lent him manuscript copies of Pushkin's *Ode to Freedom* and the writings of the poet Kondratii Ryleev, one of the five executed Decembrists. His French tutor, a Republican who had approved of the execution of Louis XVI, inspired in him a fascination with the ideas and figures of the Convention and the Terror. In this he was not untypical of his generation. He later wrote, "The cult of the French Revolution is the first religion of a young Russian; which of us did not secretly possess portraits of Robespierre and Danton?"[12] He began to study seriously, developing a fascination with the heroes of antiquity, whose civic virtues had inspired the Jacobins and the Decembrists. His approach reflected the aesthetic ideal of the Romantic age. Looking back at his youthful enthusiasm he writes: "Ancient history . . . is an aesthetic school of morality. The great men of Greece and Rome have in them that astonishing, plastic, artistic beauty that engraves itself forever on a young soul. . . . The features of Plutarch's heroes are as wonderfully graceful, open, full of thought, as the pediments and porticos of the Parthenon."[13]

With equal nostalgia he recalled his discovery, through Schiller's poetry, of the concept of the *schöne Seele* (beautiful soul). "Schiller! I bless you, to you I owe the holy moments of my early youth! . . . You are above all the poet of youth. The same dreamy gaze, fixed only on the future—'thither! thither!' [a reference to Mignon's song "Dahin, Dahin!" in Goethe's novel *Wilhelm Meister*], the same noble, vigorous, captivating feelings, the same love of humanity."[14] It was at this period that Herzen acquired a confidante in his cousin Tatiana, two years older than himself, who in her visits to Moscow became his mentor in an idealized concept of love, as portrayed in classics of sentimental literature such as Goethe's *Elective Affinities*, which they read together or discussed in correspondence, luxuriating in a pantheistic sense of unity with the cosmos. Rousseau with his cult of unfettered emotion was a favorite, although Tatiana, who seems to have been a bossy girl, drew the line at the *Confessions*, warning Herzen that it contained "impure" passages unsuitable for a boy of his age. His father intercepted the letter and wrote thanking her for her vigilance.[15]

As a soulmate Tatiana had her limitations. The sentimental self-absorption of superior beings could not satisfy Herzen's growing mood of protest. Schiller's first Sturm und Drang drama, *The Robbers*, which came into Herzen's hands during his unsystematic education, made a deep impression on him with its depiction of protest as violent (if unsuccessful) rebellion: "The band of Karl Moor led me for a long time into the Bohemian forests of Romanticism." In the Russia of Nicolas I, active resistance to evil could be perceived as an essential component of a "beautiful soul."[16] At the age of fourteen Herzen found a friend who shared this view—it was the beginning of a lifelong comradeship.

Nicolas Ogarev was a distant relative of the Yakovlevs. A year younger than Herzen, he too was a solitary child. In a memoir he wrote in the 1850s at Herzen's instigation, he describes his life before their meeting. His mother died in his early childhood; his father was a distant and intimidating figure. Cared for by serfs and female relatives, he experienced little affection. Confined indoors due to his delicate health, his main contact with the outside world was through his tutors, one of whom introduced him in his early adolescence to Schiller's works. "Schiller was everything for me—my philosophy, my civic sense, my poetry." He developed "vague longings for knowledge, poetry, and civic freedom," together with a yearning for a friend who would share his aspirations.[17]

Herzen describes the beginning of their friendship when Ogarev was brought by his tutor to spend the day with him. He was unlike any boy Herzen had met: "There was something kind, gentle, and pensive about him." By far the more self-confident and strong-willed of the pair, Herzen immediately took the initiative in their relationship, proposing that they read Schiller together. He was amazed at the similarity of their tastes. Ogarev knew far more of Schiller by heart than he did; he also knew the unpublished poems of Pushkin and Ryleev. Herzen discovered that there were no limits to the sympathy between them: "His heart beat as mine; he too had cast off from the grim shore of conservatism." This sympathy quickly developed into a passionate friendship: "After a month we could not pass two days without seeing each other or writing a letter."[18] Ogarev recalled in the 1850s: "There was no one close to me at home. My life consisted in my meetings with you."[19] Together the boys read Schiller's *Philosophical Letters*, identifying with the two friends in the work who progress in an exchange of letters from doubt and error toward "the fine goal of serene wisdom [*zu dem schönen Ziele der ruhigen Weisheit*]." On Herzen's advice Ogarev read Rousseau's *Social Contract:* "Nowhere else had I found liberal ideas expounded with such engaging force," Herzen recalled.[20]

Two decades later the friends retained the same vivid memories of that period. Ogarev writes: "Schiller, the Russian literature of the Decembrists, their fate, . . . that entire epoch we lived through together, constantly urging each other forward in . . . our striving toward the same exalted, although as yet vaguely defined goal."[21] Herzen recalled that they saw themselves as "chosen vessels," predestined to accomplish a great mission in the service of humanity.[22] Their devotion to the Decembrists fused with the cult of Schiller as they identified in fantasy with the noble rebels of his dramas. Herzen's ideal was Karl Moor, but his preference changed to the Marquis Posa in *Don Carlos*. "I imagined in a hundred different ways how I would speak to Nicolas [as Posa addresses the tyrant Philip of Spain in Schiller's play], and how afterward he would send me to the mines or the scaffold."[23] Their daydreaming culminated in the famous oath on the Sparrow Hills above Moscow; the date is not precisely known, but Herzen was at most sixteen and Ogarev fifteen.[24] Herzen describes the scene in his memoirs:

> The sun was setting, the cupolas glittered, beneath the hill the city extended further than the eye could reach; a fresh breeze blew on our faces, we stood leaning against each other and, suddenly embracing, vowed in sight of all Moscow to sacrifice our lives to the struggle we had chosen.
>
> This scene may seem very affected and theatrical, and yet twenty-six years afterward I am moved to tears as I recall it; there was a sacred sincerity in it, and our whole life has proved this.[25]

As Malia observes, that oath constitutes a historical event.[26] Among a generation that had turned its back on the lost cause of liberal reformism, Herzen and Ogarev represented the first shoots of a new humanitarian protest that would ultimately lead to Russian socialism.

* * *

In 1829 at the age of seventeen Herzen enrolled at Moscow University, following complicated negotiations conducted by his father. As an illegitimate son, he could attain noble status only through state service, rising through the Table of Ranks instituted by Peter the Great. Ivan Yakovlev obtained his son's admission into the bottom rank at the age of eight, his influence ensuring that ten years later Alexander had moved up to the penultimate rank without having served a single day. His father's intention had been that he should proceed to a career in Nicolas's bureaucracy, which would finally integrate him into gentry society, but Herzen was determined to proceed instead to Moscow University. His father having finally acquiesced, he was granted three years' leave from his fictitious service for that purpose.

View of Moscow, ca. 1825, from the Sparrow Hills, site of the oath sworn by Herzen and Ogarev as adolescents to fight Tsarist tyranny. Drawing by Auguste Cadolle.

The university, the oldest in Russia, was founded in 1755. Its initial function was to train civil servants; what learning the nobility acquired was gained through travel, reading, and salon conversations. But the alienation of the gentry from the government after 1825 conferred a new attraction on the universities as havens for independent thought. As a youth on the verge of becoming gentrified, Herzen would have been expected to enroll as a student of philology or history. Instead, he chose the Faculty of Physical and Mathematical Sciences—a decision that would have a determining effect on the subsequent development of his thought. As his memoirs explain, his reason for so doing was that he had quite suddenly developed a great passion for natural science, following his acquaintance with an eccentric cousin known as the Chemist, who lived an isolated existence in the family house, spending days and nights in his study "in a soiled dressing-gown lined with squirrel fur . . . surrounded by piles of books, and rows of phials, retorts, crucibles, and other apparatus." Though repelled by his comfortless views on philosophical questions (he was an atheist and a materialist), Herzen found him learned and witty, and took to visiting him. Seeing

Herzen in his university years, as painted by A. A. Zbruev.

that Herzen was interested in earnest in science, the Chemist sought to persuade him to give up the "empty study" of literature and the "dangerous and quite useless pursuit of politics," and take to natural science.[27] His influence decided Herzen's choice of university studies, setting him on a path that would bring him into conflict with all the major currents of political thought in his time.

CHAPTER FOUR

A Revolution in Science

It can be said that the love of the study of Nature presupposes two qualities of mind which are apparently in opposition to each other: the grand view of an intense intellectual power which takes in everything at a glance, and the detailed attention of an instinct which concentrates laboriously on a single minute detail.

BUFFON

IN the autumn of 1829 Herzen, followed by Ogarev, began his studies at Moscow University's Faculty of Physical and Mathematical Sciences. He graduated in 1833, after a year's intermission when a cholera epidemic forced the university to close. In the following year he was arrested; his personal papers were confiscated and vanished into the archives of the secret police. Apart from half a dozen letters, three of his student essays, and a copy of his final-year dissertation, the only surviving firsthand record of his life and thought in those years is a chapter in his memoirs, composed in the late 1850s. Its vivid vignettes of eccentric professors and rebellious students in the Russia of Nicolas I make engaging reading, but its value as a factual account is limited. Lidiya Ginzburg's interpretation of the memoirs as a purposefully organized reality, refracted through the consciousness of the autobiographical hero, is particularly pertinent: "*My Past and Thoughts* is about the place and role of the thinking person in an unjustly organized social reality. . . . That theme was prompted by the acute contradictions of Russian life in an era when the issue of the hero, of the Russian ideologue as the bearer of an active social consciousness, had acquired decisive significance for literature. The fate of that hero was a theme of the Russian ideological novel, and a basic theme of *My Past and Thoughts*."[1]

Herzen's account of his university years conforms to this model in setting the stage for his later career by giving prominence to his role as a ringleader, singled out for punishment after a riotous protest against a coarse, incompetent professor. He becomes a hero to his fellow students, depicted as idealists who dreamed of emulating the feats of the Decembrists. His satirical portraits of the more egregious professors convey the stultifying effect of political despotism on Russian intellectual life. We are told that Moscow University did its best under the circumstances, but the overall impression given in his memoirs is that the "excellent set of young men" in his year were largely self-taught: "Contact with other young men in the lecture rooms and the exchange of ideas and of what they had been reading did more to develop the students than lectures and professors."[2] He cites one exception to this rule: M. G. Pavlov (1793–1840), professor of agriculture and physics, who used his lectures as a platform to convey to his audience the fundamentals of the *Naturphilosophie*. Schelling's philosophy enjoyed enormous popularity among the Russian educated public, but within the universities philosophy was taught by theologians (the chair of philosophy in Moscow was abolished in 1826): thus the attraction of Pavlov's lectures for students thirsting after a coherent vision of the world that could make sense of the present and give hope for humanity and Russia in the future. Herzen writes of Pavlov in this much-quoted passage from his memoirs:

> Pavlov gave us an introduction to philosophy instead of physics and agriculture. It would have been hard to learn physics from his lectures, impossible to learn agriculture; but his courses were extraordinarily profitable. Pavlov would stand at the doors of the Faculty of Physics and Mathematics and stop a student with the question: "You want to acquire a knowledge of nature? But what is nature? What is knowledge?" This was extremely valuable; our young students enter the university without any philosophical preparation; only the divinity students have any notion of philosophy, but that is a completely distorted one. In answer to these questions Pavlov expounded the doctrines of Schelling and Oken with such clarity and style as no natural philosopher had shown before.[3]

In the absence of tributes to other teachers or any reference to his specifically scientific interests in the memoirs, the reader might assume that Herzen approached his university years primarily as an education in the German metaphysics to which his generation had turned for answers to the fundamental questions of existence. Martin Malia's view that Schelling's idealism provides "the chief key to [Herzen's] intellectual life during ten crucial years . . . approximately down to 1840" has strongly influenced the interpretation of his thought by Western historians. He observes that Herzen paid more attention to his formal studies than his memoirs imply, citing a letter in which he expresses disappointment and indignation at not graduating with the faculty's gold medal (he had to make do with silver), but he touches only very briefly on Herzen's surviving university writings on science, commenting that while they showed a good knowledge of the serious scientific literature of the period, this was all filtered through the overwhelming influence of his mentor Pavlov: "Herzen's scientific training lay essentially in the raw materials for the biology of the *Naturphilosophie*."[4]

Herzen might seem to be saying the same when he writes on the eve of his graduation: "I'm grateful for much to Moscow University. It taught me method, and method is more important than any sum of knowledge."[5] But these words reflect a very different approach to science as a tool for the understanding of history and human societies. Their meaning has been obscured by the loss of most of Herzen's papers from his university years, the misleading selectivity of his memoirs, and the tendency of Western historians to ignore the role of science, in particular the emergence of the historical view in natural science, in the development of humanistic values and ideals in nineteenth-century Russia.

What Herzen meant by his debt to his faculty will become evident in Chapter 5 when we turn to the profiles of his teachers. Questions of methodology were to be their dominant concern, reflecting a close involvement in a revolution in thought much deeper and farther-reaching than that represented by German idealism. Despite the government's best efforts, and at some danger to themselves, several of the most outstanding scientists in Moscow University were managing to keep abreast of the advances in evolutionary biology, which threatened the foundations of the political and social status quo by undermining beliefs on which 2,000 years of European culture had been built. For an inquiring and radically inclined student in the late 1820s, Moscow's Faculty of Physical and Mathematical Sciences provided an intellectual diet more challenging than could be found anywhere else in Russia.

The existence of this center of radical thought in the unpromising conditions of Nicolas's regime was the result of a long process that began with Peter the Great's determination to open Russia up to Western culture. In this there were two key factors: the prestige initially given to science by Russia's rulers as an instrument of progress, and the coincidence of the country's modernization with the development in the West of a historical approach to the natural world and to human societies. The happy conjunction of these two processes in Europe and Russia is the subject of this chapter. In the next we shall see how their reverberations in Herzen's faculty prompted the reflections on the nature of history that would become the central intellectual preoccupation of his later years: what has been assessed as the startling originality of his mature vision of history can be traced back to his grasp of a revolution that began to take shape a century before his birth.

* * *

The year after Peter's death, 1725, saw the founding of a Russian Academy of Sciences in Saint Petersburg, staffed by a number of eminent scientists imported from the West. Homegrown talent began to emerge under their leadership, but the process was slow. The vast mass of the population had no access to education, and visitors marveled at the ignorance and idleness of the provincial gentry. The aristocracy of Saint Petersburg and Moscow were more interested in the decorative aspects of French salon culture than in a serious engagement with European thought. Moscow University was founded in 1755 to meet the country's growing need for military and economic expertise; initially its scientific curriculum, designed to train technical and administrative personnel (as in Herzen's case, university study could be counted as government service and brought with it a promotion in rank), was rudimentary and incomplete, but it stimulated popular interest in science, which also benefited from the intensive translating work carried out by the Academy.

Under Catherine the Great a new generation of genuinely educated nobility began to emerge. In the early years of her reign (1762–1798) she was eager to present herself as an "enlightened" monarch, concerned to modernize Russia in the spirit of the rationalist and humanist principles of the French philosophes. Her ambition resulted in the creation of a new administrative and intellectual elite. The formal education of these young men at the hands of private tutors (sometimes followed by a spell of study abroad) tended to be restricted to the humanities, philosophy, or law, but they were also acquainted with current developments in Western science, thanks to the popular scientific journals published by the Academy and the enthusiasm of thinkers devoted to the ideals of the Age of Reason, such as the writer and publisher Nikolai Novikov.

Meanwhile the Saint Petersburg Academy of Sciences grew in strength and influence, continuing to attract distinguished foreign scholars. Its achievements in original scientific research were matched in the late eighteenth century by Moscow University's success in stimulating popular interest in science. Though its scientific curriculum, poorly funded, was rudimentary and incomplete, its graduates began to occupy important positions in the national administration, and large audiences were attracted by its extensive programs of public lectures acquainting Russians with the latest scientific ideas from the West.

A peasant uprising (the Pugachev rebellion of 1773–1774) cooled Catherine's reforming zeal, and the French Revolution put an end to it. The later years of her reign were marked by a progressively harsher suppression of advanced ideas from the West. But her initial flirtation with the Enlightenment had a subversive effect more profound than any of the political events that so greatly alarmed her. Among the philosophes to whom she introduced her subjects were two who had begun to dismantle the fundamental belief underlying the main traditions of Western thought since the Greeks: that contingent existence was the reflection of a timeless harmony and order.

The Concept of Evolution

As the biologist Ernst Mayr notes, a precondition for the eventual acceptance of the theory of evolution through natural selection was a conceptual change that involved the whole Western philosophical tradition.[6] Nietzsche described Christianity in the preface to *Beyond Good and Evil* as "Platonism for the 'people'"; the same has been said of Western philosophy well into the nineteenth century, inasmuch as it predominantly approached the phenomena of the visible world as imperfect and partial manifestations of timeless and transcendent ideas or essences.[7] Coupled with this dualism was the belief, extending back to Plato, Aristotle, and the Stoics, that there is a predetermined purpose in nature and its processes.

Modern cosmology and physics developed under the pervasive influence of Renaissance Platonism. Galileo and his contemporaries found in Plato (who, it seems, came to regard the Ideas or Forms as mathematical entities of some sort) an authority for their distinction between the appearances of nature and its underlying and enduring reality, which they represented in mathematical terms.

Newton's great triumphs in unifying celestial and terrestrial mechanics ensured the dominance of mathematics as the sole explanatory paradigm of science for the next two centuries. Faith in mathematics as the key to the underlying structure of the universe received powerful support from Cartesian dualism, which combined a crudely mechanistic conception of physical reality (the notion of the animal machine) with a rationalist metaphysics, based on the distinction between the body (a collection of matter to be explained in terms of size, shape, and motion) and the mind or soul, existing outside space and time: the latter distinction, Mayr remarks, "has plagued us ever since."[8]

In the seventeenth and eighteenth centuries, religion and science were harmonized through the deistic concept of a clockmaker God, the author of immutable laws that regulated the universe. Until well into the eighteenth century, natural history was still seen as "natural theology," its role being to describe the marvels of God's works. In accordance with the myth of the creation, naturalists assumed a steady-state world in which all species currently populating the earth had existed unchanged since the sixth day of creation, arranged in a hierarchy commonly designated by the ancient concept of a *scala naturae* or Great Chain of Being, stretching from inanimate matter upward to animals, humans, the angels, and God. But the search to reduce the universe and life within it to a minimal set of laws was increasingly frustrated by a growing fascination with diversity. Over the same period the study of the Greek classics sparked a new interest in ancient Greek culture and architecture, while the great voyages of discovery acquainted the Western world with the existence of primitive peoples and cultures and exotic animals and plants.

These factors all contributed to what can be seen as a paradigmatic change from a static to a developing view of the world, reflected in a new approach to history. Descartes and his followers had held that true knowledge was obtainable only through the methods of the exact sciences, resting on the foundation of the eternal laws of mathematics. As history was not amenable to this treatment, it tended to be regarded with condescension as a collection of stories about the irrational past.

In his pioneering work of 1725, *Scienza Nuova*, Giambattista Vico argued that the Cartesian paradigm of true knowledge excluded the human dimension of self-knowledge. There were no immutable laws valid for all peoples at all times, he claimed. Human nature was constantly evolving; societies were the products of successive stages of development and change, each with its own unique needs and character expressed in its customs, laws, morality, and art. Although Vico held that the laws governing human nature had been designed by a Creator to fulfill divine purposes, he believed these were not accessible to humans. To understand what we are in the present and what we might become, we would need to trace our growth back to its roots by close empirical study of historical facts in their specific cultural contexts.

Vico's vision of a new science of human societies ran counter to the Enlightenment's dominant faith in a fixed human nature that was able, through the universal attribute of reason, to formulate standards and ideals valid for all societies at all times. But he was an obscure and isolated figure whose ideas were largely ignored in his century. Such was not the case with the Baron de Montesquieu, a leading representative of the French Enlightenment, whose project for a new science of humankind was published in 1748, twenty-three years after Vico's.

In its defense of freedom and dignity against the forces of ignorance and superstition, *The Spirit of the Laws* reflected the dominant concerns of the Age of Reason, but Montesquieu departed radically from the universalizing ethos of the time in giving central importance to diverse and fluctuating influences, in particular the role of environmental factors—climate, topography, and other *causes physiques*—in determining the content of the laws, values, and institutions of human societies as they evolved in time. No single model of government, however perfect, could be appropriate for all peoples at all times. Montesquieu's intense interest in diversity, his fascination with exotic and unusual societies and customs, and his preoccupation with concrete detail, were a function of his method. He believed that through comparison of the myriad influences on societies and their goals one could form a sense of the limits to which reformers could go in particular cases without turning into despots. Montesquieu was not a relativist: he believed in the transcendent value of justice, but stressed that attempts to implement it in specific societies must take into account the complex interplay among natural forces, existing institutions, and human consciousness.

The use of organic metaphors for society goes back as far as Aristotle; medieval writers employed them widely. What was new in Montesquieu's thought was the notion of the development of social organisms in historical time and through natural processes which could be investigated by empirical methods. (In common with other Enlightenment thinkers, he eschewed all discussion of first causes.) Though Montesquieu was accepted in his time as one of the greatest figures of the Enlightenment, the Encyclopédistes were uneasy about some of his ideas. Voltaire dismissed his discussions of non-European habits and customs as "erroneous digressions," on the grounds that the habits of peoples not yet illuminated by the light of reason had nothing of value to teach the world. Montesquieu was sailing into uncharted waters; he was unique among the advanced thinkers of his time in challenging the faith on which new radical theories of progress were being built. In the words of Isaiah Berlin, "the whole system of values upon which the Enlightenment rested began to crumble if the very possibility of a single universal method for obtaining true answers to moral and metaphysical questions, true for all men, at all times, everywhere, . . . was doubted or denied."[9]

* * *

While Montesquieu was engaged in freeing history from the determinism of theology and Cartesian science, another thinker of equal genius and originality was transforming the study of nature, revealing that it too had a history of which the development of mankind was an integral part.

In the year following the publication of *The Spirit of the Laws*, there appeared the first of thirty-six volumes entitled *Histoire naturelle, générale et particulière*, by the great naturalist Georges-Louis Leclerc, Comte de Buffon (1707–1788). The recipient of many academic honors, Buffon was an unlikely revolutionary. David Hume described him as being less like a writer than a Marshal of France. Keeper of the Jardin du Roi, he was one of the most highly esteemed of all the philosophes (the first edition of the first of his volumes, although substantial, sold out in three weeks.) The grounds for his success had been prepared by the new fashion for the exotic and unusual. Natural history cabinets were fashionable among the noble and wealthy in England and France, and zoological and botanical gardens and popularizing lectures by amateur scientists attracted a large public. But it was Buffon who raised natural history from a hobby to the status of a science. He dominated the science of his century and secured a unique place in the history of ideas.

His *Histoire* had the distinction of being published by the Imprimerie Royale; yet the first volume was introduced by a major programmatic statement *(Discours de la manière d'étudier et de traiter l'histoire naturelle)* that challenged fundamental assumptions common to the religious and secular order of his time. The discovery of diversity had come to pose severe methodological problems for naturalists. When they began to apply Newton's combination of mathematical reasoning and close observation to questions about the origin of the earth, they were confronted with fossil evidence of geological change and extinct species that did not fit the creation story. Travelers were bringing back ever-increasing evidence of an almost limitless variety of animals and plants, while the microscope, which had been in scientific use from the middle of the seventeenth century, had revealed the existence of multitudes of organisms invisible to the naked eye. That such profusion of multiplicity could be attributed to chance was unthinkable at a period when the study of nature was still dominated by the notion of a universe designed by a lawgiving Creator, even if the latter's role were reduced to little more than the original force behind its laws. The new discoveries intensified the search for ordering and unifying principles, a "natural" system of classification that would reflect, if not the plan of creation, then the underlying rationality of the universe.

These efforts were the overriding concern of eighteenth-century natural science, and they reached their climax with the taxonomic system of Carl von Linné (Linnaeus). He approached natural history as an exercise in naming and classification, whereby he hoped to do for the earth what Newton had done for the heavens. He saw nature as a fixed and harmonious pattern of permanent structures, a "wonderful order" created by the wisdom of God.[10] He was still engaged in perfecting his "System of Nature" in 1749 when Buffon launched his manifesto in the form of the *Discours*, demanding that the quest for systems be replaced by an understanding of natural diversity. Challenging Linnaeus's static taxonomy founded on the premise of the immutability of species, Buffon based his argument on the discoveries of the new science of geology, which showed the surface of the earth to be in a process of constant change and development. Nature presents us with a world of infinite combinations, an endless proliferation of forms, grading imperceptibly into others: "a world of perpetual destruction and renewal."[11] He denied the relevance of theology to the study of nature by arguing that the human mind was not able to penetrate to first causes—a common position among Enlightenment thinkers who followed Locke in rejecting the ambitious pretensions of Cartesian metaphysics. But while the majority of the philosophes tended to adopt an eclectic mix of rationalism and empiricism, Buffon went much further in developing insights into the nature of truth and certitude that anticipated major philosophical preoccupations of the next two centuries.

It has been observed that the theoretical unity of Buffon's work consists in his break with the method and epistemology of Newtonian science, summarized in his age by Kant's dictum "There is only as much authentic science in any specific part of the natural sciences as the mathematics present in it."[12] To apply the methods of the mathematical sciences to the study of nature, he declared in the *Discours*, is "to strip the subject of most of its qualities, and to make of it an abstract entity that has no resemblance to the real being." His argument rested on a distinction between "abstract" and "physical" truth. He described the search for a coherent and perfect system as the chase after the philosopher's stone, doomed to fail because of the uniqueness of living organisms and their spatial and temporal relationships as con-

ditioned by the contingencies of climate, nourishment, and other circumstances. A species was not an abstract universal: "It can be rendered intelligible only by considering nature in the succession of time."
Life had its own laws: mathematics was of limited use to a science
whose aim should be, not to classify structures, but to discover and
understand processes and relationships evolving in historical time.
"Time is the great workman of nature. . . . Nothing can resist his
power, and those changes that at first are imperceptible, become gradually sensible, and at last are marked by results too conspicuous to be
misapprehended."[13]

Buffon had a central influence on the transformation of natural theology into natural history. The proposition that not only the earth but
its inhabitants were the outcome of a temporal process rather than the
static expression of a plan of creation was the first step along a path
that would lead to the Darwinian revolution. Hence he has been called
the father of evolution, although he was not an evolutionist himself,[14]
rejecting the hypothesis of the transmutation of species and assigning
humans a unique place in nature by virtue of their faculties of thought
and speech. His was the first serious effort to make a numerical calculation of the age of the earth—75,000 years, a conservative estimate in
his view, but far vaster than any previously envisaged. He played a
central role in what Stephen Toulmin has called "the discovery of
time," the replacement of a static Renaissance view of the world with
a developmental one that confronted humanity with uncertainties as
profound as Copernicus's reforms in astronomy.[15]

In orienting natural science away from description and toward the
study of change and development, Buffon confronted the problem of
uncertainty head-on. In the *Discours* he sketches out a methodology
for arriving at the "physical truth" of nature's operations: Beginning
with exact descriptions of the structures of animals and plants, "we
must try to raise ourselves to something greater and still more worthy
of our efforts: namely, the combination of observations, the generalization of facts, linking them together by the power of analogies, and the
effort to arrive at a high degree of knowledge." He insisted that the
truths arrived at by this difficult process are in no way arbitrary. "They
depend only on facts. A sequence of similar facts or . . . a frequent
repetition and an uninterrupted sequence of the same occurrences

constitute the essence of this sort of truth. What is called physical truth is thus only a probability, but a probability so great that it is equivalent to certitude."[16]

Montesquieu and Buffon, the two most celebrated and controversial figures of the Enlightenment, in seeking to address the instability of all being under the influence of chance and time, placed themselves at the forefront of an intellectual revolution whose implications are still being worked through in the human and natural sciences. Montesquieu transformed the study of human institutions, setting out the groundwork for the disciplines of anthropology, sociology, and comparative politics; Buffon's ideas on the influence of environment on the development of living beings inspired new thinking in such diverse fields as cosmology, the history of the earth, and embryonic development. He laid the basis for the establishment of the life sciences as distinct disciplines dealing with processes and relationships that did not permit precise predictions and were irreducible to universal laws. His insights into the influence of environment on living beings were as relevant to the emerging discipline of the philosophy of history as they were to natural science. The continuity between natural and human history is emphasized in his last work, *Les époques de la nature* (1788), which brings together his main ideas on geology, biology, and the cosmos in a detailed history of the earth and life on it.

In their fascination with diversity, their insistence on the significance of difference, both thinkers were at odds with the universalizing spirit of their time. Buffon asserts: "Accurate descriptions, without any attempt toward definitions, a more scrupulous examination of the differences than of the similarities, a particular attention to the exceptions and even to the slightest shades, are the true guides, and I will venture to affirm, the only means we possess of investigating Nature." "The more we reflect on detail," Montesquieu wrote in *The Spirit of the Laws*, "the more we will sense the certainty of our principles." Buffon affirmed that there were no absolute boundaries in nature: its progression is "always a matter of nuances." Montesquieu asserted that "everything is tied together extremely closely. . . . A great many truths do not appear until we have seen the chain that links them to others." Good sense, he affirmed, "consists very much in comprehending the nuances of things."[17]

In pursuing analogies and weighing probabilities, the methods outlined by the two thinkers demanded, in addition to reason, qualities of imagination and empathy that would be given great emphasis by the Romantics and would have an essential part in the historicism of J. G. Hamann and Herder. As Buffon put it in the *Discours*, the pursuit of physical truth required more than assiduity, attention, and a vast memory: "General views, a steady eye, and a process of reasoning informed more by reflection than by study are what is called for. Finally, that quality of mind is needed which makes us capable of grasping distant relationships, bringing them together, and making out of them a body of reasoned ideas, after having precisely determined their nearness to truth and weighed their probabilities."[18] It was due above all to Buffon that the natural sciences found themselves in the front line of the Enlightenment's campaign against dogma and superstition. Although his position in the political and intellectual elite shielded him from the extremes of censorship, he occasionally ran afoul of the religious authorities, who ordered him to remove from subsequent editions of the *Histoire* all references to the age of the earth that contradicted the biblical version of the creation. He concealed his personal religious beliefs so adroitly that there is still debate about whether he was a Christian, an atheist, or a deist.[19]

Early Effects in Russia

Buffon's skills in self-censorship and in exploiting the limits of the ideologically permissible to convey the hitherto unthinkable set a precedent of particular relevance to the French Enlightenment's poor relation in Russia in the later years of Catherine's reign, when official support for advanced ideas was replaced by deep suspicion. But this was after her early enthusiasm for the two most radical of the philosophes had already acquainted a generation with their ideas. During her short-lived determination to turn Russia into a state based on law, she had described *The Spirit of the Laws* as her "prayer book" and her faith in the progressive role of science led her to commission a Russian translation of the first volume of Buffon's *Histoire naturelle*. While the regime became increasingly hostile to progressive ideas, the Academy of Sciences continued to attract eminent scholars from the West, principally from Germany. Its most notable work in the second half of the eighteenth century was in mathematics and the natural sciences, due to the leadership of its two most distinguished members, the mathematician Leonhard Euler and the great naturalist Peter Simon Pallas, who was recognized in Europe as an equal of Linnaeus and Buffon. The bulk of Buffon's monumental work was translated by Ivan Lepekhin, one of the most gifted of a new generation of Russian scholars emerging under the Academy's auspices. The knowledge and expertise of young scholars in every branch of natural science, from botany to paleontology, mineralogy and meteorology, grew through the scientific expeditions organized by the Academy between 1768 and 1774 and led by Peter Pallas. Its achievements in original scientific research were matched in the late eighteenth century by Moscow University's success in stimulating popular interest in science. Though it was still dominated by foreign scholars, and its poorly funded scientific curriculum was rudimentary and incomplete, its graduates began to occupy important positions in the administration, and large audiences were attracted by its extensive programs of public lectures.

Alexander Vucinich has noted that throughout the reign of Catherine "the growth of the scientific spirit really outstripped the growth of scientific inquiry."[20] This was due largely to the efforts of the leading Russian representatives of the Age of Reason, a small number of intellectuals who, though not themselves scientists, were imbued with the Enlightenment's faith in the power of science to bring about social change. The three most significant of these were Yakov Kozelsky, Nikolai Novikov, and Aleksandr Radishchev, the most radical Russian thinker of his time. Kozelsky was educated at the Academy University in Saint Petersburg and in 1768 published *Philosophical Proposals*, the first systematic exposition of philosophical ideas by a Russian author. It reflected Kozelsky's scientific training and the humanism of the Enlightenment. (Under Catherine's sponsorship he had translated a number of articles by the philosophes.) A deist, he defended the autonomy of philosophy and opposed attempts to utilize it to support the idea of divine Providence. The development of science and its connection with the growth of freedom was a recurrent theme in the periodicals founded by Novikov with the aim of creating an enlightened public opinion. As one of the young men handpicked by Catherine to be future leaders of society, Radishchev had been trained in law at Leipzig University, but he had an informed interest in science, performed experiments in chemistry, and was familiar with the Academy's remarkably early research on the historical development of nature. Each of those three thinkers made some effort to derive a more general outlook and philosophical standpoint from what their exposure to contemporary science had taught them. Even though they were unsystematic about it, this was a novelty in Russia. For the first time there were people in a position to affect the development of Russian society through their influence on government and administration who understood that the natural sciences ought to be an intrinsic part of their view of the world.

* * *

Russia's rulers were not slow to perceive the new threat posed by the historical orientation in natural science. As summed up by Vucinich: "In Russia, as in the West, the historical attitude brought natural science into open conflict with religion and its official guardians, for it challenged not only the biblical cosmology but also the sacred values surrounding the *ancien régime*—it created the atmosphere in which serfdom and monarchical absolutism were shifted from divine ordinances into historical categories."[21] Church and state joined forces to defend the status quo. The fear of religious displeasure was enough to make some scientists practice self-censorship: the academician Caspar Wolff, the founder of modern embryology, refrained from publishing his daring and original ideas during his lifetime. *Les époques de la nature*, the last and most provocative volume of Buffon's great opus, published in 1788, was suppressed in Russia by the Holy Synod. The outbreak of the French Revolution put an end to Catherine's wavering between enlightenment and absolutism—the haphazard censorship of previous reigns was replaced by a wide network of professional censors, religious and secular, designed to combat ideological infection from the West.

The accession of Alexander I in 1801 seemed to promise a return to the spirit of Catherine's early reign. Encouraged by advisors who believed that Russia's progress and prosperity depended on the widest possible diffusion of Western liberal ideas and scientific knowledge, he revived the moribund Academy and created three new universities—in Vilnius, Kazan, and Kharkov—in quick succession (Saint Petersburg

University was founded in 1819).[22] New charters guaranteed the universities considerable autonomy. The school system was reformed and expanded, with central importance given to the teaching of science and mathematics. The right of admission to public educational establishments, including universities, was extended to all classes—a reform necessitated by the ever-growing need for state servants, technologists, teachers, and physicians, all of which occupations were disdained by the aristocracy.

These processes began to be reversed when Alexander succumbed to the religious obscurantism of ultraconservative advisors. The relative autonomy granted to the universities in teaching and the recruitment of staff was revoked in 1816 with the appointment of Prince Alexander Golitsyn as minister of National Education. Golitsyn was director general of the Holy Synod and saw his mission as bringing all Russian education into line with Christian morality. By the early 1820s theology was a required subject in all universities, which were instructed to teach other subjects from a religious point of view. The structure of the natural world and the political and social status quo were to be approached alike as expressions of divine wisdom operating in the universe.

Ascending the throne in the wake of the failed Decembrist uprising, Nicolas I set out to eradicate all traces of the freethinking that had inspired it. Censorship was central to this endeavor. A new decree of 1826 was so broad in its formulation—covering science and education, morality and internal security, and "the orientation of public opinion"—as to permit the banning of almost any book, including those whose grammatical errors "openly violated the rules and purity of the Russian language."[23] Subsequently revised to include much more detail, it remained in force until 1855. Its intention was to cut Russian intellectual life off from all the most important advances made in the natural sciences over the preceding century in Europe. That it failed to do so was due principally to one of the reforms carried out in the early years of Alexander's reign.

Although the universities continued to be seen primarily as a training ground for servants of the state, in the early part of his reign Alexander had considerably expanded the range of their coverage of the sciences. Moscow University's original charter had limited the teaching of natural sciences (in the Faculty of Philosophy) to physics. A new charter given to it in 1804 and subsequently extended to the other universities established a Faculty of Physical and Mathematical Sciences, which offered courses in pure mathematics, applied mathematics, theoretical and experimental physics, chemistry, mineralogy, agriculture, botany, and industrial and commercial technology.

This expansion of the sciences and their differentiation into semi-independent disciplines was the only one of the university reforms to survive the onslaughts of ultraconservative government policy over the next half-century. The same broad curriculum remained in force in Moscow when Herzen began his university studies in 1829.

For this student in particular, the range of disciplines offered by the course would more than compensate for the combined effects of the idiocies of the censors and the eccentricities of the professors. Regarding the government's chief academic watchdog, who mistrusted learning in general and science in particular, Herzen observes in his memoirs: "Prince Golitsyn was an astonishing person; it was a long time before he could accustom himself to the disorderliness of having no lecture when a professor was ill: he thought the next in seniority should take his place, so that Father Ternovsky sometimes had to lecture in the clinic on women's diseases and Richter, the gynecologist, to discuss the Immaculate Conception."[24] A shortage of native Russian professors, the pressures of censorship, and the lack of laboratory equipment (on which the Academy had a monopoly) combined to affect the university's teaching in science in ways that provided plenty of ammunition for the satirical pens of alumni of those years. The very slow increase in the number of Russians who aspired to become scientists forced the government to rely heavily on foreign professors. Most of these were competent and some were distinguished, but they had difficulty learning Russian, and their relations with their Russian colleagues were often acrimonious, hence Herzen's collective portrait of his faculty in his memoirs:

> The professors consisted of two camps or strata who peaceably hated each other. One group was composed exclusively of Germans, the other of non-Germans. The Germans, among whom were good-natured and learned men, . . . were in general distinguished by their ignorance of the Russian language and their disinclination to learn

it, their indifference to the students, their spirit of Western parti-
sanship and trade-bound routine, their immoderate smoking of cigars, and the immense quantity of decorations which they never
took off. The non-Germans for their part knew not a single [living]
language except Russian, were servile in their patriotism, as coarse
as seminarians, . . . and instead of an immoderate consumption of
cigars indulged in an immoderate consumption of liquor. The Germans for the most part hailed from Göttingen and the non-Germans
were sons of priests.[25]

Another distinguished alumnus, the famous scholar and surgeon
Nikolai Pirogov, recalling the backwardness of that period, cites professors who read lecture material written in the 1750s; many students
attended their lectures "just for laughs."[26]

But if little original research was produced in Moscow in the first
thirty years of the nineteenth century, the foreign professors performed
a great service for their Russian colleagues and students by providing
living links with the ideas currently fermenting in the West, particularly in the new science of biology, where empirical methods of the past
were giving way to new approaches to the phenomena of the living
world. In this way, as Vucinich observes, a whole generation of Russian scholars was acquainted with the debates on theory and method
that accompanied the transition of "natural history" into "natural science" and its differentiation into a number of separate disciplines.[27]

The ramshackle organization of science teaching in Moscow under
the tyranny of Nicolas I takes on a more positive light if one compares
it with what was on offer to Charles Darwin, who began his scientific
studies in the same year as Herzen, at the venerable University of Cambridge. One of Darwin's biographers notes that until the 1850s (when
the sciences became respectable enough to merit a degree), the sciences
"led a somewhat furtive life in the universities [of Oxford and Cam-
bridge], existing in the interstices of the curriculum and on the fringes
of such extracurricular subjects as hunting and fishing." It had long
been customary in both universities to regard scientific professorships
as sinecures, and total ignorance of the relevant subject was no impediment to election. One applicant for the chair of botany admitted
that he "knew very little about botany" at the time, adding, however,

that he "probably knew as much of the subject as any resident of Cambridge."[28]

In the 1820s, however, a new group of Cambridge professors experienced a sudden accession of conscience and resolved to take their duties more seriously, even going so far as to acquire a rudimentary knowledge of the subjects to which their endowments committed them and to announce their intention of delivering several lectures a year. Darwin benefited from contact with three of this new breed of scientist, all enthusiastic autodidacts who were impressively erudite by the scientific standards of the day.

The young Herzen was more consistently fortunate in his undergraduate experience. Moscow University provided him with a schooling in method that would inform his approach in later years to history and the human struggle for existence.

[CHAPTER FIVE]

Science and History

Science, even more than the New Testament, teaches us humility.

HERZEN

HERZEN'S university studies coincided with the height of a debate in his faculty on the proper relation between hypothesis and observation in science, a problem that had preoccupied thinkers since Francis Bacon's attempt to define a secular and empirical approach to knowledge that would lead humanity to dominion over nature.

Debates on this question had been a central feature of the Enlightenment as a revolution in knowledge aimed at destroying the tyranny of dogma and superstition.[1] The empiricism of Locke and Condillac completed the separation of the study of nature from theology by stressing that humans' knowledge of the external world is limited, based on sense impressions that can never explain first principles. With France leading the way, the Age of Enlightenment saw the increasing professionalization of science as an independent activity concerned with clearly defined intellectual areas and with its own institutional organizations and journals, its status enhanced by governments' appreciation of its technological utility. By the end of the eighteenth century the natural sciences had differentiated into most of the specialist fields that would develop in the next century: embryology, comparative anatomy, geology, paleontology, plant and animal physiology. The need to make methods more precise in these fields became imperative when the study of fossil beds by French naturalists provided a flood of new information that contradicted the biblical account of creation. Their astonishing successes generated vigorous polemics on the proper interpretation of the new data. From these debates, and amid fierce resistance, the Darwinian revolution would emerge.

★ ★ ★

Experimental science delivered the final blow to the literal interpretation of Genesis. In the first decade of the nineteenth century the reconstruction of extinct species from fossil bones by the great comparative anatomist Georges Cuvier (1769–1832) uncovered the vast extent of prehistorical life on earth, punctuated by sudden and violent geological catastrophes that had imperiled whole species—facts difficult to reconcile with belief in a static world brought into being by a wise and benevolent Creator. Hitherto anatomy and physiology had concentrated on the structure and functions of the human body, while naturalists had been concerned with the external features distinguishing plants and animals from each other. Cuvier heralded the advent of a new subject—biology—when in 1800 he defined comparative anatomy's task as pursuing "life and the phenomena that compose it, in all the beings that have received some parcel of it."[2] Defending the new developments in the experimental sciences from attack by theological opinion, he stressed their revolutionary significance: the epistemological independence of geology and paleontology had resulted in a new understanding of the world and man's place in it by linking natural and human history together in a common progression through time. His method reflects an important process of cross-fertilization between the new developments in the natural sciences and the rise of history as an independent discipline with a naturalistic approach to peoples and cultures.

A crucial factor in this process was Herder's *Ideen zur Philosophie der Geschichte der Menschheit* (1784–1791), one of the most significant products of eighteenth-century thought. Strongly influenced by Buffon, Herder approached human history as part of the development of the cosmos as a whole. Focusing on our biological position in the universe, he broke with Kant's idea of pure reason, arguing that, contrary to traditional belief, there was no universal human nature that could formulate ideals and standards valid for all societies at all times. Peoples were historical and temporal creatures, their cultures and languages determined by climate, environment, and other empirical and changeable circumstances. Like Montesquieu and Buffon, Herder championed diversity, claiming not that all cultures were equally valuable but that they were ultimately incommensurable—they could not be arranged in an order according to some universal schema of progress.[3]

Although there is no suggestion in Herder's zoology that the higher animals were descended from earlier and lower ones, in his emphasis on historical thinking and diversity he has been seen as the most influential of the thinkers who prepared the ground for the acceptance of evolutionary thought.[4] The weaknesses as well as the strengths of the *Ideen* would play their part in the development of the new science. Critics have remarked on the tension between Herder's naturalistic approach to the development of the cosmos and the teleological tendencies in his thought where, as Stephen Toulmin observes, "the Great Chain of Being, which up till then had been a timeless pattern of reality, acquires a time-dimension—the intellectual passage from 'lower' to 'higher' now reflects a succession from 'earlier' to 'later.'"[5] Herder accepts the doctrine that God created the universe, which he represents in vitalistic terms as a dynamic interplay of forces *(Kräfte)* in which mankind is progressing increasingly toward the goal of *Humanität:* a state of perfection in which all human powers will work in harmony.[6]

A similar search to effect a compromise between the old and the new would drive the debates on methodology that preceded the Darwinian revolution.

* * *

Buffon had been too much of an empiricist to speculate on the origins of the laws of life, but his work, read by nearly every educated European, was the major impetus behind the development of vitalism, which first appeared in the 1760s in scientific circles in England, France, and Germany as a reaction against the mechanistic explanations of natural phenomena extended to biological systems by Descartes and his followers. The vitalist approach to matter as force, power, and energy drew inspiration from the sciences of medicine and physiology of the time, especially Haller's research on muscular excitability, which could not be explained mechanically. Denis Diderot and other philosophes began to sketch out a picture of nature as an economy of dynamic forces, much more complex than Newton's laws and different in kind, that controlled the development of both living organisms and social systems. This rebellion against naive mechanistic explanations in science and philosophy marked the beginning of the Romantic Age, when writers, philosophers, and poets sought to restore a sense of unity linking the self, society, and nature that had existed before science had parted company with theology. New discoveries on the phenomena of magnetism, light, electricity, oxidation, and combustion were invoked to support the vitalistic concept of an invisible force, beyond the realm of chemico-physical laws, coursing through nature and man. With this notion the Romantics believed they had succeeded in overcoming Kant's barrier between empirical knowledge and the world of things-in-themselves. Building on Herder's work, German idealist philosophers preached a monistic vision of the universe in which matter and mind, spirit and nature, are not distinct kinds of entity but simply differing degrees of organization and development of an evolving organic whole, a single primal force or Absolute striving upward in a process of self-discovery, whose highest manifestation is achieved in human consciousness. This pantheistic vitalism was the basis of Schelling's *Naturphilosophie*, which in various forms would dominate the biological sciences in Germany for the first three decades of the nineteenth century, and which was the principal intellectual fashion among the Russian intelligentsia during Herzen's university years.

Despite differences in style and emphasis, the scientific proponents of *Naturphilosophie* shared a common view of the relation of theory to observation and experiment, based on the idealist doctrine that ideas and minds are the fundamental realities and that matter, the physical world, is governed by their laws. The primary method of science was therefore held to be speculative reasoning, whose aim was to apprehend the fundamental principles of reality from which those laws could be deduced. Because these deep truths were a priori, the role of experiment was not to validate them but rather to search for instances of their operation in nature.

The two key principles of a priori knowledge were held to be the existence of a first cause (variously designated by Schelling as God, the Absolute, or the World Soul) and unity of plan: all the processes of nature were interpreted as the unfolding of an initial purpose, the objectification of a pattern inherent in the original unity. The *Naturphilosophen* believed that the plant and animal kingdoms each developed as the metamorphoses of a primordial archetype; thus the comparative anatomist Lorenz Oken postulated a vertebrate archetype meant to represent the underlying unity of all animals with backbones.

The attempts of this movement to combine modern science with idealist metaphysics produced very mixed results. Oken's experimental contributions to comparative anatomy earned him a place in the history of biology and medicine, whereas an idealist approach to the growth of the embryo, as developed by a generation of German biologists from Caspar Wolff to K. E. von Baer, laid the foundation of modern embryology. However, the quality of their work was often vitiated by the impenetrable language in which it was expressed, their unconcern with empirical evidence that conflicted with their theories, and their overreliance on often far-fetched analogies as the basis of proof. Although they made contributions to evolutionary science, their notion of the development of nature as a purposive process generated by a spiritual reality, whose supreme manifestation was man, closed their minds to the process of discovery that began with Buffon's fascination with diversity and culminated with *On the Origin of Species.* It has been suggested that the excesses of Schelling and his followers might not have met with such enthusiasm in German intellectual circles had it not been for a general disillusionment with the desiccated vision of Newtonian science, with its mechanistic interpretation of complex organic phenomena.[7]

The development of *Naturphilosophie* initiated a new phase in the perennial debate about the proper relation of facts to hypotheses in science. Enlightenment philosophes had frequently attacked system building—"l'esprit de système"—as an obstacle to progress in knowledge; on the other hand, as Condillac put it, "Happy the man who has enough facts that he does not need to use his imagination." But the problem of methodology in natural science took on new religious and ethical dimensions when the question at issue was no longer the classification of data on structures and functions, the outward and visible signs that distinguished living things from each other, but the phenomenon of the development of life itself, including human life. In the new discipline of biology (the term was coined at the beginning of the 1800s),[8] experimental data did not point to any clear line of demarcation between the higher animals and man. This raised metaphysical issues of origins and purpose that many who had fought for the independence of science from theology were not eager to address. But was philosophical speculation not an essential component of scientific advance?

* * *

This question was central to a long-running dispute between Cuvier and his colleague Etienne Geoffroy Saint-Hilaire, a comparative anatomist of equal stature and the only eminent exponent of the *Naturphilosophie* in French scientific circles. In 1830 their differences culminated in a series of public confrontations before the Académie des Sciences. This battle between two of the leading scientists in France attracted enormous public interest, stimulated by Geoffroy's declaration that their disagreement was not about facts but about the "scientific appreciation" of facts. "It is a question of philosophy that divides us."[9] Waged over two months against the background of the turmoil in Paris that would culminate in revolution and the abdication of Charles X, the debate, seen widely as a clash between conservative and progressive attitudes to science, drew large and noisy crowds. Periodicals took sides in it according to their political allegiances, while the novelty of Geoffroy's synthetic approach and its affinities with the Romantic view of nature attracted a broad intellectual public, including the celebrated novelist, poet, and amateur naturalist Johann Wolfgang von Goethe, who declared the event more important than the 1830 revolution. Chapter 6 will show that interest in the debate was equally intense in Moscow University's Faculty of Physical and Mathematical Sciences, where Herzen's professors were deeply divided over the fundamental issues in scientific method that it raised: the relation of facts to theories and analysis to synthesis.

Geoffroy (1772–1844) was strongly influenced by the writings of the biologist Lorenz Oken and other German *Naturphilosophen*. Although he distanced himself from their mystical excesses (he himself was a deist), his philosophical or transcendental anatomy was highly speculative, based on a Platonic conception of animal form according to which all species were modifications of a single a priori plan or archetype. His theory of analogies (which had the merit of focusing on a new set of problems in comparative anatomy) held the same structure to be present in fish, reptiles, birds, and animals despite differences in appearances and milieu. Cuvier's public attack on the theory was the culmination of an unrelenting battle against the intrusion of metaphysical statements and searches for prime causes into scientific discourse. Observation and experiment, he insisted, were the sole legitimate methods in science. The introduction to the first volume of his eagerly awaited *Histoire naturelle des poissons* (1828) began with the sentence "L'histoire naturelle est une science des faits." The naturalist's role was not to formulate broad hypotheses and seek evidence to fit them but to gather "positive facts" (a favorite phrase of Cuvier's) through meticulously conducted experiments. Once sufficient facts were in place, the generalizations would follow self-evidently. Such an approach would seek an explanation for similarities of structure linking species, not in some transcendental reality, but as a pragmatic consequence of the limited options available to nature in a given set of conditions. Cuvier grouped together a number of speculative theories as products of "the imaginations of some naturalists [who are] more poets than observers."[10]

Among these he included his contemporary Jean-Baptiste Lamarck (commonly regarded as Darwin's most significant precursor), whose work Cuvier did his best to discredit. Yet Cuvier himself had contributed two of the essential prerequisites for the development of evolutionary biology through his demonstration of the existence of an extended geological timescale and his rejection of any notion of a *scala naturae* (a linear progression to increasing perfection in the natural world), his functional approach to the study of fossil strata having led him to postulate instead a treelike branching of species. He was nevertheless obdurately opposed to the notion of evolution through natural selection. The reasons for his opposition take us back to the nature of the revolution that had begun to ferment in European thought. As Ernst Mayr has remarked, the greatest obstacle to a general acceptance of a theory of evolution was the fact that evolution cannot be observed directly: unlike the phenomena of physics, it can only be inferred. But in order to draw inferences, one must start with an appropriate conceptual framework. The facts gleaned from the research by Cuvier and his colleagues could serve as evidence only once the occurrence of evolution was postulated. But the notion of evolution by natural selection ran counter to a perception of nature profoundly rooted in Western culture: "The Darwinian revolution has been called, for good reasons, the greatest of all scientific revolutions. It represented not merely the replacement of one scientific theory ('immutable species') by a new one, but it demanded a complete rethinking of man's concept of the world and of himself; more specifically, it demanded the rejection of some of the most widely held and most cherished beliefs of western man."[11]

As shown in Chapter 4, the increasing tensions in Enlightenment thought as a fascination with change and diversity began to conflict with the teleological visions of history and nature that had underpinned the values and ideals of Western thought for two millennia and continued to offer final certainties and eternal standards for knowledge, progress, and moral conduct. By the end of the eighteenth century the ancient belief in a static creation had given way to a general acceptance that humans live in a constantly changing universe. But as one commentator has observed, whereas religious and philosophical preoccupations had become much less evident, they had not disappeared—they had been incorporated in scientific reasoning. "At the beginning of the century everybody spoke of God; at the end everybody spoke of Nature."[12] Thus Herder treats the appearance of mankind on earth as the final fulfillment of the purposes of "Mother Nature." Theology metamorphosed into teleology as scientists, historians, and philosophers sought to present change and development in the natural and social world as the unfolding of an initial design.

A striking example of this development is Kant's contribution to cosmology, *On the General History of Nature and Theory of the Heavens* (1755), the first systematic exposition of the idea that the universe as a whole had developed from initial chaos. Kant presents its dynamic evolution through the destruction and creation of whole worlds as the unfolding through time of nature's plan as designed by "the great Architect of the Universe." But that this plan could include the transmutation of species Kant regarded as a "monstrous" idea. Even Buffon's groundbreaking conception of open-ended evolutionary change had not envisaged this possibility. The notion of an ascending scale of perfection culminating in man was too deeply rooted in Western religion, philosophy, and ethics for such an idea to seem credible. As Arthur Lovejoy has remarked: "Next to the word 'Nature,' 'the Great Chain of Being' was the sacred phrase of the eighteenth century."[13] But the Enlightenment's faith in steady progress (a temporalized version of the *scala naturae*) sat uneasily with the new historicism's teaching that each historical period is a unique structure corresponding in its own way to the human needs and aspirations of a specific time and place. As more became known about diversity, the notion of a universal and unchanging human nature became less convincing. Yet, as the massive resistance to Darwin's theories would show, even the most distinguished natural scientists of the time were not prepared to think the unthinkable: that all life forms had evolved through the agency of blind chance.

* * *

The case of Cuvier is of special interest as an outstanding example of the mentality with which Herzen would engage in his investigations of the fear of chance. Cuvier's theory of the branching of species, together with his demonstration of the existence of an extended geological timescale, provided for the first time a solid framework within which an evolutionary biology could develop. But he used the full weight of his scientific and administrative eminence (he was at various times inspector of public instruction, secretary of the Académie, and member of the Conseil d'État) to discredit attempts to interpret fossil data as support for a theory of organic transmutation—the first step toward a theory of evolution.

Cuvier's hostility to evolutionism is the more curious in view of his carefully cultivated image as a radical innovator. An accomplished self-publicist, he portrayed himself as "a new species of antiquarian": "I shall try to travel a road on which only a few steps have so far been ventured."[14] But there was one boundary that this intrepid pathfinder refused to cross. He presented himself as an observer who would go no further than the facts would allow; but he was also religiously conservative, and while he regarded the question of the creation of the world and the origin of man as mysteries outside the domain of science, he held that there could be no fundamental contradictions between true science and religious belief. He was committed to the idea of a fixed creation in which divine wisdom had assigned each species its place in the economy of nature, harmoniously interrelating animals with their environments. This would seem hard to reconcile with the fact of extinction, which he himself had primarily established by uncovering the fossil remains of all kinds of creatures no longer in existence, but he resolved the problem by positing periodic interventions by the Creator to tweak the workings of the overall design. He acknowledged the influence of climate, nutriment, and competition for resources in producing frequent changes in the equilibrium of the whole, including variations within species, but only within strict limits, permitting only such developments as would produce no essential change in the plan itself. He was opposed unconditionally to any suggestion that the physical environment or competition in the organic world could be causal factors in the transmutation of species. Like geological catastrophes that threatened whole species, competition destroyed creatures but could not create them. In the words of one of his biographers, "immutability was the essence of his doctrine"; he conceived of competition as "more a salubrious world-wide sanitary mechanism than a natural force leading to the emergence of new zoological forms."[15] Having postulated a lawful universe from which chance was excluded, Cuvier was forced to reject all interpretations of his data that could lead to a contrary conclusion. When some naturalists interpreted the existence of vestigial organs as indicating the beginning of transformation of one part into another or the remains of some previously developed organ, he retorted that these organs had some purpose of which we were ignorant. No law could "compel the Creator unnecessarily to produce useless forms."[16] In the entry for "Nature" in his *Dictionnaire des sciences naturelles* of 1825 he writes: "In considering the phenomena of nature in regard to their basic and universal cause . . . we also see how puerile are the philosophers who have given nature a kind of individual existence, distinct from the Creator and from the properties or forces that he has given to the creatures."[17] The tensions in Cuvier's thought reflect two very disparate influences on his early development: the systematizing approach of Linnaeus, concerned to reveal the structure of a timeless order, and Buffon's focus on diversity, process, and change. In our context he is significant as a transitional figure, a fainthearted explorer who aborted his journey when it required him to leave his familiar baggage behind. J. C. Greene puts it thus:

> In short, Cuvier was attempting the impossible task of reconciling two conflicting views of Nature. . . . In one, the particular forms exhibited in organic nature were derived from the initial blueprint of Creation; in the other, they resulted from the interactions of material bodies. In one, the conditions of existence were final causes, expressing the pre-established harmony of all created things; in the other, they were the changing configurations of the environment to which organic forms must adapt in order to survive. In one, the variety of the world was a necessary expression of divine creativity;

in the other it was the necessary product of the motions of matter in infinite time and space. That Cuvier was able to make these views seem compatible testified both to the greatness of his prestige and to the strength of the contemporary demand that the new science be reconciled with the traditional view of Nature.[18]

Another critic notes that while naturalists and geologists of the early nineteenth century made revolutionary progress in understanding how life had developed in the course of the earth's history, there were limits to how far they could go in explaining *why* the process had taken this path. It was acceptable to posit the development of evolution through a supernatural agency, or through the unfolding of a rationally ordered process aimed at producing nature's highest type—man (a notion that could coexist comfortably enough with the traditional belief in divine creation): "The one thing that no one wanted to contemplate was evolution brought about solely by everyday laws of Nature, a process all too easy to divorce from any form of teleology."[19]

* * *

Cuvier's enormous academic and political influence accounts for what has been termed the conspiracy of silence in nineteenth-century France toward theories that challenged biological and methodological orthodoxy.[20] Geoffroy's eminence as Cuvier's chief scientific rival made him an exception to this rule. Jean-Baptiste Lamarck (1744–1829), a professor of invertebrate zoology whose scientific career had begun under Buffon's patronage, was not so fortunate.

Lamarck admitted no metaphysical a priori on the origin of life. Adhering strictly to the view of eighteenth-century philosophes on the limits to knowledge imposed by the human mind, he built directly on Buffon's methodological revolution, emphasizing the nature of life as a physical fact, best studied through observation of living organisms in their interaction with and adaptation to their environment.

Lamarck's acute sensitivity to the complexity of this process has been seen as the source of many of his most original insights.[21] To develop his knowledge of the physical circumstances of life, he undertook an astonishingly wide range of studies in the disciplines of zoology, botany, chemistry, geology, meteorology, mineralogy, and astronomy. His specialization in the zoology of invertebrates, combined with his empirical studies of the earth and its atmosphere, convinced him of the development of life through infinite variations and almost infinitesimal changes over vast periods of time. The mutability of species became the basis of his approach to natural history.

Cuvier maintained that all species currently populating the earth had existed since the creation. Lamarck replaced the notion of an initial plan of nature with a hypothesis that new types and levels of existence developed from primitive beginnings as ad hoc responses to the experienced needs of living creatures and their struggle to survive amid changing circumstances.

He shared Cuvier's theory of a branching development in which no individual species could be seen as a goal, or be evaluated by the criteria of another. But he went much further in rejecting all teleological interpretations of nature, emphasizing the role of accidental environmental events in producing unexpected deviations in the development of organic forms. The history of nature was open-ended, and the earth was in a perpetual state of change, the outcome of which was impossible to predict with any certainty—hence the importance of collecting empirical data on the earth and its atmosphere.[22]

Three decades after Lamarck's death, Darwin's assumption that the variation on which natural selection operates is random would arouse a storm of horrified protest. But Lamarck had already anticipated him in his *Philosophie zoologique* of 1809, where he seeks to demonstrate that the characteristics hitherto deemed unique to the human race had evolved through the gradual historical development of organisms—that man in both his mental and physical aspects was not a special creation, but like other animals a product of time and chance. But no one else was yet prepared to confront the unthinkable. In the first half of the nineteenth century, geologists and naturalists such as Agassiz in Switzerland and Lyell in England were able to trace in ever-increasing detail the development of life on earth, but common to them all was the belief in some teleological process, whether rational or religious, from which had emerged its supreme creation: man.[23]

Lamarck was too far ahead of his time to gain recognition for the boldness and originality of his ideas. He saw himself as a philosopher, but his critics had no difficulty in pointing to inconsistencies in his thought, and his dream of an amalgamation of the sciences made him vulnerable to accusations of dealing in groundless abstractions.[24] In a condescending eulogy after his death in 1829, Cuvier dismissed La-marck's ideas as fanciful speculation. Yet they had fired the imagina-tion of a young professor of natural science at Moscow University, who began in that same year to transmit them to an exceptionally prom-ising new student: the seventeen-year-old Herzen.

CHAPTER SIX

An Education in Method

The speculative information that constitutes philosophy is possible only with the existence of the empirical data of which science is composed.

M. G. PAVLOV

WRITING in the 1860s, the historian and sociologist of science A. P. Shchapov describes the limits imposed on the teaching and study of science in Russia by the censorship decree of 1826: "A special category of 'unpublishable' books was created in the general field of Russian science and literature. . . . In the natural sciences, for example, 'unpublishable' were the treatments of the physical formation of the earth, geological eras, the origin of species, the antiquity of man, Neanderthal and other human fossils, the place of man in the organic world and his natural-historical and organic relations to apes, the importance of force and matter in nature, the physico-chemical and mechanistic explanations of nervous energy (and particularly of human mentality), reflexes of the brain, the psychopathic nature of mysticism, and many other topics."[1] Designed to protect Russian society from infection by evolutionist trends in all scientific disciplines, the decree was a belated effort to reverse an irreversible tide. As we have seen, from the late eighteenth century progressive Russians had used the new historical orientation in science to support their challenge to the political and religious status quo. Even under the tyrannical regime of Nicolas I the authorities' efforts to stem the flow of subversive ideas into Russia had limited success. The universities were starved of resources; on the other hand, the expansion of the sciences and their differentiation into semi-independent disciplines (the only one of Alexander I's university reforms to continue into the next reign) had created a core of specialist teachers closely acquainted with the latest developments in their areas, and possessing the determination, boldness, and ingenuity to circumvent the censorship in passing these on to their students.

The best Russian scientists in the 1820s and 1830s keenly followed advances in the West in the fields of historical geology, paleontology, and comparative anatomy and the debates of European anatomists over methodology and its philosophical premises. Herzen's cousin Tatiana Passek records that he told her that all the professors in his faculty were either "for or against the *Naturphilosophie*."[2] Apart from the Schellingians, who recognized the historical development of nature but gave it a vitalistic and unitary interpretation, there were two other main philosophical orientations among Moscow natural scientists, the first most notably represented by Yu. E. Dyadkovsky (1784–1841), a professor of medicine who combined a materialist philosophy with evolutionary ideas influenced by Buffon and Lamarck.[3] The second was led by I. A. Dvigubsky, portrayed in Herzen's memoirs as a relic of the past who in his capacity as rector treated him rudely when he came before him on a disciplinary offense. In fact Dvigubsky was scientifically well abreast of his time, as the editor of an important periodical, the *New Store of Natural History, Physics, Chemistry, and Economic Knowledge*, which kept a wide public up to date with the latest significant developments in science, such as Lamarck's biological transformism, Faraday's experiments in electromagnetic induction, Oersted's theories in the field of electricity, and Biot's observations on the polarization of light. His own view of change in nature had been strongly influenced by Buffon and by Caspar Wolff, whose studies of plant metamorphosis had contributed to the development of evolutionary theory.

Opposed to all the above were the narrow empiricists whose Cuvierian approach to natural history as a science of facts patiently gathered in the field produced valuable data on natural phenomena. Herzen attended the lectures of the leading figure in this group, G. I. Fischer von Waldheim, professor of zoology, and gives him some guarded praise as a "good-natured and learned" member of the faculty's German contingent.[4]

Herzen's memoirs convey the impression that the spirit of intellectual daring characteristic of the best scientists in the West had a very limited impact on Moscow University. He does, however, mention Dyadkovsky, who "probably had a good influence on the students."[5] From this single laconic phrase one could not guess that this was a figure well known to Herzen, a friend of the radical critic Belinsky, and respected by the progressive intelligentsia for his fearless expression of scientific views contrary to the orthodoxies of church and state. One of the first academics in Russia to take up the ideas of Buffon and Lamarck on the influence of environmental factors in the development of species, he defended the experimental approach as the sole path to the knowledge of nature. The founder of an entire school of thought in the Faculty of Medicine, he was dismissed from his post in the year after Herzen's graduation, on grounds of atheism. Herzen cannot have been unaware of Dyadkovsky's courage and his fate, but there was no place for either one in the artistic conception of *My Past and Thoughts*.

* * *

All these professors contributed their share to the lessons in scientific method that Herzen was to rate higher than any sum of knowledge. But he singled out two in particular for their formative influence on his thought. The first was M. G. Pavlov, whose contribution to the development of scientific thought in Russia has been obscured by Western commentators who have presented him as a mere mouthpiece for the *Naturphilosophie*.[6] A brilliant polemicist and popularizer, whose writings on the nature of knowledge addressed a broad intellectual public, he deserves more than just a footnote in histories of Russian thought. After finishing his studies in a seminary in Voronezh, he had transferred to Moscow University, where he graduated from two faculties, physical-mathematical and medical, awarded a gold medal by the first and a silver by the second. He subsequently received the title of doctor of medicine for a dissertation in Latin on embryology, and was sent abroad by the university to perfect his training in natural history and agronomy. On his return to Russia he was elected to the chair of mineralogy and animal husbandry, and from 1827 he was in charge of courses in agriculture and physics and directed an experimental farm. The textbooks he authored on agriculture established him as the founder of agricultural theory in Russia.

This polymath's lectures attracted huge audiences, both in the university and from a wider public. His range of intellectual and practical competences gave him a unique perspective on the problem central to the scientific debates of the time: the relation of philosophy to science and of theory to experiment (he was simultaneously editor of the *Russian Farmer* and the *Atheneum*, one of the periodicals that sprang up in the 1820s as the principal channels for the discussion of critical thought (although always under the ever-watchful eye of the censorship). With a sharp nose for empty rhetoric and meaningless abstractions, he demolished fashionable beliefs and dogmas with the aim of forcing his readers to think for themselves. He cannot in the usual sense be called an exponent of the *Naturphilosophie*.

Of the four Russian scientists commonly cited as the main purveyors of Schelling's philosophy in their lectures at that period, only D. M. Vellansky, who had been a pupil of Schelling and was a friend of Oken, can be regarded as a true disciple.[7] Pavlov, along with A. I. Galich and I. I. Davydov, was more selective in his borrowing, looking to Schelling's vitalistic metaphysics for what the mechanistic approach of Newtonian physics could not provide: a scientifically credible and philosophically satisfying framework in which to situate the recent discoveries in chemistry, physiology, and developmental biology concerning the processes of organic nature. In 1824 he had contributed an article, "Methods of Investigating Nature," to the Wisdom Lovers' periodical *Mnemosyne*, but the post-Decembrist generation's infatuation with *Naturphilosophie* as the answer to all questions led him to regard its claim to provide an all-embracing explanation of the nature of reality as a negative factor in the development of science. The mentality that disturbed him is well portrayed in the memoirs of one of the founding members of the Wisdom Lovers, Prince V. Odoevsky:

> My youth belongs to that period when metaphysics formed the basis of our spiritual atmosphere, as later would do the social sciences. We believed in the possibility of a general theory with the help of which it would be possible to reconstruct all the phenomena of nature, just as in the present day one believes in the possibility of a social life which would satisfy all the needs of man. However that may be, at that period nature in its entirety, along with human life, seemed fairly clear to us, and it was not without condescension that we regarded physicists, chemists and utilitarians who wallowed in brute matter. Among the natural sciences only one seemed worthy of the attention of a "philosopher": anatomy, the science of man. . . . Anatomy led us to physiology, a science still in its beginnings, of

which the first fruitful seeds appeared in Schelling, later in Oken and Carus. But in physiology we met at every step questions that were insoluble without the help of physics and chemistry, and on the other hand, much in Schelling seemed obscure to those unacquainted with the natural sciences. Thus proud metaphysicians were led to the necessity of surrounding themselves with alembics and all sorts of instruments indispensable to the study of brute matter.[8]

The attitude of such would-be scientists to their discipline is conveyed in another memoir by a pupil of Vellansky: "The ideas of the natural school [*Naturphilosophie*] . . . tended to muddle the minds of young people who were rather ill-prepared to receive them. With no knowledge of the natural sciences, these young people launched themselves into speculative fantasies, believing that they had attained the heights of knowledge by applying to everything the principles of German philosophy and intoxicating themselves with words."[9] In 1828 Pavlov exposed the pretensions of these young metaphysicians in the *Atheneum* through a satirical commentary in the form of philosophical dialogues between an eager disciple and a teacher of the "new wisdom" that, unlike the old, "resolves everything, explains everything, and leaves nothing in doubt,"[10] answering by a few propositions the questions that had preoccupied minds throughout the centuries and led to the multiplication of university faculties. His elegant satire on the vocabulary and content of Russian Schellingian discourse was not well received by an intelligentsia infatuated with German idealism, and Pavlov was forced to justify himself to his indignant critics in a subsequent issue of his journal by stressing the urgency of the problem he was trying to highlight. The passage that follows gives a flavor of the verbal style for which he was renowned:

A few years ago, certain youths with literary tastes revived the affectation of parading philosophical terms whose meaning they themselves did not understand. . . . The capricious fashion for amusement whispered now to one, now to another: this is the new philosophy! From that time the rights of common sense lost their hold and nonsense was glorified. Whole treatises appeared in Russian, which Russians themselves approached as newly discovered hieroglyphs. . . . Credulous people thought that they could detect in this impenetrable darkness the dawn of a new Enlightenment, and having previously studied nothing, began aloud to make trenchant judgments about all the sciences, concealing the paucity of their knowledge with loud words. Subject, object, infinite, finite, deductive, productive, Absolute, ideas, manifestations, echoed in all ears . . . irrespective of their relevance. Did you want to reduce someone to silence or crush them with criticism? You had only to say: that's antiquated, outdated, won't stand up to philosophical scrutiny, is not in the spirit of the new philosophy; adding a few words, such as synthetic, analytical, the higher speculation—and one's opponent has to retreat for fear of re-vealing himself as a latecomer in the field of science, were he to ven-ture to cast doubt on the nonsense arrayed in the dignity of the new philosophy.[11]

Pavlov declared his determination to combat this trend, which threat-ened to submerge Russian literature and science in "absolute darkness." His own philosophical position is summed up by a dissident voice intervening in the dialogues:

The subjects of our knowledge—that is, all that we can comprehend— are simultaneously the subjects of the sciences and philosophy, but with an enormous difference. In the sciences they are described and portrayed; in philosophy they are constructed. In philosophy their genesis is investigated. In the sciences we inform ourselves about everything that exists. In philosophy we explain how what ex-ists could have come into being. . . . Hence the empirical informa-tion that constitutes the sciences must precede philosophy: a truth that it is useful to repeat.[12]

"Science without philosophy is by no means devoid of value, but phi-losophy without science is impossible."[13] In defending empirical science with its doubts, conjectures, hypotheses, and errors, Pavlov attempted to stake out a middle position between the extremes of empiricism and idealism that dominated debates on scientific methodology. In this he was strongly influenced by the contemporary French philosopher Victor Cousin, a gifted orator whose lectures at the École Normale and the Sorbonne had made him a cult figure in Parisian intellectual circles. To the first postrevolutionary generation, in intellectual ferment after Napoleon's fall and the first years of the Restoration, his teaching seemed to offer an approach to reality that could replace the materi-alism and destructive skepticism of the eighteenth century without reverting to traditional religious beliefs. His declared aim was to reform philosophical studies in France through a method that he claimed was rigorously experimental, based on the physical sciences. In the rationalist tradition, he held reason to be fundamental to the structure of the natural world (the operation of its universal laws, discoverable through the human mind, being the source of our knowledge of humans and nature), but he sought to combine speculation with empiricism in an historicist approach to philosophical validity, arguing that the principal systems of Western philosophy, which he divided into four categories (sensationalism, idealism, skepticism, and mysticism), had all been incomplete, each neglecting one or more of the distinct but complementary capacities of human nature: will, sensibility, and reason. He claimed to have laid the foundations of a new philosophy—a "vast and powerful eclecticism"—that would harmonize in a philosophical unity all the truths embedded in previous schools of thought.[14]

Strong on rhetoric but vague in content, Cousin's philosophy of eclecticism was not highly regarded by professional philosophers, and his fame did not outlive him. In Russia in the 1820s and 1830s he was known in literary and philosophical circles as an interpreter and popularizer of German idealism, but Pavlov, who had attended his lectures in Paris, approached him from a different perspective, as an ally in his defense of the rights of empirical methods in science against the onslaught of the "new wisdom." He sought to call the Russian public's attention to the originality of Cousin's thought by publishing two of his articles on the history of philosophy in successive issues of the *Atheneum*.

The critical spirit that drew Pavlov to Cousin's ideas was his chief attraction for Herzen, as is evident from one of the few positive remarks in Herzen's memoirs on the teaching in his faculty. Commenting on its general meagerness, he adds this caveat: "It's not the function of a university, however, to give a complete training in any branch of knowledge; its business is to put a person in a position to continue to study on his own account; its work is to provoke inquiry, to teach people to ask questions. And this was certainly done by professors such as M. G. Pavlov."[15] He took a tolerant view of the fact that Pavlov's emphasis on experimental science was not conspicuously reflected in his teaching: his two-volume work *The Foundations of Physics* (1833–1836), while trenchantly critical of Oken's disregard for experimental data, was it-self more a philosophical exposition of an organicist vision of nature than a guide to the practice of physical science.[16] As Herzen remarked, it would have been difficult to learn any physics from his lectures: they were an introduction to philosophy, and extremely instructive as such.[17] Pavlov aimed to promote genuine philosophical culture in Russia by exposing the deceptions of its counterfeit version. He brought to his reflections on scientific method an intellectual independence that was rare at the height of the Russian intelligentsia's intoxication with German thought. In a tribute on his death in 1840 the biologist K. F. Rouillier, the most eminent of Russia's pre-Darwinian evolutionists, remarked: "Independence in opinions and actions, fixity of purpose in his undertakings were the distinguishing traits of his character. . . . With qualities like these there was no chance that Pavlov would have joined in the worship of some foreign celebrity."[18]

* * *

Another teacher, Mikhail Alexandrovich Maximovich (1804–1873), was an equally powerful influence on Herzen's intellectual development but is mentioned nowhere in the memoirs. Yet a reference in one of Herzen's few surviving letters points to a special relationship with this professor, whom alone he exempts from his bitter condemnation of the faculty for failing to award him its gold medal on graduation: *"Pereat academia! pereant professores!* I'll keep in touch only with Maximovich."[19]

When not entirely overlooked by Herzen's biographers, Maximovich has been given a passing mention as a former pupil of Pavlov, whom he is said to have assisted subsequently as a purveyor of Schelling's phi-losophy in his faculty[20]—a curious misrepresentation of one of the most independent-minded and iconoclastic scientists in Russia in his time, a follower of Lamarck in his anticipation of the Darwinian revolution.

Born into an old but impoverished Ukrainian Cossack family, Max-imovich entered Moscow University's philological faculty in 1818, moving two years later to the Faculty of Natural Sciences, from which he graduated in 1823. He taught at the university until 1834. Appointed head of its botanical garden and herbarium, he devoted two years to the study of the flora of the Moscow district and was the first to list the plants of the region. In 1827 he began teaching a course in botany. His position was precarious, and only in 1833 was he given a long-promised chair. He attributed his humiliations and financial struggles of the intervening years to the fact that he was not German: that nationality still dominated the teaching of science in the university. In 1834, the year after Herzen's graduation, he returned to his native Ukraine, beginning a second academic career at the new University of Kiev, initially as its rector, where he devoted himself to the teaching and study of philology, archaeology, history, and Ukrainian folklore and ethnography.

Although he had worked in the natural sciences for only eleven years, over this period he wrote more than 100 scientific works, 58 on botany, 14 on zoology; the remainder were popularizing works on natural science and general scientific questions. The brilliance and originality of his thought, the breadth of his interests, and his talent for popular exposition made him a widely known figure among the Russian intelligentsia of the first half of the nineteenth century; he was a friend of Pushkin, Gogol, and later Taras Shevchenko.

As a student he was initiated into *Naturphilosophie* by Pavlov, who simultaneously encouraged him to militate against its excesses by convincing him of the key importance of experimental methods in science, a view that, like his teacher, he conveyed to a wide public through the popular journals of the time. Thus he used a review of a book on the principles of agriculture to dismiss all theories untested by experiment as a mere "play of the imagination."[21] Speculative theories in science should be generalizations from the data of experience, not the fruit of pure contemplation on the nature of the self. In his master's thesis in the following year (1827), he stated categorically: "We know nature a posteriori," remarking in a critique of Oken's views: "Oken attempted not so much to present nature in his system as to illustrate his system by means of nature."[22]

The influence of the materialist Dyadkovsky, a colleague who became a close friend, led him to a categorical rejection of the role of speculative philosophy in scientific method. In the fervor of his campaign against idealism the young scientist turned on his former mentor, accusing Pavlov in an article of 1828 of a predilection for metaphysics that had led him close to the antiscientific views of Oken and Schelling, whose transcendent philosophy was "a brilliant hypothesis, a poetic view of nature, but not science." To reduce physics to pure speculation, he fulminates, "is to turn it into astrology, magic, and alchemy, whose deceit, secreted in the darkness of ignorance, is revealed by the light of science."[23] Entitled "On the Physics of the *Atheneum*," Maximovich's unmerited attack appeared shortly after the publication of Pavlov's critique of idealism in that journal; clearly his young colleague felt that it had not gone far enough.

Maximovich's own philosophical position, which seemed to rest on a fuzzy distinction between matter and force, was far from consistent,[24] but his hostility to *Naturphilosophie* was unwavering. In the journal *Telescope* in 1831 he takes issue with Schelling's view that all concrete phenomena are determined by the idea of nature: "By equating the universe with the Absolute . . . , Schelling falls into pantheism. Insofar as he recognizes only the Absolute as real, he comes to see everything finite as relative and insignificant, everything individual as a mere specter."[25]

Central to Maximovich's work on botany was the problem of formulating a scientific approach to questions of systematization in the plant world. He criticized Linnaeus's system for its artificiality, accused the partisans of *Naturphilosophie* of trying to force the variety of nature into a model of unity that was a construct of the human mind, and rebuked the taxonomist Jussieu for attempting to represent all of nature in an uninterrupted ascent from lowest to highest. "The plant kingdom cannot be arranged in a single line. All the intermediate links in the chain have not and cannot be found. Such a linear progression has hitherto never been found and of course never will."[26] He dismissed the creationists' interpretation of all deviations of organisms from their type as forms of degeneration: "Inasmuch as variety includes not only chance and transient forms, but also forms that are defined, consistent, even inherited, one can't call this degeneration."[27] These objections echo the basic position then being developed by Lamarck, asserting the direct effect of external conditions on the mutability of species. Maximovich was one of a small minority of scientists at that time to accept this thesis. An article of 1823 shows that in Lamarck's work, focusing on the relations between plants and their physiology in the context of the development of the entire plant world, Maximovich had found the basis of the system which he sought—one that "would present the plant world as it exists in nature itself,"[28] although he found fault with Lamarck's definition of a species, which he saw as an abstraction introduced for ease of classification, with no real basis in nature.

Maximovich produced no original theories of his own about the mutability of species, but his works were widely known and cited even outside Russia and used as textbooks by generations of Russian students. Writing to him in 1871 in the light of the great flowering of the natural sciences in Russia, for which Moscow University had done so much to prepare the ground in the first half of the century, the eminent Russian geologist G. E. Shchurovsky (who had then himself been a leader in research and the dissemination of science and can be numbered among Darwin's predecessors) described his works as "truly the most significant phenomenon of that time."[29] His greatest contribution was as a brilliant popularizer of the ideas that were transforming man's vision of nature. Numerous references to his scientific writings of the 1820s and 1830s show how eagerly they were read by the educated public. But he wrote also for a wider audience: his book on nature for the popular masses, described by the radical critic Belinsky as a "singular and remarkable attempt," went into eleven editions.[30] He took his popularizing role with immense seriousness, writing in 1832: "In the interests of Russia's intellectual enlightenment, special attention must be paid to the propagation of positive knowledge and its application to the benefit of social and individual life. The primary and stable basis of a complete system of sciences, in my opinion, must be the cognition of nature."[31] He played his part by exposing the weakness of scientific system building, undermining the theological and metaphysical preconceptions that continued to obscure the origin of species, and drawing the attention of his compatriots to the maverick French scientist who had dared to express the unthinkable. He shared Lamarck's passionate conviction that close observation of the processes and interactions of living nature must be the starting point of all theorizing, and like Lamarck prepared himself for this by a wide range of studies in medicine, chemistry, physics, and other sciences, "finding

M. A. Maximovich, professor of Natural Sciences at Moscow University.

this essential for the full knowledge of natural science," as he explains in his autobiography.[32]

* * *

Maximovich's doctoral dissertation of 1827, "On the Systems of the Plant World," reflected his awareness of the methodological issues raised by the need to investigate what Lamarck called "the power of life" without enclosing it in an artificial system of ultimate ends and purposes. Herzen's admiration of this work is expressed in a letter of

1832 to a friend to whom he is sending a copy, urging him to read "this most elegant of this world's creations: philosophical in orientation, with a noble notion of . . . the natural sciences."[33]

Herzen's preoccupation with the role of methodology in science (the central theme of his surviving student writings) reflects his debt to both of his teachers. But his receptiveness to their ideas owed much to the fact that he had arrived at the university already equipped with the knowledge that allowed him to engage with the methodological problems thrown up by the new discoveries in biology at a level of sophistication that could have been equaled by few students of his generation in Russia or anywhere else.

Here we must return to the episode in his memoirs where he describes the awakening of his passion for science: his acquaintance with his eccentric cousin, the Chemist. A convinced materialist and empiricist, the Chemist regarded all philosophy as twaddle, maintaining that the impulses of humans were "all a matter of organization, circumstances, and the condition of the nervous system in general."[34]

Skimming through the half-dozen pages devoted to their meetings, one may get the impression of an elderly, misanthropic, and deeply conservative curmudgeon, too faithful to the notions that were fashionable in his youth to accept any newfangled ideas. Such is Malia's interpretation: according to him, the young Herzen was already far too enthused by Schelling's idealism to allow himself to be swayed by a view of the universe founded on the materialism of eighteenth-century France; his long discussions with the Chemist merely provided an added incentive to pursue the study of nature, which, in true idealist fashion, he conceived in pantheistic terms.[35]

But a reading of these pages in the light of the debates taking place in France at that time leads to a different conclusion. The Chemist was certainly a curmudgeon (Herzen describes him as a second edition of his own misanthropic father), but he was not elderly—he would have been no more than thirty when the fifteen-year-old Herzen made his acquaintance. As to his ideas, Herzen makes the point that his cousin's materialism was not "the superficial and timid Voltairianism of our fathers," but the product of a different age and a different education.[36] Herzen's readers of the time would have known immediately how to place the Chemist's views from the names that follow: He held

Geoffroy Saint-Hilaire to be a mystic and Oken to be simply deranged; he lent Herzen works by Cuvier and the Swiss botanist Augustin Pyrame de Candolle, one of the creators of botanical geography.

The Chemist's fascination with the natural world "from the rocks to the orangutan," which so attracted Herzen, was scientifically wholly up to date, if emphatically *parti pris* in the current French debate on methodology. Although shocked by his materialism, Herzen was impressed by his learning and his wit; in turn the Chemist put at Herzen's disposal "his excellent collections, apparatus, herbariums, and even his guidance."[37] Thus Herzen was initiated into the discoveries by botanists, mineralogists, and anatomists on the development of life on earth that were leading toward a new vision of time and history.

He mentions that the Chemist lent him a work by Cuvier, which can be identified as the *Discours préliminaire* of 1812, where he defends the new sciences of geology and paleontology from attack by theological opinion, arguing that their epistemological independence has resulted in a new understanding of the world and humanity's place in it, linking natural and human history together in an uninterrupted chain. Man can now set out on the unaided discovery of the immense history of life: "He will have the glory of reconstructing the history of thousands of centuries before his appearance and thousands of beings that the human race has never seen!" Setting out his claim to originality, Cuvier (who liked to call himself not a natural historian but a historian *tout court*) presents his pioneering work on fossils in heroic and poetic terms:

> I shall try . . . to make known a kind of monument that is almost always neglected, although it is indispensable for the history of the globe.
>   . . . I have had to learn to decipher and restore those monuments, and to recognize and reassemble in their original order the scattered and mutilated fragments of which they are composed; to reconstruct the ancient beings to which these fragments belonged; to reproduce them in their proportions and characters; and finally to compare them to those that live today at the earth's surface. This is an almost unknown art; and it presupposes a science hardly touched on hitherto. . . . An almost general review of the present creation has given me a great collection of rules and relationships, with the result that the whole animal kingdom is revealed as subject to new laws.[38]

The argument that there was no sharp break between the development of nature and the development of our species would be a central theme of Herzen's writings on history. He would have already been familiar, if only from secondary sources, with *Naturphilosophie*'s organic vision of the universe, in which nature and mind are different aspects of an "absolute Identity," an evolving whole. But it is likely that Cuvier's *Discours* was Herzen's first direct encounter with the experimental approach that was disengaging the notion of evolution from theological and metaphysical a prioris. Imbued with the mystique of the Decembrists and the French Revolution and devoted to a cult of the heroes of Schiller's dramas, he had been on course to read history and literature at the university when he developed what he describes as his "great passion" for the natural sciences. It is not too fanciful to suppose that the *Discours* played some role in this, by showing him that poetry, revolution, and the heroism of the forerunner blasting out new paths for humanity could also be found in science, and, perhaps most important, that the disciplines of natural science and history were inextricably bound together.

That the practical implications of man's relationship with the natural world had begun to occupy Herzen's thoughts even before he began his university studies is evident from his first publications, early in 1829: translations in a scientific journal of two articles by a French epidemiologist—the first on the causes of plagues and the second on mummification of corpses in the ancient world as a protective measure against the spread of disease. Unlike the more senior contributors, he was identified only by initials, the editor introducing him as "a young enthusiast for the natural sciences."[39] In the following year Herzen would publish in Pavlov's *Atheneum* another translation from the French: an historical survey of earthquakes. In his mature writings he would cite the unpredictability of such natural disasters and their effects against the theorists of historical inevitability.

The continuity in Herzen's thought is evidenced by the title of his first surviving university essay (also his first known philosophical writing), completed in December 1832: "On Man's Place in Nature." It shows a wide acquaintance with the most advanced contemporary work in the emerging field of evolutionary thought: Cuvier, Geoffroy Saint-Hilaire, Oken, Erasmus Darwin, the creator of paleobotany Alexandre Brongniart, and Augustin Pyrame de Candolle (a chapter of whose pioneering work of 1827, *L'Organographie des plantes*, Herzen translated for publication in Dvigubsky's journal). He shows himself equally familiar with the history of the natural sciences from Bacon to Linnaeus and Buffon.

Herzen draws on this knowledge for the background to his subject: the battles between contending theories that accompanied the development of the natural sciences. The essay starts off with a pious recitation of the officially approved version of the creation, placing humans above the natural and animal world as the image and likeness of their Creator, set down on earth to understand and praise his works. One may assume that, like the ritualistic bow to the founders of Marxism-Leninism in Soviet academic works, this was a form of insurance against possible future accusations, as it is unconnected with the argument that follows. This reflects the influence of both Herzen's teachers (it contains a note of acknowledgment for a felicitous phrase borrowed from Maximovich, for whom it was probably written as an exercise), but above all it bears witness to Pavlov's success in infecting his pupil with his enthusiasm for the philosophy of Victor Cousin. "Why these endless errors, false theories and systems?" Herzen asks: "Because of incompleteness, insufficiency in method." (In a draft version of the essay, he gives Cousin credit for this view, adding his agreement.)[40] The universe is composed of two principles: idea and form, inner and outer, soul and body, indissolubly fused in reality but artificially separated by human thought, which has tended to gravitate to one or the other, to "drown in the ideal or lose itself in the real"—extremes expressed in the modern age by Descartes's speculative method versus the crude materialism of some natural scientists. In the preceding two centuries thought had moved from one extreme to another, "often flooding its path with blood." The process had reached its climax in the eighteenth century, when destructive analysis in the sphere of thought had culminated in the violence of the Revolution. Out of sheer exhaustion, mankind, "perceiving the inadequacy of all exclusive theories, has demanded the synthesis of opposites": a succinct summary of the current mood of that part of humanity for whom Herzen could speak with some authority—those European intellectuals whose hopes for the dawn of a new age, raised by the Revolution and dashed by the Terror, were now concentrated on idealist philosophy with its promise of the ultimate resolution of all conflict and dissonance. An example of this utopian mood, prevalent among the Russian intelligentsia of the time, was furnished in the same year by the future Slavophile and former Wisdom Lover Ivan Kireevsky, whose article "The Nineteenth Century" presented Schelling's thought as the philosophical anticipation of a transformed and unified European civilization in which Russia, no longer a backward and marginal nation, would play its foreordained historical role. (The journal in which it appeared was suppressed on the order of the tsar, who apparently smelled the idea of a constitutional monarchy behind Kireevsky's notion of synthesis.)

Herzen identifies with the mood of hope, which, he writes, has characterized all eras of spiritual renewal, but his attitude to Schelling struck a discordant note in the general chorus of utopian expectation. At a time when so many of his contemporaries looked to *Naturphilosophie* for the answers to the fundamental questions of science and human existence, he stands out with his critique of both sides in the battle of scientific ideologies that had recently reached its climax in France. In the sciences the division between analytical (or experimental) and synthesizing approaches was leading to "terrible mistakes." "Neither synthesis nor analysis can lead to truth, for they are two parts, two moments in a *single* act of complete cognition." "The motto of analysis is dissection into parts; but the soul, or life, exists in the whole organism, and moreover in the living organism." However, idealists are wrong to oppose the role of the senses in the cognition of nature. "Idealism is concerned only with the noumenal, but is not nature the world of phenomena? Remember Fichte, who could not distinguish between nature and his own ego. You often see that in idealism all nature is forced into one brilliant hypothesis; idealists prefer to mutilate nature rather than their idea."[41]

There are echoes of Pavlov and Maximovich here, but it is Victor Cousin who prompts Herzen's response to the question "What then is to be done?"—"Follow Bacon's rule and unite the rational method with the empirical." In the preface to his *Fragments philosophiques* of 1826 Cousin had recommended a return to Bacon's inductive method (the first attempt at formulating a methodology for modern science) as an antidote to the current tendency to corrupt the data of observation by imposing a system on them. Citing Bacon's proposal of the rational

method, "which, married to the experimental, gives excellent knowledge [*De dignitate*]," Herzen observes that his followers had distorted
his method by devoting exclusive attention to observation and experiment, whose data they then synthesized by "various artificial means,"
the end result being vulgar materialism.[42]

A few months later, in the dissertation on Copernicus's heliocentric
system of astronomy for which he had hoped to receive the faculty's
gold medal, he recommends the approaches of Bacon and Cousin,
with the proviso that empiricism and idealism, analysis and synthesis,
must be seen as "two extremes of a single method." He goes on to
present the history of mathematical astronomy from Ptolemy through
Copernicus and Kepler to Newton as the collecting of facts followed
by the deduction of universal laws, culminating in "a general synthesis,
all-embracing, wrested from Nature's mysteries," the theory of universal gravity. These three periods, he concludes, correspond to the
stages of the method he proposes. There can be no better proof in its
support: "It is at one with the laws whereby Nature brings man to fullness of understanding."[43]

Although differing from the Russian Schellingians in his description of that happy state (Newton's method with its sharp distinction
between conjectural hypotheses and experimentally established results
was deeply antipathetic to the Romantic perception of the world), Herzen
shared their expectation that it would bring with it the transformation
of human societies. As Chapter 7 will show, Herzen's scientific studies
had not diminished his interest in politics; his memoirs record his and
Ogarev's passionate interest in the July Revolution in France and the
Polish revolt of 1831 and their bitter disappointment with the outcomes. His reservations about the role of idealism in this context are
expressed in a letter to Ogarev, who had declared himself a follower of
Schelling: "That's not a bad thing, but only in part—because what
matters is the *practical application*. . . . As our *mutual acquaintance*
[Pavlov?] says, Schelling is a supreme poet, he understood the demands
of the century and created . . . a living philosophy" (his organic vision of
the universe). But the needs of the present demanded modifications in
this vision: "The reason: Schelling ended up with mystical Catholicism, Hegel with despotism!"[44]

This is the first known appearance in Herzen's writing of what was become a central theme in his later work: the despotic potential of all philosophical and political systems that laid claim to knowledge of the fundamental laws governing history and human societies. We may assume that his early perception of the basic flaw in the great idealist systems of his age owed something to Pavlov's critique of the doctrinairism of the young Russian metaphysicians and their bullying dismissal of dissenting views. Pavlov's guidance is evident too in his discovery of a philosophical antidote to the prevailing fashion—Cousin—who in turn introduced him to a figure whose name seldom appears in histories of nineteenth-century thought. In a sentence deleted from the final version of "Man's Place in Nature" he writes: "We felt it necessary . . . to distinguish Bacon from most of his followers, for it would be a bitter thing if we were to be accused of ingratitude toward the Lord of Verulam, whose memory should be sacred for posterity."[45] This awkwardly effusive tribute reflects the beginning of a lifelong admiration for Bacon's writings, from which Herzen would frequently quote to illustrate a polemical point. He was to value Bacon's method as the expression of a new humanism militating against the curbs imposed on human thought and action by narrow systems and dogmas; it was the same liberating impulse that he perceived in Cousin's eclecticism. Cousin had radical credentials: he had been under suspicion for his association with members of the Carbonari. His career was interrupted and the École Normale closed for a time in the 1820s. French police reports led to a brief imprisonment on a visit to Prussia (where he had the distinction of being released through the intervention of Hegel). He declared that on his appointment at the École Normale he had vowed to dedicate his life to the reform of philosophy, which he presents as a humanist crusade in the pursuit of unity through the harmonization of opposites.

Strong on rhetoric but vague in content, Cousin's philosophy made little impact on the thought of his time; but for Herzen the transformation of the École Normale (previously the home of a moribund materialism) under Cousin's tutelage was a significant sign of a new dawn, for which the intense intellectual activity of the preceding two centuries had been a preparation. Its motto, "Tout accepter et rien exclure," was, he writes, close to the heart of nineteenth-century man, wearied by the battle of ideas. Carried away by his theme, he concludes with a flight of fancy:

> Now man may rejoice and breathe in hope; the eighteenth century, a century of analysis and destruction, ended with that colossal, fiery eruption, so like the powerful and antediluvian upheavals that transformed the face of our planet, whose burning rocks flew through the entire world and whose bloody lava flowed from the guillotine of the Place de la Révolution to the foothills of our own Kremlin. From the ruins a new man has come forth, shaken off the dust and ... begun to build anew. He is still building, it's too early to judge him; his great work will belong to our descendants. Ours to enjoy is only the light of hope this bright ray sheds on us.[46]

There are no grounds for the view of some Soviet commentators that Herzen's reference to the violent development of the French Revolution was an Aesopian expression of sympathy for the methods of the Jacobins (elsewhere in the essay he describes "the dark and bloody terror of '93" as illustrating the perversion of noble ideas by their later interpreters).[47] This discreet expression of patriotic hope is significant as the first reference we have to the question that would dominate his thought in later decades: Russia's past and future historical path in relation to that of Europe. There are echoes here of the article in which, twelve months before, the Schellingian and future Slavophile Ivan Kireevsky had put the same question in print for the first time, defining the dominant characteristic of the postrevolutionary age as the urge to replace the destructive drive of eighteenth-century thought with an approach to historical reality that would harmonize man's reason with his spiritual aspirations. "On Man's Place in Nature" puts the same case with equal urgency, but the approach Herzen outlines is very different. Kireevsky was typical of a generation steeped in Romantic literature and thought, and looked confidently to the organicist visions of German philosophy to meet the desired end, whereas Herzen's schooling in the historical orientation in science gave him a critical perspective on *Naturphilosophie* that was lacking in those who had never submitted to the discipline of subjecting their theories to empirical testing. We have seen that he had been drawn to the natural sciences by his fasci-

nation with the new evolutionary theories and by the increasing awareness of scientists and historians that peoples and cultures are grounded
in the natural world with its constraints, its unpredictability, and its
infinite possibilities of development—all of which are alien to the absolutes of dogmatic thought. These sources, together with the lessons
in method imparted by Pavlov and Maximovich, were a powerful antidote to his contemporaries' intoxication with a misty idealism. But
they did not diminish the patriotic radicalism and the cult of the
Decembrists that had fired his adolescent enthusiasm for history.
His commitment to his studies was equaled by his devotion to the
student circle that he headed with Ogarev. In the context of their discussions he would develop an interest in the growth and transformation of human societies, which would lead him in the year of his graduation to engage with the socialism of Saint-Simon.

CHAPTER SEVEN

Science and Saint-Simonism

Those who have handled sciences have been either men of experiment or men of dogmas. The men of experiment are like the ant: they only collect and use; the reasoners resemble spiders, who make cobwebs out of their own substance. But the bee takes a middle course: it gathers its material from the flowers of the garden and of the field but transforms and digests it by a power of its own.

FRANCIS BACON

IN a letter written from exile in 1837 to his future wife Natalie, Herzen recalls his unhappy childhood. His father's oppressive nature having placed an unbridgeable distance between them, he felt "completely *alien*" in the paternal house; "there were humiliations at every step." This was why he had devoted himself so passionately to student life: "There I found comrades, *equals* who valued me."[1] In his memoirs these comrades appear as revolutionaries in the making, united by "the ever-present thought with which we entered the university, the thought that *here* our dreams would be realized, that here we should sow the seeds and lay the *foundation* of a league. We were persuaded that out of this lecture room would come the company that would follow in the footsteps of Pestel and Ryleev, and that we should be in it." If the state regarded a degree in the natural sciences as a step on the ladder to promotion in government service, a significant number of the students in his year had other concerns: "Science did not distract us from the suffering of the life around us. Our sympathy with it raised the social morality of the students to an unusual extent. We . . . said openly in the lecture room everything that came into our heads; notebooks with prohibited poems passed from hand to hand, prohibited books were read with commentaries, yet despite all that I do not remember . . . a single case of betrayal."[2]

The Seeds of Rebellion

Notwithstanding his affectionate tribute to the "splendid" set of young men in his year,[3] Herzen's closest friendships and intellectual affinities except for Ogarev were with students outside his faculty who were engrossed in contemporary Western thought in the search for solutions to the enigma of their own and their country's destiny. The effect of the 1826 censorship edict in muzzling public discussion gave an added impetus to their informal studies. Herzen's most intense experience of the joys of comradeship was within the small group of friends that became known as "the circle of Herzen and Ogarev." Loosely organized intellectual fraternities devoted to the discussion of Romantic literature and German philosophy, the circles that were formed at Moscow University in the 1830s were to be the seedbed of the Russian intelligentsia as a self-defining intellectual and moral elite, united by their alienation from the political status quo and their faith in the power of noble ideas to transform an ugly and brutal reality.[4]

As a focus for the most talented and idealistic young men of his generation, Herzen's circle had only one rival: the group gathered around Nikolai Stankevich, an exponent of Schelling's aesthetic idealism. The critic Vissarion Belinsky (who had been expelled from the university for writing a play criticizing serfdom) described the *kruzhok* (circle) as a desert island: their only refuge from a hostile and despicable society. Ivan Turgenev, in his youth a member of Stankevich's circle and later of a group formed around Belinsky, portrays it in similar terms in his memoirs: "When you look around you, you see bribery flourishing; serfdom stands as firm as a rock; the military barracks are in the foreground of life; justice is nowhere to be found, there are rumors that the universities are to be closed down, trips abroad become impossible, it's impossible even to order a worthwhile book from abroad; a kind of dark cloud hangs over the whole so-called scholarly and literary domain, while all around informers crawl and hiss; among the youth there are neither common ties nor common interests, all is fear and servility: one might as well abandon hope! But then you arrive at Belinsky's apartment, a second and a third friend arrive, a conversation starts—and suddenly you feel better."[5]

Herzen' s circle was formed gradually, on the basis of personal friendship, intellectual affinity, and mutual trust. Its principal members were eight in number. Although they all belonged to the gentry, they reflected the increasing professionalization of that class. Few of them would retain their political interests of their student years. Herzen and Ogarev were particularly close to Vadim Passek, the only member of the circle who had experienced the autocracy's vengeance at first hand, having been born in Siberia to a Polish family exiled in the reign of Paul I. He and his brother Diomid shared Herzen's concern with history. Diomid entered the engineering corps of the army, rising to the rank of major-general, and was killed in a skirmish in the Caucasus. Vadim married Herzen's cousin Tatiana Kuchina and pursued a career as a historian and ethnographer, exchanging his early radicalism for a nationalism that idealized Russia's monarchical past. Writing to his future wife from exile, Herzen would describe his former friendship with him as "the only mistake in my life."[6] Nikolai Ketcher was the son of a member of Russia's growing industrial elite. Eight years Herzen's senior, he had graduated in medicine but remained an eternal student with a passion for Schiller and for Shakespeare, many of whose works he translated. Herzen paints an affectionate portrait in his memoirs of this boisterous and eccentric figure, with whom he renewed his friendship on his return to Moscow from exile.[7] Another member of the circle, Mikhail Noskov, took up a post in the Ministry of War on his graduation. Aleksei Savich became a professor of astronomy and a member of the Russian Academy of Sciences. Nikolai Sazonov and Nikolai Satin, who, like Herzen and Ogarev, came from affluent serf-owning backgrounds, evolved into prototypes of the Russian "superfluous man" whom Turgenev would dissect in his novels. Herzen devotes some pages in his memoirs to Sazonov, a figure of "conspicuous talents and conspicuous egoism."[8] Convinced of his great destiny but incapable of sustained work, he went abroad on the eve of 1848 in search of revolutionary excitement and spent the remainder of his life in futile activity on the fringes of radical circles in the West. Arrested along with Herzen and Ogarev and sentenced to five years of exile, on his return to Moscow Satin became a prominent member of Belinsky's circle as a poet and translator. Renewing his friendship with him in that period, Herzen would describe him as having only one fault: weakness of character, his fits of melancholy being due "partly to the lack of definite goals or occupations, of anything beyond vague aspirations."[9] Of Herzen's circle, only Aleksei Lakhtin, a graduate in literature and a close friend of Ogarev, paid for his beliefs with an early death in exile in 1838.

In his memoirs Herzen stresses the circle's political orientation: "We felt a cool respect for Stankevich's circle, but could not be intimate with its members. They traced philosophical systems, engaged in self-analysis, and found contentment in a luxurious pantheism from which Christianity was not excluded. We were dreaming of how to set up a new league in Russia on the model of the Decembrists and looked upon learning itself as a means to that goal."

"We preached everywhere and all the time," he writes. "What precisely we preached, it's hard to say. Our ideas were vague, we preached the Decembrists and the French Revolution, then we preached Saint-Simonism and the same revolution, we preached a constitution, a republic, . . . but more than all else, we preached hatred for all forms of violence, for all forms of tyranny practiced by governments."[10]

Given the efficiency of the tsarist police state and the impossibility of any form of open resistance during Nicolas's reign, this picture of the circle's aims and activities does not carry conviction, reminding us once more of the dual character of *My Past and Thoughts* as a memoir and an artistic creation with a tragic hero. In the mind of the middle-aged Herzen, the image of the rebellious student had merged with the revolutionary he would become. The risks the group were taking were nonetheless substantial. With the Decembrist conspiracy still fresh in the authorities' minds, to discuss questions of philosophy, aesthetics, and science in private circles could be seen as sedition. Always on the alert for evidence of independent thought, the authorities kept a close watch on Moscow University, their zeal intensified by what was known as "the affair of the Kritsky brothers"—the discovery in 1827 of a secret society set up by three brothers, of whom two were students at the university. As Herzen notes in his memoirs, nothing was then known of their fate or of the charges against them. (One would die in prison, one would be killed in the Caucasus, where he had been sent as an army private, and the third, sentenced to exile followed by army service in the ranks, regained his freedom after twenty-eight years, at the beginning of a new reign.)[11] As another instance of the authorities' jumpiness, Herzen records the fate in 1826 of Alexander Polezhaev, renowned among his fellow students for his parodic poems. One of these earned him a personal interview with the tsar, who dispatched him to the ranks of the army.[12] In the wake of the Polish revolt of 1830 a Polish medical student was arrested on the eve of his graduation and sentenced to exile in Siberia. In June 1831 the government uncovered a secret society created by one Nikolai Sungurov on the model of the Decembrists. Among its members were four students known to Herzen's circle. The fact that the group also included two officers ignited fears of a new military conspiracy, and its members were sentenced to hard labor in Siberia or in the army. Herzen's circle got up a subscription to purchase warm clothing for the students on their journey. The grateful recipients sent back a letter of thanks, which was intercepted by the secret police; Ogarev, Ketcher, and Satin, mentioned by name in the letter, were placed under special observation.[13] In December 1833 a report was filed that Ogarev and V. I. Sokolovsky, a fellow poet and frequent participant in the carousals of the circle, had been observed singing the Marseillaise in an inebriated state on the steps of the Maly Theatre.[14]

Herzen's only comparable act of public rebellion in his student years was his participation in the "Malov affair," in which an unpopular professor was driven from the lecture room onto the street, his galoshes thrown after him. Together with five other ringleaders in the affair, Herzen was sentenced by the university senate to a spell in the university prison. The guard having been bribed to admit their comrades to their cell, they spent merry nights sustained by food, wine, and cigars. In the account in his memoirs the three days of his sentence have stretched to eight, but he is doubtless not exaggerating when he observes that the affair greatly enhanced his standing among his comrades.[15] This was already considerable; although the many commentaries of contemporaries on Herzen's personality and talents relate to his years in Moscow in the 1840s, we can recognize in them the precocious and self-willed student, fully conscious of his exceptional intellectual powers and determined to make his mark on the world. The memoirist Pavel Annenkov writes of his effect on the circles of that decade:

I was utterly stunned and perplexed when I first came to know [Herzen]—by this extraordinary mobile mind, which darted from one topic to another with inexhaustible wit and brilliance and unbelievable swiftness, which could catch in the turn of somebody's talk, in some simple incident of daily life, in some abstract idea, that vivid feature that gives it shape and life. He had a most astonishing capacity for instantaneous, unexpected juxtaposition of quite dissimilar things, and this gift he had to a very high degree, fed as it was by the powers of subtle observation and a very considerable fund of encyclopedic knowledge. He had it to such an extent that, in the end, his listeners were sometimes exhausted by the inextinguishable fireworks of his speech, the inexhaustible fantasy and invention, a kind of extravagant prodigality of intellect that astonished his audience. . . .

   With all this proud, determined, energetic intellect, Herzen had a wholly gentle, amiable, almost feminine character. Beneath the stern exterior of the skeptic, the satirist, under the cover of a most unceremonious, and extremely unreticent, humor, there dwelt the heart of a child.[16]

Herzen's gift for friendship would be exemplified in his lifelong relationship with Ogarev, much his intellectual inferior, whose slight poetic talent he loyally praised but whose irritating sentimentality must have tested his forbearance severely over the years. Annenkov describes him as always generous in his support to those less gifted than himself who sought his help or advice, which did not deter him at times from using his destructive powers on the same people at the very same time. (The coolly objective analysis in his memoirs of members of his circle is a case in point.) Ogarev would be spared from his devastating insights, due to what Herzen saw as the sacred nature of their friendship, but doubtless also to the fact that Ogarev's admiration and support were important in sustaining his faith in his own special calling. The month after their graduation he wrote to him: "You occupy an enormous place in my psyche. You and Tatiana [Kuchina/Passek] were the first beings who took the trouble to understand me when I was still a child, the first to notice then that I would not merge with the crowd—that something original would come of me."[17]

Amid the diversions of student life and fellowship, Herzen and Ogarev clung to the sense of mission that had inspired their adolescent
oath on the Sparrow Hills. As the end of their university studies approached, Ogarev exhorted his friend to write in a future memoir of
how "in that place the history of our lives began to unfold." Herzen
responded immediately with a short sketch describing how the pair had
revisited the "altar of our friendship." In a variation of the well-worn
Romantic theme of the hero and the crowd, he relates how, the experience having briefly returned them to the purity of their early youth,
they recited to each other verses of Schiller and the Decembrist poet
Ryleev. Contemplating the teeming city below, with its ignorant, depraved, venal, and irredeemably corrupt humanity, they yearned, like
Mignon in Goethe's *Wilhelm Meister*, to be absorbed in the timeless
purity of the heavens: "Dahin, dahin!"[18]

It appears that during their pilgrimage to the scene of their political awakening, the pair reverted to their adolescent longing for
an ideal freedom unsullied by the baseness of empirical reality. But
political events were pulling them back to the battle for freedom in
the here and now. In his memoirs Herzen describes their euphoria on
hearing of the revolution of July 1830 in France, followed by news of
an uprising in Warsaw: "This was not far away; this was at home."[19]
In contrast to the mystical idealism of Stankevich's circle, "a belated
and peripheral reflection of the European romantic movement" in the
words of one critic,[20] Herzen's circle was increasingly attracted to the
new philosophies of progress that were springing up in response to the
social upheaval and intellectual disarray that followed the Revolution
and the advent of industrial society.

Science and History

The great advances in eighteenth-century natural science led to a recognition of the role of environmental factors in the development of
human societies, and of an interplay between biological research and
the growth of historical thought, exemplified by the end of the century
in Herder's approach to history and human societies as part of the
development of the cosmos as a whole. Herder's view of humanity as
progressing toward a single ideal of perfection (albeit at odds with his

insistence on the uniqueness of each culture) reflected a growing demand among educated Europeans who had discarded traditional religious beliefs for a new faith to replace hope in an afterlife with the prospect of fulfillment on earth. The destruction wrought by the Revolution of 1789 and the Napoleonic wars, the political and social upheavals in France culminating in the revolution of 1830, and the stagnation of Russia under a bleak despotism intensified the need for some overarching explanation of existence that would make positive sense of the chaos of the present as a transitional stage in the passage to a state of earthly bliss. This was supplied by the concept of progress and its inevitability.

In the West, faith in the progress of human societies through knowledge, education, and the improvement of the environment stretches back to Bacon, but initially it did not involve interest in the workings of history or study of the past. It has been remarked that for the philosophes, concerned with concrete social improvements, progress was "a battle cry, not a subject for research."[21] Their interest was the future, not the past. The concept of progress as the necessary unfolding of an immanent potential originated in German metaphysics, being first fully developed in Schelling's pantheistic vision of the cosmos as a single organism in which matter and mind are simply different degrees of organization of an evolving organic whole. It was universally assumed by Romantic idealists that this movement was always upward, to ever greater degrees of perfection. The notion that political reform was a precondition of the perfecting of human existence, combined with the growth of nationalism and the Romantic vogue for local color, led to an efflorescence of historical studies in the early nineteenth century. Three French liberal historians, Augustin Thierry, François Guizot, and Jules Michelet, took the lead. In July 1820 in a series of articles in a liberal newspaper, Thierry, a Saint-Simonian, announced that the emergence of the common people on the historical stage required the creation of a new history to replace the story of kings and battles: "La meilleure partie de nos annales, la plus instructive, reste à écrire; il nous manque l'histoire des citoyens, l'histoire des sujets, l'histoire du public, de la masse [The better part of our annals, the most instructive part, remains to be written; the history of the citizens, the subjects, the public, the masses, is missing]."[22] In lectures at the

Sorbonne in the 1820s on the history of representative government and the history of Europe and France, he defined the fundamental characteristic of European society, and the source of its vigor, as the existence of diversity and conflict. Michelet (the first volume of whose monumental history of France was published in 1833) had translated Vico and studied Herder and Berthold Georg Niebuhr, a founding father of modern historiography. He emphasized the importance of the geographical conditions in which societies evolved (he had once applied for a chair of geography in Paris). He drew on all the facets of an age or culture—its art, literature, architecture, popular traditions, and legends—to create a vivid picture of what interested him above all: "le génie des temps [the spirit of the times]." All three insisted on the necessity of working closely with original documents in order to capture the unique nature of a culture or period.

The central belief of Romantic nationalism—that each country and race had its own distinctive character, its special role to fulfill in the higher purpose of all that exists—began to preoccupy cultivated Russians after the victory of 1812. The rout of Napoleon by the Russian people awakened new sentiments of national pride within the Westernized intelligentsia, which found expression in a growing preoccupation among Russian Romantics with the meaning and direction of Russian history and its relation to the West. In the dismal aftermath of the Decembrist revolt they had resorted to an inward-looking aesthetic idealism as a means of escape from the bleakness of contemporary reality, seeking to rise above the material realm of necessity and commune with the Absolute through the mediums of philosophy, poetry, and art; but by the early 1830s they came increasingly to connect their sense of alienation from their society with the position of Russia vis-à-vis Europe, seeking to elucidate their country's place in humanity's progression to its ultimate purpose. In an essay of 1833 the former Decembrist and Romantic writer Alexander Bestuzhev-Marlinsky wrote, "We live in an age of history. . . . Now history is not simply in fact, but in the memory, the mind, the hearts of the people."[23] According to the Romantics, the unique character of a people reveals itself in its history, literature, and art. But modern Russian history had begun with a brutal break with the national past, and Russian literature was as yet little more than a pale imitation of Western models. In

1829, the year in which Herzen commenced his university studies, the former Wisdom Lover and future Slavophile Ivan Kireevsky published an essay in the Moscow *Telegraph* invoking idealist organicism to put a positive gloss on these discouraging facts. Each European people had already fulfilled its mission in which its national character had been expressed: "We have one advantage that is the pledge of all the others. . . . European civilization has served as a cradle for ours. . . . Where they have come to a standstill, we are only beginning. Like the youngest sister in a great family, Russia, before her entry into the world, is already rich with the experience of others." Three years later Kireevsky returned to the problem of Russia's relation to European civilization, arguing that although the "Chinese wall" separating Russia from Europe had been breached by Peter the Great, it remained a barrier to reasoned discussion of the relation of Russian culture to European enlightenment.[24] His essay hastened the eventual suppression of the *Telegraph*, but not before intensifying the intelligentsia's interest in the issues he had addressed.

The preoccupation of Herzen's circle with Russia's historical role in the light of the philosophy of history is reflected in what Ogarev described to Herzen as "a complex correspondence" on the latter between himself and Aleksei Lakhtin in the summer of 1833.[25] Lakhtin gives Vico and Herder, Niebuhr, Michelet, and Guizot his qualified praise. They inspire him without wholly satisfying his demands: the historian "must be a prophet. He is positively obliged to reveal to me the future of mankind. If from the accumulated facts he has grasped the laws that control its movement, then do we not have the right to demand that he deduce from those very laws its vital aims, its path and, finally, its limits?" Such were Lakhtin's general preoccupations; his specific concern was Russia: "its Asiatic and European aspects, its civil structure, ideas, direction, process, development, and goal." (This letter, regarded as "full of freethinking" by the investigating commission established after Herzen's and Ogarev's arrest, formed part of the case against them.[26] Its author was sentenced to indefinite exile in Saratov.)

The interpretation of the Petrine reforms, which had inaugurated modern Russian history, posed difficult problems for the Russian intelligentsia. Under Catherine II, who considered herself Peter's direct successor, the great modernizer had been glorified in poetry and prose. The suppression of the Decembrist revolt was a stark reminder of the path that Peter's Westernization had taken.[27] Romantic writers were faced with particular difficulties: modern Russian literature from its origins in the eighteenth century was based on imitation of Western models, owing nothing to the inspiration of the masses who in the Romantic vision were the ultimate repository of a nation's individuality and creative force. In an essay of 1832 in his the periodical *The European* Ivan Kireevsky poses the problem: "When will our civilization attain the degree of development of the civilized states of Europe? What should we do to attain this goal? . . . Should we draw our civilization from our inner selves or receive it from Europe? And what is the principle of our own lives that we should develop? And what should we borrow from nations more enlightened than us?" On the answers to these questions depended "all of our ideas concerning Russia, the destiny of its civilization as well as its current state, all our hopes and all our aspirations, all our desires and all our hatreds, as well as—if we want to be consistent with ourselves—the nature of our practical activity . . . "[28]

Herzen's Response

Herzen's first known contribution to what would become one of the most contentious issues in Russian thought is a surviving fragment of an essay of 1833 in which he compares Peter the Great to a comet whose violent intrusions into the ordered motion of the planets had appeared to defy the laws of astronomy until mathematics established their place in the order of the universe. The Petrine revolution, he argued, issued from the fact that the Slavs were linked by Christianity to the rest of Europe, a living organism whose laws of development had impelled it through struggle and conflict toward a final phase of harmony. He concludes with the hope that, their fate now definitively linked to that of Europe through the victory over Napoleon, Russians would assimilate those elements of Western culture that best cohered with their national distinctiveness *(narodnost)*. Herzen promises to draw up in the second part of his essay a balance sheet of Russia's progress to date in this direction. If this was written, it has not survived. The manuscript of the first part, confiscated on Herzen's arrest the next year, was of considerable interest to his interrogators, who underlined a number of assertions.[29]

We have seen that the problem of progress and the search to find a coherent meaning in the great upheavals of the previous half-century are the leitmotifs of Herzen's surviving student writings. The natural sciences did not replace history as his main intellectual interest—they gave him a wider context in which to approach the pressing historical questions of his time and a critical method to apply to them. A few days after his graduation he writes to Ogarev of his intention to fill the gaps in his knowledge through self-education, focusing on history and political science "with the natural sciences in the background."[30]

The last phrase is significant. Despite the scientific flavor of the new historicism, with its emphasis on the study of development, its teleological approach to an evolving world tended to exclude a priori all competing interpretations. In the natural sciences in the same period, purposive explanations of the origins and development of life were fast giving way to the assaults of empirical evidence, a process in which (as already discussed) Herzen was closely interested. His project of self-education would result in the application of the methods he had learned from his scientific teachers to a critical examination of the single unquestioned faith of his century: the cult of progress. His first contribution to the great debate that would divide successive generations of the Russian intelligentsia, resonating with Kireevsky's essays, was solidly within the framework of the idealist historicism of his time. But in the next decade, as we will see, when Slavophiles and Westernizers developed their opposing visions of the "laws" of history, based respectively on religious idealism and Hegelian philosophy, Herzen would accuse both groups of indulging in vast generalizations with scant regard for historical facts. His criticism would draw on an extraordinary range of reference in the disciplines of history, philosophy, law, economics, and political theory. Its foundation was laid in the year between his graduation and his arrest.

* * *

Herzen allowed himself a few days' relaxation after his final examinations before embarking on his project, which he would document in his correspondence with Ogarev, who was spending the summer on his family's estate in Penza. It is significant that he turned first for advice on his reading to Fedor Moroshkin, a young assistant professor in the Faculty of Law, eight years his senior, whom during his interrogation he would name as a close acquaintance.[31] Moroshkin was an exponent of the historical school of law, which, as developed by Friedrich Karl von Savigny in the spirit of Romantic idealism, stressed the need to approach law as an organic process, the evolving product of the experience of peoples over centuries, reflected in popular wisdom and customary law. Herzen had written an essay in praise of Moroshkin's introductory lecture on this theme; in the fragment that survives he emphasizes its significance as a contribution to the role of German philosophy in Russian enlightenment.[32] The philosophy of law was still engaging his thoughts in the fortnight after the end of his examinations when, in the intervals between swimming, eating, and sleeping, he read an "important" work on the history of Russian law by Mikhail Speransky, who as a minister under Alexander I had attempted to rationalize the Russian legal system.[33]

Moroshkin's influence can be seen in one of the first projects Herzen formulates after he graduated: a translation (which never materialized) of Eugène Lerminier's history of law.[34] Appointed at the age of twenty-seven to a chair of comparative law created for him at the Collège de France in the wake of the revolution of 1830, Lerminier rivaled Cousin in charisma. A Germanophile, well versed in Romantic and idealist historicism (he claimed to have been the first in France to mention the name of Hegel in print), he had published a thesis on von Savigny. Moving in radical circles (he had a brief flirtation with Saint-Simonism), he devoted his lectures and articles in reviews to the message that a historical study of the development of law would lead to the discovery of the general principles of social structures, and ultimately a science of human nature as the basis of a rational society. In addition to Vico, Herder, and Michelet (already on Herzen's list, together with Thierry, and with Michelet's recently published *Histoire romaine* to use as his entrée into ancient history), Moroshkin recommended Montesquieu, a Russian translation of a German textbook on contemporary Roman law, a work by the historian Arnold Heeren *(Ideen über die Politik, den Verkehr und den Handel der vornehmsten Volker der alten Welt)*, and Malthus and Jean-Baptiste Say on political economy.[35]

After a few weeks of concentrated reading, Herzen writes to Ogarev that in the study of political science he has found his vocation: "Da bin ich zu Hause. . . . You can't imagine the degree of my activity at present. My blood is fermenting, fermenting. Study, study, and then write. Why not make sacrifices for fame when others do so for wealth, wine, or women? You, Vadim, and I together form a single whole; we'll live a purely intellectual life. Let the sciences (you understand I'm speaking in the broad sense) occupy our entire lives."[36] The process of intellectual discovery had become his consuming passion, as the sole means available to him of realizing the dream of greatness he had begun to form in his adolescence.

To launch his historical studies Herzen had chosen a representative selection of the most significant products of that cross-fertilization of historical thought with the natural sciences and idealist organicism that had begun in the previous century. His own intellectual development seemed set on a similar path. In February 1834 he drew up a program for a journal he proposed to publish in collaboration with Ogarev, Sazonov, Satin, Ketcher, and Lakhtin. In Russia, as in Western Europe during that period, journals such as Pavlov's *Atheneum* played a key cultural role in the dissemination of ideas and the creation of public opinion, and for that reason they were closely monitored by the authorities. Ivan Kireevsky's essay "The Nineteenth Century" had only recently brought about the closure of his short-lived periodical *The European*, although its subversive content was hard to discern; and a month after Herzen aired his project, the same fate overtook another leading Russian journal of the time, the *Moscow Telegraph*, for the offense of publishing a critical review of a hyperpatriotic play entitled "The Hand of the Most High Saved the Fatherland." For a youth scarcely out of university to launch himself on this perilous path required exceptional self-confidence and strength of purpose. In a letter of the previous year to Ogarev he had confessed to a yearning for fame as his "weakness,"[37] and the projected journal would serve as a platform for the public propagation of the views on the relation of science to history and philosophy that, albeit with the fervor of a trailblazer, he had hitherto conveyed only to an audience of teachers and friends. As outlined in his plan, the aim of the journal was nothing less than to establish the present condition of mankind and its prospects for the future on the basis of the principal phases of its historical development. It would consist of two sections—the philosophy of history, with literature approached as the expression of national culture; and the natural sciences, on the ground that man is part of nature: "She subjects him to her laws."[38]

* * *

The project was forestalled by the arrests of Herzen and Ogarev, but it may be assumed that their collaboration would not have been without its tensions. Their correspondence in their last years together in Moscow shows progressively sharper disparities of intellectual outlook and temperament. Herzen's portrayal of their youthful friendship in *My Past and Thoughts* has led to the belief that in their university years they followed a single path from Romantic idealism to utopian socialism. Such was not the case. While Ogarev remained attached to their juvenile Romanticism, Herzen's thought on the roles of philosophy, religion, and science in the battle for progress was evolving in a way that would lead him ultimately to an isolated position on the Russian Left. This divergence was reflected in their early correspondence as they updated each other on their progress in self-education.

Ogarev's devotion to Schelling had confirmed his belief in his poetic calling, channeling his radical inclinations into a misty Romantic idealism of the kind Pavlov feared would plunge Russian literature and science into darkness. In his rural isolation in the summer of 1833 he gives his fantasies full rein in letters to Herzen, appropriating Schelling's image of the artist as mouthpiece for the Absolute—"God lives through the life of the artist"—to convey his sense of mission as mediator between heaven and earth, expressing the infinite in finite form to the grateful few who are capable of understanding him. Poetry, he declares, is "my life, my science . . . my philosophy, my politics. . . . I don't reason, I feel. . . . To create, to be in constant rapture—that's what I desire." In his moments of inspiration, the pettiness of everyday life gives way to "a whole world of new people, fulfilling the highest demands; I live in that world like a prophet in the future."[39]

Ogarev implored his friend not to laugh at his attempts to express the undefinable in words. He was right to be apprehensive about the reception of his religious outpourings. Herzen recalls in his memoirs that he had accompanied his mother to her Lutheran church only when he had nothing better to do. His father considered the profession of religion to be a prerequisite of a cultured individual but personally refrained from its practice, although he ensured that his son fasted and received the sacrament once a year in the week before Easter, and engaged a priest to give him divinity lessons as a necessary condition for entering the university. He recalls that although he would feel a certain awe at receiving the sacrament, he would cease to give religion any thought for the rest of the year; on the other hand, in his adolescence he became greatly attracted to the social message of the Gospels.

His response to Ogarev's mystical effusions was a model of tact, praising his confession of faith as noble and profound, the work of a true poet: "I, your friend Herzen, guarantee that your name will resound." In another letter he is more outspoken: "We are different, very different," the one drawn more to contemplation, the other to the world of political activity. For all that, "there is a marvelous sympathy between us, which we share with absolutely no one else, but sympathy does not demand identity. A profound mutual understanding, each one complementing the other—that's the foundation of our friendship, whose strength will triumph over all circumstances."[40]

The bond that the two had sacralized with their famous oath on the Sparrow Hills did not prevent them from sparring on the subject of Schelling and idealism. Herzen had reminded his friend that both Schelling and Hegel had been far from radicalism in their political views: "One must look at the *application*, as *our mutual acquaintance* [probably Pavlov] points out". Ogarev for his part was scathing about the legal flavor of the reading list compiled for Herzen by Professor Moroshkin: "All glory and honor to Moroshkin's plan. Only for goodness sake don't confuse devotion to facts with scholasticism." From the heights of speculative philosophy he looked condescendingly on Herzen's interest in French eclecticism, informing him: "I'm reading Schelling's *Transcendentaler Idealismus*. Superb! . . . Now there's a poet-philosopher! No, my friend, don't you think your Cousins should straighten up and stand to attention: place au grand homme."[41]

Herzen's rejoinder was brief. Referring to the beginning of his first love affair (with Ludmilla Passek, sister of their friend Vadim), he remarks, "You have uncovered a new world in Schelling, I have found

one in love."[42] Both were preoccupied with the dream of a future perfected society, but while Ogarev awaited its coming as the unfolding
of a divine plan, Herzen was developing a more earthbound conception of progress. In the summer of 1832, citing a chapter on the Christian utopian thinker the Abbé de Lamennais in a study by the French
philosopher J. P. Damiron, Ogarev had declared himself "amazed" that
Herzen (who had also read Damiron) had not singled out "this superb
essay, so close to my cherished dream: the full perfecting of the human
race."[43] (Lamennais looked forward to an era when religion would fuse
with philosophy and belief in God would become knowledge of God.)

Herzen's reply to this letter has not survived, but as we shall see,
his interest in the new philosophies of progress focused exclusively on
their capacity to deliver social justice in the everyday world.

The Emergence of Saint-Simonism

Toward the end of the eighteenth century the notion of rational progress advanced by the philosophes was reinterpreted in terms of divine
providence in the thought of Lessing, Herder, and Kant. In France after
the Revolution the fear of social chaos led to a new emphasis on the
role of religion in integrating society. In the early nineteenth century,
traditionalists such as the Vicomte de Bonald and Joseph de Maistre
invoked the combined authority of the monarchy and the Catholic
Church, but were much less in tune with the times than Ballanche,
Lamennais, and Buchez, whose Catholicism coexisted uneasily with
an emphasis on the historical role of Christianity as an agent of social
progress. The focus of these thinkers was not on salvation in the after-
world but on the moral regeneration of human societies.

Pierre-Simon Ballanche's unfinished work *La palingénésie sociale*
attempted a universal history from the Fall to the contemporary age
in an evolutionary interpretation of Christianity as an historical process of rebirth: an ascent toward the embodiment in social relations of
Christ's teachings on human dignity and equality. He sought uncon-
vincingly to reconcile reason with revelation and secular humanism
with the dogmas of the Catholic Church, while Lamennais's increasingly radical religious humanism led him ultimately to reject the
Church's authority as interpreter of the liberating message of Chris-

tianity. The journal he founded in 1830, *L'Avenir*, bore as its motto "Dieu et liberté." The *System of Catholic Philosophy* that he was preparing was never published, replaced by an eschatological vision that he summed up at the end of the decade: "Le vieux monde se dissout, les vieilles doctrines s'éteignent: mais, au milieu d'un travail confus, d'un désordre apparent, on voit poindre des doctrines nouvelles, s'organiser un monde nouveau; la religion de l'avenir projette ses premieres lueurs sur le genre humain en attente et sur ses futures destinées [The old world is dissolving, old doctrines are fading away; but, in the middle of the confused activity and seeming disorder, new doctrines can be seen emerging, a new world forming itself; the religion of the future casts its first glimmers of light on an expectant humanity and on that humanity's future destinies]."[44]

The new role of religion in efforts to fill the moral vacuum left by the destructive criticism of the eighteenth century was highlighted in Ivan Kireevsky's essay of 1832, "The Nineteenth Century": Papists, Jesuits, Saint-Simonians, Protestants, and even rationalists, "in a word, all the religious parties who ferment in such multitudes in Europe, and who disagree among themselves on everything else, all, however, agree on one thing: *on the demand for a greater rapprochement between religion and the lives of individuals and nations.*"[45] Herzen was already preoccupied from a more secular point of view with the problem of the moral regeneration of mankind. In the following year, when his friend suggested that he add Saint-Simon to his reading list, he was quick to remind him that he himself had observed in a letter two years previously that the French Revolution had done no more than clear the ground for a new "palingenetic" age when European societies would be built on new foundations.[46] Encapsulating what would become the dominant theme of his political writings, this passage demonstrates an acquaintance (at least at second hand) with the efforts of the French utopian thinkers who sought to fill the vacuum left by the destructive rationalism of the previous century through an interpretation of the historical development of Christianity as a process of earthly redemption in accordance with the teachings of the Gospels. He is prepared to concede, however, that "Saint-Simon deserves our attention." This interchange has been seen as marking the espousal of Saint-Simonism by Herzen and Ogarev, and thereby the first step toward socialism in

Russia.[47] Although (following his principal biographers) such a view is common in Herzen scholarship, the evidence does not support it.

* * *

Often described as the founder of French utopian socialism, Claude-Henri de Rouvroy de Saint-Simon achieved celebrity only after his death in 1825, when a group of his disciples created a Saint-Simonian "Church" based on a mystical interpretation of his vision of a future society inspired by the moral teachings of the Gospel. The sect preached the future unity and brotherhood of man, symbolized in the coat worn by their leader, Barthélemy-Prosper Enfantin, which was buttoned at the back and could be opened only with the help of another. While retaining their master's faith in the progressive force of science and his notion of a planned economy, they were given to mystical fantasies and apocalyptic utterances, which together with the authoritarianism of "Père" Enfantin, led several Saint-Simonians to break with the sect. Their principal influence on their age was through their journalistic campaigns directed against the policies of the government, which they accused of having changed nothing after the 1830 revolution, and they were ahead of their time in preaching the liberation of the flesh and the emancipation of women—two themes that would be prominent in the radicalism of the next decade. Their views on sexuality scandalized bourgeois society; in a mass trial in Paris in 1832 they were convicted for offenses against public order and morality. Their leaders were briefly imprisoned, after which the movement gradually broke up.

In a much-quoted passage in his memoirs Herzen describes how he and Ogarev, casting around for ideas that would explain the present and offer hope for the future, found them in the pamphlets and tracts of Saint-Simon and his followers and in accounts of the latter's trial. Père Enfantin and his apostles had been mocked for too long:

> The time has now come to look anew at these forerunners of socialism. . . . These enthusiastic youths . . . made a triumphant and poetic appearance in the petty bourgeois world. They proclaimed a new faith; they had something to say, in the name of which to call the old order before their court of judgment. . . .
>
> On the one hand, *the emancipation of women*, . . . on the other, . . . *the redemption of the flesh*. . . . Great words containing a whole world of new relations between human beings. . . .

A new world was pushing at the door, our hearts and souls opened
wide to meet it. Saint-Simonism lay at the foundation of our convictions and remained so, unchanged in its essence.[48]

This account of the effect of Saint-Simonism on the young Herzen has
been cited as though it represented historical fact (in the words of Raoul
Labry, it was "a key passage, both for the history of [Herzen's] ideas and
for the study of Saint-Simonism in Russia").[49] Yet like many other passages in the memoirs dealing with Herzen's student years, it is part of
a heroic narrative reconstructing the past in the light of his revolutionary future. One has only to read in full his response of 1833 to
Ogarev's latest enthusiasm to find it decidedly cool. Reminding him of
the letter where two years earlier he, Herzen, had defined the needs
of the age in similar terms, he agrees that the movement deserves attention as one "experiment" in this direction, but adds: "I'm not
speaking of its current degeneration, by which I mean its religious form
(Père Enfantin) and so on. Mysticism always distorts a fresh idea. Take
the pure foundation of Christianity—how elegant and noble it was—but
look at what followed it—a dark and gloomy mysticism."[50] He suggests
that Ogarev look also at Charles Fourier's "System of Association," as
set out in an article in a contemporary French review. The oddness of
Fourier's ideas, he suggests, is justified by his aims.

   This suggestion indicates how widely Herzen's reading was
ranging as he cast around for solutions to the problem of moral renewal
which was his central concern: Fourier's notion of a future society
of cooperative communities (phalansteries) was based on a Rousseauian view of human nature directly contrary to that of Saint-Simon,
whose goal was a rational order founded on scientific principles.
Fourier held that all human passions were in principle good because
God-given. The goal was not to change human nature but to accept
it as it is and devise a means of fulfilling the totality of its desires.
Starting from his theory of the passions, of which he distinguished
twelve, he devised a concept of communities of the appropriate size
and diversity to accommodate the maximum of relationships of love
and types of labor. Work was to be organized on a voluntary basis in
a way that would avoid the monotony of single occupations, the supreme aims being happiness and pleasure. He did not call on the state

to organize his system, hoping to finance it through donations from rich men.

During the same period Herzen seems to have had a particular interest in the social theories of a fellow scientist, Philippe Buchez. During his interrogation he refers to the manuscript of an article he had written on Buchez's book of 1833, *Introduction à la science de l'histoire*.[51] Buchez had studied natural sciences in Paris, where his teachers had included Cuvier and Lamarck, before transferring to medicine, while continuing to pursue his interest in natural science through the practice of comparative anatomy. The book that had interested Herzen was the product of a variety of influences, all stemming from the intellectual ferment in the natural sciences at that time—that of Buchez's two former teachers, the work of the renowned physiologist Xavier Bichat, who had founded the science of general anatomy, and Saint-Simon's attempt at a science of society. In the "science of social physiology" that Buchez sought to sketch out, these influences coexisted bizarrely with the messianism of the Saint-Simonians. After breaking with the "Church," Buchez became, along with Pierre Leroux, one of the founders of Christian socialism. In the last chapter of his book of 1833 he concludes a historical survey of the great civilizations, or "âges logiques," of humanity with a tribute to Christianity for having bestowed on humankind a new revelation: that of the Gospels. The time had come for their message, preserved in the teaching of the Catholic Church, to be adopted as the foundation of social and political existence.

Buchez's book was probably the immediate stimulus prompting Herzen in the summer of 1833 to immerse himself in the study of Christianity's historical role in mankind's struggle for freedom. Informing Ogarev of his new enthusiasm, he exclaims: "How ashamed we should be that we have not yet come to know Christ! What nobility of spirit, especially in the Gospels of [Saint] Paul!"[52] No theological interpretation should be put on this. He was unconcerned with such questions as the existence of God or the immortality of the soul (his indifference to these matters was well understood by Ogarev, who was then engrossed in the study of pantheism, deism, ontology, and *Naturphilosophie*, begging Herzen not to respond with "a single cold word" to his admission that he believed in the existence of a Creator).[53]

Herzen's interest was in the social message of Christianity. With Christ's role as an ethical model for humanity in mind, he outlines a triadic schema in the fashion of the time. The ancient world had a one-sided conception of the citizen—the individual was swallowed up in the state. Aristotle praised slavery, the Romans were slaves in republican dress: "Mankind demanded renewal"; and then in Nazareth was born the son of a carpenter with his message of love, charity, and equality. But his teaching on the supreme value of the individual personality had been distorted, both in the mystical dogmas of Catholicism and in the philosophical revolt of the Reformation. "Now there begins a third, the *true, human* phase:—the phalanstery (perhaps Saint-Simonism??)."[54]

Again an ambivalent reference to Saint-Simon. Which, if any, of his writings (as opposed to those of his disciples) had Herzen read? The only direct source we have concerning this is the official transcript of the interrogation following his arrest. Asked to comment on the content of the letter to Ogarev in which he had cited Saint-Simon's vision of the transformation of human societies as worthy of attention, he replied as follows: "The theory of Saint-Simon . . . pleased me in some respects, especially in the historical sense. I saw in it a further development of the teaching on the perfecting of the human race. . . . Saint-Simon's main thesis is that after destruction there follows creation; these thoughts had come to me before, as I could not conceive that man lived only by destruction, of the kind we see from the Reformation to the Revolution of 1789, which destroyed the remnants of feudal society. In European customs there is still much that is outworn, which now no longer has any of its former meaning. It seemed to me that these remnants should be replaced by a morality issuing from new principles, as I say in the letter."[55]

This summary of the appeal of Saint-Simonism as a response to Herzen's philosophical preoccupations rings true, as does the distinction he makes between the theories of the master and his disciples. Questioned on the suggestion in his letter to Ogarev that Saint-Simonism might represent the third and final phase of Christianity, he responded that, as indicated by the two interrogation marks that followed it, he was referring only to Saint-Simon's teachings and not to those of his followers, whose practices, he emphasizes, were at odds with his conception of a new Christianity. At the same time he claimed that his knowledge of the former derived from "journals and various fragments."[56]

It has been argued that it would not have been in his interest to admit to a more precise acquaintance with Saint-Simon's ideas,[57] but there is no reason to doubt his assertion. Saint-Simon's turbulent life, punctuated by imprisonment under the Terror, successive financial crises, a spell in a mental asylum, trial and acquittal on charges of subversion, and an attempt at suicide that left him blind in one eye, was not conducive to the orderly production of scholarly treatises. His work consists largely of pamphlets and short booklets, some of which were handwritten because he could not afford the printing costs; two were published only a century after his death. Public recognition came late in his life: many of his writings had a limited circulation, and fewer still would have reached Russia, via Riga, to end up in the French bookshops on Moscow's Kuznetsky Bridge. With his intense interest in French thought, Herzen would have been familiar with the periodicals that reflected the efflorescence of ideas under the July monarchy. These—particularly the *Globe*, which became the organ of the Saint-Simonians after 1830, and the *Revue encyclopédique* (then under Pierre Leroux's direction), whose article on Fourier he had brought to Ogarev's attention—would have been Herzen's main source for Saint-Simon's thought at that time. Despite the paucity of primary sources at his disposal, Herzen's comments to Ogarev and his responses to his inquisitors show that he had read enough of Saint-Simon to draw a clear distinction between his faith in progress through the growth of solid knowledge about man and nature and the mystical fantasies of the Saint-Simonian sect. This distinction is not observed by his own principal biographers.[58] If he had had access to the central texts in which Saint-Simon expounded his system, he could not have failed to perceive its close affinities with the vision of progress to which his own studies were leading him. Saint-Simon had devoted his life to a task on which Herzen had only begun to embark: the search to formulate a new humanism, grounded in the methods of the natural sciences, that could deliver mankind from the prejudices and false hopes that prevented it from exploiting its power over nature for the common good.

Although Saint-Simon's thought seems to have had no specific influence on Herzen in this respect, it is relevant to the present study for two reasons. First, a survey of Saint-Simon's central ideas should lay to rest a long-standing misconception about the philosophical origins of the Russian socialism that Herzen was to pioneer. Second, it places Herzen's search for a "method" in the context of a distinctive group among proponents of theories of progress in the late eighteenth and early nineteenth centuries in France—those who used the methods and successes of the natural and physical sciences as their point of departure in the search to establish a "science of man."

* * *

The leading Enlightenment figure in this regard was Condorcet, a mathematician by training, who argued that although the truths derived from observation, whether in the realm of natural science or human behavior, were only probabilities, through a calculus of probabilities one might measure their degrees of certainty sufficiently to trace a pattern of progress in the past (interpreted as the gradual emancipation of human society through the growth of the sciences and the arts) and build a model of its continuation in the future. His theories, expressed in his *Esquisse d'un tableau historique des progrès de l'esprit humain*, were the main inspiration for nineteenth-century positivism, as developed in the social theories of Saint-Simon and Auguste Comte.

Saint-Simon too was trained as a scientist, first at the École Polytechnique, where he completed courses in physics and mathematics, and then at the École de Médecine, where he transferred to study physiology as the most suitable starting point for the development of a theory of "social physiology," as he called it. In his approach to scientific method, as well as in acknowledging his debt to Condorcet, he saw himself as the heir of Bacon and of Descartes, who, following Bacon's plan, "organized the scientific revolution . . . drew the dividing line between ancient and modern sciences, and planted the flag around which the physicists rallied to attack the theologians. He tore the world's sceptre out of the hands of imagination and placed it in the hands of reason. He established the famous principle: *Man should believe only those things avowed by reason and confirmed by experience*—a principle that crushed superstition and changed the moral face of our planet."[59] Bacon had defined as the "true and lawful" goal of the sciences: "that human life be endowed with new discoveries and powers."[60] Saint-Simon laid equal emphasis on the philanthropic role of the scientist as the agent of progress, dedicated to the improvement of human life on earth. At his own expense he organized public courses in science taught by some of the foremost young scientists in Paris. In late middle age he described how as a young man he had defined his vocation: "To study the advance of the human mind in order subsequently to work for the improvement of civilization: that was the aim I set myself. From that moment I devoted myself to it totally; I consecrated my entire life to it."[61]

He represented his utopia as the crowning stage of an historical process he interpreted as an alternation between "organic" epochs of construction, when individuals were united by a common bond of faith or culture, and "critical" epochs whose function was to destroy outdated institutions and values. The two great constructive periods were classical antiquity, represented by Greco-Roman civilization, and medieval Christianity. Christianity's failure to adapt to a new age of science had led to a period of destructive criticism, which Saint-Simon saw as a necessary preparation for the coming third epoch, based on mankind's great advances in science. The eighteenth century's destruction of outdated institutions and values had cleared the ground, but at the cost of humans' sense of unity: the coming new order required a new unifying conception of man, which Saint-Simon undertook to provide.

In contrast to the theocrats, as the neo-Catholics came to be called, he presented his vision of social transformation as a scientific construct based on empirical observation of the achievements of the applied natural sciences in the nineteenth century and the emerging industrial society, whose forces and processes, he argued, would be best accommodated through the diffusion of power in a system of corporate cooperation embracing the "productive" elements of society— entrepreneurs, producers, and workers—which he collectively termed "les industriels," directed by an elite of managers chosen for their professional expertise. Moral guidance would be provided to the new society by scientists and artists as a spiritual force to replace the vacuum left by the decline of religious belief. This functional system based on selection by merit would end the domination of "les oisifs," the old privileged classes, and promote the well-being of "la classe la plus nombreuse et la plus pauvre" by increasing production and ensuring that rewards were distributed in accordance with the contribution of each to the common good. There would be no conflict or exploitation in the new society, which would be founded on a natural hierarchy of abilities. Power politics would be replaced by "the science of production,"[62] an echo of Bacon's prediction that the progress of the arts and sciences would lead to the replacement of dominion over men by the rule of men over things.

Historians of socialism are divided on whether Saint-Simon's system of corporate cooperation can be described as such.[63] He failed to anticipate the exploitative aspects of industrialization and the ensuing class conflict, and was close to contemporary French liberals such as Benjamin Constant and J-B. Say in his faith that the wealth created by industry would advance the interests of society as a whole. But while he shared their utilitarian concept of the goal of morality as the greatest happiness of the greatest number, he differed from them in his literal interpretation of this precept, as applied to "la classe la plus nombreuse et la plus pauvre": "The direct aim of my enterprise is to improve as much as possible the condition of the class that has no other means of existence but the labor of its hands."[64] The liberals' failure to perceive the weaknesses of the parliamentary system as a means to that end and their lack of interest in social welfare led him to break with them. In a fragment written in the last year of his life, he stated that the most direct way to bring about an improvement in the moral and physical well-being of "the proletarian class" was to provide state funding for the provision of productive work for all, to disseminate education as widely as possible, and to provide that class with the leisure and interests to develop their faculties.[65]

The originality of Saint-Simon's attempt to apply the methodology of the natural sciences to a "science" of social organization has often been obscured by a misinterpretation of the "New Christianity" he began to formulate in the last year of his life, and a failure to make a clear distinction between his thought and the messianic authoritarianism of his disciples, the Saint-Simonian sect. He was consistent in presenting his vision of social transformation as a scientific construct based on empirical observation of the progress of industry and the achievements of the applied sciences in the modern age. He saw the advance in knowledge as the driving force behind the "critical" periods that had discarded outworn philosophical and moral systems in the past—thus theology had gradually lost ground and theism had been replaced by positivism as a result of the advance in the empirical study of nature and man. He urged scientists, artists, and all who were devoted to the process of enlightenment to assume the role of the moral vanguard of society, and attempted unsuccessfully to garner support for his project of a new encyclopedia of knowledge that would complete the work of the *Encyclopédie* of Diderot and d'Alembert by replacing theology with a system of "terrestrial morality" in harmony with positive science. He sought the collaboration of Europe's most distinguished scientists in constructing a philosophy of social organization based on a general synthesis of the sciences. But although a few scientists, including Cuvier, responded positively, he was unable to get the support he sought from the scientific community.

In his later life he gave increasing significance to the historical role of religious sentiment in creating the moral unity he saw as the basis of social cohesion. But this was not a retreat from his positivism. On the question of the existence of God he declared: "This belief is not in opposition to any observed fact; but the existence of God is not itself an observed fact, and this is sufficient reason for us not to include the science based on that idea among the positive sciences." It was not, however, his intention "to destroy beliefs that have been very useful for such a long time, and can still be very useful."[66] Thus, on the ground that the principles of charity and fraternity, which would serve as the basis of public education under the direction of scientists, were identical to the Christian message, he called on Christians to join in the call for the changes in social organization "required by the progress of enlightenment." This utilitarian approach to the Christian religion is reflected in his "New Christianity." It was not a replacement for "terrestrial morality" but a response to the perceived need to endow scientists with the spiritual and moral authority previously exercised by the Church. He had come to believe that this moral guidance could be delivered most effectively by an organized Church with its own rituals and body of beliefs. He lived only to complete a few pages on the subject; his project was continued in a very different spirit by his disciples.

Saint-Simon's legacy eludes definition. He combined the Enlightenment's faith in reason with a Romantic insistence on the importance
of imagination and feeling in the perception of reality. Commonly
regarded in his lifetime as an interesting eccentric, he had a seminal
influence on the development of sociology, socialism, and industrial
ideology. Utopian though they undoubtedly were, his hopes for the
future were built not on mystical faith but on the achievements of
modern science. In his own century his influence extended to such
disparate figures as John Stuart Mill, Heine, George Sand, Berlioz,
and Liszt, as well as the humanistic strand of socialism represented
by Pierre Leroux and P.-J. Proudhon. Saint-Simon's humanism was
the single common factor attracting liberals, socialists, writers, and
artists to his thought. As he put it, "The essence of my life's work is to
afford all members of society the greatest possible opportunity for the
development of their faculties."[67]

*　*　*

It is to this aspect of Saint-Simon's thought that Herzen was referring
when, asked to comment on his letter to Ogarev of 19 July, he told his
interrogators that what attracted him was Saint-Simon's teaching on
the moral perfecting of the human race, coinciding with his own hopes
that the destruction of the last century would clear the way for a purer
morality founded on "new principles."[68] He is unlikely to have missed
the summary of his ideas as presented by his followers in 1830 in the
Revue encyclopédique, a French periodical with a wide circulation
among the Russian intelligentsia. It began as follows:

> All the bonds of attachment are broken; everywhere there are com-
> plaints or fears; nowhere can joy and hope be seen; mistrust and ha-
> tred, charlatanism and cunning reign in general relations and are
> equally expressed in private life. This disorder we observe in politics,
> which divides us in the name of power and freedom; in the sciences,
> devoid of any mutual links . . . in industry, where so many sacrifices
> are offered on the altar of fierce competition; finally, in the fine arts,
> which shiver in their drabness, deprived of bounteous inspiration. . . .
> In the face of this terrible crisis we ask these disunited, isolated
> people locked in mutual combat—has not the time come to create
> new bonds of love, teaching and activity, which would unite them,
> inspire them to proceed peacefully, in an orderly way, lovingly to the

service of all and give society, the globe itself, the whole world, the character of unity, wisdom and beauty?

The technocratic aspects of Saint-Simon's teaching had little relevance to the concerns of a Russian living under a system still based on the preindustrial economy of serfdom, but a passage such as the above would have resonated fully with the aesthetic ideal of moral self-fulfillment Herzen had formed under the influence of Schiller—the harmonization of sentiment with reason, to be achieved through the all-round development of human potential. On the ethical role of experimental science as a means to this end there are striking parallels between Herzen's thinking and Saint-Simon's. Both assign a key significance to Bacon's inductive method as marking a turning point in the moral development of European societies, away from the reign of prejudice and superstition and toward a new respect for sensuous reality and the physical world. Saint-Simon's image of scientists as the moral leaders of society was anticipated long before by Bacon, who replaced the scholastic ideal of the contemplative life with an insistence on the philanthropic role of science as devoted to the improvement of the human lot, speaking at times of scientists as a priesthood in their dedication to this goal.[69] The social responsibility of scientists and philosophers is the leitmotif of the essay "On Man's Place in Nature," where Herzen calls to mind the "terrible mistakes" of those one-sided visions of the world that have flooded humanity's path with blood. Bacon's insights in this regard will be a recurring theme in Herzen's later writings, as we shall see.

* * *

The surviving writings from Herzen's years at Moscow University demonstrate how far removed his approach to knowledge was from the stereotype of the Russian idealist of the 1830s, as satirized by Pavlov—the youths who "believed themselves to have attained the heights of knowledge by applying to everything the principles of German philosophy." Perpetuated by his principal biographers,[70] this image is belied by the essays and letters that reflect the remarkable breadth of his thought, based on an astonishing range of reading in philosophy, history, and science from the ancient to the contemporary world, a body of knowledge into which he introduced a kind of coherence with the help of the method he had acquired in his scientific studies. His aim was ambitious—to diagnose the malady of modern societies and provide a prescription for their cure. "The world awaits renewal." But whence would that come?

He began debating this question with Ogarev in the summer of 1832. To Herzen's suggestion that this role might be fulfilled by the recently founded United States of America, Ogarev had responded that, given the strength of political opposition and the growth of enlightenment in France, the initiative would fall to the French.[71] Herzen rejected this view on the ground that they had been too deeply corrupted by the excesses of the Revolution. Nor was England a likely candidate, egoism being the dominant trait of English life and politics. Where then should one look? "Boldly I say: Germany."[72]

Given the pair's preoccupation with French radical thought, Ogarev would have had reason to be surprised. But the legacy of the German Enlightenment was part of the cultural air Herzen breathed.[73] He was effectively bilingual: he spoke German with his mother; one of his two nurses had been German, and in his adolescence their role had been taken over successively by two male Germans fulfilling the dual function of tutors and servants. His youthful idealism had been shaped by Schiller's poetry and plays, and he had entered university at the height of the Russian intelligentsia's infatuation with German Romanticism. Although he rejected the Romantic escapism of Stankevich's circle, he maintained a strong critical interest in contemporary German writing, as shown by an essay written in prison in 1834, focused primarily on the fantastic stories of E. T. A. Hoffmann. While acknowledging the mesmerizing power of Hoffmann's imagination, he deplores his detachment from the great issues of the age. Herzen singles out only one of Hoffmann's contemporaries for praise, referring approvingly to a critique of the Romantic movement emanating from the "poisonous pen" of Heinrich Heine.[74] The work in question, a substantial study entitled "The Romantic School," is characterized by Heine's mocking wit and spirit of revolt.

Herzen's optimistic prediction to Ogarev in the autumn of 1833 may be explained by the fact that he was then engaged in translating a report written for the French government by Victor Cousin on the condition of public education in the German states. (The translation was completed a year later, but its publication was forestalled by his arrest.)[75] Cousin's highly positive picture would have heightened his interest in the potential of the country that had undergone significant changes in the direction of enlightened absolutism after the Napoleonic Wars, "the country of the Vehmic courts, of the Burschenschaften" (the student societies whose motto was "Alle für einen, eine für alle!" [All for one, one for all!] and who took part in public demonstrations in sympathy with the French revolution of July 1830). "Superficial people," he writes to Ogarev, "are amazed that Germany is not clearly following the current [constitutional] trend; but what is this current trend? Une transaction entre la féodalité et la liberté [a deal between feudalism and liberty], a contract between master and servant: but we need neither masters nor servants."[76] This was the first hint in his writings of his future anarchist sympathies.

He promised to develop these thoughts in an article "for friends"; it was never written, nor did he ever return to his hopes for Germany. On the other hand (as Chapter 11 will show), the view of freedom to which he devoted the most profound writings of his mature years would owe much of its inspiration to four German thinkers: Schiller, Goethe, Hegel, and Feuerbach.

CHAPTER EIGHT

Prison and Exile

Providence knows where it is leading us, and by what paths.

HERZEN TO HIS FUTURE WIFE N. A. ZAKHARINA, 1837

IN *My Past and Thoughts* Herzen presents his brief love affair with Ludmilla Passek as overshadowed by the pair's prescient anticipation of his impending fate. Modeling themselves on the hero and heroine of a melodramatic novel by the French writer Saintine, they "dreamed together of the future, of exile, of prisons . . . and I used to fancy how she would accompany me to the Siberian mines."[1] A letter to Ogarev at the height of this relationship conveys a very different anticipation of the future: "I'm terribly happy. I have everything, a *comrade*, friends, and *her*, who loves me madly; and I know that I have the spirit and the will to guarantee me a sphere of activity, and fame. What else do I need?"[2] Absorbed in his plans for the journal, which promised his circle a leading position in the philosophical debates of the time, he was wholly unprepared for the catastrophe that engulfed them in July 1834.

It began with the arrest of a group of students accused of singing seditious songs about the imperial family at a drunken supper party set up by a provocateur. None of Herzen's circle had been present, but because Ogarev's name had been mentioned by one of the accused, he was arrested. His seized papers included letters from Herzen, which led in turn to his own arrest on 21 July, followed by the arrests of Satin, Lakhtin, and Sokolovsky, author of some of the offending verses. Ever on the lookout for signs of sedition, the authorities' vigilance had recently been sharpened by an outbreak of fires in Moscow, whose perpetrators were never caught. The leading investigator of the "affair of the libelous songs" informed Count Benckendorf, chief of gendarmes, that of those arrested, Herzen and Ogarev merited special attention—the papers seized from them included "certain writings and letters that give cause to conclude that they have some kind of intention."[3]

On the tsar's orders an investigative committee designed to deal with offenses against the state was set up to examine their case. Their interrogations took the form of written questions and answers. Herzen's first appearance before the committee, three days after his arrest, was relatively brief. He replied in the negative to a series of questions: Had he translated any forbidden works, expressed in writing anything "contrary to the Christian religion or to decrees of the state," belonged to or known of the existence and aims of any secret society?[4]

Required to give the names of his acquaintances and the contents of their discussions and correspondence, he supplied a litany of names, including his father, senior government officials, and professors, as well as his contemporaries, with all of whom he had discussed matters of literature, science, and philosophy. He later wrote that he responded to his questioners with "evasive and empty phrases,"[5] but this is not wholly the case. Asked if he had participated in "free and even impudent conversations directed against the government," he replied, "My friends and I had conversations about the government. I criticized some institutions and, most frequently, the straitened circumstances of the landowners' peasants, pointing to the arbitrariness of the taxes levied by their masters and the burden of work and considered that this situation was harmful to industry." This is Herzen's first known reference to the inhumanity of serfdom, the abolition of which would be the central goal of his political propaganda as an émigré in the 1840s and 1850s. His interrogators had not asked for his opinion on the subject; to volunteer this criticism of the economic basis of the regime was an act of ill-considered candor. He seems to have sought immediately to palliate its effect by adding that, as shown by his critical remarks on constitutional regimes in the papers they had seized, he regarded autocracy as "definitely" superior to "mixed governments."[6]

His second interrogation a month later was based on a meticulous examination of the letters, manuscripts, and literature (fifty-four items in total) seized on his arrest. As a result his case was deemed serious enough for the appointment of a new commission, personally approved by the tsar. The session began with the demand that he explain his freethinking opinions on the Russian system of government, in particular two instances of "oppositional tendencies"—a reference in his essay on the period from Peter the Great to the French Revolution as an example of the way in which history progresses through conflict and destruction, and his expression of hope (expressed in a letter to Ogarev) for a new revolution that would eliminate the need for "masters and servants." He responded that his reference to the Revolution concerned its destruction of feudalism, and that the phrase in his letter related only to constitutional systems, which he saw as perpetuating feudal relations; as Hegel had shown, the relation between monarch and subject was of a different order. The evident thinness of this defense prompted Herzen to conclude it with the caveat that at the time of writing he was "somewhat carried away" by new philosophical ideas, and was no longer in "complete" agreement with the opinions he had then expressed.[7]

There was no such evasiveness in his answer to the next question. This demanded an explanation of the letter in which he had agreed with Ogarev that Saint-Simonism "deserves our attention." Citing the relevant passage in full, his inquisitors asked what precisely he had meant in describing the French Revolution as only a preliminary step toward the renewal of European societies. He replied that he was referring to moral renewal.[8] We have seen that this answer was a fair summary of his thinking on the subject of Saint-Simon.

Sifting diligently through his papers for evidence of membership in a secret society, the commission had discovered a list of names and numbers referring, as Herzen explained, to the distribution of complimentary copies of his recently completed translation of Victor Cousin's book (whose publication was forestalled by his arrest). He was unable to furnish any specific reasons for possessing a copy of the official account of the sentences given to the Decembrists. Combing his correspondence for evidence of conspiratorial intent, the Third Department had come up with three particularly suspect passages: a comment to Ogarev that together with Vadim Passek "we form a single whole," Ogarev's complaint that at the age of eighteen he had still to "create something," and a prediction by Ludmilla Passek that he would fulfill his destiny "at the head of a multitude of noble young men." Herzen explained the first comment by the circle's common dedication to the sciences, the second by the daydreams characteristic of youth.

Ludmilla Passek's prediction was trickier to explain, but the example of Professor Pavlov seems to have come to Herzen's aid: he replies that both his friends and his professors knew of his ambition to continue his studies with the goal of attaining a professorship in natural sciences, which he would combine with "contemporary German philosophy," thereby captivating the young.[9]

The tsar was kept informed of the progress of the two interrogations. In his report to the Third Department in September, the committee's chair, Prince S. M. Golitsyn, wrote: "[Herzen] is a very young man with a fervid imagination and with talents and a good education. He did not take part in the singing of libelous songs, but is noticeably infected with the spirit of the times. This is evident from his papers and his answers. However, up till now we have not uncovered any sign of evil intent nor any links with ill-intentioned people." On the basis of this assessment one might have expected Herzen to be freed with a stern warning. But the final report submitted by Golitsyn in January 1835 on Herzen and those of his circle who had been charged with him added an afterthought that was to seal his fate: "Although they show no sign of a real intention to change the state order and their opinions . . . are no more than the dreams of a fervid imagination, . . . if ingrained over time, they could nevertheless give rise to an intellectual disposition to undertake acts contrary to order." He therefore recommends that Herzen, "not having participated in singing or listening to seditious songs and involved in the inquiry only through his mode of thought," should not be subjected to further imprisonment but sent into government service in some distant province under strict supervision by the authorities.[10]

Herzen spent six and a half months in prison before being summoned at the end of March 1835 to hear his sentence along with the other members of his circle caught up in the same investigation. All would be condemned to periods of exile. To Herzen's great indignation, his offense was stated as participation in the affair of which the investigation had cleared him. He was forced under protest to append his signature to the document connecting him with the drunken supper party, which remained the source of all subsequent official references to his case. He was sentenced to exile for an indeterminate period in the city of Perm in the borderlands of western Siberia, a destination that was almost immediately changed to nearby Vyatka.

* * *

Composed nearly two decades after the events, and imbued with contemptuous loathing for the regime that had persecuted him, the chapters of Herzen's memoirs relating his arrest and imprisonment are an artistic reconstruction in which personalities and events are viewed through the hero's satirical lens, an approach amply justified by the records of his interrogations and sentencing. Factual gaps and inaccuracies in the narrative do not detract from the credibility of his account of the ordeals that brought about his transformation from young idealist into mature revolutionary.

The ordeals began in the early hours of 21 July with the arrival at his father's house of a small detachment of Cossacks and police, armed with an order for his arrest signed by the military governor-general of Moscow. His mother and the servants wept; his father blessed him and put a little icon round his neck: an enamel of the head of John the Baptist on a plate. "What was this—example, advice, or prophecy?"[11]

He was taken initially to an ordinary prison, but as the son of a nobleman and a political prisoner he enjoyed certain privileges: a cell to himself and permission to receive up to a bottle of wine a day from his home. But from his cell he could hear the moans and screams of those arrested on suspicion of involvement in the Moscow arson attacks as they were thrashed to extract confessions. Nearly twenty years later he recalls, "It was awful, intolerable. I dreamed of these sounds at night, and woke up in a frenzy, thinking that these sufferers a few paces away from me were lying on straw, in chains, their backs torn and beaten, and in all probability quite innocent." Much of Herzen's revolutionary journalism in emigration would be devoted to describing specific cases of the brutality and lawlessness of the Russian regime. His first direct exposure to it inspired this passage in his memoirs:

> To know what Russian prisons, Russian courts and police are like one must be a peasant, a house-serf, an artisan or a *meshchanin* [town workman]. Political prisoners, of whom the majority belong to the nobility, are under strict custody and are brutally punished, but their fate bears no comparison with that of the common people. With them

the police does not stand on ceremony. To whom can a peasant or an artisan go subsequently to complain? Where can he find legal redress?

So great is the brutality, savagery, arbitrariness, and corruption of the Russian courts and the Russian police that a simple man who is brought to judgment fears not the sentence of the court but the process of law itself. He waits impatiently to be sent to Siberia—his martyrdom will end with the beginning of his punishment. Let us now remember that three-quarters of people seized by the police on suspicion are freed by the courts, and they have passed through the same tortures as the guilty.[12]

Herzen's account of his interrogations conveys vividly what Martin Malia has described as the moral tone of Nicolas's rule, in which "the trappings of a benevolent paternalism vainly attempted to conceal an arbitrary exercise of power which recognized no rights for the individual independent of the needs of the state and the will of the emperor."[13]

Herzen describes the false solicitude of his interrogators, who urged him for the sake of his father's health and his future career to throw himself on the tsar's mercy, demonstrating his penitence by naming those who had led him astray. No members of his circle availed themselves of this fatherly concern.[14]

After his first interrogation he was transferred to a cell in a former monastery that had been converted to hold political prisoners. He would remain there until his sentencing. His brief account of the months spent in this cell, stressing the monotony of the daily prison routine, is significant for what it omits. He relates that after a few weeks he was given a supply of paper, ink, and a candle to allow him to read at night, his only permitted reading matter being "some little books of no account [koe-kakie knizhonki]"[15] and, at his request, an Italian grammar. There is no mention of the content of the books or of the use he made of the paper, although we know that in prison he began an essay on the fantastic stories of E. T. A. Hoffmann and two tales: The German Traveller and A Legend (all of which he reworked during his exile). He was closely enough acquainted with the subject matter of the first two, German Romanticism and Goethe, to be able to write from memory (he had devoted some of his first weeks after graduation to refreshing his knowledge of Goethe), but the third was based directly on one of the "little books" he read in prison: the lives of the Eastern saints—the *Cheti-Minei*.

In his last months of freedom he had come to perceive the lives of the early Christians as a source of inspiration for a future social order. From letters he managed to smuggle out to his future wife it is evident that in prison they became for him a model for fortitude in the face of persecution.

The daughter of one of his father's brothers by a serf, Natalya Zakharina led a lonely and unhappy life deprived of family affection, as the ward of another relative, Princess Khovanskaya. Six years her senior, Herzen had befriended her, a friendship cemented by her sympathy in the days before his arrest, when he had been tormented by ignorance of Ogarev's fate. When they found means of corresponding after his own arrest, she became his eager confidante, his "sister." In his seventh month of captivity he writes, "I've made myself at home, become used to being a convict, an outcast from society, a state criminal." But he rejects the thought that he and Ogarev may be fated to finish their lives in oblivion—"Why then did nature endow us with these ardent souls, craving action and fame, if only to mock us? . . . But no! In my breast there burns a strong and living faith. Providence exists!" Reading the *Cheti-Minei* is sending him into "transports of delight"—"What divine examples of selflessness! What people!"[16]

Two months later the account in the New Testament of the Last Supper leads him to reflect on the "powerful poetry" of sorrow, as Christ prepares to sacrifice himself for mankind. "But where is *our* Christ? . . . Surely we're not pupils without a teacher, apostles without a Messiah?" He was ready to endure worse sufferings than those now inflicted on him, but not the cold indifference with which society regarded him and his fellow prisoners. "I'd rather they hated us—that would still be preferable." When the apostle Peter arrived in Rome in chains, the populace ran to greet him: "Who will . . . accompany us? Perhaps only laughter. The Commission accused me of Saint-Simonism; I'm not a Saint-Simonist, but in many things I feel wholly at one with them. There's no true life without faith."[17]

Prisoners were allowed only religious or improving literature in their cells (Herzen was able to convince his jailers that the Italian grammar came into the second category), but his choice of religious reading was not just a way of filling time. The subject matter of the *Legend* and its numerous references to specific passages from the Epistles and Gospels reflect an intensification of his interest in early Christianity, prompted by his personal predicament. In the summer of 1833 the figures of Christ and his followers had attracted him as historical models for the moral renewal of society. Now, desperate to find some redemptive meaning in the disaster that had struck him, he tries to interpret it as a test of his faith in a divine providence presiding over human affairs. Without identifying with the excesses of Saint-Simon's followers, he is at one with them in seeking a mystical explanation of the disorder of contingent existence.

His letters to Natalie show that his religious reading provided the main comfort of his prison life. Why therefore conceal this fact under the reference to "little books of no account"? The answer may be found in the nature of the memoirs as an epic account of the formation of a great revolutionary. Herzen began to write the chapters dealing with his early life in 1852, three years after completing *From the Other Shore*, with its passionate and sustained attack on all forms of faith, religious or secular, that sought to explain present suffering as a necessary prelude to the attainment of future bliss. There he would emphasize the strength of humans' attachment to teleological visions of history and individual destinies that were unsupported by experience. It is evident that his mature insights into the human need for metaphysical comfort owed much to his own experience, but such self-revelation would have been inconsistent with the artistic and didactic goals of *My Past and Thoughts*. In his first years of exile he found consolation in a surrogate form of religious faith, focused on the notion of a higher destiny chosen for him by Providence, and nourished through an earnest and exalted correspondence with his future wife, who responded in kind. The memoirs gloss over this episode, attributing his lapse into "mysticism" to the influence of a fellow exile and the devoutly religious Natalie. Fortunately, a voluminous correspondence has survived to fill this gap.

* * *

On 10 April 1835 Herzen set out for Perm in a carriage escorted by a gendarme. Cold and drenched after a stormy crossing of the Volga on a raft, he was forced to spend a night in Kazan in wet clothes on a table in the posting station. He fired off a letter of protest instantly to Count Apraksin, general of the gendarmes, which resulted in permission to put up at a hotel for three days in Kazan before resuming his journey.[18] On the road to Perm he was exposed to the traveling conditions of less privileged prisoners, as his carriage passed a multitude in chains on their way to Siberia on carts or on foot. He subsequently wrote to Natalie, "Those terrible faces, that terrible noise, the harsh light of dawn and the cold morning wind filled my soul with such icy horror that I turned away shivering—those moments will remain in my memory for my entire life."[19]

After three weeks in Perm, where he made the acquaintance of a number of Poles exiled for their part in the insurrection of 1830, he was transferred to Vyatka to take up a post as an official in the provincial administration. In letters to Ketcher and Natalie he looks back on his first months in the post. He did no serious reading. His mornings were spent on official business and the afternoons mostly squandered on the "empty life" of the Vyatka salons. His personal wealth and position in Moscow society made him a center of attention for the town's social elite, a position that he confesses he had enjoyed, but that led him into a regrettable sexual liaison: "les devoirs de la société of a small town force everyone to commit follies." The principal folly in question was an affair with Praskovia Medvedeva, an attractive young woman unhappily married to an elderly functionary. When he died unexpectedly and she was free to remarry, Herzen took fright and extricated himself from the relationship. In a letter to Natalie confessing the liaison, he managed to reduce his sense of guilt by offloading most of the responsibility for his behavior onto those who had encouraged it: "the crowd!"— henceforth his collective name for Vyatka society: "I gave you my confidence once, unclean people, and you used it to soil me."[20]

The Romantic opposition of the hero and the crowd was a satisfying way of interpreting his current misfortunes. A few days later he reflects that he is not to blame for the distress caused to his parents by his banishment: "God endowed me with a soul that towers above the crowd— my guilt consists solely in this."[21] The society whose attentions had so recently gratified him had turned into "a kingdom of darkness and turpitude." "It is truly horrible to see trivia, nonsense, and gossip engulfing all of [provincial] life, . . . and to be forced to take part in it

Drawing of Herzen in Vyatka, 1836, by Alexander Witberg.

all!" He is surrounded by "repulsive monsters"—from the bureaucratic machine, "sucking the people's blood through a thousand unclean mouths," to the governor, Tyufiaev, coarse, dissolute, and
wielding his power like a Turkish pasha.[22] His fellow clerks are dismissed in his memoirs as mostly persons of no education and no moral
principles, for whom cheating the authorities and exploiting the peasants was a way of life. He recalls yearning for his Moscow prison cell
with cockroaches as his sole company—"instead of these vulgar re-

View of Vyatka at the time of Herzen's exile there as a provincial official.

marks, dirty people, petty ideas and coarse sentiments, a deathly still-ness and undisturbed leisure."[23] Nowhere, he assures Natalie, could one encounter a lower representative of the human species than in a backwater like Vyatka. "In the capital at least the externals are respect-able but here everything is on show; there they sweep up the dirt, here it is knee-high!"[24] All that could be said for his current situation was that it was giving him a closer knowledge of Russia and its system of government, which might turn out to be useful in the future.

In the autumn of 1835 his circumstances improved. Following a government decree on the collection of statistics throughout the re-gions of the empire, a committee was established for this purpose in Vyatka—and Herzen, whose superior education marked him out from the other clerks, was selected to serve on it, a task that, as he wrote to Natalie, was better suited to his aptitudes. Moreover, he was permitted to work on his own at his residence, which, thanks to his father's fi-nancial resources, was a comfortable rented house with the services of a family valet brought from Moscow. But these privileges, together with considerable leisure for writing and reflection, did nothing to alleviate the misery of separation from his friends. "Where are you all?" he writes to Sazonov and Ketcher. "It's as though I once glimpsed you in a dream, but reality is the chancellery, the absence of intellectual activity and, worst of all, the absence of poetry."[25] He is oppressed by the fear that he may die without achieving any of his aspirations, "a Don Quixote *sui generis*," fit only as a model for the role of doomed genius in some fashionable novel of the time.[26]

He was saved from despair by a combination of religion and romantic love.

* * *

He had turned to Christianity in his first months in prison in the search for some providential meaning that would make sense of the disaster that had overtaken him and give him hope ("One cannot live without faith"). With the prospect of indeterminate exile, the need for faith became even more pressing. In December 1835 he wrote to Natalie that he had encountered a "messenger from heaven"—the exiled architect Alexander Witberg, who introduced him to Masonic mysticism.[27]

This was Herzen's first engagement with a strand of thought that from the second half of the eighteenth century had attracted Russian intellectuals disillusioned by the excesses of Enlightenment rationalism but not prepared to return to traditional forms of religious belief. In Russia, as in England at that time, the dominant form of Freemasonry was deistic and socially oriented, combining the goal of moral self-perfecting with belief in the universal brotherhood of man, to be attained in a future golden age. Its foremost representative, the writer and satirist Nikolai Novikov, was a dedicated reformer, committed to the Enlightenment's ideals of tolerance and individual freedom; his educational and publishing activities led to his imprisonment under Catherine II, whose persecution of the movement in the 1780s drove it inward, toward concern with the life of the soul. Mystical Freemasonry enjoyed only a brief period of popularity in intellectual and court circles in the first quarter of the nineteenth century, at the time of Alexander I's addiction to various forms of mysticism and occultism, but the sources that had inspired it—the writings of the mystics Jakob Boehme and Louis-Claude Saint-Martin, most of which had been translated into Russian—continued to occupy a prominent position in Russian thought. Their faith in the soul's capacity for direct insight into the secrets of nature and communion with the Divine without the mediation of reason or ecclesiastical doctrine, together with their notion of humanity and nature as manifestations of a single fundamental force, contributed to the religious and mystical character of early Romantic philosophy, most notably Schelling's *Naturphilosophie.* "Lyubomudrie" (love of wisdom)—the word used by early Russian idealist philosophers to signal their independence from the French philosophes—was originally a mystical Masonic term.

Alexander had commissioned Witberg to design and build a great cathedral on the Sparrow Hills to commemorate the victory over Napoleon. His visionary project, infused with Masonic symbolism, came to grief when mysticism fell from favor on the accession of Nicolas, who was strongly averse to esoteric doctrines and secret societies. Unjustly charged with mismanagement of funds, Witberg was disgraced, ruined, and after a trial which dragged on for a decade, exiled to Vyatka.

Though Witberg was almost twice his age, Herzen immediately found him a kindred spirit, describing him in letters to Ketcher and Natalie as a Colossus with an artist's soul, "a great man in a petty age" who had dedicated his life to a noble dream and suffered persecution for it.[28] Herzen devotes a chapter of his memoirs to this man, with whom he would reside for the remainder of his time in Vyatka, and under whose influence he plunged into the study of occultism and Christian mysticism with the same thoroughness and enthusiasm he had brought to the study of history, asking his friends to supply him with Swedenborg's *Arcana Celestia* (a line-by-line commentary on Genesis and Exodus), the work of Einemazer [?] on magnetism, and everything they could find on "alchemy and its adherents, Paracelsus, the Neoplatonists of the time of Apollonius Tyaneus. I beg and implore you."[29] In prison he had seized on the image of Christ the Redeemer and a vague notion of Providence as sources of comfort and hope ("There is no true life without faith"). In his current situation, amorphous Christianity would not do; stronger consolation was required. He found it in the certitude of mystics that their insights into the divine and preordained order of the universe represented a higher form of knowledge than that of philosophy or science. He writes to Natalie how at the end of an exhausting day reading spiritual literature as preparation for "an article about *religion* and *philosophy*," he opened a work by the Christian theosophist Karl von Eckartshausen and came upon a passage from scripture on love as the foundation of all being. Why did the text fall open at just that place? Was it chance? "Nonsense, there's no such thing as chance—(that's an absurdity, invented by unbelief)."[30] Eckartshausen's name was missing from the list Herzen had sent to his friends; his works would have been readily available in Witberg's library. A very influential exponent of early German Romanticism, his work in natural philosophy and Christian theosophy influenced contemporary mystical thinkers. His writings were particularly popular in France and in Russia, where they were disseminated by Novikov's publishing enterprise. One of his greatest admirers was Alexander Labzin, a prominent Russian mystic under Alexander I until he ran afoul of the Orthodox hierarchy and was exiled to Siberia, where he died in 1825. Labzin, who had devoted himself to translating and publishing Eckartshausen's works, was a close friend of Witberg, who describes his relationship with him and his fate in autobiographical notes written in collaboration with Herzen.[31] One may assume that the variety of Christian theosophy into which Witberg initiated Herzen drew heavily on Eckartshausen's thought, which had strong affinities with Schelling's *Naturphilosophie*. He had a close interest in the workings of nature, interpreting the latest discoveries in the natural and physical sciences as confirmations of the existence of a single divine force—the ultimate ground of all being, whose development he interpreted in terms of a vitalistic pantheism that, like Schelling's World Soul, laid claim to the authority of science. Such mystical notions of the perfectibility of nature and man harmonized neatly with the cult of romantic love Herzen developed in a vast correspondence over three years with his cousin Natalie: religious mysticism and idealized love were to be his lifelines in Vyatka.

* * *

This extraordinary epistolary relationship (over 600 double-sided pages) was the expression of a love affair that was, in Malia's words, "quite the equal of anything imagined by the most resourceful of any of the romantic writers of Germany."[32] The correspondence between "brother" and "sister" that had begun during Herzen's months in prison continued after his transfer to Vyatka. By the end of 1835, loneliness, uncertainty about his future, and remorse over his conduct with Medvedeva had made him increasingly receptive to Natalie's "sisterly" devotion and her fervent faith in a benign Providence presiding over them both. In December he responded with a declaration of love, which was fervently reciprocated. The pair conceived their relationship in mystical terms, as the quasi-sacramental union of two souls. In the ensuing correspondence Natalie is invoked as "my reward for all my sufferings, my saint, my deity"; a "holy virgin" sent to lead Herzen, like Dante's Beatrice, into paradise. He links their love with his friendship, sealed on the Sparrow Hills, with his other ideal of holiness, Ogarev, as clear evidence of "the finger of Providence" directing his life.[33] He tells her that he dreams of their future reunion with all the awe with which a Christian approaches the sacrament of holy communion. Not to be outdone, Natalie describes herself as a lamp burning before his icon; he congratulates her on the poetry of the image. Although he represents himself as a "fallen angel" (a reference to his treatment of Medvedeva, the subject of a confession to Natalie at the outset of their new relationship), he takes for granted his spiritual ascendancy over his beloved: "Without you I am morally depraved, a man without a heart, a Byron, contemptuous of all mankind. Without me you are the beginning of a divine song, which goes no further, you are lips open but mute, a gaze directed toward the emptiness of a misty steppe. . . . Who but I would have dared to continue the poem, give speech to those lips, say to the eyes: 'Look at me' "? In her response to his need for redemptive love, she had surrendered her independent identity: "You are wholly absorbed into me; you no longer exist [tebia net bolee]."[34] In the light of their future marital tragedy, this passage has a prophetic ring.

As Malia observes, Herzen's protracted self-flagellation over Medvedeva in his correspondence with Natalie served only to increase his self-esteem.[35] By deifying the new object of his affections, he endowed her with the power to forgive his "sin," while not relinquishing his preeminence in their relationship. In October 1836 he explains that while her life had attained "its goal and its summit" in their love, his was not yet complete: he had still the obligation to assume his role in "universal life" through work for the good of mankind.[36] By the following year (his last in Vyatka) the idyll of romantic love had taken second place to the thirst to make an impact on the real world. "People with ardent souls don't exist for their private lives alone. I'm already twenty-four years old, and . . . I have still not divined what Providence has decreed for my life." Neither a literary career nor state service attracts him. The first is too far removed from day-to-day existence; as for the second, "How much humiliation, how many years will there be before my service can be of use?"[37] These, he tells Natalie, are the questions currently occupying his mind. Six months later, as rumors begin to reach him of an imminent end to his exile, he tells Natalie of an insistent inner voice—Providence perhaps—commanding him to become a man of action. At the end of December he was transferred from Vyatka to the town of Vladimir, around 200 kilometers northeast of Moscow.

* * *

From the quantity of his epistolary effusions on the love of two "beautiful souls," it might be assumed that Herzen passed most of his exile in Vyatka in a cloud of Romantic self-absorption and religious exaltation, to the neglect of his official duties. In fact these were the source of insights and experience on which he would draw long after his mystical fantasies had been forgotten.[38] Toward the end of his stay in the town, he wrote to his Moscow circle that while they knew nothing of Russia outside the capital, Vyatka had taught him a great deal about it. Their generalizations were based on books, whereas he had arrived at them through direct observation of events and juridical facts. "You see, I've become an empiricist."[39] His administrative duties initiated him into the workings of the bureaucracy and what passed for law in Russia, while the travels he undertook in his capacity of compiler of statistics (which would remain his principal duty after he was transferred to Vladimir) gave him broader insights into the nature of autocracy and the ignorance and helplessness of its victims, which would serve him well when, two decades later, he would attempt to influence the course of Russian history from the London offices of *The Bell*.

His impressions of the Vyatka administration were not entirely negative. Progress was being made in education; libraries were being established, although the pages of the books and journals they contained remained largely uncut, and the government's initiative in collecting data on the region was hobbled by chaotic disorganization. His official travels imbued him with a sense of Russia's vast potential. A visit to Kazan inspired patriotic musings on Russia's future as a meeting point between East and West. Siberia struck him as "a wholly new country" without a history, with all the potential of a *"sui generis* America"[40]— apparently the first allusion in his writings to the notion of historical youth that would become a central component of his "Russian socialism."

His work on the statistical committee demanded a less imaginative approach to history. His ethnological survey of the Finnish tribes and Russian peasants of the Vyatka region, printed in an official gazette, has survived. A section on the history, religion, songs, customs, and dress of the former is followed by a discussion of the latter's distinctive characteristics, resulting from their centuries-long isolation from their counterparts in European Russia—their nomadic tendencies, archaic syntax, and pronunciation, and the unusual architecture of their dwellings. Later, as editor of the statistical section of the *Vladimir Regional Gazette,* he would produce a similar report on the peasants of that region, calling for substantive study of their legends and traditions, the ancient churches and monuments of the area, and the documents contained in monasteries, all sources from which the narrative of their daily life was constructed. He urges that no detail of this be lost to history. The Vladimir peasants "have very many peculiarities, both in their inner lives and their occupations; and every peculiarity, of whatever kind it may be, is a precious fact, and should be recorded the more carefully as they are being gradually effaced through time."[41] Herzen would return to this theme in an editorial in the *Gazette* in February 1839. Pointing to the extraordinary richness of the area in historical treasures and memories, he urges readers to contact him with any information relevant to its history and topography. "At the present time all over Europe, the greatest attention is being given to amassing the smallest details of the life of the common people, the principal repository of ancient beliefs and traditions. This has come about through the current state of historical science, which seeks to recreate the past in its entire body and soul."[42] As a model of this approach he cites a study of the period of William the Conqueror by "the great Augustin Thierry," and the historical research of the contemporary Russian ethnographer Ivan Sakharov.[43]

During the 1830s, impelled by the Romantic movement and the Slavophiles, ethnographic studies had made considerable progress in Russia. In France the impetus for their development had come from liberal historians such as Thierry, a former secretary of Saint-Simon, who focused attention on the potential of the common people as the source of progress and pioneered the study of primary sources. Thierry had been on the historical reading list Herzen had drawn up on his graduation; but it was only when misfortune forced him into daily contact with the bedrock of Russian society, as a recipient of their complaints and requests and a witness of their arbitrary treatment at the hands of the bureaucracy, the landowners, and the courts, that its history and way of life became a matter of real interest to him. While researching his report on the Vladimir peasants, he wrote to Ketcher, requesting him to search out an issue of the *Revue des deux mondes* containing Thierry's essays on French historians and on Nero, "which must exist in Moscow."[44]

Statistical surveys gave Herzen a practical training in patient observation and the gradual accumulation of empirical facts, which he would later use to good effect against idealized images of the popular masses constructed by radical intellectuals. While praising Sakharov's reconstruction of the national past, he insists on the equal importance of studying the contemporary customs and rituals of the Russian peasantry. He welcomes the government's effort to advance popular enlightenment by setting up public lectures in physics and chemistry, observing that in the nineteenth century the practical importance of a knowledge of nature and its forces should be self-evident to all—a view that would become central to his thought in the following decade.

Herzen's reports belie the image conveyed in his letters of the self-obsessed adept of Counter-Enlightenment mysticism. He took part in setting up a public library in Vyatka, and one of his last official duties there was to make a speech at its opening. The core of his speech was a passionate defense of progress through the accumulation of knowledge and experience:

The book is the spiritual bequest of one generation to another. . . .
The entire life of mankind has successively accumulated in the
book: tribes, peoples, states have vanished, but the book remains. It
has grown up with mankind, in it are crystallized all the teachings
that had excited minds, all the passions that had inspired hearts; in
it has been inscribed that enormous confession of the life of mankind, that enormous autograph, which we call universal history. But
in the book is not only the past; it forms a document whereby we
enter into possession of the present, into possession of that sum of
truths and efforts, discovered through sufferings, sometimes drenched
in bloody sweat: it is the program for the future. Hence, we will respect *the book!* It represents that part of the thought of mankind that
has attained a relative independence, it is the trace it has left behind
in its transition into another life.[45]

Herzen's deliverance from Vyatka was the result of a visit to the
town by the tsarevich Alexander, attended by the poet V. A. Zhukovsky
and the statistician K. I. Arsenev. Herzen was given the responsibility
of preparing an exhibition of the artifacts of the region in their honor,
and (no doubt by virtue of his superior education) selected to comment
on the exhibits, after it had been established that the august visitors
would not object to being addressed by a convicted criminal. Zhukovsky, who had known some of the Decembrists, took an interest in
the young exile, and he and Arsenev persuaded Alexander to intercede
with his father for a mitigation of his sentence. At the beginning of
January 1838 Herzen was transferred to Vladimir, within easy reach of
his friends in Moscow. His isolation was at an end.

CHAPTER NINE

Awakening

We looked to philosophy for everything under the sun except pure thought.

IVAN TURGENEV

WHILE Herzen fretted in his Vyatka isolation, an epoch-making event occurred in Moscow. As Russian Romantics of the late 1820s sought refuge from a hostile world through the cult of their inner life, an eccentric ex-army officer had been preparing a philosophical time bomb that would shatter their metaphysical calm.

Petr Chaadaev, who was associated in his youth with the Decembrist movement and was a close friend of Pushkin, had abandoned his army career to devote himself to philosophy. His *First Philosophical Letter*, written in 1829 and inadvertently passed by the censor, was published in the *Telescope* in 1836. The government reacted instantly. The censor was dismissed, the journal banned, and the editor exiled to Siberia. Chaadaev was pronounced insane by order of the tsar and placed under medical supervision. The Russian educated public in general greeted the *Letter* with shocked indignation.

The cause of the furor was Chaadaev's ferociously pessimistic interpretation of his country's past, its present state, and its future prospects. He traced the origin of its predicament to the Schism of 1054, which had tied the Russian Church to the moribund culture of Byzantium. Russia's separation from the West was completed by two centuries of Mongol rule, a time of "cruel and humiliating foreign domination whose spirit was later inherited by our national rulers." While Europe was experiencing the cultural and moral flowering of the Renaissance, Russians were living "a dull and somber existence . . . in which the only thing that animated us was crime, the only thing that pacified us was slavery." Without traditions to revere or ideals to emulate, "we have taught the world nothing, added not a single idea to the mass of human ideas, contributed nothing to the progress of the human spirit. And we have disfigured everything we gained from that progress."[1]

Chaadaev's criticism did not spare the intelligentsia, whom he sought to disabuse of the belief that with the aid of Western philosophy they could transcend the reality around them and achieve wholeness and inner freedom. He argues that Europeans do not acquire their notions of duty, justice, right, and order from literature or science. Embedded in the history and traditions of their society, these are part of their physiology, absorbed at an early age through the practices of their daily life, along with the air they breathe. But Russians, like illegitimate children, enter the world without a patrimony. Belonging to neither East nor West, they possess the traditions of neither. "What has long constituted the very basis of social life in other lands is for us only theory and speculation. . . . The very things that elsewhere provide the necessary framework of life, within which all daily events are so naturally ordered, this condition, as indispensable to a healthy moral existence as good air is to a healthy physical existence, is completely lacking." He stresses that he is speaking not of moral principles or philosophical maxims, "but simply of a well-ordered life, those habits and routines of the intellect that give ease to the mind and impose a regular movement on the soul."[2]

Look around you, he invites his reader: "We all resemble travelers. Nobody has a definite sphere of existence, we have no proper habits, no rules for anything, not even in our domestic life; there is nothing to which we can be attached, nothing that would awaken our sympathy or affection—nothing durable, nothing lasting; everything passes, everything flows, leaving no traces either without or within us. In our own houses we seem to be guests, in our families we look like strangers, in our cities we look like nomads, even more than the nomads who graze their herds in our steppes, for they are more attached to their deserts than we to our cities." In the moral sphere his countrymen were still in a state of "chaotic fermentation . . . similar to the eruptions of the globe that preceded the present state of the planet." A culture based exclusively on borrowing and imitation had kept them at the stage of children who had never been made to think for themselves. All their knowledge remained on the surface of their being: "There is among us no inner development, no natural progress; new ideas sweep out the old because they do not arise from the latter, but land on us from heaven knows where. Because we accept only ready-made ideas, the indelible traces that a progressive movement of ideas engraves on the mind and that gives ideas their force makes no furrow on our intellect. We grow, but do not mature; we advance, but obliquely: that is, in a direction that does not lead to the goal." There are lost souls everywhere, he observes, "but in Russia it is the common characteristic."[3]

Chaadaev's critique was based on an interpretation of the historical process derived from French Catholic thinkers of the Counter-Enlightenment such as Pierre-Simon Ballanche and the early Lamennais. He held that the flowering of civilization in Europe under the tutelage of the Catholic Church was leading toward the ultimate rule of justice and harmony in a kingdom of God on earth. Russia's religious isolation had excluded her from this process. What was instinct for Europeans would have to be driven into Russian heads by hammer blows.

Although Chaadaev's metaphysics and philosophy of history isolated him from the main currents of Russian intellectual life, his analysis of the Russian intelligentsia's predicament touched too many raw nerves to be ignored. The *Letter's* appearance has been described as the most significant intellectual event inside nineteenth-century Russia. It raised publicly for the first time the questions that would define the debates between Slavophiles and Westernizers and their twentieth-century heirs. Its immediate effect was to produce almost universal outrage. The bleakness of Chaadaev's conclusions repelled even those who accepted that Russia had much to learn from the West. (He suggested that the single great lesson Russia might give the West in return was the presentation of an example to be avoided.)

Two notable exceptions to the chorus of indignation were the poet Lermontov (whose sardonically entitled novel of 1840, *A Hero of Our Time*, was the first depiction in realist prose of a Russian "superfluous man"), and Herzen, who describes in his memoirs the arrival by post in Vyatka of the issue of the *Telescope* containing Chaadaev's verdict on his country. He was struck by the bitterness of "this somber indictment" of Petrine Russia, the first to break the silence imposed on the country after 1825: "Chaadaev's *Letter* was . . . a shot ringing out in the dark night. . . . Whether it was a signal, a cry for help, news of the dawn, or news that there would be no dawn—it was all the same, one had to wake up."[4]

The chapter of Herzen's memoirs containing this account was written nearly two decades after the event. In the intervening years he would devote much of his writing to reflection on the wounds inflicted on the intelligentsia's psyche by its sense of alienation and the consequent distortion of its grasp of reality. Chaadaev's *Philosophical Letter* was crucial for his awakening to the Russian realities from which he had taken refuge in his cult of ideal love. But this process was slower than the memoirs suggest. It was only when he came back into direct contact with members of his Moscow circle, whose dreams of self-fulfillment alternated with destructive bouts of self-analysis, that he began to form an objective assessment of the psychological roots of his generation's thirst for certainties and to stake out a position of sober realism that would set him apart from Slavophiles and Westernizers alike.

* * *

The beginnings of this development occurred in Vyatka as Herzen contrasted the "empiricism" born of his involvement in the day-to-day government of the province with the daydreams of the Moscow intelligentsia. It accelerated from January 1838 after his move to Vladimir. He had visits from his brother Yegor and two of his closest friends, Ketcher and Sazonov, and having established very cordial relations with the governor and his wife, was assigned the agreeable duty of editing the *Vladimir Province Gazette*.

His first concern on arriving in Vladimir was to arrange his marriage with Natalie. His father and her guardian were both opposed to the match, for reasons that are unclear. In March, with Ketcher's help, he made a secret visit to Moscow for a brief reunion with Natalie. Two months later Ketcher spirited her out of Moscow to Vladimir, where with the governor's permission and the sanction of the bishop of Vladimir and Suzdal, the pair were married in a country church with Ketcher and a local Uhlan officer as witnesses. They settled down to a peaceful provincial life in Vladimir, where their first child, Alexander (Sasha), was born in June of the following year. "What shall I tell you about our life?" he writes to Ketcher in August 1838. "There is nothing to *tell*. A bright, sky-blue stream of harmony."[5] In March 1839 Ogarev came to visit the couple with his wife of three years, Maria Lvovna. It was the first reunion of the two friends since 1834, and their first meeting with each other's wives: they invested the occasion with religious significance. Herzen and Natalie welcomed Maria as a "sister," a lofty soul communing with them in an ideal love. As Herzen described it at the time: "I had kept a crucifix that Nick had given me at our parting. And the four of us threw ourselves on our knees before the divine sufferer and prayed, thanking him for the happiness he had sent us after so many years of suffering and separation. We kissed his nail-pierced feet, kissed one another, saying: 'Christ has risen.' " Herzen later wrote to Ogarev that this was "one of those supreme moments of life, at which it would be fitting for a person to die."[6] Unfortunately Ogarev's wife proved unsuitable for the role allotted to her. Herzen recalled in retrospect that she had looked at the proceedings "with some astonishment," and she subsequently told him that the scene had struck her as "affected and childish."[7] Soon he was reporting to Natalie that he had lost all respect for her: rumors were circulating in Moscow about her conduct. The couple would separate four years later.

This brief reversion to the Romantic exaltation of his youth marked the end of the mystical reveries that had occupied Herzen's Vyatka years. These he subsequently attributed to Witberg's influence, combined with "separation, exile, the religious exaltation of the letters I was receiving."[8] The energy applied to the theme of two souls united in contemplation of the Absolute was now transferred to the search for "reality" that had come to preoccupy his friends. He was able to order from nearby Moscow books and "progressive" literary and philosophical journals, such as the *Moscow Observer* (then edited by Vissarion Belinsky) and the liberal Parisian *Revue des deux mondes*. He resumed his long-interrupted historical studies with passionate enthusiasm, bombarding his friends with comments on his reading and lists of his requirements. A letter to Ketcher two months after his arrival in Vladimir shows him preoccupied with recent history, with an emphasis on French politics since 1789. A romanticized history of France by the contemporary historian Henri Martin, which gave pride of place to heroes and their myths, struck him as intellectually confused; the recently published six-volume *Mémoires, correspondance et manuscrits* of the

Natalya Alekseevna Zakharina, Herzen's wife. Charcoal sketch by an unknown artist, Paris, 1848.

liberal royalist general Lafayette he found mildly interesting, and he dismissed as tedious the memoirs of Napoleon's brother Lucien. But the main focus of his attention was on the French Christian socialists who had attracted his interest first in the months before his arrest. He inquires whether the projected history of the French Revolution edited by Buchez together with Prosper-Charles Roux has yet been published,[9] and urges Ketcher to read *Les affaires de Rome* by Lamennais. Published in 1836, this "very interesting" work expressed Lamennais's final disillusionment with the Catholic Church as the terrestrial organ of the Christian message (hoping for a reconciliation between the Church and progressive social doctrine, he had gone to Rome to plead his case in person to the Pope, who had responded with an encyclical denouncing the liberal tenets of his journal *L'Avenir*): "What fire, poetry, enthusiasm," Herzen observes.[10]

In August he pronounced himself "enraptured" with the *Encyclopédie nouvelle*—a popular journal the former Saint-Simonian Pierre Leroux had co-founded as a vehicle for his philosophical and religious interpretation of the malaise of his age.[11] Though it was only a brief episode in Herzen's intellectual development, the influence of the religious and social ideas of Leroux and his friend and disciple George Sand nevertheless played a significant role in his transition from religious mysticism to socialism.

The essence of Leroux's thought is contained in two essays in the *Revue encyclopédique*, the organ of the dissident Saint-Simonians from 1831, when he became its director.[12] They convey the flavor of the polemical style that had seduced Herzen. In the first, entitled "Aux Philosophes," Leroux announces the end of the age of philosophy: the age of religion had taken its place. The Enlightenment and the French Revolution (based on its principles) had destroyed the historical authority of institutional Christianity, but built nothing on its ruins. The new generation of radical enlighteners were as retrograde as those of the past. The order they sought to create could never be more than an illusion: "Calm on the surface; anxiety, confusion, moral, intellectual, and material disorder in society as a whole. The sand of the desert can remain immobile beneath a heavy, storm-charged atmosphere without ceasing to be dust. Society has been reduced to dust, because men are dissociated, because no bond unites them, because man is a stranger to man. And it will remain so until a common faith enlightens minds and fills hearts."[13]

Leroux insists that in order to transform human communities into durable organisms, the religion of the future must draw on the richness of humanity's historical experience, adopting the democratic teachings of early Christianity without the dogmas and rituals of the historical church, and evolving along with the progress of human knowledge. In his second essay, "On Individualism and Socialism," he argues that the new society must navigate between the Scylla and Charybdis of these two extremes. While individualism builds the freedom of the few on the exploitation of the majority, the proponents of socialism, "marching bravely toward what they call an organic epoch, do their utmost to find a way of burying all liberty, all spontaneity under what they call organization." Among the "tyrannical theories" in this category Leroux cites Saint-Simon's notion of organizing society into "regiments of *savants* and regiments of *industriels*." Modern society remained in "perplexity and incertitude, simultaneously attracted and repelled by two opposing magnets . . . liberty or equality, individuality or association." Leroux traces this dilemma back to the Declaration of Rights of 1789:

> There you will find the principle of society formulated in the most energetic and absolute way, with the aim of universal equality; but two lines above you will find formulated, equally in the most forceful and absolute fashion, the principle of the individuality of each person. And nothing to unite or harmonize these two principles . . . nothing to reconcile these two rights, equally infinite and boundless, these two adversaries which threaten each other, these two absolute and sovereign powers who each extend to the heavens and invade the entire earth. . . . You cannot prevent yourself from recognizing them, because you feel their legitimacy in your heart; but you know at the same time that, both born out of justice, they will wage a terrible war on each other. Thus Robespierre and the Convention were constrained to proclaim them both, and then the Revolution became the bloody theater of their battle. . . .
>
> We are still at the same stage, with two loaded pistols facing in opposed directions. . . . Our perplexity will cease only when social science succeeds in harmonizing these two principles, in satisfying both our tendencies. Then this anguish will give way to an immense contentment.[14]

This utopian hope was in line with the spirit of the age, but at odds with Leroux's insistence on an ineradicable conflict between the human drive toward social solidarity and the individual's urge for self-realization. In this latter perception he was ahead of his time. When in the next decade Proudhon asserted that conflict between the individual and society was not a temporary aberration but "the very condition" of social existence, his would be a lone voice on the political scene: Marxists and Hegelians alike looked forward to a resolution of all social conflicts in a final synthesis. But Leroux's recognition of the "infinite and boundless" nature of the two conflicting drives, each equally grounded in the notion of justice, suggests that he saw their future harmonization not as a final state but as a historically conditioned process of adjustment in terms similar to those of Proudhon, who would exhort his fellow socialists to see the dissonance and harmony of human faculties as reflecting not two distinct periods in history, but rather "two aspects of our nature, always opposed, always in process of reconciliation, but never entirely reconciled."[15]

Leroux's *Encyclopédie* presented Herzen with a humanistic socialism founded on Christian principles of charity and fraternity (Leroux describes its ethos as "solidarité")—a "new Christianity" stripped of the authoritarian elements in the neo-Catholicism and Saint-Simonism of his age, and also of the dogmatism of idealists whom Herzen had accused of forcing the diversity of the world of phenomena into "a single brilliant hypothesis." "A marvelous monument to the knowledge of the nineteenth century!" he enthuses to Ketcher.[16]

When his attention was caught by Leroux, he was already engrossed with the theme of Christianity's historical role, which had first attracted him in the summer of 1834. In the spring of 1838 he began a play entitled *Licinius*. He relates in a fragment of his memoirs how it was inspired by his reading of Tacitus: "Panting, with a cold sweat on my brow, I read the terrible tale of how the Eternal City had passed away in writhing and convulsions, with the ravings of the dying." He had turned for relief to the *Acts of the Apostles:* "Side by side with Rome, somber, bloodstained, corrupt, consumed by passions, I saw the poor commune of the persecuted preachers of the Gospel, and realized that it had been entrusted with the regeneration of the world; side by side with a decaying world, whose entire wealth consisted in memory and the past, was the sacred repository of good tidings, of faith, of hope in the future."

He describes his fascination with the theme: "For a long time I meditated on the period preceding their encounter. There exists a special atmosphere of alarm and unrest, of tormented aspiration and fear when the future, pregnant with a whole world, is striving to unfold . . . , when a great storm is imminent; when its inevitability is obvious, but silence still reigns—the present is hard to bear in such moments. Horror and longing fill the soul, it is difficult to breathe, and the heart, filled with melancholy and expectation, beats more strongly."[17] His interest in this subject antedated by some years his reading of Tacitus. In *My Past* he recalls the strong impression made on him in his early youth by a French novel, *Arminius*, depicting the confrontation between ancient Rome and the new barbarian world, "full of untried strength and chaotic aspirations." He had begun to write a few scenes in this genre, "which were critically examined in 1834 by the police commander Tsynsky."[18] The plot was simple: Licinius, a patrician youth, dies oppressed by his sense of a world expiring around him. He is miraculously brought back to life by St. Paul, who, carrying the Christian message to Rome, meets his funeral cortege on the Appian Way; abandoning his family and friends, the youth joins the apostle's little band of followers to work for the regeneration of mankind.

The role of Christianity in mankind's historical struggle for freedom remained a central preoccupation of Herzen's months in Vladimir. Hence his enthusiasm for the novels of Leroux's devoted friend and follower George Sand. In March 1838 he urges Natalie to read a translation of her novella *Lavinia*, which had just appeared in a Moscow journal. He asks Ketcher to send him all of Sand's novels—despite her repellent habit of smoking cigars, he wrote, "I love her with all my heart."[19] To another friend he writes that he is "tremendously attracted" to a character in Sand's novel *Mauprat*: a cenobite and rustic philosopher who prophesies the coming of an age of equality among mankind: "There will no longer be valets or masters, villains or lords. . . . The wicked will be swept away by the wind of the Lord."[20] He is equally impressed by her novel *Spiridion*, dedicated to Leroux, whose *Revue encyclopédique* Sand described as "la seule expression complète du progrés de notre siècle."[21] In this Romantic exposition of Leroux's doctrine, a monk disillusioned with the official Church finds a new source of faith in a manuscript hidden in the tomb of a medieval saint, prophesying a "religion of the spirit" that will regenerate human societies by presenting the Gospel's message of charity and fraternity as an ideal to be realized in the world.

In Vladimir over the spring and summer of 1839 Herzen worked on a second drama on this theme: *William Penn*. He writes to Witberg that the subject of his new poem will be "Christianity as a social, progressive *religion*, Quakerism in fact."[22] In his comments on the work two decades later, he writes that at the time he had known little about English history, or the character of Penn and the community he had set up in Pennsylvania. His concern had been not historical verisimilitude but "another kind of truth"—"the break between 'two worlds, two moral outlooks,'" epitomized in Penn's rebellion against the English Church and the social structure on which it rested, and his dream of a new fraternal community, founded on virgin soil. The play ends in Pennsylvania with the elderly Penn's disillusionment with the new community's failure to live up to his hopes, a dénouement owing something to Herzen's reading of Tocqueville's *On America* a year earlier. To Ketcher he had expressed skepticism about Tocqueville's view that America would head the transition to a *genuinely* new world: "A cold, calculating country."[23]

He includes the outlines of these two plays in his memoirs for their biographical interest as exhibiting the last remnants of the religious outlook that had sustained him during his first exile and the beginnings of its transition to socialism.[24] His choice of historical subjects also masked a political message that would not have escaped his readers. In an analogy with the trial of the Saint-Simonians (which, Herzen observes, would have been still fresh in their memory in 1838), the young Penn, brought before a family council to renounce his social ideals, responds not as a defendant but as the judge of his accusers.

The range of Herzen's preparatory reading for the plays reflects the extent to which his mind remained focused on analogies between the past and the present. Among the works cited in his letters are Arnold-Herman Heeren's social and economic study *Ideen über die Politik, den Verkehr und den Handel der vornehmsten Volker den alten Welt*, a new translation of Tacitus's *Life of Agricola*, and Wolfgang Menzel's *Geschichte der Deutschen bis auf die neuesten Tage*. Repeatedly he asks Ketcher to send Thierry's articles on systems of government in France from the sixteenth century to the Revolution, recently published in the *Revue des deux mondes*, and thanks him for Georg Wilhelm von Raumer's *Geschichte Europas seit dem Ende des fünfzehnten Jahrhunderts*. He could not promise to return this in less than a month:

one could not be expected to deal quickly with "six volumes of a *German work.*"[25]

His interest in Hegel's historicism seems to have been aroused in February 1839 by a history of German philosophy by A. Barchou de Penhoën. Intrigued but unsatisfied by the work ("the French don't know how to write about philosophy"), he asks Ketcher for "something by the Hegelians" as well as more works on history; Hegel himself he had not yet read. A week later he writes to another friend that he has been reading intensively, including extracts from Hegel. "There is much that is great there, but it doesn't grip one's entire soul. There's more poetry in Schelling." Two weeks later Ketcher received the impatient demand: "Give us *Hegel.*"[26] A fortnight later Herzen writes that he has ordered the new edition of Hegel's works. These would have presented a significantly greater challenge than von Raumer's opus. Perhaps this is why there is no further mention of Hegel in Herzen's correspondence during his time in Vladimir. Inspired by the radicalism of an exiled Pole, his route to Hegelianism would be very different from that of his Moscow friends.

History and Philosophy

In the summer of 1839 Herzen writes to Witberg that he is deeply engaged in the study of history and philosophy, and that he had been writing an essay on the nineteenth century as a link between the past and future when he came across a work published in Berlin on the same theme. "Imagine my delight to find that on all the main questions I was in astonishing agreement with the author."[27] The work in question was *Prolegomena zur Historiosophie* by the Polish Left Hegelian philosopher Count August von Cieszkowski.

In Russia as in Germany, Hegel's variety of idealism had a strong appeal for intellectuals estranged from their society and disillusioned with the consolations of Romantic fantasy. Like Fichte and Schelling, Hegel sought to solve the problem of alienation by revealing the fundamental identity of the human subject with the creative force of the universe: the Absolute, World Spirit, or God. But he accused previous idealist and Romantic thinkers of perpetuating the sickness they sought to cure by locating the Absolute in a transcendent "beyond" that could be apprehended only by those endowed with exceptional powers of aesthetic intuition or spiritual insight. He shared the faith of Kant and the Enlightenment in reason as the source of human autonomy, but he made the further claim that the structure of speculative thinking is identical with the structure of ultimate reality or "Being," which could therefore be fully understood and expressed in the universal language of reason and logic. The aim of philosophy was to make humans "at home in the world." Hegel's Absolute is an infinite rational subject whose goal is the achievement of full self-comprehension. Humans are the vehicles of this search, and "world history" is the process whereby they advance to self-knowledge and freedom through the growing awareness of a larger rational order to which they belong. Hegel saw the most urgent task of his age as the combination of moral autonomy with the recovery of a lost sense of community. This reconciliation was to be achieved through a perfected form of the constitutional state embodying the universal principles of reason, and through a system of checks and balances that would harmonize individual will with the general will of the community. Political crises in France, England, and other European states and the emergence of a radical movement in Germany led Hegel to emphasize the conservative tendencies in his philosophy toward the end of his life, regarding the Prussia of his time (in which popular representation was respected more in theory than in practice) as the vanguard in the progression to the Hegelian state as "the actuality of the ethical Idea."[28]

Hegel's system began to acquire a significant following among German intellectuals when the political reforms and cultural regeneration of the first decade of the nineteenth century failed to fulfill the Romantics' eschatological hopes for a suprahistorical transformation of the world. In place of the illusory consolations of "subjective" idealism he seemed to offer a sober realism that took full account of the obstacles to human self-realization presented by the objective world. Intellectuals preoccupied with the dissonances in their experience found a historical explanation of their predicament in his description of the "unhappy consciousness" that arose when humans began to sense a rift between their life in nature and society and their spiritual calling and to seek fulfillment by retreating from their human reality with the help of a succession of religious and philosophical doctrines.

Hegel appeared to offer more solid grounds for hope than previous philosophers; his dialectical vision of development through conflict and negation presented the dichotomies of the modern consciousness as a logical and necessary stage in the progressive deepening of humans' understanding of the self and the world that was leading to "absolute knowledge" of the rational harmony underlying chaotic appearance. As Hegel put it: "To recognize reason as the rose in the cross of the present and thereby to delight in the present—this rational insight is the *reconciliation* with reality that philosophy grants to those who have received the inner call to *comprehend*."[29] These words are borne out in the ecstatic accounts in which German converts to Hegelianism described their experience as "rebirth" and "salvation"—sentiments that would soon be echoed by Russian intellectuals on whom the psychological pressure of alienation was particularly acute.

Hegel's thought began to be studied in Russia only in the mid-1830s, a decade after the formation of a Hegelian school in Berlin. There were two main reasons for this: the passion of Russian Romantics for Schelling's philosophy of nature and philosophy of art, and the absence of authoritative interpreters of Hegel's formidably difficult prose. The first Russian propagators of Hegelianism in the 1830s were the Stankevich circle. By 1835 Stankevich had come to see philosophy divorced from history as sterile and embarked on a systematic study of Hegel, having acquired a complete set of his works. He extolled Hegel's view of the state as the "the sole refuge from subjective caprice," the only sphere in which humans could achieve self-realization.[30] In 1837, before Bakunin and Belinsky began to take this position to its absurd extreme, Stankevich had left for Germany, where he joined a growing number of young Russians who, attracted by the reputation of Germany's most famous philosopher, had come to Berlin to attend lectures on his thought. Most were preparing for university professorships; among them were two future Moscow professors, P. G. Redkin and D. A. Kryukov, who as popularizers would do for Hegel what Pavlov and Vellansky had done for Schelling, Redkin as professor of law and Kryukov as professor of classical philology and ancient history. Their respective disciplines were significant. Hegel's vision of the development of law and the modern state as the historical unfolding of rational necessity gave Russian intellectuals a means of coming to terms with realities they could not avoid. A pupil of Redkin in the 1840s records that his courses "forced us to see an inner evolution in the phenomena of this world, and to recognize a continuity in that evolution. They showed us that nothing arises just by itself and that there are laws one cannot transgress. We were full of enthusiasm."[31] Boris Chicherin, the future leading exponent of Russian Hegelian liberalism, records: "We learned to see in the state not merely an external form, the guardian of security, but the supreme goal of the development of law, the realization of the principles of liberty and justice in the supreme union that, without swallowing up the personality, . . . directs it to the common good."[32]

While the future pioneers of Russian liberalism were struggling to integrate the contemporary Russian state into Hegel's schema of rational progress, Herzen was approaching Hegel from a very different direction. Cieszkowski was one of the principal representatives of the "old" Left Hegelians, so called because, unlike the variety that came to prominence in the 1840s, they did not reject Hegel's speculative method a priori. Instead they sought to incorporate it into a blueprint for radical reform, adopting his diagnosis of the age as one of crisis and transition impelled by humans' acute sense of the deep divisions in consciousness, but arguing that these divisions could not be healed by speculative thought. A product of the "old world" of dualism, it could explain history only *post factum* and could not shape the future. With Hegel philosophy had reached its culmination: by uncovering the laws of history it opened the way to a new era of the "philosophy of action" where the divisions in the human consciousness would be overcome, not by thought, but by will, through a synthesis of thought with action for which Cieszkowski coined the term "praxis."

Cieszkowski's personal experience of "homelessness" (he was forced into exile after participating in the Polish revolt of 1830–1831) predisposed him to an activist approach to social change. To his fellow Hegelians he emphasized the importance of Charles Fourier, whose system he described as "a considerable step forward on the path to the concrete realization of organic truth," and he seems to have been influenced by Saint-Simon.[33] Although he saw Fourier as utopian in his failure to address the problem of the transition from the present to his ideal, there are echoes of the Saint-Simonians' "new Christianity" in his own eschatological vision of the human community of the future. Hegel had argued that his philosophy presented a new conceptual understanding of the relationship between God and man that was expressed unclearly in the Christian dogmas of Christ's incarnation, death, and resurrection. Cieszkowski maintained that the form of speculative thought was also inadequate for the expression of absolute Spirit. He looked forward to a future when the relationship between the human and the divine represented in Christian faith would be actualized through the identification of human purposes with God's will in the practical ethical interaction of a "divine-human" community, or universal church.

There was good cause for Herzen's elation on discovering the *Prolegomena*. Cieskowski's triadic view of progress would have seemed to him a direct echo of the schema he had set out in his letter to Ogarev in the summer of 1833 in the expectation of the imminent beginning of "a third, the true human phase," initiated perhaps by Fourier's phalanstery. Resuming his study of history after a gap of six years, Herzen found himself in close sympathy with one of the most radical philosophers of the age, which would be a source for the coming conflicts with his Moscow circle.

The Moscow Hegelians

The mood among the Moscow intelligentsia at the end of the 1830s was very different from what it had been when Herzen was removed from its milieu in 1833. Seven more years of Nicolas's rule had severely tested their faith in fulfillment through cultivation of the inner world of the spirit, and they had begun to look for answers to their questions in the philosophy of history. The Romantic nationalism preached by Ivan Kireevsky had grown into the Slavophile movement, which maintained that European civilization had been undermined fatally by the forces of rationalism and individualism. Russia alone had preserved the principles of Christian fellowship through its Orthodox religion: to heal the divisions in Russian society and avoid the fate of the West, the enlightened elite had only to return to the people's religion and its traditional ways. Those who became known as Westernizers saw no attraction in this idyll and began to experience a sense of self-estrangement no less tormenting than the physical exile imposed on dissenters by the Third Department.

After Stankevich's departure abroad, the Westernizers' circle was dominated by the critic Belinsky and the former army officer Mikhail Bakunin, who took over Stankevich's role as the principal exponent of idealism there. Belinsky (who knew no German) thanked Bakunin for explaining the thought of Fichte, which "has convinced me for the first time that ideal life alone is real, positive, concrete; and that so-called real life is negation, illusion, nothingness, emptiness."[34] This belief proved impossible to sustain. In September 1837 Belinsky confesses to Bakunin that he is still far removed from life in the Absolute, "but I do not despair of approaching it."[35] But one month later he admits defeat: he had constructed a fantastic world for himself and his return to reality was a bitter awakening.

Bakunin was going through a similar crisis. His extravagant fantasies of self-realization had been fueled by Fichte's voluntaristic idealism, according to which the external world exists solely as the field for the moral striving of the finite ego. But the obstacles opposed to this vision by empirical reality began to impinge on his consciousness. Hegel's famous dictum in the Introduction to the *Philosophy of Right*—"What is real is rational, and what is rational is real"—came to his aid. This gnomic phrase is open to both radical and conservative interpretations; Bakunin's version, in an introduction to a translation of Hegel's *Gymnasial Speeches*, can be seen as the first manifesto of Russian Hegelianism. Printed in the *Moscow Observer* (a journal of which Belinsky had just become editor) in April 1838, its interpretation of Hegel's phrase was more extreme than that of any of his German commentators. Bakunin argued that as the expression of God's will, reality was rational and necessary. His generation's suffering was caused by the baneful influence of the French Enlightenment and the "subjective systems" of modern philosophy which had led them to reject it in the name of "fantastic, arbitrary, imaginary worlds." "Abstract, spectral, alien to all reality," they frittered away their time in empty chatter instead of leading useful lives as "strong and real Russians, devoted to tsar and country." He expresses the hope that the next generation will attain reality through submission to "our beautiful Russian life": "Reconciliation with reality in all regards and in all spheres of life is the great task of our time."[36]

Bakunin instantly found a disciple in Belinsky, who responded: "I look upon reality, which formerly I had so despised, and tremble with secret delight when I discover its rationality, when I see that . . . nothing in it can be rejected or reviled." In a letter to Stankevich he describes his reaction to Bakunin's version of Hegel: "A new world opened up before us. 'Might is right and right is might.' No, I cannot describe to you with what emotion I heard those words. It was a liberation. I understood the meaning of the downfall of empires, the legitimacy of conquerors; I understood that there is no crude material force nor conquest by sword or bayonet, nothing arbitrary, nothing accidental. . . . The word Reality became for me the equivalent of the word 'God.' "[37]

In 1839 he published two review essays using works celebrating the battle of Borodino as vehicles for a glorification of the Russian autocracy and state. The distinction between reality and illusion had become an obsession to which he returned in another review in January 1840: "Everything that is particular, contingent, and irrational is *illusion*, . . . *appearance* and not *essence*. Man eats, drinks, dresses himself: this is the world of illusions because his spirit plays no part in it. Man feels, thinks, knows himself to be an organ and a vessel of spirit, a finite particularization of the general and infinite: that is the world of *reality*."[38] His correspondence with his friend Vasilii Botkin reflects a growing despair as he struggles to maintain a position at odds with his moral instincts. A fierce outburst in a letter of October 1840 marks the battle's end: "I curse my vile effort at reconciliation with a vile reality! . . . For me now, the *human individual* is above history, above society, above mankind."[39]

Belinsky's repentance was expressed with the same intensity as his recently held beliefs. "My God! What loathsome abominations I have expressed in print, with all the sincerity, all the fanaticism, of profound, preposterous conviction. . . . Only think, what zigzags my path has followed."[40] His intellectual career is a prime example of the "chaotic fermentation" that Chaadaev perceived as characteristic of Russia's lost souls. "You know my nature," he tells Botkin. "It's always in extremes and never hits the center of an idea." There follows an analysis of the

effects of alienation on the Russian psyche that is the equal of Chaadaev's in its sharpness of perception:

> Do you see: we became friends, quarreled, made peace, quarreled
> again, fought each other, loved each other passionately, lived, fell in
> love, according to theory, by the book. . . . Our cherished and con-
> stant dream was to raise all our lives . . . to the level of reality—and
> what became of that? The dream was a dream and will remain so; we
> are phantoms and will die phantoms, but that is not our fault and we
> have nothing with which to reproach ourselves. The ground of any
> reality is society. . . . Man is great in word and deed but only when
> he is a Frenchman, an Englishman, a Russian. But are we Russians?
> No, society regards us as unhealthy growths on its body, and we re-
> gard society as a pile of dung. . . . Society lives by a certain sum of
> certain convictions, in which all its members are united, . . . un-
> derstand each other without saying a word. This is why in France,
> in England, in Germany, people who have never seen each other
> before . . . can be conscious of their kinship, can embrace and shed
> tears, some on a square during a rising against despotism for the
> rights of mankind, others at the unveiling of a monument to
> Schiller. . . . We are people without a homeland—no, worse, . . . we
> are people whose homeland is a phantom: Is it surprising that we our-
> selves are phantoms? . . . There are people whose life . . . is devoid of
> all content, but we are people for the boundless content of whose lives
> neither our society nor our age has ready-made forms. Form without
> content is triviality . . . content without form is a deformity, often
> striking in its tragic grandeur, like the myths of the ancient Ger-
> manic world.[41]

Gone is the vision of the circle as a refuge within which it was possible to live a self-sufficient and productive moral and intellectual life,
inspired by an ideal of perfection. Herzen's memoirs contain a deeply
affectionate portrait of Belinsky, who in the 1840s became a close
friend. In his dauntless consistency and "bitter skepticism, won
through suffering" Herzen saw an echo of Chaadaev's relentless exposure of unwelcome truths—a path he himself would follow after win-
ning his personal battle against the temptations of utopian hope.[42]

* * *

In July 1839 Herzen was pardoned (Ogarev had been pardoned two
months earlier). At his father's insistence his first months of liberty

were devoted to an urgent practical matter. As an illegitimate son, he could inherit Ivan Yakovlev's considerable fortune only by rising to the civil service rank of collegiate assessor, which automatically conferred noble status. The governor of Vladimir, whose intervention had secured his pardon, had recommended him for promotion and transfer to Saint Petersburg. Over the next months he made several trips to the capital for lengthy negotiations, which (eased by his father's bottomless purse) enabled him to bypass the queue for promotion to the desired rank. In March 1840 he finally left Vladimir to take up an appointment in the Ministry of the Interior.

These activities were a tedious distraction from his consuming interest: the life of the Moscow circles. Indirect contact with them through visits from his friends had been no compensation for firsthand participation in the clash of personalities and ideas. In a letter to Ketcher requesting books he adds: "And another thing . . . as much literary gossip as you can fit in."[43] He spent the last week of August and all of September 1839 in Moscow, but his reunion with Ogarev in Vladimir was not the prelude to a joyful reintegration into the brotherhood of his old circle. Its remaining members—Satin and Sazonov (both of whom had been pardoned) and Ketcher had gravitated to Belinsky's circle.

Herzen recalls that his new acquaintances treated him and Ogarev with some condescension, combining respectful indulgence to returned exiles with the hint that they were men of the past: the circle represented the present, and their interpretation of Hegel was not open to question. When Herzen broke off relations with Belinsky over his insistence that the tyranny under which they lived was rational, the chorus was on Belinsky's side.

Herzen paints a memorable portrait of the Moscow Hegelians when friendships were made or broken on a point of interpretation of a paragraph in the master's *Logic, Phenomenology, Aesthetics,* or *Encyclopedia:*

> They discussed these subjects incessantly: there was not a paragraph in the three parts of the *Logic,* in the two of the *Aesthetics,* the *Encyclopedia,* and so on, that had not been subject to desperate disputes for several nights in succession. People who loved each other quarreled for weeks at a time because they disagreed about the definition

of "all-embracing Spirit," or had taken as a personal insult opinions on "the absolute personality and its *existence in itself.*" Every insignificant pamphlet on German philosophy published in Berlin or other provincial or district towns, if there was a mere mention of Hegel in it, was ordered and read to tatters. . . .

. . . Our young philosophers distorted not merely their phrases but their understanding. . . . Everything that *in reality* was direct, every simple feeling, was raised into abstract categories, and returned from them without a drop of living blood, a pale algebraic shadow. . . . A man who went for a walk in Sokolniki Park went in order to surrender himself to the pantheistic feeling of his unity with the cosmos; and if on the way he chanced upon a drunken soldier or a peasant woman who got into conversation with him, the philosopher did not simply talk to them, but defined the essential substance of the people in its immediate and contingent manifestation. The very tear that welled up the eye was strictly referred to its proper classification, to "Gemüth" or "the tragic in the heart."[44]

The internecine strife within Herzen's circle was the background to his soul-searching with regard to his generation, the results of which he conveyed in a long letter to Ogarev on returning to Vladimir after his second visit to Moscow. Neither they nor Satin, Ketcher, nor Sazonov, he maintains, had reached that stage of maturity at which knowledge and beliefs form a stable and harmonious basis for action. They were all eternal youths, dilettantes whose projects rarely came to fruition: "How often, for instance, have you and I wavered between mysticism and philosophy, between some indeterminate artistic, scholarly, or political callings? That, my friend, is not the way to creativity and success." The reason was clear: lack of intellectual preparation and discipline. "We have all studied badly, fill the gaps with anything to hand and are ready to act before we have tempered our sword and learned how to use it." Ogarev had informed him that he was reading very little but writing a great deal: a fatal inversion of priorities, in Herzen's view. Leavening his criticism with praise of Ogarev's poetic sensibility, he attributes his friend's "theurgical-philosophical dreams" to laziness and weakness of character, urging him to follow his example: he was studying history, and Hegel was next on his list. "There's much that I still need to clarify in my outlook."[45] On the positive side, prison and exile had given them both a wide experience of life that would inform their future activity. The years of ordeal were over; the time had come for serious study and practical action.

The letter to Ogarev took Herzen three weeks to write; it represented a formal farewell to the compensating illusions of the past and a new determination to exploit the narrow possibilities of his given reality: "I'm glad that I've managed to analyze us both with such detachment," he writes, "because time will not wait for us."[46]

His resolve was soon to be tested by a new ordeal.

CHAPTER TEN

The Discovery of Chance

There is no such thing as chance. Chance is an absurdity, invented by unbelief.

HERZEN IN 1836

SEVEN months after his transfer to Saint Petersburg, Herzen was again arrested, this time on a charge of spreading rumors harmful to the state. He was confronted with a letter to his father in which he had repeated gossip about a policeman who had robbed and murdered a citizen. He protested that the story was the talk of the town, but the tsar had personally decided that in view of his past record Herzen should be banished again to a place selected by the Minister of the Interior (Herzen as a civil servant being ultimately under his direction). Herzen benefited from the rivalry between the minister and the political police: the minister showed his view of the absurdity of the charge by promoting him to the highest rank consistent with his length of service and inviting him to choose his place of exile. His choice fell on Tver or Novgorod, the two provincial cities closest to Moscow and Saint Petersburg. In June 1841 he was appointed a councillor in Novgorod, where he took up residence with his family in July. He would remain there for less than a year. In April 1842 he was granted permission to resign from the civil service because of his wife's ill health. Meanwhile Natalie had written to the empress begging her to plead Herzen's case with Nicolas; as a result he was permitted to return to Moscow in July to live under police supervision, which continued until shortly before his departure from Russia in 1847.

In the five years between his second banishment and his emigration, a succession of frustrations, humiliations, disillusionments, and bereavements stripped away all the props on which he had previously relied for comfort, hope, and meaning in his life. From these disasters he emerged neither broken nor embittered, but with a new vision of the self as morally independent of all external powers and circumstances. Before he left Russia he had already laid the groundwork for the view of freedom that would receive its most compelling formulation in *From the Other Shore*.

* * *

The conditions of Herzen's second banishment were not severe. Friends from his circle visited him regularly, and in the autumn of 1841 he was permitted to spend a month's leave in Moscow. His official duties in Novgorod were light, if stultifyingly dull—provincial governors rarely invited their councillors to discuss policy. "Before everyone lay a pile of papers and everyone signed his name: it was a signature factory."[1] Before his departure he had given Ogarev a list of the projects with which he intended to occupy his time: the continued study of "Hegel and the Germans," a work on the Petrine revolution, and an introduction to world history for children. Nothing came of the last two projects, but, as Chapter 11 shows, his study of Hegelianism would bear fruit in his major philosophical works of the 1840s. The freedom to devote most of his energies to intellectual activity, however, was no substitute for the creative engagement with external reality—which, he was now convinced, was his only path to self-fulfillment. On hearing that Ogarev had departed on an extended tour of Europe, he comments in the diary he began in Novgorod, "So he's off to Rome and Paris, and I'm still here with a chain on my feet. I feel an inner necessity to travel to a big city, I need people. . . . My nature is eminently sociable—I'm destined for a tribune, a forum, as a fish is for water."[2]

The new blow was all the more cruel because it came at a point in his life when he had become intensely aware of the passing of time and the slightness of his achievements. The first entry in his diary, on his thirtieth birthday, reads: "Half my life is gone. Twelve years of childhood, six of youth, and eight of persecution, victimization, exile."[3] The mood in which he began his second sentence was very different from that of the first. Promoted against his will to a post for which others would have had to beg and bribe, he no longer sought the hand of Providence in the brutal ironies of Russian life. He writes to Ketcher that he has no regrets about rejecting the solace of former illusions: the pain of their loss is not a death agony but the pangs of birth. When Ogarev, echoing the reigning doctrine of their new circle, wrote counseling resignation in face of the inexorable movement of history, he met with a stinging reply: resignation might be the appropriate reaction to a fatal illness or a natural disaster, "but resignation as a response to a blow in the face is something I do not comprehend, and I'm as much attached to my anger as you are to your quiescence." Ogarev had urged Herzen not to despair of universal progress just because of a "particular case" (his own), advice that Herzen attributes to "that false monkish theory of passivity that in my opinion is your besetting sin. True Christians could regard all that was done to them with indifference: life for them was an inferior staging-post on the road to the Kingdom of God, where labors will be rewarded. We don't look at life like that. Our faith is too shaky, we see weakness in what they regard as strength." He proposes to face life with "proud, unbending stoicism," rather than a meek acceptance of its shabby tricks.[4]

In July 1840 Herzen had made peace with Belinsky, who, after an intense moral crisis culminating in discussions with Herzen in Saint Petersburg, had replaced his conservative Hegelianism with a fiery humanism, denouncing all theories that viewed individuals as means to universal goals. On the eve of his departure to Novgorod Herzen urges Ketcher to follow Belinsky's example and renounce his "absurd reconciliation with reality," and tells Ogarev that he is starting to experience the positive effect of the latest blow. Thanks to their circle's addiction to metaphysical debate, he had been in danger of drowning in abstractions, "in the manner of the nineteenth century,"[5] but the rage he felt at his second banishment had put an end to any tendency he might have had to remain in the sphere of abstract thought.

Stoical realism was Herzen's dominant mood in Novgorod. In the diary that he began writing there he contemplates the alternatives facing him: "Surely I'm not to regard my life as over, surely everything that excites and engrosses me—my eagerness to work, all my need to express myself—will not remain buried under a heavy stone until I become accustomed to muteness, until my needs subside?" No, he is certain that he will not follow that path, and equally sure that he will not revert to a life of philosophical contemplation or the "insane bliss" of faith in divine providence. Only stoicism, combined with a smoldering anger, will carry him through the years ahead: "My shoulders are breaking, but they still bear their burden."[6]

This resolve would be tested severely in the years to come. The first casualty was the idyll of romantic love. In his memoirs Herzen recalls how in the first year of his marriage he had lived in the present without a care for the future, in the belief that his predestined union with Natalie would provide a secure haven from the buffetings of Russian life. This illusion was dispelled by his second banishment. His gnawing bitterness increased Natalie's natural tendency to melancholy, and the death of a newborn child in February 1841 undermined her delicate health so much that Herzen petitioned unsuccessfully to be allowed to spend his exile in the south of Russia. Another child died at birth at the end of the year and a third followed at the end of 1842; meanwhile every minor illness of their son Sasha brought new terrors to the parents. Herzen attributed his wife's frailty and the deaths of his children directly to his persecution by the government, but for the disaster that struck the couple after their move back to Moscow in the summer of 1842 he had only himself to blame. Following the convention that there should be no secrets between them, he confessed to Natalie that he had committed a sexual indiscretion with the family maid. He expected that his expression of sincere repentance would be met with understanding and forgiveness, confident that she would see the incident as he did—a deplorable but momentary surrender to physical passion that in no way affected the deep bond between them. But he had not reckoned on the success of the sentimental education she had received at his hands. Her delicate mental equilibrium was shattered by the news, which she interpreted as the desecration of their sacred love, and no assurance of repentance could convince her that Herzen still loved her. In his diary he records a succession of agonizing scenes extending over many months, in which Natalie in floods of despairing tears attributed her husband's unfaithfulness to her own inadequacies, while Herzen's self-castigation alternated with a growing resentment at the disparity between the punishment and the crime. Their relations regained a precarious equilibrium, but Natalie's health, undermined by difficult pregnancies and the deaths of their infants, caused Herzen alarm.

At the same time his sense of self-worth was steadily eroded by his powerlessness before a regime that reduced him to the status of a slave. His relief on returning to Moscow in 1842 was tempered by the fact that he was still officially under surveillance. "Again I'll be surrounded by spies."[7] His diary records the corrosive effect of constant dependence on the whims of the authorities. As he and Natalie began to toil in Novgorod over the letter that would persuade the empress to intercede for them while their friends in Moscow cast around for a suitable emissary to present the petition in person, he reflected bitterly: "All this together is offensive to an unbelievable degree; my dignity as a human being, together with the dignity of all other human beings, is trampled in the mud by this lawlessness." Over the next five years he became an unwilling expert in the art of petitioning. In 1843 he approached Benckendorf, the chief of gendarmes, for permission to take Natalie to Italy to recover her health. Met with a refusal, he broods: "What constant, consistent, malevolent persecution! . . . A slave's cap lies heavy on the head; being deprived of rights is a suffocating state, and there's no foreseeable end to it." On hearing that two censors had been arrested for permitting the publication of a short story containing unflattering physical descriptions of functionaries of the Ministry of Communications and Public Buildings, he reflects, "We are sinking ever deeper and deeper into some primitive state of military despotism and arbitrariness." Hearing of a new decree permitting travel abroad only to those aged over twenty-five and to women only when accompanied by their husbands, he comments, "I'd like to read this edict in print, to have material proof that such an outrageous contempt for rights could exist in the mid-nineteenth century."[8]

In the summer of 1844 he began directing his persuasive efforts toward another arm of the bureaucracy, approaching the censorship committee with a request for permission to found a new literary review. While awaiting a decision he busied himself with raising funds for his project and gathering material for the first issue. His diary over the next six months records his growing anxiety at the absence of a response from the authorities. An official refusal arrived at the end of the year.

His mood was not improved by letters from Ogarev, who left Russia in 1843 to spend nearly four years meandering around Europe, whence he sermonized his friend on the moral defects of the life of fear and dissembling from which he had temporarily escaped. Herzen commented grimly in his diary: "Ogarev writes that it's impossible to live at home in Russia. We know that rather better than he."[9] All he sought now from the Russian government was permission to go abroad. It would be two more years before this was granted.

"What a terrible time—one's strength is exhausted in fruitless battle, one's life drains away, and not a single drop of joy, a single hope of imminent relief—nothing." Such despairing comments abound in Herzen's diary of the mid-1840s, but they are only part of the story. He found ways of exploiting the narrow margins of freedom at his disposal to engage in an extraordinary burst of concentrated and fruitful intellectual activity. When Ogarev, who had revitalized his interest in the natural sciences during his wanderings abroad, wrote that he was thinking of moving to Berlin or returning to Moscow to devote himself to serious study, Herzen replied tartly: "Why this dependence on geography? Wherever you're cast by fate it's possible to apply yourself to work."[10]

He acted on his own advice: Belinsky's position as literary critic for the journal *National Notes* gave him the opportunity at last to express his ideas in a public forum (albeit under the constraints of a watchful censorship). Between 1842 and 1847 he published there, along with a constant flow of short articles, stories, and reviews, two lengthy cycles of philosophical essays—*Dilettantism in Science* and *Letters on the Study of Nature*, and his novel *Who Is to Blame?* He feared in particular for the fate of his essays: the censors might either ruin them or refuse to pass them altogether. In civilized countries, he reflects in his diary, writers apply their talent to expressing their ideas. In Russia they must use it to disguise them.[11]

Failure to do so could have catastrophic consequences. Herzen came perilously close to disaster when the critic Faddei Bulgarin (who worked as an informer for the secret police) singled out his novel in a report to the Third Department entitled "Socialism, Communism, and Pantheism in Russia in Recent Times," informing his masters that in the first instalment "the nobility is depicted as depraved, while the teacher, who is a doctor's son, and the illegitimate daughter of a peasant girl are models of virtue." The head of the Third Department, General Dubelt, added to the report his opinion that the entire novel was "reprehensible."[12]

Herzen knew the danger he was courting. The day before publication of his essay on Romanticism in the cycle *Dilettantism in Science* he reflects: "If the censors don't mutilate it, it could have a significant effect—possibly a third banishment? That will be a bitter blow, but I'm ready for it."[13]

The Superfluous Man: Confrontation with Chance

The work for which Herzen was prepared to sacrifice so much was shaped by the new mood of realism with which he had arrived in Novgorod in July 1841.

His diary records that the practical problems of reestablishing his household after his return to Moscow gave him only a brief respite from "the eternal voice of grief, the wail of indignation, the wail of a spirit straining for a form of life that is full, human, and free." Reading Gogol's *Dead Souls*, published in that year, made him want to weep for his benighted land: "Our sleep has been long and heavy. Why did we wake up too soon? We should have gone on sleeping, like everything around us." The existence of a Russian intellectual, constantly prevented from writing what he wanted to write and constitutionally incapable of writing what he was allowed to write, was "a monotonous jeremiad of indignation."[14] But as Chaadaev had shown, indignation eloquently expressed could awaken thought in those who were still sleeping, and it was to this task that Herzen addressed himself in his last years in Russia, seeking to reveal his compatriots to themselves by stripping away the illusions and false hopes that obscured the horror of their situation.

Freed from surveillance through the intervention of a powerful friend, Chaadaev had become a familiar figure in the Moscow salons. Herzen first encountered him on his return to Moscow from Vladimir. He had no sympathy with Chaadaev's religious interpretation of history, but the closeness of their respective diagnoses of the psychic malaise of their compatriots is evident from the following passage in Herzen's diary, written the day after one of their discussions:

> Will future generations understand and value all the horror, all the tragic side of our existence? . . . Will they understand why we are idle, why we pursue all sorts of pleasures . . . ? Why we haven't the energy to apply ourselves to any substantial task? Why in moments of de-

light we do not forget our melancholy? . . . Was there ever such a time for any country? Perhaps Rome in the last days of its existence?—but no. They had sacred memories, a past, and ultimately those who were offended by the state of their homeland could find peace in the bosom of the new religion that had appeared in all its purity and poetry. But we are worn down both by the emptiness and chaos of the past, and the lack of common interests in the present.[15]

He concludes these reflections with an ironical sally against the Slavophiles: One can't argue with those who contend that Russian history is developing in an original way. Their Romantic nationalism and Chaadaev's religious conservativism were two sides of the same coin. Through their uncompromising opposition to the existing order, the best and noblest of his compatriots had closed off all avenues of activity that could wholly engage their intellect and emotions. This unnatural divorce from the life of their society inclined them to an egotistic idleness, Romantic fantasies, and every sort of self-indulgent eccentricity. Oppressed by the monotony of their lives, in their youth they placed their hopes on a future where their every desire would be satisfied, but by middle age they discovered that the future would bring nothing but more persecution, more inactivity and boredom. Unable to realize their potential and test the limits of their abilities through action, they tormented themselves with dreams, "that surrogate for real passions," theorizing about emotions instead of experiencing them, inventing sorrows and nursing them. The very sight of Chaadaev makes Herzen shudder. A man of such exceptional qualities and nobility of character is forced to waste his powers as a salon philosopher, in "petty arguments . . . a false substitution for real words and deeds." He observes that practical intellects are rare in Russia: "We are either animals or ideologists, like my sinful self. We either do nothing at all or everything under the sun."[16] All his generation on entering adulthood led the lives of one or another of the characters of Gogol's novel. Among the debauched, the corrupt, and the empty dreamers, the only active person was Chichikov, a swindler of limited horizons. Those who rose above the norm—Pushkin, Lermontov, and many lesser individuals— were doomed to perish because there was no place for them in the world of dead souls. Herzen defines the dominant malaise of the century as the divorce between theory and life, but rejects the Romantics' view that their alienation is the mark of their status as a spiritual elite. To some degree, their predicament was of their own making.

This is the dominant theme of the novel *Who Is to Blame?*, which he began writing during his Novgorod exile. The first attempt at a rounded portrait of the Russian "superfluous man" who was to take center stage in Turgenev's novels, as fiction the work is not an outstanding success. The plot is rudimentary and the serf-owning nobility who comprise most of the secondary characters are all monsters, scarcely credible in their uniform beastliness. But the three main characters in the love triangle that forms what action there is are drawn from life: from Herzen's observations of his own and his circle's spiritual malaise. The strengths and weaknesses of the best of his generation he put into the principal character, Vladimir Beltov.

Beltov's background reflects the ugly lawlessness of Russian life. His mother, like Herzen's wife, was the product of a landowner's liaison with one of his serfs. Trained to earn her living as a governess, she was dismissed after her employer's son attempted to seduce her. She subsequently married him, but her humiliations had turned her into a neurotic. Her son was endowed with an energetic nature and an encyclopedic mind, open to all contemporary issues, but when we first encounter him at the age of thirty we are told that he had put none of his gifts to use. His education at the hands of a Swiss tutor, a pure-hearted follower of Rousseau, had ensured that he would be unable to come to terms with Russian reality. Equipping him with "a shining set of ideals," his mother and his tutor had fashioned him into an abstract model of a man, as Rousseau had done with Émile—a development that continued within his student circle at the university. In the company of half a dozen youths full of extravagant dreams and hopes, and entirely ignorant of life outside the lecture room, Beltov acquired a set of values wholly alien to the milieu in which he had to live. Aspiring to play a role in public affairs, he entered the civil service, but found its procedures an insult to his intelligence and embarked on a search for an occupation that would absorb his energies, only to find himself

> in a country completely unknown to him, so foreign that he could in no way adapt to it; he could not empathize with a single aspect of the life seething around him. He did not have the ability to be a good

landowner, an excellent officer, a zealous official; and in reality that left only the profession of idler, gambler, or the fraternity of debauchees. To our hero's credit it must be said that he was more drawn to the last category than to the others, but even here he could not feel at home; he was too civilized, and these gentlemen's debauchery was too corrupt, too coarse. He struggled with medicine and art, caroused and gambled, and then went off to foreign parts. It goes without saying that he found no satisfactory occupation there; he studied without system, studied everything under the sun; he astonished the German specialists by the many-sidedness of the Russian mind; he astonished the French by his depth of thought, and while the French and Germans accomplished much, he accomplished nothing.[17]

His learning did not bring maturity. "At the age of thirty, like a sixteen-year-old boy, he was still *preparing* to begin his life, not noticing that the door to which he was drawing nearer and nearer was not that through which the gladiators enter but that through which their bodies are carried out."[18] After a decade of aimless wandering, he returns to his estate to make one final effort to engage in meaningful activity by standing as a candidate in the elections to the noblemen's assembly in his province. But even here he fails; the local officials (whose corruption and philistinism Herzen depicts with savage wit) dimly perceive that he constitutes an indictment of their way of life, and block his election. His future as a landowner is equally open to doubt. Having resolved to spend his mornings reading the latest works on economics, he stretches out on a sofa to immerse himself in Byron's *Don Juan*. His last hope of fulfillment, in a relationship with the novel's heroine (an idealized version of Natalie), who alone perceives and values his positive qualities, is lost when she refuses to leave her husband for him. There are elements of Ogarev in the husband, whose Romantic dreaminess is contrasted unfavorably with Beltov's latent energy, but Beltov's life promises to be no less futile: the future stretches before him as "a grey mist, a dreary, monotonous continuation of the present."[19]

The novel (with cuts by the censor) first appeared serialized in 1845–1846 in *National Annals*. While acknowledging its literary defects, Belinsky lauded it for its feminism and its powerful indictment of Nicolas's Russia. In spite of the cuts, it was the most outspoken critique of serfdom to appear in print in the 1840s, but the central focus of the book is the fate of the principal character, into whom Herzen put much of himself and his fears of what he might become. Doctor Krupov, a character who reappears in Herzen's later works as a psychiatrist who claimed to have proved insanity to be a generic characteristic of mankind, suggests that Beltov's predicament is due in part to too much money, too little willpower, and unfamiliarity with hard work. But the author points to a mitigating circumstance—the early frustration of his dreams of civic activity. "Nothing in the world is so attractive to a fiery, active nature as participation in current affairs, in the history being played out before one's eyes. He who has allowed dreams of such activity to enter his breast has rendered himself useless for all other fields of action." Herzen here is speaking for himself, and Beltov's ultimate fate as a "useless person" seemed very likely at that period to be his own.[20] When the novel was published in book form in 1847, he presented a copy to Chaadaev, with a dedication taken from the *First Philosophical Letter:* "Let us not aspire to the existence of pure intelligences; let us learn to live sensibly within our given reality." Chaadaev's description of a generation who came into the world without patrimony and whose memories go back no farther than yesterday is directly echoed in the work:

> Happy is he who continues something begun by others, who inherits some task; he becomes accustomed to it at an early age, does not waste half his life in choosing it, concentrates, limits himself, in order not to dissipate his energies; and he is productive. We Russians most often start with nothing, inheriting from our fathers only personal property and real estate, and even of these we are poor guardians. Hence, on the whole we are not impelled to do anything, or if we are, it's as if we start out on a vast steppe: you're free to go wherever you like, in any direction—it's up to you; only you'll never arrive at any destination. Hence our many-sided inactivity, our busy idleness.[21]

The time for Romantic refusal to bend to empirical reality was past, but there remained the problem of constructing a stable vision of that reality in its social and historical dimensions that would permit an individual to make the best use of his talents within the given possibilities. Chaadaev (and after him the Westernizers) believed that the

Russian intelligentsia's salvation lay in accepting these principles ready-made from their elder and wiser European brothers. Herzen's observation of the ideological confusions of his time, though, began to persuade him that the challenge of constructing their moral outlook from first principles was one that Russians should not avoid. In an essay of 1843 he argues that the obsessive self-questioning of their generation is characteristic of all transitional periods. Their forefathers could find answers to all questions by appealing to their traditional authorities. The criticism that had demolished these authorities had cleared a space, but at a cost: people had become terrified by the perception that they might have to take the place of Providence and assume responsibility for their own destiny. Like Faust, they were sometimes ready to reject the spirit they had called forth, sensing that their hearts and heads could not cope with it. "But the problem is that this spirit does not emanate from Hell or from another planet but from the human breast, and there's no place to which it can disappear."[22]

The thought of dispensing with the authorities on which one had traditionally relied for reassurance, Herzen wrote, strikes terror into the soul. That was nevertheless the course he took.

* * *

In a diary entry of 1843 Herzen muses on the beliefs of the Slavophiles, the Catholicism of Chaadaev and Prince Ivan Gagarin (a member of one of Russia's oldest aristocratic families, who had recently entered a Jesuit monastery in France), and the proliferation of other varieties of religious fervor among the Moscow intelligentsia. They were all, he observed, rooted in the same desperate need to find firm principles and absolutes that would fill the moral vacuum of Russian life. "The terrible awareness of how vile our reality is ... makes people seek reconciliation in anything at all, in any nonsense or self-delusion, if only in order to exercise their minds, to divorce themselves from that reality and find reasons for its vileness."[23]

He spoke from experience. These were the grounds on which, five years earlier, he had tried to stifle his increasingly nagging doubts about the beneficent role of Providence, writing to Natalie: "What if, after all the torments and sufferings, no triumph ensues? ... But why then, if some person is destined to do nothing but live through his time, why in the depths of his soul does there cry a voice that cannot be silenced: 'You're stifled and cramped, you have strength, create a realm of action for yourself, open wide life's narrow boundaries, lay down a new track on its path, spread the fire that is in your soul, share your thoughts and feelings with others?' Why?" Faced with the suffering of two Vyatka friends stricken by fatal illnesses, he had sought to persuade himself that such tragedies had a redemptive meaning. "No, I firmly believe in the strict consistency and intelligibility of Providence. Don't these same sufferings cleanse their souls and lead them more directly to heaven? . . . Why is one means chosen and not another? We must believe that the one that is chosen in the one that best leads to the goal; doubt is already a crime. But how to find the fortitude to suffer calmly and to give thanks with the same prayer for a knife through the heart and a flower thrown by an angel? How? That is the whole problem. Again we return to the bitter cup and the prayer in Gethsemane. But I admit that I don't possess that strength. I endure, but not always without a murmur."[24]

On the eve of his second exile he finally relinquished his faith in Providence, as a form of weakness to which he was determined no longer to succumb. He would greet each subsequent ordeal with this resolve. After the death of his second child in 1841 he writes to Ogarev: "How can one not grieve when before one's eyes matter battles with spirit, and spirit is vanquished and mindless forces gain ascendancy over life?"[25] But he insists that while he cannot accept the consolations of religion, neither will he curse the malignancy of fate. He will always resist the wrongs inflicted by human wills because they offend human dignity, but it is as absurd to take offense at the tragedies created by natural forces as it is to rail against bad weather.

He found this stoical acceptance of dependence on contingency exceedingly difficult to sustain. His helplessness in the face of a succession of illnesses and bereavements in the family that had been his sanctuary against the onslaughts of the outside world led to bitter outbursts in his diary. At times he feels a nihilistic despair in the face of the "terrible whirlpool of chance" that sucks in human life, and his impotence before the "blind but powerful force" to which all that is personal and individual is subject. "Threatening possibilities," "dark dreams" fill him with horror and fear: "The fragility of all that is holiest and best in life is enough to drive one mad. But what is not subject to loss can't satisfy us completely." Each of Natalie's pregnancies gives rise to an agonizing alternation of hope and fear. When a short period of domestic calm is shattered by a sudden illness, he reflects that the little happiness given to human beings is only sufficient to prevent them from destroying themselves in despair. "Grain upon grain, like sand, with infinite labor, with sweat and blood, man lays down his treasure—and then suddenly chance intervenes and destroys with a single senseless blow all that was achieved with such suffering." In the summer of 1844, after a sudden and frightening storm had overtaken his family in a wood, he notes in his diary, "How helpless and pitiful is man in such circumstances! How can one be reconciled to such a state of dependence?"[26]

His preoccupation with the role of blind forces was so intense as to alarm his friends. Ogarev wrote to Ketcher from Berlin in February 1845 that Herzen was tormented by a fear of chance disasters.[27] But what his circle interpreted as a fall into depression was an increasing engagement with the philosophical problem that would dominate his mature life. A few days after the death of a third child, he recorded in his diary a discussion with the Slavophile philosopher A. S. Khomyakov. He noted that Khomyakov's greatest strength—his gift for logical abstraction—was also his greatest weakness. He had little grasp of the relation between ideas and the world of facts. Logic, concerned only with the universal and the inevitable, excluded the element of chance; but concrete existence—"the fact *des Daseins*"—necessarily contained an aspect of contingency: "One may leave contingency aside in theory, but one can't do so in practice. . . . A human fetus should develop into an adult: the inevitability of this is inherent in the concept of the embryo—but chance cuts the thread of life, and the fact does not exist. Hence, chance is an essential component of the fact."[28]

"I have never felt more acutely," he wrote to Ogarev on the eve of his second banishment, "the necessity for the translation—no, the development—of philosophy into life."[29] The effects of his encounter in 1842 with the humanism of the Hegelian Left will be the subject of Chapter 11, but an equally important factor in the development of his thought (although rarely mentioned by his biographers) was the revival of his interest in natural science, reflected in a bold assertion derived (without attribution) from an essay by his university mentor M. G.

Pavlov: "that philosophy without natural science is as impossible as natural science without philosophy."[30]

A Return to Science: Evolutionary Theory

In search of an answer to the questions that tormented him, on his return to Moscow Herzen set out with characteristic thoroughness to bring himself up to date with developments in the sciences that had passed him by during his long preoccupation with his inner world, combining a formidable amount of reading with systematic attendance at a lecture course in comparative anatomy, which, he confides to his diary, "reveals to me each day a multiplicity of new facts, along with thoughts, views, etc., on nature." He had come to the conclusion that the method of zoological classification of Cuvier and his followers was erroneous. Citing the botanist Augustin de Candolle's geographical method of classification, he points out that "one can't arrange any realm of nature in a straight line of development; it scatters around and advances toward higher types in a multitude of directions."[31]

One of the founders of botanical geography, de Candolle was the first botanist to draw attention to the importance of the role of geographical distribution in the variation of species. Herzen had seized on a question of particular importance in the development of evolutionary theory. An increasing number of naturalists had come to observe that in many species, populations in different habitats differ from each other, and that much of this variation can be interpreted as adaptive responses to their environment. The role of contingent conditions in the mutation of species would be one of the cornerstones in Darwin's theory of natural selection. Because M. A. Maximovich had already emphasized that facet of the view of nature due earlier to Lamarck, it is not surprising that Maximovich's former student Herzen was drawn to the same concept in his search for means to make sense of human dependence on chance.

He keeps his friends abreast of his studies, informing Ketcher that as well as attending lectures, he is "reading Carus and Co." Carl Gustav Carus, a German physiologist who corresponded with Goethe and Humboldt on art and nature, was the author of works on zoology, entomology, and comparative anatomy whose greatest claim to fame would be to have originated the concept of a vertebrate archetype, a groundbreaking idea in the development of Darwin's theory of evolution. "You may laugh," Herzen writes, "but you'll be foolish to do so."[32]

He had infected Ogarev (then in Berlin) with his enthusiasm—and, as he expected, his philosophical circle regarded them both with condescending amusement. Ketcher wrote to Herzen that they must be demented to study the natural sciences "at this time, when the social sciences, political economy and history are so vitally important."[33] Herzen retorted that their criticism was absurd: "I'm studying physiology because in our age there's no philosophy without physiology, and since the loss of the *Jenseits* we need a foundation in the *Diesseits*." Ogarev echoed his protest: "I can only conceive of science as 'world history,' in which nature plays too important a role to be expunged."[34] Herzen assured his friends that while logic had brought him back to the natural sciences, this did not mean that he was neglecting the humanities: along with studies by two eminent German scientists—the anatomist Karl Ernst Bock and the physiologist Karl Friedrich Burdach—he was reading Pierre-Joseph Proudhon's *De la création de l'ordre dans l'humanité, ou Principes d'organisation politique*, which he strongly recommends to Ketcher, together with *Qu'est-ce que la propriété?* ("a delicious work").[35] Published respectively in 1843 and 1840, these two works are among Proudhon's earliest expositions of his idea of a social order based on mutual associations flexible enough to mitigate the contradictions of existing society without enforcing conformity to some absolute ideal. As Chapter 12 will show, Herzen was already meditating on the potential of the Russian peasant commune in this regard. But another reason can be inferred for his enthusiastic response to Proudhon's thought. The French socialist's rejection of all metaphysical absolutes and theories of society not grounded in the contingent needs of the present harmonized perfectly with the developments in evolutionary science that had found their way to the center of Herzen's attention.

* * *

In the decade between Herzen's graduation and his return to the study of the natural sciences, the historical dimension of the study of life had been mapped out with ever-increasing amounts of data. The old debate begun by Linnaeus and Buffon still rumbled on, but the classification

of species based on the assumption of their immutability was yielding
to an acceptance of change and process, backed by the study of environmental factors in the transformation of species. Darwin's notebooks
show that he found Lamarck a significant source of inspiration in the
late 1830s, on both the general theory of evolution and its specific
mechanisms. As Cuvier had foreseen when he defined himself as a historian, the boundary between natural and human history was van-
ishing fast. Herzen's particular interest in chemistry and anatomy
shows a keen awareness of their current philosophical significance
at that stage in the development of biological thought. He was much
impressed by a history of chemistry, *Leçons sur la philosophie chi-
mique,* by the French chemist Jean-Baptiste Dumas—"an extraordinarily remarkable book," he notes in his diary. "Chemistry is the real
support of empiricism; its importance is only now beginning to be
realized. Without chemistry there is no physiology and hence no
natural science." The latter had hitherto paid serious attention only
to the morphology of living things, and not to the causes of change
and development: he cites Goethe's *Metamorphosis of Plants* (an early
classic of plant morphology much admired by the German *Naturphilosophen*). Modern chemistry had been born toward the end of the
eighteenth century with Lavoisier's close observations of the processes of change in the chemistry of living matter; thereafter it had
only to "grow in facts and observations, awaiting the possibility to
make the transition from crude empiricism to speculative empiricism."[36] In his university essay "On Man's Place in Nature," Herzen
had identified the age-old antagonism between empirical and speculative approaches to the natural and historical world—the human
tendency to "drown in the ideal or lose one's way in the real"—as
the source of some of the worst calamities of history. After nearly a
decade of submersion in the ideal, he resumed his search for man's
place in nature, once again with the question of method as a central
concern.

The enthusiasm and commitment with which he returned to the
scientific and philosophical preoccupations of his student years is reflected in an essay entitled "The Public Lectures of Professor Rouillier," published in December 1845 in the journal *Moscow News.* A
graduate of Moscow's Medical-Surgical Academy, Karl Rouillier was

appointed professor of zoology at Moscow University in 1840. His breadth of interest and expertise, encompassing zoology, geology, paleontology, and questions of evolution, was comparable to Lamarck's. He remained aloof from both sides in the contemporary battles between empiricists and *Naturphilosophen*, insisting on the importance of building theory upon experiment—the method that Herzen had defined as more precious than all the knowledge acquired in his university career.

Extending the concept of experiment beyond the laboratory to observation of the natural world in a ceaseless process of development, Rouillier was one of the pioneers of the comparative historical method in the study of biological phenomena—later to become known as ecology. He conducted extensive investigations of fossils in the field, and his emphasis on the study of animals in their natural habitat led him to a critical reworking of the ideas of Lamarck and Geoffroy. In an essay entitled "Doubts about Zoology as a Science," published in *National Notes* in 1841 and undoubtedly known to Herzen, he questioned the theory of the immutability of species. Without explicitly defending evolutionary ideas, he popularized them nearly a decade before the publication of *On the Origin of Species*, in his books and lecture course, which attracted large numbers of Moscow's intellectual elite. When the guardians of official ideology became aware of what was happening, his books were withdrawn from circulation, he was forbidden to give further lectures to the public, and the Minister of Enlightenment ordained that his university lectures could be delivered only in the presence of the rector or dean of the faculty.[37]

An attempt to set Rouillier's ideas in the context of the development of biological thought since Buffon, Herzen's essay was intended to serve as the introduction to a future article on the completed course.[38] This was never written; the reason may be inferred from a bitter reflection in his diary of November 1844 on the imperative for a Russian writer to be schooled in the cunning distortion of his meaning, forcing the reader to make guesses: "I'm reproached for the obscurity of my articles: that's unjust—I deliberately make them obscure."[39] Rouillier's ideas were so close to the unthinkable that he could not have discussed them without bringing the wrath of the authorities down on them both. Instead he marshals his argument around the question of methodology, beginning with an exhortation on a theme dear to Maximovich—that the dissemination in society of accurate and practical knowledge of the natural sciences is one of the most urgent needs of the age. Citing Rabelais and Francis Bacon on the value of knowledge derived from direct observation of nature as a weapon against all forms of scholasticism, he affirms: "No other branch of knowledge so much trains the mind in taking firm, positive steps, in submission before the truth, in conscientious work and, what is even more important, in honest acceptance of the consequences, *whatever these may turn out to be.*" Education should start with the natural sciences in order to cleanse the minds of the young of prejudices; only then, armed with the methods they had learned, should they be introduced to the world of history, whose study leads directly to involvement in contemporary questions. The fruits of the great achievements in the natural sciences had so far remained within academic walls, without affecting the education of cultivated Europeans. This remained "an education in memory rather than reason, words rather than concepts, style rather than thought, authorities rather than independent action: as before, nature is supplanted by rhetoric and formalism. Such an education leads almost always to intellectual arrogance, to contempt for all that is natural and healthy and a preference for all that is fevered and strained; thoughts and judgments as before are injected like smallpox at an age of spiritual immaturity: on attaining the age of reason man finds the trace of a wound on his arm together with a sum of ready-made truths, and setting out with them on his journey, accepts them good-naturedly . . . as a completed process."[40]

There is no more efficacious remedy for this condition, Herzen affirms, than the dissemination of knowledge of the natural sciences "from that viewpoint to which it has currently developed"—a discreet reference to the latest evolutionary theory. He continues to maneuver with Aesopian skill: The "great discoveries" that are following in such quick succession and the truths they reveal do not pass into general circulation. If they do attain publicity *(glasnost)*, this is only in a distorted form. The French have done most for the popularization of the natural sciences, but their efforts, impeded by the need to make concessions to their audience, are unable to penetrate the "thick crust of prejudices." "Our imagination is so corrupted and imbued with metaphysics that we have lost the power to convey the events of the physical world directly and simply without introducing . . . false ideas, mistaking metaphors for the real thing, separating in words what is united in reality." This false language had infected science itself; hence the significance of the new view of life and nature in the natural sciences as reflected in Rouillier's lectures—a view "equidistant from vulgar materialism and from dreamy spiritualism."[41]

Herzen remarks that the lecturer's choice of subject (to use Rouillier's own term, the "psychology" of animals and their modes of life) was courageous. He was proposing a new narrative of life based on the clear recognition of the premise that there were no absolute boundaries between the sciences of zoology and psychology. It then became the business of comparative anatomy and physiology to trace the development of consciousness in the animal world to its appearance in humans and thereby "in the arteries of history." Although the scientific study of animal psychology had scarcely begun, this narrative raised intensely interesting questions on all sides. At stake were the most profound truths of natural science, "and even philosophy."[42]

Although Herzen leaves it to his readers to reflect on the nature of these questions, his daring was no less impressive than Rouillier's. The proposition that man was not a wholly separate creation was so abhorrent to so many that even in the *Origin* Darwin would not spell it out directly. Only in 1871, in *The Descent of Man*, did Darwin suggest explicitly that man had descended from apelike ancestors.[43]

Herzen had said enough to alert the livelier minds in Moscow to the fact that attendance at Rouillier's lectures would be worth their while. The rest of his essay is a brief exposé for a popular audience of the history of biological science and its gradual transformation from Linnaeus's system of botanical classification into the new sciences concerned with life as process. He stresses the importance of Buffon's pioneering studies of animals in the fullness of their existence in their native habitat. (The great naturalist's historical significance in Herzen's eyes can be deduced from a phrase in his diary: "the eighteenth century . . . the age of Voltaire and Buffon.")[44] He remarks that Buffon had a great advantage over most contemporary naturalists in that he knew nothing about natural science, but although free of the scholastic prejudices of his age, he lacked the methodology to give a scientific form to his study of nature. It was Cuvier's comparative anatomy that forged a new path for zoology, but his descriptive approach encouraged his followers to view the organic world of "headlong process" as a changeless realm of final results. The embryological experiments conducted by Geoffroy brought zoology nearer to its ultimate goal: a shift from morphology to physiology and the chemistry of living nature. Herzen was acquainted with the work of Karl von Baer, the founder of comparative embryology, quoting from his study of 1828, *Über Entwicklungsgeschichte der Thiere: Beobachtung und Reflexion* (On the Developmental History of Animals: Observation and Reflection), which laid the foundations for a systematic study of animal development. Focused on the nature of life and raising questions ultimately resolvable only by philosophy, every serious new publication in the natural sciences, Herzen asserts, is evidence of "tireless activity" linked by unity in aims and spirit. Among those whom he cites as giving the natural sciences a new empirical direction focused on the processes of life are the French physiologist and neurologist François Magendie; the German chemist Justus von Liebig, who did pioneering work in applying chemistry to plant and animal physiology; J. B. Dumas, whose experiments with Prévost in Geneva on the process of fertilization played an important role in animal biology; and Moritz Wagner, an explorer, collector, and geographer who had devoted three years to the exploration of Algeria, adding support to the theory of geographic speciation by comparing closely related but different species of fauna on the different sides of rivers and of mountain ranges.

A notable absentee from the list is Lamarck, whose *Philosophy of Zoology*, the chief inspiration of Maximovich, is one of the most striking examples of the achievements of evolutionary thought before Darwin. Herzen's daring had its limits.

"A Practical Philosophy"

As an introduction to the philosophical significance of evolutionary theory, Herzen's essay is an impressive example of the kind of scientific popularization for which he put so strong a case. But the primary beneficiary of his research was himself—his studies on nature had enabled him to come to terms with the destructive role of chance in his own life. Two months before his philosophical discussion with Khomyakov he published an essay that, he notes in his memoirs, stemmed from his reflections on the domestic dramas that had destroyed his faith in the role of Providence in his marital life. Its subject was the plot of a play he had just seen, a marital triangle with a tragic ending. This had ensued because the characters' happiness, based on their private lives and loves, was wholly at the mercy of chance.

> All the individual side of human life is buried in a dark labyrinth of contingencies, intersecting and interweaving with each other: primitive physical forces, dark urges, chance encounters, each have their place. They can form a harmonious choir, but equally can result in dissonances that can tear the soul apart. Into this dark forge of the fates light never penetrates: the blind workmen beat their hammers aimlessly, not answering for the results. . . .
>
> There is something about chance that is intolerably repellent to a free spirit: he finds it so offensive to recognize its irrational force, he strives so hard to overcome it, that, finding no escape, he prefers to invent a threatening fate and submit to it. He wants the misfortunes that overtake him to be predestined—that is, to exist in connection with a universal world order; he wants to accept disasters as persecutions and punishments: this allows him to console himself through submission or rebellion. Naked chance he finds intolerable, a humiliating burden: his pride cannot endure its indifferent power.[45]

One cannot avoid the blows of chance by retreating into a world of the imagination, but one can lessen their destructive power by opening oneself up to the actual world of reason, science, art, and the universal concerns of contemporary society. "To exist is the greatest good," and the apotheosis of life is to extend the boundaries of individual existence through loving contact with one's human and natural surroundings: such is Herzen's new philosophy. In a diary entry of 1844 he insists that precisely because the future is so greatly dependent on chance factors that we can neither predict or control, we should place "enormous value" on the present. "Instead, we treat it carelessly, sacrificing it to dreams of a future that will never be organized according to our conceptions but rather in some haphazard fashion, giving us more than we expect, and trampling on our most justifiable hopes."[46]

His diaries and letters of the 1840s show him struggling to maintain this position against both the pressures of his environment and his own tendencies to pessimism and despair. "Mankind's life is an endless bitter battle. No sooner are obstacles overcome, peace arranged on one side, than on the other enemies arise from under the earth or fall from the sky, ruining the calm enjoyment of life and the harmony of its development." He observes that to renounce a goal-directed approach to reality is enormously difficult in an age whose distinctive characteristic is "reflection." "We don't want to take a step without reasoning it out, ceaselessly we stop, like Hamlet, and reflect, reflect. . . . There's no time left to act: we chew over the past and the present ceaselessly, over everything that has happened to us and to others, looking for justifications, explanations."[47]

When his son Sasha suddenly falls ill, Herzen muses on the precariousness of human life. "Man lives by minutes, in bands of light between which there are dark, drab transitions, a cloudy dimness. . . . These rare instants are the fulfillment of life's promises, its demands, its truth. . . . This is a great deal, if we know how to take advantage of it. But in reality these moments fly by unregarded, followed by a foggy, dank mist of triviality, which stretches on and on."[48]

The commonsense doctor in Who Is to Blame? describes the inability to surrender oneself to the present and the tendency to let spontaneous enjoyment be clouded by fears of future disaster as "a kind of madness . . . one of the most widespread moral epidemics of our time." It was a disease to which Herzen was no more immune than his friends. He confesses to them that his constant admonitions are as much for his own benefit as for theirs, that when not prey to Romantic gloom about the past, he was subject to cowardly fear about the future: "My enjoyment often fades before the chilling thought: perhaps I shall lose it tomorrow." The life of his circle vindicated his new vision of reality while making it more difficult to sustain in practice. The intense emotional and intellectual fulfillment it afforded was constantly threatened by the precariousness of its existence. After a happy evening with Vasilii Botkin and the historians Timofey Granovsky and Konstantin Kavelin ("What a noble group of people, what love binds them together!"), he reflects: "There is much that is beautiful in the present, one must grasp it, grasp it all and revel in it: friendship, wine, love, and art—that's what it means to live."[49]

The passages in his diary embracing the self-sufficiency of the present read like short sermons addressed to himself. With Natalie one evening in the last gloomy months of his exile in Novgorod, he hears a peasant singing. What is the purpose of the song? Nothing more than the expression of the spontaneous joy of existence: "If one looks deeply into life then, of course, the supreme good is life itself, whatever the external circumstances may be. When people come to understand that, they will also come to understand that there is nothing more foolish than despising the present for the sake of the future. The present is the true sphere of existence. Every instant, every pleasure must be grasped, the spirit must constantly open itself, absorb all that surrounds it and pour its own being into its surroundings, The aim of life is life itself. Life in that form, at that stage of development at which a creature finds itself. Thus the aim of man's life is human life."[50]

An unusually cold and wet summer, attributed by astronomers to changes on the surface of the sun, prompts reflections on the unpredictability of the natural world and the fragility of the life it sustains: "Can anyone guarantee that some change in the sun won't produce a cataclysm over the whole surface of the earth, and that then we shall perish along with the animals and the plants, and a new population will appear in our place, adapted to a new earth? We possess only the present, and even that we aren't capable of valuing."[51] Anticipating the Darwinian revolution, this rejection of cosmic determinism would receive its extended development in *From the Other Shore*.

In his diary for December 1844, while acknowledging his struggles to live up to it, Herzen sums up his personal credo in an attack on those idealists who see the vulnerability of beauty and all that engages human affections as a reason to disparage them. Quoting Schiller, "Nur wenn er glühet, labet der Quell, [A source is only a living spring if it glows]" he demands: "What sort of colorless, arrogant and miserly personality is he who can stifle the demand for love in his soul, because the object of his love can die, betray him, etc.? . . . One must seize the present, realize in oneself all one's potential for bliss, and by this I mean both social action and the bliss of knowledge, as well as the bliss of friendship, love, family feelings; and then what will be will be—the responsibility is not mine. He who has hidden his talent in the earth so that it shall not be stolen, shall have to answer for it."[52]

In December 1843 Herzen's second son Nikolai (Kolya) was born, followed a year later by a daughter, Natalie (Tata). Both children were healthy. Informing Ketcher of the unfamiliar calm that has descended on his personal life, he observes that he has rarely—perhaps never— experienced such a sense of complete and tranquil possession of the present: "One must learn to value such spells in life—that is, to be capable of surrendering fully to them—a sort of anxious restlessness makes people give insufficient value to the present, or value it only when it is past." Still in this mood of calm acceptance at the start of 1845, he communicates his credo to Ogarev and Satin in what he describes as "a small exercise in practical philosophy," attempting to capture in words the state of consciousness to which he aspires:

> We are terribly guilty before the present: with us everything is either memory or hope, *sui generis* abstractions; meanwhile life flows through our fingers unremarked. . . . In fact the present is never self-contained: all our past life is reflected and preserved in it. But that past must not weigh the present down—I'm speaking not so much for you as for myself. . . . When I'm not subject to melancholy Romantic *Grübelei*, I'm subject to cowardice in the face of the future; my pleasure often fades before the chilling thought—perhaps it will be gone tomorrow. Anything can happen. If one thinks like this one should sit with folded arms and with feet tucked up beneath one; nevertheless, the thought does occur to me. Man can least of all be reconciled to the precariousness, the fragility, of all the most precious things that he possesses. It's a simple matter: the more stable a thing, the more like stone, the more removed it is from our affections . . . because what is lasting is unmoving, unfeeling, while what is fragile is process, movement, energy, *das Werden*. The highest manifestation of life is weak because all its material strength has been spent on reaching that height. A flower will be killed by a cold wind, but its stem will hold fast. You can't shatter a muscle with your hand, but the brain? . . .
>   One must realize all possibilities, live on all sides—this we are taught by the encyclopedia of life.[53]

He rejects responsibility for the potential consequences of his "practical philosophy" on grounds of the unpredictability of the conditions and collisions of life, which, he tells his Hegelian friends, can be grasped better through a knowledge of chemistry than by philosophical logic.

* * *

Herzen's emphasis on the dominant role of chance in human life invites comparisons with the pessimism of Nietzsche—or his predecessor, Schopenhauer, who made the first sustained assault on nineteenth-century historical optimism in his treatise of 1819 *The World as Will and Representation*, depicting human history as a blind struggle for existence dictated by the unconscious will to power. But Herzen's mature philosophy was based on quite different foundations. As we shall see in Chapter 16, a far more apt comparison would be with "the greatest of all historical scientists," as Darwin has been described.[54]

In a letter of 1843 to Ogarev (quoting a remark he attributes to Hegel, that an intelligent, sane person, on being told that twice 2 equals 4, will not be scandalized that it doesn't equal 3, or be distressed because it doesn't equal 5), Herzen observes, "I've long ceased to place ideology above factology."[55] His notion of chance was rooted not in idealist metaphysics but in the latest advances in evolutionary science, which were pointing to the concept of adaptation by natural selection. The opponents of these advances argued that this led to the unthinkable conclusion that mankind and the natural world were the outcome of pure chance. But as Ernst Mayr has stated, this word can be misleading when applied to Darwin's theory: "Natural selection has been particularly puzzling to the physical scientists, because it is so different from physical theories and laws. It is neither strictly deterministic nor predictive but probabilistic with a strong stochastic element. Whether one likes or dislikes such an undisciplined process is irrelevant. The fact is that it occurs in Nature."[56] The confusion can be avoided if, like Stephen Jay Gould, one substitutes the word "contingency," a central principle of all history, for chance: "An historical explanation does not rest on direct deductions from laws of Nature, but on an unpredictable sequence of antecedent states, where any major change in any step of the sequence would have altered the final result. The final result is therefore dependent, or contingent, upon everything that came before—the unerasable and determining signature of history." Contingency is "the affirmation of immediate control by immediate events over destiny, the kingdom lost for want of a horseshoe nail." To acknowledge its role in the development of nature

> is not to ignore the role of invariant laws in determining the forms and functions of organisms and the way in which they evolve: the question is one of scale, or level of focus. . . . Invariant laws of Nature . . . set the channels in which organic design must evolve. But the channels are so broad relative to the details that fascinate us! . . . When we set our focus upon the level of detail that regulates most common questions of the history of life, contingency dominates and the predictability of general form recedes to an irrelevant background.[57]

Gould draws attention to the famous exchange of letters with the Christian evolutionist Asa Gray in which Darwin makes this central distinction between laws in the background and contingency in the details: The universe, Darwin affirms, runs by law, "with the details, whether good or bad, left to the working out of what we may call chance."[58]

Herzen would combine the notion of chance in this Darwinian sense with a radical humanism, drawing on a number of sources to shape the concept of limited but real freedom that he would oppose to all teleological narratives of history and human life.

CHAPTER ELEVEN

From Bacon to Feuerbach: Nature and Time

The blows of chance remain the same: what has changed is the breast on which they fall.

HERZEN

By the mid-1840s the battle set in motion by Chaadaev's *Philosophical Letter* had reached fever pitch. The opposing parties waged their polemics in the Moscow salons and in their respective journals. The principal Slavophiles included Konstantin and Ivan Aksakov (former members of Stankevich's circle), Yurii Samarin, Petr Khomyakov, Ivan Kireevsky (a former member of the Society of Lovers of Wisdom and, along with Aleksei Khomyakov, the main contributor to the Slavophile philosophy of history). Their philosophy drew heavily on the mysticism of the later Schelling and on thinkers of the European Counter-Enlightenment—Romantic conservatives such as Franz von Baader and Friedrich Schlegel, who argued that empirical reasoning was incapable of grasping the true nature of reality, which could be understood only through poetic intuition, supernatural revelation, and religious faith. Chaadaev's glorification of Western civilization and his denigration of Byzantine Orthodoxy provoked this group into spelling out the anti-Westernism implicit in their thought, first formulated uncompromisingly by Khomyakov in an essay of 1838–1839, and then more moderately in a reply by Ivan Kireevsky.[1] They argued that European societies were artificial constructs devoid of moral content and held together by formal, legal structures inherited from the rationalistic civilization of ancient Rome. This soulless rationalism had corrupted the Catholic Church through its association with secular power, and through the philosophy of the Enlightenment followed by the French Revolution it had created the atomized societies of Western Europe— aggregates of individuals linked merely by external rational bonds based on abstract theories of rights. Russia could escape a similar fate only by remaining true to its Orthodox Christianity, which, uninfected by the individualism and rationalism of the West, was preserved in the faith of the Russian peasantry and the structure of their communes, whose members were bound together not by external, legal sanctions but by bonds of Christian brotherhood (sobornost)—the social manifestation of the spiritual essence of Orthodoxy. Only the return of Russian society to its religious roots, the Slavophiles believed, would heal the inner discord of Russia's superfluous men. Their doctrines offered an escape from grim reality by transforming its defects into virtues. When viewed in the rosy glow of Romantic conservatism, Russia's backwardness and stagnation were proof of its spiritual superiority over the West. However, the Slavophiles stopped short of justifying the contemporary autocracy, which they saw as a Western invention superimposed on the patriarchal structure of pre-Petrine Russia.

Their main opponents, Belinsky and his circle, were profoundly influenced by Hegelian rationalism and universalism. Individual differences—such as those between the radical democrat Belinsky and the liberal professor Granovsky—were submerged in a common vision of progress as the emancipation of the personality from uncritically accepted traditions and beliefs, a process headed by the most advanced countries of the West. Granovsky's Hegelian vision of history as the progression to rational freedom infused his historical scholarship to such an extent that a series of public lectures he gave in 1843 on the recondite subject of the Merovingian and Carolingian kings—attended, according to the memoirist Annenkov, by the entire educated population of the city—took on the character of a political event. While keeping within the permitted boundaries for public expression, he made out of the narrow terrain assigned to him "a flowering oasis of knowledge." His descriptions of the brutal despotism of the feudal system had a clear application to the Russia of his time. "When, at the conclusion of his lectures, the professor addressed the audience directly in his own name, reminding it how huge a debt of gratitude we owed Europe, from where we had received, without paying any price, the blessings of civilization and a truly human existence, which it had attained through bloody toil and bitter experience, his voice was drowned out by a burst of applause resounding from every corner of the auditorium."[2] Herzen describes what may be seen as the first expression of public opinion in Nicolas's Russia: "Everyone leapt up in a kind of intoxication, ladies waved their handkerchiefs, others rushed to the platform, pressed his hands and asked for his portrait. I myself saw young people with flushed cheeks shouting through their tears: 'Bravo! Bravo!' "[3]

Herzen has left his own deeply affectionate portrait of Granovsky, whose great strength he describes as the moral influence of his humanism and independence of thought.[4] But their friendship would be clouded by the rift in the Westernizers' circle that occurred as Herzen staked out the position that was to set him apart from all the major currents of opinion in the progressive thought of his time.

Herzen and Hegel

In Novgorod at the beginning of 1842 Herzen had embarked on his long-planned study of Hegel, his expectations formed by his reading of Cieszkowski. He was not to be disappointed. In February he asks A. A. Kraevsky, the editor of *National Notes,* to let Belinsky (whose celebrated revolt against Hegel had taken place two years before) know that he has read the *Phenomenology of Spirit* "thoroughly," and that he "should swear only at [Hegel's] followers, . . . and not attack the great shade himself." "Toward the end of the book it is as though you are entering a sea—limpid and deep, you are carried along on the breath of the Spirit—*laschiate ogni speranza*—the shores disappear; one's sole salvation is within one's breast . . . but then fear is dispelled, there is the shore, the beautiful leaves of fantasy have been plucked, but the succulent leaves of reality are there. The Undines have vanished, but a full-breasted maiden awaits. Excuse me, I am not completely coherent, but such was my reaction."[5]

The Hegel whom Herzen believed he had discovered was very different from the mature philosopher who was the subject of the metaphysical debates that he mocks so entertainingly in his reminiscences of his Moscow circle. He recalls in his memoirs that when he started to study Hegel in earnest, he began to distinguish the famous Berlin professor, who made no protest when his philosophy was used to justify Indian quietism and Prussian Christianity, from the "real Hegel" of the early works: in particular, the *Phenomenology*. "A person who has not *lived through* Hegel's *Phenomenology* . . . who has not passed through that furnace and been tempered by it, is not complete, not modern. . . . Hegel's philosophy is the algebra of revolution; it emancipates man in an extraordinary way and leaves not one stone upon another of the Christian world, of the world of tradition that has outlived itself."[6]

★ ★ ★

What was there in this work that made so powerful an impression on Herzen? Published in 1807, this is the earliest and most radical of Hegel's major writings. Completed as Napoleon's army was sweeping away Germany's *ancien régime*, it reflects the hopes aroused in his generation by the French Revolution's promise of a new world built on the principles of reason and the rights of man. But the work is also permeated with the sense of a profound crisis in European culture. Hegel had shared the disenchantment of the other prominent intellectuals of his period when the Revolution, whose impact he described as a "glorious mental dawn,"[7] degenerated into violence followed by terror and dictatorship. Along with the Romantics Schelling, Schleiermacher, Novalis, and the Schlegels, he believed that the ideals of freedom and autonomy could be put into effect only through the cultural and spiritual education of society, and that the speculative tradition of German philosophy equipped it uniquely for the role of mentor to modern man. But he added that philosophy could fulfill this role only if it changed drastically its approach to the nature of truth, abandoning the search for eternal and universal values and truths in favor of a historicist approach to philosophical doctrines as the products of human thought in specific cultural contexts. This was not a radical break with the past: Hegel's early works show him to be well acquainted with the historicism of Montesquieu and Herder, and like them he maintains that philosophical doctrines are not, as Kant had held, the product of a timeless reason, but instead the expression, criticism, and defense of the values of specific cultures at specific historical periods. In the famous phrase of the preface to his *Philosophy of Right:* "Philosophy is its own age comprehended in thought."[8]

Like Herder, he combined an emphasis on the uniqueness of each historical period and culture with a teleological vision of progress. Retrospectively the history of cultures could be seen as a process leading to the full development of the consciousness of freedom, although the modes of thought and being that are transcended in this process are not discarded—their partial insights would be incorporated in the fuller comprehension that succeeds them. The *Phenomenology*'s style is notoriously obscure; Frederick Beiser has commented on the problematic nature of Hegel's metaphysics in this work, as seen from the standpoint of contemporary philosophy with its legacy from Kant: "Hegel seems to fly in the face of every stricture upon the limit of knowledge, blithely speculating about such obscure entities as 'Spirit' and 'the Absolute.'"[9]

Hegel emphasized that his term "absolute knowledge" referred not to a supernatural entity but to the immanent purpose of history, a whole of which individual humans are parts; but this interpretation fits uneasily with the famous passage in the introduction to his *Philosophy of History* on the "cunning of Reason" which uses human passions to work toward its goals, through an ascending dialectic culminating in the end of history when God, or the World Spirit, comes to full self-consciousness in an ethical community whose relations are structured on reason.[10] Commentators have pointed out that the notion (adumbrated in the *Phenomenology of Spirit*) of the perfecting of the modern European state seems to require the foreclosure of the future and the end of alienation, transcending the finitude that is the condition of human existence and thereby negating Hegel's own definition of the human subject as self-transforming in historical time.[11]

* * *

In view of his belief in the role of contingency in history and his aversion to "abstract" thought that had alienated him from the Moscow Hegelians, Herzen's enthusiastic reception of the *Phenomenology* seems surprising, even if one takes into account that his initiation into Hegelianism had been through Cieszkowski's activist interpretation. There is strong reason for suspecting that his reading of the *Phenomenology* was much more selective than he makes out. The source of his enthusiasm was not so much the text itself as the preface, whose relation to what follows it is problematic. The work was intended initially as an introduction to his system, but Hegel's priorities seem to have changed in the course of its composition. It has been suggested that the work consists of two texts with no clear connection—a historical theodicy alternating with an account of the faculties involved in humans' perception of the external world.[12] This latter theme is the subject of the preface. Hegel describes it in an announcement accompanying its publication: "In the preface the author explains . . . what seems to him the need of philosophy in its present state; also about the presumption and mischief of the philosophical formulas that are currently degrading philosophy, and about what is altogether crucial in it and its study."[13] His discussion revolves around two themes: the contemporary age as an epoch of transition to a radically new perception of the self and its relation to the world, based on a historicist approach to beliefs and values; and the magnitude of the struggle and sacrifice required for the human consciousness to come to terms with this vision and make it the foundation of moral and social practice. As we have seen, Herzen's philosophical reflections were already focused on the same two issues. His highly emotional account to Kraevsky of the experience of reading Hegel reflects his personal identification with the trauma of the journey into unknown territory whose path is indicated in the preface.

The background to Hegel's argument is the mood of European society less than two decades after the French Revolution: weariness with the crumbling remnants of the past combined with a vague apprehension of something unknown—signs of "a time of birth and transition to a new period."[14] A far-reaching revolution in all forms of culture was in the making. The task ahead was to elevate philosophy to the status of a science. Hegel shared the German notion of science *(Wissenschaft)* as including the systematic study of history, art, religion, and other fields of human activity; true philosophy would mirror the structure of the world as a single intelligible system and embrace the other sciences when their concepts had been purified. Hegel illustrates the difficulty of the path to this goal by means of a critique of the two approaches to knowledge and truth most prevalent in his time: Romantic subjectivism and schematizing formalism.

He is contemptuously dismissive of the "empty depth" of Romantic philosophy—"an intensity void of content." Its cult of intuition and mystical inspiration constantly excites expectations that are never fulfilled. "Whoever decides to shroud the worldly multiplicity of his existence and of thought in a fog to attain the indeterminate enjoyment of this indeterminate divinity . . . will easily find the means to impress himself with his enthusiasm and thus to puff himself up." By "mono-chromatic formalism," his second target, he has principally in mind Schelling's less able followers whose method "juggles abstractions, argues back and forth," pigeonholing everything under the sun by reducing it to a lifeless schema—"for example, subjectivity or objec-tivity, magnetism, electricity, . . . east or west, *et al.*" This process "gives only the table of contents; the content itself, however, it does not furnish."[15]

A leitmotif of the preface, Hegel's critique of these two one-sided approaches to knowledge serves to clarify the singularity of his own approach to philosophy. (Walter Kaufmann observes that in his attack on formalism he seems to go out of his way to ridicule views com-monly attributed to him.)[16] True science in Hegel's interpretation demands the "exertion" of conceptual thinking *(die Anstrengung des Begriffs)*, but this does not have the transcendental connotations of Schelling's idealism. Hegel's "Concept" is the ground of all being, but its essence is fluid, existing only in concrete time and place. The bud and the blossom that supplants it are "elements of an organic unity . . . in which the one is as necessary as the other." To comprehend who and where we are now, we must strive to attain a form of comprehension that enters into past forms of consciousness as though they were our own (Herder's concept of *Einfühlung*) in order to understand the con-crete circumstances that brought them into being as well as the phi-losophies that opposed and superseded them. Empathy is an essential quality of the true philosopher.[17]

Hegel stresses the difference between his historicist approach and conventional opinion on the nature of truth—the "formal" thinking that holds that truth can be formulated in fixed propositions of eternal validity—an approach appropriate to mathematics but not to the study of the human mind, where sharp distinctions and dogmatic oppositions succeed only in removing flesh and blood from the bones, leaving out the "living essence of the matter." A "concrete and copious fullness" in the formulation of general principles is the first stage of a process leading us into the experience of their subject matter—"the seriousness of life in its fullness," the proper basis for knowledge and judgment.

Conceptual thinking captures the fluidity of all forms of existence, embracing the dimensions of time and process in empirical reality. "The true is . . . the Bacchanalian whirl in which no participant is not drunken." "Formal" thought stands outside and above its object; Romantic subjectivism shies away from what does not conform to its wishful thinking. True "scientific" understanding demands that we "surrender to the life of the object," respecting the concrete individuality of each stage in the odyssey of mind.[18]

Hegel repeatedly insists on the magnitude of the transformation in humans' relation to the external world demanded by his "science," a journey from the familiar into the unknown. His generation found themselves at the beginning of a far-reaching revolution in thought and culture, the prize for the toil of many generations following "an immensely tangled path"[19] (as Hegel put it in a famous phrase: "Der Weg des Geistes ist der Umweg [The path of Spirit is a roundabout path]"). Humanity had already accomplished a long and painful journey through time and space to attain the goal of rational self-consciousness. The task now facing it was more arduous: to make "fixed" thoughts fluid. But there could be no shortcuts on the way to understanding what constitutes knowledge. "The length of this way must be endured, for every moment is necessary." The goal of this labor is the surrender of comforting illusions and unreal expectations through a self-reflective and self-critical acceptance of the historicity of one's own ideals and values: "Reasonableness is a becoming."[20]

As described to Kraevsky, Herzen's breathless reaction to Hegel's ponderous prose might seem overdramatized; but the passage in his memoirs describing the life-transforming effect of reading the *Phenomenology* shows him to have been right to sense its importance as a turning point in his intellectual development. Hegel's account of the struggle involved in achieving the full development of self-consciousness explained and validated Herzen's own painful odyssey from the consolations of mystical idealism (or, as Hegel put it in the preface, "the arbitrariness of prophetic speech that despises . . . scientific procedures").[21] In his efforts to come to terms with the role of chance in human life, Herzen's studies in the natural sciences and Hegel's historicism were mutually reinforcing. Although he never elaborated on its nature or extent, Hegel admitted the role of contingency in history,[22] distinguishing in the preface between mathematical truths, consisting of "fixed, dead propositions," and historical truths, which concern "particular existence and the accidental and arbitrary."[23]

If the language of the preface often calls to mind Professor Pavlov's parody of idealist discourse,[24] it is frequently lightened by striking images encapsulating key philosophical points in a way in which Herzen, himself an expert in this technique, must have relished. To cite two examples, both on the methodology of the formalists: The trick behind their wisdom is easy to master, its instrument being "no more difficult to handle than a painter's palette on which there are only two colors, say red and green, one if a historical piece is wanted . . . the other for landscapes." On the arduous journey that conceptual thought has to undertake in tracking the stages in the phenomenology of the Spirit, Hegel remarks: "Above all, it will differ from that enthusiasm which, as shot from a pistol, begins immediately with absolute knowledge, having done with other standpoints simply by declaring that it will not deign to take notice of them." He also enlivens his text with one-liners, such as "What is familiar is not known simply because it is familiar."[25] One of Herzen's principal tactics in *From the Other Shore* would be to confront his readers with the underlying implications of their traditional assumptions and received beliefs. The immediate effect of his reading of the *Phenomenology* was in shaping the form and content of the two cycles of essays that were to be his major works of the 1840s. But first he completed his Hegelian education with his discovery of Feuerbach.

Herzen and Feuerbach

The attempt by the Hegelian school to clarify the relation between Hegel's historicism and his philosophy of religion led to deep divisions in the movement after his death. A Lutheran, Hegel maintained that the self-knowledge of Reason was manifested in Christianity in symbolic form, but he was ambiguous about the question of whether his philosophy preserved the truths revealed by Christianity or superseded them. On the one hand, he presents belief in a God (or Absolute Reason) apart from the world as an expression of unhappy consciousness. On the other hand, he was not a pantheist: in his lectures on the philosophy of religion he rejects the view that "all is God."[26] Dissension over the relationship in his system between the Absolute and existing political and religious realities led to the consolidation of the group of radical intellectuals known as the Left (or Young) Hegelians. This process took place against a background of political unrest in Germany, where the reverberations of the July Revolution in France had led in some states to a strengthening of moderate liberalism and the emergence of a radical republican movement. Both were repressed by Metternichean reaction, but social unrest and the alienation of the educated elite from the political order produced a sense of crisis and transition that infused the theological debate about what Hegel meant by God.[27]

The political radicalism of Cieszkowski's notion of a future "human-divine" community could not easily be reconciled with the concept of a transcendent God. Divisions within the Hegelian school were accentuated by reactions to the publication in 1835–1836 of the theologian D. F. Strauss's notorious *Life of Jesus*, which used demythologizing techniques to present the Gospel narratives as projections of human imagination and desires. It was Strauss who, in response to the polemics over his book, first divided the Hegelian school into factions of left, right, and center.[28] From an atheistic stance the former theologian Bruno Bauer attacked Strauss's critique of Christian culture as halfhearted, but Ludwig Feuerbach's "unmasking" of all forms of religious belief went farther than both in its work of demolition, marking the birth of a wholly new secular humanism that equated human liberation with the rejection rather than the realization of Christian values.

As a student of theology Feuerbach had attended Hegel's lectures, which destroyed his faith in the literal truth of biblical revelation. Abandoning his theological vocation, he devoted himself to Hegel's philosophy but became increasingly disturbed by the inconsistencies in his position on the Christian religion. Published in 1841, Feuerbach's *Das Wesen des Christentums (The Essence of Christianity)* presents theological discourse and speculative philosophy as the agents of mankind's self-alienation. Feuerbach argues that monotheism's "God," Spinoza's "substance," Kant's concept of reason as the source of morality, Fichte's "absolute ego," Schelling's "absolute identity," and Hegel's "absolute mind" are all objectifications of man's essential nature, which he projects onto a transcendent "other," abasing himself as object before this mythical entity. All the divine attributes are latent human powers, limited in individuals but infinite in the human species-being and manifested progressively throughout history. "Man's knowledge of God is knowledge of himself, of his own nature. . . . What presents itself before thy consciousness is simply what lies behind it." Religion had subverted man's moral sense by encouraging him to devote to the worship of God the powers and dispositions that would otherwise be dedicated to the improvement of human existence. "The secret of theology is anthropology." With this discovery history had reached a turning point at which humanity could begin to reappropriate its own alienated nature. A truly humanist morality must have as its guiding principle "Homo homini deus est [To man, man is God]."[29] The goal of history was not the self-comprehension of the Absolute in humans and nature, but the actualization of the individual's essential intellectual and affective qualities, to be accomplished not through the pursuit of a supernatural redemption but in loving community with all other humans actively striving for autonomy and the fulfillment of their potentialities in a new cultural order.

"God is the idea of the species . . . a universal being, the totality of all perfections, freed from all limits which exist in the consciousness and feeling of individuals."[30] The infinitude of this being, Feuerbach explains, is realized "in infinitely numerous and varied individuals." We seem here to be back in the realm of the Absolute, but Feuerbach seeks to mark his distance from Hegelian metaphysics by grounding man's universal nature as a "species being" in his concrete, sensuous existence—his most distinctive contribution to Left Hegelian humanism. The emancipated human being of the future will be not merely the reflective rational consciousness of Hegelian philosophy, but a creature of flesh, blood and passions. Feuerbach defines human nature as "reason, will, affection": "I feel: and feel feeling . . . as belonging to my essential being, and . . . as a glorious, divine power and perfection." He argues that all true comprehension of reality demands the combination of the individual's sensuous and rational powers. But, accustomed to view the world through "the deceptive vapours of

mysticism," we are wont to shrink from natural objects and processes which remind us disagreeably of the way in which external
reality obstructs our subjectivity. Hence the denigration of physical
reality and the sensual side of man that is characteristic of religious
alienation: contempt for the flesh and suspicion of sensual pleasure
has been a feature of Christianity throughout its history. "Where the
heavenly life is true, the earthly life is a lie; where imagination is all,
reality is nothing." Through contemplation of the divine and infinite
humans seek to free themselves from the "painful bonds of matter,"
the limitations of their individual existence: but fear of limitation is
fear of life. "All real existence . . . is qualitative, determinative existence."[31] Personality, individuality, and consciousness are "nothing"
without nature; and nature is nothing without corporeality. "The body
alone is that negativing, limiting, concentrating, circumscribing force,
without which no personality is conceivable. Take away from your personality its body and you take away that which holds it together. The
body is the basis, the subject of personality. Only by the body is a real
person distinguished from the imaginary one of a spectre. What sort of
abstract, vague, empty person would we be if we had not the property
of impenetrability, if in the same place, in the same form in which
we are, others might stand at the same time? Only by the exclusion
of others from the space it occupies does personality prove itself to
be real."[32]

* * *

At the end of May 1842, four months after Herzen began his study of
Hegel, Ogarev arrived in Novgorod on his way abroad with copies of
Dead Souls and *The Essence of Christianity*. While Gogol's masterpiece induced deep gloom, Feuerbach had the opposite effect. Herzen
describes his reaction in his memoirs: "After reading the first pages I
leapt up with joy. Down with the trappings of masquerade; away with
the stammering allegory. We are free men and not the slaves of Xan-
thos; there is no need for us to wrap the truth in myth."[33] This was
not a farewell to Hegel, whose significance as the greatest demythologizer of his age he would continue to uphold, while noting that the
great man had taken fright at the consequences of his own thought,
leaving it to others to spell it out. Feuerbach (who in response to the
clamor aroused by his book would describe himself as "nothing but *a*

natural philosopher in the domain of mind"\[34\] offered an original and inspiring approach to the problem of method in philosophy and science which had preoccupied Herzen in his student years. In the preface to the second edition he explains:

> I unconditionally repudiate *absolute,* immaterial self-sufficing spec-
> ulation, that speculation which draws its material from within. I
> differ *toto caelo* from those philosophers who pluck out their eyes
> that they may see better; for *my* thought I require the senses, espe-
> cially sight; I found my ideas on materials which can be appropriated
> only through the activity of the senses. I do not generate the object
> from the thought, but the thought from the object. . . . I am an ide-
> alist only in the region of *practical* philosophy, that is, I do not re-
> gard the limits of the past and present as the limits of humanity, of
> the future; on the contrary, I firmly believe that many things . . . that
> with the short-sighted pusillanimous men of today pass for flights of
> imagination . . . will . . . in the next century,—centuries in individual
> life are days in the life of humanity,—exist in full reality. . . . The
> "Idea" is to me only faith in the historical future, in the triumph of
> truth and virtue; it has for me only a political and moral significance;
> for in the sphere of strictly theoretical philosophy I attach myself, in
> direct opposition to Hegelian philosophy, only to *realism,* to materi-
> alism in the sense above indicated.[35]

Feuerbach based his anthropological approach to progress on the "striking proofs" of the latent potential of species presented by con-temporary physical and evolutionary science, combined with the evi-dence of history and psychology for the role of society and culture in augmenting human powers. From this perspective he describes the his-tory of mankind as "a continuous and progressive conquest of limits which at a given time pass for the limits of humanity. . . . But the future always unveils the fact that the alleged limits of the species were only limits of individuals."[36]

He was alone among the radical Hegelians of the 1840s in seeing the primary task of the movement as the popularization of the concep-tion of "species consciousness" that had emerged from their deconstruc-tion of religious and philosophical illusions: until this self-understanding took root in the popular consciousness, political action would be prema-ture. In Russia, where the latter option was inconceivable, Feuerbach's priorities offered at least a hope of philosophical progress. There are echoes of *The Essence of Christianity* in Herzen' s retort to Ketcher that philosophy could no longer exist without a foundation in physiology, and in his essay in the same year on Karl Rouillier's lectures on evolution, urging the widest possible dissemination in Russian society of the methods and discoveries of the natural sciences to counteract the corrupting influence of metaphysics on the intellect and the imagination.

Feuerbach's chapter on the human attachment to the idea of Providence must have resonated especially strongly with Herzen, whose faith in that concept had made his years of exile bearable. Belief in Providence, Feuerbach writes, "is belief in a power . . . in opposition to which all the power of reality is nothing. Providence cancels the laws of Nature; it interrupts the course of necessity, the iron bond which inevitably binds effects to causes." By exempting man from a connection with the universe, Providence convinces him of the infinite value of his existence—"a conviction in which he renounces faith in the reality of external things; it is the idealism of religion." In the inmost depths of his soul man would rather there were no world to limit his subjectivity: "for where the world is, is matter, and where there is matter there is weight, resistance, space and time, limitation and necessity. Nevertheless, there *is* a world, there *is* matter."[37]

Those who seek to escape from this dilemma can find refuge in the fundamental dogmas of Christianity as "realized wishes of the heart": "The essence of Christianity is the essence of human feeling. It is pleasanter to be passive than to act, to be redeemed and made free by another than to free one oneself, pleasanter to make one's salvation depend on a person than on the force of one's own spontaneity; pleasanter to set before oneself an object of love than an object of effort; pleasanter to know oneself beloved of God than merely to have that simple, natural self-love which is innate in all beings; pleasanter to see oneself imaged in the love-bearing eyes of another personal being than to look into the concave mirror of self or into the cold depths of the ocean of nature."[38]

Herzen was soon to encounter those depths in the tragedies of his personal life. One may assume that Feuerbach was not far from his mind when in his essay of 1845 he stressed the value of training in the natural sciences in inculcating the acceptance of fundamental truths about humans' place in nature and in history, no matter how unwelcome they might be, and whatever painful consequences this might entail. The need to disengage such truths from the accretions of consoling myths, along with the sacrifices involved in the process, were to become the leitmotifs of his mature political writings. Meanwhile in his last years in Russia Hegel's historicism, reinterpreted in terms of Feuerbach's naturalistic anthropocentrism and infused with his own growing radical impatience, was to serve as the stimulus for a form of humanism that would set him at odds with Slavophiles and Westernizers alike.

"Dilettantism in Science"

In March 1841, while awaiting news of where his second exile was to be spent, Herzen wrote to Ogarev that his fury at the authorities' treatment of him, together with Belinsky's radical rhetoric, had saved him from losing his way in the sphere of abstract thought "in the manner of the 19th century" by reviving his thirst for practical action. "I have never felt more acutely the need for the translation—rather the development—of philosophy into life." In Russia only one path was open to him: to follow the example of Feuerbach and the professors of Moscow's Faculty of Physical and Mathematical Sciences in undermining the traditional beliefs that provided the philosophical support for the existing order. On his return to Moscow in 1842, he notes in his diary: "I want to write some propaedeutic words addressed to those who want to study philosophy, but are confused about the aim, justification, and methods of science."[39] The result was *Dilettantism in Science*, a cycle of essays that took him a year to complete.

For the essays to reach a broad public (they would be published in successive numbers of *National Notes* between January and December 1843) they had to be passed by the censorship overseen by the official in charge of education in the Moscow region, Count S. G. Stroganov, whose criteria tended to be unpredictable. Fortunately, the last essay of *Dilettantism* was safely in print when Stroganov demanded that Herzen remove all mention of Hegel's name from his article on the first of Granovsky's public lectures on the Middle Ages, due to appear

in the journal *Moscow News*. He surmised that the reason for this
"Hegelophobia" was a combination of pressure from the Slavophiles
and the Metropolitan of Moscow, who had pronounced Hegel's views on
religion to be in contradiction with the doctrines of the Orthodox
Church.[40] This was only the partial truth, as he discovered in a meeting
with Stroganov which sheds light on the haphazard nature of tsarist
censorship. Herzen had complex relations with Stroganov, whom he
liked and respected, and who had interceded unsuccessfully with
Benckendorf on his behalf during his second exile, when he had sought
permission to travel to Italy to restore Natalie's health. He recognized
the virtues of Belinsky and the positive role of *National Notes* in Russian culture, and disapproved of the rantings of the Slavophiles' journal,
the *Muscovite*, while at the same time maintaining close relations
with its contributors. Herzen believed that his influence on education
was on the whole beneficent; his comments on Stroganov in his diary
depict a good man wholly confused, torn between his love of European
culture and his desire to preserve the status quo. He records Stroganov's
response in their meeting over the question of the naming of Hegel:
"I . . . shall oppose Hegelianism and German philosophy with every
possible means. They contradict our theology. Why do we need a dichotomy—two different dogmas: the dogma of revelation and the
dogma of science? I don't even accept that tendency which proclaims
the reconciliation of science with religion; the bedrock is religion."
He concluded that if he did not get his way, he would resign from
his post or close down a few Faculties: "You and the others will probably call me a barbarian, a vandal."[41] One must remember, Herzen
observes charitably, that Stroganov had spent his life in the army
and among the high aristocracy, neither milieu being distinguished
for a contemporary education of high quality. While this interview
had no negative repercussions, it serves as a reminder of the precariousness of Herzen's position, and of his courage in entrusting to
print anything that might conceivably serve as a pretext for further
punishment.

He was, however, careful in expressing the thirst for political action that inspired these essays only in Aesopian terms to an audience
he knew would be able to read between the lines. What his message
might have been without these constraints can be conjectured from

comments consigned to his diary over the period in which the essays appeared.

From the spring of 1842 it reflects a close interest in the political radicalization of the Young Hegelian movement, whose philosophical journal, the *Hallische* (later *Deutsche*) *Jahrbücher*, was edited by Arnold Ruge, the most influential activist of those who went beyond Feuerbach in extending the critique of Hegel to his political thought. The movement had initially subscribed to Hegel's view that Prussia would develop into the embodiment of historical Reason, but their liberal hopes were shattered by the repressive measures of Friedrich Wilhelm IV, who came to the throne in 1840, and the journal began to demand the replacement of the remnants of feudalism in Germany with civic emancipation and a rational state in accordance with the principles of the Enlightenment, as the ultimate fulfillment of the demands of reason. In June 1842, an article by Ruge in the *Jahrbücher* prompts Herzen to reflect on the heroism demanded by consistency with one's principles: Hegel's attachment to the status quo (*das Bestehende*), which had led him to absolutize the Prussian state, would have led him also to disown the Young Hegelians, " but the fact is that they were *truer* to him than he was himself."[42]

An entry of August that year is devoted to Ruge's journal, which Herzen credits with moving German philosophy out of the lecture room and into life. Through its agency thought had "taken on flesh," thereby acquiring the power directly to influence events. Reflecting that the *Jahrbücher*'s social and revolutionary ethos represented a great step forward in the political education of Germany, Herzen is impressed with the "astonishing nobility" of an article attacking the established churches as bulwarks of the status quo, in which the author declares his readiness to suffer the likely consequences of his criticism: "It's not long since Germans started speaking this language . . . *Se muove, se muove!*" Another contributor poses the question straight out: "one must decide, once and for all: 'Christianity and monarchy or philosophy and the Republic!' ": here was the voice of Germany, launched into political emancipation along with its characteristic depth and solidity of thought and despite its traditional quietism.[43]

In January 1843 Herzen reacts with strong enthusiasm to the style and content of "Die Reaktion in Deutschland," the most radical article to date in the journal (and likely to have been the immediate cause of its suppression that same month): "a resounding, open, triumphant proclamation by the democratic party" whose author, one Jules Elysard, he declares to be the first Frenchman to have understood Hegel properly. As he discovered some days later, Jules Elysard was the pseudonym of his former antagonist Bakunin, who had made a remarkable political volte-face after his departure for Europe. The article (which Herzen considered to have washed away his former sins)[44] began with the assertion that the realization of liberty was now first on the agenda of history. In Bakunin's version of Hegel's dialectic, the coming conflict between the "party of negation" and the supporters of the existing "positive" order would result in a revolutionary transformation without precedent in history; "a new heaven and a new earth . . . in which all the discords of our time will be resolved in a harmonious unity."[45] Two years later, *a propos* a letter from Bakunin in the French journal *La réforme*, citing as his reason for emigrating the need to escape the tyranny of the Russian regime and suggesting the possibility of a revolution in his country in the near future, Herzen comments: "Here's the language of a free man; it strikes us as absurd. . . . We're used to allegory, to bold words *intra muros*, and we're amazed by the free speech of a Russian, just as a person immured in a dark hovel is astonished by the light."[46]

A rumor (which proves to be unfounded) that Bakunin had been arrested in Switzerland along with some Swiss communists prompts some positive reflections in the diary on utopian communism, as preached by the Swiss tailor Wilhelm Weitling, extracts from whose writings cited in an official report strike Herzen as forceful and eloquent: reminiscent of the preaching of the apostles, his evangelical communism contains along with some nonsense, some strongly worded truths. Herzen notes that communism is spreading fast among Swiss and German workers: "Their principles are known: Eine vollkommene Gesellschaft hat keine Regierung, sondern eine Verwaltung [A mature society has no government, only an administration]—organization of work, de facto equality, war against property etc."[47]

Thus, as he prepared his Hegelian essays for the censor's approval, Herzen was confiding to his diary views that ranked him among the most intransigent of Hegel's radical interpreters. After attending a lecture in which the Hegelian Professor Redkin attempted to reconcile the concept of Absolute Spirit with Christian theology, he comments: "There is nothing more amusing or more annoying than the *juste milieu* in any affair: it's a statistical exercise in which all the effort is spent in maintaining equilibrium, leaving no strength for any kind of action; it is Austrian politics. . . . Bakunin expressed the bitter truth when (in "Die Reaktion in Deutschland") he wrote that people *du juste milieu* are like the Polish Jews who were hanged by both Russia and Poland."[48] The irony would not have escaped him: *Dilettantism* and the cycle of essays that followed were the product of a compromise between what he would wish to have written and what he was permitted to say.

* * *

Herzen recalls in his memoirs that he began work on *Dilettantism* at the height of the "philosophical ardor" aroused in him by Feuerbach's work, starting (so his diary records) with an assiduous reading of Hegel in order to comprehend and convey the "living" truth of his philosophy. Looking back twenty years later on his polemics with Russian conservative Hegelians, he writes: "When one has grown used to Hegel and mastered his method, one begins to perceive that he is much closer to our viewpoint than to that of his followers. . . . He was so in his early works, he was so everywhere where his genius had taken the bit between its teeth and forged ahead, oblivious of the Brandenburg Gate." While working on the essays he returns repeatedly in his diary to the problem of the two Hegels, reflecting that the great philosopher's attachment to the existing order would have held him back from admitting even to himself all the consequences of his principles. "He feared as much to talk in this way as others would have feared to listen to him."[49]

The conflict between the two Hegels runs through the argument of *Dilettantism*, which follows loosely the structure of the preface to the *Phenomenology of Spirit*, beginning with a description of the malaise of the age: "We live on the border between two worlds." The old beliefs had been shaken, but retained their hold on the affections. The new promised great fruits in the future but gave no comfort to the heart: hence the moral confusion prevailing in society. Herzen uses Hegel's critique of the respective approaches to knowledge of Romantic dilettantes and schematizing formalists as the template for the ensuing discussion of his contemporaries' philosophical delusions. In his concluding essay, with reference to the strengths and weaknesses of Hegel's analysis, he puts the case for the philosophy of action in terms that will be clear to his readers.

As he planned *Dilettantism* Herzen recorded in his diary his intention to point to the harm done by "good people who *love* to philosophize. The enemies of science are not as dangerous as all the semi-pietists, semi-rationalists."[50] The dilettante is defined in the essays as "the most harmless and useless of mortals; he spends his life in conversation with wise men from all the centuries, disregarding material occupations." Who knows what they discuss? "It's not clear to the dilettantes themselves, but they find a kind of comfort in their semi-darkness." Dreamy souls, they approach philosophy with a vague hope that it will provide reconciliation and reassurance, "proofs for their convictions, and all their hypotheses, consolation in their misfortunes, and God knows what else."[51] As portrayed in his memoirs, several members of his own circle fit this description perfectly, but the type makes only a only a fleeting appearance in the published work. Herzen had admitted that he had no idea in advance how the cycle would turn out: by the time of writing, he had come to concentrate his attention on a variety of dilettantism more toxic than the superfluous man, but more dangerous to attack in print.

Without changing his overall title, he disposes of philosophical dilettantism in the shortest of the essays: leaning heavily on Hegel's philosophy of history, he traces the development of Romanticism from medieval man's sense of dissonance between spirit and matter, passing through Scholastic mysticism into a movement born in a confrontation with classicism, and now, he emphasizes, safely consigned to the past. By the 1840s the Romantic movement whose subjectivism had been Hegel's principal target had indeed run its course, but it had a significant afterlife in the religious philosophy of the late Schelling, and among the Slavophiles whose outlook had been formed in the milieu of the Lovers of Wisdom. As portrayed in Herzen's diary this group displays all the traits of Hegel's model of the Romantic dilettante. In an entry of July 1842 he remarks: "The Slavophiles . . . are as absurd and as dangerous as the pietists. There's absolutely no way of communicating with them in word or print. . . . Religious people . . . often resort to this trick: 'Yes, that's so according to reason, but reason can trip up.' Thus the Slavophiles: 'Yes, that may be so according to the Europeans, but it's not our way.'" He laments the fate of Ivan Kireevsky, who before the closure of his journal had been a Westernizer: broken by despotism, he had rushed for salvation into "the gloomiest forest of mysticism."[52]

The Slavophiles make one brief appearance in the introduction to the essays in the guise of "our home-grown dilettantes" who, objecting to contemporary Western philosophy on pietistic, moral, patriotic, and sentimental grounds, make an exception for certain ideas which they adopt without reference to the historical context in which they evolved.[53] The reason for Herzen's reticence on their subject was self-preservation: with its indirect critique of religion, this was the essay most likely to earn him a third spell of exile. But he was acutely aware of the danger posed by the Slavophiles as supporters of the status quo in Russia, reflecting in his diary at the end of 1842 on the fanaticism of that "deranged trend": "With each new day Slavophilism brings forth new luxuriant fruits . . . along with hatred and contempt for the West goes hatred and contempt for freedom of thought, for law, for all manner of guarantees, the whole of civilization. Hence it goes without saying that the Slavophiles range themselves on the government's side, and they don't stop there." The authorities were short of educated spies to expose every thought issuing from independent minds, or detect a hidden meaning in a scholarly article; the Slavophiles had begun to do it for them, their *Muscovite* taking on the role of political informer by pointing out the subversiveness of Belinsky's contributions to the rival *National Notes*. "And why do they do this? From conviction, not for gain."[54]

The ostensible target of the last essay in the cycle, "Buddhism in Science," was the schematic approach and ponderous language of the scholarly caste of conservative Berlin professors who, following the letter rather than the spirit of Hegel's philosophy, had interpreted the phrase "what is real is rational" as a call to reconciliation with the darkest sides of contemporary life. Suppressing all sentiments of sympathy and compassion, they covered the chasm between life and thought with a thin layer of dialectical *fiorituri:* "like Buddhists they regard . . . destruction in the infinite as freedom and their goal, and the higher they rise in the icy sphere of abstractions the more they feel at peace."[55] Facts do not impress them: if asked why at this supreme stage of existence workers in Manchester and Birmingham are dying from hunger, they will reply that this is mere contingency. This tirade is an echo of Herzen's polemics against the excesses of Belinsky and Bakunin in their Right Hegelian period; few German professors were guilty of such extremes, but examples far from home were useful in distracting the censor from the radical message the essay was intended to convey as a vehicle for the promulgation of the philosophy of action.

Botkin had described the introduction to this essay as Herzen's *Sinfonia Eroica*. In his diary he accepts the tribute: written with fervor and poetic inspiration, it links philosophy organically with all the burning questions of contemporary society, expressing in coded language "all that ferments in my breast."[56] Here he addresses for the first time in print a theme which was to be central to his mature political thought: the difficulty of coming to terms with the lack of an overarching goal in history and human life, and making this acceptance the basis of human dignity and self-fulfillment.

He starts by contrasting the aridity of formalists and the faint-heartedness of those for whom philosophy is an agreeable pastime with Hegel's notion of the struggle and self-sacrifice involved in accepting the historicity of human existence and values. "Science demands the whole person, holding nothing back, ready to sacrifice everything and to receive as a reward the heavy cross of *sober knowledge*."[57] A year had passed since Ogarev had brought the *Phenomenology of Spirit* to Herzen in Novgorod; the passage below shows how profoundly Herzen had been affected by Hegel's warning of the magnitude of the struggle involved in breaking with the historical past to place mankind's self-knowledge on new foundations:

> One must live philosophy through, not assimilate it formally. To suffer through the phenomenology of spirit, to bleed with the heart's hot blood, to shed bitter tears, grow thin from skepticism, feel pity and love for many things . . . , and surrender everything to truth— such is the lyrical poem of education in science. Science becomes a terrible vampire, a spirit, which cannot be banished by any invoca-

tion, because man has called it forth out of his own breast and there is nowhere for it to hide. One must abandon the pleasant thought of engaging at a certain time of day in conversation with philosophers to educate the mind and decorate the memory. Terrible questions cannot be avoided: wherever the unfortunate one turns, they are before him, written in fiery letters by the prophet Daniel, . . . and he lacks the strength to withstand the bewitching force of the abyss which beckons man toward it by its mysterious danger. A serpent keeps the bank; the game, which began coldly with logical truisms, quickly turns into a desperate contest; all the cherished dreams . . . , hopes for the future, faith in the present, benediction of the past, all in turn appear on a card . . . All is lost.[58]

Of the players who stop at this point some, consumed by doubt, will resort to moral nihilism; others, more complacent, will make do with a "soulless atheism." But for those who, having parted with their final thaler, are prepared to wager their own existence on the truths of science and philosophy, the game changes: "he who loses his soul *will find it.*"[59] Full acceptance of the "living truth"—the contingency and impermanence of all being as a product of time and chance—demanded in turn full involvement in the joys and sorrows of transient life: only by expressing their beliefs through action could humans realize their true potential. Despite his genius Hegel had lacked "the heroism of consistency, the self-sacrifice involved in accepting truth in all its fullness and at whatever cost." Hence the ambivalence in his philosophy. His thought constantly broke free from the fetters imposed on it by his mode of life, habits, and professional calling: he conceived of the life of the Idea as a "Bacchanalian whirl" of endless movement. At the same time he had remained too closely bound to the culture and values of his own time to spell out the conclusions that followed from the principles he could not refrain from proclaiming, exemplifying the observation in the introduction to his *Philosophy of Law:* "as each person is the product of his time, so is philosophy an epoch caught in thought."[60] His contribution to the future age had been to complete his predecessors' work in defining the path to self-knowledge: he had done no more than hint that the freedom attained by this understanding must be translated into action. The years were now passing with the speed of centuries. In Germany new questions were being raised in books and journals about the relation of philosophy to life: "For-gotten by science, the individual personality has demanded its rights, demanded a life palpitating with passions and satisfied only by cre-ative, free activity. After negation completed in the sphere of thought it has come to desire negation in other spheres."[61]

Herzen had found the consistency he sought in Feuerbach's view of humans as species-beings subject like all others to the laws of nature, whose only hope of self-realization lay through the maximum exercise of their powers of sense and intellect in their given historical environ-ment. Feuerbach's anthropotheism is the key to the coded language of some of the more obscure passages in this essay, which echo his view of humans' immortality as consisting in their effect on the future of the species through their actions in the present. In the process of ab-stract thought, Herzen explains, humans subject their individuality to the universal laws of reason: here "man is eternal, *but he is not him-self*, . . . in the realm of the heart man is at home, but transient. In a rational, morally free and passionately energetic act . . . man is eternal in time, infinite in finiteness, a representative of his species and him-self, a living and conscious organ of his age." The role of science is to submit the empirical world to the laws of logic, but man also possesses "creative reason"—will, which demands that he play an active role in his time and place. "In this consists his universal calling—*his conditio sine qua non*."[62]

The influence of Feuerbach's naturalism can be seen in Herzen's growing interest in the role of contemporary discoveries in biological science in challenging the speculative method of idealist philosophy and its teleological assumptions about man and human societies. In the same essay, completed in the spring of 1843, he cites Buffon: "La nature ne fait jamais un pas qui ne soit en tous sens." Nature achieves all that is possible, "knocks at all gates, creating endless variations on the same theme. In this is contained the poetry of life."[63] Nature has no table of ranks, hence the failure of all attempts to order its creations in a single ladder of progress. Each stage of development in nature is an end as well as a means, a link in a chain, but also complete in itself. In the diversity and multiplicity of its paths through time, the develop-ment of mankind is a continuation of the history of nature, made more complex by the existence of consciousness and thereby of moral freedom:

> Each individual fulfills his own calling *in his own way*, leaving the stamp of his individuality on events. Nations . . . do the work of all mankind *as their own work*, thereby endowing their actions with aesthetic wholeness and fullness of life. Nations would be something pitiful if they saw their whole lives as only a stage toward an unknown future; they would be like bearers who have only the weight of the burden and the toil of the journey, while the golden fleece that they bear is for others. Nature does not act thus with her unconscious children. . . . All the more so, in the world of consciousness there can be no stage that does not carry its own satisfaction. . . . Each stage in history, absorbing and actualizing the *entire* spirit of its time, contains its own fullness—in a word, its personality, seething with life. Nations, sensing a calling to step forward onto the stage of world history . . . have shown strengths that no one would have ventured to suppose they possessed and which they themselves did not suspect: steppes and forests surrounded by dwellings came into being, sciences and the arts have flourished, gigantic labors have been carried out to prepare the caravanserai for the Idea that was in gestation. . . . But these were not external abodes for the Idea, but rather its own flesh, without which it could not be realized. . . . Each phase of historical development has had its end in itself, and hence its own reward and satisfaction. The ideal for every epoch is itself, cleansed from chance accretions, a transformed image of the present. It goes without saying that the more all-embracing, the richer the present, the more universal and valid its ideal.[64]

Seven years later, a new version of this passage would introduce the view of history presented in his essays in *From the Other Shore*.[65] In the last pages of *Dilettantism* Herzen can do no more than hint at the liberating potential of the convergence between philosophy and the sciences, which he sees as prefigured in Feuerbach's philosophy. Abstract thought must constantly submit itself to the test of the "concrete truth" of contingent existence: "However original and exhaustive certain definitions may be, they melt in the fire of life and, losing their one-sidedness, flow into its broad, all-engulfing stream. . . . Thought must take on flesh, descend into the marketplace of life, unfold in all the richness and beauty of transient existence without which there can be no absorbing action, pulsating with life." He ends with a visionary picture of humanity emerging from the gates of the temple of science in proud awareness of its creative freedom in an unprogrammed world: *"omnia sua secum portans."*[66]

"Letters on the Study of Nature"

While composing *Dilettantism* Herzen had resumed the study of natural science interrupted by his years of prison and exile. He was gratified to be informed by a student attending Professor Glebov's course in comparative anatomy that the essays had been immensely popular among his comrades, who had had no difficulty in reading between the lines, rushing to get their hands on every installment as soon as it appeared.[67] In February 1845 he was present at Glebov's dissection of a living dog. His initial revulsion was soon replaced by fascination with the physical revelation of the organs containing the mystery of life. He noted that the Slavophiles were waging a fierce campaign against comparative anatomy.[68] Science was increasingly encroaching on ground to which the Church claimed exclusive rights (in his memoirs Herzen recalls being told by the censor that the Metropolitan of Moscow had complained that his essays were being read by students in the seminaries as well as the university and the secondary schools).[69] In the same year he attended Karl Rouillier's epoch-making lectures on evolutionary biology. His belief in the effectiveness of this discipline (when properly understood) in training the mind to approach ethical and social questions is the inspiration behind *Letters on the Study of Nature* in which, armed with the insights of evolutionary science and Feuerbach's anthropocentric naturalism, he returns to the question of scientific method that had preoccupied him in his student years.

In July 1844 he began work on the *Letters*, whose publication in *National Notes* started in the following April.[70] Over twice the length of *Dilettantism*, they were Herzen's most ambitious philosophical work, based on the contention that philosophy could no longer exist without a firm basis in the physical sciences: they must share a common method, consisting of a combination of empiricism with speculation.

Modeled on the approach used in Hegel's lectures on the history of philosophy (which he read in preparation for his project),[71] they trace the
development of thought on mankind's relation to nature from the ancient world to the modern age. His declared intention was to make
the principal questions posed by the contemporary natural sciences
more accessible to a general audience by exposing stock concepts,
false assumptions, outworn prejudices, and half-truths—"the whole
arsenal of rusty and useless instruments that we have inherited from
scholasticism."[72]

He begins with a stirring picture of the astonishing progress made
by the natural sciences in his century, enumerating with lyrical enthusiasm advances the eighteenth century could not have even predicted.
Starting from modest beginnings, organic chemistry, geology, paleontology, and comparative anatomy had produced fruits surpassing
the most daring hopes, throwing new light on all other areas of
knowledge:

> Obedient to the powerful voice of science, the world of the past is
> rising from its grave to bear witness to the revolutions that accom-
> panied the development of the earth's surface; the ground on which
> we live, this gravestone of past life, is as it were, becoming trans-
> parent; the stone burial vaults have opened, the interiors of rocks
> have not managed to preserve the secrets they guarded. Not only have
> half-calcified skeletons, reduced almost to ashes, once again grown
> flesh; paleontology is seeking to uncover the law of relations between
> geological epochs and their entire organic population. Then all that
> was once alive will be resurrected in human understanding, wrenched
> from the sad fate of total oblivion, and those whose bones have been
> reduced to ashes, whose phenomenal being has been wholly effaced,
> will be resurrected in the radiant abode of science, where the tem-
> poral is laid to rest and becomes immortal.[73]

The world visible only to the microscope was also being forced to yield
its secrets. The physiologist had joined forces with the chemist in exploring the threshold of life, while the applied sciences were generating
ever new devices to ease human existence. Though there was much
cause for exultation, all areas of natural science seemed prey to a mood
of unease, a sense of something left unsaid. In search of what Bacon
had called the *magnum ignotum*, philosophers had ranged themselves

against scientists, the former delivering mysterious prophecies from some unattainable height, the latter refusing to venture beyond the bounds of experience. The two camps had developed in mutual distaste and mistrust, each nourishing its own prejudices and invoking its own phantoms: essence divorced from existence versus the "forces of life." The source of this enmity was dualism. The pride and glory of scholastic thought, it had separated the inseparable: genus and individual, life and the living, thought and the thinking subject, empiricism and speculation, analysis and synthesis. The hostility of empirical science to the arrogant self-sufficiency of philosophy was understandable, but threatened to reduce its discoveries to a mere inventory of facts. Herzen predicts that the fast-growing accumulation of data on the origins of the physical world will ensure that both sides will soon have to address seriously the question of the relation of thought to being and philosophy to science. Fifteen years later the publication of the *Origin of Species* would open such a debate; its ultimate resolution has not yet been achieved.

Herzen is dismissive of the capacity of *Naturphilosophie* to bridge the gap between the warring parties. Bypassing his intuitive insights into the nature of truth, Schelling's followers had adopted his "mystical somnambulism" as the basis of a narrow formalism.[74] Even Carus and Oken, for all their contributions to physiology, were not exempt from this criticism—the *Naturphilosophen* could not take credit for any of the most significant recent developments in natural science. Herzen notes approvingly that Cuvier had warned the Paris Academy of Science against the influence of theories from beyond the Rhine and that Victor Cousin in his lectures had been even more insistent on the danger presented by the spread of idealism from Germany to France. "The French are gifted with so true a view of things that they can't be led astray"[75]—an opinion Herzen would revise in 1848.

He had been impressed by the extent of Hegel's treatment of nature in his *Encyclopedia,* which he had read in preparation for his work on the *Letters.* He applauded it in his diary as the first example of a scientific account of the content of natural science because it signaled a break with the dualism of German philosophy.[76] But he observes that Hegel still gave unqualified precedence to reason as the fundamental self-determining principle of all reality, independent of its individual determinations in time, treating history and nature as "applied logic." Echoing the concluding pages of *Dilettantism*, Herzen extends Hegel's metaphor of the Bacchanalian whirl of the temporal to embrace the life of nature. There is no "stone wall" between the two: the former is an essential continuation of the latter, and neither can be comprehended in abstraction from history.[77] Nor, he believes, can the current conflicts between scientists and philosophers be understood without reference to their historical embryology, which he traces through three phases: ancient philosophy, scholasticism, and the modern age. He acknowledges his debt to Hegel in this respect, but there is a fundamental difference between their approaches.[78] Hegel presents the history of philosophy as a necessary logical process of ascent toward the "absolute truth" embodied in his system; Herzen views Hegelianism as a stage in a more untidy process whose goal is the harmonization of philosophy with science through a shared understanding of the relation of human consciousness to the natural and historical world. Hence, he deviates from Hegel not only on the modern era, but on the significance he gives to what he sees as an underlying quality of realism in the ancient Greeks' approach to nature, reflected in the physical atomism of Leucippus and Democritus and epitomized in the genius of Aristotle.

The *Letters* were justly criticized by Belinsky and others for their obscurity, which is not wholly explicable by the need to escape the censor's attentions; Herzen's assiduous reading of Hegel clearly had its effect on his style.[79] The lucidity and the forthrightness of his introductory chapters resurface only when he moves on to a thinker whom Hegel had considered undeserving of serious attention: Francis Bacon. While giving Bacon credit for spearheading the revolt against medieval scholasticism, Hegel had contended that the esteem in which Bacon was held for this was "greater than can be ascribed directly to his merit." The mode of reasoning by proceeding from facts and experience was common among cultivated men, and Bacon was no more than such a man, with clear perceptions, but devoid of "the power of reasoning through thoughts and notions that are universal." In Hegel's view the English were notably deficient in this power, hence the modest role he accords Bacon in the world-historical scheme: he is "leader and representative of that which in England is called philosophy and beyond which the English have not yet advanced, for they appear to constitute that people in Europe which, limited to the understanding of actuality, is destined, like the class of shopkeepers and workmen in the State, to live always immersed in matter and to have actuality but not reason as object."[80]

In his student essay of 1832, "On Man's Place in Nature," Herzen had argued that the contemporary battle between theorists and experimentalists in the natural sciences could be resolved by combining the two approaches through Bacon's inductive method. The revival of his interest in science led him to an enthusiastic rediscovery of Bacon. In August 1843 he copies into his diary one of Bacon's aphorisms directed against ' "idols"—the prejudices, superstitions, and habits of the mind that give rise to false representations of the world: "All idols must be renounced and put away with a fixed and solemn determination, and the understanding thoroughly freed and cleansed; the entrance into the kingdom of man, founded on the sciences, being not much other than the entrance into the kingdom of heaven, wherein none may enter except as a little child." Bacon's method, he insists, *"in no way"* resembles the narrow empiricism of some French and English natural scientists.[81]

In March 1845 Herzen observes that, compared to "systematizers" such as Descartes (the essence of whose thought could be encapsulated in a short summary), Bacon demanded intensive study. "One encounters almost on every page, quite unexpectedly, something strikingly new and strongly expressed."[82] In his essay on Rouillier's lectures at the end of that year, he stressed the historical significance of Bacon's *Instauratio Magna*. His method had borne fruit in the work of another genius— Cuvier's ability to reconstruct an antediluvian animal from a single bone was a triumph of Baconian induction. In his 1832 essay Herzen had expressed a hazy hope that a transformation of human societies would ensue from the application of a Baconian approach to knowledge. Viewed from the standpoint of the mid-1840s, when science had joined forces with philosophy in an assault on the traditional barriers to knowledge and human endeavor, this expectation seemed not unfounded.

Herzen maintains that Hegel had failed to appreciate Bacon's importance as the Columbus of science. Hegel's four-volume *Lectures on the History of Philosophy* allotted less than a dozen pages to Bacon.

Herzen devotes two of the *Letters* (nearly a quarter of the entire work) to him—the first contrasting him with Descartes, the second abundantly supplied with quotations from Bacon's writings and followed by Herzen's translation of sixty of the aphorisms in which Bacon had distilled the essence of his thought.[83] (He urges his own readers to read Bacon for themselves: "Everywhere you'll meet . . . ideas of striking truth and breadth.") He informed his editor, Kraevsky, that the first of the two essays seemed to him the best in the series so far. One thing he knew for certain—no similar argument was to be found in any contemporary history of philosophy.[84] This went as follows: Although Bacon shared the credit with Descartes for freeing philosophy from the authority of tradition and scholastic metaphysics, Descartes's protest was made from the standpoint of pure thought, whereas Bacon's reflected the disobedience of life, "which looks on all forms of one-sidedness with a smile and goes its own way." The question of the relationship of thought to being was approached by Descartes logically and transcendentally, by Bacon through observation and experiment. Descartes's distinction between mind and body (the latter explained in terms of matter and motion) was scholastic dualism in logical form, resulting in the subsequent bifurcation of philosophy into materialism and idealism, both equally one-sided in their approach to phenomena. "Idealism . . . has recognized only the universal, the generic, essence, human reason abstracted from all that is human; materialism, equally one-sided . . . denied the existence of universals, held thought to be a compartment of the brain, experience the only source of knowledge, and truth to be found only in . . . tangible and visible things. It has recognized the existence of rational persons, but not of reason or mankind." Herzen may exaggerate this dichotomy in the thought of his time, but the three aphorisms he chooses to illustrate his point read like a critique of the methodological debates in mid-nineteenth century evolutionary science:

> There are some minds more able to observe, make experiments, study details, gradations; others on the contrary strive to penetrate to the most hidden resemblances in order to draw general concepts from them. The first, lost in details, see only atoms; the second, floating in generalities, lose sight of everything that is particular, replacing it by phantoms . . .

... Neither atoms nor abstract matter devoid of all determination is real; what are real are *bodies, as they exist in nature.* ...

One must not be carried away in either direction: so that consciousness may be deepened and broadened, each of these attitudes *must in turn pass into the other.*[85]

Herzen contends that although the movement in physical science that had led to the achievements of Newton, Linnaeus, Buffon, and Cuvier can be traced directly back to Bacon, he cannot be held responsible for the narrow empiricism of some contemporary natural scientists, citing another aphorism: "Our path and method consist in this, to deduce not facts from facts and not experiments from experiments, as empiricists do, but from facts and experiments—causes and axioms and inversely, from causes and axioms—new facts and new experiments. This path is not smooth; it leads now up, now down, ascends to new axioms, descends to individual phenomena."[86]

Elsewhere in the *Letters* Herzen refers to this method as "speculative empiricism."[87] He had come to adopt this description for his own standpoint, possibly inspired by a passage in an 1841 essay in which Feuerbach defines his opposition to Hegel's philosophy as follows: "Hegel opposes the finite to the infinite and the speculative to the empirical, whereas I ... find the infinite in the finite and the speculative in the empirical."[88] Some of Herzen's citations from Bacon would not have seemed out of place in *The Essence of Christianity*—for example, Bacon's condemnation of "that ingrained, haughty and harmful opinion that the grandeur of the human mind is diminished by an extended and frequent occupation with experiments and details pertaining to the feelings and possessing a material definition." Herzen observes that Bacon regards philosophy that does not lead to action as worthless: "He sees knowledge and action as two facets of a single energy." More "modern" than Schelling or even Hegel, the early seventeenth-century philosopher-scientist is transformed in Herzen's eyes into a precursor of Feuerbach's anthropotheism, his protest against scholasticism inspired by "that disobedient element of life which looks with a smile on all manner of one-sidedness, and goes its own way."[89]

It appears that Herzen's extended encomium to Bacon temporarily sapped his creative powers. The last of the eight essays, entitled "Realism," consists of sketchy and disjointed comments on eighteenth-century philosophy, singling out (as a reductio ad absurdum of Bacon's thought) Locke's empiricism and Condillac's theory that sensation alone provides the foundation of knowledge. After a brief reference to similar excesses on the part of post-Cartesian idealism, he brings the cycle to an abrupt conclusion with the pious hope that the insights of the two great founders of modern philosophy will be reconciled in a single coherent vision, whose foundations have already been laid by Hegel. He wrote to Kraevsky that he had intended to finish off with an essay on Leibniz and Spinoza but felt a certain apprehension about it, as even the liveliest account of the history of philosophy could not prevail over the abstractness of the language they used.[90]

Wisely, he abandoned that project. Even if one takes into account the constraints imposed by the censorship, it is clear from the *Letters* that analysis of philosophical abstractions was not Herzen's métier. He was at his best in the destruction of idols, including those at whose shrines he himself had worshipped. His two "propaedeutic" works are interesting above all in what they reveal of the intellectual path already leading him toward the distinctive humanism that would set him at odds with all the major ideologies and political groupings of his time in Russia and the West. The Chemist, Maximovich, Pavlov, Rouillier, Hegel, Bacon, Feuerbach—all played their roles. Two names remain to be added at this stage: Goethe and Schiller.

* * *

In the *Letters* Herzen stresses that (although sketched out by Bacon and Hegel) an approach to historical reality that could grasp its unifying principles without falsifying our representations of the visible world was still an ideal for the future. But an anticipation of that ideal already existed in the creative arts.

On his graduation he had announced to Ogarev that his first occupation would be the study of Goethe's works. Goethe's poetry and dramas were familiar to him from his adolescence, when he had wept over *The Sorrows of Young Werther*.[91] The breadth of his acquaintance with Goethe's oeuvre is reflected in the epigrams with which he decorates his own writings, and the multiplicity of references to Goethe's novels and plays in his two cycles of essays of the early 1840s. While composing them, he came to regard Goethe's scientific writings as exemplifying the perception of reality that he himself was seeking to define. Rejecting conventional scientific methods of classification, dissection, and analysis, Goethe was concerned with processes: The emergence of new forms through the interplay of forces, all of whose manifestations (from inorganic matter to the highest forms of human creativity) must, he insisted, be perceived as part of a single living totality. His approach was unscientific by any commonly recognized standards—the rigorous testing of inspired intuitions by evidence and logic that Herzen admired in Bacon's inductive method was anathema to Goethe. The result of a few dissections, his idealist explanation of the structure of vertebrates (including man) as the product of an underlying essence, an archetype *(Urbild)*, was emulated by the *Naturphilosophen*, who held him in high esteem.

Herzen seems to have passed over this affinity in his enthusiasm for the style of Goethe's forays into natural science, epitomized for him by a fragment entitled "Nature." This he translates at the end of one of his *Letters*, emphasizing its rapturous tone: "Every word breathes love of existence, intoxication with it." On reading Goethe's treatise *On the Metamorphosis of Plants*, he notes in his diary: "What a giant! the poet was not lost in the naturalist."[92] Goethe attracted him primarily as an artist embodying a state of psychic harmony that was supremely difficult to define in terms of abstract argument. (Goethe readily accepted a contemporary's definition of his thought as "object-thinking" [*gegenständliches Denken*].)[93]

But Herzen's admiration for Goethe was not unqualified. He declares that he is prepared to kneel before the creator of *Faust* but not to respect his politics: "Goethe recognized the paltriness of his century, but was incapable of rising above it."[94] Moreover, Goethe was indifferent to the social issues of his time and hostile to all attempts to subvert the established order. In the third essay in *Dilettantism in Science* (published in 1843) Herzen writes, "We continue to stand before his threatening and majestic shade with the deep respect which with which we stand before the obelisk of Luxor—a great monument of some different epoch, majestic, but bygone, not ours!"[95]

Herzen and Schiller on Moral Freedom

Disillusionment with Goethe was accompanied by a fresh perception of Friedrich Schiller's significance. In the winter of 1840, in his first printed work after his pardon the previous year—an autobiographical fragment disguised as a fictional narrative—Herzen records that he had turned his back on Schiller as the poet of adolescent dreams. But, he notes, "I soon came to my senses, blushed at my ingratitude, and with burning tears of repentance threw myself into [his] embrace."[96] This transformation was of very recent date. In November 1839, elated at the prospects opened by the end to his banishment, he had reproached Ogarev for clinging to the Schillerian dreams of their youth. Schiller was obsessed with the ideal of perfection: "That is why it seemed to him 'und das Dort wird nimmer hier'—but it *is* 'hier'—one must not neglect the possibilities of self-fulfillment in the here and now."[97] But a few months later in *Dilettantism* he stresses that Schiller's mature works were not Romantic, but "purely *humanist*"—his main affinities were with his own age.[98] In the intervening months it seems that Herzen had discovered Schiller the philosopher. It is likely that he had in mind *On Grace and Dignity*, the 1793 work in which Schiller took issue with Kant's dualistic vision of the moral life, which, in presupposing a sharp distinction between duty and inclination, presented virtue as the result of an endless struggle with the self. Schiller argued that Kant's model of the psyche did not fit our human reality—our natures could not be broken so neatly into parts. For us to be fully human, our inclination should be not "the oppressed partner in the moral order" but a participant on equal terms in the decisions of our will.[99]

While working on *Dilettantism* in the summer of 1842 Herzen had extended his critique of formalism to relations between the sexes in an essay inspired by a contemporary French drama in which a marital triangle ends in disaster for all three participants. As represented by the state and the established church, the formalist approach to the characters' predicament would be to demand the sacrifice of individual happiness to the concept of duty, whether religious or secular, as embodied in the marriage contract. The characters in the play are no less one-sided: their lives circumscribed by their emotions, they are wholly exposed to the impersonal force of chance. Only by broadening their horizons to include the common interests, pleasures, and sorrows of their time can they cease to be entirely dependent on "the dark labyrinth of contingencies, which intersect and interweave with one another."[100]

The essay is headed by a quotation from *The Essence of Christianity:* "The heart sacrifices humanity to the individual, reason—the individual to humanity. A person without a heart has no home; family life is based on the heart; reason is man's *res publica*." But there is also a clear echo of Schiller in Herzen's comment on the formalist attitude to the institution of marriage: "Thus, marriage for marriage's sake. The supreme development of such a marriage will be when husband and wife cannot tolerate each other and fulfill their marital duties *ex officio*."[101] Schiller had mocked Kant's equating of moral freedom with successful self-coercion in a satirical quatrain: In a philosophical discussion taking place in Hell, a disciple admits to his mentor that he is disposed by inclination to do good to his neighbor—Where is the virtue in this? The reply is: "You must endeavor to despise your neighbor, so that you may perform with revulsion what duty commands you to do." Subsequently in his *Letters* on nature Herzen quotes the verses in the original German in the course of a digression on the strange habit of moralists to see virtue specifically in the unwilling performance of duty.[102]

Schiller and Feuerbach might seem strange bedfellows, but they shared the anthropological approach to morality that Herzen had imbibed from his studies in science. Significantly in this regard, Schiller was trained in medicine, and his early medical writings (such as his dissertation *On the Connection between Man's Animal and Spiritual Natures*) reflect the empirical approach to the relation between body and mind then being pioneered by such figures as the Swiss physiologist Albrecht von Haller.

As Herzen was to discover in the summer of 1843, Schiller, like Feuerbach, saw the adoption of a truly humanist morality as the *sine qua non* of historical progress. In July of that year he notes in his diary that he has chanced on "a great and prophetic work . . . far ahead of its time." In the following year in a commentary on Granovsky's public lectures he refers to it again, as "a colossal step forward in the development of the idea of history."[103]

The work in question was Schiller's *Letters on the Aesthetic Education of Man*, the final fruit of his debate with Kant on the nature of the moral life. Published in 1795, it was the result of his reflections on why the rational principles on which the French Revolution was founded had led to the monstrous excesses of the Terror. He argues that humans can be at odds with themselves in one of two ways, according to which of their two fundamental drives (sense drive and form drive) is dominant. "Savages" are dominated by their crudest instincts, whereas "barbarians," deriving their rules from principle alone, tend toward unfeeling brutality. The former category he sees as exemplified by the French revolutionary mobs, the latter by the ideologues of the Terror. He attributes the Revolution's failure to achieve its liberating goals to what would later be described as alienation—the fragmentation of the human psyche through the specialization demanded by the ever-increasing complexity and differentiation of modern societies. One activity represented an exception to this rule. The contemplation of beauty as "living shape" simultaneously engages the senses and the urge for form, activating a third component of our psyche, the "play drive," which by its existence proves "the compatibility of our two natures, the practicability of the infinite being realized in the finite, hence the possibility of the sublimest humanity." We emerge from the contemplation of beauty in a state Schiller describes as one of "active determinability"—a state from which "we shall with equal ease turn to seriousness or play, to repose or to movement, to compliance or to resistance, to the discursions of abstract thought or to the direct contemplation of phenomena."[104]

Although praised by Hegel on its publication, Schiller's work made little impact in his time. Its title laid it open to misinterpretation. He was not advocating a turn away from politics to art and self-cultivation. He does not question Kant's distinction between beauty and the good, seeing his own prescription as a necessary but not sufficient condition for moral freedom—an intensification of our sense of what it means to be human, impelling us to live to our full potential. It is not an all-purpose formula or a way of freeing ourselves from moral choices, even less from moral conflicts: sometimes sacrifices will be needed because of issues or situations that transcend the self. He sees personal wholeness in terms of a continuing effort at modulation of our drives in response to the situations we encounter, neither blindly following instinct nor holding rigidly to rules and principles. An aesthetic education is his name for the development of a sense of relationships, valid for all human activities and guiding us at each relevant level—physical, intellectual, moral. As such, it was the antithesis of the Romantics' fixation on the myths of an ideal future or a lost past. But it also coincides exactly with the remedy proposed by Herzen in the "exercise in practical philosophy" he recommended to his friends as a cure for the disease of "reflection" that bedeviled them all, stunting their personalities: to cultivate the ability to surrender oneself to the joy of a moment undimmed by the thought of its passing, through an aesthetic openness to the infinite variety of human experience and to beauty in forms as diverse as the pleasures of friendship or the song of a peasant heard in the distance.

* * *

The subject of Schiller's treatise might seem far removed from the political activism of the German Left Hegelians to which Herzen had recently responded with such enthusiasm. But Schiller's image as the poet of an ideal freedom has obscured a more down-to-earth reality. He described the work as his profession of political faith, the construction of true political freedom being "the most perfect of all the works to be achieved by the art of man."[105] Like his great friend Wilhelm von Humboldt, he was a liberal who believed that the role of the state was to safeguard and promote the rights of the individual. He argued that a state has two ways of relating to the humans who compose it: "either by the ideal man suppressing empirical man, and the State annulling individuals; or else by the individual himself becoming the State, and man in time being ennobled to the stature of man as Idea." Reason demands unity, but nature demands multiplicity: both of these laws make their claim upon man. By subordinating the sensuous drive unconditionally to the rational, Kant had not resolved the problem. A political constitution that achieves unity only by suppressing variety will lead only to uniformity, never to harmony, "and man goes on forever being divided." As the French Revolution had shown, as long as humans remained at odds with themselves, states would alternate between tyranny and insurrection, with the issue always decided by blind force. There was only one way to escape from this cycle: "Wholeness of character must . . . be present in any people capable, and worthy, of exchanging a State of compulsion for a State of freedom."[106]

Schiller admitted that human endeavors to reach this condition might never produce more than an approximation. He simply desired that humans should make use of the approach, even if—as was likely—they were setting themselves "a task for more than one century." This caution about the speed of change, so much at odds with the optimism of his age, came from his conviction that the fundamental obstacle to progress was the fear of freedom. History showed that humans are consistently more inclined to submit to external authorities rather than assume the burden of responsibility for their own development:

> The old principles will remain; but they will wear the dress of the century, and Philosophy now lends her name to a repression formerly authorized by the Church. . . .
>
> . . . Fearful of freedom, which in its first tentative ventures always comes in the guise of an enemy, we shall either cast ourselves into the arms of an easy servitude or, driven to despair by a pedantic tutelage, escape into the wild libertinism of the natural state. Usurpation will invoke the weakness of human nature, insurrection its dignity; until finally blind force, that great imperatrice of human affairs, steps in and decides this pretended conflict of principles as though it were a common brawl.[107]

As T. J. Reed has observed, though Schiller's constant use of the word "Ideal" in his writings suggests a visionary dreamer, "in context the word is never vacuous, but always dense with a desired reality of a very earthly kind."[108] The works of Schiller the dramatist and philosopher are embedded in history, culminating in his account of the French Revolution's failure to live up to the Enlightenment's utopian expectations, which had been based on the faith that the principal barriers to human freedom were ignorance and oppression by rulers and systems of government. Half a century before Feuerbach's celebrated deconstruction of the essence of Christianity, Schiller had located the mainstay of political and moral oppression in the fear of freedom: humans' need to ground their being and their conduct in some principle outside themselves.

* * *

The fear of freedom was to be a dominant theme in Herzen's mature writings. His first publication on the subject was an essay that appeared in *The Contemporary* in 1847, a tirade against the persistent tendency of humans to subject themselves to moral authorities of their own creation: "There is no universally valid idea from which man has not

woven a rope to bind his own feet, and if possible, the feet of others as
well, so that the free product of his creativity becomes a punitive power
over him; no true, genuine relationship between people which they
have not turned into mutual enslavement. Love, friendship, tribal loyalty, and finally even *love of freedom* have served as inexhaustible
sources of moral oppression and servitude. . . . Humans are eternally
on their knees before one or the other—the golden calf or duty imposed
from outside. . . . It doesn't enter their heads that there is also something within them worthy of respect."[109] There follows a paean to
egoism, conceived in Feuerbach's sense as the striving of the human
species to fulfill its potential. The egoism of a developed individual,
Herzen argues, is noble—the source of his love of science, of art, of his
neighbor, of the inviolability of the individual. People conscious of their
human dignity will act nobly because it is natural for them to do so,
rather than from a sense of duty or fear of punishment. "To tear egoism
out of a person's breast is to tear out his vital essence, the salt of his
personality." Returning to one of his favorite themes, Herzen attributes the moral confusion of his age to the unexamined heritage of
scholasticism. "Our morality is still in feudal dress, albeit now faded
and tattered," its arms rusted and blunt. It was no longer even logically consistent, maintaining the precepts derived from religion but
placing abstract duty as their source. Having set off from the safety of
a shore, people had taken fright at the endless vistas before them and
the possibility of going in any direction. "We lack the courage either
to return to the outlook of the Middle Ages or to reject it completely;
we still blush to think that we have bodies without believing that we
are spirits."[110]

While Feuerbach's role in establishing Herzen's view of freedom is
not disputed, Schiller continues to be seen only as the idol of his dreamy
adolescence.[111] Yet the *Aesthetic Letters* were far more significant than
Schiller's poetry and plays in the formation of that view. It would take
yet another century for the *Letters* to be generally perceived as an original contribution to the philosophy of history.[112] Herzen's prescience
in this regard stemmed from his personal odyssey as a Russian *intelligent* in search of an approach to reality that would reconcile the demands of his intellect with his senses. Along with the empiricism of

the natural sciences, Hegel's historicism, and the species consciousness propounded by Feuerbach, Schiller's antidote to the fear of freedom would serve as inspiration for the distinctive humanism Herzen began to develop in the 1840s and on which his mature political philosophy would rest.

CHAPTER TWELVE

Man in the Middle

I'm not a teacher but a fellow seeker. I won't presume to say *what must be done*, but I think I can say with a fair degree of accuracy *what must not be done*.

HERZEN

IN May 1845 Herzen noted in his diary: "My position is a strange one, a sort of involuntary *juste milieu* on the Slavic question: the Slavophiles see me as a man of the West; to their opponents I am a man of the East. It follows from this that these one-sided definitions have no place in our time."[1]

The ideal of inner wholeness that he had formed from his disparate sources was the measure by which he judged and found wanting the ideologies and personalities of the two warring factions whose dispute dominated Russian intellectual life in the 1840s. They were the chief models for the one-sided intellectual types of *Dilettantism in Science*. In the process of contending with his own inner demons he refined his critique of these categories, working toward an ideal of the intellectual personality that would combine the positive insights of both.

* * *

The ties of friendship and common values linking Herzen with his Westernizer circle were subjected to increasing strain by the gulf between his radicalism and their moderate reformism. This tension did not come to the surface until 1846, but was already implicit four years earlier in his criticism of Hegel for lacking the courage of his convictions. The virtue of a total engagement of the personality in "suffering through" to the truth and accepting all its consequences was to be a leitmotif of his political writings. He comments feelingly in his diary on the sufferings of those whose thought was endowed with a "terrifying logic"—wherever it might roam, it could find nothing immutable on which to come to rest. Observation of his friends convinced him that this was not a problem that tormented them. He deplores Ogarev's weakness in not ending a failed marriage, and when after the birth of his second son Granovsky tells him that he had prayed for Natalie's safe delivery, he reflects that this was not an example he could have followed: in decisive moments he looks for strength only to himself, facing terrifying prospects with "a savage and ferocious consistency," like a duelist waiting with gloomy fortitude to see whether or not the bullet will pierce his breast.[2]

Only one other member of Herzen's circle was "no coward in the matter of consistency"—Belinsky, who always set his commitment to his beliefs above all other priorities, including personal relationships, and had not hesitated to switch from one ideological position to its opposite when logic seemed to require it. Herzen was fascinated by this "man of extremes." "I love the way he talks, his discontented appearance, even his oaths." In his intolerance of dissent Herzen likens him to Robespierre—for such people "men are nothing, convictions everything"—but Belinsky presented such a welcome contrast to the Hegelian liberals that Herzen was prepared to be indulgent to his excesses: "One may love him or hate him; there is no middle way. I love him sincerely."[3]

Herzen's view of the meaning of consistency became more nuanced in his later years. In his memoirs he accuses the Russian intelligentsia en masse of a predilection for extremes. "We advance in a fearless front . . . to the limit and beyond, in step with the dialectic, but out of step with truth."[4] But in the Russia of the 1840s any steadfast commitment to ideas that had not received full official sanction could be said to have its merits. He admired such commitment in the Slavophiles; his intellectual disdain for the movement was counterbalanced by a growing fascination with the personalities of its leading ideologists. In November 1841 he wrote to Belinsky, "In Moscow I've been fighting Slavomania all the time, and in spite of everything I swear people are better off there. They have interests that they are happy to argue about for days." There is a hint of admiration in his remark that they are so angry with German philosophy that "they don't want to know even in general terms what it's all about."[5]

In spite of this severe impediment to dialogue, Herzen spent considerable time in the years 1842–1843 in debates with the Slavophiles.

His affinity with them has been ascribed to their common roots in the Moscow aristocracy (in a letter to his friend Ketcher he describes Samarin as "un parfait honnête homme").[6] But his diary (the most revealing source we have for his relations with the two warring camps) shows that it was above all the strength of their beliefs that fascinated him. He was particularly attracted to Ivan Kireevsky ("a fine, strong personality"), as fanatically attached to his beliefs as Belinsky and just as intolerant, arrogant, and rude in their defense—defects that for Herzen were redeemed by the struggles he had gone through in his search to comprehend Russia's destiny. Kireevsky's "one-sided" views were not without poetry: they might be absurd, but they had been bought with "blood and tears."[7] Subsequently Herzen noted disapprovingly that he had watered down his fanaticism in favor of a more eclectic approach to the question of Russia and the West. His brother Petr was "a head higher than all the Slavophiles, because he alone has adopted their foolish ideas with all their implications . . . but precisely because of his consistency the foolishness disappears, leaving a tragic grandeur in its wake."[8]

He frequently expressed astonishment that the considerable philosophical abilities of Slavophiles such as Samarin were devoted to the exposition of "pitiful Orthodox theories and exaggerated Slavism"[9]— evidence of how despotism could destroy the best talents, forcing even men like Ivan Kireevsky to seek refuge in mysticism. Herzen's predilection for philosophical discussions with the Slavophiles (which enraged Belinsky and alarmed his other friends) is explained in his diary by his pleasure in testing his dialectical abilities against worthy opponents; but there was more to it than that. However different their solutions, they shared a similar view of modern man's main predicament—an inner disharmony that could be healed, not by political reforms, but only by a fundamental transformation of social relationships. Their approach to the problem of personal wholeness was much closer to his own than the legalistic historicism of the Westernizers. It was partly through his engagement with the Slavophile solution that Herzen would begin to situate his ideal of inner harmony in a historical context, but his diary shows that in his debates with them on history and the nature of progress their respective differences were much more evident than their affinities: "history—as the movement of mankind toward liberation and self-knowledge, toward conscious action—does not exist for them."[10] They saw the entire development of Europe as a malignant abnormality, its cultural strivings as petty bustle, its achievements as empty glitter.

Herzen's opposition to the Slavophile view of history focused on the theme of human rights. He notes how through a series of liberating upheavals Europe had progressed from feudalism to a new world, opened up by the French Revolution, the first step in the rule of law. These conflicts expressed the strength and vitality of the European organism, in contrast with the stagnant Orthodoxy of the Slavs, their "remoteness from all humanity's concerns." In the West, the clash between church and state had been a force for progress; the Russian church had merely submitted slavishly to the temporal power. In Europe, autocracy had been "the disease of a single century"; in Russia it was officially proclaimed as the aim of the state, for which the population was a mere means.[11] Hence their slavish mentality, reacting to oppression with either apathy or revolt (a reference to the *Pugachevshchina*, the great peasant revolt of 1773–1774, the specter of which continued to haunt the country's rulers). Russians could only marvel at the English, with their "majestically calm" consciousness of their rights, protected by public opinion—a phenomenon unknown in Russia, where the question of rights was the subject of such confusion that the masses had on occasion resisted the development of the electoral principle, while the government treated demands for legality as rebellion. The "raving Slavophiles [*slavianobesnuiushchie*]" had no comprehension of the meaning of European history. "Hatred of the West is open hatred of the whole process of development of the human race, because the West, as the successor to the ancient world . . . is the whole of humanity's past and present. . . . Hence, hatred and contempt for the West go hand in hand with hatred and contempt for freedom of thought, for law, for all guarantees, for all civilization." In this the Slavophiles were at one with the government. In everything, Herzen concludes, the distance between Russia and Europe is immeasurable. "The soil of Europe is holy; blessings on her, blessings!"[12]

Herzen's personal relations with the leading Slavophiles were eventually soured by what he saw as their "primitive" intolerance. Repeatedly he characterized their views as inhumane—a term that stood for the opposite of all that his ideal of personal development implied. Their tactics in enlisting the government's support in their battle with the Westernizers led to the final break between the two groups after they attempted to have Granovsky's dissertation suppressed on grounds that it denied the existence of a town sacred to Slav tradition—proof in Herzen's view that Slavomania had reached the stage of "comic madness." Where, he wonders, will this "deranged" tendency lead? It was clear from their behavior that if these fanatics ever got to power, they would make haste to burn him and his friends at the stake.[13] In June 1844 he recognized that the gulf separating the Slavophiles from the defenders of Western enlightenment was unbridgeable, and in February of the following year in a letter to Samarin and at a ceremonial meeting between himself and Granovsky on one side and Konstantin Aksakov on the other, he made a dignified termination of his personal relations with the group.

The end of these contacts coincided with the beginning of a more serious engagement with Slavophile ideas. Recalling their farewell meeting, he described Aksakov as "noble, pure-hearted, but one-sided."[14] This last epithet he would come to apply to fantasizing Slavophiles and rationalizing Westernizers alike, while integrating in his theory of socialism the incomplete truths he considered each group to represent.

Ideas from French Socialism

The Russian variety of socialism was to be built on promising French foundations: a notion of the moral renewal of human societies as developed by the first generation of socialists from Saint-Simon to Proudhon. In the decade following the revolution of 1830, which saw the entrenchment of the political and economic power of the bourgeoisie under the July Monarchy, French socialists turned from ultimate goals to questions of economics and political tactics. In his work *La destinée sociale* Fourier's most important disciple, Victor Considerant, declared: "Those who pursue social happiness by the exclusive route of parliament and constitutional transformation are pursuing a chimera and dreaming of utopia."[15] The idea of workers' associations had begun to spread in France after 1830. Louis Blanc's work of 1839, *Organisation du travail,* for the first time established as a central policy of socialism the organization of labor as a political force. In 1840 Proudhon's *Qu'est-ce que la propriété?*, with its inflammatory message "Property is theft," sketched out the consequences of a social revolution based on a transformation of the concept of ownership.

It took some time for Herzen to transfer his attention from the German Left Hegelians to these developments in France. The first signs of this shift are comments in his diary in February 1843 on the desperate situation of the working class under Guizot's government as reflected in an account in the French press. An unemployed worker in Lyon was driven to theft in order to buy food and medicine for his sick wife: facing arrest, the couple attempted suicide but were revived in order to stand trial for their crime. Such reports, Herzen observes, reflect the degradation of contemporary society, which rates property more sacred than human life. How to escape from the horror of this form of existence? Events would shape the details, but the general direction was clear—toward a form of communal association as first proposed by the Fourierists.

On completing *Dilettantism* Herzen set to work bringing himself up to date with French socialism. In the summer of 1843 he immersed himself in Louis Blanc's *Histoire de dix ans,* a multivolume account of how the bourgeoisie—a category with which Herzen was as yet unfamiliar—had taken control of the revolution of 1830 with the connivance of Louis-Philippe. He is fascinated by Blanc's exposition of how France—the foremost liberalizing force in Europe—had betrayed its admirers: the political domination of the bourgeoisie was merely feudalism by another name. On finishing the third volume he looks back with affectionate condescension at the "poetic" socialism of the Saint-Simonians: "They didn't have the full solution. . . . The necessity of a social revolution has now become clear." He pronounces *La destinée sociale,* with its "pitiless" exposure of the wounds of contemporary society, incomparably more energetic and broader in conception than anything previously issuing from the school of Fourier.[16]

An approving diary reference in February 1843 to the venom of Proudhon's attacks on the injustices of the existing order is the first mention we have of the thinker whom Herzen would eventually rank alongside Hegel as one of the two key influences on his thought. He seems at this point to have known of Proudhon's ideas only from secondary sources (in July he asks Ketcher to forward his pamphlets to him in the country). He did not obtain a copy of *What Is Property?* until December of the following year. Proudhon attacks two extremes on the question of property: unbridled individualism as propounded by English economists who equated private enrichment with public good, and its communistic opposite, according to which all human faculties and talents were the property of the state, which had the right to do with them as it saw fit in the general interest. The middle position, toward which he maintained all human societies were gradually progressing, was a form of "free association," characterized by a system of exchange in which the products and rewards of labor would be distributed equitably amongst the producers. He abstained from elaborating further on the nature of this system: like all the other human sciences, the science of society "will forever be incomplete; the depth and variety of questions it embraces are infinite."[17] His own century could hope to do no more than begin the transition to a new order by clarifying its methods and goals and removing the prejudices that hampered its realization.

Herzen urges Ketcher to read this "great work," and to sit down with Belinsky and study Proudhon's 1843 book, *De la création de l'ordre dans l'humanité,* which he describes as "pure delight [*ob'edenie*]."[18] Echoing Comte's view of the historical stages in human understanding, Proudhon argued that with the advance of science, religion had lost its former role as the prime mover of progress toward a just moral order. Along with its concern with causality, philosophy's fascination with substance was in the process of being replaced by description of the relations between things, which Proudhon calls "la série." To discover a série is "to perceive unity in multiplicity, synthesis in division." Proudhon predicts that the "loi sérielle" may provide the means of overcoming Kant's epistemological division between experienced reality and things-in-themselves—a hope unsupported by the rigmarole of his argument, which offers no further elucidation of the nature of his "law."[19]

Philosophically overambitious and much muddled, *De la création* has been commonly judged to be Proudhon's worst work; he himself admitted freely that he was not a born philosopher. But Herzen observes that when reading Proudhon, like Leroux and other "philosophizing Frenchmen," one has to "force one's way through" to the serious meaning across a thicket of apparent nonsense (niaiseries).[20] (The notion of série can be read as a failed attempt to add philosophical weight to the approach to empirical reality that Herzen had come to define as speculative empiricism.) What delighted Herzen was not Proudhon's theorizing but his iconoclasm. Herzen sees the defects of Proudhon's argument as redeemed by his boldness in engaging with speculative thought, exposing the weaknesses in the concepts of causality and substantiality, which were the stock-in-trade of idealism. He concludes that the best part of the work is Proudhon's insistence, while giving credit to its contribution to mankind's moral development in the past, that religion has no role to play in the future. He objects, however, to Proudhon's prediction of the same fate for philosophy: idealism, yes, but not Spinoza, Hegel, and even Kant?

With all its defects, Herzen judges De la création to be an "extraordinarily remarkable phenomenon."[21] Through his discovery of Proudhon he seems to have relived the sense of liberation he had experienced three years before on opening Feuerbach's The Essence of Christianity. Having moved from religious socialism to what he called "anti-theism," Proudhon was the only French socialist to echo Feuerbach's critique of religious alienation, while maintaining that his followers had not gone far enough in their critique of mankind's self-imposed subjection to transcendent powers and were still clinging, in defiance of historical experience, to the hallucination of a collective ego. Herzen would have been attracted strongly by Proudhon's opposition to all theoretical prescriptions for the shape of a future social system, whose "flesh," Herzen writes in his diary, will only be revealed by events.[22] His repeated use of this metaphor, with its echoes of the Phenomenology and The Essence of Christianity, reflects the continuity of the intellectual preoccupations drawing him to ideas that challenged the universalizing systems of the age. Reading the Fourierist Considerant, he finds even the phalanstery, designed to ensure the maximum of individual self-fulfillment in work and personal relations, "rather cramped" in its prescriptivism. It required that children be separated from their parents for the purpose of "social education," evidence that Fourier understood nothing of the nature of a mother's love. "To remove her children by force is barbaric and in contradiction with a system promoting the development of all the passions."[23] But he approved positively of the fact that in Fourier's system women's horizons would no longer be limited to the family.

With the exception of Proudhon, whose conservative view of the role of women betrayed his peasant origins, the early French socialists all signed up to the new feminism, whose prophetess was George Sand, militating against the degradation of women in the patriarchal monogamous family, and the hypocrisy of bourgeois moralists who supported an institution that depended for its survival on the acceptance of prostitution and social tolerance of adultery. The rehabilitation of the flesh proposed by Fourierists and Saint-Simonians was intended to meet women's actual needs and wants. Their principal concern was women's sexual liberation, but Herzen had strong reasons for insisting on a second priority. He reflects in his diary: "Why do women in general not devote themselves to burning social issues, but lead an exclusively private life? Why are their torments and their joys restricted to the strictly personal? Socialism will produce a change in this regard."[24] He wrote this after five months during which Natalie, obsessed with a sense of personal guilt for Herzen's "fall" from the heights of romantic love, had tormented herself to such a degree that he feared for her life. Conceived as the voluntary cooperation of the members of society in its common purposes, socialism could be expected, among its other merits, to be the antidote for the disease of morbid introspection to which Herzen refers in his diary as *Grübelei*.

In an account of the origins of Russian socialism widely accepted by Western historians, Martin Malia has presented Herzen's emphasis on the moral dimension of French socialism rather than its economic theories (such as they were) as reflecting his demand for "the total realization of the promises of 'enlightenment' and 'humanism,' the complete destruction of the 'old' world and the inauguration of the 'new,' without any gradual transitions, compromises, or half measures"—the culminating stage of a self-centered intellectual progression starting in adolescence with a Romantic cult of self-fulfillment through art, friendship, and love followed by Schelling's and Hegel's pantheistic visions of self-realization.[25] The present account of Herzen's intellectual trajectory from Romantic fantasies of personal self-fulfillment to socialism has diverged significantly from Malia's, which ignores the role of Herzen's scientific studies in this process. As previous chapters show, Herzen approached these as an invaluable training in a method equally applicable to the natural and historical world: the scrupulous submission of hypotheses to the tests of observation and experience. At the same time the pressures of unremitting persecution made it hard to resist the attraction of a philosophical interpretation of his generation's sufferings as the necessary prelude to a historical catharsis in which the conflicts of what Hegel called the Unhappy Consciousness would be resolved in a higher harmony. The intensity of his inner struggle between empirical and teleological approaches to contingent reality was reflected in the last essay of *Dilettantism*, completed in the year in which he began to turn his attention to the socialist potential of the Russian peasant commune. We shall return to the involuntary self-revelation in that essay as a key to understanding the development of Herzen's socialism in the 1840s.

A Russian Socialism

The first record we have of the renewal of Herzen's interest in socialism at the end of his Vyatka exile is his enthusiastic reaction (cited in Chapter 9) to the body blow aimed by Pierre Leroux at the optimism that had inspired the French Revolution. Leroux had maintained that, as historical experience showed, liberty and equality were not two words for the same thing, but two "adversaries" that could be induced to coexist only in a precarious truce. Proudhon's *Contradictions économiques* makes a similar assault on radical optimism. Herzen's conception of personal wholeness was leading him in the same direction. The notion of the commune he drew from his French sources was not an ultimate ideal, but rather a form of association sufficiently flexible to adapt to changing needs and situations. His first formulation of a socialist program—in a diary entry of 1843 responding to the account of the attempted suicide of the Lyon worker—is Proudhonian in its avoidance of prescriptiveness. He asks, How can one put an end to such horrors? There can be no complete theoretical answer. Only events and circumstances will reveal the precise form a new order should adopt, but what its general lines should be is already clear. "Social control of property and capital, communal life [*artel'noe zhitie*], organization of work and rewards and the establishment of the right to property on different principles. Not the complete destruction of personal property, but a form of its investiture in society that will give the government the right to take general measures and directions."[26]

In future years Herzen's view that there was no one best form of government, suitable for all nations at all times, was to alienate him from every variety of Russian political opinion. An early example of his thinking in this direction is his response in the diary to a French historian's account of the Restoration following Cromwell's Commonwealth in seventeenth-century England. He agrees with the author that the class divisions in England would have made the transition to a republic impossible. Cromwell's own power had depended on the conservative interests of a single class. A divided state must have a central unifying power, "otherwise there will be mob rule or a *régime de terreur*."[27]

* * *

Herzen's use of the Russian term for productive associations within the commune is the first indication we have of his interest in the socialist potential of the Russian peasants' traditional mode of life. In May 1843 he records a conversation with a Prussian ethnographer, Baron August von Haxthausen, who was engaged in a study of the Russian commune, which, as a remnant of a social structure long since vanished elsewhere in Europe, he believed should be preserved in the interests of social stability. Haxthausen astonished him with his knowledge of the peasants' way of life and their relations with the landlords, the police, and government officials, and he was impressed by the argument that development of the commune's existing structure was much preferable to its abolition in the name of progress, which would only render the peasants more vulnerable to political and economic oppression. In June, when Herzen returns to the subject of the commune as a stick with which to beat the Slavophiles, Haxthausen's view of its potential has taken root in his mind. He is prepared to admit that it may serve as the embryo of a future development, while not ignoring (in an echo of Proudhon's emphasis on the connection between ownership and rights) the fact that its present structure is a sign of Russia's backwardness: "In the same way the Bedouin's right to property does not have the egotistic character of the European's; but [the Slavophiles] forget, on the other hand, the absence of all self-respect, the stupid endurance of all kinds of oppression. . . . Is it surprising that the right to property in the sense of personal possession is not developed in our peasant, when his strip of land is not his strip, when even his wife, daughter, son, are not his? What property does a slave have; he is worse than a proletarian, he is a *res*, an instrument for working the fields. . . . Give him legal rights, only then will he be a man. Twelve million people *hors la loi. Carmen horrendum.*"[28] Reading Louis Blanc, he reflects that the current struggle in Europe for the recognition of human dignity and rights is the outcome of a long process of development, culminating in the "great initiative" of the French Revolution, a fact the Slavophiles seem incapable of comprehending. "In the future the Slavs are probably destined to do great things, but what have they done in the past with their stagnant Orthodoxy and their alienation from all that is human?"[29]

The caveat here is significant: three months earlier he had completed the fourth and final essay "Buddhism in Science," where he invoked the notion, central to Romantic nationalism, of historical youth and age to suggest that it might be Russia's "calling," by virtue of its late appearance on the historical scene, to lead Europe toward a new order harmonizing individual self-fulfillment with social goals. His dreams then had been based on an idealized image of himself and his circle; his subsequent discussions with Haxthausen seem to have prompted him to see the equally Romantic populism of the Slavophiles in a more positive light. In November of that year he records a "long and extremely interesting" conversation with Samarin: "[The Slavophiles] say that the fruit of European life will ripen in the Slav world": Europe having completed its task through the negation of the existing order in the name of a vision of socialism, it would fall to the Slavs to turn that vision into reality. He makes no further comment other than to reject the "fanatical" belief that the future of the Slavs is linked with the historical triumph of the Orthodox Church, but he returns to the subject two months later: The Slavophiles are mistaken in believing that the future potential of their race signifies superiority over the West in the present, but there are grounds for their view that that potential contained a response to the great historical questions currently preoccupying Europeans.[30]

This argument bears the hallmarks of Herzen's intensive reading of Hegel's history of philosophy in the course of work on his two cycles of essays. Put in less opaque language, thanks to Hegel's dialectic and some prompting by Haxthausen and the Slavophiles he had come to attach considerable significance to the fact that the masses had been virtually untouched by the Petrine revolution, which had replaced a traditional patriarchal structure by a government founded on universal rational principles and thereby alien to the common people. He returns frequently to this theme in his diary. Reading the Marquis de Custine's account of his recent travels in Russia, he was struck by the felicity of Custine's image of an *"empire de façades"* and his perspicacity in discerning a rich promise in the "rough, primitive features" of the enslaved masses. He was equally impressed on reading Mickiewicz's lectures on Slavic literature to the Collège de France: this Polish Slavophile represented the "true and beautiful" facet of Slav nationalism. While emphasizing yet again the poverty of contemporary Slav culture, Herzen now detects a "profound foresight" in the fact that the newly united Rus took as its emblem the Byzantine eagle whose twin heads faced in opposing directions, symbolizing the break between state and people: "calm, submissive, but indifferent to the state, the people has been shivering in its villages, as if awaiting something."[31] In the course of reflections on universal history Herzen attempts to formulate the "great prophecy" that might be contained in the people's indifference to the state. The West's legacy to the future is the concept of personality enshrined in the *Déclaration des droits de l'homme:* "But did we have the right to say that the future epoch, whose banner will not be the individual, but the commune, not freedom, but brotherhood, not absolute equality, but the organic division of labor, does not belong to Europe? That is the whole question. Will the Slavs, impregnated by Europe, realize Europe's ideal and join a decrepit Europe to its life, or will Europe join us to its rejuvenated existence? The Slavophiles are quick to decide this question, as if it were a matter settled long ago. There are pointers, but they are far from the whole solution."[32] The Slavophile solution ignored an essential element, the immense positive significance of the Petrine period of Russian history as "severance, criticism, and negation," introducing a dynamic of development rooted in the paradox of Peter himself, a civilizer devoid of humanity who had instituted a system "both worse and better" than the dynasties of Europe—a revolutionary tyranny that had allowed the Russian state to make gigantic strides, revealing to the world the enormous potential it would have if the despotism that reined it back were removed.[33]

Herzen continues to stress his principal difference with the Slavophiles. It was Peter's Westernization that had set Russia on the path of development that would now allow it to exploit its national potential. He points out that apart from brief awakenings during the Time of Troubles at the beginning of the seventeenth century and the popular resistance against Napoleon in 1812, the common people had as yet given no evidence of independent potential or constructive capacities. He finds no hints of the future in the daily life of the countryside and the peasants' passivity in the face of oppression. "History has not absorbed all the people's capacities into its fabric; it has left it as a fertile soil for growth, nothing more than that."[34]

His hopes are surrounded with caveats. He observes that the Slavs are everywhere "serfs, obedient, passive serfs."[35] The primitive democracy of the commune on which the Slavophiles based their faith had flourished at the earliest stage of Russia's development. In this sense the Bedouins were democrats; all patriarchal societies rested on communal and family principles. The Slav commune had reached its highest level of development with the Montenegrins, who enjoyed a patriarchal democracy that had stoutly resisted the Russian government's attempts to establish its influence in their territory. Herzen clearly regarded the Russian commune as significant less for what it was than for what it was not. Its centuries-old isolation and stagnation had preserved it from contamination with the entrenched values of private wealth and privilege that now blocked progress in the West, but the driving force for its development had to come from the intelligentsia—those products of Peter's revolution who identified with Western ideals of justice and human rights. He supports his argument through a manipulation of Hegel's historical dialectic, emphasizing that the principles of spontaneity and consciousness had been separated in Russian society as nowhere else in Europe. At the same time, a revolutionary despot had imbued the development of the Russian state with a dynamic unique in Europe, where the conflict had slowed down, its lines no longer so clear, and where the organism might be in need of rejuvenation from an outside source. It is hardly surprising, he declares, that the mute world of the Slavs is increasingly engaging Europe's attention.

This optimism was not new. From his travels in the vastness of Siberia he had brought back a sense that Russia, like America, possessed a potential untrammeled by the weight of history, and his reading of Tocqueville had persuaded him that Russia had the advantage in this respect. On the eve of his second exile he wrote to Ketcher of his plan to compose a series of essays on Peter the Great's revolution. These never materialized, but the paradox of the reforming tyrant continued to absorb him as a means of putting a positive gloss on the predicament of his generation. He explains to Ketcher that their role as the first representatives of a purely European culture in their country was to bring the Petrine era to a close, by completing the "humanization" of Russia that Peter had begun—the prelude to a new period of organic development, in which for the first time their country would play a positive role in Europe. "Our position vis-à-vis Russia and Europe is strange, *une fausse position,* but it was contained in the *idea* of Peter's revolution, and all its harshness and sorrow was essential: by these sorrows we redeem ten centuries of isolation from mankind."[36]

He had begun his Novgorod exile in that year with the resolve no longer to seek a providential meaning in his tribulations. The habit of a decade was nevertheless hard to drop. Romantic nationalism offered a new, if tenuous, source of optimism. When Belinsky, alarmed by his continuing relations with the Slavophiles, rebukes him for consorting with the "Philistines," Herzen accuses him of failing to perceive the grain of truth in the *fatras* of their absurdities. "He does not comprehend the Slav world; he regards it with despair, he's unable to *sense in advance the life of the coming age.* But this presentiment is what heralds the advent of the future. To despair is to destroy the fruit in its mother's womb." He invokes the most skeptical of all Russian Westernizers in his support: "Chaadaev once made the marvelous remark that one of the greatest characteristics of the Christian vision is the elevation of hope into a virtue along with faith and charity. I wholly agree with him." The intelligentsia above all are duty bound to express "the hope that is a part of grief . . . firm hope in an apparently hopeless situation. . . . Faith in the future of one's people is one of the conditions for bringing that future into being."[37]

Eight months later he writes in his diary: "We have fallen beneath the burden of our century and our country; we have no future. We have brought with us from the past only love for individuals and skepticism."[38] Made at the bleakest period of his struggle with the blows of chance, this reflection bears witness to the intensity of Herzen's sense of alienation in the first half of the 1840s. Crushed by the deaths of his children, perpetually threatened by a new sentence to prison or exile, ideologically at odds with the circle that had been his sole refuge from a corrupt society and a tyrannous regime (Ogarev, his most intimate friend, spent most of the decade abroad or on his country estate), the first Russian socialist experienced an isolation and impotence of a kind unimaginable to his Western counterparts. It was one thing to preach heroic acceptance of the limitations placed by empirical circumstances on the realization of human ideals, another to resign himself to the strong possibility that the country and the age into which he had chanced to be born would deny him the participation in social action that he had come to see as the only means of humans' self-fulfillment as species-beings. A central preoccupation of Herzen's writings in the 1840s was the problem of the nature of the self. His reflections on the Russian peasant are no exception.

The Russian Peasant as Noble Savage

Herzen asserts repeatedly in his diary that Slavophile theories about the virtues of the commune are based on a disregard for the social reality of the peasants' existence. It is curious, therefore, that no reflections are to be found in his writings of the 1840s on an issue one would expect to be of close interest to him: the potential of the commune's existing structure as a basis for the free association proposed by French socialists. In the countryside in the summer of 1844, he writes: "I am constantly observing here the lowest class, with whom we are in daily contact."[39] But the fruits of these observations as recorded in the diary are remarkably thin. On the peasants' customs, values, and aspirations he has almost nothing concrete to say, apart from noting peasants' pitiful apathy in the face of injustice and their childlike faith in the power of prayer to avert misfortune. On the details of the structure and functions of the commune his diary and letters are equally silent. His discussions with Haxthausen seem to have brought no revival of the brief interest in ethnography that had been sparked by his official duties in Vyatka and Vladimir as collector of local statistics.

In his memoirs he combines faint praise of the Slavophiles with strong censure—although they had opened his generation's eyes to the native elements in Russian culture, they had also blinded them. "It is the Slavophiles' fault that for so long we failed to understand either the Russian people or its history; their icon-painter's ideals and incense smoke hindered us from perceiving the realities of the people's mode of life and the foundations of village existence."[40] With regard to Herzen, at least, the facts are somewhat different. The Russian countryside first appears in his writings as a backdrop to his pantheistic fantasies of self-aggrandizement. At the age of sixteen he relates in a letter to his cousin Tatiana how he would throw himself down under a tree on his family's country estate alone with the great sweep of nature, declaiming Schiller and dreaming that he was in a Bohemian forest.[41] To the adolescent Herzen, the countryside was a stage on which the beautiful soul could contemplate his union with the cosmos and his isolation from crass humanity. An early autobiographical fragment records how at the age of eighteen he first read Rousseau's *Confession*, followed by the *Contrat social*, and came to idolize its author, attracted above all by one event in his life: "his poetic retreat from the crowd to Ermenonville . . . ; he seemed to me a kind of sacrificial lamb, bearing the sorrows of all the humanity of the eighteenth century."[42] He named his own favorite refuge on his father's estate after Rousseau's village, and when in 1843 he returned there after a lapse of thirteen years, he saw in the local landscape the sacred repository of his youthful ideals and dreams: "Various phases of my life flashed vividly before me—here was the tree where I sat as a child, the road along which as a youth I went to pay court to the village beauty, expending enormous energy on a frivolous intrigue. . . . I was sad to leave—only in the presence of that river, those lime walks, can I be vividly transported back to those times when all life lay before me and my soul was bright and fresh."[43]

Writing in the 1850s, Herzen dates his hatred of all forms of brutality and subjugation to the time when, as a solitary child playing in the servants' hall, he observed firsthand the evils of serfdom. But it was principally his personal frustrations as a gentry *intelligent* that inspired his adolescent rebelliousness. When his work as a government official in Vyatka brought him into direct contact with the situation of the peasants, his initial reaction seems to have been not compassion but the fastidious revulsion of a Europeanized aristocrat confronted with barbarous masses. A memoir of 1836 on the subject of Russian legislation since Peter the Great begins: "In the social sphere . . . the progressive element is the government, not the people."[44] Instances of official cruelty and abuse of power abound in his reminiscences of this period, but at that time the peasants' sufferings were peripheral to his polarized vision of reality, which consisted of a persecuted hero and the despised "crowd" of Vyatka society. The only reference to the peasants in his self-admiring correspondence with Natalie during his Vyatka years is in response to her description of her emotions on attending a peasant's christening. He congratulates her on the "saintliness" of her perceptions, which coincide with his own: "I love the common people, I love them." They are morally flawed, their characters warped by oppression and ignorance, "but through all this crust one glimpses a childlike, simple soul, even something good."[45] But while urging a closer study of the peasants' life and customs in his official reports, he showed little personal inclination in that direction. It is to illustrate the predicament of his caste that they figure first in in his diary, at the beginning of his second year of exile in Novgorod: "Our isolation, the lack of sympathy shown to us by all sides, is hard to bear. We do not want to extend our hand to the masters, the officials, and indeed they look on our kind as madmen, while the Orthodox peasant—to whom, for whom, on whose behalf, any morally noble person is ready to do God knows what—is (when not engaged in open war with us, in which he enmeshes us in a net of deceit) silent and suspicious. . . . I have very frequent experience of this: when he sees you doing something out of simple calculation, it's another matter, but when you do something from pure goodwill, he shakes his head and fears that you are tricking him."[46] Herzen's disappointment at the peasants' lack of sympathy for his suffering is indicative of the degree to which renewed victimization had returned him to a preoccupation with his own inner world. It is only back in the intellectual life of Moscow, when his indignation is aroused by French socialists' accounts of the desperate situation of the proletariat, that his thoughts turn to the equally dismal plight of the Russian peasant. Halfway through his reading of Louis Blanc's *Histoire de dix ans*, he is moved to reflect:

> But one has only to look around one. . . . The poor, poor Russian peasant. . . . Looking at their lives, it seems monstrously criminal to live in luxury. This peasant of this region never eats meat, he has hardly enough bread to survive; the better-off ones eat cabbage. Every day he and his family fend off death from starvation—there's no thought of laying in reserves. If his horse or cow dies, that's the end of him. Next to their poor strips are the rich fields of the landlord, tilled by their hands. . . . We marvel at the gladiators; but in the next century won't people marvel at us, at our ferocious cruelty, our lack of humanity? In what way are we better than the colonists in Surinam, the English in India? No, we are worse, because our peasants aren't savages; they humbly, sadly bear life's heavy cross. . . . Their future prospects are the whip, starvation, the corvée . . . , the recruiting officer.[47]

Life on the family estate retained its attraction as a "purer, nobler existence" than that of Moscow, where his few friends provided little shelter from the "stupid, vile crowd." But a new element now intruded on his rural meditations: "When I look at the poor peasant, my heart bleeds, I am ashamed of my rights, ashamed that even I am partly responsible for preying on their lives."[48] When during their meeting in May 1843 Haxthausen asks him to define a model of the relationship of the peasant to the landowner, "an algebraic formula, so to speak," Herzen finds the question nonsensical. "If the relationship of a village commune to the landowner changed with its size, with the quantity of land or other conditions, one could conceive some sort of norm. This is not the case. The state of commune X depends on whether its landlord is rich or poor, is in state service or not, lives in Petersburg or in the country, runs his estate himself or through a manager. Here precisely we have that pitiful and disorderly element of chance that stifles all development."[49]

He begins to cull from newspaper reports instances of the barbarity of his own class. Soldiers had been ordered to fire on a deputation of peasants who had come to protest to a provincial governor about the injustices committed by their landlord; a number were killed. A landlord who beat a peasant to death was acquitted on the ground that "people of the same age as the deceased peasant can endure incomparably more severe punishments."[50] Repeatedly he observes in his diary that theories about the virtue of the commune ignore such social realities, remarking that the more closely one observes the horror of the present state of society, the more grotesque the Slavophiles' complacency appears. *Who Is to Blame?* and *The Thieving Magpie* (a story he first published in 1848) satirize the injustice and brutality of Nicolas's regime through a gallery of Gogolian grotesques: corrupt, parasitic, and heartless officials, and landowners who relieve the boredom of their idle lives by erotic conquests over their female serfs and liberal use of the whip. The reader is reminded of the punishments these all-powerful despots could administer on a whim. Sons could be sent off to the army to pay for the transgressions of their fathers, discarded mistresses were married off to the nearest peasant, while every serf faced the terror of the unknown: into whose hands would he fall after his master's death?

But the main focus of Herzen's indignation in these works is not the physical sufferings of the masses, but the affronts inflicted by the gentry on the dignity of those who, like himself, were only ambiguously noble. His memoirs record his bitterness at the humiliation inflicted on his wife by the old Moscow princess who brought her up as her ward. Lyubonka (an idealized version of Natalie), the heroine of *Who Is to Blame?*, is constantly shocked by the indelicacy of her landowner father and his wife in reminding her of her good fortune in being rescued from life in the servants' quarters. Beltov's mother, a peasant educated by her mistress and trained as a governess, is similarly humiliated when her employer's son attempts to seduce her. The same predicament faces the heroine of *The Thieving Magpie*, a member of a troupe of serf actors, when she is sold to a new master. These peasants are depicted as representing true nobility in contrast to their persecutors. Lyubonka's refinement of spirit is stressed;

the peasant governess, dismissed by her employer and reduced to destitution, writes the man who has ruined her life a letter that is a masterpiece of indignant rhetoric (and that so affects the aristocratic would-be seducer that he proposes marriage and is accepted). The serf-actress resists her tormentor; the narrator to whom she recounts her story is profoundly impressed by the nobility and grace of her demeanor.[51] With their refined sensibility, Herzen's heroines are no more peasants than the shepherdesses of the sentimentalist novels of the eighteenth century. Peasants of the uneducated variety make only a marginal appearance in these works, but we are given to assume that they too have an inborn distinction: Lyubonka reflects that the local peasant children have "such fine faces—open-hearted and noble!"[52] Herzen's satires propagate the myth of the noble savage so beloved of the Romantics—a projection of their yearning for a state of consciousness that would harmonize primitive spontaneity and the values of a refined culture. His criticisms of the Slavophiles show him to have been acutely aware of the illusoriness of this goal and the Romantic nationalism that it spawned, but the need for compensation was as strong in him as in them. His first hopes for Russia's future in the 1830s had been supported by a trust in the primitive vitality of the Russian people, and the same link between personal frustration and nationalist dreams appears in his diary in the next decade. In the summer of 1843 he rejoices in the peace of the countryside: "And this simple, good people. I have fallen in love with them. A wonderful people. How much hope there is in these intelligent, free-and-easy, bold faces!" He is similarly inspired by the boatmen who sail past his window in Novgorod on feast days "with tambourines and song, . . . cries, whistles, uproar. Germans would not even dream of such carousing; and then in storms, what bravery, audacity."[53]

"*In potentia* there is much in the Russian soul."[54] Transposed into the discourse of Romantic nationalism, drunken revelry is a token of that primitive "immediacy" Herzen had speculated might be the Slavs' contribution to the renewal of European culture. Concerned to distance himself from the Slavophiles, he remarks that his patriotic hopes are "not simply Romantic dreams 'ins Blaue': they are rooted in reality."[55] But whatever their objective status, their function at a period of acute crisis in his life seems to have been to bolster his sense of personal worth and purpose through identification with a force that was the bearer of idealized values. The consequent transformation in his self-image as a Russian *intelligent* is strikingly illustrated by his citation on two different occasions of the same lines from Goethe's poem: "Dich stört nicht im Innern, / Zu lebendiger Zeit / Unnütztes Erinnern / Und vergeblicher Streit [You live in the present, undisturbed by vain memories or senseless quarrels]." In January 1844, in the midst of gloomy reflections on Natalie's sufferings and his guilt of the previous year, he cites these "marvelous" lines as an admonition to modern man in general and his Russian friends in particular to abstain from useless reflection and learn to live in the present.[56] In his review of Granovsky's lectures on European history six months later, he repeats the same lines to convey the Russian intelligentsia's freedom from the attachments, regrets, and ancient enmities that bound Europeans to the past: they were entering into dialogue with the West in the name of a universal order in which particularistic interests, whether Romano-Germanic or Slav, would be replaced by common goals.[57]

The Loneliness of the Superfluous Man

On his return to Moscow at the beginning of the 1840s Herzen had been quick to diagnose the Romantic nationalism of the Slavophiles as a symptom of the malaise of the Russian superfluous man. That he was soon tempted to view this nationalism as an antidote is indicative of the intensity of the loneliness and sense of impotence that kept him on the verge of despair in that decade. The camaraderie of the kruzhok, which Belinsky had described as a desert island, turned out to be no refuge against harsh realities. Herzen describes a typical session together: "We argued, argued, and as always, ended with nothing, with cold remarks and witticisms. Our situation is hopeless because it is false, because we are superfluous to the people's needs, and we are condemned to suffering and despair."[58]

His bitter self-absorption is reflected in his indifference to the humanism of the new realist school of Russian literature that began to emerge in the second half of the 1840s with Belinsky's enthusiastic encouragement. Dostoevsky's novel *Poor Folk* appeared in January 1846; Turgenev's long poem *Parasha* had been highly praised by Belinsky in

1843; his *Notes of a Huntsman,* widely interpreted as an attack on serfdom, began its publication as a series of short stories in 1847. In a letter to his brother, Dostoevsky rates Herzen as one of the most remarkable of contemporary Russian writers; Herzen's opinion of Dostoevsky on meeting him in Saint Petersburg is tersely conveyed in a letter to Natalie: "I can't say he made a particularly pleasant impression."[59] He is similarly unimpressed on meeting Turgenev, describing him sourly to Ketcher as "a superficial nature, with a desire to be noticed and a *fatuité sans bornes*—but such people seem almost geniuses to Belinsky."[60]

Compared with the prospect of a wasted life, the dreams of the "poor, pitiful Slavophiles"[61] had their attraction, but as we have seen, attraction alternated with revulsion, messianic hope with sober realism. In the spring of 1843, after a gap in his diary, Herzen writes that in the preceding fortnight he had nothing to record except a thirsty yearning for "some kind of fullness of life,"[62] alternating with an all-consuming skepticism. After his last long conversation with Samarin he records that he shares the Slavophiles' belief in the existence of a deep conflict in the human psyche, "which allows reflection to destroy what fantasy accepts, while on the other hand, by lulling thought to sleep, opens the way to imagination." But while Herzen's goal was a shifting balance between these drives, the Slavophiles looked forward to the healing of all inner divisions in a society in which reason would be subordinated to Christian faith, a delusion that "borders on fanaticism."[63] The Russian peasant commune, in which the idea of nationalism merged with that of democracy, has been described by Martin Malia as the most significant point of contact between Herzen and the Slavophiles.[64] But as later chapters will show, Herzen was attracted to the notion of communal association, not as a recipe for the final resolution of social conflict, but as a structure flexible enough to effect a balance between the demands of social cohesion and individual liberty in response to the needs of a given historical context. The Slav commune attracted his interest because its primitive structure might provide the basic building block for such an experiment. The millennial passivity of the Slav peasant was an obstacle in this regard. Therefore Herzen's national expectations focused on the intelligentsia—imbued, thanks to Peter's Westernizing revolution, with the notion of individual freedom. It on was their "redemptive" sufferings, rather than the virtues of the Russian peasant, that in moments of Hegelian optimism he placed his best wager for the future.

But Herzen could never console himself for long with ideologies of compensation. In its rejection of comforting illusions, the last entry in his diary in October 1845 is bleak in the extreme. He notes that it repeats what he wrote in the first entry, three years before: "We live in a terrible epoch for Russia, and there is no way out to be seen. . . . We have lost respect in Europe; Russians are regarded with anger, almost with contempt. Russia is becoming the representative of all that is retrograde: a material force used to check the course of European development—and how else should one see her? . . . And, like these three years, more and more years will pass, and we shall grow old, and shall see more clearly that our life has been wasted."[65]

Herzen's flirtation with Romantic nationalism is commonly viewed as the principal development in his thought during his last years in Russia. But his insights into the illusions of Romantic compensation were considerably more original and more significant. Nor are they vitiated by the fact that he himself was prone to these illusions. Indeed, it can be argued that if his own need for a faith had not been so intense, his analysis of the lure of utopian constructs could not have been so discerning. In his attraction to historiosophical doctrines he was typical of his time; the Hegelian Westernism of the Russian liberals was as messianic in its way as the nationalism of their opponents. Where Herzen differed from both groups was in his insights into what he called the "one-sidedness" of all ideologies as means of making sense of historical reality, and his use of the method he described as speculative empiricism as a means of achieving a sense of process—a grasp of living form undistorted by rigidity of principle. Hence his attraction to the two French socialists who held the heterodox view that there could be no single formula for an ideal society, no permanent reconciliation, only at best an uneasy and shifting process of mutual accommodation, between the goals of liberty and equality. His most original contribution to Russian thought in the 1840s was this critique of goal-directed visions of history, his contention that the contingent element in life, which constantly subverts attempts at rational ordering or prediction in public and private existence, should be welcomed as freeing the psyche from the sterile fears and hopes of anticipation, releasing intellectual, affective, and aesthetic energies that allow us to exploit the maximum potential of the only reality we possess.

When in emigration he could at last express his ideas in freedom, he would draw on his experience as the man in the middle in the doctrinal battles over Russia's historical destiny to propose an approach to the problem that broke with all the historiosophical thought of the time: to evaluate both the national and the Europeanized strands of Russian culture in terms of, not their conformity to a predetermined goal, but their intrinsic richness and potential for development—to reconcile and accommodate rather than to order and exclude.

* * *

After Ogarev's return to Russia in 1846, Herzen's circle gathered to spend the summer together at a country house Herzen had rented near Moscow. In this close confinement the tensions among them erupted in an open argument between Herzen and Granovsky over Herzen's atheism. The quarrel was patched up, but with the exception of Ogarev and Belinsky, who was absent in Saint Petersburg, it was clear that the circle did not sympathize with Herzen's views on the heroism of consistency. This rift lent added urgency to Herzen's desire to escape from Russia. Once again he applied for permission to go abroad on grounds of his wife's ill health. After enlisting the support of powerful persons, including the governor of Moscow, he was permitted to visit Saint Petersburg in October 1846 for an interview with the head of the Third Department, General Dubelt, who had recently condemned Herzen's novel. Surprisingly, his request to be freed from police surveillance was granted in the following month, and he was given permission to travel abroad for medical reasons.

His escape from the morass of Russian life was appropriately made via the border post named "Black Mud" (Chernaya Gryaz)—after an equally appropriate tragicomic episode with a bumbling Gogolian inspector when his passport was apparently lost and he was told he should go back to Saint Petersburg and apply for a new one. A gendarme eventually found the passport where the inspector had folded it inside the papers of another member of his party.

Here in March 1847, accompanied by Natalie, their three children, and his mother, he bade farewell to a little group from his Moscow circle, their differences temporarily set aside. He would later describe his joy at breaking free from the stifling atmosphere of the circle, where friendship and love were rooted in shared sorrow and frustration: "I was beckoned to by distance, space, an open battle and free speech: I sought to test my strength in freedom."[66]

His first free act was to purchase, in the German town of Königsberg, a number of cartoons of Nicolas the First.

Ogarev

One of those missing from the group that accompanied Herzen to the Russian border was his closest friend and future collaborator in emigration. Ogarev tends to figure as little more than a footnote in histories of Russian socialism—Herzen's "ideological shadow," as Malia puts it.[67] His absence from Moscow in the 1840s—being at first abroad and then on his country estate—perhaps explains why he appears rarely in accounts of the intellectual ferment of those years. Yet his correspondence with Herzen and his circle shows that at this period he was the most radical of them all. He began to address the reality of Russian backwardness while Herzen in Vyatka was still exclusively absorbed in his private idyll of romantic love. When his friend turned to idealizing the common people as a source of hope for the future, Ogarev had already embarked on a pioneering experiment designed to transform the lives of real peasants in real communes.

Observing his fellow landowners in the province of Penza, where he was living out his exile in the 1830s, Ogarev poured scorn on his liberal friends' faith in the gentry as agents of progress, reminding them that those few who had begun to free their house serfs were doing so not from enlightened principles but because in a declining economy they no longer wished to have to feed them; on the system of serfdom in general they were at one with the government, voicing no objections to its inhumanity.[68] In the following year, to the alarm and disapproval of his neighbors, he set about freeing 4,000 serfs together with land on his estate, an example he proposed to other members of his circle. None followed his lead. (Herzen had no influence on his own family's estate until much later, and then only in the narrow time interval between taking legal possession of his inheritance following his father's death and the government's sequestration of the estate after he had left Russia.) Before leaving in 1841 for an extended stay in Europe, Ogarev busied himself on projects for a village school, a polytechnical college, and a factory on the estate, financed by his substantial inheritance. Due to his inexperience and his absence abroad, this first experiment, manipulated by the more resourceful peasants to the detriment of the majority, had very limited success, but on his return to Russia in 1846 he was to repeat it on a more ambitious scale on another estate, Staroe Aksheno.[69]

He spent the intervening years mainly in Berlin, initially applying himself diligently but with little success to the study of Hegel. He soon discovered his limitations in this area. After a long tussle with the *Encyclopedia* he confessed to Herzen that he was baffled by Hegel's exposition of the relation of thought to being: "If you've made some sense out of this, please write." He decided to emulate his friend (then engaged in composing his *Letters on Nature*) by attending lectures on the natural sciences, combined with further study of the *Encyclopedia*. After three more months of increasing mental confusion, charted in a lengthy letter to Herzen, he abandoned his struggle with metaphysics: "Give me . . . concrete science." Stimulated by Herzen's engagement with the natural sciences, he embarked on what he admitted might be a lifelong task: to familiarize himself with the disciplines of anatomy, embryology, chemistry, and geology, explaining to a skeptical Ketcher that these sciences were an essential link in a chain leading to the goal of all knowledge—the nature of humans and their world.[70]

In February 1847 Ogarev states his profession of faith in response to Granovsky's criticism of his atheism: The hereafter is an empty abstraction. The meaning of life on earth consists of individual humans in their specific historical surroundings. The mainspring of human activity consists in striving to resolve those questions, both individual and universal, with which each human is confronted through the development of history and of human logic. Whether or not they believe in the future triumphs of the humanity is irrelevant.[71]

He was then already acting out his credo in Aksheno. The questions with which his personal place in history confronted him continued to trouble him during his years in Europe. In a letter to Herzen, sandwiched between a severe critique of Schelling's *Naturphilosophie* and faint praise of Hegel, is the following passage: "Friend! Have you ever felt the whole burden of inherited property? Did you ever find the morsel you put into your mouth bitter? Did you feel humiliated before yourself, helping the poor with the money of others? How deeply do you feel that only personal labor gives the right to enjoyment? Friend, let's become proletarians. Otherwise you'll suffocate."[72]

On his return to Aksheno he built a laboratory to pursue his studies of the living world, but his most ambitious experiment was conducted outside its walls. He remained on his estate for the next decade, working to transform it into a profit-making enterprise for the mutual benefit of himself and his former serfs, turning them into specialized hired workers on his farms, in greenhouses, a distillery, and small factories for the production of paper and sugar. Shortly after his arrival he drafted a detailed plan for a polytechnical school that would provide training from basic literacy to specialized trades and would also replace the peasants' traditional fatalism with a sense of personal dignity and independence. Its graduates would be required to remain at least four years in the district as "peasant propagandists," passing on their skills and independent outlook to others.[73] Sending a copy of his plan to his Moscow friends, he requested them to find a suitable teacher to set the project in train. Nothing came of this ambitious scheme (discovered by the police during a search of Aksheno, his draft ended up in the files of the Third Department). But several of his projects were carried through on a much smaller scale, despite some stubborn resistance from the peasants themselves.

Ogarev's reports to his friends on his dealings with the peasants reflect a deep empathy with their situation, combined with a dispassionate view of their mentality rare among the intelligentsia of his time. Both sentiments are expressed in a letter to Granovsky describing a selection of army recruits from among the local peasantry, at which as a landowner he was required to be present. "You would find it hard to imagine how distressing this spectacle is. My chest contracted, I felt dizzy, I thought I would burst into tears, or fall in a faint. . . . After half an hour I got used to it, and understood that the majority of the members [of the recruiting commission] present have to remain completely indifferent arbiters of the fate of these naked people, with their expressions of fear or despair, surrounded by weeping women or trembling old men."[74]

But Ogarev was not inclined to idealize these victims of the regime. He follows this account with the comment that the idiocy of the mass of the people has to be seen to be believed. The resistance he encountered in the first year of his efforts to improve the peasants' situation tempted him to lose faith in the efficacy of practical activity: "I feel engulfed by a kind of chaos . . . and am truly happy when I get home and can escape into a calculation on the crystallization of carbon . . . or . . . with the maximum of detail, dissect a sheep." He deplores the slave mentality engendered by the traditional commune, and complains of the difficulty of improving the peasants' lives without "planters' methods of persuasion." His efforts to replace the institution of the corvée with paid labor met with deep suspicion. "One has to have enormous patience . . . to put up with the stubborn irrationality of the commune, which insults one at every step." He writes to Herzen that he is moderating his consumption of wine: "I'm beginning to be repelled by everything barbarous. Probably because every day here I can observe barbarity and see how it dulls a human personality and prevents it from expanding in vividness and clarity." Three months later he concludes a detailed exposition to Herzen of his economic projects with the comment, "If you can't put up with the boredom, the revulsion, the grief with which you are assailed by skirmishes with stubborn inertia and ignorance, you will naturally give up agriculture and quit the countryside, never to give it a second glance." Nevertheless, his first months in Aksheno culminate, not in disillusionment and retreat, but in the reaffirmation of his resolve. His isolation, the lack of trained workmen for his factories, "sap one's strength, one feels sick at heart, but I've decided to stand firm whatever happens, and I'm convinced that the result will be worth it."[75]

He kept to his resolution for a decade, despite renewed persecution by the regime when his activities drew the attention of the local and Saint Petersburg authorities. Together with three other Penza landowners—his neighbor A. A. Tuchkov, who had been close to the Decembrists, N. M. Satin, a member of Herzen's and Ogarev's circle in the 1830s, and I. V. Selivanov, a contributor to the *Contemporary*—he was arrested in February 1850 and brought to Saint Petersburg. The authorities were unable to find proof for a charge of organizing a "communist sect,"[76] and he was freed under police supervision. When a new search a month later uncovered suspect documents and forbidden literature, the surveillance was increased. It was intensified again in 1853 when he was suspected of disseminating a revolutionary proclamation from the press Herzen had founded in London. Three years later he would leave Russia illegally to join Herzen.

The courage, tenacity, and self-discipline with which he pursued his solitary pioneering enterprise does not fit with his common image as Herzen's shadow, a naive and amenable Romantic—"poor Nick," as his future wife (subsequently Herzen's mistress) would describe him in her memoirs. This image was largely of his own construction. He had a compulsive tendency to self-chastisement, a constant theme of his letters to Herzen. He confesses that he is "weak, indecisive, impractical"; he was born with "an impressionable soul, but not one that makes an impression."[77] Commentators have tended to take him at his word. Noting that Ogarev titled one of his longer poems "The Confessions of a Superfluous Man," Malia remarks on the aptness of the epithet: "There was something passive and dependent in Ogarev's nature, a lack of will and purpose of his own. He needed to be led and directed, and all his life he submitted gratefully to the tutelage of more masterful natures . . . most of all Herzen."[78]

His friend's self-denigration (as well, perhaps, as a certain pique at being outdone by him in radical initiatives) may help to explain Herzen's tepid reaction to the letters in which Ogarev kept him informed of his progress. As a fervent admirer of Feuerbach's naturalistic approach to human societies, he might have been expected to respond enthusiastically to this experiment in social transformation. Ogarev was no more gifted as a natural scientist than as a philosopher (he complains that the progress of his studies is hindered by his inability to grasp the basics of mathematics and chemistry), but his concern with achieving what was practically feasible within given empirical conditions distinguished him from most Russian thinkers of the period, whose gaze was fixed on more all-encompassing visions of social transformation. Ogarev firmly believed along with Feuerbach (whom he had brought to Herzen's attention in 1841) that the secret

of philosophy was anthropology, or, as he put it himself, that speculation must be grounded in direct observation of empirical reality.
"I've come to find abstractions unbearable," he wrote to Ketcher in
1845; "all I want is the science of the living world." When he was dis-
heartened with the lack of progress with his reforms, he turned for relief to "concrete science"—anatomy and physiology.[79] As he explained
to Herzen after a very detailed description of his dissection of a ram's
head, he took advantage of the limited possibilities his environment
offered for scientific research by using the bodies of farm animals as a
means to a deeper understanding of the processes of life.[80]

During the decade Ogarev devoted to his Aksheno experiment he
kept Herzen informed of its development. He was increasingly dependent on loans from his friend to continue it. Herzen responded gener-
ously, having assured himself that his loans would be secure ("I believe
this affair will make a profit," he wrote from abroad to his financial
agent),[81] but he seems to have had at most a lukewarm interest in the
specific aims of the project, to judge from his only surviving comment
on the subject, in a letter of 1847. Ogarev had set out the economic un-
derpinning of his plans in a letter consisting largely of meticulously
detailed pages of facts and figures, remarking that he was confident
that Herzen would not be bored with these calculations: it was essential to include the material aspect of a theory in order to have a full
grasp of the whole. His enthusiasm met with a condescending and plat-
itudinous response: "On your economic theories I can say nothing,
because I have a poor knowledge of the subject; what I like most about
them is how vividly they reflect your lively and practical nature. To
be at one with one's time, to choose precisely that aspect of one's milieu where creative work is possible, and to make that work important—that sums up the character of a practical person."[82]

Ogarev's practical nature was expressed in his forthright response
to a tirade against the West in which Herzen summarized his reaction
to the failure of the 1848 revolution and the subsequent carnage he had
just witnessed on the streets of Paris—events that, he declared with
passionate eloquence, signaled the death of an entire civilization. Given
Herzen's desire to escape the dying West, Aksheno had acquired a new
charm. Russians, he maintained, are more fortunate than the Europeans whose culture they share; by nationality they resemble the bar-

barian invaders of ancient Rome—part of a "young and new world."
Thus, "long live Staroe Aksheno and the life of the Russian countryside"; he might even go back to settle in the district.[83]

Ogarev was unimpressed by this onset of Slavophilism: "I don't
share your gloomy view of things, I don't look with desperation on the
West and I don't think it would be very pleasant to settle somewhere
between Moscow and Aksheno. Each of us in our own small corner
has to put up with all sorts of vileness—that doesn't make anything
easier, but there are still no grounds for despondency." Herzen's comparisons of the events in France with the death of the ancient world
strike him as empty rhetoric. There was no harm in studying the latter,
it could be a pleasant way of passing the time. But what would Herzen
deduce from it—Vico's law of the recurrence of historical cycles? What
good would that comparative anatomy of history do him? "After all, the
data are different." He recommends instead a study of the historical
organism in its current form, citing in this regard Proudhon's *Contradictions économiques*, which had inspired him with "a mass of ideas,
which little by little I'll put into order." And he continues his letter
with what for him are the matters of real significance. He is not content with his existence, but is working as hard as he can. It has been a
terrible year for agriculture; without Herzen's loan he might have
gone bankrupt. "There is an enormous amount of work to be done,
my friend. . . . I'm not sparing myself, but every minute is terribly
important."[84]

In one of his first letters describing to Herzen his experiences with
his peasants he had remarked: "You don't know the Russian countryside, you don't know its daily life, its needs and its potential."[85] In his
view the peasants' most immediate need was to be weaned away from
the passive mentality formed by centuries of slavery in the traditional
communes in which Herzen was tempted to see the seeds of future development. Ogarev's transformation of his estate followed no ideological blueprint, but the intention behind his reforms, encompassing
health, education, and technical training, coincided with Proudhon's
view of the aim of social and economic progress: the achievement of
"a general equation of our contradictions" through a new form of communitarian socialism to which each would contribute according to
his capacities, and where initiative and expertise would be rewarded

appropriately without detriment to the well-being of the less endowed. Embarking on his project, he writes to Herzen of his determination neither to be an absentee landlord nor to assume "the ugly position of an aristocratic planter." A Russian landowner should aim simply to be "an industrial producer"—leader of a workforce whose prosperity, like his own, would depend on their joint efforts.[86] He approached this enterprise with great seriousness, informing his Moscow friends that he intended to gain hands-on experience of all the functions in his factories, from laborer to foreman, as well as the construction of simple buildings, and river boats for the transport of the products of his distillery—could they send him the appropriate technical handbooks?[87]

His project was cut short by the renewed persecution that ultimately drove him abroad. In 1856 he left Russia illegally with his second wife (the daughter of his neighbor Aleksei Tuchkov) to join Herzen in London and begin a partnership in which their very different qualities and experiences would combine to realize their youthful dream of playing an active role on the historical stage.

* * *

While Ogarev grappled with the realities of the Russian countryside, Herzen in France was witnessing firsthand the progress of the revolution whose coming he had anticipated so eagerly. His initial reaction to its outcome, reflected in his despairing letter to Ogarev, was followed by a painful process of self-searching aimed at expelling the lingering remnants of utopian hope from his view of history and freedom. This process, culminating in his most powerful work, is the subject of Chapters 15 and 16.

CHAPTER THIRTEEN

A Conservative Revolution

Outside us everything changes, everything vacillates. . . . Twilight descends and no guiding star appears in the sky. We shall find no haven but within ourselves.

HERZEN, *FROM THE OTHER SHORE*

THE events Herzen witnessed in his first three years in the West were crucial in the transformation of his intellectual protest into the concept of "Russian socialism," which became the first banner of radical opposition to the autocracy and survived to contest the 1917 revolution with the Marxists.

Equally significant, perhaps, was an exchange of ideas that did not take place, due to the mutual antipathy between Herzen and Marx, whose *Neue Rheinische Zeitung* propagated the rumor in 1848 that Bakunin was a Russian government spy, and who suspected Herzen himself of being a nationalist engaged in plotting the revitalization of Europe through the invasion of Russian barbarian hordes. On the other hand, Herzen developed an intellectual affinity and a warm personal relationship with the anarchist Pierre-Joseph Proudhon. Like Proudhon, he would found his socialism on a radical critique of notions of power, authority, and freedom that were then as prevalent on the political Left as on the Right. Integrated into the Russian populist tradition, this critique would form the basis of its opposition to Marxism.

Commentators continue to be divided over the question of its significance and value. Did it derive from a prescient judgment on the values of centralized societies? Or was it no more than the compensatory blustering of a sense of national inferiority, backed up by an intellectually flimsy Romantic idealism? With regard to Herzen himself, the question has focused on the violence of his reaction to the failure of the 1848 revolution in France. Was it a foregone conclusion, based on anti-Western prejudices already formed in Russia, or the result of frustration at the failure of the Provisional Government to realize his ideals? The two principal studies of Herzen in English are opposed on the question.[1] Soviet and many Western commentators have repeated the mixed verdict of Marxist historiography on the relation of realism to fantasy in Herzen's reaction to 1848, as expressed in Lenin's pronouncement that although as the aristocratic product of a preindustrial society Herzen failed to appreciate the economic forces at work in the conflict, his revolutionary intransigence and opposition to the bourgeoisie place him in the camp of revolution: "He stands in the line that leads from the Decembrists to the Bolsheviks"—a judgment echoed faithfully by Russian scholars of the Soviet period.[2]

These conflicting views of the objective validity of Herzen's political theories are often based on partisan assumptions about the nature and development of socialism. In his study of Proudhon, K. Steven Vincent identifies the ways in which such assumptions have hindered our understanding of pre-Marxist (or "utopian") socialism, due to the influence of Marx's and Engels's critiques of the socialist programs of their contemporaries for failing to recognize essential socioeconomic divisions and to understand the march of history. Many liberal historians, while strongly critical of Marx's own achievements in this regard, nevertheless maintain that his socialism was more "scientific" than that of his predecessors. The historicist view that his predecessors "foreshadowed" Marxism has led to emphasis on their economic theories at the expense of the ideal of moral regeneration, which was of primary importance for them; their concern with unattainable moral ideals has been seen as evidence of the movement's immaturity. But it is in the nature of moral ideals to be unrealizable. Proudhon would insist repeatedly that their role was to be a yardstick for measuring progress toward goals that could never be attained in their entirety. The question to be asked is whether or not the consensual vision of society they reflected was impracticable. The classic Marxist response is that they were "reactionary" because they ran counter to the "true" path of progress through the intensification of conflicts between the forces and relations of production. Another historicist argument, retrospectively conflating the actual with the possible, infers the impracticability of the utopian socialists' ideals from the fact that they had such little success. Neither approach is compatible with the role of the intellectual historian, who needs to empathize with his subjects to the extent of comprehending their conceptual world, the historical context in which they developed their ideas, and the discourse in which they framed them.[3]

This belaboring of the seemingly obvious is a necessary preliminary to the analysis, in Chapters 14 to 16, of the formation of Herzen's political philosophy. His position as an aristocrat from a preindustrial society, his interest in the ideas of the early French socialists, the importance of a moral ideal in his thought, and finally his agrarian socialism, deeply hostile to the communism of Marx, have made him a natural target for attempts at ideological typecasting of the kind outlined above. Designed to fix Herzen's place in some particular intellectual "tradition," these attempts are by their nature peculiarly insensitive to the cast of mind of a thinker who was centrally preoccupied with the distortions of reality induced by ideological thought. Herzen would remark frequently that his contemporaries' inability to place him in relation to the warring ideologies of his time was due to the inappropriateness of their categories when applied to his ideas. Chapters 15 to 17 will discuss the development of his socialism in terms of the goals he set himself and the historical context in which he operated. They will present his continuing struggle against the attractions of metaphysical absolutes as the key to the understanding of his responses to 1848.

Although Herzen shared his generation's yearning for an overarching and redemptive meaning to their stunted existence, his education in the methods of the natural sciences had equipped him with a critical perspective on theories and ideals that would become the basis of an empirical approach to the nature of history and the future of Russia. This approach had remained unelaborated as he grappled with and occasionally succumbed to the pressures that made "Buddhists" or "dilettantes" of his Russian circle. Chapters 14 and 15 will treat Herzen's first years in the West as a crucial stage in the odyssey that began with his scientific training under Maximovich and Pavlov and would culminate in the definitive statement of his moral and social philosophy in *From the Other Shore*.

* * *

Herzen's impressions of his first two years in Europe were chronicled in three cycles of letters, the first of which, *Letters from the Avenue Marigny*, were printed in *The Contemporary*, the principal periodical of the Westernizers.[4] His description of his journey from the Russian border to Paris seems aimed at reigniting his polemics with that group. Ironic condescension toward the West is its dominant note. Europe appears to him as a fascinating museum, every epoch of European civilization having left its traces like geological strata along the banks of the Rhine. But there was no need for a Russian to feel ill at ease among these foreign splendors. By wedding Russia to Europe, Peter the Great had given his nation rights of inheritance; it could benefit from Europe's past without being oppressed by it. For Europeans the present was the roof of a multistoried house; for Russians and North Americans it was the foundation on which the future would be built: "In this end is our beginning." Citing once again Goethe's lines on the good fortune of a young nation unencumbered by the futile memories and arguments of the past, Herzen transports his readers from Cologne, whose buildings embodied the entire architectural history of Europe, to the Russian countryside, the scene of a historical drama only beginning to unfold. The actors are familiar from his earlier writings—the Russian state, imbued with dynamic movement by Peter's reforms; the peasant, untouched by its history; and the link between the two—the intelligentsia, whose faith in the value of their national distinctiveness had been strengthened by Western philosophy. The history of the Russian people lay in the future. "It has proved its potential through the minority that has faithfully followed the path marked out by Peter—it has proved it through us!" The inference would seem to be that by producing Herzen and his generation, European civilization had fulfilled its historical calling and had now outlived its usefulness—a point that we are told is immediately evident to the Russian traveler. An hour's journey from the Russian border is enough to find oneself in "a wholly different world: a world of the past, a world of loss, of memories, of bereavement." There is no feature of European life that a Russian armed with the correct historical insight cannot interpret as a sign of decay, not even the crisp white cloth adorning the table in the impeccably clean waiting room at the first German coach station across the border. A love of cleanliness and order are, Herzen explains, signs of an aging civilization that ascribes great importance to external forms. The Russian tramples such forms underfoot in his breathless rush toward the future. Western man has the advantage of well-elaborated and stable rules; the Russian's advantage lies in "fresh forces and aspirations."[5] According to Pavel Annenkov, Herzen's Moscow friends found his satire amusing though slightly overdone, in the style characteristic of one determined not to give the impression of an awestruck tourist.[6] In his private letters to them he could be more positive: "I am simply in love with Cologne." The elegance of Brussels was "beyond all description."[7]

Paris in 1847

His final destination was Paris. "We have grown used to linking the word 'Paris' with memories of the great events, the great masses, the great individuals of 1789 and 1793. . . . The name of Paris is tightly bound with all the finest hopes of contemporary man, and I entered it with a beating heart, with that timidity with which people once arrived in Jerusalem, in Rome." Recorded in a *Letter* dated June 1848, these expectations are likely to have been exaggerated, the more sharply to contrast them with what, as he claimed in retrospect, he actually found on his arrival at the end of March 1847: a city and a culture "in the final stages of moral decay, spiritual exhaustion, vacuity and triviality."[8]

The best contemporary source for Herzen's time in Paris is Pavel Annenkov, who was well acquainted with the main figures in the Russian circles and had been living in Paris for some time when Herzen presented himself at his door—a typical Moscow inhabitant with long hair, a long frock coat, and no beard, soon to reappear as a typical Western gentleman, with short hair, a short jacket, and a beard of fashionable cut. His wife underwent a similar transformation: the quiet, dreamy romantic became "a resplendent tourist," not out of place in a city of world renown.[9] The couple led a life in Paris appropriate to Herzen's rank and fortune. Natalie's letters to their Moscow friends reveal their predilection for oysters and champagne in the fashionable cafés of the Palais Royal, while Herzen comments knowledgeably on the quality of French cigars (five times more expensive and three times inferior to the Russian equivalent) and wine (he bemoans the absence in Paris of the widow Clicquot's champagne, currently being produced exclusively for export). He treats his circle to a satirical dissertation on a besetting concern of his class, the servant problem. The French had found a way of solving one of the dilemmas of modern life: how to dispense with personal servants without going to the primitive extreme of Rousseau's natural man. The answer was the Parisian concierge, who catered for the needs of all the tenants in his block. He could be summoned to clean clothes and boots, to polish, wash, dust, and light the fires, fetch tobacco, wine, beefsteaks and cutlets, deliver letters and journals and receive visiting cards. True, he would not be amused to be summoned to the fifth floor to fill one's pipe or to bring a handkerchief from the next room; but one of the moral benefits of education was that it weaned one away from the more preposterous habits of one's motherland. Cooks could be dispensed with, thanks to the prevalence of cafés where coffee could be drunk over the morning papers, and the ubiquity of excellent restaurants; nor did one need a personal coachman; there were boys everywhere who in exchange for a sou would call a cab, and, when one alighted, place a board under one's feet if the ground were wet. As a result one could have all the convenience of being served without the mutual constraints and corruption of the master-and-servant relationship.

Annenkov observed that the political ferment of Paris at that time, with its plethora of parties and opinions, the polemical wit of its press, the concern of its theater and literature with contemporary issues, produced on Russian visitors at the time the effect of an oasis discovered after long wanderings over a desert steppe. From his first days in Paris, having established himself in an apartment on the Avenue Marigny, Herzen was in his native element. "He immediately threw himself into that glittering sea of bold hypotheses, pitiless polemic and passions of every possible kind."[10] His first cycle of letters from Paris draws on sources available to any cultivated tourist: street life, the theater, the press, and literature.

He reveled in the luxury of a comparatively free press, describing the passion for news in Paris as "a kind of sickness."[11] As if on a drinking spree, one would succumb to the temptation of just one small paper, then another, until one had devoured a whole dozen. If this diet resulted too often in the depressing symptoms of a hangover, it was also highly stimulating: Herzen greatly admired the radical journalism of the day for the boldness of its attacks on the existing system, in particular the iniquities of laissez-faire economics and bourgeois rule.

His knowledge of both derived mainly from the account of France under Louis-Philippe by Louis Blanc, whose view of the wholly negative role of the bourgeoisie he had adopted. The economic complexities of their role in a modern society did not concern him; his opposition to them was above all on moral and aesthetic grounds. His first personal encounter with them took place on his journey from the Russian border to Berlin, where he shared a carriage with German merchants who shocked him with their "hidebound philistinism," the narrow meanness of their outlook and aspirations.[12] That was to remain, in essence, his opinion of the bourgeoisie, and he was soon to find ample support for it in the Parisian radical press. The fourth of his *Letters from Paris* highlights the ferocity of its daily revelations about the financial and sexual scandals of prime minister Guizot's administration.

The French socialists who had contributed to forming his ideas in the early 1840s—notably Sand, Leroux, Considerant, and Proudhon— were then in Paris, and one might have expected him to have been eager to make their acquaintance. But on his own admission, he left Paris in the autumn of 1847 having made no contacts in the city's political or literary circles. The reason given in his memoirs was that no direct opportunity presented itself, and he had no desire actively to seek one out:

> I thought it unseemly to frequent literary or political circles simply to gaze at celebrities. In addition, I had very little liking for the tone of condescending superiority that the French employ with Russians: they approve and encourage us, praise our pronunciation and our wealth; we put up with all this and come to them like supplicants, sometimes half-apologetically, rejoicing when from politeness they take us to be French. The French shower us with words; we can't keep pace with them—we're still thinking of how to answer them when they've already passed on to something else. . . .
>
> To get onto another footing with them one has to *impress*—for which one needs various rights that I did not then possess.[13]

Such considerations cannot account for his failure to acquaint himself directly with some of the radical working-class groups that had sprung up in Paris in the 1840s. He explains this with the argument that the "invisible Paris" of workers and secret societies was inaccessible to foreigners;[14] but this was not the case. Bakunin, who had been in Paris since July 1844, had attended meetings of such groups, and several of

the German communists were in touch with French working-class radicals. Herzen had come upon Bakunin and a member of his student
circle, Nikolai Sazonov, soon after his arrival in Paris. Bakunin was
by then deeply involved in Slav nationalist politics—he was shortly to
be expelled from France at the request of the Russian ambassador after
a speech, on the anniversary of the Polish insurrection of 1831, calling
for an alliance between Russian democracy and Polish nationalism
against the tsar. Herzen seems to have taken no interest in any of these
activities. His personal contacts with the lower classes were confined
to observations in the course of his perambulations in the Paris streets,
which convinced him of the instinctive dignity and goodness of their
natures. He recounts to his circle one such incident. A small boy drops
a bag of silver pieces, which scatter over the street. Workers rush to
comfort the weeping child, retrieve his money, count it, and return it
to him; the poorer a man was in Paris, the farther removed he was from
the corruption of the bourgeoisie.

The principal source of Herzen's sociological observations was the
theater. He was an assiduous playgoer, explaining in a letter to a
Moscow friend, the actor Mikhail Shchepkin, that the theater was nowhere more tightly bound with the life of a city than in Paris. Its
twenty-two theaters were full to capacity every night, and the great
majority of plays, ingeniously constructed but devoid of genuine passions, faithfully reflected the middle-class audience's attachment to the
values of order and decorum. In addition the vaudeville existed for the
titillation of the bourgeois paterfamilias. Absent from both categories
was the slightest reference to "contemporary questions"—the seething
waves of protest beneath the surface calm of the city's life.[15]

He found this at last in a small theater on the outskirts of Paris, in
a play by the French socialist journalist and playwright Félix Piat, *The
Rag and Bone Man.* It impressed him so greatly that he envisaged the
possibility of having it staged in Moscow. His third *Letter* consists
of a blow-by-blow account of the action, in a world of "hunger and
poverty, . . . cellars and attics, a world of gloomy self-sacrifice and violent crimes."[16] The main protagonist, characterized by untutored
wisdom and self-sacrificing love, befriends an orphaned seamstress but
cannot save her from being wrongfully convicted of infanticide through
the intrigue of a wicked baron. Herzen takes the reader carefully

through the intricacies of the plot; this meticulously detailed summary of a melodrama whose characters strain all credibility is the closest he gets to an analysis of the psychology of the Parisian worker for the benefit of his Russian readers.

A recurring theme of *Letters from the Avenue Marigny* is nostalgia for an idealized aristocracy whose "social religion" was founded on patriotism, courage, and honor.[17] Here too, Herzen's sociological musings were inspired by the theater, where he saw this noble ethic reflected in the grace and harmony of Racine's plays. Regrettably, he reflects, it was doomed through its Romantic one-sidedness: its failure to address the practical question of material prosperity. Perceiving that its end was inevitable, the French aristocracy elected to perish in glory— Herzen's generous interpretation of 4 August 1789, when in a move to avert revolution the nobility prompted the Constituent Assembly to declare the abolition of its feudal privileges.

Herzen's critique of the West was greeted with indignation by his Moscow circle, who objected especially to his aesthetic and ethical criticism of the bourgeoisie. Botkin wrote to Annenkov: "Herzen has no clear conception of the old aristocracy about which he is so enthusiastic, or of the bourgeoisie that he so despises. . . . God grant that we should have such a bourgeoisie!"[18] But as his fourth letter from the Avenue Marigny (composed in September 1847) reveals, Herzen also employed his time in Paris to follow the current political scandals and form a perceptive analysis of the gathering storm. His source was the unaccustomed luxury of a free press, with its daily exposures of madness and depravity. Papers of all sizes and political tendencies descended daily on the city like a flock of locusts, "devouring events before they have a chance to mature, . . . rag and bone men, marauders, marching step by step in the wake of the great army of historical advance."[19] The overwhelming mood they reflected was profound discontent with the existing order, along with total incapacity to define the desirable ends or means of change. Romantics and idealists complained that the noble visions inspiring progress in the past had been replaced by questions of political economy; but the future of all peoples depended on these questions, which must be addressed if great ideals were to be more than pious platitudes or instruments of bloody destruction. France had proceeded from one extreme to another, in a version of Vico's *corsi e ricorsi* of history, replacing political faith with money as the linchpin of society. Where the Revolution had sacrificed humans to ideas, the bourgeoisie sacrificed ideas to itself, transforming the theories of Adam Smith into a means of uncovering the laws of the increase of wealth, equating economics with commercial guile—the art of producing maximum profit with a minimum expenditure of capital. Science had delivered a bludgeon into their hands, with both ends of which the consumer was belabored—on the one hand a reduction in wages, on the other a rise in the price of products. Drawing their legislators from their own ranks, they had turned exploitation of the masses into a system protected by the full force of the government, reducing life to a means of minting money, and the state, the courts, and the army to instruments for the preservation of property.

Four months of reading the Paris press had not enhanced Herzen's view of the opponents to the status quo. He pronounces the parliamentary opposition and the radical press alike as strong on indignation but weak on positive measures, relying on palliative solutions or seeking to breathe new life into old ideals, while the utopias of the Left were too abstract to appeal to the people: radical economic theories would never penetrate the cast-iron fortress of their habits and traditions. Most curious of all was the fact that the new theories sought to free humans from poverty and exploitation merely in order to engulf them in a commune: "To comprehend . . . the full sanctity, the full breadth and reality of the individual's rights *and not to destroy society, not to shatter it into atoms*, is the most difficult of tasks. It has never been resolved by any historical systems in the past; for that one needs a great maturity, which mankind has not yet attained."[20] This quotation encapsulates the criterion by which Herzen was to measure all the social theories of his age.

The *Letters* do not support the widespread interpretation of Herzen as having arrived in the West a fully fledged messianic nationalist.[21] In September 1847 he remarks that there is nothing easier than to expose the "dark and sordid" side of contemporary France: The political opposition is devoted to that task, with the eager assistance of an uncensored press. But the present situation should be viewed from the historical perspective of the great ideals of 1789. France was still exhausted by a difficult birth, of which Europe continued to reap the benefits without having suffered the pain; this should not be forgotten. Fetid air was not France's native milieu. "It demonstrates this through a universal indignation, and is not accustomed to be indignant to no avail." This optimism is combined with a sally against the nationalist messianism of the Slavophiles. There was nothing desperate or hopeless in the present situation—France would still extricate herself without earthquakes, fire from heaven, floods, or plague: apocalyptic images dear to "the newly invented East, which speaks with a primitive glee about everything wrong with the West, in the belief that hatred of one's neighbor equates with true love of one's family; that the misfortune of others is the best consolation in one's own grief."[22] This passage was omitted from the edition of the *Letters* published after the defeat of 1848.

Italy and 1848

In the autumn of 1847 Herzen left for Italy, where he would remain until May 1848. In the first of four letters written between the end of December 1847 and the beginning of March 1848 he explains that he had needed to escape from the overwhelming atmosphere of depression: "Death in literature, death in the theater, death in politics . . . the walking corpse of Guizot on the one hand and the childish babble of a grey-haired opposition on the other." He repeats that France would recover without recourse to drastic measures, but he had no wish to sit at her bedside while she battled with an attack of insanity. "I wanted to rest, I wanted the sea, the warm air, luxuriant verdure, and a people less exhausted and sick at heart."[23]

Arriving in Italy at the height of its struggle against tyranny and foreign occupation, he was overwhelmed by the energy and optimism of the Risorgimento, which, he told his Russian readers, had revived his faith in mankind. A backward, miserably poor people, subjected to centuries of oppression, humiliation, and foreign invasion, had miraculously found the strength to resist not only its native tyrants but also one of the great imperial powers of Europe in the name of political independence and civil rights. While the rest of Europe had embraced the goal of a centralized state, Italy (with the exception of the monarchies of Naples and Piedmont) had remained feudal in structure and federal in outlook. Herzen was impressed by what he saw as a sense of independence reflected in an elegance of bearing inherent in all Italians from the nobility to the most destitute. He pointed to the significance of the people's militias in each principality and the absence of the uniforms symbolizing the role of armies as instruments of the state. In Italy every clod of earth, every little town, had its individual character. Nowhere else could one find such a dislike of centralization. The concept of federation was inherent in the nature of Italians: the only rights to which they laid claim issued from their municipal commune.

He suggested to his friends that the Risorgimento demanded a rethinking of the standard norms of progress based on the countries of northwestern Europe. It returned his own thoughts to a subject eclipsed by the excitement of his first encounter with the West: the potential of the Russian peasant commune. He remarked that the peasants of central Italy were as far removed from the dispirited rabble of a modern state as was the Russian peasant from the values of the bourgeoisie. Nowhere except in Italy and Russia had poverty and toil done so little to destroy the courage and nobility reflected in the faces of the common people—inspired, he maintained, by a secret idea that would be fully revealed only when the time was ripe, but that meanwhile inspired a passive resistance to all assaults on their independence. He recalls how, as he traveled through France to Italy, his "Slav soul" had grieved at the sight of the high stone walls separating gardens from fields, arrogantly asserting the exclusive rights of property. In western Europe the village commune was merely an administrative device for the policing of society: "Long live . . . the Russian village: its future is immense."[24]

Herzen would return to that theme only after the events of 1848.

* * *

On the streets of Rome in March of that year, Herzen had his first and only experience of participation in a revolutionary crowd. In his memoirs he describes the intoxication of those days. "All Italy awoke before my eyes; the whirlwind that swept everything up bore me along too: all Europe took up its bed and walked—in a fit of lunacy that we took for an awakening." A republic had been declared in Paris and there was news of fighting in Milan, where an uprising had begun against the Austrian government in Lombardy, and a rumor had spread that the king of Piedmont had declared war on Austria. Herzen and the women in his party, mingling with the excited crowd, were invited to join the head of a procession to the Piedmont embassy, where the news was confirmed. The Russians stood together with the nationalist leader Cicerouacchio on the balcony of the embassy looking down on the excited crowd. Herzen read a special symbolism into this moment. In France he and Natalie had met with indifference, if not hostility: "Here the aristocratic proletariat, descendants of Marius and the ancient tribunes, greeted us warmly and sincerely. We were accepted by them into the European struggle." His Romantic rhetoric matched the occasion. In his sense of empathy with the crowd, transcending national and cultural differences in a common revolutionary purpose, he must have experienced something close to that synthesis of intellect and emotion in which, as he had put it in his Hegelian essays, humans act as both species and individual, at one with their age and with themselves. Looking back on these moments in 1855 he writes, "It seems now that all this was a drunken fever? Perhaps, but I don't envy those who were not then possessed by that graceful dream."[25]

In his intoxication with the Risorgimento Herzen seems to have remained in ignorance of the chain of events in Paris that had led from political banquets and street demonstrations to the abdication and flight of Louis-Philippe and the declaration of a republic on 24 February. He notes in a brief postscript to a *Letter* from Rome, dated one week later: "There is talk of an important uprising in Paris; the affair began with a reform banquet. There's nothing in the newspapers about it." That night, he reports, he saw a huge crowd gathered in the center of Rome, shouting "Evviva, evviva la Repubblica francese!" Or had this been merely a dream?[26] In his last *Letter* from Rome, dated 20 April, the new French republic gets only a brief mention as a spur to the Italian battle for independence. The drama unfolding in France, the catalyst for a wave of revolutions in Europe, took second place for him to the events in Italy, which, he wrote to Annenkov, seemed to be leading to an entirely new kind of republic, devoid of all forms of centralization.

Paris in 1848

Herzen was in no hurry to leave Rome, and he didn't arrive in Paris until 5 May. As he was to discover, 1848 in France was a year of conservative revolution, dominated from the outset by liberal republicans with a hazy allegiance to the ideals of 1792: civic virtue, natural rights (including the absolute right to individual property), and universal suffrage (denoting not enfranchisement of the masses, but wider representation of the property-owning classes). The constitutional monarchy of Louis-Philippe, which had replaced the Bourbons after the revolution of 1830, had moved increasingly to the right, harassing the republican opposition and forging a closer alliance with the Catholic Church. A severe agricultural and economic crisis began to develop in 1845, causing extreme misery in the countryside and substantial unemployment among the new industrial working class in the cities. The parliamentary opposition attacked Guizot for encouraging materialism and profiteering and demanded a more democratic franchise; most were in favor merely of extending the property franchise. In mid-1847 they began garnering public support through a nationwide banquet campaign that subverted restrictions on public assembly. Workers politicized by radical republicans and the socialism of Louis Blanc, Auguste Blanqui, Considerant, Cabet, and Proudhon joined the street demonstrations in Paris following the government's decision on 21 February to ban further banquets. After three days of street scuffles and barricades, Louis-Philippe abdicated and a list for a provisional government was drawn up. Of the eleven people listed, two— Louis Blanc and Albert Martin, a worker—were socialists. The five ministers elected included one token radical, Alexandre Ledru-Rollin, editor of the journal La réforme, organ of the radical republicans in the 1840s. The aristocratic poet Alphonse de Lamartine, who headed the government until the June uprising, had been a royalist under the Restoration.

This inauspicious coalition appointed a "Luxembourg Commission" to investigate and alleviate the condition of the working class, legalized workers' committees, permitting them to negotiate with employers, and set up "national workshops"—a public works program for the unemployed that bore a distant resemblance to Louis Blanc's concept of the replacement of private enterprise by industrial self-government through social workshops. Conflict with the radicals began in April when the National Guard halted a march by radical republicans and socialists demanding the postponement of elections for a National Constituent Assembly, to give time for their candidates to canvass in the provinces, where the vote would be crucial. The government went ahead with the April date, with a predictable result: the politically uneducated peasantry, suspicious of urban republicans and guided by local notables, voted en masse for the most conservative candidates. In Paris candidates from the trade committees were neither sufficiently well known nor politically organized to make an impression on the electorate. Moderate republicans and crypto-royalists (many of whom had served under Louis-Philippe) each won a third of the 900 seats, while the extreme Left gained less than a hundred.

On 15 May the Assembly was invaded by a demonstration of workers organized by the extreme Left in favor of intervention in Poland, where rebels were being bombarded by Austrians and Prussians. The government retaliated by dissolving the Luxembourg Commission, arresting prominent radicals—including Blanqui, the recognized leader of the extreme Left—and placing Louis Blanc under indictment; other leaders of the Left went into hiding. The authorities followed this up by ordering the abolition of the National Workshops as a potential seedbed of revolution. This issue became the focus of opposition to the regime. Petitions were submitted, to which the government responded by announcing that the unemployed would have the choice between being drafted into the army or sent to the provinces to drain swamps. Following two days of protest meetings, demonstrators began to build barricades in the poorer neighborhoods in the east of Paris. After three days of violent street fighting, the uprising was crushed by the combined forces of the National Guard and the regular army, which bombarded the barricades with artillery, blowing up entire houses. Ferocious reprisals were carried out on the surviving insurgents: 3,000 of those captured were shot on the spot, 12,000 were imprisoned, and 4,500 were deported to Algeria.

The insurrection resulted in a comprehensive defeat for the Left in France. A number of political clubs and trade unions were closed, and the government was reorganized, headed by the former minister of war, General Eugène Cavaignac, who had led the forces that suppressed the insurrection. In a reshuffled Assembly the conservatives, reorganized as the self-styled "Party of Order" (otherwise known as "Union libérale"), set out to restrict democracy. Some leading socialists were arrested, others fled abroad. A new constitution specified a president,

Insurgent barricade in the Faubourg St. Antoine quarter of Paris, at the edge of the
Place de la Bastille, July 1848.

to be elected by universal suffrage. The limitations of this process became evident when to general surprise the winner of the election was
a little-known mediocrity, Prince Louis-Napoleon Bonaparte, a nephew
of the former emperor. The real power was exercised by the conservatives, who were determined to complete the rout of the revolution. A
new Legislative Assembly elected in May 1849 contained about 450
conservatives against an opposition of 250: somewhat fewer than 200
radicals led by Ledru-Rollin, plus assorted "Constitutional" republicans. In June the intervention of French troops to forestall a restoration of Austrian power in northern Italy culminated in a French attack
on Rome, which caused the fall of the Roman republic and the restoration of the pope. On 13 June a demonstration in Paris organized by the
radicals against this betrayal of republican values was suppressed by
the army. A number of radicals were arrested and charged with attempting a coup d'état. The conservatives' fear of a mass electorate

was reflected in a law of May 1850 which disenfranchised all males with judicial records, all with less than three years' residence, and all who could not prove their residence through the tax records—a means of reintroducing a property qualification.

On 2 December 1851 Louis-Napoleon seized personal power in a coup d'état. Three days later, republican resistance in Paris was crushed.

* * *

It has been argued that Herzen's rejection of the Second Republic was a foregone conclusion, that he had arrived in France already a fully formed anarchist and a Russian nationalist, his hopes for the potential of the Russian commune bolstered by his Italian experiences. But it was French "associative socialism"—the ideas of Buchez, Louis Blanc, and Proudhon, and not Russian peasant anarchism—that had sparked his first hopes of a social revolution that would transform modern societies. At the beginning of May it was still far from clear that these figures would have no influence on the shape of the new republic. Indeed, Louis Blanc's concept of industrial "social workshops" (with a similar organization for agriculture) had proved so popular among French workers in the 1840s that the Provisional Government had adopted the name as a cover for its efforts to channel and control working-class discontent. It was the near exclusion of socialists such as these from the Provisional Government that had aroused Herzen's sense of foreboding when, still in Rome, he read the list of those elected. The name of the Romantic poet and onetime royalist Lamartine augured nothing good. Armand Marrast (editor of the moderate republican paper La nationale) was known as an intriguer. Then came a succession of unknown lawyers. Only Ledru-Rollin inspired some hope. Louis Blanc and Albert Martin had nothing in common with the rest. After the June defeat Herzen recalls his euphoria in May 1848, when on entering France again he was addressed as "citoyen." In Paris he observed freedom "in all its republican expanse—posters, newspapers, pamphlets, gatherings on the streets; everywhere there was muscular republican life."[27] He is likely to have been exaggerating his initial elation, the better to convey the extent of his subsequent disillusionment with the revolution, a process chronicled in a continuation of his Letters, which he now addressed only to his Moscow friends, explaining that he had no further wish to disguise his views for the sole satisfaction of having them printed. Direct responses to the unfolding of events, driven alternately by anger and despair with occasional flickers of utopian hope, they have none of the intellectual consistency or calm reflectiveness of his subsequent philosophical analysis of the revolution's defeat in *From the Other Shore*. Their importance lies in what they reveal of the making of that work, as the culminating stage in the transition from the Romantic idealism of his early youth to the sober acceptance of the limits of the historically and humanly possible that he had described in Hegelian terms as suffering through to the truth. He had represented the difficulty of the sacrifices involved in a poetic passage in *Dilettantism* reflecting his acceptance of the absence of a transcendent purpose in his personal life, but he had then not yet lost hope for mankind in that respect—hence the millennial impatience with which he had greeted the beginnings of revolution in Europe as a confrontation between supporters of the old world and representatives of the new.

His second series of *Letters* from Paris begins with the announcement "We have been deceived." He interpreted the failed attempt by the Paris populace on May 15 to unseat the members of the Assembly as a revolt against the state in all its historical forms: "the great protest of Paris against the obsolete claim of legislative assemblies to absolute power, which has always and everywhere been a cover for monarchy, reaction, and the whole decrepit social order." The events of that day "tore the blindfold from my eyes: no room for doubt remains—the revolution has been defeated, and the republic will be defeated in its turn."[28] His subsequent comments on the process that led to that defeat have none of the ironic detachment of the *flâneur* from the Avenue Marigny. He followed closely the debates in the Assembly and the commentaries in radical pamphlets and the press, familiarizing himself with the public personae of the chief actors in the revolution, from the smooth-talking but ineffectual liberal Lamartine to the socialist Ledru-Rollin and the revolutionary firebrand Blanqui. He was present as an observer on the Paris streets during the May demonstration and with Annenkov on June 24, as the barricades were being set up (the two were briefly detained by the forces of order as possible *émeutiers étrangers*.)[29] The fruit of this involvement was a series of acute insights into the mix of conspiracy and confusion that led to the June days, alternating with departures into fantasy where he blames the Provisional Government for its failure to realize his ideal.

* * *

A fortnight before the outbreak of fighting in June, Herzen records some sharp perceptions on the unpreparedness of the major participants in a revolution that had been sparked off by a spontaneous expression of working-class anger supported by a few socialist intellectuals:

> It was a clap of thunder that suddenly realized aspirations long stored up, but far from mature. On 23 February neither Louis-Philippe, nor Guizot, nor the ministers, nor *La réforme*, nor *La nationale* [the two principal Republican papers], nor the opposition, nor even the people who built the first barricades, foresaw how 24 February would end. They wanted reforms—they made a revolution; they wanted to sack Guizot—they sacked Louis-Philippe; they wanted to proclaim the right to hold banquets—they proclaimed a republic. . . . How did this happen? . . . A handful of people belonging to secret societies, courageously fighting on the barricades, backed by the noble instincts of the Paris workers, proclaimed a republic and gave all Europe such a shock that it is still impossible to predict how this universal ferment will end.[30]

The newly liberated populace had then fallen into the hands of a group who knew nothing of their needs and desires and had not faced death in their name. They took their places because there were people bold enough to nominate them—not on the barricades but in the offices of a newspaper, not on a battlefield but in a crowded chamber. Giving the masses no time to draw breath, they appeared before them not as candidates but as a ready-made government, pulling in two opposing directions, Ledru-Rollin seeking to consolidate the revolution, Lamartine to put a brake on it. He and his supporters were alarmed by their success: "They were used to everyday parliamentary opposition, to harmless banquet toasts to revolution and daring newspaper articles . . . and now suddenly they had conquered a kingdom and were sitting on a throne. . . . The first thought that entered their heads was to oppose the revolution."[31] Their immediate goal was to rein in the people, restore internal order, and allay the fears of foreign powers; their choice of means varied from the monarchical to the socialist, with occasional resemblances to the first Revolution's Committee of Public Safety.

Herzen's September *Letter* catalogs the fatal blunders of the Provisional Government, compounded of error and betrayal, that had led to the June Days. It had failed to hold elections either immediately after the February revolution (when popular feeling would have ensured a majority of radical deputies) or with a sufficient delay to allow the radical forces to consolidate themselves. It had neglected to dismiss those who had held office under the previous government. The resulting domination of those who feared the proletariat far more than the reaction ensured the ultimate triumph of the latter. "They wanted somehow or other . . . to keep the peace; and they achieved their goal. They were afraid to break with the old order; they had no new, constructive ideas about the state. Hence that unpleasant and discordant hesitation between various tendencies. Now we would have a law based on socialism, now a command of a purely monarchical nature. In some measures we could see a pale imitation of the Committee of Public Safety, while others retained all the character of a constitutional monarchy. . . . [They] had not given a thought to what should distinguish a new republic from an old monarchy."[32] The principal lesson of the last three terrible months, he concludes, is that while a republic that clings to the "monarchical" principle of reverence for power may appear more decorous than a monarchy, it is in essence no different. It had been thought that through the principle of universal suffrage the French Republic had thoroughly democratized itself, but those elected by this principle had immediately assumed the powers of sultans. Writing to his circle, he cites the case of the committee created by the Constituent Assembly to investigate the demonstration of 15 May and the June uprising; the overwhelming majority of its members were conservatives. When the source and extent of its remit were questioned, the Senate replied that it was invested with the powers of the Assembly, which had the autocratic right to constitute it in the way it had done. "If this is not *l'état c'est moi*, . . . the principle on which slavery and despotism are based, then where has it been more harshly expressed? While government continues to proceed from the principle that . . . the law is above the individual, the representative of power above the citizen, that the minority may be crushed by the majority if that majority is the result of universal suffrage, governments will continue to imagine that the text of laws is religious dogma. . . . They will be aggressive, violent, and monarchical."[33] His principal charge against the Provisional Government was that it had diverted the revolution from what he held to be the inevitable destination of a "true" republic: an anarchist federation of communes. He argues that it had not rejected the two main demands of the February revolution—universal suffrage and "l'organisation du travail" (Louis Blanc's slogan for the transformation of labor relations called for by the socialists)—but had interpreted the first in such a way as to exclude the second. If universal suffrage is not to be an optical illusion, it must be preceded by the dismantling of the centralized state and all its ministries. "The point is emphatically not that the people should gather once a year, choose a deputy and revert again to the passive role of the governed: . . . the commune should be allowed to elect its own government, the region too; all those proconsuls who receive their sacred rank through ministerial consecration must be abolished—only then could the people make genuine use of its rights and in addition, choose its central deputies efficiently."[34]

Herzen's admiration for the Italian peasants and the Paris proletariat had encouraged him in the belief that his ideal coincided with the aspirations of the French masses. But he soon discovered that that was not the case. The April elections had shown that outside the working-class districts of Paris and Lyon, support for any form of socialism was negligible in France. He had ascribed this fact to the Provisional Government's failure to counter the propaganda of the rich landowners and bourgeoisie; but after the June Days he concluded that the French nation was not ready for the kind of republic of which socialists and workers dreamed; it needed to be educated into an understanding of its rights. In his anger and frustration he fell back on what, in a retrospective view of his life, he would describe as the "first religion" of his generation of young Russian democrats: the cult of Rousseau and the Jacobins of 1793. He insists that the revolution could have been saved if the Provisional Government, with the support of the Paris workers and invested with dictatorial powers, had installed new institutions and begun to train the populace in their use (an echo of Rousseau's view that the fundamental goodness of human nature had been so corrupted by society that humans might have to be "forced to be free"). Sadly, it had lacked the revolutionary nerve of a Danton, demolishing the past without a backward glance, "raging and reveling in destruction."[35]

Nostalgically Herzen recalls the Committee of Public Safety, which had installed the Terror. The only contemporary figure on the Left who shared their energy and faith was Blanqui, who was to spend most of his life in various prisons as a consequence of his dedication to revolutionary violence. "Blanqui is a revolutionary for our century"—he had understood that what was required was no less than the wholesale destruction of the existing order. Herzen writes admiringly of the oratorical gifts that had led to his arrest in May 1848. "He inspired the masses, his every word a condemnation of the old world and a call for its execution."[36]

This bloodthirsty yearning for a shortcut to freedom—the antithesis of the arduous path to moral autonomy that Herzen had marked out in his philosophical essays—was a visceral reaction to the slaughter of the June Days, whose traumatizing effect on him would be conveyed in *From the Other Shore*. "To sit in one's room with hands folded . . . to hear all around one, from near and far, shots and cannon fire and screams, the beat of drums, and to know that nearby blood is being shed, people are being stabbed and slaughtered—this is enough to kill one, to drive one insane." Two days later he and Natalie heard the sound of regular gunfire—the firing squads. "Moments like this make one hate for an entire decade, seek revenge all one's life. *Woe to those who forgive such moments!*"[37]

The rage and grief produced in Herzen by this catastrophe in the home of revolution, following so soon on the hopes aroused by the spread of liberation movements through Europe, found immediate expression in an impotent thirst for retribution. Five years earlier, he had welcomed an appeal to violence by another firebrand, Bakunin, who had ended his call for the liquidation of the entire political order in Europe with the phrase "The urge for destruction is also a creative urge." At that time, newly returned from a second period of exile and faced with the prospect of permanent muzzling by the regime, Herzen had expressed envy of this "free man" openly calling for the consignment of all such governments to perdition. Now once again his sober insights into the illusions of Romantic utopianism were not proof against the need to escape from an intolerable reality, as with the collapse of his hopes of socialism in Europe he transferred his attention to Russia's future, resuming his attempts to establish a *juste milieu* between the two warring camps on the issue. In a letter to Ogarev of October 1848, returning to the antithesis over which he had brooded in his last years in Russia, he compared the current state of Europe to the death throes of ancient civilization, with the youthful world of the Slavs in the role of modern barbarians from the East. His friend having declared himself unimpressed by his argument, a month later he backtracks. Without forsaking the Romantic metaphor of historical youth and age, he insists to his circle that he is no Slavophile. Contingency, "an element incomparably more important in history than is believed by German philosophy," will play a role in determining whether the primitive elements of socialism in Slav cultures will be invigorated by Europe's deathbed legacy of socialism or will expire, like the vestiges of communal life among the Germanic peoples. Infancy was as much subject to the hazards of chance as old age. The European proletariat had not reached the stage of development required for a peaceful entry into possession of the fruits of civilization, but they were not prepared to be patient. "Therefore the explosion will be terrible. In [17]93 the Terror and all that came with it was carried out by bourgeois and Parisians; imagine how it will be when the entire proletariat of Europe gets to its feet." Russia was in an even worse predicament than Europe in that it could progress only by renouncing two legacies from the past: the barbarism of the pre-Petrine era and the Westernizing despotism that had succeeded it.

"*Signori*, how infuriating it is that history is not logic; yes, history is *Naturgewalt*, embryology, which has not the slightest interest in our categories."[38] In his essays on science Herzen had emphasized the strength of human resistance to this idea, so much at odds with the spirit of the age. His personal struggle with the temptations of utopian hope now entered a new phase as he began to envisage the possibility of influencing developments in Russia. He had witnessed the power of the press in France as a channel for the dissemination of radical ideas, and in a poignant farewell address to his friends in March 1849 announced his decision to remain in Europe in order to act as his country's uncensored voice abroad. Russia was known in Europe only as a primitive and threatening despotism. Conscious of their cultural inferiority, Russians had hitherto been inexcusably modest about the merits of the peasant commune; it had taken a German to point them out to Europe. It was now time to draw attention to the resemblance between the primitive existence of the Russian masses and the ideal to which European socialism had been striving: "We are advancing toward socialism as the Germanic tribes advanced to Christianity."[39]

Forestalling a further charge of Slavophilism, he stresses the obstacles posed by Russia's backwardness to this ideal. The fruit of Europe's long civilization, respect for the individual and the right of free speech had survived centuries of oppression by church and state. Russia had no such tradition, nor could the virtues of the commune compensate for this lack. The Russian people would have to go through an arduous process of education in order to awaken from the inertia, compliance, and servility instilled by the commune in its historical form. Growing up under a regime of terror, small circles like his own had managed to retain their inner independence, but to infect the population with this spirit, action was needed in the public domain. Why had the uprising of 14 December 1825 so deeply affected the youth of Russia? Because it took place in the capital on Saint Isaac's square. Such public demonstrations, along with freedom of speech in the press and in university lecture halls, had become unthinkable. Protest could only begin from abroad—the role Herzen now intended to assume as Russia's tribune in the West. His qualifications were not impressive. After a year in Paris he remained almost unknown in French radical circles. Having dominated his circle in Moscow, his amour-propre held him back from seeking acquaintance with prominent figures on the French Left whose political horizons did not extend to his benighted country. His main radical contacts in Paris were Bakunin and Sazonov, a former member of his Moscow circle who had established himself in the West; through them he met other European émigrés, including a friend of Bakunin, the German radical poet Georg Herwegh, who had organized a legion of German democrats in March 1848 to link up with republican insurgents in Baden. Chaotic planning had resulted in an ignominious retreat in which the expedition was overtaken by the Prussian army. Herwegh escaped back to Paris, his reputation tarnished by tales of his comic failure. On his return he and his wife Emma became the Herzen family's closest friends, with tragic consequences for Herzen and Natalie.

"I'm far from despair; quite the contrary—my hopes for Russia's future have never been higher."[40] This expression of unbounded optimism seems here to have fulfilled the same compensating function as Herzen's desperate declarations of faith in Providence during his Vyatka exile. In the months following the defeat of 1848, Annenkov and other friends returned to Russia under pressure from the government, and with no involvement in a common cause to distract him from the memory of what he had seen and heard in the June Days, he was overtaken by homesickness, writing to his friends in August of his overwhelming love for Russia: "Sometimes I dream of returning, dream about our impoverished landscapes, . . . our peasants, life at Sokolovo—and I long to throw myself into your arms, like the prodigal son, stripped of everything, with all hope gone." His unhappiness found expression in bouts of xenophobia. In a long letter to Granovsky in May 1849 he describes himself as surrounded by "total chaos, the ugliness of a society in the process of disintegration and decay." Sometimes Granovsky's features, even small details of his dress, appear to him as vividly as if he were about to embrace him—a truly "Russian nature." Even though after a long spell of semi-isolation he had acquired a number of "more or less interesting" acquaintances in Paris, all of them, French, German, and Italian, were so lacking in the "broad nature" of his countrymen, that he despaired of them. He admitted only one exception to this rule—the man whose betrayal of his trust was soon to destroy his personal happiness, his friend Herwegh, "an individual, not parochial like the French, not a lymphatic abstraction like the Germans, not a repellent creature of habit like the English."[41]

The seven years between 1848 and his death were the darkest period of Nicolas I's reign. Spurred on by the discovery of the Petrashevsky circle—a society devoted to the discussion of ideas, in particular those of French socialism—the political police and censorship combined their efforts to prevent revolutionary contamination from the West by stamping out all independent thought. Herzen later recalled those

years, when his sense of isolation was compounded by personal tragedies, as the worst time of his life. There was no news from Russia;
his circle had ceased to write to him, and after he ignored an official
order to return, Russians traveling abroad feared to visit him. The Russian government in contrast had conceived a lively interest in him.

The street demonstration of 13 June, organized by the radical opposition in the Assembly (known as the Mountain, after the Jacobins
of the 1790s) in protest against the participation of French forces in the
fall of the Roman Republic, achieved a disappointingly small turnout
and was swiftly dispersed by a troop of dragoons. Among the protesters
was Herzen, in a group of foreign radicals. He subsequently castigated
the ineptness of the organizers and the absence of any clear aim among
most of the participants, whom he dismissed as mere "choristers of revolution."[42] The Mountain, he observed, had fled without giving birth
even to a mouse.

The authorities used the occasion as a pretext for arresting prominent radicals, including several of Herzen's acquaintances (Ledru-
Rollin escaped to London, where he would spend more than twenty
years in exile). One of those detained revealed that he had met Bakunin, Ivan Golovin (a radical Russian émigré), and the German communist Hermann Ewerbeck at Herzen's apartment. This information
was passed to the tsar via the Russian Embassy in Paris, which had
requested help from the French in tracking down Russian nationals
who threatened the security of the state. Ignoring a demand that he
present himself at the embassy for questioning, Herzen borrowed
the passport of a Wallachian citizen and was safely in Geneva when
the seizure of his papers from his mother's Paris apartment, followed
by investigations of his radical contacts by the Third Department,
resulted in a personal command from the tsar to return to Russia
forthwith.[43]

Escape to Geneva

With a new constitution safeguarding civil liberties, the Swiss confed-
eration was a magnet for political refugees from the upheavals of 1848.
Under its radical president, James Fazy, the canton of Geneva was

especially sympathetic to those seeking to escape the reaction else-where in Europe. Herzen was impressed by the informality of his re-ception by Fazy, and the fact that the policeman summoned to prepare his residence papers wore neither uniform nor epaulettes, but he found the European Left no more congenial in this new setting than they had been in Paris. Herwegh had come to join him in Geneva (together with Natalie and their children Sasha and Tata), and he began to be known in the émigré community, greatly expanded by Germans fleeing the suppression of the uprisings in Frankfurt and Baden, but with few exceptions he pronounced them not worthy of attention. He acquired no new friends among republicans after explaining to them that they had failed because their cause was not worthy of success; even Mazzini, he tells his Moscow circle, frowned on hearing this news.[44] In the same letter he expresses his longing to return to Russia, the stony ground whence an immense future would spring: "But the vintage is not yet ripe—if only a shred of that humanity that comes from a long exposure to enlightenment had found its way into the be-havior of our Russo-German bureaucracy, I would return."[45] His sole remedy for depression was the beauty of the Swiss countryside and the "practical philosophy" he had preached to his circle in Moscow. From abroad he repeats that advice to his introspective friends. "Grasp every passing moment, especially if it is full of poetry, pleni-tude, passion." To live in fear or hope about the future is futile at a time when chance is making nonsense of all calculations and fore-casts. But he could not repress his sense of urgency. In September he writes: "Where can I go, what lies ahead—America or England? I have no idea."[46]

Meanwhile events were preparing the way for what he had defined as his future calling. An opportunity presented itself in February 1849, when the Polish refugee Chojecki ("Charles Edmond") requested his collaboration and financial aid in setting up a journal addressed to European democracy, *La Tribune des peuples*, a project conceived by Adam Mickiewicz. Herzen declined the invitation after hearing a speech by Mickiewicz calling for the liberation of Poland by the army of Louis-Napoleon Bonaparte. A similar project hatched by Mazzini and some other eminent refugees ceased to interest him when he realized that he would have no influence on editorial policy. But the idea of an international radical publication had nevertheless taken root in his mind as the means of accomplishing his self-appointed mission, when he was enticed out of his Swiss solitude by a proposition from a socialist even more isolated than himself: Proudhon.

CHAPTER FOURTEEN

A Glowing Footprint:
Herzen and Proudhon

The one man in France who still had something to say.

Herzen on Proudhon

I call a cat a cat, and I don't believe that I gain much by saying that
that animal is a differentiation of the Great Whole.

Proudhon (on reading Hegel)

Proudhon was the only European socialist with whom Herzen was
to have close relations; yet their collaboration would be brief, and it
revealed significant differences in their approaches to the practical
problems of revolutionary change. Consequently, Proudhon is commonly regarded as merely one among several socialists who influenced
Herzen at the outset of his revolutionary career. The most detailed
study of their relationship to date concludes that his influence was as
"a guide rather than a teacher."[1] But Herzen himself was categorical
on this question. In an obituary of Proudhon in 1865, he salutes him
as his mentor.[2] "I am obliged to you more than you think. You and
Hegel together are responsible for half my philosophical education,"
he had written to him in 1851, addressing him in another letter three
years later as "the only *autonomous* thinker of the Revolution."[3] Elsewhere he describes him as a modern Samson, "shaking the edifice
of Europe from the depths of his prison cell."[4] (Convicted of sedition
for articles ridiculing Louis-Napoleon, Proudhon was then serving a
three-year sentence.) They shared a view of individual freedom that
marked them out from all their radical contemporaries; the root of
this divergence was their understanding of the nature of the self.
Herzen would see his encounter with Proudhon's ideas as crucial in
his passage toward "another shore," the image he chose to convey his
rejection of the comforting illusions that mask the limitations of finite

existence. Focusing on Herzen's debt to the French socialist at a pivotal point in the evolution of his view of freedom will help to disentangle his view from the differing interpretations that have been placed on it.

A Fellow Humanist

The two issued from very different backgrounds. Proudhon was born in 1809 into a family of peasant stock. A bursary enabled him to attend the Collège Royal of Besançon, where the teaching was strongly religious in flavor. His parents' poverty forced him to leave before his final examinations, and at the age of eighteen he became an apprentice printer, a trade at which he worked for many years; he would always see himself as a member of the working class. His rebellious spirit and the influence of his Catholic background drew him to the French Christian socialism of the 1830s and early 1840s. He was a voracious reader, with particular interests in linguistics, philosophy, and theology. His desire to devote himself to writing was fulfilled in 1838 when an award from the Besançon Academy provided him with an income for three years.

De la célébration du dimanche (1839), his first extended work on social issues, contained his anarchist program in embryo. It was followed in 1840 by *Qu'est-ce que la propriété?*, which proclaimed the historical institution of property to be the root of all social injustice. Echoing other religious socialists of the time, Proudhon castigated the official Church for appealing to divine authority to justify the status quo and called for a return to the message of the Gospels. By the mid-1840s he had moved from religious to secular socialism, but his thought retained its strong moral cast. From a much more humble social background than the other students at the Collège Royal, he recalled in his later writings the humiliations of his early life, remarking that the starting point of his defense of the individual's dignity and moral autonomy had been his personal experience of the distinction between classes and the dehumanizing effects of poverty.[5] By contrast, Herzen's early humanism sprang from a Romantic individualism combined with the influence of the Gospels. By the end of the 1830s both thinkers had begun to look to history and philosophy for an explanation of the causes of the abuse of human dignity in the past and present and a formula for their elimination. Both found inspiration in the Young Hegelian humanism that had challenged Hegel's vision of history as the progression of Absolute Spirit. Proudhon's grasp of German philosophy was severely limited by the fact that he had no training in philosophy, did not know German, and had to rely on translations and interpretations; moreover (as his notebooks reveal), he looked to philosophy less to widen his horizons than to confirm his existing opinions.[6] But his acquaintance with Young Hegelian thought, rare among French radicals of the time, would be the intellectual basis of his common ground with Herzen. Herzen had drawn attention to the threat to individual autonomy represented by Hegel's identification of the laws of history with the laws of logic. Proudhon made the same point in less temperate terms: "I don't let myself be fooled by Hegel's metaphysics and formulae. I call a cat a cat, and don't believe that I am much advanced by saying that that animal is a differentiation of the Great Whole, and that God arrives at consciousness of himself in my brain." By constructing the history of Mind through logical reasoning instead of empirical observation, he argued, Hegel was able "to legitimize and explain what is false and inexplicable—for example, property."[7]

Both men deplored what they saw as the misuse of reason and logic by idealist philosophers to distort reality and sanction what observation and experience showed to be unjust, maintaining that the only reliable basis on which to build a defense of human autonomy and rights was the individual's moral sense. It was this that Herzen opposed to the abstractions of Fichte, Schelling, and the Old Hegelians. Proudhon found in Kant a justification for doing the same, declaring that the categorical imperative was a "purely human" Absolute: "not a commandment by a superior authority . . . but . . . the soul's foundation, constituting its highest power and supreme dignity." The fundamental principle dictated by conscience is reciprocity—as expressed in the Gospel precept *"Do unto others as you would have them do unto you."*[8]

The principle of reciprocity, as Proudhon understood it, was incompatible with all traditional notions of political power. Tracing the historical development of human societies in *What Is Property?*, Proudhon succumbs to the fashion of the time, summing up his argument in a "Hegelian formula" with community—the earliest form of social

existence—as thesis, and property as antithesis: "We have only to discover the third term: *synthesis,* and we shall have the solution we
seek."[9] There was, however, little that was Hegelian in Proudhon's
vision of conflict and synthesis. His version was based on his view of
man's moral nature, and it would isolate him from all the socialist
groupings of his time.

He differed from Marxists and utopian socialists alike in denying
that a revolutionary improvement in mankind's social conditions
would eventually lead to its moral perfection. He adopted Feuerbach's
notion of religious alienation, but rejected the Young Hegelians' view
that the conflicts of the religious stage of mankind's development
would ultimately be transcended. There were, he argued, no empirical
grounds to support the notion that humans' natural state was one of
harmony; on the contrary, all the available evidence suggested that
human nature, before it is tamed through education, is inherently
"ferocious." "This work . . . has eternally to begin again for all the
individuals born on this earth. . . . The theory of the excellence of the
passions is complete nonsense."[10] The eradication of social evils was
only part of the moral process of taming the passions with the help of
art, science, and industry—an unceasing battle of mind with animal
instincts. Socialists were wrong to believe that egoism would be replaced as a motivating force in human societies by the drive to "association." These are simply "the two facets of our nature, ever adverse,
ever in the process of reconciliation, but never wholly reconciled."
Monopoly is eternally confronted by competition, property by social
solidarity. If one of these forces is stifled by its opposite, society moves
toward oppression, whether by a caste or a collective. The injustices of
systems based on property ownership had led to a revival of the idea of
"community" in its modern form of communistic socialism, but
these two modes of social organization were opposites only in appearance. Socialist collectivism represented the errors of individualism and
the despotism of property in an inverted form: "Property is exploitation of the weak by the strong; community is exploitation of the strong
by the weak." Along with his possessions, the individual becomes the
property of the state, which imposes a deadening uniformity on talent
and initiative. Mankind continued to believe that there was no alternative to these two models of society—a "deplorable error."[11]

Proudhon's third model was set out in the substantial two-volume *Système des contradictions économiques*, published in 1846. A phrase in his conclusion encapsulates his theme: "Antinomy is the very law of life and progress, the principle of perpetual motion."[12] He argued that contemporary social thought was polarized into the extremes of "tradition" and "utopia," an economic liberalism equating private profit with public good and preaching unrestrained competition, and a socialism that rejected the existing order root and branch in the name of a system existing only in the realm of fantasy. What was required was "a general equation of all our contradictions" according to the principle of reciprocity. Otherwise described as "mutualism" or "progressive association," it was his answer to the problem he had defined in his first important work: "To find a state of social equality that is neither community nor despotism, nor parceling out, nor anarchy; but liberty in order and independence in unity."[13] His solution sprang from a contemporary reality with which he was closely acquainted—mutual aid organizations of skilled workers, which in the face of official hostility grew in popularity and radicalism in the early 1840s, and had come to attract the interest of radical intellectuals (the right to association would be one of the principal demands of 1848). As an employee of a shipping business in the mid-1840s, Proudhon became familiar with the cooperative associations of the Lyon silk workers, aimed at ending their dependence on merchants by ensuring a just price for their products. He held that social change was best achieved not through political reform but by the formation of mutualist societies for production and consumption and a system of exchange in which economic value is based on labor, to be serviced by a people's bank funding credit at low rates, which would eliminate the parasitic role of capitalists and financiers (Saint-Simon's "oisifs"). As they gained in social and economic power, these associations would, he expected, effect a peaceful revolution; the power of the state would dwindle until it became (as in Saint-Simon's conception) an organization for the administration of things, its role reduced to providing services that were beyond the competence of individual associations. While property in the sense of sources of capital and rent would cease to exist, individual ownership would be permitted; initiative and competition would be sustained through competitive relations between associations.

Proudhon was utopian in his hope that cooperative associations could ultimately prevail over the forces of capitalist competition, but he refused to indulge in the notion of a final state of harmony that all human societies were destined to attain, defining progress as "the negation of all immutable forms and formulas, of all doctrines of eternity, impeccability, and of all permanent order, not excepting that of the universe."[14] The moral content of his socialism has been likened to Kant's moral ideal: a criterion by which to judge human behavior.[15] He opposed the hardening of insight into dogma among the German communists, earning their enmity through the manner of his response to a letter from Marx inviting him to join his international socialist organization:

> By all means let us work together to discover the laws of society. . . . But for God's sake, when we have demolished all a priori dogmas, do not let us think of indoctrinating the people in our turn. Do not let us fall into your compatriot Martin Luther's inconsistency. As soon as he had overthrown Catholic theology he at once, with constant recourse to excommunications and anathemas, set about founding a Protestant theology. . . . Let us not make further work for humanity by creating another shambles. . . . Let us not set ourselves up as apostles of a new religion, even if it be the religion of logic or of reason. Let us welcome and encourage all protests, . . . let us never consider any question exhausted, and when we have used our very last argument, let us begin again, if necessary, with eloquence and irony. On this condition I will join your organization with pleasure, otherwise I will not.[16]

On the question of systems he declared: "I do not have one, I do not want one, I formally reject the assumption. The system of humanity will not be known until the end of humanity. . . . What interests me is to identify its path and if I am able, to mark it out."[17] To represent that path as a shifting balance between inherently irreconcilable forces was to underline the relative and conditional nature of his own social prescriptions, a fact of which he was acutely aware. He stressed that workmen's associations were not absolute goods, as they placed limits on individual liberty and initiative; they must be seen as pragmatic responses to the needs of individuals or groups in particular circumstances. In some cases these needs might be better met by other arrangements (such as personal contracts). He objected even to the principle of association when elevated into a dogma by his fellow socialists: "Let humanity perish sooner than the principle! That is the motto of the Utopians, as of the fanatics of all ages."[18] He warned of the threat posed to individual liberty by a modernized version of primitive communism: there was no greater danger for society than to shipwreck once more on that rock. Philosophically reborn as atheistic humanism, this ancient dream claimed to satisfy the deepest yearnings of humanity—yet, Proudhon argued, the vision of human nature on which it rested was a lie. His critique of it would have passed unnoticed were it not for Marx's counterattack on him a year later, but it deserves attention for its insight into the authoritarianism hidden in the liberating philosophy of the Young Hegelians. In Proudhon's lifetime it would be echoed by only one other prominent socialist—Herzen.

The French Feuerbach

Proudhon devoted the prologue and the final chapter of the first volume of *Contradictions* to a lengthy discussion of the hypothesis of God, for which he made no apologies, arguing that the science of economics was only the practical application of philosophical theories of the existence of God, the nature of certitude, and the destiny of humanity. His attitude to religion in the early 1840s had earned him the admiration of German radicals, one of whom, Karl Grün, called him the "French Feuerbach."[19] Following Comte's triadic schema of historical development, he viewed his age as a period of transition from religion to philosophy as the source of humans' understanding of their place in the world; in the final stage, this role would be filled by science. But while echoing Feuerbach on the religious alienation of man, he rejected the Young Hegelians' belief that humans would progress toward perfection by reappropriating the attributes they had traditionally projected onto a divinity, professing himself unimpressed by this new religion "in which people vainly seek to interest me by telling me that I am its God."[20] On the evidence of history and psychology, the attributes of perfection, infinity, and absolute harmony habitually ascribed to the divinity were not the potential of human nature, but fundamentally contrary to it. Change, progress, and conflict were essential to our being: "We live, think, feel only through a series of oppositions, shocks, internecine war; our ideal is thus not infinity but equilibrium." Atheistic humanists would retort that they idealized not fallible individuals, but humanity, conceived in the totality of its manifestations, "as if all human generations, reunited in a single instant, formed a single person, infinite and immortal." To discover "real" man, one must quit the dimensions of time and space, which goes back full circle to religious alienation, with mankind subjected to a new invisible master, its own collective ego. Radical humanists would argue that their transcendental vision of humanity anticipated a new social reality, qualitatively different from all that had gone before, but this was mere rhetoric, based on a confusion of the finite with the infinite. The progress of human societies through the forces of reason and science was a self-evident fact, but at no stage of civilization had this process involved a metaphysical leap of the kind envisaged by the builders of utopias. "However excellent the future condition of humanity may be, it will be nonetheless the natural continuation, the necessary consequence, of what has gone before."[21]

Humanity's ideal of happiness was "permanent youth, serenity of soul, absolute dominion over ourselves, faultless knowledge, unfailing love, omnipotence, immortality."[22] But the brief span and physical limitations of terrestrial existence allowed humans the sole fulfillment of making a finite contribution to the edifice of science and human happiness. Proudhon argued that the most pernicious source of superstition in his age was atheistic humanism's deification of mankind, whose vices were attributed to the constraints imposed on it in the past. Inevitably man would come to recognize that he is neither God, nor saint, nor sage, and would throw himself back into the arms of religion. "In the last analysis, all that will have been gained by the rejection of God will be the resurrection of God."[23] He expressed regret that his attack on atheistic humanism had estranged him from "the most intelligent of contemporary socialists"—the school of Feuerbach; but his tone was not conciliatory. He dismissed their revolution in philosophy and sociology as a reaffirmation of the authoritarian status quo. Atheistic self-deification "is merely the final echo of the old religious terrors: under the name of *humanism* it rehabilitates and consecrates mysticism, brings superstition back into science, habit back into morality, community—that is, inertia and privation—into political economy, the Absolute and the absurd back into logic."[24]

* * *

Proudhon found it easier to expose the inconsistencies of atheistic humanism than to construct a philosophically consistent humanism in its place. He rejected thoroughgoing materialism, which he saw as a mere variation of the theological argument. Both postulated an absolute order that left no place for individual autonomy. Whether that order was predicated on an omniscient Creator or blind necessity was of small significance. Theories of historical determinism were no more than a covert reaffirmation of the doctrine of Divine Providence, while the theological and transcendental conclusions the Young Hegelians drew from their radical critique were an unconvincing attempt to capture the attributes of divinity for mankind. Not atheism but "anti-theism" was the necessary premise for the defense of individual moral autonomy. True virtue, he declared, is "to fight against religion and against God."[25]

He argued that the evidence of history showed that if God existed, his qualities not only would be unattainable by humans (as creatures whose nature is defined by change and conflict)—they would also be hostile to humanity. By projecting onto a deity qualities antithetical to their own, humans had constructed a being that was not only their opposite but also their enemy. What was one to make of a Providence that endowed man with false and contradictory beliefs and then punished him for his errors with bloody catastrophes? Proudhon insisted that he was proposing, not a rejection of humanism, but its logical extension: war against all absolutes not open to the scrutiny of reason. Progress conceived in this way consisted in a series of victories over the concept of divinity.

But to accept Feuerbach's contention that the image of God has been engendered by human needs was not to deny the objective possibility of an Absolute. To do so, Proudhon contends, would be to accept that the world is governed by blind fate: it was to fill this moral emptiness that the atheist was forced to deify mankind. To escape the negative consequences of religious and atheistic dogmatism alike, he resorts to an ingenious third alternative: "I need to admit the hypothesis of God. I'm no longer able to agree with any other hypothesis because of the consequences I anticipate from the divinization of man."[26] The empirical nature of human consciousness suggested this to be a legitimate conclusion. "We are full of divinity, *Jovis omnia plena*; our monuments, our traditions, our laws, our ideas, our languages and our sciences all are infected by that indelible superstition, outside which it is not given to us to speak or to act, and without which we do not even think." The tenacity of religious belief throughout history, the distinctions inherent in human consciousness between intelligence and necessity, matter and spirit, the subject of thought and its object, were compelling evidence of an eternal dualism. Religion had converted belief in God into passive obedience to kings and priests, but the assertion of human independence from these earthly powers was insufficient to exclude the possibility of some infinite sphere of existence. In philosophical speculation our reach continued to exceed our grasp, while the progress of science had revealed nature to be "a magical laboratory, from which anything can be expected." The most advanced conclusions of reason lead us back to a primordial unknown, a "secret affinity," suggesting some as yet inconceivable harmony between finite and infinite.[27] In a letter of 1843 he writes optimistically, "Far from destroying what religion inspires of honest, heroic, mysterious sentiments and sublime hopes, it is only a question of giving these sentiments a scientific, positive base, which would transform them, purify them, and lift them out of the domain of theologians."[28] Although this remained a possibility, it was also undeniable that human life as we experience it represents an "antithetical stage" of existence in which freedom and intelligence can be asserted only through confrontation and conflict with our sense of the infinite and its manifestations in religion. Thus, Proudhon concludes, "practical atheism must be the law of my heart and my reason."[29]

This extraordinary philosophical construction (whose kinship with the "Godfighting" [*bogoborchestvo*] of Dostoevsky's Ivan Karamazov has been noted)[30] has puzzled most commentators on Proudhon. It has been argued that some of his "antinomies" (for example, his representation of the deity as both a transcendent being and a projection of human needs) are in fact contradictions; and efforts have been made to follow the twists of his philosophical maze with the aim of defining which of these two positions he actually held—resulting, in the case of two of the principal studies of Proudhon, in opposing conclusions.[31]

Pierre Haubtmann contends that Proudhon's argument rests on a confusion. The God he depicts is the God of Islam or the Old Testament, not of Christianity, which is not a religion of fatalism. The evils he attacked sprang from the distortion of Christian teaching by the established Church. Proudhon did not really believe in his anti-theism: it was forced on him by the necessity of fighting the German humanists with their own weapons. Hence the ingenious logic that purported to be more consistent with Feuerbach's dialectic than Feuerbach himself (and which, by representing the process of salvation as a battle with the Creator, appealed to Proudhon's combative temperament). K. S. Vincent, on the other hand, sees what he terms the philosophical confusions in Proudhon's argument as evidence of an agonizing struggle with the remnants of his religious beliefs, ultimately resolved by a clear rejection of transcendent sources of ethical and social values.

Neither interpretation does justice to the originality of Proudhon's position. Anti-theism was certainly a direct reflection of Proudhon's inner conflicts over the question of immortality and the existence of God (with which his notebooks show him to have been preoccupied in the mid-1840s). But he saw his ambivalence as a particular instance of a universal human predicament, which he describes as a discord between the actual capacities of humans and the age-old notion of a future perfect society—"a contradiction between humanity and its ideal." He rightly believed himself to be original in drawing attention to this "fundamental antinomy" in an age of utopian hope.[32] The fact that his perceptions, when not ignored, have been largely misrepresented owes much to the tortuous and inflated rhetoric in which they were too often conveyed. Proudhon was very much an amateur philosopher, competing with his sophisticated German contemporaries in that field to convey insights whose source was observation and experience rather than analytical reason. He anticipates the derision of the Young Hegelians and Marxists defensively: "Am I to blame if . . . the mere suspicion of the existence of a Supreme Being is already regarded as the mark of a feeble intellect, and if, of all philosophical Utopias, it's the only one the world will no longer tolerate?" But he insists that a sense of infinity is an integral part of human conscious-ness, and thereby a legitimate object for discussion and hypothesis. Much of this discussion is a poetically immediate expression of the conflicts of the creature whose reach exceeds his grasp, whose finite reason confronts infinity in science, whose sense of unbounded poten-tial is contradicted by meager achievement, who experiences an "in-comprehensible emptiness" when he denies God and seeks him in man, but equally rebels against the notion of transcendence as an insult to his reason and a denial of his autonomy; and who in despair is driven to imagine a malevolent deity who, having made us "contradictory . . . in our thoughts, contradictory in our words, contradictory in our actions," laughs to hear us gravely discuss the meaning of justice and injustice.[33]

There is no coded certitude in this text. The intensity of psychic conflict in modern man, his obsessive yearning to be otherwise con-stituted than he is, had led all Proudhon's socialist contemporaries to conclude that the moment of transformation was close. Proudhon's originality was to draw from the same evidence the contrary conclu-sion, to argue on both logical and empirical grounds that all theories—from the myths of the golden age to the "scientific" socialism of Marx—that deduce from present conflict the promise of future har-mony, dominion over oneself and nature, have no empirical foundation whatsoever. Theories refusing to take into account existing socioeco-nomic contradictions and the conflicts in the psyche that generate them "were summed up long ago by Plato and Thomas More in a single word, UTOPIA—that is, no-place, a chimera."[34] Polemical ne-cessity forced him to mount his attack on utopia with the help of the only human yearning totally discredited on the Left—an irony that, as he foresaw, would lead to the misrepresentation of his argument. That argument, far-reaching in its implications, is that the belief that the true fulfillment of humans lies in being otherwise constituted than they currently are is the ideological source of all forms of reli-gious and political despotism.

Herzen and Proudhon on Freedom

Anti-theism was an attack on utopian visions of human potential. It was also a working hypothesis to defend the alternative conception of the human psyche on which Proudhon's anarchism was based. This conception was the source of his differences with contemporary socialists, and, as will be argued below, of his affinities with Herzen. As a preliminary to the discussion of their relationship, it will be useful here to summarize the parallels between Proudhon's view of individual freedom and the one Herzen had formulated independently before his departure from Russia.

The two shared a view of the personality as bearer of moral and spiritual values that sprang from the Romantics' revolt against Enlightenment rationalism. Two main influences had molded their concept of freedom: the religiously tinged humanism of early French socialism and the Young Hegelian demand for the liberation of humans in their concrete sensuous existence from the thrall of philosophical abstraction. But both rejected the Fourierist belief in the inherent virtue of the passions. Like *Dilettantism in Science* (published a year earlier), *Contradictions économiques* sets out an approach to human self-fulfillment equally distinct from the constructs of rationalist universalism and from the cult of feeling.

Proudhon argues there that human nature in the raw is a "constellation of potentialities" whose realization depends on the exercise of individual choice.[35] While maintaining that the struggle between moral imperatives and "animal" instincts is a permanent feature of social existence, he rejected all conventional views—religious, conservative, and radical—of its nature, expressing equal contempt for the Christian notion of self-perfection as the practice of self-hatred in the hope of eternal life ("precisely the opposite to what reason prescribes"), and the ideal of *communauté* as preached by the socialists for "the iron yoke it imposes on the will, the moral torture in which it grips the conscience, the inertia into which it plunges society, and . . . the stupid uniformity in which it enchains the free, active, reasoning, unsubmissive personality of man."[36] Such a notion of moral obligation was repellent to the conscience. "Man is quite willing to submit to the law of duty, to serve his country, to oblige his friends, but he wishes . . . to give service through reason, not on command, to sacrifice himself through egoism, not servile obligation. If it is a duty to support the weak, man wants to perform this duty out of generosity. . . . Equity is sociability raised by reason and justice to the level of an ideal."[37]

There are close parallels here with the model of moral life with which Herzen was already familiar from his reading of Schiller's *Aesthetic Education*. Proudhon distinguishes between justice—the essential moral basis of social intercourse—and equity, variously defined as *humanitas*, urbanity, or *politesse*: the form the universal human instinct of solidarity takes in an intellectually and morally developed individual. It is equity that makes it "at one and the same time a duty and a pleasure to aid the weak . . . , to treat him as an equal, to give just tribute of recognition and honor to the strong without becoming his slave."[38] Pleasant and agreeable to all, equity can make distinctions between ranks, virtues, and capacities without causing offense. Without compromising justice, equity can enhance it with the qualities of aesthetic taste, love, esteem, and the human capacity to idealize. Proudhon's argument echoes Schiller's distinction in his debate with Kant between moral dignity and moral grace, the latter to be achieved through the cultivation of imaginative empathy as the ally of the will.[39] It is to the aesthetic sense of equity that he looks to maintain the delicate balance in a future society whereby genius and talent will neither be used to exploit others nor smothered by egalitarian mediocrity.

To sum up: in an age that saw the birth of modern historicist doctrines and secular teleologies, Herzen and Proudhon were distinguished by their struggle to confront the question of humans' nature and potential without superimposing their personal goals and values on the historical process. Proudhon's religious roots and Herzen's search for a redeeming significance in the sterile existence of his generation predisposed both to rebel against what Proudhon called the "emptiness" of a world with no transcendent purpose. But their humanism was incompatible with all contemporary attempts to justify or explain present suffering as a stage in the advance to future bliss. They had developed their ideas in vastly different circumstances—Proudhon in the process of conflicts in person and in print with opponents of all political persuasions, Herzen in solitary reflections or discussions within his small circle on philosophy, science, and history. But Herzen's "speculative empiricism" and Proudhon's "practical atheism" were attempts to confront the same dilemma. They had each come independently to believe that humans could realize the maximum of freedom possible for their species only when they ceased to aspire to a form of perfection contrary to their nature. Both of them would maintain this belief in the face of increasing hostility from the radical movements of their time.

* * *

In the aftermath of 1848 Proudhon's views on the ends and means of social transformation had succeeded in alienating him from radicals and moderates alike. In contrast to both groups he described himself as a defender both of progress and conservation.[40] In terms of practical tactics, this meant the attempt to work for social reform through a resolution of the conflict between social groups and classes. He believed that the bourgeoisie could be shown that their economic interests were not at odds with those of the workers: they had a common concern in eliminating the economic parasitism of the "oisifs." But the cooperation of the bourgeoisie in the process of social transformation had much more than tactical importance for him—the principle of individualism they represented was an essential ingredient of his concept of liberty. He attached such importance to their past contribution to the realization of individual liberty that he dedicated his book *Idée générale de la révolution* to them: "It is you . . . who for eighty years have proclaimed . . . all the revolutionary ideas: freedom of worship, freedom of the press, freedom of commerce and industry; you who, through your skillful constitutions have reined in the altar and the throne; you who have established on indestructible foundations equality before the law, legislative control, the publication of state accounts, the subordination of the government to the country, the sovereignty of opinion."[41]

Although he would excoriate the bourgeoisie for betraying these ideals in their support for the suppression of the revolution, he believed that without their influence the masses were likely to jettison the principle of individual freedom in the name of equality. "The people have no conception of municipal, departmental, corporative liberties, of individual guarantees of freedom. . . . They enjoy accomplishing the big things: centralization, indivisible republic, unitary empire. For the same reason, the people are communistic."[42] In his work of 1845, *The Holy Family,* Marx had praised Proudhon as the first thinker to have demonstrated the inhumanity of the concept of property. But in his response to Marx's invitation to join his organization, Proudhon had declared his opposition to the arbitrary violence of revolution as the means of social reform: "I would rather burn property little by little than give it renewed strength by making a Saint Bartholomew's Day bonfire of property owners."[43] He expands on this theme in *Contradictions*, arguing that a communist revolution would turn citizens into the property of the state. Marx retaliated in 1847 with *The Poverty of Philosophy*, the first published statement of his historical materialism and a violent attack on Proudhon's "idealist" and "unhistorical" approach to class conflict, as characteristic of the class ideology of the petty bourgeoisie.

If Marx saw the concept of reconciliation as the cornerstone of Proudhon's theory of progress, moderate reformers identified Proudhon with the notion of "permanent revolution," a phrase he had used at a banquet of socialists in 1848 to convey his view of history as a process of perpetual adjustment between the forces of progress and conservation, individual liberty and social solidarity.[44] Removed from its context, it served to reinforce his reputation as an agent of destruction. He was unsparing in his criticism of his fellow socialists, including Louis Blanc, who shared his view of existing workers' associations as models for the future organization of society but believed these should be overseen by a watchful state to stamp out the evils of egoism and competitiveness, which he saw as corruptions of human nature. Rather than accepting men as they are, Proudhon wrote, "M. Blanc requires men made expressly for him."[45]

Turning to full-time political journalism in 1844, Proudhon condemned the Left's emphasis on political objectives to the detriment of social reform. After February 1848 he urged the Provisional Government to address the economic causes of the current crisis through the formation of "progressive associations." His journalism was highly popular among the Paris working class (he was to be involved with four papers after the February revolution, all of which would be suppressed by the government), but after his election to the Constituent Assembly in June 1848, his isolation among French radical theorists became complete. Although even after the suppression of the June rising he continued to urge conciliation between the working class and the bourgeoisie, the attention of the French press and political parties was concentrated exclusively on his attacks on religion and his calls for the abolition of the state and the current property structure. Louis

Caricature of Pierre-Joseph Proudhon as destroyer of property and subverter of the established order.

Blanc, who held that the state should play a key role in the transition to socialism, defined Proudhon's anti-statist views as "the code of tyranny by chaos."[46]

The two most notorious phrases of his writings—"Dieu, c'est le mal" and "la propriété, c'est le vol"[47]—were constantly quoted in papers whose cartoonists depicted him as a bloodthirsty monster; as he

noted in 1849, he had become "l'homme-terreur" of the French bourgeoisie. He wrote with relish that he had been attacked on all sides: by
communists for criticizing community, by proprietors for criticizing
property, and by politicians for calling for anarchy.[48]

His enemies simplified him in accordance with their personal de-
monologies, while his few sympathizers were hard put to locate his
"system of contradictions" anywhere on the existing political spectrum. Bakunin suggested that there were "two Proudhons: *a reformist
lawyer*, well combed and clean-shaven, and *a true proletarian revolutionary*."[49] Proudhon himself reveled in the role of iconoclast: "I shall
not cease to pursue the truth through ruins and rubble. I hate work
that is half done, and you may be certain . . . that if I have dared to
place my hand on the sacred ark, I won't rest until I have lifted off its
lid."[50] His sacrilegious attack on the arks of rationalist certitude and
atheistic humanism earned him the enmity of the Left, but his positive
ideas were built on firmer ground than those of his critics. Ridiculed by
Marx and Engels as contrary to the march of history, his concept of
workers' associations was inspired by structures already in existence in
large industrial towns in France. At that period it would have been
hard to predict the extent of their growth, although Proudhon's hope
that they could come to dominate the country's economy, replacing
traditional relationships of power and subordination rather than
becoming infected by them in their turn, presupposed a faith in
humans' ability to learn from their mistakes that is unsupported by
historical experience. His reputation never recovered from Marx's
venomous distortion of his thought, but unlike the facile constructs
of "scientific socialism," his views on the nature and limits of freedom
were well in advance of his time. He did not exaggerate in claiming as
his greatest achievement to have illuminated "the dual face of things."[51]

* * *

Herzen's admiration for Proudhon's empirical approach to social change
had grown along with his conviction of the importance of the methods
of the natural sciences as tools for the study of history. In 1848 he describes *Contradictions* (which he had just finished reading) to his
Moscow friends as "the most serious and profound work to have appeared in France over the last decade."[52] He was already familiar with
Proudhon's concept of mutual associations; what was new in *Contra-*

dictions was his colorful attack on the delusions of his fellow-socialists, in which the iconoclasm that had so enchanted Herzen in Feuerbach's *Essence of Christianity* was extended to the earthly paradise to which the doctrinaire Left aspired.

Bringing his Moscow circle up to date with the revolutionary events that had preceded his arrival in May 1848, Herzen describes Proudhon as belonging to no political parish, a solitary figure pasting manifestos on the barricades in the February days.[53] Proudhon had been opposed to the republicans' banquet campaign, commenting in his notebooks, "Political reform will be the result, not the means, of social reform."[54] Following the February revolution he set down his position in *Solution du problème social*, published in three installments in a paper he had launched as a mouthpiece for his views. He insisted that universal male suffrage—the banner of the republicans in the Provisional Government—was incapable of resolving the fundamental problem of social injustice. A democracy that relied on this device was merely a "disguised aristocracy": in a true Republic, "every citizen participates directly in legislation and government, as he participates in the production and circulation of wealth. . . . The Republic is a positive anarchy."[55] He concluded his manifesto with his conception of an equitable exchange of commodities between cooperatives of producers and consumers, serviced by a people's bank.

Proudhon's insistence on the primacy of economic and social issues over politics isolated him from other French radicals. In the elections of April 23 he stood unsuccessfully for several constituencies, commenting bitterly in his notebooks, "In Lyon the communists have revenged themselves by eliminating me, in Besançon it is the propriétaires. . . . In Paris I owe the absolute silence concerning me to the rancor of the journalists and of the statesmen of the provisional government."[56] In a complementary election to the Constituent Assembly in June he managed to gain a seat, which he used as a platform for his views on the importance of the social question. Maintaining his stance as an outsider aligned with no political party, he achieved notoriety by presenting a proposal to its Finance Committee to resolve the economic crisis by requiring property owners to give up a third of their rents received, half of which would go to the tenants, the other half to the state. Condemnation of the proposal having been approved enthusiastically by the Assembly, he responded in a speech lasting three and a half hours, calling for the abrogation in France of the absolute right to property as the implementation of a principle implicit in the character of the February revolution. "In case of refusal we ourselves will proceed with the liquidation without you." Asked for elucidation of the two pronouns, he explained that it was obvious: he identified himself with the proletariat and his opponents with the bourgeoisie.[57] Marx would subsequently comment that although it showed how little Proudhon understood what was happening, his speech "deserves the highest praise. After the June rising it was an act of high courage."[58] Following uproar in the chamber, a motion of censure was passed condemning Proudhon's suggestion as "an odious attack on the principles of public morals."[59] The vote was 689 in favor (including Pierre Leroux and Louis Blanc) and only 2 against: Proudhon and a working-class representative from Lyon.

In the wake of the June Days, Proudhon was the only radical exempted from Herzen's critique. Herzen was impressed by his fearless and increasingly isolated protests against the savagery of the government's reprisals. He had dared to ask for publication of the numbers of those killed in the fighting or massacred as prisoners—without result, as Herzen tells his circle. In August, in a bitter letter describing the terror that had engulfed Paris—"there can now be no conciliation, no truce"—he promises to send them Proudhon's notorious speech to the Assembly. On embarking on his collaboration with him in the following year, he writes to his friends, "You have a right to ask: Who stands on the same shore as you? If there were no one, there would be no harm, and the truth would not thereby cease to be the truth. However, I can add one name to the list of *virorum obscurorum*—Proudhon's name." Even incarcerated in his prison, he was more effective than the most radical of the refugees of 1848. "Proudhon is the true incarnation of the revolutionary principle in France."[60]

A Treaty with a Barbarian

Herzen had first met Proudhon in Paris in 1847 at the lodgings of Bakunin, whose interest in Hegel Proudhon shared. (Their discussions on philosophy were reputed to often last throughout the night.) Apart from two chance meetings in that year, Herzen had no personal contact with him again until August 1849, when Proudhon, then in prison, approached him through a go-between (the Polish émigré Karl-Edmund Chojecki), offering him the chance to collaborate in a new paper, *La voix du peuple*, in return for supplying the caution money required by the authorities.

Herzen replied after a silence of nearly three weeks, agreeing to provide the required sum in return for full rights as co-editor in sole charge of the paper's foreign section, pointing out the advantage his collaboration would bring, "knowledge of other peoples not being your compatriots' strong point."[61] This cool reaction to an overture from the man he so much admired was, as his memoirs reveal, dictated by a very vulnerable amour-propre. "I wanted to show [Proudhon] from the very first that he was not dealing with a mad *prince russe* who was giving the money from revolutionary dilettantism, and still more from ostentation, nor with an orthodox admirer of French journalism, deeply grateful for their accepting 24,000 francs from him, nor finally with a dull-witted 'bailleur de fonds,' who imagined that providing the guarantee for such a paper . . . was a serious business investment. I wanted to show him that I knew well what I was doing, that I had a definite objective, and therefore wanted to have a definite influence on the paper."[62]

In a response that was a model of diplomacy, Proudhon expressed agreement with Herzen's demands while making it clear that he himself would retain full responsibility for the paper's "general direction," reassuring Herzen that as they were at one on fundamental principles, he did not anticipate having to question his views.[63] Honor having been satisfied, Herzen opened his soul to him in a "confession" accompanying the signed contract: "Do you know, Sir, that you have signed a treaty with a barbarian . . . all the more incorrigible in that he is such not only by birth, but by conviction." As a true Scythian, he intended to imbue the foreign section of the new journal with his profound and all-embracing hatred of the dying civilization of old Europe and his pleasure at the prospect of its imminent demise. The revolution had failed because it had not deserved to succeed: its protagonists had not freed themselves from the religious and monarchical traditions of the past. Liberty born in the arms of such midwives would not be worth having. "Let's rather have barbarism to refresh our slack-ened morals, our effeminate souls." He expresses confidence that his bloodthirsty rhetoric will find favor with Proudhon:

> I know only one free Frenchman: yourself. Your revolutionaries are reactionary, they are men of the old world, they are not free, they are Christians without knowing it, monarchists even when fighting monarchy!
>
> You have raised negation to the level of a science . . . you have been the first in France to say that there is no salvation within the boundaries of this putrefying world, that all that it has produced is infected with an aristocratic spirit, with slavery, contempt for indi-viduals, injustice, monopoly. . . . For this reason I believe that you will sympathize with my barbarian way of seeing things—at least, I flatter myself that this is so.[64]

Only two months before, in a gloomy letter to Ogarev from the isola-tion of his Geneva exile, Herzen had identified with those Roman phi-losophers who, equally repelled by the corruption of the ancient world and the barbarism of its conquerors, had chosen to live out their lives in isolation. By offering him a role in the unfolding of events, Prou-dhon's proposition encouraged him to see himself in a more positive light as a reincarnation of the barbarians from the East who had rein-vigorated the declining West. But he had spectacularly misjudged his correspondent. As he had made clear to Marx, contrary to his reputa-tion as "l'homme-terreur," Proudhon consistently opposed violence as an instrument of political change. While sympathizing with the insur-gents' aims, he had called for conciliation in May and June 1848, opposing the concept of class war with his faith in the peaceful trans-formation of societies through the economic organization of the masses. His new paper was intended to convey the same message. To Chojecki's letter outlining the project he had added a postscript whose significance seems to have escaped Herzen, emphasizing its function in keeping the public informed of political developments: "Il ne s'agit plus d'agiter le peuple avec du pathos, mais d'éclairer la bourgeoisie elle-même sur ses propres intérêts. [It's no longer a question of stirring up the people with emotionalism, but of enlightening specifically the bourgeoisie about its own real interests.]"[65] As he had emphasized in a chapter on competition in *Contradictions*, his concept of revolution did not include physical force. It demanded constant renegotiation of the balance between the satisfaction of the individual ego and the requirements of social existence, through the development of bonds of mutual interest between groups and classes in society. Human life was "permanent war"—war against need, nature, other humans, and the self—but there was no reason why the engagements should be bloody.[66] Herzen's ignorance of this aspect of his thought adds weight to the suspicion that in reading Contradictions, Herzen had paid attention primarily to what has been described as its "astonishing display of anti-religious fireworks."[67]

When Herzen's fulsome tribute met with no immediate response, he concluded bitterly that he had made the mistake of addressing a great economist as an ordinary man, remarking to Herwegh (who had become his partner in the negotiations) that so long as Proudhon kept to their contract, he would not insist on his friendship. The eventual reply was a model of tactful restraint. Herzen having mentioned his own ongoing essays on the philosophical significance of 1848, Proudhon informed him that he had written a similar work (his Confessions d'un révolutionnaire). Herzen would be disappointed not to find in it the "verve barbaresque" to which German philosophy and the proximity of northern races had accustomed him. (Proudhon's Hegelian discussions with Bakunin in Paris had familiarized him with the notion of the creative force of the urge for destruction.) But he should remember that Proudhon was writing for the French, "who for all their revolutionary fire are, one must admit, far inferior to their role." He assured Herzen that he entirely shared his opinion of the doctrinairism of French and German "so-called" republicans. "I also think like you that a peaceful, methodical advance by means of imperceptible transitions, such as pure economic theory and the philosophy of history would wish, is no longer possible for the revolution: we must make fearful leaps. . . . But as journalists announcing social catastrophes, we should never present them as inevitable or just . . . , or we shall be hated and persecuted. After all, we have to live."[68]

This interchange reflects the cultural distance between the two. On the question of the practical application of political philosophy, Proudhon had a head start over Herzen. Grounded in personal experience of the lives of those whom he championed, his view of the limits of the possible had been shaped by public debate and direct observation of the clash of contending interests and goals in a complex capitalist economy dominated by a bourgeoisie. The primacy of economics over politics and plans for the organization of credit, aimed at transforming the concept of property from a divisive to a unifying force in society, were central themes of his writings in 1848–1850. Such concerns were alien to a persecuted intellectual from a backward country, fresh from the hothouse of his circle and convinced of the power of ideas to transform human societies. Herzen had shown scant concern with the contemporary realities of peasant life in the Russian commune, confessing to Ogarev his lack of interest in practical economic matters. A year in the West had not changed his priorities. In his *Letter* of June 1849 he protests against the tendency to reduce socialism to questions of material well-being. Economic questions "represent only one aspect of an entire world view that seeks to eradicate along with the abuse of property . . . all monarchical and religious elements in the courts, in government, in the entire structure of society, and above all, in the family, in private life, around the fireside, in behavior, in morality."[69] Proudhon would have endorsed this view, but with the proviso that these goals could be pursued only through the uphill process of economic reform. Having arrived in Paris from Italy with extravagant hopes of a revolution in human minds, Herzen's immediate recourse from despair was the Romantic notion of historical death and rebirth, which had been a source of meaning and hope in his personal life since his first encounter with it in early adolescence in an obscure French novel depicting the death of the classical world and the rise of the new Christian era. The opening phrase of *Dilettantism*—"We live on the border between two worlds"—had indicated a sense of alienation so extreme as to demand a full-scale transformation of human societies, an expectation reflected in his reaction to the revolutions of 1848. As he cast around for some grounds for continuing hope in the ensuing carnage, it would have seemed not unreasonable to him to interpret it as the birth pangs of a new world, with socialism performing the function previously fulfilled by Christianity.

But Proudhon was not dealing with another Bakunin. Whereas Bakunin was to build a revolutionary career on a cult of violence as the means to a millenarian goal, Herzen's bloodthirsty imprecations were the short-lived effect of his traumatized reaction to the horrors he had seen on the Paris streets in June, a point he makes twenty years later, in the course of a powerful condemnation of Bakunin's cult of destruction. "Standing next to corpses, next to houses destroyed by shells, listening in a fever to prisoners being shot, with all my heart and all my mind I invoked wild forces to exact revenge and to destroy the outworn, criminal social order—invoked them, without even giving much thought to what would replace it."[70] His letter to Proudhon was composed while these impressions were still vivid in his mind, and the bravado of the self-image that failed to impress his correspondent can be seen as a form of compensation for his actual impotence and irrelevance as an spectator in a battle in which he could play no part. In his letters to Moscow, while still clinging to the notion of a new world, he had become increasingly careful to surround his antithesis between old Europe and the youthful Slavs with caveats, followed in a letter to Herwegh in July 1850 by a sober appraisal of his own divided identity as a Europeanized Russian, fluctuating between two cultures and torn between incompatible sets of values. Citing from one of his as yet unpublished essays on 1848, he describes himself as one of the last links between the "old world" and the world that was in the process of emerging, "belonging neither to the one nor the other. As people who have rejected the past, who have doubts as to the future—at least the immediate future—we have no refuge, no sanctuary, no cause in the contemporary world. . . . What are we to do?" To start a new life in some distant country would be no solution. "Don't we belong despite ourselves to this world which we hate, with its vices, its virtues, its passions, and its habits? What would we do in virgin lands—we who can't spend a morning without devouring a dozen newspapers? It must be admitted, we would make poor Crusoes."[71]

Herzen's preoccupation with his role as a revolutionary intellectual in the aftermath of 1848 was the culmination of a process that had begun in his Vyatka exile when he had opened the journal containing Chaadaev's indictment of his generation. He had been one of the few among them who had been prepared to recognize himself in the image of "lost souls" in a chaotic state of fermentation in their search to construct a stable intellectual and moral identity from first principles. His efforts to confront the unadorned truth of the gulf between the real and the ideal were reflected in his treatment of his alter ego, the antihero of

Who Is to Blame?—a work long in gestation and completed only on the eve of his departure for the West. His tendency to wishful thinking was constantly subverted by his powers of observation, honed by his scientific training and his unusual capacity for self-criticism, which did not spare the sanctified image of the alienated *intelligent:* such a person, he had observed in a diary entry of 1844, was ready to grasp at any nonsense just in order to fill the terrible void of Russian life.[72]

Thus it is not surprising that Proudhon's gentle rebuke had its intended effect. In a letter of December 1851 Herzen praises his role as a peacemaker in 1848: "You did everything possible to point out to [the French public] . . . the means of salvation, of transition, organic solutions . . . When you said 'development,' it heard 'destruction.' . . . It took your words for war cries."[73] His admiration for Proudhon survived his disapproval of Proudhon's attempts to build bridges with the bourgeoisie and his disappointment at the result of their collaboration in the *Voix du peuple.* To Emma Herwegh he had expressed his irritation at what he saw as the paper's excessive concentration on French politics at the expense of its foreign section: "So I was right, he only wanted to get the caution money. One more lesson."[74] But his participation had served its primary purpose. Before the paper was suppressed he had published seven articles in it, including a long essay, "La Russie," designed to draw the attention of Western democrats to the Russian people's potential. He had also cemented a friendship with Proudhon that was to give him strong support in the tragedies of his personal life. Although they were not to meet again after 1859, they maintained an affectionate correspondence that ceased only after Proudhon censured Herzen's support for the Polish uprising of 1863, which he saw as inspired by an outdated nationalism devoid of progressive social content. Two years later in an obituary for the man whom he describes as his teacher, Herzen writes that Proudhon's strength lay not in the healing of wounds, but in the dissection of corpses: "Above all he set everything in motion . . . stirred everything up, discarding conventional expressions of respect, concepts sanctified by custom, and ceremonial that is unquestioningly accepted."[75]

* * *

What united the two thinkers was far greater than the sum of their differences. As Proudhon remarked during their negotiations, they were both "missionaries" for a single idea.[76] Their shared preoccupation with the nature of the self had led each to a view of individual freedom in stark contradiction with the visionary utopias that dominated radical thinking in their century, anticipating insights that would emerge from painful experience in the next.

Herzen is said to have told the editor of Proudhon's *Voix du peuple* that there were only two works of real importance in the nineteenth century: Feuerbach's *Essence of Christianity* and Proudhon's *Contradictions*.[77] He was alone among his radical contemporaries in giving much greater significance to the second. While commenting severely on Proudhon's traditionalist attitude to women's role in society (as expressed in his work of 1858, *De la justice dans la révolution et dans l'église*), he gives strong praise to what he sees as the rare audacity of its attack on the shibboleths of the age: "[*De la justice*] rejects . . . not only the gross dualism of religion but also the cunning dualism of philosophy; it is free not only from heavenly phantoms, but also from those of the earth . . . the sentimentalization of humanity and the fatalism in the concept of progress. It contains none of those endless litanies about brotherhood, democracy, and progress that are so pitiful and wearisome in the midst of dissension and violence. Proudhon has sacrificed the revolution's idols and its rhetoric in the cause of understanding what revolution means, and has moved morality onto its only true foundation: the human heart, which recognizes reason alone and has no other gods."[78]

A similar revolt against dualism had inspired the search for a "method" that had been a dominant theme in Herzen's thought from his early university years. Feuerbach's naturalism had inspired his demand in *Dilettantism* that thinking about history should take on flesh; in exposing the residual dualism in Young Hegelian philosophy, Proudhon gave a new impetus to his search to deliver himself from phantoms in all their diverse forms. The reading of Proudhon, Herzen wrote in *My Past and Thoughts*, "provides one with a special method, sharpens one's weapons and supplies not results but means. . . . In most sociological works the ideals advocated, which almost always are unattainable in the present or boil down to some one-sided solution, are of little significance; what is important is what, on the path to their attainment, is seen as the *question*."[79]

He attributed Proudhon's "fearful power" to his willingness to tackle what he had come to call the "concrete truth" of contingent existence. "He is as much the poet of dialectics as Hegel, with the difference that one stands on the peaceful summit of the philosophical movement, while the other is engulfed in the turmoil of popular commotions and the hand-to-hand fighting of political parties." Proudhon's insistence that he had no system "puzzles his fellow-countrymen, who are accustomed to a moral at the end of the fable, to systematic formulae, to classifications, to abstract, binding prescriptions."[80] To a Russian correspondent he remarks that Proudhon had left the French of all political persuasions "far behind him."[81] He savored the aptness and wit of Proudhon's ripostes to the insults thrown at him from all sides, declaring his derisive pamphlets against Louis-Napoleon to be "pure poetry of anger and contempt." He recalls the uproar with which the "parliamentary rabble" greeted one of his speeches: "Even there Proudhon succeeded in rising to his full height, and leaving in the midst of the wrangling a glowing footprint."[82]

Proudhon has a special place among those whom Herzen regarded as his teachers, providing him at the outset of his revolutionary career with a living model of the approach to history and society he had been seeking to define since his earliest meditations at Moscow University on the relation between the natural and human worlds. The influence of *Contradictions* is evident in the following diatribe of September 1848 against "the French," a collective epithet for some of his former heroes.

> There is no people in the world who would perform so many feats, shed so much blood for freedom as the French, and there is no people who understand it less, seek less to realize it in reality, in the public square, in the courts, in their homes; they are content with words, they publish proclamations where they should change their mode of life. The French are the most abstract and the most religious people in the world; their fanatical attachment to ideas goes hand in hand with lack of respect for the human personality, with contempt for their neighbors. The French turn everything into an idol, and woe to him who will not bow before the idol of the day. The Frenchman fights heroically for freedom and will unhesitatingly drag you to

prison if you don't agree with his opinions. Louis XIV used to say: 'L'état c'est moi'; the Republic showed in practice that it regarded the government to be the state. The tyrannical *salus populi* and the bloody, inquisitorial *'pereat mundus et fiat justitia'* are inscribed in the consciousness of royalists and democrats alike. . . . The French elevate every truth to a dogma; they have been thought to be irreligious . . . because they are frivolous and accustomed to Voltairean blasphemy, but side by side with Voltaire is there not Rousseau, whose every word is religious . . . ? The French have in no way freed themselves from religion. . . . Read George Sand and Pierre Leroux, Louis Blanc and Michelet—everywhere you'll encounter Christianity and Romanticism, transposed onto our morals and customs; everywhere there is dualism, abstraction, abstract duty, obligatory virtues, official, rhetorical morality without any relation to practical life.

In this ferocious blast against the home of revolution Herzen condemns French radical intellectuals en masse for clinging to a Romantic otherworldliness whose rhetoric never confronted the reality of the fight for freedom. For the French, freedom of thought and speech was a noble caprice rather than a real demand. "I would as little vouch for the freedom of the press if the democrats gained power as I would now." It was only their "lively nature" that had preserved this nation from permanent slavery. "Having lost nine-tenths of what they had gained through bloodshed, in about another fifteen years they will once again build barricades, strew the streets with corpses and astonish the world with their heroism, in order once again to lose what they had won."[83] (His prediction was off by less than a decade: the Paris Commune would erupt in March 1871.)

Two Radical Ironists

Herzen's highest praise for Proudhon was reserved for the conclusion to *Confessions of a Revolutionary*, written from prison in 1849, in which Proudhon distributes equal blame for the revolution's defeat to the socialists who had lost precious time in chaotic demonstrations and the gossip and intrigues of their clubs and sects, and the republicans in the Provisional Government who had failed to address economic questions and reaped a terrible civil war. In the passage that made the strongest impression on Herzen, he defines the salient characteristic of both groups as a doctrinaire earnestness which excluded all forms of self-questioning:

> What our generation lacks is neither a Mirabeau, nor a Robespierre, nor a Bonaparte: it is a Voltaire. We're unable to judge anything from the viewpoint of an independent and mocking reason. Slaves to our opinions and our interests alike, by taking ourselves too seriously, we become stupid. We convert knowledge into pedantry; instead of liberating the intelligence, it stupefies it. Wholly devoted to our loves and our hatreds, we can laugh neither at others nor at ourselves; in losing our wit, we have lost our freedom. . . .
>
> Liberty, like Reason, . . . manifests itself only through constant disdain of its own creations; it perishes as soon as it begins to worship itself. That is why in all ages irony has been the mark of philosophical and liberal genius, the . . . irresistible instrument of progress.
>
> Irony, true liberty! You free me from the desire for power, the tyranny of parties . . . respect for routine, the pedantry of scholars, adulation of important persons, the machinations of politicians, the fanaticism of reformers, superstitious fear of this great universe, and adoration of myself. . . . You were the familiar demon of the Philosopher, when he unmasked at one stroke the dogmatist and the sophist, the hypocrite and the atheist, the Epicurean and the cynic. . . .
>
> Sweet irony! . . . You give grace to beauty and piquancy to love; you inspire charity through tolerance. . . . You allay dissension and civil wars; you make peace between brothers, you heal the fanatic and the sectarian. . . .
>
> Come, sovereign: shed on my co-citizens a ray of your light: light up their souls with a spark of your spirit, so that my confession may reconcile them and the inevitable revolution be accomplished in serenity and joy.[84]

The stance conveyed in this passage is that of the "liberal" ironist as defined by Richard Rorty: "the sort of person who faces up to the contingency of his or her own most central beliefs and desires."[85] In a letter to Emma Herwegh, Herzen describes it as representing "the most sublime poetry . . . the profoundest understanding of reality, of life."[86] Its powerful impact on him is understandable in light of the preference for "factology" over ideology that he had acquired painfully in Russia. Hegel, Feuerbach, and evolutionary science had all helped to bring about his personal acceptance of the impermanence of human ideals; Proudhon's mocking acquiescence in his role as a pariah on the French left impressed on him the heroism required to voice such a view in radical circles. In his memoir of Proudhon he recalls how his language had offended the French Left, who, like judges in a Russian court, rejected views not couched in an official form. "Their criticism stops short before their symbolic texts, such as the *Contrat social*, or the Declaration of Human Rights. Men of faith, they hate analysis and doubt . . . they cannot tolerate an independent mind."[87]

As expounded in *Contradictions*, Proudhon's ironist outlook drew no comments from his contemporaries. The work is still known mainly through Marx's attack on it in *The Poverty of Philosophy*. In setting it alongside Hegel's *Phenomenology* Herzen showed himself in advance of his time. Well into the twentieth century it was generally believed by both liberal and radical theorists that there was one right way, a single rational formula for the final resolution of social conflict and the establishment of a just and harmonious society, the only barriers to its achievement being ignorance, superstition, and ill will. The dismal records of totalitarian democracy and laissez-faire liberalism have led to increasing emphasis in political philosophy on the distinction between "positive" and "negative" liberty—the first representing freedom to lead a way of life conforming to one's rational nature, to be achieved through participation in a community sharing the same goals and values; the second denoting freedom to act on one's own terms, with the minimum of coercion and constraint. Liberal theorists have come to recognize what Bernard Williams has described as the "permanent possibility" of conflict between the values of liberty and equality, and the consequent need for continual adjustment of the balance between "freedom to" and "freedom from" in response to circumstances.[88]

Herzen's conception of the relations between the individual and society was already advancing in this direction when a crucial further impetus was supplied by Proudhon's model of socialism as an unstable equilibrium reconciling individual ambition and initiative with collective goals through the cultivation of *humanitas*—"the distributive justice of social empathy"—an ideal Proudhon believed to be prefigured in existing workers' associations in France. His model of "liberty in order and independence in unity" evokes Schiller's vision of the ideal state as "removed alike from conformity and confusion."[89] The resemblance would not have escaped Herzen.

* * *

Proudhon's importance for Herzen was not as a theorist of anarchism, but as a living example of what in his essay "Buddhism in Science" he had described as the willingness to bear "the heavy cross of sober knowledge"—the consequences of accepting the overwhelming empirical evidence of the contingency and impermanence of all being. Hegel had pioneered this path but lacked "the heroism of consistency," the quality Herzen most admired in his second teacher. In *My Past and Thoughts* he declares that a person who had not *"lived through* the *Phenomenology* and the *Contradictions*, "who has not passed through that furnace and been tempered by it, is not complete, not modern."[90]

His first references to Proudhon's thought in 1845 coincide with the period of his most intensive immersion in the study of the natural sciences. "In our age there is no philosophy without physiology" had been his response to the amused incredulity of his circle. The erosion of faith in a providential order forced humans to turn to the structure of the visible world for answers to the question of how one should live. (He had gone on to recommend to his friends two of Proudhon's works: *On Property* and *On the Creation of Order in Humanity.*) At the end of that year he exposed himself to considerable personal risk by publishing his essay on the evolutionary theorist Karl Rouillier, whose questioning of the theory of the immutability of species had incurred the wrath of the Russian authorities; an education in natural science, Herzen had suggested, should be an essential preparation for the study of history and society. His temerity in publishing his essay on Rouillier's ideas indicates the strength of his belief in the significance of evolutionary biology as a method of training the mind in acceptance of the evidence of observation and experiment, however unwelcome this might be. As the only contemporary political thinker who conformed to this model of "submission before the truth," Proudhon had a unique influence on him. Herzen's formal studies in natural science had ended with his departure to the West, but combined with that influence, they would bear fruit in his philosophical summing up of 1848, as we will see in Chapter 16.

CHAPTER FIFTEEN

Toward Another Shore

The time for political eclecticism is past: one must take up one's
stand on either one shore or the other.

HERZEN, *LETTER FROM PARIS*, JUNE 1849

The development of my thought has deprived me of almost all community of ideas with my contemporaries.

PROUDHON, 1846

HERZEN'S immediate concern in the wake of 1848 was to assume his
self-appointed role as interpreter to the West of his country's history
and socialist potential. Written in the form of a letter to Georg Herwegh, his first contribution, "La Russie," appeared in Proudhon's paper
in November and December 1849, followed in April 1850 by an open
letter to Mazzini. An extended historical account entitled "On the Development of Revolutionary Ideas in Russia," completed in 1849, was
first published two years later in German. "The Russian People and
Socialism" (a response to a hostile article on Russia by the French historian Jules Michelet) was first published in a much truncated form in
a Paris paper in November 1851. The complete version was confiscated
by customs at the French border after its publication in Nice; a second
French edition published in Jersey survived. The need to escape the ever
more savage censorship imposed by Louis-Napoleon's regime was to
be a prime factor in Herzen's move to London in 1852, by which time
he had established himself as the principal representative of Russian
democracy abroad and had distilled the lessons of 1848 into the confession of faith he would describe as the best of all his works.

The common theme of these essays is summed up by the epigraph
introducing his survey of Russian history: "Dich stört nicht im Innern /
Zu lebendiger Zeit / Unnutzes Erinnern / und vergeblicher Streit [No
useless memories and vain struggles distract you from the living

reality of the moment]"[1]—a quotation from Goethe on America that had originally struck him in 1844 and which he had used to taunt his Westernizer friends in the first of his *Letters* from Paris. He argued that while the Germano-Latin peoples had devoted all their forces to producing two successive civilizations, Russia had scarcely entered the mainstream of history with its potential as yet untapped, putting it in a position to build on the achievements and learn from the mistakes of its European elders. Back, it would seem, to the role of "man in the middle" he had played in the conflicts of Slavophiles and Westernizers. But the metaphor is misleading: he was fundamentally opposed to both sides on one issue. His rejection of all forms of historical determinism would be the starting point for his defense of his vision of Russia's socialist potential.

He launches on a vigorous attack on the dominant historiosophical fashion of the age: "that fatalism that . . . speculative philosophy has imported into history as it has into nature. What has existed certainly had reasons to exist, but that in no way means that all other combinations were impossible; they became so through the realization of the most probable chance, that's all one can concede. History is far less determined than is usually believed."[2] Distancing himself equally from Slavophile mysticism and the Hegelian liberals' view of the march of history toward the constitutional state, he emphasizes the role of contingency in the survival in Russia of the peasant commune, a primitive form of social organization swept away by the progress of civilization in the West. "Russia's past has been poor, its present is monstrous."[3] It was true that this condition conferred no right to a better future. But there was also no reason Russia should copy all the phases of Europe's development, all the more so because by pure chance she had emerged on the European stage with her native communes intact at a period when "anticommunal" civilization had begun to take its first steps toward social revolution. Michelet, one of the most prestigious names identified with the radical opposition to the rule of Louis-Napoleon, had poured scorn on the passivity and primitive communism of the Russian peasant; Herzen retorts that in their century there were no questions more serious than that of the just distribution of land. Citing Haxthausen in his support, he asserted the significance—as a means of avoiding the mass pauperization afflicting

European societies—of the commune's rudimentary system of sharing out the land among those who worked on it; but he is careful in these essays to mark his distance from the "depraved dialectic" of the Slavophiles, who viewed the absorption of the individual by the commune as an expression of spiritual togetherness.[4] To Michelet he makes the point that it had taken a European (Haxthausen) to perceive its potential, and in conclusion to his account of the growth of oppositional thought in Russia he remarks on the coincidence between the awakening of interest in it among the Russian intelligentsia and the development of socialism in the West as an answer to the rampant individualism in modern societies. "Europe has not resolved the antinomy between the individual and the State, but at least it has posed the question. Russia is approaching the problem from an opposing direction, but has also not resolved it. In confronting this question we stand on a ground of equality." Europe could learn from the structure of the Russian commune, but its existence had not preserved the peasants from serfdom. Their traditional passivity in the face of oppression could be overcome only through contact with Western notions of rights. "We tremble for [the commune], because there is nothing secure without individual liberty."[5] The absence in Russian law of the concept of individual rights had been turned by the state to its advantage. Citing a study on the subject by two prominent liberals in *The Contemporary*, the Westernizers' journal at the time, Herzen echoes their conclusion: "Russian history has been the development of autocracy and authority, as the history of the West is the history of the development of liberty and rights." Basing their response on Slav chronicles, the Greek Catechism, and Hegelian formalism, the Slavophiles had maintained that the presence of the Holy Spirit in the Byzantine Church had ensured a remarkable harmony in pre-Petrine Russia between prince, commune, and individual. "They have preached disdain for the West, which alone could light up the abyss of Russian life; in other words, . . . a return to the past, which, on the contrary, we need to repudiate in the name of a future that will henceforth be common to East and West."[6] But he is equally dismissive of the constitutional guarantees on which Russian liberals placed their hopes. "The masks have fallen, we now know exactly what French republican liberty and German constitutional liberty are worth. . . . All existing governments, from the most modest canton in Switzerland to the autocrat of all the Russias, are mere variations on one and the same theme."[7]

A large part of the *Letter* addressed to Herwegh is devoted to the structure and traditions of the commune as a "moral personality . . . responsible for each and everyone," apportioning land according to individual needs and giving each of its adult members an equal voice in its affairs. He quotes Haxthausen: "Each rural commune in Russia is a little republic, self-governing for its internal affairs, which knows neither personal property nor a proletariat; which long ago raised a feature of socialist utopias to the status of a *fait accompli.*"[8] Those who leave the land to work in trades in the cities retain their rights in the commune, forming workers' associations patterned on its structure. Citing Haxthausen's comment that the temporary nature of individual possession in the commune deterred the peasant from making long-term improvements in the land assigned to him, Herzen retorts that advances in agriculture for the benefit of individual farmers in the West could scarcely be considered just compensation for the plight of a vast and starving proletariat. To Michelet he underlines the inner strength that had enabled the Russian peasant to preserve his way of life intact under the servitude of the Petrine state. "He has submitted to that degrading yoke with a despairing passivity, I admit, but has *never been prepared to believe* either in the rights of the seigneur, nor the justice of the tribunal, nor the equity of the administration. For nearly two centuries his entire existence has been nothing but mute, negative opposition to the actual order of things; he endures oppression, he submits to it, but he takes no part in what goes on outside the rural communes."[9] This inner autonomy was the source of the "strength, agility, intelligence, and beauty" that had astonished Custine and Haxthausen. But the self-sufficiency of the commune had its negative side, unremarked by Haxthausen and its Slavophile admirers: it stifled initiative. "There is too little movement in the commune . . . no impulsion from outside to stimulate progress, no competition, no inner struggle producing variety and movement; in giving the individual his share of land, it frees him from all care."[10] It was powerless against the incursions of the state: to survive, it must undergo a revolution. Russia's future depended on a force stronger than either the commune or the government—the intelligence, strength, and resilience that had enabled the Russian people to survive the rule of the Mongols, the German bureaucracy imported by Peter I, the tyranny of serfdom, and the rampages of Napoleon. Here the intelligentsia had its contribution to make, although only as a means, "a fermenting agent . . . conduits between the Russian people and revolutionary Europe."[11] He insists on this modest role. The commune with its socialist potential was solely the product of the peasants' inner life.

The intelligentsia, nevertheless, are crucial to Herzen's attempts to convince European democrats of Russia's socialist potential. He describes their emergence among the Westernized elite after the failure of the latter's constitutional hopes in 1825, when the self-searching in the works of Pushkin, Gogol, and Lermontov, the propagandist mission of Belinsky's radical criticism, and Chaadaev's trumpet call galvanized a new generation prepared to confront the reality of their predicament, alienated both from the "empire de façades" and from a population who knew them only as their exploiters. In response to Michelet's dismissive comments on the Russian intelligentsia and the "amusing" pretensions of nascent Russian literature, he retorts that the self-analysis and self-accusation of Russian poetry and the "pathological anatomy" conducted by her novelists stand alongside the peasant commune as evidence of Russia's vast potential. "Sadness, skepticism, and irony: these are the three chords of the Russian lyre."[12]

"The great indictment drawn up by Russian literature against Russian life, that total and ardent negation of our own faults, that confession with its horror at our past, that bitter irony that makes us blush for our present—this is our salvation, the progressive element of the Russian nature." He describes Belinsky as an embodiment of this new freedom: inspired by a boundless love for freedom of thought and a hatred of all that encroached on it, independent of public opinion, deferring to no systems, traditions, or authorities, and denouncing all he considered reactionary without regard for the anger of his friends or the revulsion of more tender souls.[13] Herzen affirms that the moral straitjacket imposed on Europeans by their long history and traditions was alien to thinking Russians, who could feel no allegiance to the values of either ancient Muscovy or Saint Petersburg imperialism. Having imported Western culture into Russia, the autocracy had had a reason for existing only as long as it pretended to persist in such a noble role. This deception was now played out. The government that had broken faith with the people in the name of civilization hastened a century later to break with civilization in the name of absolutism. Although the mass of the population were passively obedient to their oppressors, they remained faithful to an alien way of life and values. "In Russia behind the visible state there is no invisible one . . . no unattainable ideal that never coincides with reality, while always promising so to do. There is nothing behind the palisades where a superior force holds us in a state of siege. The possibility of a revolution in Russia comes down to a question of material strength"[14]—a factor that, along with the existence of the commune, made it an exceptionally propitious ground for a social revolution.

A propaganda exercise designed to secure sympathy and support from Western democrats for the cause of revolution in Russia demanded some varnishing of the truth, but Herzen exceeds the bounds of credibility in the following passage: the most eloquent and passionate in all his addresses to the West.

> The thinking Russian is the most independent man in Europe. What could restrain him? Respect for the past? . . . But does not the modern history of Russia begin with a total rejection of our national identity and traditions? . . . On the other hand, the past of you Western peoples serves us as a lesson, and no more; in no way do we consider ourselves executors of your historical testaments.
>
> We accept your doubts; your faith does not inspire us. You are too religiose for our taste. We share your hatreds; your attachment for the heritage of your ancestors we do not comprehend. We are too oppressed, too wretched, to be content with a demi-freedom. You are held back by ulterior motives, by scruples; we Russians have neither ulterior motives nor scruples, but for the moment we lack strength. . . .
>
> It is this, Sir, that is the source of our irony, of the rage that exasperates us, gnaws at us, impels us forward, leads us sometimes to Siberia, to torture, exile, an early death. We dedicate ourselves without hope; from disgust, from boredom. There is truly something senseless in our lives, but there is nothing banal, nothing stagnant, nothing bourgeois.
>
> Do not accuse us of immorality because we do not respect what you respect. Can one reproach a foundling for not respecting his parents? We are free because we begin with ourselves. The only thing traditional in us is our organism, our nationality: this is a matter of

our blood and our instinct and in no way an arbitrary authority. We are independent because we possess nothing; there is almost nothing for us to love; all our memories are filled with bitterness and resentment. Civilization and knowledge were handed to us at the end of a whip.

What then have we to do with your traditional duties, we . . . the disinherited? And how could we freely accept a faded morality, neither Christian nor humane, that has no existence outside rhetorical exercises and speeches for the prosecution? . . .

. . . We bear too many chains imposed on us by force to wish to add others to them through our own choice. In this regard we are the exact equals of our peasants. We obey brute force; we are slaves because we lack the means to break free; nevertheless we will accept nothing from the enemy camp.

Russia will never be Protestant. Russia will never be *juste milieu*.[15]

As a portrait of his generation, this passage carries scant conviction. (Herzen's addresses to the West skim over such issues as Belinsky's intolerance of all who did not agree with him, the Westernizers' admiration for bourgeois culture, Chaadaev's and Gogol's religious conservatism, and the Slavophiles' allegiance to pre-Petrine values.) The revolution he hoped would transform the Russian commune into a model for a new kind of society had only one proponent among the intelligentsia of his generation: himself. Ogarev, his future collaborator in furthering the cause from London, was still deep in the Russian provinces, grappling with the financial problems involved in the liberation of his serfs. Bakunin, the only active revolutionary of Herzen's generation, had dabbled briefly in Slav nationalism before his arrest in Germany in 1849 and subsequent deportation to Russia to serve ten years of prison and exile. Like the image of the barbarian from the East with which he had sought to impress Proudhon, Herzen's portrayal of the "thinking Russian" served to put a positive gloss on the isolation and impotence of the Russian intelligentsia. "We are free from the past because our past has been empty, impoverished, narrow,"[16] he had written in his dissertation on Russian history for the benefit of his Western audience. This confidence was belied by his fits of self-analysis as he struggled to define his own identity and values as a Westernized Russian. To the German communist Moses Hess, who had accused him of a detached attitude to the crisis in Europe, he responds that his role of spectator has been predetermined by his nationality. "I belong physically to another world." He could observe the cancer consuming western Europe with a certain indifference, confident that the future was with the East.[17] But writing to Herwegh only four months later, he identifies with the predicament of those radicals who reject the old order while fearing that the values they hold most dear will be jettisoned by the new, "at least in the near future."[18] "A stranger at home and a stranger abroad"—Herzen's description of the antihero of *Who Is to Blame?* encapsulates his own sense of alienation following the defeat of 1848, as he began to come to terms with the possibility that his ideal of socialism might not coincide with the aspirations of the masses.

He had not entirely lost hope in France's revolutionary potential, as evidenced by his elation when republicans made strong gains in complementary elections to the National Assembly in March 1850: "The great question of the future has been wholly transformed. France is becoming democratic before our eyes."[19] But expectation gave way to resignation as he moved toward the conviction that the only force capable of eradicating the old order in France was communism. As the socialism of revenge, it had particular appeal for the French masses, who, he tells a Russian correspondent, should not be idealized. They were impelled, not by notions of democracy and individual freedom, but by a burning sense of social injustice that would drive them to destroy indiscriminately the good along with the bad in the old world.[20]

The coup d'état of 2 December 1851 provoked a response of apocalyptic gloom in the last of his *Letters* from France and Italy: "Everything is over—representative republic and constitutional monarchy, free press and inalienable rights, an open court and an elected parliament. . . . Wherever you look, on all sides, there is the smell of barbarism: from Paris and Petersburg, from above and below, from palaces and workshops. What will complete it, deliver the final blow: the decrepit barbarism of the scepter or the violent barbarism of communism, the bloody saber or the red flag?"[21] In this mood of nihilistic despair, even Russia seemed to hold out no hope. To Proudhon he wrote, "France—relapsed into childhood, and Russia—not yet emerged from it—both subject to an ignominious yoke, have sunk to the same level. Russia has achieved nothing, France has lost everything." Despotism would prepare a fertile ground for the spread of communism; only England, the bastion of conservatism, would remain outside this general development as a "a magnificent example of the civilized, Christian, and feudal world."[22]

With the prospect of no audience for the role in which he had cast himself, his immediate future became Herzen's main concern. He had returned to Paris from Switzerland in December 1849 for the complicated negotiations required to secure the return of his large fortune, which had been sequestered by the Russian government in 1848. He made a fictitious sale of his property to the banker Baron James de Rothschild, who secured transfer of its value to Paris by threatening refusal of a loan for the tsar then under negotiation. On Rothschild's advice, Herzen invested his money judiciously in property and American bonds to secure his family's future and serve as a source of funds for the cause of revolution in Russia. It also helped pay for his acquisition of citizenship of the Swiss canton of Fribourg, which had shown itself friendly to political refugees. During these negotiations he was ordered to leave France at the request of the Russian government, an order invalidated by his new citizenship. He was now protected against possible extradition proceedings, but reluctant to remain in Paris. In April 1850 he wrote to the German democrat Johann Jacoby of his increasing aversion to its political milieu, divided between ferocious reactionaries and moronic democrats. "What's in gestation here is hard to say: either a degrading despotism or a no less arbitrary communism. It's a time when the individual must break either his heart or all the ties that attach him to his contemporaries. Let's save ourselves rather than aspiring to save the world."[23]

A solution was proposed by Herwegh, his only close friend among the revolutionary émigrés. Since 1848 he and Natalie had developed an affectionate relationship with Herwegh and his wife Emma, despite Herwegh's capricious and petulant nature, a frequent subject of reproach in Herzen's correspondence with him. After his break with him, Herzen recalled that Herwegh had exerted increasing pressure on him to quit the infected air of Paris in order to share with the couple "a communal existence, pure and serious, far from humanity," that would anticipate the harmonious life of the future.[24] Herzen was strongly attracted by the notion of an aesthetic education in the spirit of Schillerian humanism in preparation for a social existence built on Proudhon's principles of reciprocity and mutuality, but observation of Herwegh's coldness toward Emma led him to doubt his friend's suitability for this experiment. He recommended that the two couples set aside any fantasy of a retreat to an isolated existence together. Repulsive though he found Paris, he intended to remain there. "This is the only way to save us—from ourselves." A tense correspondence ensued, in which Herzen responded to Herwegh's continued pressure with a critique of his domineering nature, telling him that communal life as they both envisaged it was impossible "without the complete freedom and autonomy of the persons concerned." The real significance of this long correspondence, he wrote, was simple—before committing themselves definitively to the project, he and Natalie wished to alert Herwegh to aspects of his character that were ill-suited to it. In reply to what was presumably a heated rejoinder from Herwegh, he calls for a cessation of recriminations between them. "It is unseemly to sink into this subjective analysis when we are witnessing this somber tragedy that threatens to engulf the world."[25] The following day, in a mood of depression, he agreed to Herwegh's proposal. The increasing suppression of dissent under the party of order had convinced him that it was unsafe to remain in Paris, and he forecasts gloomily that two generations will pass before the advent of socialism. Natalie had already expressed ecstatic approval of the project. "Two little maisonettes in the south of France. . . . Imagine if Ogarev and Natalie would come to complete our little commune, our sacred commune. . . . Oh, it would be so beautiful, so beautiful, so beautiful!!!"[26] The two couples eventually found a large house in Nice (then a part of Piedmont), where they moved at the end of June 1850, the Herweghs occupying the upper floor and paying Herzen a nominal rent. The domestic tragedy that ensued from this arrangement would overshadow the rest of Herzen's life.[27]

Family Tragedies

Herzen's isolation in his Geneva exile had ended in July of the previous year when Herwegh arrived with Natalie, leaving Emma and the Herwegh children behind in Paris. The three had lived together as a single household, occupying their free time with excursions into the environs of Geneva, which Natalie described in rhapsodic letters to Emma. On a visit to Montreux, unaccompanied by Herzen, who was preoccupied with his publishing projects, Natalie and Herwegh declared their mutual love. At the end of 1849 Herzen left with Natalie for Zurich, where their deaf-mute son Kolya was attending a special school for his condition; he then departed to deal with his financial affairs. He described his parting with Herwegh as a highly emotional moment, his friend "repeating again and again declarations of the most enthusiastic and passionate affection. . . . That was almost the last minute when I still really loved this man." Herwegh then proceeded to Zurich to join Natalie. Her gushingly affectionate references to him in her letters to Herzen, alone in Paris, began to arouse his suspicions, which he conveyed to her in a "sad but calm" letter, followed by a request for an open discussion of the situation.[28] Her fervent denials, followed by an immediate return to Paris with the children, were sufficiently reassuring for him to continue corresponding with Herwegh on the possibility of a communal existence, although his letters had lost their former warmth, drawing attention with increasing asperity to Herwegh's defects of character and neglect of his wife. The liaison between Herwegh and Natalie continued after the move of the two families to Nice in the summer, Herzen's suspicions increasing until the drama's denouement in January 1851, when he confronted Natalie with the demand to make a final choice between Herwegh and himself. If she chose for him to remain, Herwegh must leave. Natalie tearfully professed her exclusive love for Herzen, and the revolutionary hero meekly quit the house the next morning, avoiding a confrontation with Herzen and sending placating messages via Emma. This was only the beginning of a chain of events that would culminate in Natalie's death in May of the following year.

Herwegh was a remarkably handsome man with the aura of a martyr in the fight for freedom, a Romantic poet whose self-centeredness and haste to take offense could be interpreted as the sensitivity of a superior soul. Natalie had retained the lessons of her correspondence with Herzen during his Vyatka days: her playfully affectionate postscripts to his letters to Herwegh show her cloaking her infidelity in the image of the pure friendship of sensitive spirits in which husband, lover, and herself communed as equal partners. Her diary and love letters to Herwegh reflect her reading of George Sand, from whom (again at Herzen's instigation) she had absorbed the doctrine of the divinity of love and its self-sufficiency as a guide to human conduct. The awakening brought about by Herzen's grief and humiliation was a shock from which she never recovered.

Herzen describes their life together in the months after Herwegh's departure: "Everything bore the traces of the storm. . . . What was most tormenting of all was that the thread of life was broken . . . nothing sacred was left. If all that had been had been, nothing was impossible. How many times we came into dinner alone in the evening and, neither of us touching anything, and not uttering a word, left the table, wiping away tears. . . . Idle days, sleepless nights . . . , anguish, anguish. I drank whatever came to hand."[29] Natalie's adultery with his closest friend had destroyed the hope inspiring his move to Nice. Back in Paris alone in June he writes to his Moscow friends that he is overcome by gloomy apathy. "I'm doing absolutely nothing, I wander from café to café and read the newspapers, nothing more than that."[30]

In July came further humiliation when he discovered through his friend Sazonov in Geneva that Herwegh's version of his family drama, depicting him as a tyrannical husband denying his wife the freedom to rejoin her lover, was circulating among émigrés in Switzerland. Natalie had continued to correspond with Herwegh (while protesting her faithfulness to Herzen, she was still unable to come to terms with the destruction of her vision of ideal love). Herzen knew of the correspondence and wrote to her, insisting on the truth. She set off to meet him after writing her last letter to Herwegh, expressing contempt for his behavior and her intention to destroy unread any further communications from him. His trust in her restored, Herzen recalled the three days they spent together before their return to Nice as their second honeymoon. He was to look back on the peace of the four months that followed as "a triumphant ending to my personal life."[31]

In the middle of November the steamer bringing Herzen's mother, Kolya, and the boy's tutor to join the rest of the family in Nice capsized. All three were drowned. Natalie, who was pregnant again, never recovered from the blow. Two weeks later came news of the coup d'état in Paris. To family friend and fellow émigré Maria Reichel, Herzen wrote: "We had scarcely begun to get used to the terrible loss of 16 November, when suddenly not a family, but a whole country goes to the bottom and with it, perhaps, the century in which we live."[32]

At the end of December Natalie fell gravely ill with pleurisy. She was recovering soon after the New Year of 1852 when a letter arrived from Herwegh, who had worked himself into a rage over the return of his unopened letters to her. He accused Herzen of having forced her to betray her lover, taunting him as a cuckold and challenging him to a duel. In a long letter detailing Herwegh's betrayal and circulated among the émigré community, Herzen stated his reason for rejecting Herwegh's challenge: his treachery and deceit were crimes to which the only appropriate response was trial by his fellow democrats in a "court of honor." Writing to Maria Reichel, he implores her to understand that this was not just a personal tragedy: it brought into question the entire revolutionary cause. "I regard myself as a *new* man . . . and here I am making the experiment of punishing a scoundrel without the courts and the duels of the old world: by the sole force of democratic opinion." If he were not supported by his fellow democrats, would this not be a sign that their movement was deficient, not only in political strength, but also in inner moral fiber? The recipients of his call for support, including Proudhon and Mazzini, offered warm sympathy but took no practical steps to realize his wish. He would subsequently observe bitterly to his Moscow circle, "I am only to blame in that I believed too naively in the new society. I wanted to show the world how a person propagating our principles should act." At the same time he mentions another aspect of the situation as he sees it: "Two Russian natures wrestling with Western depravity."[33]

The principal victim in the affair was Natalie, who, still in precarious health, was enlisted to participate in the public shaming of Herwegh by contemptuously repudiating his version of their relationship in a letter to him whose style betrays Herzen's hand,[34] and which he circulated among his supporters. Her health continued to decline, and she died on 2 May after giving birth prematurely to a son who did not survive.

* * *

In one of his admonitory letters to Herwegh before their move to Nice, Herzen had stressed his wish that his criticism should not impact on their friendship. Only two others—Ogarev and Natalie—had occupied such an important position in his life: "Do you think I could be so frivolous as to part with you?"[35] His sense of isolation after Herwegh's betrayal was compounded by the fact it deprived him of the only role that had seemed left to him with the fading of his hopes for political progress. A year after his arrival in Nice he wrote, "I had long thought it possible at least personally to begin a new life, to retreat into oneself, to withdraw from the crowded marketplace. It is not possible—if there is just one person around you with whom you have not broken all ties, the old world will return through him, along with its vice and debauchery, its cunning and its treachery." Writing to Maria Reichel in April 1852, he was driven for the first time to admit to moments of doubt in the convictions that had hitherto guided his private and his public life, describing a sudden yearning for the feeling of security promoted by tradition—for example, through attendance at the imposing Easter rituals of the Russian Orthodox Church. Otherwise, "There will be nothing for our children to commemorate; we have reduced their lives to the prose of digestive functions and the boredom of reason."[36]

After the destruction of his "commune" his prognostications on the future of Europe became ever more pessimistic. He was repelled by the "democratic orthodoxy" of those French radicals who, forced into exile, remained true to the republican ideals of 1789, ignoring the people's demand for a social revolution. "They have set up their own radical inquisition. . . . Ideas and thoughts satisfying their requirements have rights of citizenship and public expression, others are declared heretical and deprived of a voice: these are the proletariat of the moral world, they have either to keep silent or seize their place through might and main, through an uprising."[37] It was the more painful, therefore, to have to acknowledge his own roots in the old order, as he now does for the first time, in one of the most deeply felt passages of all his writings:

It would seem time to stop and reflect: above all, to study contemporary life more closely and cease . . . to persuade oneself and others of
facts that don't exist and to avert one's eyes from those that do; time
to cease taking large crowds at demonstrations for a ready-made army,
seeking the people's voice in newspaper articles written by ourselves
or our friends, and public opinion in a narrow circle of friends who
meet daily to repeat the same things. . . .

However we may protest or bemoan the fact, we belong through
our lives, our habits and our language, to the same literary, intellectual, and political milieu that we renounce. It is not within our
power to transform our theoretical break with it into a practical one:
we are too deeply enmeshed in that life to bring it to an end. . . .

Naturally, it seemed to us that this self-liberation was the first
step, from which full and free deeds would ensue. But in fact our
anger is our deed: on it we spent the best of our strength, uttered the
best of our words. Even now we can be strong only in battle with the
pedants and pharisees of the conservative and revolutionary world. . . .

The people do not need what we have to say. . . . The people
scarcely know the phantoms against which we fight; our battle does
not concern them, their anger is different from ours. . . . They await
not books but apostles, people whose faith, will, convictions and
strength are as one. . . .

. . . We are both the corpse and the killers, the disease and the
dissectors of the old world—that is our calling. . . .

The death of the world that has outlived its time will engulf us
too: there is no escape, our damaged lungs can only breathe infected
air. . . . But, disappearing along with it we'll still rain on it our most
vicious blows and, expiring amid destruction and chaos, will joyfully
welcome the new world—which will not be our world—with the
words: "We who are about to die, salute you, Caesar!"[38]

Composed in December 1851 in the wake of Louis-Napoleon's coup
d'état, his last *Letter* from France and Italy ends with the bleak prophecy
that the ultimate victory in the battle between two varieties of barbarity would lie with communism; the forms it would take would
vary according to historical contexts, but they would all destroy the
old order together with its culture. "You grieve for civilization? So do I.
But not the masses, to whom it has given nothing except tears, hard-
ship, ignorance and humiliation."[39]

This vision of the imminent future in Europe contained no conceivable role for Herzen himself. A few days previously he had written to Proudhon of his intention to quit Nice. Switzerland (of which he was now a citizen) was a possibility, "but I have little confidence in that fossilized republic—'free as the mountains,' the Swiss say; yes, and 'sterile as the mountains.'" His choice fell on England, the last home of true conservatism: "She alone will remain as a magnificent example of the civilized world, the Christian and feudal world."[40]

A Move to England

In the summer of 1852 Herzen set off for England with his son Sasha, leaving his two younger children in Paris in the care of Maria Reichel and her husband, Adolph. On 25 August he arrived in London, which was to be his base for the next twelve years.

His first impressions of England were positive. He pronounced London to be the sole city in Europe worth inhabiting, characterized by an almost religious respect for the individual—the ideal environment in which to educate Sasha. Even the police did not inspire the fear they generated in Europe: when a policeman knocked at his door, he was pleasantly surprised to learn he had come only to return Botsvin (not a straying Russian member of his household, but his lost dog, inventively named after Lord Byron's "poor dog, in life the firmest friend," Boatswain). But his attitude to England as reflected in his letters to friends soon began to swing between ironic ambivalence and exasperation. In 1857 he declares that notwithstanding the inanities of its combination of feudalism and Toryism, England is the only country where one can reasonably live. On the extraordinary enthusiasm of the reception given to Garibaldi by the London crowds on his visit in April 1864, he comments, "An amazing country, foolish and great, trite and eccentric, an ox with the manners of a lion." But already by 1860 he had become "bored to death" with England.[41] He began to form vague plans to move to Switzerland or Brussels. His sense of rootlessness was reflected in the frequency of his moves around the city; during their twelve years there his family occupied fifteen houses in succession.[42] He was, however, much gratified by the attention he attracted in progressive circles in London, informing Maria Reichel that he had received a "dithyramb" from the editor of *The Leader*, a liberal paper with radical tendencies; his long essay on the history of revolutionary ideas in Russia was in the process of translation into English, and he was being assailed by requests from journals for more essays on the subject. In February 1854 he was invited by the American consul to attend a dinner in honor of Washington's birthday; to his place card was added "the Russian republican." At this dinner he made the acquaintance of Garibaldi.[43]

Again he attracted general attention when he was invited to speak as the representative of "the Russian revolutionary party" at a gathering of leaders of European socialism organized in London by the English Chartists on the seventh anniversary of the revolution of February 1848. He was duly elected to their committee—"the first fruit of migrations and exile," he wrote to Michelet. The London *Times* reported that the speech of the "Russian gentleman" was welcomed with enthusiasm.[44] He maintained links with the Chartists through William Linton, the founder of their journal *The English Republic*, which printed a number of his articles in translation. But he neither sought nor received attention from notable English thinkers of the time. Two exceptions were Robert Owen, to whom he was introduced by an English acquaintance, and Thomas Carlyle, who sought him out after reading a French translation of "The Development of Revolutionary Ideas in Russia." Herzen enjoyed debating with a man known as the Scottish Proudhon for his attacks on rationalist theories of progress, and urged Maria Reichel to read his history of the French Revolution: a work bordering on genius, "but with a *graine de folie*."[45] Despite Carlyle's opinion of him as "an estimable man of sense,"[46] an exchange of letters between them showed little meeting of minds. Declaring tsarism far preferable to anarchism, Carlyle remarked that Russians possessed a "talent for obedience" that had elsewhere gone out of fashion. Herzen responded that without the talent to resist when forced to act against one's conscience the world would still be at the stage of contemporary Japan.[47]

Herzen's circle in London consisted of exiles like himself. He forged a close friendship with the Italian revolutionary Aurelio Saffi, exiled after the fall of Rome in 1849. Another friend was Carl Schurz, "the best of all the German émigrés," who had escaped in 1849 after the failure of the Baden rising.[48] In his memoirs Schurz (subsequently a Union major-general in the American Civil War) evokes soirées spent in Herzen's hospitable house:

> He poured forth his thoughts and feelings with an impulsive, sometimes poetic eloquence, which, at times, was exceedingly fascinating. I would listen to him by the hour when in his rhapsodic way he talked of Russia and the Russian people, that uncouth and only half conscious giant, that would gradually exchange its surface civilization borrowed from the West for one of national character; the awakening of whose popular intelligence would then put an end to the stolid autocracy, the deadening weight of which held down every free aspiration; and which then would evolve from its mysterious depths new ideas and forces which might solve many of the problems now perplexing the Western world. But, in his fervid professions of faith in the greatness of that destiny, I thought I discovered an undertone of doubt, if not despondency, as to the possibilities of the near future, and I was strongly reminded of the impression made upon me by some of Turguéneff's novels describing Russian society as it entertained itself with vague musings and strivings of dreary aimlessness.[49]

CHAPTER SIXTEEN

View from the Other Shore

There is no absurdity that cannot be inserted into the mold of an empty dialectic in order to endow it with a profound metaphysical significance.

HERZEN

Garbage in, garbage out.

UNKNOWN PROGRAMMER, CIRCA 1971

HERZEN'S new acquaintances did not distract him from his main preoccupation. He recalls in his memoirs how, arriving in England in a state of "terrible, inexpressible weariness," he had welcomed the solitude of his rented house. "The emptiness around me strengthened me and gave me time to collect my thoughts."[1] This process involved a return to the past and its lessons.

* * *

He began work on his memoirs and the revision of his philosophical reflections on the 1848 revolution—a cycle of essays composed between 1847 and 1850, collectively entitled *From the Other Shore* and first published in their entirety in a Russian-language edition of 1855.[2] In his preface to that edition he would claim that he had never written anything better and probably never would: a claim that deserves attention. By the time the volume appeared, he had embarked on the role that would occupy the rest of his years in England, as a political propagandist responding to day-to-day events in Russia in his campaign for peasant emancipation.

This new role has been seen as a regrettable derogation from his earlier philosophical preoccupations.[3] But it can be better understood as a practical application of the lessons on method he would set out in *From the Other Shore*.

In the dedication to his son introducing the work, he describes it as "a monument to a struggle in which I have sacrificed much, but not the courage of knowledge . . . [the] protest of an independent individual against an obsolete, slavish and spurious set of ideas, against absurd idols that belong to another age, and that linger on meaninglessly among us, a nuisance to some, a terror to others."[4] The most considered expression of his mature moral and social philosophy, the essays have elicited a bewildering variety of interpretations. The Soviet editors of his collected works rate them as characterized by "profoundly contradictory evaluations of reality and the paths of historical development"; Martin Malia, too, pronounces them "the most confused and . . . paradoxical of all Herzen's writings."[5] Comparisons have been made with the ethical anarchism of Max Stirner, the existentialism of Kierkegaard,[6] and Nietzschean pessimism and amoralism. Parallels have been drawn with Sartre and Camus,[7] while, straining credibility to its extreme, prominent representatives of the Russian religious renaissance of the early twentieth century sought to claim him as a precursor.[8]

In contrast with all the above, in his introduction to the first English translation of the work Isaiah Berlin emphasizes its originality as "a moral and social philosophy . . . possessing affinities with views fully articulated only in our own time."[9] This chapter will take a similar approach, presenting *From the Other Shore* as anticipating that transformation in the understanding of the nature of history that would follow the greatest scientific revolution of the modern age. Highly quotable, *From the Other Shore* features in studies of Herzen mainly as a source of isolated citations. Yet taken together the essays form a sustained argument, the mature fruit of a preoccupation with the relevance of natural science to philosophy that had led him via chemistry, evolutionary biology, and the historicism of Hegel and Feuerbach to a fascination with the role of contingency in history and human life. When he began to compose them at the end of 1847, it was still generally considered axiomatic that historical development and natural evolution were two different types of process, each with its own laws and goals. This belief would be exploded scientifically a decade later, with the publication of *On the Origin of Species*. The first edition of the *Origin* sold out on the day it first appeared, and the Darwinian revolution began.

* * *

As the philosopher John Dewey has remarked, the theological clamor that attended the publication of the *Origin of Species* concealed the true nature of the crisis in systems of knowledge and representation that it brought about. The issue was not primarily between science and religion, but within science itself. It is now generally accepted that the farthest-reaching implications of Darwin's theory of natural selection lay in its challenge to teleological thought in all branches of intellectual endeavor. The notion of species change and the descent of man from apes had been discussed before Darwin. What was new was the hypothesis that evolution was, not a goal-directed process, but instead the by-product of adaptive responses to changes in local environments. Half a century later Dewey (whose pragmatism claimed direct descent from Darwinian methodology) stressed the magnitude of the intellectual revolution that Darwin had set in motion. "The conceptions that had reigned in the philosophy of nature and knowledge for two thousand years . . . rested on the assumption of the superiority of the fixed and final; they rested upon treating change and origin as signs of defect and unreality." Philosophy, science, and religion were rooted in the idea (inherent in the Greek formulation of the term *species*) that knowledge of individual phenomena meant referring their peculiarities to a general regulative principle: the phenomenal world could be rendered intelligible and given sanction and worth only by reference to concepts of ultimate purpose and design. These conceptions, part of the familiar furniture of the mind, were made redundant by a new logic. With some exaggeration, Dewey maintained that philosophy after Darwin "forswears enquiry after absolute origins and absolute finalities in order to explore specific values and the specific conditions that generate them."[10] Of course, elements of such a logic had existed as a skeptical strand in European science at least since Bacon's time. In the immediate pre-Darwinian era, as Gertrude Himmelfarb has observed, every possible doubt about the meaning and purpose of life had been expressed: "What the *Origin* did was to focus and stimulate the religious and nihilist passions of men. Dramatically and urgently, it confronted them with a situation that could no longer be evaded, a situation brought about not by any one scientific discovery, nor even by science as a whole, but by an antecedent condition of religious and philosophical turmoil."[11]

When the Darwinian revolution broke out, Herzen would be at its center in London. All around him in lecture halls, academies, learned journals, and the popular press, raged a debate over questions to which he had already given more than a decade of reflection since his first university essay, "On Man's Place in Nature." The originality of the view of history he had formed in that process can be appreciated best in the context of the issue of chance that lay at the heart of the controversy over *On the Origin of Species.*

Contingency versus Design

The question dividing Darwinian and anti-Darwinian parties in England and the Continent was less the origin of species than the origin of man. Darwin himself wished to avoid discussion of this subject "as so surrounded with prejudices."[12] (*On the Descent of Man* was published only in 1871, by which time his ideas had been broadly accepted by the scientific community.) But the continuity between animals and humans was clearly implied in the argument of the *Origin,* and scientists expressed a surprising degree of unanimity with the clerical establishment in their opposition to the new theories. Darwin's most ardent supporter, T. H. Huxley, later declared: "There is not the slightest doubt that, if a general council of the Church scientific had been held at that time, we should have been condemned by an overwhelming majority."[13] Even those who accepted that Darwin had killed off the old conception of the immutability of species often refused, like the Catholic *Dublin Review,* to condone the expansion of his theory to "such unreasonable lengths"[14] as to include man. Behind the resistance to Darwinism there was what Himmelfarb describes as a "primitive and pervasive revulsion" against the idea that human beings were no more than the culminating stage in a natural order encompassing primal matter and savage beasts; hence George Bernard Shaw's ironic opinion that though Darwinism could not be disproved, no decent-minded person would accept it.[15]

Acutely aware that he was treading on hallowed ground, Darwin had concluded the *Origin* with a reassuring reference to "the laws impressed on matter by the Creator": "As natural selection works solely by and for the good of each being, all corporeal and mental endowments will tend to progress toward perfection."[16] But when others equated natural selection with the intervention of a purposive power, he would reject that theory as "rubbish"—if all variations were designed to lead to the "right" end, natural selection would be superfluous.[17]

As the furor over the *Origin* died down, Darwin began to express himself with increasing forthrightness on the question of design. In an 1867 work he affirms that "no shadow of reason can be assigned for the belief that variations . . . which have been the groundwork through natural selection of the formation of the most perfectly adapted animals in the world, man included, were intentionally and specially guided."[18] In the *Origin* he contends that adaptations which, when viewed with hindsight, appeared to be goal-directed, are the outcome of "many complex contingencies" such as changing physical conditions and the nature of other competing inhabitants.[19] Believing in "no fixed law of development," Darwin marvels at the ignorance and presumption that leads us to invent overarching designs to explain the extinction of a single organic being. In the dynamic equilibrium of living things, the forces are so nicely balanced that, "while the face of nature remains uniform for long periods of time . . . assuredly the merest trifle would often give the victory to one organic being over another."[20] Any such fluctuation would set in motion adaptive changes whose extent had no necessary limits and whose direction could not be plotted in advance. Hence the irrelevance to Darwin's scheme of the two dominant interpretive categories of teleological thought: perfection and progress. Natural selection precluded universal standards of perfection, requiring instead that each organic being be "as perfect as, or slightly more perfect than, the other inhabitants of the same country with which it comes into competition."[21] The notion of perfection was qualified further by the existence of independently evolving and functionally similar solutions to complex problems, such as flight. Darwin did not reject the notion of biological progress (which he tended to identify with increasing complexity) but gave it a relativist interpretation. If, as he believed, evolutionary change tended to a maximum of economy in the use of resources, a retrogressive development—such as the loss of eyes in cave-dwelling animals—could increase the chances of survival of a particular organism. Nature in the Darwinian scheme was not a fine-tuned instrument created by the Divine Artificer for the ideal performance of its allotted tasks, but rather a collection of contingent structures adapting themselves with the help of whatever improvisations lay to hand in a never-ending process of crisis management. The cherished myth of Creation's plan was thus replaced by an undignified scramble, in which Darwin had the audacity to include the human species. In the democratic world of nature, where the sole criterion of fitness is the ability to reproduce, it is (as he reflects in his *Notebooks*) "absurd to talk of one animal being higher than another. *We* consider those, where the cerebral structure / intellectual faculties most developed, as highest. A bee doubtless would where the instincts were [most developed]."[22] Nor are human attributes so distinctive as to justify placing man in a category apart. "The mental faculties of man and the lower animals do not differ in kind, although immensely in degree."[23] One of Darwin's most revolutionary hypotheses (for which, he notes, he was "much abused")[24] was to attribute the origin of the moral sense, as well as the historical variations in value systems, to demands contingent on socialization: "The imperious word *ought* seems merely to imply the consciousness of the existence of a persistent instinct, either innate or partly acquired, serving humans as a guide."[25] The process of humanization was not nature straining upward to create her most perfect work, but the cumulative result of ad hoc modifications dictated by immediate needs: "What a chance it has been . . . that has made a man!"[26]

Darwin seems sometimes to have been tempted to draw back from the abyss that this discovery opened up. It has been pointed out that in arguing against belief in designed adaptations, he "retained the rhetoric of deliberate, piecemeal design": as used in the *Origin*, his central metaphor (natural selection) often carries voluntaristic and anthropomorphic connotations.[27] In later editions he emphasizes that by the term "nature" he meant "only the aggregate action and product of many natural laws."[28] However, while his earlier ambivalence helped reassure those who sought to superimpose human values on natural processes, Darwin never gave support to the social Darwinists who attempted to justify their models of social progress by appealing to the principle of the struggle for existence. When the efforts of German "scientific socialists" in this regard were brought to his attention, he dismissed them as "foolish."[29] The Darwinian revolution was neither so tidy nor so abrupt a break with former mentalities or methodologies as it has sometimes been made out to be, but its logic led irresistibly in one direction. As Robert Young admirably puts it, Darwin and the evolutionists on whose ideas he built "together, by a confused mixture of metaphysical, methodological and scientific arguments which depended heavily on analogical and metaphorical expressions . . . brought the earth, life and man into the domain of natural laws."[30]

* * *

"We superimpose upon [nature] a sentimental personality and our passions; we become oblivious to our metaphors, and take the turns of phrase we use for reality. Unaware of the absurdity of it, we introduce our own petty household rules into the economy of the universe for which the life of generations, peoples, of entire planets, has no importance in relation to the general development."[31] When the essay containing this passage was published, the *Origin* was still a bundle of notes. The parallels between nature and history that Herzen drew in *From the Other Shore* strikingly anticipate ideas that Darwin would express with much greater circumspection in his scientific writings. Two years before embarking on the essays, Herzen had declared to his incredulous circle, "There is no philosophy without physiology," proceeding in defiance of the censor to give public praise to Karl Rouillier's pioneering achievement in erasing the boundaries between the natural sciences and human history. *From the Other Shore* would use the same approach in dealing with the events of 1848 and their aftermath.

The Cross of Sober Knowledge

Darwin would admit subsequently that in the first edition of the *Origin* he had not been entirely able to free himself from the prevalent teleological habits of thought. Herzen records in his memoirs that when he began his cycle of essays in 1847 he was not yet reconciled to the vision of history they would present: "I still frantically and obstinately sought *a way out*."[32] The struggle and sacrifice involved in bearing "the heavy cross of sober knowledge" had been a constant refrain in his writings of the 1840s. He sees the events of 1848 as forcing a final choice between the "bliss of lunacy" and "the unhappiness of knowledge," confessing in the essay dated July 1848:

It is hard to part with thoughts that we have grown up with, have become accustomed to, thoughts that have comforted and consoled us. . . . Men are afraid of their own logic and having summoned the Church and the State, family and morality, good and evil, to face logic's judgment, they then try to save the remnants, the fragments of the past. Having repudiated Christianity, they cling to the immortality of the soul, to idealism, to Providence.

. . . The world will not know liberty until everything religious and political is transformed into something simple, human, susceptible to criticism and denial. . . . It is not enough to despise the crown, one must give up respecting the Phrygian cap; it is not enough to consider *lèse-majesté* a crime, one must look at *salus populi* as being one.

It is time for man to put the republic on trial, along with its legislation, its system of representation, all our notions about the citizen and his relations to other citizens and the State. There will be many executions: things nearest and dearest will have to be sacrificed—merely to sacrifice the detestable is not the problem. This is the whole point: to surrender what we love if we are convinced that it is not true.[33]

Herzen recalls that in *From the Other Shore*, "I pursued the last idols I had left. With irony I avenged myself on them for the pain and the deception."[34] This struggle to achieve consistency in his view of freedom is reflected in the dialogical form of three of the essays, with something of Herzen on each side. This technique impressed Dostoevsky, who told Herzen on a visit to London that what he liked most about the work was that his opponent was also very clever—"Many a time he has driven you into a corner."[35] Herzen warns the reader not to look for solutions in his book. "In general modern man has no solutions." He insisted to his Moscow friends that it should be seen, not as a systematic treatise *(ne nauka)*, but rather as a fermenting agent, "a flail against nonsensical theories . . . it angers people and makes them think."[36]

In the first essay, composed on the eve of the 1848 revolution, he is accused by his companion, an impatient believer in progress, of aloof detachment from the unfolding events. He replies that his calm reflects not indifference but acceptance of the fact that the historical process has its own embryogenesis, "which does not coincide with the dialectic of pure reason." "You are looking for a banner," he observes, "I am trying to lose one." We must cease to believe that humanity lives under some special dispensation: its path, like nature's, was subject to deviation and disease. It could continue for millions of years, or end tomorrow in a geological cataclysm. "In nature, as in the souls of men, there slumber countless forces and possibilities, under suitable conditions they develop . . . or they may fall by the wayside, take a new direction, stop, collapse. The death of one man is no less absurd than the end of the whole human race. Who guaranteed the immortality of a planet? It will be as little able to survive a revolution in the solar system as the genius of Socrates could the hemlock. . . . On the whole, nature is perfectly indifferent to the result. . . . She, having buried the whole human race, will lovingly begin all over again, with monstrous ferns and reptiles half a league long, probably with certain improvements suggested by new surroundings, new conditions."[37]

His companion protests, if such is the nature of history, we have nothing to live or to die for. "Why all these efforts?" he demands. "The life of peoples becomes mere idle play, it piles grain on grain, pebble on pebble, until once again everything comes tumbling down to earth and men begin to crawl out from under the ruins, to clear a space and build huts for themselves out of moss, boards and fallen capitals, only to achieve, after centuries of long effort, destruction once more. It was not for nothing that Shakespeare said that history was a tale told by an idiot, signifying nothing."[38]

This interchange anticipates the famous exchange of letters between Darwin and the Christian evolutionist Asa Gray, who feared that Darwin's theory could be held to imply that the world was shaped entirely by pure chance. Darwin's reply acknowledges the existence of laws that may or may not have been expressly designed, and that direct the broad channels of life, "with the details, whether good or bad, left to the working out of what we may call chance."[39] Herzen makes the same distinction: "Nature has hinted only vaguely . . . at her intentions, and has left all the details to the will of man, circumstances, climate, and a thousand conflicts." His friend has been misled by "categories not fitted to catch the flow of life. Think carefully: is this end that you seek—a program, an order? Who conceived it, who declared it? Is it something inevitable or not? If it is, are we mere puppets? . . .

Are we morally free beings, or wheels in a machine? I prefer to think of life, and therefore of history, as an aim attained rather than a means to something else."[40]

There follows a philippic against the cult of progress preached by almost all the radical thinkers of the age, with the notable exception of Proudhon. Here is Herzen at his polemical best:

> If progress is the end, for whom are we working? Who is this Moloch who, as the toilers approach him, instead of rewarding them, only recedes, and as a consolation to the exhausted, doomed multitudes crying "morituri te salutant" can give back only the mocking answer that after their death all will be beautiful on earth. Do you truly wish to condemn all human beings alive today to the sad role of caryatids supporting a floor for others some day to dance on, or of wretched galley slaves, up to their knees in mud, dragging a barge filled with some mysterious treasure and with the humble words "progress in the future" inscribed on its bow. . . . An end that is infinitely remote is not an end, but . . . a trap. An end must be nearer . . . at the very least, the laborer's wage, or pleasure in the work done. Each epoch, each generation, each life had, and has, its own fullness; and en route new demands grow, new experiences, new methods. . . . This generic growth is not an aim, as you suppose, but the hereditary characteristic of a succession of generations. . . .
>
> The struggle, the reciprocal action of natural forces and the forces of will, the consequences of which one cannot know in advance, give an overwhelming interest to every historical epoch. If humanity marched straight toward some kind of result, there would be no history, only logic. . . . If there were a libretto, history would lose all interest, become unnecessary, boring, ludicrous.[41]

Hence Herzen regards it as "comforting" that promising developments can be cut off prematurely, legitimate hopes unrealized: "To me these losses are proof that every historical phase has its complete reality, its own individuality, its own good that is peculiar to it alone and that perishes along with it."[42]

In the first essay he likens himself to a surgeon, cutting away dead flesh to save a patient from a chronic illness. In the dialogues that follow he assumes the persona of a naturalist on the model of Krupov, the commonsense doctor in *Who Is to Blame?* He observes that modern Europeans are reconciled to the insubordination of nature, but centuries of romantic beliefs have convinced them that in history man can do as he likes. Returning to a metaphor he had used in *Letters on the Study of Nature*, he insists there is no stone wall between the two. "The development of nature passes imperceptibly into the development of mankind, . . . these are two chapters of one novel, two phases of one process. . . . Part of everything that takes place in history is influenced by physiology, by dark forces. It is true that the laws of historical development are not opposed to the laws of logic, but their paths do not coincide with those of thought, just as nothing in nature coincides with the abstract norms constructed by pure reason. . . . Has anyone ever given serious thought to the physiology of social life, of history as a truly objective science? No one: neither conservatives, nor radicals, nor philosophers, nor historians."[43] The hallowed phrases we use to describe human virtues disguise a simple physiological truth: "Man is an animal with a remarkably well organized brain. Therein lies his power." Lacking the tiger's litheness, the lion's strength, and the acuteness of their senses, "he discovered within himself infinite cunning and a multitude of tame qualities which, together with a natural inclination to live in herds, placed him on the first rung of social life." Among these qualities is a strong inclination to obedience, a trait equally observable in the animals domesticated by the human race. "The wolf eats the lamb because it is hungry and because the lamb is weaker, but the wolf doesn't demand slavery from the lamb, the lamb doesn't submit; it protests with cries, with flight; man introduces into the animal world of savage independence and self-assertion an element of loyal and humble service, the element of Caliban. That alone made possible the development of Prospero. And here again is the same merciless economy of nature, her calculation of means, whereby an excess in one direction is paid for by unfulfillment in another, so that having stretched the neck and front legs of the giraffe to fantastic lengths, she stunts its hind legs."[44]

"A long life in society develops the brain." The fact that over many generations a certain tendency toward freedom had developed in some privileged strata of society had led Rousseau to utter his "famous absurdity": "Man is born to be free—and is everywhere in chains!" What, Herzen asks, "would you say to a man who, nodding his head sadly, remarked that 'Fish are born to fly—but everywhere they swim'?" A pathologist would argue that up to the present, slavery had been the dominant condition of human development. "You," he tells his companion, "when speaking of history and nations, speak of flying fish, whereas I speak of fish in general."[45] The power of heredity and contingent circumstances had turned the teachings of early Christianity and the revolution of 1789 into instruments of violence and oppression. The tiny cohort of flying fish who love beauty and cherish individual freedom have no grounds for presuming that their values will become generally accepted. The mass of humanity at whose cost their development had been achieved were still in the throes of "*Naturgewalt,* instinct, dark forces and passion."[46] Ignoring the unique physiology of the human race and driven by a belated sense of guilt, the liberals of 1848 had preferred to invent the people rather than observe them. Men of books, journals and clubs, they resembled the early naturalists whose study of nature was confined to the herbarium and the museum. They had constructed a fictitious people out of memories of things read, arraying it in a Roman toga or a shepherd's cloak and setting it up as the idol of a new political religion, expecting "that every peasant should suddenly become a political person . . . and that this new Cincinnatus should now concern himself with general issues."[47] If they had studied the people in the village and the marketplace, they would not have been surprised to see them voting for Louis-Napoleon. To them the word "Republic" meant only the imposition of a new tax, whereas the name of Bonaparte appealed to their national pride, evoking victories celebrated in popular song and story. We now know, Herzen observed, that it is not enough to print an illustrated edition of the *Droits de l'homme* for humans to become free. A century after Rousseau and half a century after the Convention, the masses were still blind to the concepts of individual liberty, free speech, and the Social Contract: the revolutionary ferment that inspired the European proletariat came from hunger. While the liberals were playing with revolution, those masses had emerged, demanding their share of life's bounties. "Is it that you don't see . . . the new barbarians marching to destroy? . . . It is they . . . whose muttering we hear above and below us, in garrets and in the cellars, while we sit on the *piano nobile,* 'over pastry and champagne,' talking of socialism."[48]

Herzen predicts a long night for Europe, followed by a new spring in which socialism would play a major part. But it would be foolish to expect that our ideals will materialize in the form in which they take shape in our minds. The Gospels were not fulfilled according to the expectations of the early Christians; what had followed were ages of revolution and reconstruction, in all of which Christianity had a dominant role. "Life realizes only that aspect of an idea that falls on favorable soil, and the soil in this case doesn't remain a mere passive medium, but gives its sap, contributes its own elements. The new element born of the conflict between Utopias and conservatism enters life, not as the one or as the other side expected it—it enters transformed, different, composed of memories and hopes, of existing things and things to be, of traditions and pledges, of belief and science, of Romans who have lived too long and Germans who have not lived at all, united by one church, alien to both."[49] Civilization, he observes, "dreams the apotheosis of its own being, but life is under no obligation to realize such fantasies and ideas. . . . Roman civilization was higher, far more humane than the barbarian world, but in the very confusion of barbarism were the seeds of things not to be found in the civilization of Rome, and so barbarism triumphed despite the *Corpus Juris Civilis* and the wisdom of Roman philosophers. Nature rejoices in what has been attained, and reaches beyond it; she has no desire to wrong what exists; let it live as long as it can, while the new is still growing. That is why it is so difficult to fit the work of nature into a straight line: Nature hates regimentation, she casts herself in all directions and never marches forward in step."[50]

The future of socialism would involve the same combination of abstract doctrine and existing fact. It "will develop in all its phases until it reaches its own extremes and absurdities. Then once again a cry of denial will break from the titanic chest of the revolutionary minority, and again a mortal struggle will begin, in which socialism will play the role of contemporary conservatism and will be overwhelmed in the subsequent revolution, as yet unknown to us. The eternal play of life, ruthless as death, inevitable as birth, the *corsi e ricorsi* of history, the *perpetuum mobile* of the pendulum."[51]

This prediction was made in an age when thought was dominated by visionary utopias of all political colors, and when communism was declared by Marx to be "the *definitive* solution of the antagonism between man and nature, and between man and man . . . the conflict between existence and essence, between objectification and self-affirmation, between freedom and necessity, between the individual and species. It is the solution of the riddle of history and knows itself to be this solution."[52]

* * *

In the essay "Omnia mea mecum porto," written in 1850, Herzen reflects on the consequences for his own future role of the lessons learned from 1848. He identifies with an image that had begun to occupy his mind since the June days: the Roman philosophers who, faced with the clash between two worlds and declining to choose between the corruption of the old and the destructiveness of the new, had withdrawn into isolation somewhere on the shores of the Mediterranean. Humans are freer than is usually believed; a large part of our destiny lies in our own hands. There are no eternal rewards or punishments: "Indeed, the truly free man *creates* his own morality."[53]

This last phrase has been cited in support of the view of Herzen as a precursor of existentialist anarchism and Nietzschean nihilistic pessimism. According to Malia, *From the Other Shore* "dissolved all rational values and schemes, whether of 'science' or of socialism . . . thereby his philosophy ended in universal negation and the world became in a sense absurd."[54] Herzen was indeed much admired by Nietzsche.[55] However, some of Nietzsche's tributes were based on a misconception. Herzen consistently situates moral freedom within the boundaries of historical development: his argument is not that the world is meaningless, but that humans have historically been seeking its meaning in the wrong place. The physician who is his mouthpiece declares himself to be neither an optimist nor a pessimist; he is more modest than both in his respect for the physiology of social existence. "I watch, I examine, without any preconceived notion, without any prepared ideas, and I am in no hurry to reach a verdict." As shown by the fierce opposition a few years later to *On the Origin of Species*, to situate humans in the processes of the natural world was to challenge centuries of faith in the uniqueness of their nature and destiny. "As a social being, man strives to love." Like Darwin, Herzen sees the moral sense as a product of socialization, built up by physiology and inheritance as well as the "physiologico-moral" element—education.[56] Contrary to the pessimists' belief, the movement of history is neither random nor determined: among the forces that fashion it are human reason and moral ideals.[57] "The future is created by the combination of a thousand causes, some necessary, some accidental, plus human will, which adds unexpected dramatic *dénouements* and *coups de théâtre*." It is this unpredictability that gives history its interest. "All is *ex tempore:* there are no frontiers, no itineraries. There exist conditions, sacred discontent; the flame of life and the eternal challenges to the fighters to try their strength." History, like nature, improvises, "she rarely repeats herself . . . she uses every chance, every coincidence, she knocks simultaneously at a thousand gates. . . . Who knows which may open?"[58]

Herzen discerns an upward movement in this process, but his conception of progress is not to the liking of his idealist friend. As each generation builds on experience stored in the memory of the species, new demands and methods arise. "Some capacities improve at the expense of others; finally, the cerebral tissue improves. . . . Why do you smile? . . . Yes, yes, indeed, the substance of the brain improves." Comparing the skull of an ancient bull with a modern domesticated one, Goethe had established that while the latter had grown more fragile, the volume occupied by the brain had increased. "Why do you consider man less capable of development than a bull? This generic growth is not an aim, as you suppose, but the hereditary characteristic of a succession of generations."[59] The wonder was not that mankind had not progressed further, but rather that on the whole it did so little evil. While individuals could not but reflect their time and environment, their moral autonomy developed in inverse proportion to their dependence on their milieu. At some periods those who outpaced the majority might find fulfillment in a common cause; at others they might be condemned to isolation, irreconcilably at odds with their society. But it did not follow that they should abjure their stage of development.

> If there is something in you . . . that will stir others profoundly, it will not be lost, such is the economy of nature. Your strength, like a pinch of yeast, will . . . ferment all that comes under its influence; your ac-

tions, thoughts, words will take their place without any special effort. If you have no such strength or strength of a kind that has no
effect on contemporary man, that is not a great misfortune either for
you or for others. . . . We do not live to entertain others, we live for
ourselves. . . .

Instead of assuring the people that they passionately want what
we want, it would be better for us to ask whether they want something different, or whether they want anything at all at this moment,
then . . . to leave in peace, without doing violence to others or wasting
ourselves. *Maybe* this negative action will be the beginning of a new
life. In any case, it will be a virtuous act.[60]

From the Other Shore was much in advance of its time in its two-
pronged attack on the optimism of radical theories of progress and
on the philosophical pessimism that had begun to challenge it, pioneered by Schopenhauer's critique of metaphysical systems that
presented empirical reality as the incarnation of an a priori moral or
rational order. Published in 1818, his treatise *Die Welt als Wille und
Vorstellung* (*The World as Will and Representation*) began to attract
general attention only in the wake of the defeat of radical hopes in
1848. Nietzsche would later acknowledge his debt to Schopenhauer
as a precursor, paying tribute to his boldness "in confronting suffering and monsters that other philosophers only pretended to
fight."[61]

Schopenhauer himself frequently emphasized the courage and
pioneering integrity of his response to the problem of human freedom
in a world without transcendence, and the ruthlessness of his exposure of the self-deception of previous philosophies. He argued that
true being was a timeless will of which individual consciousness
was an aberration. Human history was a blind struggle for existence
which set the individual against the species in an endless and insa-
tiable pursuit of egocentric aims. We should reject the fantasy of progress in favor of the only goal attainable by humans: self-knowledge.
The highest mode of understanding is the turning of the will away
from the world in renunciation of the limitations of finite being:
"The vanity of existence is revealed in the whole form existence
assumes: in the infiniteness of time and space contrasted with the
finiteness of the individual in both; in the fleeting present as the

sole form in which actuality exists; in the contingency and relativity of all things . . . Time is that by virtue of which everything becomes nothingness in our hands." He represents the "scornful mastery of chance" as playing a purely destructive role in the "tragicomedy" of world history: "It is nature's way of declaring: 'the individual is nothing and less than nothing. I destroy millions of individuals every day for sport and pastime; I abandon their fate to chance, to the most capricious and wanton of my children, who harasses them at his leisure.' "[62] The prodigality with which nature, as Herzen puts it, "pours the whole of herself into the present moment,"[63] the infinite variety and resourcefulness of the evolutionary adaptations of animals, are for Schopenhauer the most compelling of demonstrations of the futility of all transient existence: "We cannot help asking what comes of all this, and what is attained by animal existence that demands such immense preparations. And there is nothing to show but the satisfaction of hunger and sexual passion and . . . a little momentary gratification, such as falls to the lot of every individual animal, now and then, between its endless demands and exertions. If we put the two together, the inexpressible ingenuity of the preparations, the untold abundance of the means, and the inadequacy of what is thus aimed at and attained, we are driven to the view that life is a business whose returns are far from covering the cost."[64]

One may assume that Herzen was well acquainted with Schopenhauer's philosophy.[65] "Is the game worth the candle?" his pessimist bitterly demands; the same phrase recurs in Schopenhauer's work as a refrain accompanying his insistence on the worthlessness of an existence in which "the present is always inadequate, . . . the future is uncertain, and the past irrecoverable."[66] Herzen brushes aside his friend's outpourings of despair as "the tantrums of a sulky lover." What you want, he tells him, "is that the world should, out of gratitude for your devotion, dance to your tune and, as soon as you realize it has its own step and rhythm, you feel angry. . . . You haven't the curiosity to watch it doing its own dance." To look at the end and not at the action itself is "the greatest of errors. Of what use to the plant is its bright, gorgeous flower, its intoxicating scent that will pass away? None at all. But nature is not so miserly, and does not disdain what is transient, what lives only in the moment."[67]

He dismisses the pretensions of philosophical pessimism. As a supposedly pioneering attempt to confront the implications for human freedom of a godless world, it was merely the latest historical manifestation of religious alienation. There are echoes of Proudhon's *Contradictions* in the pages he devotes to this "strongest of all the chains by which man is fettered": "The submission of the individual to society, to the people, to humanity, to the Idea, is merely a continuation of human sacrifice. . . . All religions have based morality on obedience, that is to say, on voluntary slavery. . . . The individual, who is the true, real monad of society, has always been sacrificed to some social concept, some collective noun, some banner or other. For whose sake this was done, to whom was the sacrifice made, who profited by it, who was liberated at the price of the individual's freedom, no one ever asked. Everyone sacrificed (at least in words) himself and everyone else."[68]

With its fear of the natural and yearning for some unattainable bliss, dualism was Christianity "raised to the power of logic":

> Its chief method consists in dividing into spurious antitheses that which is in fact indivisible . . . in pitting these abstractions one against the other, and then effecting an artificial reconciliation between what was always joined in inseparable unity . . .
>
> As Christ tramples upon the flesh, thereby redeeming the human race, so in dualism idealism sides with one shadow against another, granting spirit the monopoly over matter, species the monopoly over the particular, sacrificing man to the state, the state to humanity. . . . Our language is the language of dualism; it has destroyed all simple notions; our imagination has no other images, no other metaphors . . . our entire morality originates from this same source. This morality demanded constant sacrifice, ceaseless heroism, endless selflessness. That is why its rules were hardly ever obeyed. . . . Christianity, dividing man into, on the one hand, something ideal and, on the other, something animal, has confused his understanding. Finding no way out of the struggle between conscience and the passions, he has become so used to hypocrisy . . . that the contradiction between the word and the deed does not disturb him.[69]

The time had come to examine "these rhetorical exercises . . . composed of *réchauffé* Christianity, diluted with the muddy water of rationalism and the sugary flavor of philanthropy":

> What is the meaning of all these elucubrations against egoism and individualism? . . . Of course men are egoists, because they are individuals. . . . We are egoists—and therefore we fight for independence, for well-being, for the recognition of our rights, that is why we thirst for love, seek action and cannot deny those same rights to others without obvious contradiction. . . .
>
> The fact is quite simply that egoism and social sense (brotherhood and love) are not virtues or vices. They are the basic elements of human life, without which there would be no history, no development, but either the scattered life of wild beasts or else a herd of tame troglodytes. Kill the social sense in man—and you will get a savage orangutan; kill egoism in him, and he will become a tame monkey. . . . The real point is not to fulminate against egoism and extol brotherhood, but to unite freely and harmoniously those two ineradicable elements of social life.[70]

While few practiced the selflessness demanded by the "moral gibberish" of dualism, even fewer had the courage to attack it: "Is it so strange that after this we are unable to organize either the inner or the outer life, that we demand too much, sacrifice too much, scorn the possible, are indignant because what is impossible scorns us." The credibility of this approach to the physical world was evaporating with every new advance in science: "We want alchemy, magic, but life and nature go their ways indifferent, submitting to man only to the extent to which he has learned to work by their very methods."[71] 1848 had dealt a deathblow to idealist determinism, but as Herzen subsequently observed, its teleological vision was acquiring an afterlife in existential pessimism: "In general we know best, in nature, in history and in life, the gains and successes: we are only now beginning to feel that the cards are not so well stacked as we had thought, because we ourselves are a failure, *a losing card.* It grieves us to realize that the idea is impotent, that truth has no binding power over the world of actuality. A new kind of Manichaeism takes hold of us, and we are ready, *par dépit,* to believe in rational (that is, purposive) evil, as we believed in rational good—that is the last tribute we pay to idealism."[72]

"Our language is the language of dualism." This was scarcely an exaggeration. Toward the end of the next century Stephen Jay Gould would observe that we are scarcely beginning to come to terms with the implications of Darwin's discoveries for our understanding of *Homo sapiens*. In the popular imagination the march of progress remains "*the* canonical representation of evolution," reinforcing a comforting view of the inevitability and superiority of the human race.[73] But, as Darwin reassured the Christian evolutionist Asa Gray, contingency was not to be confused with randomness and the destruction of all meaningful notions of truth, objectivity, and freedom.

The first essay of *From the Other Shore* is headed with an epigraph from Goethe: "Ist's denn zu grosses Geheimnis was Gott und der Mensch und die Welt sei? / Nein, doch niemand hoert's gerne, da bleibt es geheim [Is the nature of God and Man and the world really such a big secret? No, but nobody takes it in willingly, so that's why it stays secret]." The realist in the dialogue there describes his idealist friend's pontificating attitude to the world as "not merely vanity—it is immense cowardice. . . . Pain distracts, absorbs, comforts. . . . Yes, yes, it comforts, and above all, like every occupation, it prevents men from looking into themselves, into life."[74] This reproach was the product of a decade of painful introspection that had led him to the conviction that humans preferred to ascribe their misfortunes to a universal world order rather than the "terrible whirlpool" of chance. "The aim of life is life itself." His sermons on that theme to his friends and to himself in the mid-1840s anticipate the dialogues of *From the Other Shore*.

"The brain has grown one-sidedly because of idealism." Herzen concedes that the notion of a special destiny (diagnosed as a neurological disorder by the doctor in *Who Is to Blame?*) is so deeply entrenched in humans' sense of what we are that it is strongly resistant to rational argument or empirical evidence. "You think that doubt . . . is easy?" he asks his questioner in the last dialogue of *From the Other Shore*. "But can you know what a man, in a moment of pain, weakness, exhaustion, might not be ready to give for a belief? But where will you acquire it?"[75] As Dostoevsky had perceived, there is no final resolution of the confrontation in the work.

The sense of isolation brought on by his opposition to the system builders of his age had led Herzen to compare his predicament to that of Roman philosophers in the early Christian era. But a more inspiring role model was to be found in Proudhon, who had been ostracized by the liberators of humanity for "the immoral statement that the republic is for man, not man for the republic."[76] The fearless eloquence and wit of his responses to the abuse hurled at him from all sides had impressed Herzen profoundly in 1848. The two had been brought together by their focus on a common target—religious and philosophical dualism as the intellectual ground of political oppression, and by their rejection of all systems purporting to supply final answers to perennial questions.[77] The core of the argument in *From the Other Shore* was already contained in the two cycles of essays Herzen had completed while still in Russia (key metaphors of which reappear in the later work)[78] and the "exercise in practical philosophy" he had communicated to his friends in the mid-1840s, urging them to stop yearning after unattainable goals, accept the limitations of contingent existence, open themselves up to the present, and exploit its potential to the full.

Proudhon's tutorship in practical politics was now to be crucial for setting him on the path he would take in his remaining years in Europe. In a memoir on Proudhon published in 1859 he wrote: "In most sociological works the ideals presented, which almost always either are unattainable or boil down to some one-sided solution, are not significant; what matters is what, in arriving at them, is seen as the *question*." Proudhon's "fearful power" lay precisely in the destructive force of his attacks on hallowed traditions: "He is as much the poet of dialectics as Hegel is, with the difference that one stands on the tranquil heights of philosophy and the other is thrust into the turmoil of popular disturbances and the hand-to-hand fighting of parties."[79]

"We do not build, we destroy; we do not proclaim a new revelation, we eliminate the old lie." These words from the introduction to *From the Other Shore* could equally well have been written by Proudhon, as could the following lines from one of its dialogues: "Could you please explain to me why belief in God is ridiculous and belief in humanity is not; why belief in the kingdom of heaven is silly, but belief in utopias is clever? Having discarded positive religion, we retain all the habits of religion, and having lost paradise in heaven we believe in the coming paradise on earth."[80]

London building, now with commemorative plaque, where the Free Russian Press was housed.

In his penultimate essay, written in Zurich in 1849, Herzen declares his intention to remain in Europe in order to continue his struggle against "the pharisees of the conservative and revolutionary world." But "to whom shall we talk? . . . About what? . . . I really have no notion, only that this is something stronger than I."[81]

He would find the answer in the establishment of his Free Russian Press.

CHAPTER SEVENTEEN

The Living Truth

We cannot remain in our present state of chaos—that is clear; but in order *consciously* to escape from it, we need to resolve another question: Is the European path of development the only possible and inevitable one, so that each people, wherever it lives, whoever its ancestors may have been, must follow it, just as an infant must cut its first teeth . . . ? Or is this path itself a particular instance of development, a part of the universal human canvas which was generated and shaped under particular, individual influences . . . ? And in this case wouldn't it be strange for us to repeat the whole long metamorphosis of Western history, knowing in advance *le secret de la comédie?*

HERZEN

IN his memoirs Herzen reflects on the destruction of his personal and political hopes between 1848 and 1852:

Our historical vocation, our achievement, consists in this: that through our disillusionment, our sufferings, we reach resignation and humility in the face of the truth, and spare future generations from that grief. By means of us humanity is attaining sobriety; we are its hangover, we are its birth pangs . . . but we must not forget that the child or the mother, or perhaps both, may die by the wayside, and then—yes then—history, in its prodigal way, will begin a new pregnancy. . . . *E sempre bene*, gentlemen!

We know how Nature disposes of individuals; later, sooner, with no victims or on heaps of corpses, it's all the same to her; she . . . goes her way, or any way that chances. Tens of thousands of years she spends depositing a coral reef, every spring abandoning to death the ranks that have gone too far ahead. The polyps die without suspecting that they have served the *progress* of the reef.

We also shall serve something. To enter the future as an element in it does not yet mean that the future will fulfill our ideals. Rome did not bring into being Plato's republic, nor the Greek idea in general. The Middle Ages were not the development of Rome. Contemporary

Western thought will be incorporated into the flesh of history, will have its influence and its place, just as our body will pass into the composition of grass, of sheep, of cutlets, and of humans. That sort of immortality is not to our taste, but what can we do about it?

Now I am accustomed to these thoughts, they no longer frighten me. But at the end of 1849 I was stunned by them, and in spite of the fact that every event, every encounter, every contact, every person vied with each other to tear away the last green leaves, I still frantically and obstinately sought *a way out,* . . .

I was unhappy and perplexed when these thoughts began to come to me; I tried by every means to escape from them. Like a traveler who had lost his way, like a beggar, I knocked at every door, stopped passers-by and asked the way, but every encounter and every event led to the same result, to *humility before the truth,* to self-sacrificing acceptance of it.

Three years ago I sat at the bedside of a sick woman and saw death drawing her slowly step by step to the grave. That life was my entire wealth. Darkness spread around me, I was a savage in my dull despair, but I did not comfort myself with hopes, did not betray my grief for a moment with the stultifying thought of a meeting beyond the grave.

All the more therefore, I shall not be false to myself over the general questions [of society].[1]

The resolve Herzen expressed in the last sentence of this passage was to be the guiding principle of his efforts to influence political developments in Russia during the last two decades of his life. The "Russian socialism" he preached in those years has commonly been seen as a utopian construct.[2] It was, on the contrary, a consistent attempt to apply to the situation in Russia the respect for the physiology of history so alien to the radical dreamers of 1848. "Life realizes only that aspect of an idea that falls on favorable soil"—the leitmotif of *From the Other Shore,* this conviction would set him at odds with ideologists of Left and Right alike.

The Notion of the Prosaic Worker

When Herzen turned his attention back to Russia after the collapse of revolutionary hopes in the West, it was with a concrete and limited objective. In December 1852, four months after his arrival in London, he mentioned in a letter to Maria Reichel "a wonderful project now turning in my mind—to begin agitation for the emancipation of the peasantry."[3] In February 1853 he broke the silence imposed on his compatriots with his Free Russian Press, founded with the help of Polish émigrés in London who had already established a means of channeling illegal literature into Russia: a censorship-free forum for all sections of Russian society to voice their views on the current state of Russia and its future. This move he described in a letter to the Polish émigré committee in London as "the most revolutionary action a Russian can undertake at the present time."[4] In a manifesto entitled "To My Brothers in Russia" he invited his countrymen to send him anything written in the spirit of freedom, from scientific and factual articles to literature and poetry, including the recent works of Russian writers then only passing secretly from hand to hand.[5] Its first publication contained an address to the Russian gentry in which Herzen exhorted them to obey the spirit of the times and free their serfs before this was either imposed on them from above or brought about by an uprising from below. He was overjoyed by news of the death of Nicolas I on 2 March 1855: "I felt as though several years had rolled off my shoulders."[6] In the days that followed he conceived the idea of founding a periodical review named the *Polar Star*, after the review published by the Decembrist Ryleev. Its first number was timed to coincide with the twenty-fifth anniversary of Ryleev's execution. Calling for contributions, he announced: "We have no system, no doctrine; we extend our invitation equally to our Europeans and our Pan-Slavists, to the moderate and immoderate, the careful and the careless. . . . As far as means are concerned, we open all doors, summon all arguments," excluding only those in support of a continuation of the status quo.[7] Seven small volumes appeared between 1855 and 1862; an eighth followed in 1869. Herzen's contribution to the first of these was an open letter to the new tsar, Alexander II, urging him to inaugurate his reign by freeing the serfs and granting free speech.

The Free Russian Press did not go unrecognized in England. Early in 1855 the London weekly *The Athenaeum* published a generous and historically informed article assessing the likely future significance of Herzen's project:

> Are many of our readers aware that there is a Russian press in London? . . . A veritable Russian press,—printing Russian books in

the Russian language, for the purpose of circulation in Russia? Such is the fact. . . . . Moreover, it is free. No censor suggests its issues, no police controls its types. . . . We think our readers will agree with us, that the existence of such a press is of some importance. Much of the best literature of Russia is a contraband literature—existing only in manuscript,—and therefore liable to serious accidents. Whatever the moral nature of that literature . . . it is most desirable that it be preserved. . . . Such a literature is a necessary phase in the growth of a nation,—and ought to be preserved with the jealous care which we bestow—or ought to bestow—on those documents of our own history which record its intellectual struggles.[8]

This reads as a remarkably modern judgment, even now.

In April 1856 Ogarev arrived unexpectedly in London from Russia with his second wife, Natalie (the daughter of his Aksheno neighbor, A. A. Tuchkov), and they set up house with Herzen. Seventeen years Herzen's junior, Natalie became infatuated with him soon after the couple's arrival in England, and Ogarev acquiesced in their relationship, which was to produce a daughter, Lisa, followed by a twin boy and girl (Ogarev remaining the nominal father). But their union was not to be happy. Natalie's highly unstable nature, expressed in frequent outbursts of hysteria, alienated Herzen's elder children and cast a cloud of gloom over the household. Alternating between extremes of guilt and resentment over the ambivalence of her position, she constantly threatened to go back to Russia together with her children.

With Ogarev's encouragement, in July 1857 Herzen founded *The Bell (Kolokol)*, which until its demise a decade later appeared first monthly, and within a year fortnightly, in order to cope with an ever-increasing flow of material. Under Nicolas, contributions to the London Press from Russia had been sparse, but with the beginning of the new reign the all-pervasive atmosphere of fear gave way to a mood of optimistic expectation and a general consensus, with the new tsar's wavering support, on the need for fundamental reforms. Alexander's intention to embark on the liberation of the serfs became known at the end of December 1857 with the publication of an edict requiring the nobility of one province to meet for discussions on the form emancipation should take. Herzen responded in the *Bell* with an article praising the tsar for opening a new era for Russia,[9] but warning that the end of serfdom would be only the first step in the task of delivering the peasants from the power of rapacious landlords and the arbitrariness of officials. The question of the emancipation of the peasantry with adequate land was to be at the center of his efforts to influence the new reign. To a Polish correspondent who questioned his preoccupation with a "mere" economic measure, he responded: "as if the economic question is not the main, the vital, the only source of salvation."[10] To reduce the religious and political questions over which so much blood had been shed to questions of economics was the principal challenge facing the contemporary world. In 1847 he had confessed to Ogarev his lack of interest in economic matters: the political catastrophes of the next decade in Europe had reversed his priorities.

* * *

Conceived as a forum for public discussion on the way forward after emancipation and smuggled into Russia in large numbers, the *Bell* or its content reached all sections of Russian society.[11] In response to his request for contributions, Herzen was deluged by letters from every part of the empire with details of the corruption and brutality of individual landlords and officials, financial and administrative scandals, and ferment among the peasants. Secret official documents arrived at his London desk, along with the protests and programs of revolutionaries, liberals, and conservatives, some of which he published in two collections entitled *Voices from Russia*. The products of his press were avidly read (not least in the highest government circles, whose members were often less informed than Herzen about the internal state of their country). Thus, from London he presided over the birth of public opinion in Russia.

As a starting point for discussion he set out a three-point "minimum program": emancipation with land, the abolition of corporal punishment, and an end to censorship (he subsequently added a fourth: openness in court procedures). Five years later he recalled the modesty of those demands: "We confined ourselves to the wish for the rough iron chains to be removed from the Russian people, so that its development could become possible."[12] On ultimate goals the *Bell* was silent at this period: Herzen's unspoken hope was that his program would set his country on the path to the Russian socialism whose principles he believed to exist in embryo in the structure of the village commune.

His promise that the *Bell* would resound in response to all instances brought to its notice of abuse of power by the authorities resulted in a rapid rise in its circulation throughout Russia. With the prospect of change in the air, the *Bell*'s London offices became a popular port of call for Russians on European tours. "We were the fashion," Herzen recalls in his memoirs.[13] In a tourist guidebook he was mentioned as one of the attractions of his area of London. But this popularity proved to be relatively short-lived; over the next seven years he would alienate Russian liberals by rejecting their view that Russia's destiny was to follow the most advanced countries of the West in their progress toward a form of liberal democracy, while he would antagonize the Left by refusing to regard a socialist revolution as the only way forward. He was eventually compelled to close the *Bell* for lack of readers, and the combined hostility of liberals and the Left forced him into a political isolation so great that his death would pass almost unremarked in his own country. According to a common interpretation of this phase of his life, his philosophical outlook did not equip him for the role of leadership he sought to assume. He has been portrayed as an idealist who proved intellectually and temperamentally unsuited to the compromises of principle demanded by the day-to-day politics into which he plunged after 1855.[14]

Herzen's standpoint in the *Bell* presents a different picture when approached without the benefit of historical hindsight. In the ideological disarray of the early years of Alexander's reign, it could be plausibly maintained that a combination of circumstances gave strong credibility to Herzen's belief that the peaceful transformation of the country could be accomplished best through the development of the democratic principles that inspired the peasant commune, whose dismantling would expose the vast mass of the population to the dismal situation of the European proletariat. At that time the peasants in their communes numbered around 23 million, almost three-quarters of the total population of the central Russian provinces. His defense of the commune set him against the liberal Westernizers who associated communal possession with socialism. He would insist that his aims, unlike theirs, were grounded in current reality. "Our banner is very prosaic," he wrote to Garibaldi in 1863; it was based on the "social religion" of the Russian people—their recogni-

tion of the inalienable right of every member of the commune to possess a determinate part of the land. In this letter he envisages an era in
which the educated minority would apply their knowledge and libertarian ideals to the task of securing the future of the commune and its
rights to land as a safeguard against the creation of a proletariat on a
Western model, or "state communism"—the death of individual liberty.[15] The ultimate goal to be desired was the replacement of the
Petrine bureaucracy by a National Assembly (*zemskaya duma* or
zemskii sobor)—following the model of the nationwide consultation
between tsar and people, based on representation without distinction
of classes, that had restored order in Russia after the Time of Troubles
at the beginning of the seventeenth century, and that was linked in the
popular mind with an image of the tsar as the protector of his people
against the depredations of landlords and officials.

He would defend his position on empirical grounds against his opponents from the Left and Right alike. Pointing out to his liberal critics
that their admired Western counterparts had proved unable to solve the
problem of mass destitution, he suggested they take note of J. S. Mill's
speculations on the advantages of communal landownership in that
regard before dismissing its Russian variety as the relic of a primitive past.[16] Russia had the opportunity to exploit a historical
contingency—the survival of a tradition embodying in embryo principles that the most advanced Western social theory had only begun to
embrace. At the beginning of 1864, amid a wave of triumphalism on
the Right following the defeat of the Polish uprising, he stubbornly
repeats his message. The task facing Russia was not of the kind that
called for faith to defy logic in pursuit of an abstract ideal. "We want
to remove obstacles, dismantle unnecessary barriers, untie hands,
liberate thought; we negate precisely what is negative, what hinders,
cripples and oppresses us. . . . None of this is utopian, all the basic
elements . . . are to hand: *the Russian people's way of life and the
knowledge of the West*; in their combination lies our strength, our
future, our advantage." His opposition to the Left's faith in a quick fix
of Russian society through revolutionary violence was grounded in
the experience of 1848, which had convinced him of the limitations of
political change as a means of social transformation. But he was
equally far from the nationalist messianism that has been attributed

No. 2.   THE BELL   AUGUST 1, 1857.

REGISTERED AT THE GENERAL POST-OFFICE FOR TRANSMISSION BEYOND THE UNITED KINGDOM.

КОЛОКОЛЪ

ПРИБАВОЧНЫЕ ЛИСТЫ КЪ ПОЛЯРНОЙ ЗВѢЗДѢ.

VIVOS VOCO!

(ВТОРОЕ ИЗДАНІЕ)

Выходятъ два раза въ мѣсяцъ въ Лондонѣ,
цѣна 6 пенсовъ. Получается въ Вольной
Русской Типографіи — 2, Judd Street,
Brunswick Square, W. C.

ЛИСТЪ 2.

1 Августа 1857.

У Трюбнера & Со. въ книжной лавкѣ,
60, Paternoster Row., и у Тхоржевскаго,
39, Rupert Street, Haymarket, London.
Price six-pence.

I.

РЕВОЛЮЦІЯ ВЪ РОССІИ.

"Господа, лучше, чтобъ эти перемѣны сдѣлались
сверху—нежели снизу."

(Александръ II—Рѣчь къ московскому дворянству.)

Мы не только наканунѣ переворота, но мы вошли въ него. Необходимость и общественное мнѣніе увлекло правительство въ новую фазу развитія, перемѣнъ, прогресса. Общество и правительство натолкнулись на вопросы, которые вдругъ получили права гражданства, стали неотлагаемы. Эта возбужденность мысли, это безпокойство ея и стремленіе вновь разрѣшить главныя задачи государственной жизни, подвергнуть разбору историческія формы, въ которыхъ она движется—составляетъ необходимую почву всякаго кореннаго переворота.

Но гдѣ же знаменія, обыкновенно предшествующія революціямъ,—все въ Россіи такъ тихо, такъ подавлено и еще больше съ такимъ добродушнымъ довѣріемъ смотритъ на новое правительство, ждетъ его помощи, что скорѣе можно думать, что вѣка пройдутъ прежде, нежели Россія вступитъ въ новую жизнь.

Да на что же эти знаменія? Въ Россіи все шло инымъ порядкомъ, у нея былъ разъ коренной переворотъ, его сдѣлалъ одинъ человѣкъ—Петръ I. Мы такъ привыкли съ 1789 года, что всѣ перевороты дѣлаются взрывами, возстаніями, что каждая уступка вырывается силой, что каждый шагъ впередъ берется съ бою—что невольно ищемъ, когда рѣчь идетъ о переворотѣ: площадь, баррикады, кровь, топоръ палача. Безъ сомнѣнія возстаніе, открытая борьба, одно изъ самыхъ могущественныхъ средствъ революцій, но отнюдь не единственное. Въ то время, какъ Франція съ 1789 года шла огнедышащимъ путемъ катаклизмовъ и потрясеній, двигаясь впередъ, отступая назадъ, метаясь въ судорожныхъ кризисахъ и кровавыхъ реакціяхъ, Англія совершала свои огромныя перемѣны и дома и въ Ирландіи и въ колоніяхъ, съ обычнымъ флегматическимъ покоемъ и въ совершенной тишинѣ. Весь правительственный тактъ Торіевъ и Виговъ состоитъ въ умѣньи упираться, пока можно, и уступать когда время при-

шло. Такъ какъ Робертъ Пиль—переходомъ своимъ на сторону свободной торговли, одержалъ экономическое Ватерлоо, для правительства; такъ одно изъ будущихъ министерствъ вступитъ въ сдѣлку съ Чартистами и дастъ интересамъ работниковъ—голосъ и представительство.

На нашихъ глазахъ переродился Піэмонтъ. Въ концѣ 1847 года управленіе его было іезуитское и инквизиторское, безъ всякой гласности, но съ тайной полиціей, съ страшной свѣтской и духовной цензурой, убивавшей всякую умственную дѣятельность. Прошло десять лѣтъ и Піэмонтъ нельзя узнать, физіогномія городовъ народонаселенія измѣнилась, вездѣ новая, удвоенная жизнь, открытый видъ, дѣятельность; а вѣдь эта революція была безъ малѣйшихъ толчковъ, для этой перемѣны достаточно было одной несчастной войны и ряда уступокъ общественному мнѣнію со стороны правительства.

Артисты-революціонеры не любятъ этаго пути, мы это знаемъ, но намъ до этаго дѣла нѣтъ, мы просто люди глубоко убѣжденные, что нынѣшнія государственныя формы Россіи никуда негодны,—и отъ души предпочитаемъ путь мирнаго, человѣческаго развитія, пути развитія кроваваго; но съ тѣмъ вмѣстѣ также искренно предпочитаемъ самое бурное и необдуманное развитіе—застою николаевскаго status quo.

Государь хочетъ перемѣнъ, хочетъ улучшеній, пусть же онъ вмѣсто безполезнаго отпора, прислушается къ голосу мыслящихъ людей въ Россіи, людей прогресса и науки, людей практическихъ и жившихъ съ народомъ. Они съумѣютъ лучше николаевскихъ бургравовъ не только ясно понять и формулировать чего они хотятъ, но сверхъ того съумѣютъ понять за народъ его желанія и стремленія. Вмѣсто того, чтобъ малодушно обрѣзывать ихъ рѣчи,—правительство само должно принятся съ ними за работу общественнаго пересозданія, за развитіе новыхъ формъ, новыхъ органовъ жизни. Ихъ теперь, ни мы не знаемъ, ни правительство не знаетъ, мы идемъ къ ихъ открытію, и въ этомъ состоитъ потрясающій интересъ нашей будущности.

Петръ I носилъ въ себѣ одномъ ту непредвидѣнную, новую Россію, которую онъ осуществилъ сурово и грозно противъ воли народа, опертой на самодержавную власть и личную силу. Нынѣшнему правительству не нужно прибѣгать ни

Early issue of *Kolokol* [*The Bell*], complete with one-line concession in English to local Post Office regulations.

to him, warning that without an injection of Western notions of freedom, the commune would be exposed to the "ravings" of the Slavophiles.[17] In advance of the Emancipation he had admitted in the *Bell* that the search for conscious purpose and direction in Russia's native institutions was met with a "terrifying silence." In the following year, disillusioned with the tsar's tergiversations, he comments: "The fatal strength of the contemporary reaction in Russia . . . is so difficult to overcome because it rests on two strong granite strongholds—*the stupidity of the government and the immaturity of the people.*" Was the commune's present structure merely a relic of Russia's backwardness? If not, how best could it be combined with Western concepts of individual liberty? He admits that these are open questions, on which he invites his readers to reflect.[18]

His own standpoint on these questions was set out in an essay published in the *Bell* in the wake of the Emancipation of 1861. He puts the question: Possessing only the façade of European culture, superimposed on primitive national traditions, what were Russians now to do? Continue the process of Westernization or develop their native culture? "It would naturally be best of all to do both. But one can't be simultaneously a Sicilian grandee and a Jacobin, just as when moving from town to country one can't preserve all the conveniences of the town."

Not all the youthfulness and brilliance of the life of ancient Greece was transmitted to Rome, not all the refinement of the ancient world was carried through into its Christian successor; not all that was graceful in aristocratic Europe survived into bourgeois Europe. Each epoch possessed its own hallmark, its aesthetic exclusiveness. Like all other phenomena in nature, the development of human societies followed no single or predictable upward path: "There is no table of ranks in Nature, no transition from class to class; otherwise all animals would long ago have attained the rank of humans and a socialist Atlantis would be flourishing on the island of Ceylon and the banks of the Euphrates. . . . Each species represents a progressive development on the one hand, and on the other a limit; namely, obstacles that it was unable to circumvent. This impotence in no way prevents another species, perhaps more poorly organized in some other aspect, to overcome precisely that obstacle."[19] Herzen interprets the failure of the revolutions of 1848 as a demonstration that the West had reached just such a limit in the juridical and economic structure of the modern bourgeois state, impediments to fundamental change that did not exist in Russia, where the publication in April 1861 of the Edict of Emancipation could be seen to have opened the way to a form of democracy no longer attainable in the West.

He had organized a celebration in London to mark that event, which vindicated the eight-year-long campaign of the Free Russian Press. It was to culminate in a toast to the "tsar-liberator," but on the same day news came of a massacre by Russian troops in Warsaw. The dinner went ahead but the toast was not pronounced.

A Cacophony of Voices

The behavior of the government's advisors and the peasantry alike immediately before and after the Emancipation seemed to support Herzen's long-held contention that the one truly conservative element in the Russian "empire of façades" was the peasants' belief that the land was theirs, to be held in common ownership. The main representatives of gentry conservatism were in considerable disarray, bombarding the government with conflicting advice on the nature and extent of the reforms of law and local government whose implementation was due to start in 1864. A. Koshelev and Yu. Samarin, the Slavophile authors of a land reform model presented to the government, were divided over the question of whether the interests of the nobility and the masses were served better by an autocracy or by the development of bureaucratic absolutism. The Hegelian liberal Chicherin preached the virtues of French centralism, while in his journals *The Russian Messenger* and the *Moscow Gazette* and in private memoranda to the government the archconservative Mikhail Katkov castigated the bureaucratic rationalism he saw as the legacy of the Petrine institution of service gentry, arguing that society could be cemented into an organic unity only through the development of an aristocracy of wealth on the English model. Katkov was known to have the ear of the minister of the interior, P. A. Valuev—hence Herzen's caustic remark in the *Bell* that the *empire de façades* was so foreign and so vacuous that it needed a Katkov to explain to it what it should be defending and preserving.[20]

The peasantry meanwhile had shown no hesitation. They interpreted the first rumors of emancipation as a promise to free their communes from all obligations to the landlord and the state. When the terms of the Emancipation Edict, promulgated in the spring of 1861, failed to deliver this freedom, widespread disorders broke out. The peasants were baffled by a manifesto whose bureaucratic language was impenetrable not only to the illiterate but to many of those instructed to interpret it to them. The circulars that followed, dealing with the transitional period of limited obligations (the product of many compromises), were even more muddled and obscure. Many peasants, convinced that the tsar had given them "liberty and land," rose against the local authorities. Some held the manifesto to be a fake, substituted by officials for a document in which the tsar had given them "true liberty"; others sought out those who could explain the text in a way that satisfied them.[21] One such interpreter, the peasant Anton Petrov of the village of Bezdna in Kazan province, was hailed as a prophet when he announced that it was the tsar's will that the peasants defend their land and freedom against all attacks. Peasant communities in that region and surrounding provinces refused to work on landlords' properties and began to meet in assemblies in order to elect their own administration. A company of soldiers sent to Petrov's house was met by a mass of 5,000 people who refused to disperse. Fifty-one were killed and many more wounded before Petrov could be arrested.

The Bezdna uprising was the most serious of the disturbances following the promulgation of the Edict; others followed on a decreasing scale through 1862 and 1863, as the majority of peasants began to resign themselves to the limits and conditions of their liberation. But the nature of those protests seemed to vindicate Herzen's view that the peasantry conceived of freedom as life within autonomous and democratically administered communes. While the radical journalist Nikolai Chernyshevsky campaigned in Saint Petersburg against the redemption fees imposed on the peasants, peasant protesters had more immediate concerns: the abolition of the corvée and other obligations, and the right to run their communities and elect their leaders without interference from the state bureaucracy. Only in very few cases did they demand all the land (even Anton Petrov believed that the landowners should be allowed to retain a third of their existing holdings).

There were no recorded attempts to seize landlords' houses and estates; the peasants merely refused to work on them. As Franco Venturi put it, the entire peasant class was inspired by a desire for isolation: "What the peasants meant by their dreams of 'true liberty' was mainly the complete separation of their community from the landlord, the breaking of all ties between them and hence the *obshchina* closing in on itself."[22]

If the peasants' isolationism confirmed Herzen's predictions, it posed an immediate problem: how to construct that bridge between intelligentsia and people on which the development of "Russian socialism" depended. He insisted that for this there was no alternative to the step-by-step method of the "prosaic worker." "The first priority," he explained to Garibaldi, was "to clarify what we want, what we are able to achieve and what the people actually desire."[23]

To this end the *Bell* put its support behind a project that had a strong resonance in Russian history: the convocation of an assembly in which the people could express their demands freely and elect their representatives without distinction of classes. This idea had support in radical quarters, as shown by an anonymous leaflet *Velikorus* (Great Russia), widely distributed in Moscow and Saint Petersburg in 1861. It also found favor among the nobility, some of whose regional assemblies passed votes for national representation. The most famous instance was that of the 112 nobles from the province of Tver who in an address to the tsar at the beginning of 1862 renounced their privileges as a shameful form of parasitism. Declaring that the reforms could not be successful unless they were undertaken after consultation with the people, they petitioned Alexander to summon "an assembly of delegates elected by the country without distinction of class for the purpose of creating free institutions" on the model of the *zemskii sobor*.[24]

The power of this myth was brought home to Herzen by a peasant, Petr Martyanov, who arrived at the *Bell*'s offices in the autumn of 1861 to seek publicity for injustices done to him by his former master. During his stay in London he wrote a letter to Alexander, which was published in the *Bell* in May 1862. Sharply criticizing the bureaucratic structure of the state, it called on the "people's tsar" to assume his rightful place at the head of a *zemskii sobor*.

Herzen with his children Sasha, Olga, and Tata, London, late 1850s.

This institution was still strong in folk memory; it appealed to the Romantic conservatism of the Slavophiles, while liberals could interpret it as a form of constituent assembly. At the same time, by insisting that there be no discrimination between social estates (a characteristic lacking in the historical prototype, which had had a disproportionate presence of boyars and service gentry), radicals could present it as a means of avoiding the defects of liberal parliaments. Herzen had therefore seized on it as a central plank of his propaganda immediately

London studio photograph of Herzen and Ogarev, 1860.

after the Emancipation, in the hope that its chemistry would bring about a synthesis of two disparate cultures and stages of development. To Garibaldi he speculates that in such a popular forum the religious sects of Old Believers would emerge as the most energetic representatives of "the people's idea," while the "contemporary, scientific idea" would be represented by a very mixed milieu—the lowest ranks of officialdom, students, officers, sons of priests, and nobles who (like those of Tver) believed that the gentry as a privileged caste had lost its raison d'être.[25]

In propaganda addressed to all sections of Russian society, Herzen and Ogarev assiduously promoted the concept of a National Assembly. In 1861 Ogarev, together with a young radical, N. N. Obruchev, wrote an appeal entitled "What Do the People Need?" Couched in popular language, it maintained that in order to secure the land for the people, it was necessary that taxes be apportioned and collected by the peasants themselves, through leaders they had elected.

The government ignored the pressures for an assembly. Public opinion (as represented by the nongovernmental press) had little, if any, influence on the provisions of the Statutes of January 1864, which created a system of limited local representation (the *zemstva*) that did not encroach on the principle of absolutism. It became clear that the tsar's priority was not to listen to his people, but to silence their demands both in Russia (where student demonstrations were met with military force) and in Poland, where in 1860 discontent had developed into public unrest. At the end of 1862 the government ordered a levy of recruits in Poland in a special decree aimed at removing the most militant elements from the population. Herzen acknowledged angrily that his policy of persuasion had failed.

In January 1863 the Polish insurrection broke out. The nationalist reaction in Russia, in which the liberals sided with the government and the Right, shattered the fragile consensus between liberal and radical opinion on the idea of an assembly. Herzen could now do no more than try to keep the concept alive. He advanced it again in an appeal to the tsar in 1865; but by then there were few in Russia who believed that deep divisions could be healed by such means. In the *Bell* in December 1866 he justified the standpoint that had led to his political isolation, arguing that it had been based on the factual situation after the death of Nicolas I. On the one hand, the peasantry—the vast majority of the population of Russia—were unanimous in their age-old belief that possession of the land in common ownership was their natural right. On the other, educated society had resembled a masked ball featuring a bewildering variety of costumes: a mixture of liberals and democrats, doctrinaire Hegelians, adherents of traditional absolutism, Slavophile Orthodoxy, and Western political economy.[26] A year later he recollects that his call for an assembly had met with wide support among the gentry as well as the peasantry, who still adhered to the pre-Petrine image of the tsar as their defender against injustice: based on representation without distinction of classes, a National Assembly was the only way of defining the true needs of the people and the state of the country. "It is also the only means whereby we can emerge without revolutionary convulsions, terror, horror, and rivers of blood, from that long preface known as the Petersburg era."[27]

In July 1867, when intensifying measures of repression had effectively closed off the *Bell*'s main channels of communication with Russia, Herzen was compelled to suspend its publication. On announcing this, he declared, "We have called and shall continue to call with all our strength for the convocation of a *National Assembly.*"[28] But by then he had scant hope that his voice would be heard.

The Marketplace of Life

In the conclusion to his study of Herzen's career, Edward Acton attributes Herzen's ultimate isolation to a failure to "grasp the nettle of revolution." In the face of ever-increasing evidence that the government would not permit the social change that he desired, Herzen continued to resist the demand of Russian radicals that he put his authority behind a call for an uprising, on the grounds that to incite the masses prematurely to revolt would result in either a destructive peasant *jacquerie* or the dictatorship of an intellectual elite.[29] Acton's view that this conviction was not empirically based is questionable in the light of Herzen's familiarity with the history of Russian peasant uprisings ("senseless and merciless," in Pushkin's summing-up)[30] and his observations of the behavior of the French masses in 1848, which had led him to assert that in history, as in nature, disparity between stages of development was a "physiological fact."

In the absence of any realistic alternative means to bring about social change in Russia in the 1860s, Acton argues, Herzen's opposition to revolution lost him the respect of the Left, depriving him of any effective role in Russian society. This approach is retrospective rather than contextual. Herzen did not enjoy the hindsight that permits the historian to make firm assertions about the true nature of a system of government that would remain fundamentally unchanged until 1917. The first five years of Alexander II's reign gave reasonable grounds for the hope that his predecessor had been Russia's last autocrat. This hope would finally be extinguished only after the Polish revolt (whose failure Herzen had predicted). Herzen has been viewed as deserting his true calling as a thinker when he turned his attention to day-to-day politics in his home country,[31] but in his own perspective the contrary was the case. As he had maintained constantly during his years in Russia, his was a philosophy of the everyday. The truth resided not in timeless absolutes but in the continuous flow of transient existence: "Thought must take on flesh, descend into the marketplace of life." When he founded the *Bell* in order to respond to events while they were still on the wing, he was not turning his back on his philosophy but seizing the chance to act it out. When early in the new reign he was accused in a Polish émigré journal of using his Free Russian Press to concentrate on the fate of the commune instead of directing all his efforts to the destruction of the autocracy, he responded in a cycle of letters published in the *Bell* between January 1859 and April 1860, explaining that his day-to-day preoccupation with events was in total conformity with his beliefs. The time for discussions over abstract principles had passed. Prophets and visionaries were essential for the purpose of keeping ideals alive in societies where movement was frozen, but in Russia this had ceased to be the case: from the preface and the epigraph "we have moved into the *text*." The skills now needed were those of "prosaic workers," among whom he numbered himself. "We are seeking to act in our own time, here and now, in Russia. This obliges us not to force new questions on the age, but to attempt to master those that have already arisen." It was not enough to have mapped out a final destination for the Russian troika. "We have to determine precisely *which* stage of the journey we are at, and what ruts and bridges are to be found at this precise stage." Seduced by the poetry of distant ideals, his Polish critics had scant concern for the ready-made (albeit primitive) example of socialism existing in his country—the peasant commune. Herzen suggests that they find his preoccupation with this humble and imperfect institution "somewhat earthbound."[32] They were offended by his attempts to encourage the tsar's inclinations toward reform—their democratic orthodoxy forbade all praise of rulers—but the time had come to approach history from a physiological viewpoint, without the addition of religious and civic symbols of faith and catechisms. The Poles suspected that his defense of the commune was linked with the hope, shared by liberal nationalists, of a Slav federation in which Russia would occupy the dominant position. They were mistaken: *"I am even less a patriot than I am a liberal."* He had no belief in the special calling of peoples: like the fate of any individual, the destinies of peoples and states could change along the way, "but we have a right, basing ourselves on the elements to hand, to reach conclusions about the future according to the theory of probabilities."[33]

The accusations he would encounter from all quarters concerning the question of Russia's future had been anticipated in the dialogues of *From the Other Shore*, where he presents himself as a demythologizer after the manner of Proudhon, whose political journalism he was to describe as a groundbreaking experiment in articulating the "living truth," not in the tranquillity of a philosopher's study but amid "the hurly-burly of popular commotions."[34]

It was on just such a task that he had embarked in the new reign. As the deliberations of the committee set up by the tsar to establish the terms of the Emancipation dragged on, the Russian intelligentsia began to divide into mutually hostile camps—liberals who feared the reforms would go too far, and radicals who feared they would not go far enough. The former included Konstantin Kavelin and Boris Chicherin (both members of the committee); pitched against them was a new radical generation, the "men of the sixties," whose intellectual leaders cultivated an aggressive journalistic style reflecting their intransigent opposition to all compromise with the existing order. The

Bell's approach (alternately encouraging Alexander's liberating tendencies and warning him of the consequences if he reneged on his promises) would find favor with neither group. Once again Herzen became the "man in the middle," the focus of attacks from both sides. In response he would devote some of his finest writing to the intellectual and moral challenges of life on the other shore.

CHAPTER EIGHTEEN

In Defense of Inconsistency

People like truth to be tidy; they prefer not to see grass growing around the back. . . . But real truth has three dimensions, and all three are essential to its existence.

HERZEN

The beliefs we have most warrant for have no safeguard to rest on, but a standing invitation to the whole world to prove them unfounded. If the challenge is not accepted, or is accepted and the attempt fails, we are far from certainty still; . . . if the lists are kept open, we may hope that if there be a better truth, it will be found when the human mind is capable of receiving it; and in the meantime we may rely on having attained such approach to truth, as is possible in our own day. This is the amount of certainty attainable by a fallible being, and this is the sole way of attaining it.

JOHN STUART MILL

THERE is a version of the March of History that places Herzen's polemics with the Russian liberals of his time at the head of a chain of events leading to the final suppression of freedom in his country. Those polemics have been cited as a paradigmatic example of a crucial turning point in the history of developing societies: the parting of the ways between pragmatic moderates, who preach peaceful evolution through compromise with the existing order, and radical visionaries, who seek a shortcut to freedom through revolution. In Russia the sequence of events has been seen as the following: The brief period of unanimity with which educated society welcomed Alexander II's reforming intentions ends when Herzen rejects the moderates' request that the *Bell* cease to carp at the tsar's delay in spelling out these intentions. The intransigence of his criticism of the government helps to radicalize the young generation, who soon outstrip him in revolutionary fervor. In the early 1860s the threat posed by the latter to Russia's stability creates a backlash in the form of a new conservatism that, in struggling against the Left, acquires many of their qualities, including a tendency to all-or-nothing positions and a contempt for liberal gradualism. Meanwhile, the young radicals attack Herzen for being less than wholehearted in his support for drastic change, and Left and Right begin to fragment into warring sects over questions of ends and means.

With this splintering apart, the basic debate among the intelligentsia was, in the words of Richard Pipes, "a dialogue between radicals and conservatives who could agree on nothing except their common loathing of the sensible, pragmatic men of the middle."[1] Who were these admirable people? To call them liberals is to use a term that needs to be hedged around with qualifications.

The origins of Russian liberalism, in its broadest and least contentious sense, lay in the moderate Westernism of the 1840s, which combined faith in reason, science, and individual liberty with fear of the more radical social doctrines emanating from the West. Liberalism emerged as a significant current of thought only in the second half of the 1850s, when public discussion of political questions became possible in Russia. Small informal groups of academics, writers, and a few enlightened bureaucrats (such as D. A. Miliutin, who became deputy minister of the interior in 1858) began meeting in Moscow and Saint Petersburg with the aim of defining and influencing Russia's future political course.[2] Their main forum was the journal *The Russian Messenger*, founded in 1856 and edited by Mikhail Katkov. In the first years of the new reign these circles produced a number of articles on economic and administrative questions and draft proposals for the reform, with warnings of the dire consequences that would ensue if the government lost control of the process it had set in motion.

Although the liberalism of many among this group shaded into a monarchical conservatism, their motives tended to be pragmatic. Some of them were "men of the forties"—former members of the *kruzhki* who had rejected the Hegelian metaphysics of their youth. Like Belinsky, they came to view Hegel's system as idolatry of abstractions (the memoirist Pavel Annenkov was among those inspired by Feuerbach's humanism to reject metaphysical speculation in favor of a more empirical approach to political realities). But other leaders of their generation never made that transition, preferring the certainties of the

Hegelian dialectic of progress. From this group came the self-appointed philosophers of Russian liberalism, who were to head the attack on Herzen and the *Bell*.

It has been argued that although it was conservative in comparison with the liberal tradition associated with John Stuart Mill, the Russian tradition was liberal in its own context. The English had no monopoly on classical liberalism; the conditions of political and cultural backwardness prevailing east of the Rhine favored another "classical" tradition that, rather than regarding the state as a potential threat to individual liberty, emphasized its role as the chief guardian of freedom for the individual.[3]

Herzen's principal ideological opponents in the early years of the new regime came from this group. Western historians have given prominence to their critique of Herzen's radicalism, but significantly less attention to the texts in which Herzen deconstructs the pragmatic self-image of the theorists of Russian liberalism, to reveal—behind their appeals to reason and to history—Hegelian metaphors rooted in the yearning for liberation from the limiting constraints of time and chance.[4]

Against the deterministic rationalism of this group Herzen mounted a defense of inconsistency, drawing for support on a text whose vision of freedom has strong resemblances to his own: Mill's treatise *On Liberty*. Like his affinities with Proudhon, his commentaries on Mill (as we will see) defy all attempts to fit his thinking into a conventional political paradigm. If he is to be associated with any retrospectively constituted tradition, it is with a small minority of thinkers who opposed the deterministic systems of post-Enlightenment rationalism while keeping an equal distance from the limitless subjectivism of Romantic revolt, and who began to map out new approaches to problems of history and society free from teleological assumptions. Like Mill, Herzen stressed the importance of the inductive methods of the natural sciences as a corrective to thinking that approached such problems from the narrow perspective of predetermined goals. His challenge to the Russian liberals' doctrine of progress was based on analogies between processes in history and nature, and an emphasis on the role of contingency in both realms—which would receive formidable endorsement from the Darwinian revolution of 1859.

Darwin's *On the Origin of Species* raised a question that has haunted social theorists ever since: Are moral freedom and responsibility possible in a world dominated by contingency and without a final design? I shall seek to demonstrate that in his polemics with the Russian liberals, Herzen anticipates this question and gives a compellingly argued answer: Freedom is possible *only* in such a world.

Liberalism and the State in Russia

The liberal theories that concern this chapter were born in 1843, when Granovsky's celebrated lectures at Moscow University invoked the authority of Hegel to demonstrate that Russia was a European country and hence destined to follow the West's progress toward the optimal form of social existence: the modern state, defined in Hegel's *Philosophy of Right* as the embodiment of Reason in the world. Hegel's concept of the state as the goal of world history was the basis of the so-called *étatist* school of Russian historiography, which, through the writings of two of Granovsky's pupils, Konstantin Kavelin and Boris Chicherin, furnished nineteenth-century Russian liberalism with a concept of freedom more commonly associated with the doctrines of both the Left and the Right.

It is true that, as John Plamenatz has written, "no liberal is only a liberal."[5] The concept of the "night watchman" state—the ideal of a classical liberalism concerned to defend the individual against the encroachments of state power—has been much criticized for separating the individual artificially from his social context. In debates about the limits of the state's role in defining, promoting, and safeguarding goals and values deemed essential for the development of human potential, the boundaries between liberal, radical, and conservative doctrines have become progressively blurred. There exists, nevertheless, a well-founded consensus that if liberalism means anything at all, it must exclude the most original of modern theories of the state—that of Hegel's *Philosophy of Right*.

Hegel's theory of the state is grounded in his ontological vision of man as the vehicle through which Spirit—the rational necessity underlying all phenomena—comes to embody itself in the world and thereby to comprehend its own laws. This process takes place through the progression of human societies toward ever more rational forms. In Hegel's thought, the Kantian ideal of the autonomous, self-directing individual is achieved through society and history, reaching its perfection in and through a community whose foundation is reason. His state is the expression of man's moral nature, "the actuality of the ethical Idea," embodying in its structure (a system of representation that mediates between the interests of civil society and the "objective" goals of the state) the subordination of subjective interests to the universal will. In the identity of the personal and the universal will, expressed in acts of obedience to law, Hegel held, right and duty coalesce.

Despite Hegel's emphasis on law and the protection of rights such as freedom of conscience, his divinization of the state has traditionally been seen as incompatible with liberalism. In an interesting defense of Hegel, Charles Taylor attributes this view to the "atomistic prejudices" of Anglo-Saxon liberals who are repelled by the concept of "positive liberty" based on the recognition of man's social nature and grossly misinterpret Hegel's theory as a justification of the sacrifice of individuals to the Moloch of the state. In Taylor's view, the growth of communitarian social theories (which blur the distinctions between positive and negative liberty) reflects an awareness that, as Hegel puts it, in obeying the state "the individual is not serving an end separate from him; rather, he is serving a larger goal which is the ground of his identity, for he only is the individual he is in this larger life. We are beyond the opposition of self-goal and other-goal."[6] To attempt a political classification of so original a construction as Hegel's theory of the state is, as Taylor contends, a laughable exercise. But there is no doubt as to where that theory stands with regard to the distinction between the concepts of freedom, which was of central concern to Herzen. It is misleading to imply, as Taylor does, that the common unease about the implications of Hegel's system springs merely from the fact that it is based on a concept of positive liberty. Many varieties of that doctrine, by acknowledging the contingency of the communities within which individuals define their identity and purposes, provide loopholes for individual initiative and opposition. No such loopholes exist in the seamless whole of Hegel's doctrine, in which all freedoms flow from the recognition of necessity. In the development of history, morality, and the state, there is one right way whose principles, inherent in the structure of the world and in human nature, make all rebellion against it not merely unlawful but senseless. This internalization of formulas of necessity is what makes Hegel's state such a nightmarish construction—liberal in its emphasis on the rule of law and the safeguarding of rights, but not admitting the possibility of change or development as a result of the exercise of those rights. The form of representation and mediation is absolute and final, the functions and relations of each of the three *Stände* (aristocratic, peasant, and bourgeois—Hegel's system did not allow for further differentiation) defined according to the laws of the articulation of Spirit in the world. "Philosophy [will] . . . lend her name to a repression formerly authorized by the Church": thus Schiller predicted what one liberal thinker has described as the "magical transformation" of Kant's theory of rational autonomy into the deification of a collective entity with which the rational self is identified.[7]

It has been observed that there are liberalisms of harmony and liberalisms of dissonance.[8] The former see rational consensus as the ultimate goal of social organization; the latter emphasize the need for flexibility in institutions to accommodate the diverse ways in which individuals seek to fulfill themselves. But while consensus-oriented liberal movements have been influenced by Hegel's organicist vision, Hegel's ontological legitimation of the state has attracted only one such movement of any significance: the Russian.

* * *

In the 1840s Hegel's thought served Russian academic jurists and historians as an organizing paradigm for interpretations of Russia's past and predictions about her future path.[9] These theories varied considerably. None was characterized by dialectical rigor, but all were strongly teleological, based on the belief that history was a purposive progression toward the rational state, and that Europe and Russia would ultimately converge on this common goal. The foundations of the étatist school of Russian historiography were laid by the young Moscow historian Konstantin Kavelin in an essay of 1847, which presents the central features of Russian history as the development of the "principle of individuality" characteristic of modern European societies, at the expense of the primitive "patrimonial" principle. But whereas in Europe (according to Hegel's triune schema) the instrument of this development had been civil society, in Russia, Kavelin argues, it had been the state. In their battle against the patrimonial principle in the name of the "Idea of the state," Ivan IV (the founder of the centralized Muscovite state) and Peter the Great were the two towering figures in Russian history. Kavelin interprets the *oprichnina*—the private-army-cum-secret-police with which Ivan terrorized his country—as a revolutionary force that freed the tsar (and thereby the state) from the tutelage of the hereditary nobility, replacing these with functionaries promoted on merit, a process that was completed by Peter's establishment of a nobility whose ranks were determined by state service.[10]

The violence of the Petrine revolution could plausibly be justified in the name of "rational" progress; the atrocities of the demented sadist Ivan could not. There was no shred of historical evidence to support the contention that, whether consciously or not, Ivan's killings served the purpose of replacing the patrimonial principle by the principle of personal worth. One commentator has drawn attention to the bizarre resemblance between Kavelin's apologia for Ivan and those made for him by Soviet historians at the behest of a later tyrant.[11] But at least those historians had no choice in the matter; it remains a mystery why Kavelin, by all accounts a gentle, humane, and civilized man, should have had the eccentricity to venerate such a monster.

Whatever the psychology behind them, Kavelin's views are logically consistent with the premises of his étatist philosophy. If the modern state represents a historically inevitable progression from primitive patrimonial relations, all that furthers the destruction of these relations is *eo ipso* progressive; and once forces opposed to the ruler are identified in this schema with the outgoing phase of history, the interests of the ruler become logically identical with the interests of the state. Kavelin's idealization of Ivan and Peter is supported by another Hegelian notion (previously invoked by Granovsky for similar ends): that of great historical individuals, chosen by Providence to realize the aspirations of the incoming historical phase.

Although one prominent Westernizer pronounced that it would have been "incomparably better had it not been written from the Germano-philosophical point of view,"[12] Kavelin's essay established his reputation as an effective polemicist against the Slavophile version of Russian history. His status as a historian ensured him a dominant place among those greeting the reforming intentions of a tsar who seemed to embody the state as agent of progress. His memorandum of 1855, "On the Emancipation of the Peasants in Russia," figured prominently in discussions on this subject in liberal circles of the time. It emphasized the social and economic advantages of a post-reform free-enterprise economy based on private ownership of land, making the point that the terms of the Emancipation should safeguard the interests of the gentry while not being so detrimental to the peasantry as to create a landless proletariat. In a second essay, published in 1859, he suggests retaining a limited form of communal tenure alongside private land ownership as a counterbalance to the excesses of uncontrolled capitalist development and a safety net for the weakest sections of the population, who might otherwise be seduced by socialist propaganda. The spirit of liberal compromise characterizing Kavelin's economic views on the eve of the Great Reforms contrasts with his firm assertions that the latter were the business of the government alone: the intelligentsia's role was to cooperate with initiatives from above, not to set about creating its own.

In urging restraint on Russian educated society, Kavelin was supported by Russian liberalism's other leading theoretician, Boris Chicherin, a figure whose position has been difficult for later commentators to assess. His insistence (encapsulated in his slogan "Liberal measures and strong government") on the importance of continuity and tradition as counterweights to reform made him despised by many liberals in his day, yet it has won him the admiration of some historians who see his quarrel with Herzen as an archetypal conflict between two political temperaments: one moderate and pragmatic, the other doctrinaire and extreme.[13] There was indeed such a conflict, but Chicherin was not the pragmatist. His calls for restraint, prescient though they may seem in a post-1917 perspective, were rated more accurately by his liberal contemporaries: they sprang from a vision so doctrinaire and abstract that even his fellow-Hegelians thought he had gone too far in identifying the real with the rational.[14]

Kavelin, Granovsky, and the conservative Hegelian jurist P. G. Redkin had been among Chicherin's mentors during his studies in jurisprudence and history at Moscow University in the mid-1840s. The description in his memoirs of his conversion to Hegelianism is reminiscent of Herzen's portrait of the "Buddhist," at ease only in the icy sphere of abstraction. He describes himself as "completely captivated by the new worldview that revealed to me with surprising harmony the supreme elements of Being." The shock of the European upheavals of 1848 convinced him of the profound truth of Hegel's doctrine that only those ideals can be realized that correspond with the given stage in the historical development of consciousness. It became clear to him that the entire history of Russia to date had been a preparation for its crowning achievement: the completion, in the ripeness of time, of the rational state. Henceforth he would dismiss radical ideals as "the delirium of overheated minds" unable to cope with reality. Historians from Western liberal traditions may not always have appreciated that for Chicherin "reality" denoted "the actual representation of Spirit, working out its self-definition according to the eternal laws of Reason inherent in it." He had come to understand that all contingent processes formed part of "a single living picture"[15]—to which, it went without saying, only those versed in the conservative version of Hegel's dialectic held the key.

From this position of privileged knowledge Chicherin lectured Russian society on what its expectations should be. In the first years of the new reign he warned against premature hopes of constitutional freedoms: it would take several generations for the Russian people to reach the level of consciousness appropriate to those. He developed this argument in a book of 1866, *On Popular Representation,* which was received coolly by the Russian public. As the jurist A. D. Gradovsky commented in a review, in Chicherin's methodology "the form [of government] is the main thing—something exalted and unique that the people can achieve only after generations. The characteristics of this form having been stated, there is nothing easier than to raise it to such a height that its attainment will always be impossible for a given nation."[16]

The Russian autocracy, too, was far from Hegel's ideal. But when Chicherin urges his fellow citizens to submit to it, he does so with arguments borrowed from Hegel's discussion of the rational state in the *Philosophy of Right.* In his inaugural lecture as professor of jurisprudence at Moscow University in 1861, he defines obedience to the law as the primary condition of liberty, adding in an article written at that time that "the absolute meaning of the law confers absolute meaning also on the . . . person who submits to it." The duty of obedience, he insists, applies equally to "bad" laws.[17] This last argument made no sense in the context of Hegel's moral justification of law, but was perfectly clear to the government, which forbade all public criticism of his lecture. An anonymous letter to the *Bell* denounced it as "a philosophy of slavery."[18] The Russian educated public inclined to the same view: Chicherin had already acquired the reputation of a reactionary through his attitude to the student disturbances earlier that year. In Saint Petersburg the police and army violently suppressed a peaceful demonstration against the new university regulations, which represented a return to the policies of Nicolas. Kavelin resigned along with his fellow professors in the Faculty of Law in protest against the government's methods. Chicherin (in a letter written for circulation among senior officials) commented that, while the repressive edicts had been misguided, the government had been too hesitant in its suppression of the ensuing unrest. As Chernyshevsky commented, he had come to comprehend the duties of the police "in a light more absolute than the police itself."[19]

In Chicherin's thinking the Russian autocracy and the rational state seem all too often to coalesce. His defense of the status and privileges of the Russian nobility and bureaucracy is based on Hegel's definition of the role of these bodies in the ideal state. Even his fellow Hegelians came to doubt whether his unconditional support for the authority of the state was compatible with liberalism. Responding to a derogatory review of Tocqueville in which Chicherin praised the centralism of the French state as more "rational" than the decentralized government of England, Kavelin described his theory of the state as a "new Baal . . . to which he offers bloody sacrifices."[20]

Liberalism Meets the Free Russian Press

These misgivings did not prevent Kavelin from making common cause with Chicherin in an effort to persuade Herzen to change the line adopted by his London press. In this Kavelin took the lead. Six years younger than Herzen, he had known him in their Moscow days. An intermittent correspondence between them, begun after Herzen's move to London, is tinged with reverence on Kavelin's side. Herzen responded with affection to this gentle, cultivated man from the intellectual milieu to which he was still bound by strong emotional ties. Kavelin was among the first to act on Herzen's request for material from Russia for publication by his Free Russian Press, providing him in the early years of the new regime with a flow of documents and articles discussing current problems. Though moderate in tone, these were still felt to be beyond the limits of what the censorship would permit. In 1856, Herzen published the first of nine collections of such material under the title *Voices from Russia.* The first volume opened with a letter signed "a Russian liberal"—an anonymous joint protest by Kavelin and Chicherin against the line taken by Herzen's journalism.[21]

Writing to Kavelin shortly before his death in 1855, Granovsky had dismissed Herzen's political journalism as the expression of a childish urge to play the Slavophile before a European audience consisting of a few French refugees whom he sought to dazzle with the myth of a Russian political opposition (a reference to his response to Jules Michelet).[22] Adopting a similar tone, the "Russian liberal" claimed to represent the opinion of the vast majority of educated Russians in condemning Herzen's current views and activism, while expressing respect for his undoubted literary talents. As Herzen himself had acknowledged ("in your only sensible political article"—his letter to Alexander II expressing his hopes for the new reign), an epoch of reform had begun. His press should seek to promote this process by providing a forum for responsible debate on the issues involved, thereby helping to reopen channels of communication between tsar and people that had been blocked by Nicolas's bureaucracy. Conspiracies were a thing of the past: Russian educated society firmly believed that progress could be brought about only from above. But Herzen had chosen to present Proudhon's anarchy as the ideal for the human race (a reference to a discussion of Proudhon's theories in an article by a Russian émigré that had recently appeared in the *Polar Star*). He had mistaken his audience: "Your revolutionary theories will never find a response in Russia, your bloody banner . . . inspires us solely with indignation and revulsion." Herzen's fantasies were of "absolutely no practical interest" to his countrymen: "In the most daring conversations I have not heard anyone inside Russia utter a word about necessity of a secret society or a revolution, *or the limitation of autocratic power* or anything like that." (All this flight of fantasy from the "Russian liberal" is followed by an editorial question mark; the letter was printed with a brief comment by Herzen expressing disagreement with its contents and protest at the offensive tone of some of the remarks, where Chicherin's hand is particularly in evidence.)

Apart from the Emancipation already announced by the tsar, the hopes expressed in this letter were modest: a "cautious reform" of the censorship and bureaucracy, in accordance with the "law of gradualism"—interpreted in Hegelian rather than pragmatic terms. The authors argue that Herzen could justify his faith in socialism only if he could prove that it represented "an inevitable consequence of what has gone before, the ripened fruit of the rational development of human societies." But the opposite was known to be the case: communal association belonged to a primitive stage of historical development, long since superseded. All Herzen's errors flowed from one source, his failure to perceive "the law of gradualness" imbuing all phenomena: history advances gradually from one imperfect stage to the next, with each stage moving closer to perfection.

In private correspondence over the next two years, Kavelin and Chicherin attempted to convert Herzen to their ideological position. A letter from Kavelin gives an interesting insight into the methods of action he perceived to be consistent with the "law of gradualism." He emphasizes the *Bell*'s importance as the only public forum for discussion of the burning issues of the day. These do not include political questions, "in which our society has little interest"—what does concern it is the incompetence and corruption of the bureaucracy. Indeed, Herzen would do well to found a paper in the French language, available only to the educated classes and therefore more acceptable to the government. Its "merciless criticism" of bureaucratic incompetence and corruption (if made from "the most moderate point of view") would have a "fearsome" effect, giving Russia "the medicine it now needs." In a sequel to this masterpiece of craven ferocity, Kavelin repeats his demand for the "merciless" exposure of bureaucratic wrongdoing, while imploring Herzen not to criticize the tsar or any member of the imperial family: "You can and *must* weigh every one of your words and acts.' "[23]

Chicherin added his voice to Kavelin's. In the autumn of 1858, after visiting London in an unsuccessful attempt to persuade Herzen to change the policy of the *Bell*, he wrote urging him to moderate his tone. Herzen responded to his critics in an article in November of that year. He notes that he has been attacked from all sides: by "liberal conservatives" for being too severe on the government, by "red democrats" for believing in the tsar's good intentions, by Slavophiles for being a Westernizer, by Westernizers for being a Slavophile. The main charge from dogmatists of all political persuasions was one of inconsistency: "in winter we complain of the cold, in summer of the heat." The problem was that history itself tended toward inconsistency. Nicolas's reign had followed a single pattern; but Alexander's, swinging between reaction and reform, did not. Only on the final goal (liberation of the peasants with land) could there be no compromise; the means would depend on circumstances. In appraising these, the *Bell* identified with no single party or doctrine, but sought to reflect the hopes and doubts of those who had no voice. Carried away by the passion of the moment, it had on occasion misjudged the direction of events, but this was the fate of all those involved in the conflicts that were the life of history, as opposed to those who, secure in their doctrinal fortresses, took it on themselves to read its funeral oration.[24]

In October the *Bell* had printed without comment an anonymous letter from one of the voiceless ones, calling on the peasants to sharpen their axes and rid themselves of serfdom at one blow. This was not the kind of opinion the liberals wished to include in their forum. The letter, together with Herzen's riposte to his critics, provoked a bitter attack from Chicherin, which Herzen printed in the *Bell* in December that year under the title "Act of Indictment." In a remark calculated to inflame the proponents of rational progress, Herzen had claimed that Russia's path of development would be a matter for "the poetic caprice of history." Chicherin took the bait, pompously admonishing Herzen for the frivolity of his indifference to the means of political change. In a reference to the by then notorious "axe" letter, he accused the *Bell* of making "frenzied appeals to wild forces, to the club and the axe, as poetic caprices that it is wrong to prevent." He pressured Herzen to see his "very great obligation" to support the government's initiatives for reform, reminding him that Russians have not yet acquired the "manly virtues" of a mature civil society, first among which are patience and respect for law: "Our society must earn the right to freedom through rational self-control." Instead, by encouraging it to make premature demands, Herzen was justifying in advance any repressive measures the authorities might see fit to take. "If a sick man, instead of calmly and patiently undergoing his treatment, . . . opens his own wounds, seizes a knife to cut off the limb that is causing him pain, there is no other course to follow—he must be bound hand and foot."[25]

Chicherin's letter was a fair summary of the Russian autocracy's views on the duties of a subject, a point to which Herzen drew attention in an introductory note: unlike previous criticisms of the *Bell*'s policies, Chicherin's came from the opposing camp—that of the bureaucracy. This view was shared in the overwhelming majority of the responses to Chicherin's letter that found their way to London. Among them was a rambling contribution from Kavelin, comparing Chicherin's "soulless" doctrine unfavorably with Herzen's "warm heart and ardent love for good and truth." Without the enthusiasm that Chicherin held in such contempt, the *Bell* might not have made its "mistakes" (on the nature of which Kavelin concurs with Chicherin), but it would also not have awakened Russian society. In a private letter to Chicherin, Kavelin reveals that his own attitude to Herzen's propaganda had changed since their joint protest to the *Bell* in 1856. He accuses Chicherin of misrepresenting Herzen's position by citing the "axe" letter as evidence of revolutionary intent. Why did he not quote other passages in other issues of the *Bell*, where the editor and his correspondents pressed for peaceful reform as a way to avoid the dire consequences of revolution? In this Herzen was at one with most progressive people. By painting him as an apostle of destruction, Chicherin was playing into the government's hands: "In exalted circles everyone is delighted by your letter. 'The liberal party has finally decided to break with the revolutionaries': that is the stereotyped phrase with which your letter is greeted in the palaces and high administrative spheres. Is this what you wanted, Boris Nikolaevich? The only reproach they make against you is that you did not present your fine and noble letter, before its publication, to the government for approval; the government would have approved it without fail."[26] These sentiments were generally shared by progressive Russian opinion. Ivan Turgenev and Pavel Annenkov were among seven prominent signatories to a letter to Chicherin declaring support for Kavelin's letter. Even some bureaucrats inclined to the same view. The censor A. V. Nikitenko wrote in his diary that Chicherin's letter of protest was even more damaging to society than Herzen's radicalism: "It seems to justify harsh measures, and invite them."[27]

Nikitenko's reaction and Kavelin's change of tack reflect the confusion of a society that, as its masters hesitated between reform and reaction, found it increasingly difficult to define the boundaries between moderate liberalism and radical dissent. These were the people whom Herzen saw as opponents, but whom he still had faint hopes of persuading that the gap between Russian reality and Western liberal theories demanded a pragmatic approach to the historical material that lay to hand. But in Chicherin (as he records in a description of their meeting in London) he sensed from the first an enemy.[28]

* * *

As both protagonists understood perfectly, Herzen's quarrel with Chicherin represented a head-on collision between two intellectual types fundamentally opposed on the question of the ends of life. In his letter to the *Bell* Chicherin had challenged Herzen to reveal how he saw himself—"as a political figure, directing society along a rational path, or an artist, observing the chance play of events." Herzen presented his own interpretation of these two types in the draft of a letter setting out "a general definition of our opposing points of view." In his portrait of Chicherin we can recognize the Russian "Buddhist" whose defense of the rational reality of Nicolas's regime he had satirized in the early 1840s.

One cannot argue with Chicherin, he concedes—he knows a great deal and knows it well:

> You confidently await the rational development of events in confirmation of the program revealed by philosophy. You cannot be at odds with the present; you know that if the past was *thus and thus*, the present is bound to be thus and thus, and lead to such and such a future; you reconcile yourself to it through your understanding and your interpretation of it. To you has fallen the enviable lot of a priest, consoling the grieving with the eternal truths of your philosophy and with your faith in them. All these advantages are bestowed on you by your doctrine, because doctrine excludes doubt. . . . Doctrine ap-

proaches truth from a specific point of view. . . . But doubt seeks to free itself from all points of view, looks all around, turns back on its tracks, often paralyzing all action through its humility before the truth. You, my learned friend, know precisely in what direction to go, how to lead; I do not know.

Chicherin's secular version of religion had replaced the poetic qualities of its predecessors with "the red tape of officialdom, the idol of the State with the tsar at the top and the hangman at the bottom." "Aware of the necessity of suffering, doctrine stands like Simeon Stylites on a pedestal, sacrificing all that is temporal to the eternal, living particulars to general ideas. In short, doctrinaires are above all historians, while we, along with the masses, are your substratum; you stand for history *für sich*, we—for history *an sich*. . . . You bury us, and after our death you reward and punish us; you are our doctors and priests; but it is we who suffer and die."[29]

Chicherin's slogan "Liberal measures and strong government" would seem to categorize him as a liberal conservative. But he had a very narrow view of civil rights, believing that public speech and the press should be carefully supervised by the government, that in Russia political rights should be a remote ideal. Once the government had embarked on reform, he was quick to condemn those who questioned its speed or proposed alternative agendas: the second part of his slogan invariably took precedence over the first. It can be claimed that this was sound realism in a country that lacked a stable middle class as a foundation for civil society; but Chicherin's pessimistic assessment of the Russian people's civic potential is in marked contrast to his categorical defense of the historical rationality of the Russian state, whose laws he had equated with the moral purpose of mankind. In his memoir on their meeting, Herzen had called Chicherin's theories a "philosophy of bureaucracy." His insights into his opponent's mentality are supported by the following extracts from two of Chicherin's private letters.

In March 1863 there was fear in bureaucratic circles that the steps taken by the government against the insurgent Poles might spark off a war with the Great Powers. Chicherin wrote to his brother (who was then an aide to the foreign minister) that in the current crisis, "I would even consider a war useful. The Crimean War was necessary for the government; a new war is necessary for society, and afterward not a trace will remain of the insanity that has affected part of Russian youth. . . . I fear only that the government, trusting neither itself nor the people, will prove too weak." By mid-October, when Russian military forces were engaged in suppressing the revolt, Chicherin recommends to his brother that they should be encouraged to show no mercy: "I hope that in the future we shall also make no concessions, . . . that for the next ten years the Poles shall live under terror so that they may be convinced that they are completely in our hands. . . . In my view, there can be only one solution [to the Polish question]: the complete impotence of Poland with respect to Russia. . . . For this to happen we must smash anyone who approaches us with any sort of demand. Russia cannot permit any other solution of the Polish question."[30]

Herzen's intuitions, on first hearing the "fearful, repellent conceit"[31] in the timbre of Chicherin's voice, had been sound: Chicherin's passionless character was his most frightening quality. He was isolated because his time had not yet come. In 1861 the autocracy, morally and politically wavering, had been less than satisfactory in its response to his demand that it be not timid in its treatment of its subjects. Chicherin's faith in the state as arbiter of moral purposes has more in common with Leninism than with liberalism. In the two letters quoted above we recognize a type with which subsequent centuries have been more familiar than the nineteenth: a type that can recommend the mass extermination of human beings calmly and dispassionately, without the shadow of a moral scruple, secure in the knowledge that they are history's instruments and, when the need arises, its executioners.

* * *

Preempted by Chicherin's indictment, Herzen's letter was not sent. (He included it in his memoirs, next to a pen portrait of the cold and arrogant young man who had called at the offices of the *Bell* in the autumn of 1858.) But he developed its main theme in a series of essays entitled "Russian Germans and German Russians" (an allusion to the descendants of those who were dispatched to Germany by Peter I to study Western principles of statehood), which appeared in the *Bell* over the last three months of 1859.[32] Recommending them to his son for the

Imaginative painting by S. V. Gerasimov of Russian peasant unrest following the equivocal 1861 proclamation of the freeing of the serfs.

clarity with which they expressed the line taken by his paper, he predicts that as a result "our doctrinaires" will be after him in full cry. "But I won't trade my instincts on the nature of truth for their learned opinion."[33]

* * *

His final break with the liberals came only after they gave their support to the Russian government's reprisals against the Poles in 1863. Until then Herzen maintained cordial (if distant) relations with individual liberals, such as Ivan Turgenev. His personal regard for Kavelin was such that he would dedicate to him one of his finest works, the essay "Robert Owen." Their relations ended in 1862 when Kavelin refused to recant over a pamphlet Herzen saw as a paean to the Russian gentry.[34] But "Russian Germans" essays show that by the end of 1859 he had already come to recognize the futility of seeking a fruitful dialogue with those who believed that Russia's path of progress had been mapped out in advance. The tone of the essays did not encourage friendly discussion. Herzen declares that the main threat to the peasant commune after its liberation will come not from the government but from persons well versed in political economy and legal theory and devoted to the principles of Prussian bureaucracy and French centralism. (The allusion to Chicherin's aversion to Tocqueville would have been plain to his readers.) More practical than the nobility, more honest than the bureaucrats, these individuals were thereby more dangerous than both. Opposed to venality and abuse of power, in favor of "reasonable freedom and moderate progress" (a reference to two of Chicherin's favorite phrases), "they will reconcile us with all that we despise and hate." Their modest civilizing efforts would strengthen the bureaucratic order and hasten the dissolution of the commune, a process that would bring violence and famine in its wake. By the best prognosis, "in a century and a half their improvements will lead to the state from which Prussia is seeking to escape."

The Russian Silence

Herzen admits that the search for evidence of conscious purpose and direction in Russia's native institutions is met only with a "terrifying silence." The historical existence of the masses, formless and fluctuating, is strewn with the clutter of inchoate aspirations and aborted developments. The difficulty of interpreting the Russian silence is compounded by the fact that the educated classes read that silence in translation. Our German training, Herzen argues, has blunted the sympathetic intuition that might have allowed us to make sense of the data before us. Accustomed to dealing with completed processes, testaments, inscriptions, and sarcophagi, when confronted with the chaos of Russian life, we follow the example of Peter the Great, "bending and fracturing facts we do not comprehend in order to make them fit our foreign criteria." Centuries of scholastic dualism had taught Western thought to classify and to stereotype, to read rather than to observe. Its philosophies were not equipped even to formulate, much less to solve, the problem of finding new bottles for new wine. (Hence, Herzen suggests, the Slavophiles' understandable, if misguided, attempt to ransack Orthodox theology for concepts for which Western philosophy had no adequate expression.)

Reverting to a major theme of his essays of the early 1850s, Herzen questions the Russian liberals' central assumption—that the path pioneered by Europe was obligatory for all nations. Like some dubious anthropologist seeking to base his discipline on the biography of a single individual, Europe "resolves everything in the world by analogy with itself." The ideal of its philosophers and economists was a modified version of the contemporary European state, while the Prussian philosopher Hegel had proclaimed the Prussian *Rechtsstaat* to be the goal of human progress. For all their appeals to objectivity and the authority of science, this was the tradition to which the ideologists of Russian liberalism belonged. Their language betrayed them. They were scandalized because people like him wanted to *"go back"* to the commune, on the supposition that only primitive peoples like the commune: "Educated peoples like state order."

Russian Germans, Herzen concludes, are profoundly mistaken about the nature of science (his all-embracing term for philosophy and the human and physical sciences): "There is no absolute science. . . . In the real world, science is always conditioned: as the refraction in human consciousness of the phenomenological world, it shares the fate of that world; it moves, grows and retreats along with it, in constant interaction with history. Hence, its development has the same engrossing interest, the same elements of poetry and chance, suffering and enthusiasm, as the historical process. Its *relative* truth is always deflected from a straight line by its refraction in the brain and is colored by its environment, all the more so when the subject of its investigation is dear to us." The Western tradition of thought that Herzen censures so severely in these essays nevertheless provided him with two formidable allies against the Hegelian liberals, thinkers whose instincts on the nature of truth and consequent defense of inconsistency were remarkably close to his own. An issue of the *Polar Star* published in the same month as the last essay of "Russian Germans" contained a review of John Stuart Mill's *On Liberty* and a chapter on Proudhon from Herzen's memoirs. In that chapter Herzen contrasts Proudhon's thinking—"developing, varying in aspect, reflecting events"—with the sluggishness of thought characteristic of religion and doctrinairism: "a willful narrow-mindedness, a definitive circumscription . . . that rejects everything new that life offers. . . . The real truth must lie under the influence of events, must reflect them, while remaining true to it-self, or it would not be the *living truth*, but an eternal truth, at rest from the tempests of this world in the deathly stillness of sacred stag-nation." In a footnote to this passage Herzen cites "an excellent expres-sion in regard to these truths settled once and for ever: 'the deep slumber of a decided opinion.' "[35] The quotation is from *On Liberty*, which, by a happy coincidence, had just been published.

Toward the end of his life Herzen remarked that because Russians tended to have far more respect for Europeans than for other Russians, he had always attempted, when he particularly wished to be taken se-riously, to place his ideas under the protection of a European nanny.[36] The nannies in question were two: Proudhon and Mill, whom he cites throughout the 1860s as authorities on the deficiencies of liberal de-mocracy. Mill's writings appear to have come to his attention only after some years in England; his first published reference to them (recom-mending them to readers of the *Bell*) occurs in 1857. He seems never to have met Mill. An attempt by a mutual friend to arrange a meeting between them in 1859 was frustrated by Mill's departure abroad; he was to spend little time in England during Herzen's years in London. Al-though, unlike Proudhon, he was neither a friend nor a mentor to Herzen, there is a remarkable affinity between their visions of freedom. But while Mill's insights into the defects of liberal democracies are a landmark in political thought, Herzen's reflections on the same sub-ject tend to invisibility because they have been routinely lumped to-gether with the patriotic outpourings of the Slavophiles. In the words of one critic: when compared with his earlier philosophical writings, Herzen's Russian socialism represents "an astonishing descent from the sublime to the ridiculous."[37] But we have seen that Herzen him-self conceived these later works as an attempt to pursue the practical consequences of his denial of a cosmic order that defines the purposes of rational human beings. If his thought is to be set retrospectively into any tradition, then his place is surely among that small number of thinkers who distanced themselves equally from both sides in the battle between forms of rationalist foundationalism and irrationalist doctrines of self-creation. Mill was one of this number. He had the fate that Bacon forecast for all those who question the dominant metaphors of their time—to be sentenced by the tribunals that they themselves have put on trial. Treated with far greater respect by his countrymen than Herzen was by his, Mill has often been not much better understood. The excursion into his thought that follows offers an added perspective on Herzen's conflict with Russian liberals over the nature of freedom.

Herzen and John Stuart Mill

Mill came to his unorthodox views on freedom by the same path as Herzen: through painful reflection on the emotional cost of his preoccupation with philosophical abstractions. The young Herzen had diagnosed his generation's search for the rational meaning of finite existence as "a kind of madness."[38] Mill has left us his famous account of his breakdown in 1826, when at the age of twenty he concluded that his education in the spirit of Benthamite utilitarianism had turned him into "a mere reasoning machine." Cultivation of the feelings—not as a substitute but as a corrective for the habits of rational analysis—became a central point of his ethical and philosophical creed.[39] As he wrote to Thomas Carlyle in 1834, the utilitarian goal of the greatest happiness of the greatest number continued to be his ultimate aim, but he now believed that "this end can in no other way be forwarded but . . . by each taking for his exclusive aim the development of what is best in *himself.*"[40] This in turn Mill believed could be achieved only by what he describes as "the maintenance of a due balance among the faculties."[41] His view of liberty, like Herzen's, rested on a Schillerian model of the individual's relations with himself.

He acknowledged the primacy of reason in determining moral goals and controlling selfish and irrational impulses, but maintained that this was best achieved by forming character through an aesthetic education that makes feeling reason's ally, furnishing images of noble conduct for emulation, and developing our imaginative empathy with particular individuals and cases. This, he insists, is a more secure foundation for morality than the habit of obedience to general principles, the great majority of good actions being intended "not for the benefit of the world, but for that of individuals, of which the good of the world is made up."[42] Rejecting, like Schiller, the view that all acts of self-renunciation are necessarily virtuous, he maintained that social utility is best served by those in whom the cultivation of feeling has created a disposition to do good that is independent of any system of sanctions and prescriptions. The formation of character in this way would, moreover, constitute a safeguard against the excessive ascendancy of systems that, in the name of service to humanity, threaten to "interfere unduly with human freedom and individuality."[43]

On Liberty, like the *Aesthetic Letters*, is structured around the opposition between a dualistic and an aesthetic vision of the individual's relations with himself. In Mill's nightmarish picture of Victorian society, the stern rigor of moral attitudes founded on Kantian dualism and Christian asceticism have combined with the zeal of reforming rationalists to secure the ascendancy of "conglomerated mediocrity." Tocqueville had remarked on the part played by Puritanism in enforcing moral conformism in the United States; in England Mill calls attention to the influence of the "pinched and hidebound" types of character favored by the more mean-minded varieties of Protestantism, whose power was reflected in such monstrosities as sabbatarian legislation. Social reformers, too, seemed bent on making people "all alike," regulating their thoughts and actions by a common set of rules and maxims. The growth of mass communications and the standardization of the conditions of material existence were moving society in the same direction. Spontaneity and eccentricity were frowned on as obstructions to the right way of doing things; this "liberticide" was favored even by heretics and dissidents who occupied themselves "rather in inquiring what society ought to like or dislike, than in questioning whether its likings or dislikings should be a law to individuals." Mill insisted that he was seeking to define an incipient tendency. It was as yet insufficiently perceived that the term "self-government" had come to denote "not the government of each by himself, but of each by all the rest." The collective tyranny of popular sovereignty offered fewer means of escape than other kinds of oppression, "penetrating more deeply into the details of life, enslaving the soul itself." The personality divided against itself submits unprotestingly to the yoke of uniformity. Hence the famous principle of *On Liberty*: "The sole end for which mankind are warranted, individually or collectively, in interfering with the liberty of action of any of their number, is self-protection. . . . The only part of the conduct of any one, for which he is amenable to society, is that which concerns others. In the part which merely concerns himself, his independence is, of right, absolute."

Mill was well aware of the heretical status of his principle. It might, he wrote, seem a truism that "the only freedom which deserves the name, is that of pursuing our own good in our own way," but no doctrine was more directly opposed to the general tendency of existing opinion and practice. Such a view had been held only by a minority of thinkers in any age, and in his own, "few persons, [outside] of Germany," would not be amazed to find so high a value attached to individuality. In asserting his "very simple principle,'" Mill stood like Herzen on a lonely shore. Like Herzen's essay "Omnia mea mecum porto," *On Liberty* hits out in all directions, presenting a view of human autonomy clearly distinct from all the mainstream varieties of idealist metaphysics, rationalist determinism, and Romantic doctrines of protean self-creation.[44] It is significant that of those thinkers who anticipated his ideas, Mill finds it "appropriate" to mention only one: Schiller's admired friend and correspondent, the Prussian scholar and statesman Wilhelm von Humboldt. *On Liberty* is headed by an epigraph from Humboldt's book *The Sphere and Duties of Government:* "The grand, leading principle, towards which every argument unfolded in these pages directly converges, is the absolute and essential importance of human development in its richest diversity."[45]

It has been said of Humboldt that he enlarges one's sense of what a liberal theory may be.[46] The same is true of Mill. His mental breakdown having taught him that human needs were too complex to be explicable in terms of any unitary system of rational purposes, he began to seek illumination from mutually exclusive doctrines—a procedure that, as Isaiah Berlin has commented, was "greatly daring" in one brought up in a puritanical Benthamite radicalism.[47] The ideological contest between the eighteenth and nineteenth centuries came to seem to him a battle between half-truths. Following Goethe's motto of "many-sidedness," he turned to idealist philosophies of history, rejecting their metaphysical *a prioris* but using their dialectical vision of an evolving truth to deepen his sense of the creative potentials of an unprogrammed world. (A few years later the young Herzen, exasperated by the incompleteness of idealist and materialist explanations of reality, would follow a similar path.) Respecting no ideological boundaries, Mill found inspiration in sources as diverse as the Saint-Simonians' revolutionary views on the relations of the sexes, and the conservatism of Carlyle, from which he benefited "not as philosophy to instruct, but as poetry to animate."[48] Asked to explain his system, he retorted that he neither had nor aspired to have one. Instead, like Proudhon and Herzen, he had a method, whose basic premise can be summed up in Schiller's dictum: "Reason does indeed demand unity, but Nature demands multiplicity; and both these kinds of law make their claim upon man."[49]

Much of what Mill's critics took to be his inconsistency derived from his efforts to maintain in his thinking a dynamic equilibrium between these competing orders of law. In this he believed, like Herzen, that science was on his side: the inductive methods of the natural sciences supported moral instinct and aesthetic insight by demonstrating the incompleteness and provisionality of all generalizations about contingent phenomena. Hence, while sharing Auguste Comte's optimism about the possibility of a future science of society, he viewed the range and competence of such a science very differently from Comte, whose ideal of a society ruled by a body of scientist-philosophers seemed to him both despotic and unscientific. "It is one of M. Comte's mistakes that he never allows of open questions"[50]—his love of system and certainty was at odds with his positivism. Observation showed human nature to be, not an unchanging totality of characteristics, but a not necessarily consistent thing of "extraordinary pliability" whose achievements were built on historically accumulated experience.[51] By plotting regularities in that experience, science could make increasingly accurate predictions, but it should not presume to extrapolate the future form of society from the present. A true science of society would be experimental, not prescriptive.

It is as experiments, always open to revision and rejection, that Mill approaches all social theories, including his own. Herzen predicted that socialism would generate demands it could not satisfy; Mill regarded representative democracy as a question of "time, place, and circumstance." He saw nothing sacred in the principles of the liberal political economy of his time. In revised editions of his *Principles of Political Economy*, written with Harriet Taylor, he speculates on the advantages of communal systems of ownership and production; their attempts to reconcile the principles of individual liberty and social justice led the two to class themselves "decidedly under the general designation of Socialists," while distancing themselves equally decidedly from all forms of collectivism. With this exception, Mill welcomed all "experiments of living" (such as those of Robert Owen's followers) that, by offering alternative models of organization, could shake society out of the complacency that he saw as the greatest danger facing modern democracies.[52]

Given Mill's perspectivist approach to political institutions, it is unsurprising that his work contains no formulas for the conduct of representative government, other than the general principle of the necessity of counterbalances to the ascendancy of any single power or elite. On the definition of the areas of competence of government, he offers only one "simple and vague" rule—that the interference of government should never be admitted except "when the case of expediency is strong."[53] He warns against the folly of premature attempts to introduce enlightened reforms in the face of the resistance of opinions that, however intellectually discredited, continue to form the moral framework of most lives. All of Mill's writings on politics and society flow from those insights into the moral self that his personal crisis had given him. That self was not, he believed, an unchanging rational core that orders the rest according to universal norms; it was (to use Proudhon's term) "an agglomeration of potentialities," from which each person creates a unique individuality. Thus, while attaching great importance to the role of education in developing the imaginative empathy that he saw as the basis of social cohesion, he strongly opposed any centralized system of instruction that would force people into a standardizing mold. "It is essential that different persons be allowed to live different lives. . . . Whatever crushes individuality is despotism, . . . whether it professes to be enforcing the will of God or the injunctions of men."[54]

* * *

"Thanks be to those who after us confirm with their authority what we have said, and with their talent clearly and forcefully hand on what we have feebly expressed." Nicely balancing modesty with a claim to precedence, Herzen's review of *On Liberty* greets Mill as one of the few

"serious" minds in western Europe who have come to share those notions about fossilized opinions and ideals that he had expressed in
1849.[55] Then he had been scolded for presuming to criticize his elders
and betters; now a similar pessimism has been expressed, not by some
"angry socialist exile" like Proudhon or himself, but by a man of "enormous, well merited authority," a celebrated political economist "long
versed in affairs of state and theories deeply thought out, accustomed
to regard the world calmly, like an Englishman and a thinker." Denied
intellectual respectability outside a narrow circle of radical émigrés,
Herzen recognized in Mill a fellow heretic who, unlike himself, could
not be patronized by liberal intellectuals.

In his autobiography Mill expressed regret that the desire to compromise with common opinion had on occasion made him suppress
"the more decidedly heretical part of my opinions, which I now look
upon as almost the only ones, the assertion of which tends in any way
to regenerate society."[56] Herzen's first printed reference to Mill, two
years before the appearance of On Liberty, shows a keen sense of this
predicament. In a survey of current Western publications in the Bell
he refers to Mill's work, along with new positivist approaches to the
natural sciences, as spearheading an attack on all forms of idealism by
"bringing the realm of theology and mystery down to the level of
nature and history." But he notes the enormous distance between
this approach and what popular opinion will tolerate, and the consequent hypocrisy of the scientific popularizers of the time, who
water down their message "so as not to scare the crowd and to have
a full auditorium."[57]

Herzen had no such reservations about On Liberty. His review exploits the piquancy of the situation, inviting his readers to reflect on
the strangeness of the fact that, ten years after his own much-derided
critique of the aesthetic poverty and moral despotism of bourgeois culture, a thinker in a country renowned for its political freedoms should
find it necessary to publish a book "in defense of liberty of thought,
speech and the individual." "Can there be any idea in the world more
impoverished than that of order?" Herzen had inquired of Proudhon
after Louis-Napoleon's coup of 1851.[58] Mill's answer to this question
was so much in sympathy with his own thinking that the notion of
"conglomerated mediocrity" would become a refrain of Herzen's com-

mentaries on Western democracies. His review gives much emphasis to Mill's warning that progress is not a universal characteristic of human history. Were the despotism of custom to become institutionalized in European societies, they could reach a state of inertia so complete that Europe would become another China, with one difference—the bitterest drop in Mill's cup of wormwood—the European bourgeoisie would continue in its restless pursuit of change and fashion. In proscribing singularity, the spirit of conformism did not proscribe change, "provided all change together."

Herzen seizes on Mill's image of a new China to develop the analogy between historical and evolutionary processes that had long been a central feature of his writing on history. He notes that Mill is describing something akin to the formation of "herd types," the ultimate result of a long succession of struggles and achievements. "The antediluvian beasts represent a kind of heroic age in this *Book of Being:* they are the Titans or paladins; they diminish in size, adapt themselves to a new environment and, as soon as they attain to a type that is sufficiently skillful and stable, they begin to repeat themselves in conformity with their type, to such a degree that the dog of Ulysses in the *Odyssey* is as like all our dogs as two drops of water. And that is not all: has anyone said that political and social animals, not only living in a herd but possessing organization of some sort, like ants and bees, established their anthills or nests out of hand? I do not think so at all. Millions of generations lay down and died and perished before they built and stabilized their *Chinese* anthills." In human societies, Herzen suggests, an analogous process occurs when the active—"historic"—part of a people reaches a form of social organization that suits it and gives up the struggle for something better in favor of preserving what has been attained. To maintain this state of equilibrium requires neither wars, nor revolutions, nor eccentric individuals. On the contrary, passive absorption in the herd is a prime condition for self-preservation. There are signs that Europe is approaching such a state: "Individuals do not step out of the ranks because there is not sufficient occasion. For whom, for what, or against whom are they to come forward?" This, Herzen says, is not a question that Mill addresses. Frightened by the moral worthlessness of his environment, Mill seems to want people with the mentality of shopkeepers: "to turn, from

some poetic necessity, by some spiritual gymnastics, into—heroes!"
Instead of remonstrating with the sick man, we should admit the
pathological fact: the absence of the kinds of ideals that were the creative inspiration of Europe from the Middle Ages to the eighteenth
century. Catholicism, Protestantism, science, and revolution had all
played their part in this respect:

> Where is that sacred monomania, that *magnum ignotum*, that riddle
> of the Sphinx of our civilization? Where is the mighty conception,
> the passionate belief, the burning hope, that could temper the body
> like steel and bring the soul to such a pitch of obduracy as feels nei-
> ther pain nor privation but walks with a firm step to the scaffold or
> the stake?
>
> Look about you: What is capable of heartening individuals, up-
> lifting peoples, shaking the masses? The religion of the Pope with
> his Immaculate Conception of the Mother of God, or the religion
> with no Pope and its abstention from beer on the Sabbath Day? The
> arithmetical pantheism of universal suffrage or the idolatrous wor-
> ship of monarchy? Superstitious belief in a republic or in parliamen-
> tary reforms? . . . No, no: all this pales, ages, and is bundled away, as
> once the gods of Olympus were bundled away when they descended
> from heaven, dislodged by new rivals risen from Golgotha.
>
> Unfortunately our blackened idols do not command these sources
> of inspiration, or at all events Mill does not point them out.

Herzen notes that *On Liberty* is unaccountably silent on one question:
"On what principle are we to wake the sleeper? In the name of what
shall the flabby personality, magnetized by trifles, be inspired, be made
discontented with its present life of railways, telegraphs, newspapers,
and cheap goods?" If no such principle can be found, Mill's nightmare
will take different forms in all those countries where the benefits of
education and technology have prepared the ground for a new, improved
version of China. England will retain her trade and may even extend
her freedoms, the growth of obligatory custom providing a more effective rein on the will than legal sanctions. France will perfect its martial centralization until it becomes a new Persia. "The transition . . .
will take place imperceptibly; not a single right . . . will be lost, not one
freedom will be diminished; all that will be diminished is *the ability
to make use of those rights and this freedom.*"

In Herzen's interpretation of Mill's scenario, the human urge for liberty is in danger of withering away like an organ rendered superfluous by the evolutionary process. The only hope of a different path of development lies in those for whom that organ still performs a vital function as the instrument of struggle with a hostile environment: the working masses. The idea of social revolution might recover from its recent defeat to become that *idée fixe* that could steer Europe to new destinies. But he suggests that the chances for this are slight. To pursue his metaphor, it was not an adaptation profitable to Europe's governing classes.

Herzen's "Mill on Liberty" makes no reference to his hopes about the potential of the Russian commune. He used the weapon that had fallen so conveniently to hand to concentrate his fire on what he had come to perceive as the major impediment to all constructive discussion about Russia's post-Emancipation options: the "fanatical" faith of the liberals that their favored political option was the desired and destined goal of all mankind.[59]

CHAPTER NINETEEN

What Is History?

*Qu'est-ce que c'est donc l'histoire? . . . Providence, hasard, ironie,
ou fatalité?*

IVAN TURGENEV TO PAULINE VIARDOT, 13 MAY 1848

I'm not a fatalist; I don't believe in any form of predestination, not
even the notorious "perfectibility of mankind."

HERZEN TO TURGENEV, 1856

HERZEN'S polemics with Chicherin and Kavelin were followed by an
extended debate in private correspondence and in print with Ivan Turgenev, who once described himself as "an old-fashioned liberal in the
English . . . sense."[1]

The relationship between the two dates from the months Turgenev
spent in Paris in 1848–1849, when he became a friend of the Herzen
family. He and Herzen corresponded intermittently in the 1850s, and
met twice in London; their last encounter, followed by a rift in their
friendship, was in 1862. Each admired the other's humanism; Herzen
welcomed Turgenev's *Sketches from a Huntsman's Notebook* as a
powerful attack on serfdom. Both were intensely interested in the phenomenon of intelligentsia introspection (described by Turgenev as
"our strength and our weakness, our downfall and our salvation"),[2] and
they valued each other's insights into the tensions between the Russian intellectual's iconoclasm and his need for faith. Herzen sent Turgenev chapters of his memoirs for comment, while Turgenev sent him
drafts of his own fictional chronicles. Their affinity was based above all
on their common suspicion of doctrines, systems, and utopian faiths,
which led both to distance themselves from all the political ideologies
and groupings that began to take shape in the first years of the new
tsar's reign. But their differing interpretations of the social and political realities of those years soon drew them into opposing positions,
each believing the other to have compromised his basic principles.

Their rift developed slowly. They were in agreement in seeing the two priorities of the new era as the abolition of serfdom and the granting of individual rights. As preparations for the Emancipation gained momentum, Turgenev (under strict anonymity) sent Herzen's London press leaked information on the state of government thinking on the question, together with documentation of abuses of power by the new regime. He was among those liberals who signed a protest against Chicherin's public attack on Herzen, but he disapproved strongly of what he saw as Herzen's worship of the Russian peasantry, which he perceived as a radical variation on Slavophile utopianism. He urged him to refrain from direct criticism of the tsar for fear of discouraging him from any Westernizing reforms. Russia, he wrote, was not a Venus de Milo and did not differ much from her western European sisters, "except, perhaps, that she is a little broader in the beam."[3]

Their debate developed in the context of the polarization between liberal and radical opinion under Alexander II. The government's silencing of radical protest about the terms of the reforms was increasingly supported by those who regarded themselves as liberals but believed that only a show of force by the government could avert the catastrophe of a peasant revolt—hence the almost universal approval in that quarter for its bloody suppression of the Polish rising of 1863. Herzen and Turgenev defended their vision of a complex reality against the narrow intransigence of both the Right and the Left. Nevertheless, the two men's sympathies lay with opposing camps, and each was strongly critical of the political company the other kept. Turgenev pleaded with Herzen to distance himself from Bakunin (who, after escaping from Siberia in 1861, had arrived in London eager to use the Free Russian Press to print incendiary pamphlets) and from Ogarev. Herzen disapproved of both Bakunin's propaganda and his influence on Ogarev, but he would not tolerate Turgenev's attack on his co-editor. There were no grounds, he affirmed, for confusing Ogarev's journalism with Bakunin's demagoguery. Turgenev chose to do so because he had a grudge against the younger generation—he was snapping at the older because it was closer to hand.[4]

This reference was to Turgenev's quarrel with the radical critics Nikolai Chernyshevsky and Nikolai Dobrolyubov, who had become joint editors of the literary journal The Contemporary in which

Turgenev had been publishing his work, and who treated him there with insolent contempt. He then switched to a journal edited by the increasingly chauvinistic Mikhail Katkov. His association with this man was a target of Herzen's sarcasm. When Turgenev sought his opinion of his novel *Fathers and Sons* (whose depiction of the conflict between the liberals of his own generation and the self-designated "new people" of the 1860s had succeeded in offending both camps), he replied that the work was marred by a desire to settle scores with Chernyshevsky and his group. Its portrait of a young radical highlighted the rudeness and arrogance characteristic of the type, while revealing nothing of those radicals' inner life or the experiences that had made them what they were.[5] Turgenev (who pointed out that his liberal friends had reproached him for idealizing the same character) was deeply offended by this charge of tendentiousness. Their relations deteriorated further in 1863 after the Russian Senate summoned Turgenev to give evidence to its inquiry into the connections between Russian radicals and the editors of the *Bell*. Greatly alarmed, Turgenev succeeded in obtaining permission to send written answers to its questions on his dealings with Russian exiles and Herzen in particular. He stressed his estrangement from Herzen, whose political views, he claimed, were repudiated by all "sensible Russians"—whose love of freedom was inseparable from their loyalty to the tsar.[6] After being subsequently compelled to attend the Senate inquiry in person, he was officially exonerated in June 1864. In January of that year Herzen had commented in the *Bell* on reports about "a certain white-haired Magdalen (of the male sex), who wrote to the tsar that she had lost sleep and appetite . . . , tortured by the thought that the tsar did not yet know of the repentance that has overcome her, as a result of which *'she has broken all contact with the friends of her youth.'*" Turgenev wrote to him expressing his distress at being thus pilloried for having done no more than state that he did not share Herzen's views, claiming (not entirely truthfully) that he had not repudiated his former friend. Herzen in turn expressed disbelief, while noting coldly, "We were never particularly close." As evidence of the gulf between them he mentioned the presence of Turgenev's name on a list of subscribers to a fund for Russian soldiers wounded during the suppression of the Polish rising. Turgenev (along with most of liberal society) had considered the Poles' bid for freedom to be senseless and futile; Herzen noted that the *Bell*'s defense of the Poles' cause (an attempt, as he put it, to save something of his country's honor) had been condemned by the "slavish majority" to which Turgenev, to his shame, belonged. After this exchange, their relations ceased until May 1867, when Turgenev sent Herzen a copy of his latest novel. Herzen rebuked him for continuing to publish with "a vile informer" (Katkov). Turgenev replied in his defense that Katkov's journal was the only one everybody read. He reminds Herzen that as men of the 1840s they had more in common with each other than with the next generation, a view that Herzen did not dispute. Asking Turgenev to pass on some of the current gossip in Russian society, he adds "I suppose we have been forgotten."[7]

*　*　*

It occurred to Herzen after Turgenev's visit in 1856 to use their discussions as a vehicle for expounding his view of history in his preferred dialogical form. In the following year he published a long essay in the *Polar Star*—"Another Variation on an Old Theme"—in the form of a letter to an anonymous friend (Turgenev had asked not to be identified by name).[8] He starts by summarizing the reproaches of Turgenev and other Russian liberals—that his criticism of the West undermined the faith in enlightened values so necessary to Russia at this juncture, and his defense of the commune made common cause with the reactionary philosophy of the Slavophiles.

Herzen cites these charges as evidence that the liberal Westernizers were just as obsessed as the Slavophiles with old scholastic controversies over questions such as the precedence of races and the nationality of truth. Neither side had perceived that these debates had been rendered irrelevant by the new life fermenting in Russia at a unique turning point in her history: the eve of an economic upheaval of immeasurably vaster scope than the recent political revolutions in Europe, its agreed-upon goal being a fundamental revision of the rights of ownership and of the workers' relation to the means of production.

Always concerned to stress the empirical basis of his hopes of a separate path of development, as the Emancipation loomed ahead Herzen took particular care to distance himself from the intelligentsia's two main ideological camps. Chicherin had enraged the Slavophiles by publishing an article claiming that in its modern form the Russian commune had been created by the rulers of Muscovy as a means of attaching the peasants to their masters and the land.[9] In his essay "Another Variation" Herzen observes that the commune's origins were of no importance in comparison with the fact of its present existence as a component of that historical material from which a new political and social reality was about to be fashioned. This must draw on the science and the humane values of the West, but not on its institutions, which were in profound contradiction with those values. He stressed that his conviction was based not on a set of theories but on first-hand observation of the deepening antagonisms in European societies and their failure to heal the wounds of 1848. The outcome of their struggles promised to be neither speedy nor positive. In these circumstances should one not cast around for different models of development? Only two merited consideration. America's achievements had resulted from the transplanting of elements of an old culture onto a new soil; Russia's colonizing feats of the preceding century in European Russia, Siberia, and the Amur region revealed the same youthful energy and plasticity, but in a nation free from those prejudices that had paralyzed western Europe. Herzen recapitulates to Turgenev the grounds for his belief in the possibility of a separate path for Russia: on the one hand, the absence of an entrenched economic and legal order supported by a strong middle class; on the other, the survival of the commune with its democratic system of election. "This is why, dear friend . . . in the midst of the dark night that is falling on the sick and weary West, I turn aside from the death agonies of the great warrior whom I respect, but whom I cannot aid, and gaze with hope on our native East, inwardly rejoicing that I am a Russian."

As so often when Herzen writes on this theme, his hopes seem rather more robust than the evidence produced in their support. The colonial expansion that he reads as evidence of the Russian people's untapped strength was achieved through the military might of a governing system he held to be alien to its national traditions. Yet his hyperbole had a practical aim. He could not hope to convince Turgenev, but he sought to reach a wider audience, to persuade as many of his countrymen as would read his smuggled journal that the way forward preached by the liberals was neither the only option nor the best—that it was possible to strike out in a new direction away from old, discredited formulae. Hence his "passionate impatience": "In Russia I see a chance at hand, I feel it, I touch it; there is no such possibility in western Europe—at least, not at this juncture."

He insists that his intention is not (as Turgenev believed) to close minds, but to open them by weaning Russia's Westernized elite away from its vision of history as the movement along a single track to a universal goal. People tended to believe that history followed a linear path because they saw only the ready-made results—the successful experiments, not those that had been aborted at the start or discarded along the way. Like their counterparts in nature, these unsuccessful historical forms had lived out the fullness of their own existence and passed on an inheritance, not to their children, but to strangers: "the mammoths and the ichthyosauri to the elephants and crocodiles, Egypt and India to Greece and Rome." Such was the untidy unpredictability of natural and historical processes, which "plod along, from day to day and from age to age, losing their way, opening up new paths, amazing us now by their speed, now by their slowness, now by their intelligence, now by their stupidity, pushing in all directions, but entering only where the gates are open." If, as Herzen believed, such a gate was now opening in the East, what would follow would be the same largely unpredictable brew, as those elements of Western civilization that retained most creative vitality—its science and its social theories—entered new combinations with the native elements of another soil. If Russia failed to grasp the opportunities opened by the new era, other countries—America, Australia, or even a regenerated Europe—would soon leave it far behind. "But is it really possible that after setting one foot on the beaten track, [Russia] will once more sink down into the bog, having given the world the spectacle of enormous strength and a complete incapacity to use it? Something prevents the heart from accepting that! How painful are these doubts, how painful this loss of time and energy!"

History as Embryology: "Robert Owen"

Herzen's approach to history as a complex process of embryology would make him particularly receptive to *On the Origin of Species* when it was published in London in November 1859. He sent a copy to his son, who had embarked on a career in the natural sciences. To readers of the *Bell* he cited the *Origin* as an eminent exception to the spirit of pietism prevalent in English intellectual circles. The most enthusiastic of Darwin's defenders, T. H. Huxley, sought to propagate the new theories as widely as possible through popular lectures to working men; Herzen recommends that one such series be translated into Russian, in view of its "sound and simple language."[10]

With his close interest in the natural sciences, Herzen was likely to have attended several lectures of the pietistic variety during his years in London (including, perhaps, those of the eminent exponent of evolutionary biology, the geologist Charles Lyell, who welcomed Darwin's theories as scientific confirmation of the notion of an a priori plan: "the amount of power, wisdom, design or forethought" required for evolution being at least as great as that required for a multitude of separate acts of creation).[11] A Darwinian *avant la lettre*, Herzen was better equipped than most to appreciate that the new theories had edged providential design altogether out of the cosmic scheme.

In December 1860 he completed a long essay inspired by his meeting in London with the English socialist Robert Owen, whose personality had made a deep impression on him. He dedicated it to his friend and ideological opponent Kavelin, sending a copy to Turgenev with the message: "I want you very, very much to read it; it's a bold and, it seems to me, successful piece." He attached great importance to the work; in the last year of his life he would look back on it as one of his best.

A successful mill owner turned socialist, Owen set up a factory and school on exemplary communitarian principles in the Scottish hamlet of New Lanark, following this philanthropic exercise with a full-scale attack on the existing social and economic order, organized religion, private property, and the institution of the family. His ideal was a system of cooperative socialism based on networks of small, predominantly agricultural units, within which liberty for all would be harmonized, in some undisclosed fashion, with full equality. His nebulous schemes were firm on one point: once society was reorganized according to rationalist and egalitarian principles, it would become clear that humans were by nature both rational and benign. The dismal failure of his later attempt to create such a community in

New Harmony, Indiana, did not affect his serene optimism, reinforced in his old age by spiritualism. In one of his last works he foresees a peaceful revolution engineered by the departed spirits of good men and women.

Herzen recalls that when he met him in 1852, Owen was nearing the end of his life as an isolated and seemingly pathetic figure, reviled by the English clergy and regarded by liberal opinion with condescending pity as a harmless madman. Still smarting from Chicherin's admonitions, Herzen declared Owen's passionate rantings to be less repulsive than the calm superciliousness of those who held their beliefs to be eminently rational. Owen had transgressed the commandments of their civic credo by maintaining that in matters of morality and education, punishment and coercion were not the best methods of developing human potential. If he *were* mad, it would be because, with the indestructible faith of the eighteenth century (known so curiously as the age of unbelief), he held mankind to be on the threshold of adulthood, making the mistake of all prophets and reformers in believing that simple truths are easily understood. The failure of Owen's groundbreaking experiment in socialism is Herzen's starting point for a return to the principal themes of *From the Other Shore* in the light of the Darwinian revolution anticipated by that work.

Darwin's discoveries lent formidable authority to Herzen's long-held view that the human faculty of reason was a chance, marginal, and terrifyingly fragile development in the history of life—a point he makes vigorously in his essay "Robert Owen." "Quantitatively, reason must always give way; it will always carry less *weight*; like the Northern Lights it shines over great distances, but it scarcely exists." All civilizations had had their prophets and accusers protesting against moral and social bondage, but none of their utopias had been realized. North America provided a frightening example. Nowhere had conditions been more propitious for the development of a free and rational state. "Everything that old Europe dreamed of: a republic, a democracy, a federation, . . . the whole lightly tied together by a common governmental girdle with a weak knot in the middle." The result: persecution and slavery in the southern states, while the North bore the burden of a public opinion founded on the intolerance of Puritans and Quakers. In milder forms one came across the same phenomenon in European democracies such as England or Sweden: "The freer a country is from government interference, the more fully recognized its right to speak, to independence of conscience, the more intolerant grows the mob. Public opinion becomes a torture-chamber: your neighbor, your butcher, tailor, family, club, parish, keep you under surveillance and perform the duties of a policeman. Can only a people incapable of *inner* freedom achieve liberal institutions? Or does not all this mean that a State constantly develops demands and ideals which the better minds fulfill by their activity, but the realization of which is incompatible with life in a State?" There were no simple answers to these questions. The old order of things still had many solid sources of support—among them, fear of the mob (the educated classes were prepared against their convictions to walk on a leash themselves provided that the masses be not released from it), and the fear of freedom. "The fear that children have when they begin to walk without leading-strings . . . the habituation to those mandates steeped in sweat and blood, to those boats that have become arks of salvation." People will accept and believe anything, submit to anything, sacrifice much, "but they recoil in horror when through a chink between two religions . . . there blows in on them the cool wind of reason and criticism."

Owen had believed that it was sufficient to demonstrate the absurdity of a custom or conviction for it to be discarded. But history had developed by means of absurdities—peoples had set their hearts on chimeras, built cities and created beauty as a result. For absurdities they had gone willingly to their deaths and executed others. "Life goes by as a series of optical illusions, artificial needs, and imaginary satisfactions. One dream yields to another; the sleep becomes lighter but is never quite gone. In all these thousand and one nights of history, a little education is achieved, a few awaken, but they are unable to rouse the rest. Their appearance demonstrates without the slightest doubt humans' capacity to evolve a rational understanding. But this does not answer our question: Can this exceptional development become general? The guidance given us by the past does not favor an affirmative verdict."

It was wrong to believe that simple truths were always easy to understand: "It is positively simpler to breathe air than to breathe water, but for this one must have lungs, and where are they to be evolved in a fish, which needs a complicated respiratory equipment in order to obtain a little oxygen from water? Their environment does not permit, does not challenge them to develop lungs. . . . The moral density, the moral composition in which Owen's hearers grew up called forth their spiritual gills; breathing a purer and thinner medium necessarily caused them pain and revulsion." This was not, Herzen insists, merely a figure of speech: "Here is a true analogy of identical phenomena at different ages and in different strata." The delirium of history was a magnificent prolongation of the plasticity of nature. "There is no haste in nature: she could lie for thousands and thousands of years in a trance of stone, and for other thousands twitter with the birds, scour the forests with the beasts or swim in the sea as a fish"—the development of the brain needs and takes time.[12]

It should be remembered how novel—and for many, how shocking—such comparisons were in 1861. Ten years later, Darwin's explicit analogies between human and animal behavior in *The Descent of Man* would expose him to the charge of moral nihilism: the London *Times* asserted that a similar "loose philosophy" was then fanning the flames of the Paris Commune.[13]

Echoing the dissenting voices in *From the Other Shore*, a questioner protests: If mankind's most advanced ideals stand so little chance of realization, what then is the point of history? Herzen's response, querying the "mercenary" demands of those who look to history for confirmation of their hopes, is familiar from his earlier essays; but his argument is developed in some of his finest prose, exploring the nature of human intervention in history through a series of vivid images conveying the inner tensions and the creative freedom of an attitude that approaches the predicament of human contingency in a Schillerian spirit of aesthetic play.

To the questioner demanding what moral can be drawn from his view of history, he replies *"liberation from deceit—that is the moral"*:

> In return for all we have endured, for our broken bones, our bruised heart, our losses, our mistakes, our delusions—at least to decipher a few letters of the mysterious script, to understand the general sense of what is going on around us. . . . That's a very great deal! The childish rubbish we are relinquishing no longer interests us: it is dear to us only from habit. What is there to regret in that? The Baba Yaga

or the Vital Force, the fairytale of the Golden Age behind us or of unending progress ahead? The miracle-working phial of St. Januarius
or a meteorological prayer for rain? The secret design of conspiratorial chemists or *natura sic voluit?*

For the first moment it is frightening, but only for one moment.
Everything around one oscillates and speeds past. Stand motionless,
or set out wherever you like: there is no barrier, no road, no authority
of any kind. . . .

Both nature and history are *going nowhere,* and therefore they are
ready to go *anywhere* they are directed, *if this is possible*—that is, if
nothing obstructs them. They are composed *au fur et à mesure* of an
immense multitude of particles meeting, attracting, and repelling
each other. But man is by no means lost as a result, like a grain of
sand on a mountain, [he] is neither more subject to the elements nor
more rigidly bound by necessity; by understanding his predicament, he grows into a helmsman, proudly ploughing the seas with
his vessel, making the bottomless wave serve him as a path or
communication.

Having neither program, nor set theme, nor inevitable denouement, the disheveled improvisation of history is ready to go along
with anyone; anyone can insert his line of verse into it, and if it is
sonorous, it will remain *his* line, until the poem is torn up, as long
as the past ferments in its blood and memory. A multitude of possibilities, episodes, discoveries, in history and nature, lies slumbering
at every step.

Herzen does not exaggerate the fear and disorientation of those who
sensed that science and philosophy were in the process of destroying
the foundations of order and meaning in human societies. The *Times*
reflected a widespread apprehension when it predicted that, should Darwin's mischievous ideas ever become widely accepted, "morality
would lose all elements of stable authority."[14] In 1866 Herzen speculates in the *Bell* that the Russian government must have suspected
Darwin's influence somewhere behind Karakozov's plot to kill the tsar:
it had banned his works, along with those of the natural scientists Moleschott and Vogt.[15]

In the controversy over the *Origin,* many expressed the sense of
being adrift in a vast, purposeless, and unfeeling universe. People had
come to fear their own logic and to cling to remnants of the past.

Having repudiated Christianity, they found refuge in idealism or Providence: thus Herzen had accounted for the survival of faith in inevitable progress after the catastrophes of 1848. Darwin's ambivalences on the question of purpose and design have been attributed to the fact that the idea of progress was too central to his age to be easily and tidily dispensed with. His correspondence suggests that the conflict of logic with traditional and cherished beliefs was particularly intense in his thought around the time of the publication of the *Origin:* "The mind refuses to look at this universe, being what it is, without having been designed; yet, where one would most expect design, viz. in the structure of a sentient being, the more I think on the subject, the less I can see proof of design." "I cannot think that the world, as we see it, is the result of chance; and yet I cannot look at each separate thing as the result of Design." He confessed that he was in "an utterly hopeless muddle" on the question. But chance progressively edges out design in Darwin's metaphors until, in an autobiographical fragment of 1876, he summarizes his personal views: "There seems to be no more design in the variability of organic beings, and in the action of natural selection, than in the course which the wind blows."[16]

Herzen, who attached great importance to the metaphors we use in describing the world, would have approved of this one. In the conclusion to his essay "Robert Owen" he uses a succession of vivid images to familiarize the reader with the novel proposition that to deny a final purpose in nature and history is not (as Darwin seems to have feared) to reduce mankind to being the mere product of brute force: there is hope after teleology.

The fact that nature is not for us does not mean that she is against us: "Nature never fights against man; this is a trite religious slander. She is not intelligent enough to fight: she is indifferent. . . . Nature cannot thwart man unless man thwarts her laws; as she goes on with her work, she will unconsciously do his work for him." Through science and reason we can influence and change the flow of circumstance as a navigator exploits the elements. But we tend to forget that in history we are simultaneously pilot, boat, and wave, inextricably meshed in processes we seek to control. It is this that offends the abstracting and systematizing intellect: "In history it is easier [for the individual] to be carried along passively by the current of events or to burst into it with a knife and a shout: 'General prosperity or death!,' than to observe the ebb and flow of the waves that bear him, to study the rhythm of their fluctuations, and thereby to discover for himself endless fairways." We yearn for maps to direct our journey, not understanding that only if history is not determined can human beings be regarded as objects of serious interest. If the cards are stacked in advance, and the future mortgaged before its birth, if history is simply the *mise en scène* of some plot conceived before it began, then we should at least be given wooden swords and shields: "Surely we are not to shed real blood and real tears for the performance of a charade by Providence?"

With the Russian étatist school in his sights, Herzen comments that at least the religious concept of predestination has its aesthetic side: the drama of the rebellious Lucifer, the banished Adam and the redeeming Christ. But the secular notion of inevitable progress toward the modern state had replaced the poetic images of religion with the logical absurdity of a historical *arrière-pensée:* "Fatalism in its transition from church to school has lost all its meaning, even the verisimilitude that we demand of a fairy tale."

In *From the Other Shore,* Herzen had declared that the transience and unrepeatability of individuals and their ideals was a comforting demonstration that every historical phase had its own individuality as an end in itself. To this proposition, central to his differences with the Russian liberals, he devotes the concluding pages of "Robert Owen." Is it not simpler than believing that man lives to embody an idea, to grasp that he lives "solely because he was born," that his sphere of activity is the present, which in no way stops him from receiving a heritage from the past, or bequeathing something to the future? Idealists find this too simple and demeaning a view of human life—they cannot bear to recognize that the only source of significance in the momentary flicker of our individual lives is the fact that while we are alive,

> we are for all that ourselves, and not puppets destined to suffer progress or embody some homeless idea. We must be proud of not being needles and threads in the hands of fate as it sews the motley cloth of history. . . . We know that this cloth is not sewn without us, but that is not our aim, not our assignment, not the lesson set us to learn,

but the consequence of the complex mutual guarantee that links all existing things by their ends and beginnings, causes and effects.

And that is not all; *we can change the pattern of the carpet.* There is no master craftsman, no design, only a foundation, and we are alone, quite alone.

His questioner objects: If people do not believe that they are serving some higher end, surely they will sit back and do nothing? Herzen retorts that if the crushing fatalism of religion and the cheerlessness of doctrinairism did not make people fold their arms, "then there is no reason to fear that this may be done by a view that rids them of these slabs of stone. A mere sniff of life and its inconsistency was enough to rescue European peoples from religious pranks like asceticism and quietism, which had perennially existed only in word and never in deed: surely reason and consciousness will not prove to be weaker?"

Instinct and conscious understanding together tell us that although we are not independent of our natural and historical environment, neither are we subjugated to it: "Humans are a long step ahead of the apes; their aspirations do not vanish without a trace: they are clothed in words, embodied in images; they are preserved in tradition and handed on from age to age. . . . At our backs, as behind the wave on the shore, is felt the pressure of the whole ocean—of the history of all the world; the thought of all the centuries is in our brain at this moment; there is no thought except in the brain, and with that thought we can be a power." Each individual can be an *"irreplaceable reality."* Herzen emphasizes these words from the concluding paragraph of his essay to encapsulate his vision of human freedom and dignity. The price we pay for the chance to insert our own verse into history's improvisation is the absence of a rational pattern of development—but the role of contingency in history does not reduce the latter to a random process. The accumulated experience of generations, by destroying delusions about the world and allowing us to make inductive assumptions about the future on past evidence, gives no grounds for setting up progress as an idol, but it can supply us with a theory of probabilities on which to base predictions and ideals.

"When we perform an induction, we know what we are doing, basing ourselves on the permanence of certain laws and phenomena, but admitting the possibility of their infringement." Herzen underlines that his own hypotheses about the future of Russia represent no more than such a theory. "Aspirations alone guarantee nothing: we are fearfully emphatic about the difference between the possible and the inevitable." Bourgeois democracies may yet take flight in new directions; the most poetic nations turn into shopkeepers. Who knows how many possibilities may perish, aspirations be aborted, developments deflected? But there is one incontrovertible fact about the historical process: each individual in his particular time and place has his unique contribution to make to it. "Now do you understand on whom the future . . . depends? On *you and me,* for instance! That being so, how can one sit back and fold one's arms!"

Turgenev, to whom Herzen sent a copy of the essay, fails to respond to its challenge to his growing pessimism. A few months later Herzen writes to Turgenev that he has not yet received his reaction, "despite my having asked you a dozen times."[17] When the silence continues, Herzen moves the argument onto his friend's home ground. A phrase from "Robert Owen," "ends and beginnings," reappears as the title of the cycle of eight essays in which he argues that Turgenev's political credo is incompatible with the latter's own values as artist, moralist, and observer of human behavior.

Herzen versus Turgenev on History

Addressed once again to an unnamed friend and published in the *Bell* between July 1862 and February 1863, the essays *Ends and Beginnings* were prompted by a second series of discussions that took place during Turgenev's visit to London in the latter half of May 1862. Their content may be deduced from Turgenev's letter to a mutual acquaintance remarking that his main objection to the platform of the *Bell*'s editors was that "while despising the educated class in Russia—almost trampling it in the mud, they assume the existence of revolutionary or reforming principles in the people," while in fact the opposite was the case:[18] the capacity and motivation for genuine reform existed only among a minority of the educated elite, by whom Turgenev meant those Westernizers who, like himself, were committed to civilized and liberal values.

The essays are a patchwork of argument, reminiscence, portraits, anecdotes, reported conversations, and digressions from digressions; but the haphazardness of their structure is as deceptive as their lightness of tone. The form is tailored to the content of the argument. Its dominant theme is Herzen's vision of history as a meandering, shapeless, and inconclusive process, constantly prone to aberrations and easily deflected from its inchoate purposes. Against this background he develops the critique of the current bourgeois culture sketched out in his review of Mill's *On Liberty*, exploiting Europe's present and recent past as a rich seam of evidence against Turgenev's Eurocentric view of human achievement.

He notes that they both agree on the universal significance of the West's cultural past. The problem is that his friend and critic wishes to go much further, maintaining that only the mode of life of the European upper classes, as evolved in the historical past, is in harmony with the aesthetic needs of human development—a view hard to reconcile with the fact that those aspects of Western art and culture that they both valued most dearly were in decline. Herzen had no quarrel with the importance Turgenev gave to art in life, but maintained that it was precisely the inner freedom characteristic of aesthetic play and essential for genuine creativity and moral growth that was now under threat in western Europe. True, its museums and galleries were overflowing with artistic treasures. "But in all this where is the new, living, creative art, where is the aesthetic element in life itself?" Art is not fastidious: "It can depict anything. . . . From the savage, menacing fantasy of Hell and the Day of Judgment to the Flemish tavern with the back view of a peasant, from Faust to Faublas, from the Requiem to the Kamarinskaya; all lie within art's competence. . . . But even art has its limits. There is a stumbling block that neither the violinist's bow nor the painter's brush nor the sculptor's chisel can overcome; art, to hide its [own] impotence, mocks it and turns it into caricature. That stumbling-block is *petit-bourgeois vulgarity.* The artist who excellently depicts a man completely naked, covered with rags, or so fully dressed that nothing can be seen except armor or a monk's cassock, is reduced to despair before *a bourgeois in a frock coat.*"[19] "Art, which is preeminently elegance of proportion, cannot endure the measuring-tape." In the cramping milieu of petty bourgeois decorum, punctual and precise, shunning extremes and superfluity both in virtue and vice, art "withers . . . like a green leaf in chlorine." Where now are the kind of ideals that inspired great acts and great art? The French Revolution had replaced the crucifix with the Phrygian cap, but "the optical illusion deceives no more." After the terrible events of 1848, "the Utopia of the democratic republic volatilized, just like the Utopia of the kingdom of heaven on earth. *Emancipation* has finally proved to be as insolvent as *redemption*." The bourgeoisie mutters incoherent phrases about progress and liberty—but "is there in all the arsenal of the past a standard, a banner, a word, an idea for which men would now go out to fight, that they have not seen disgraced and trampled in the mud?" Not, surely, that of universal suffrage? "No; no man of our time will go out to defend a single dethroned idol with the radiant self-sacrifice with which his forefather went to the stake for the right to sing psalms, with the proud self-confidence with which his father ascended the guillotine for the sake of the One and Indivisible Republic." Only one faith continued to find adherents and inspire political parties: nationalism, a phenomenon Herzen sees as "not merely a backsliding from the Revolution, but a backsliding from Christianity." Aspirations common to all mankind had ceded to a heathen patriotism: the classification of humans by nationalities was increasingly becoming the wretched ideal of a world that had buried the Revolution.[20]

The spiritual leveling of modern Europe was a consequence of the economic supremacy of the middle classes. "It is clear that the man at the helm of this world will be the merchant, and that he will set his trademark on all its manifestations. The absurdity of an aristocracy of birth and the misery of a proletariat by birth will be equally helpless against him. The government must die of hunger or become his shop assistant; . . . the lawyers, judges, notaries, etcetera, will be under his yoke."[21] Herzen's attitude to the bourgeoisie had changed little since the day in 1847 when he had recoiled from the German merchants who shared the carriage bearing him from Russia. Now he recalls the horror and disgust that he felt in his first years in the West when faced with the "continually moving, swarming crowd," the "deadly sameness" of the apartments offered him for rent, the standardization of goods to conform to criteria of quantity and cheapness that excluded those of aesthetic finish or personal taste.[22] There is something in this attitude of what Malia has described as "aristocrat's reaction to a world of shop-keepers,"[23] but other critics have called attention to the farsighted-ness of some of Herzen's observations on what has come to be known as mass culture.[24] His concern was with the phenomenon identified by Mill: a "conglomerative mediocrity" enforced by the tyranny of the crowd. The bourgeoisie interested him not as an economic category but as an ethical type: the antithesis of his aesthetic ideal of man. Together with the supremacy of the middle classes, he writes, "there will de-velop the degradation of the whole of moral life, and [John] Stuart Mill, for example, was not exaggerating in the least when he talked of the narrowing of men's minds and energies, of the obliteration of individ-uality, of the ever increasing shallowness of life, of the constant exclusion from it of general human interests, its reduction to the in-terests of the countinghouse and bourgeois prosperity."[25]

But this would not in the least deter the vast multitude who aspired to the manners, ideas, and customs of the middle classes. At the cost of surrendering their individuality, they would be better fed and clothed: true, an immense step forward, but achieved at a great price. Herzen suggests that Turgenev's defense of the bourgeois state is based on fear of the kind that inspired those artists and literary men in France in 1848 who supported political and civil forms in which they did not really believe, but that kept in check the discordant forces that threat-ened their peaceful, ordered lives. "For the sake of this mess of pot-tage *well served*, we yield up our share of human dignity, our share of compassion for our neighbor . . . and give our *negative* support to a re-gime that in its essence repels us."[26]

Herzen sees the compromises that creative, freedom-loving individ-uals make with the status quo as an instance of the agonizing state of wavering and uncertainty that had characterized Europe since 1848. "To me it is evident that western Europe has developed up to certain limits . . . and at the last moment has not had the spirit either to cross them or to be satisfied with what it has gained." The radical minority was proving incapable either of devising forms consistent with its ideal of human autonomy, of renouncing that ideal, or of frankly accepting the modern bourgeois state as a form of life, as suitable for Europeans as Chinese civilization was for China. Yet scrutiny of modern history suggests that the latter might be the case:

Yes, my dear friend, it is time to recognize with calm and humility that *bourgeoisie* is the final form of western European civilization, its coming of age—*état adulte; this* closes the long series of its dreams; with this there ends the epic of its growth, the romance of its youth, everything that has brought so much poetry and disaster into the life of nations. . . . By their painful labor the nations of the West have earned their winter quarters. Let others show their mettle. From time to time, of course, men of the old leaven, of heroic times, of other geological formations—monks, knights, Quakers, Jacobins—will appear again, but their transient appearance will not be able to change the prevailing tone.

The mighty elemental hurricanes that tossed up the whole surface of the European sea have been transformed into a quiet sea-breeze, not perilous for ships but furthering their coastal voyages. Christianity has shoaled and calmed down into the still, stony haven of the Reformation; the Revolution, too, has shoaled into the still, sandy haven of liberalism. Protestantism, a religion stern in trifles, has found the secret of reconciling the Church, which despises earthly goods, with the rule of commerce and profit. Liberalism, stern in political trifles, has learned even more artfully to unite constant protest against the government with constant submission to it.

With so indulgent a Church, with such a tame Revolution, the Western world has begun to settle, to find its equilibrium: everything that hindered it has been drawn gradually into the solidifying waves, like insects caught in amber.[27]

This hypothesis of Europe's final form is based on the evolutionary analogies that Herzen had begun to pursue in his reflections on Mill's image of Europe as a second China. In history as in nature, he argues, a species tends to reach a plateau when its development is consolidated in a certain direction: "the mollusc is not importunate to become a crab, the crab a trout, or Holland Sweden."[28] Wherever human swarms and ant heaps attain a certain level of contentment, progress slows down, imagination dims, and ideals fade. With England and France at its head, western Europe appeared to be moving toward such a state. But no living equilibrium is stable or immutable; every species is in a sense a deviation from some anterior balance and may develop its own unsuccessful deviations that distort or kill the organism, releasing its elements to form new combinations. The adaptive deviation represented by the phenomenon of a bourgeoisie may yet prove to be a "final form" in this sense, precipitating a transmutation of the organism. History presents us with a formation caught in the very act of becoming. Some parts of the human race have attained an appropriate form; others are struggling to create it; yet others, like the bed of a sea that has only just dried up, lie ready to be seeded. All these processes are too dependent on contingent factors to permit firm conclusions about their outcome. Herzen is at pains to distance himself from those organicist visions of historical death and rebirth that fed the fantasies of Romantic nationalism. Unlike the neat dialectical schemas of idealist historiosophy, the process he depicts is untidy, unpredictable, with no clear boundaries, and susceptible of infinite variations as chance hollows out new channels for development. He observes that the decline of the ancient world and the rise of Christian Europe present us with every form of historical death, of the transmigration of souls and of birth. His comments on the direction of current events are qualified by the reflection that in history, as in nature, "there are no sharp limits nor irreversible decrees." One could not assert with certainty that China or Japan would continue for much longer in their isolated existence, "that some word will not fall like a drop of yeast among those sleepy millions, and rouse them to a new life." But it did not follow that, after careful observation, one had not the right to make certain predictions about historical processes. A fisherman may conclude with some confidence that, if the sky is clear and there is no wind, there will be no storm within the hour: "It is only this right that I seek in my scrutiny of modern history."[29]

If Herzen was guilty of exaggeration, it was the same kind of exaggeration as Mill's contention that modern democratic societies were moving toward "liberticide." Both men sought to dramatize the moral consequences of those ways of conceptualizing the world that had come to pervade notions about the individual's relations with himself and with society. They saw modern man as schooled by Christian dualism and rationalist universalism to accept conformity as a virtue and leveling, standardization, and rationalization as imperative social goals. Both maintained that the development of democratic institutions and mass communications imbued with these values had resulted in the narrowing of horizons, in the progressive elimination of what Herzen called the "aesthetic element" in individual and social existence—the development of many-sided individuality through the love of originality and diversity, creative experimentation, and the pursuit of virtue as moral beauty. But even though Mill's project of a long-term moral and aesthetic reeducation was consistent with his empirical approach, Herzen's belief that new beginnings already existed close to hand was hard to present as anything other than a leap into utopia.

In the first essay in *Ends and Beginnings* he attempts to forestall this objection by frankly admitting the slender basis for his hope regarding Russia:

> In our country . . . people and institutions, culture and barbarism, the past that died centuries ago and the future that will be born in ages to come—all are in ferment and decomposition, collapsing and being built up; everywhere there are clouds of dust, posts and rafters. Indeed, if one adds to our virginal ways of communication our government officials' well-matured methods of profiteering, to the mud of our roads the filth of the life of our landowners, to our winter tempests the Winter Palace, together with the generals, the cabinet ministers, the sideboards and the Filarets, the 'gendarme vanguard of civilization' consisting of Germans, and the rearguard with axes in their belts, elemental in their might and their immaturity, one must be possessed by a violent *passion or a violent madness* to plunge of one's own free will into this whirlpool, which tries to redeem all its confusion by means of rainbows of prophecy and great visions, constantly cutting through the fog and constantly unable to disperse it.[30]

In an autobiographical excursion in the fifth essay, he recalls how after Herwegh's betrayal he had felt himself to be living through the tragedy portrayed in the novel that had affected him deeply in his youth—the destruction of individual lives by a conflict between two worlds, such as had occurred in the first centuries A.D.: "the one . . . corrupt and effete; the other savage as a wild beast of the forest, but full of untried strength and chaotic impulses"[31] He had not changed his views of the aptness of the comparison with Russia and the West, despite the continuing viciousness and depravity of Russian mores at home and abroad.

He points to the remarkable fact that the coarse and cruel milieu of the Russian gentry had produced the moral nobility of the Decembrists; broken into culture by rough-and-ready methods, Russia's educated classes were profoundly unattractive in their rawness, but the malady had not the deeply rooted, fatal depravity that affected their contemporaries in western Europe.

A decade after the events, Herzen was still incapable of seeing that to an uninvolved observer Herwegh's treachery was not a historical indicator of the first magnitude. In reliving the tragic events of that time, he reverts to the language he had used when faith in Russia and disgust with the West had been the sole means of restoring his self-esteem. His subsequent reflections on Russia's future contain little on the subject of innate Russian virtues, emphasizing instead the absence of the entrenched institutions and social codes that elsewhere reinforced a dualistic vision of the human personality and the world. The fifth essay strikes a discordant note in a work that, in its play of feeling, imagination, reason, and empirical observation, comes close to Herzen's model of what historical thinking should be. The occasional lapses in his ironic self-awareness may remind us of the point he made so often: that such thinking involves an unremitting struggle against the consolations of illusion.

Realism Confronts Pessimism

Turgenev had intended to respond to *Ends and Beginnings* in a series of essays in the *Bell*, but, preempted by an official warning not to contribute to a banned publication, he was constrained to conduct his side of the polemic in his private correspondence with Herzen.

He concentrates his attack in one main volley following the publication of Herzen's sixth *Letter:*

> You have made an extraordinarily subtle and sensitive diagnosis of contemporary mankind—but why does this have to be Western mankind and not "bipeds" in general? You are like a doctor who, having analyzed all the symptoms of a chronic illness, announces that the cause of all the trouble is that the patient is a Frenchman. An enemy of mysticism and absolutes, you mystically abase yourself before the Russian sheepskin coat and see in it a great paradise, the new and

original social forms of the future—*das Absolute,* in a word; that same Absolute that you make such fun of in philosophy. All your idols have been shattered, but one cannot live without an idol, so let's raise an altar to this new, unknown god . . . and once again one can pray, and believe, and wait. This god behaves quite differently from what you expect: you argue that this behavior is temporary, chance, forcibly imposed on it by an external power. Your god loves to the point of idolatry what you hate, and hates what you love,—your god accepts precisely what you reject in his name—you avert your eyes, stop up your ears—and with that ecstasy peculiar to all skeptics who have grown sick of skepticism—with that special, ultrafanatical ecstasy, you keep talking about "spring freshness, blessed storms," and so on. History, philology, statistics—all count for nothing with you: facts count for nothing—not even, for instance, that indubitable fact that we Russians belong linguistically and racially to the European family, "genus Europaeum," and consequently, by the invariant laws of physiology, must proceed along the same path. I have yet to hear of a *duck* which, belonging to the genus *duck,* breathed through gills like a fish. Meanwhile, your spiritual pain, your weariness, your thirst to place a fresh snowflake on your parched tongue, makes you hit out at everything that should be dear to Europeans and therefore to us: civilization, legality, finally revolution itself; and, having filled young heads with your half-fermented socialist-Slavophile brew, you send them out drunk and confused into the world, where they will stumble on their first step. . . . Do one of two things: either serve the revolution and European ideals as you did before, or, if you have indeed become convinced of their bankruptcy, have the courage and daring to look the devil in both eyes, say "guilty" in the face of all European mankind—and don't make explicit or implied exceptions for some newly coming Russian Messiah in whom you actually have as little faith as you have in a European one.[32]

Penetrating in its insight into the tension between Herzen's skepticism and his faith, Turgenev's criticism nevertheless caricatures the latter. Essays such as "Russian Germans" and "Robert Owen" show that Herzen needed no reminding that the silence of the Russian people could be interpreted in different ways, and that the survival of the commune was an indicator into which one should not attempt to read too optimistic or unambiguous a message. Turgenev's contention that the people should be given freedom to choose from the menu of Western culture seems much more libertarian in spirit than Herzen's desire that the shape taken by the reforms should nudge them toward developing their native institutions. But Herzen may be seen as rather more realistic than Turgenev in his fear that if those institutions are destroyed, the peasants' choice from the Western menu would be restricted to the meager dishes on offer to the landless proletariat.

Turgenev's reference to invariant laws prompted Herzen to round off his polemic with an attack on the deterministic assumptions common to all varieties of Russian liberalism. In the final letter of *Ends and Beginnings* he puts Turgenev's critique almost word for word into the mouth of a visitor to the *Bell*'s offices. He takes issue with this "learned friend" (the mode of address he had used with Chicherin) on the status of his "physiological law"—reminiscent, he suggests, of the "typically Muscovite invention of various institutions and regulations in which everybody believes, which everyone repeats, and which in fact have never existed." "The general plan of development allows for an endless number of unforeseen deviations, such as the elephant's trunk and the camel's hump. There are any number of variations on the single theme of the dog: wolves, foxes, harriers, borzois, water spaniels and pugs. . . . A common origin by no means conditions an identical biography. Cain and Abel, Romulus and Remus, were brothers, but what different careers they had! . . . Every form of Christianity has similarities in the organization of the family, the Church, and so on, but it cannot be said that the history of the English Protestants has been very similar to that of the Abyssinian Christians, or that the Most Catholic Austrian army resembles the extremely Orthodox monks of Mount Athos."[33]

Contrary to the view of his stern critic, the fact that ducks had lungs did not destroy his case. There was evidence that ducks had had a tendency toward gills at one stage in their evolution: the development of lungs had been a response to new conditions and possibilities. The *genus Europaeum* contained peoples who had grown old without fully developing a bourgeoisie; there were others whom the bourgeois system suited as water suits gills. So why should there not be a nation for whom the bourgeois system would be a transitory and unsatisfactory situation, like gills for a duck? Why should it be "a wicked heresy, a defection from my own principles, from the immutable laws of creation and rules and regulations, human and divine," to not regard the bourgeois state as the final and predestined form of Russian society?[34] The fact that Russia had evolved late and separately from the rest of Europe suggested that it would develop institutions of its own, under the influence of the past and of borrowings, its neighbors' examples, and its own perspective. The possibilities and directions were multiple, depending on accidents of time, place and development, conditions and habits of life, individual traits of character. In the United States, a new breed of the "European variety" had been formed before our eyes. If a fresh soil were enough to make a new nation out of old peoples, why should a nation that had developed under completely different conditions from those of western European states repeat Europe's past—"and that, too, when it knows perfectly well what that past leads to?" It was one thing for a narrow and sterile government to impose a straitjacket on the Russian people. "But here we have not the government, but mandarins of literature, senators of journalism, university professors preaching to us that such is the *immutable law of physiology:* we all belong to the *genus Europaeum,* and must therefore repeat all the old follies in a new way."[35] Herzen's readers would have had no difficulty in identifying his targets: Turgenev, Kavelin (who held the rank of senator), and Chicherin, a professor at Moscow University—a trinity of liberal civilizers.

* * *

"There are in nature and life no monopolies, no measures for preventing and suppressing new biological species, new historical destinies and political systems—they are limited only by practical possibility. The future is a variation improvised on a theme of the past."[36] This reprise of the dominant metaphor of "Robert Owen" links the end of Herzen's polemic on Russian liberalism with its beginnings. Nations and individuals best fulfill their potential when they seek not to act out a script but to improvise unrepeatable selves from the materials to hand. This proposition was tightly argued in *From the Other Shore* and "Robert Owen." In *Ends and Beginnings* the method is different. By constant repetition in the course of the loose meanderings of casual conversation, interspersed with references to personalities and events of the time, Herzen aims to accustom the reader to an idea that centuries of

cultural conditioning have made offensive to the intellect and the emotions. All the images and metaphors of the work serve one purpose: to
subvert assumptions that the structure of reality reflects the way we
organize our thought, that nature and history represent a linear ascent
from primitive to advanced, simple to complex—a process in which
order dominates over diversity and systems, laws and rules are ranked
above the singular, unrepeatable phenomena of contingent existence.
He notes his opponents' unease at the way he puts contingency at
the center of the historical stage. We can discern the stern figure of
Chicherin among "the bond-slaves . . . attached to the factories of
learning and the foundries of scholasticism," who wrathfully denounce
such nonsense, appealing to the universal laws that keep historical
development on track. To this contention Herzen replies that one has
only to glance into any hospital

> to see how living organisms *go off the track*, develop in their devia-
> tion . . . distorting and sometimes killing the whole organism. The
> unstable equilibrium of every living creature oscillates and to some
> extent accommodates deviations; but one more step in the same di-
> rection, and the badly tied knot that binds them together is untied
> and the elements released form new combinations.
>
> The universal laws, of course, remain the same, but may lead to
> opposing results: in obedience to the same law, fluff floats in the air
> and lead falls.
>
> In the absence of a fixed plan and fixed date, of a yard-measure
> and a clock, development in nature and history, far from being un-
> able to deviate, is continually *bound* to do so, conforming to every
> influence by virtue of its irresponsible passivity, resulting from the
> absence of precise aims. In the individual organism the deviation
> sometimes lets itself be known by pain, and the warning of pain often
> comes too late. Complex, composite organisms stray from their path
> and are borne downhill, rendered insensible to their path or its danger
> through the change of generations.[37]

By calling such deviations diseases, we perpetuate the illusion that
they are unnatural, exceptions to the normal order of things. We resist
the perception that disease and abnormality are less exceptional than
a "normal" condition, "which is the algebraic formula of an organism,
an abstraction, a generalization, an ideal assembled from different

particulars by the exclusion of what is accidental." It is because norms and generalizations have so much greater status in our thinking than the accidental and the particular that we are constantly "startled by the unexpected, caught unawares, rebel against the inevitable, struggle with the irresistible, pass by what is coming into being, and apply all sorts of alleopathies and homeopathies to that which has one foot in the grave."[38] Herzen recalls the monumental effort made in the first half of the nineteenth century to harmonize and integrate all branches of human knowledge. In history, philosophy, science, law, and even religion, the rational progress of humanity was mapped out with certainty. Then came 1848. If war blazed up again—"and that depends on a thousand accidents, on one well-timed shot"—the scholars would be at a loss to interpret this further deviation from history's beaten track. "Where is humanity going, since it despises such authorities? . . . Apparently not where we expected it to go. And, indeed, it is hard to tell where one will end up, traveling on a globe that a few months ago nearly crashed into a comet."[39]

If this view of history allowed for optimism, it was not in the form of the messianic hopes that Turgenev ascribed to Herzen. *Ends and Beginnings* repeats the message of his earlier essays on the nature of history: We can exploit our freedom only by first coming to terms with the narrowness of our area of maneuverability in the interstices opened up by contingency in natural laws. Navigation is a matter of knowing the currents of the sea and the constantly shifting equatorial winds, without seeking to correct them. "To recognize the inevitable is a source of strength."[40] The vision glimpsed through the fog is not a final destination but a propitious configuration of circumstances to be made to work in our favor while the chance is still there.

* * *

Herzen's polemic with Turgenev had begun in 1856 with this urgent call; it ends with the recognition of opportunity missed, in a somber foreword added to the first separate edition of *Ends and Beginnings*, which appeared after the suppression of the Polish uprising in the summer of 1863. He had intended, he writes, to add two or three letters in which the "beginnings" would be more precisely defined, but events had forestalled him—"they set to producing their own commentaries and their own deductions." Some of his assumptions about "old" Europe and "young" Russia had had to be revised. "Everything that had long ago faded in the old world, from the miter and the sword of chivalry to the Phrygian cap—has appeared once more in its poetic brilliance in rebellious Poland." On the other hand, Russian society's support for the government's reprisals revealed how deeply it had been corrupted by the Saint Petersburg regime. "We had thought that our literature was so noble, that our professors were such *apostles*—we were mistaken." In the tragedy now unfolding, everything was confused—neither people nor parties could be recognized. "One cannot help recalling the image of Dante's wrestlers, in which the combatants' limbs were not only intertwined but by some metamorphosis successively transformed into each other." This did not mean that the hidden seed had been uprooted; only that before it could sprout, much blood would have to flow. "Why will it flow? Why, indeed? But what can be done, if humans get no more sense? Events move rapidly, but the brain develops slowly. Under the influence of obscure motives, of fantastic images, peoples move half-awake through a succession of insoluble antinomies; they fight among themselves and, having elucidated nothing, they arrive, fifteen hundred years after the terrible destruction of the Roman world, at the times of Germanicus and Alaric, transferred into the manners of the nineteenth century."[41] These gloomy reflections echo the key ideas of the essay "Robert Owen," which foresaw no early awakening from the delirium of history. They can be seen to contradict Herzen's hopes of new beginnings only if these hopes are interpreted (as they were by Turgenev) as a claim for exemption for a Russian Messiah. But Herzen claimed no such exemption. On the contrary, he presents us with the reminder that in the future, as in the present, the odds are always loaded in favor of ignorance and prejudice, that the ground gained with great effort today may be lost again tomorrow: "History rises and falls between prophets and Knights of a Sorrowful Countenance."[42]

He had been eager for Turgenev's response to "Robert Owen"; an artist could have been expected to react positively to a historical discourse that broke radically with Enlightenment and Hegelian rationalism. But Turgenev maintained a significant silence. Chicherin had sneered at Herzen the artist, observing the "chance play" of events; Turgenev, too, felt that his friend's imaginative gifts would be put to better use elsewhere, helpfully suggesting that he devote himself to writing his memoirs. He was, as Herzen came to understand in the course of their debate, no less doctrinaire than Chicherin in his insistence that history was not an improvisation open to creative intervention—the aims and ideals of the masses are as yet unknowable, but he is nevertheless confident that they do not include those positive tendencies Herzen claims to discern. He does not contest Herzen's suggestion that the European ideals dear to them both are fading into the past; he finds fault, not with Herzen's diagnosis of the moral and aesthetic decline of modern culture, but with his view that this process may not be universal or irreversible. As an antidote to Herzen's hopes about Russia's future, he recommends the philosopher whose influence had come to pervade his novels: "You should read Schopenhauer more attentively, my friend."[43]

Herzen responds that his correspondent has thereby revealed the authority behind his tirade: "a nihilistic idealist, Buddhist and philosopher of death." Had Turgenev noticed that under that blighting influence he, too, was becoming a nihilist? He had been accused of insulting the younger generation by introducing that term in *Fathers and Sons* to denote their rejection of values sanctioned by tradition. Herzen remarks on the contrast between their "nihilism of *energy and anger*" and "the most utter nihilism of weariness and despair'" expressed in Turgenev's November letter.[44]

Returning to the topic some years later, he would characterize Turgenev's attitude as a "haughty folding of the arms,"[45] the stance recommended by the narrator of *Enough!*, a work Turgenev had begun while *Ends and Beginnings* was in process of publication, and whose tirade against history's monotonous repetitiveness can be read as an oblique response to Herzen's perception of new beginnings. (The first manuscript of the story is headed "Some Letters without Beginning or End.") But he refused to be drawn by Herzen on the contradictions between his private philosophy and his public defense of liberal values, rejecting Herzen's charge that he regarded his country with despair. "I see a tragic side to the fate of *the entire European family* (including, of course, Russia)," but this still did not make him a nihilist: "I'm nevertheless a European—and I love the banner, I believe in the banner under which I came to stand in my youth."[46]

This was Turgenev's parting shot in a debate commonly interpreted as a straightforward and robust defense of the principles of freedom embodied in Western democracies against a misty vision of a Messiah in a sheepskin coat—although it might reasonably be asked what precisely political freedom and progress meant to a man who confided in a letter to a friend that the most perfect symbol of human existence was the image of flies beating themselves against a pane of glass.[47] When the final installment of *Ends and Beginnings* mocked the stultifying determinism of his concept of the "invariant laws of physiology," Turgenev did not protest. "Old Goethe was right: der Mensch (der *europäische* Mensch) ist nicht geboren frei zu sein," he would remind Herzen when they resumed their correspondence after a gap, in 1867. He was prepared to concede that the European Peter was at death's door; but it did not follow that the Russian Ivan was in any better shape.[48] This was the tragedy referred to in his deeply ambivalent confession of faith in the European banner: The pettiness and futility of most human aspirations and achievements (not least those of the Western bourgeoisie) were part of an immutable cosmic order that stood in profound opposition to the highest human values. Not even the greatest achievements of reason and science had the power to release mankind from its suffocating sack and move history in new and unpredictable directions. As Herzen had suggested at the outset of their debate, Turgenev's commitment to the culture and institutions of western Europe was principally motivated, not by hope, but by fear of something worse—he believed that, however corrupt and unjust, the order at which western European states had arrived represented the best form yet devised of protection against those blind, deterministic forces that shape human lives. But he would have agreed with Schopenhauer on the miserable inadequacy of any such protection: that even when favored by fate, human happiness "is yet a hollow, deceptive, frail and wretched thing, out of which neither constitutions, legal systems, steam engines, nor telegraphs can ever make anything that is essentially better."[49]

He had been irritated by Herzen's reference to Schopenhauer, protesting that he had done no more than mention him, yet found himself accused of bowing to his authority.[50] He rightly felt vulnerable on this point, and it may seem odd that Herzen did not probe more deeply and more publicly into the intellectual premises of an opponent who had recommended that he cure his tendency to idealize reality by immersing himself in German metaphysics; but to discuss Turgenev's personal philosophy in print would have been to identify him. It is possible, however, to reconstruct the debate over first principles that was forestalled by the Russian police and Turgenev's evasions. In one sense it had already taken place. As expressed in his published works, and (more frankly) in his private correspondence, Turgenev's vision of the sameness and absurdity of the historical process is identical in all significant respects with that of the opponent in *From the Other Shore,* who concludes that history is a tale told by an idiot, signifying nothing.

Turgenev would cite the same passage from Macbeth in the course of a similar tirade against what he described as history's "unnecessary game."[51] The same bleak view lies behind his advice to Herzen to have the courage to look the demon of doubt "in both eyes," seeking no exemptions from the common fate of humanity. But in the dialogues of *From the Other Shore* the charge of cowardice is thrown back at Herzen's interlocutor, whose petulant anger with a world that will not dance to his tune reveals his stubborn attachment to a fantasy that imbues physical reality with a direction and aims coinciding with our heart's desire. Conducted by an intelligence that refuses to be deceived by false hopes, the search for an absolute meaning leads logically to the most utter nihilism; for, as Herzen notes elsewhere in that work, "if one looks for the final aim, then the purpose of everything living is—death."[52]

This was the conclusion Turgenev had reached with the help of the philosopher for whom the march of history was a funeral procession. Schopenhauer viewed physical existence as "only a constantly prevented dying, an ever-deferred death. . . . Every breath we draw wards off the death that constantly impinges on us. . . . Ultimately death must triumph, for by birth it has already become our lot, and it plays with its prey only for a while before swallowing it up."[53]

"Death is like a fisherman who has taken a fish in his net and leaves it in the water for a while. The fish continues to swim, but the net is on it and the fisherman will take it when he wants," said Turgenev in his novel *On the Eve.*[54] The "sentence of condemnation" that, as Schopenhauer observes, nature imposes on every will-to-live[55] was for Turgenev the most immediate of realities. From the mid-1850s he poured out his despair in letters to intimate friends, comparing life to a fortress, constantly besieged by death; the inevitability of the outcome deprives the battle of much interest. Life cannot be other than a tragedy:

after all, "we are all condemned to death—you could hardly have any-thing more tragic than that!"[56] In a memoir on the controversy aroused by *Fathers and Sons* he seems belatedly to admit to the charge he had so indignantly denied in his correspondence with Herzen, recording that a certain witty lady (his friend, Countess Lambert) had remarked to him that the book's title should have been *Neither Fathers nor Sons*, "and you're a nihilist yourself!"[57] Life, according to Schopenhauer, "swings like a pendulum between pain and boredom";[58] Turgenev's most intimate letters, over three decades, do much the same. *Taedium vitae*, the intrinsic worthlessness of an existence imminently to be an-nulled by death, is their dominant theme. In 1877 he writes to Gustave Flaubert: "Après quarante ans, il n'y a qu'un seul mot qui compose le fond de la vie: *renoncer* [After forty years, there's only a single word for the core of life: renunciation]."[59]

Here, then, is the "nihilism of weariness and despair" that Herzen detected behind Turgenev's profession of faith in Western values. To his most trusted correspondents he gives frank expression to his lack of hope in the improvement of mankind. Garibaldi's campaign for Italian independence inspires this comment to Countess Lambert: "So there's still enthusiasm on this earth? People can still sacrifice them-selves, rejoice, behave like madmen, be filled with hope? I'd like at least to take a look to see how it's done." But, he reflects, it would be too late: what passion he still had now flowed into his writing.[60] It was passion of a very masochistic sort. His essay "Hamlet and Don Quixote" (on which he was working when he made this comment) presents mankind with a choice between deluded hope and clear-sighted awareness of the pathological deformity of human nature.

Herzen sees Turgenev's dilemma as self-imposed. The despair he presented as the lot of all self-awareness was merely the result of the disdainful rejection of a world that contradicts our "fantastic imagin-ings." Like the disappointed idealist in *From the Other Shore*, Turgenev had chosen to assume a stock role that was once tragic but was fast becoming ridiculous.

* * *

Their debate took place at a turning point in their century, when prov-idential and rationalist theories of progress were being undermined radically by both science and the unceasing political turmoil of Europe.

In a peculiar attempt to console Countess Lambert on the death of her only son, Turgenev informs her that her grief is proof to him that earthly existence is all dust and ashes; those who lack faith (among whom he counts himself) "possess nothing."[61] His attitude to the young Russian radicals, whose trials he followed closely in the 1870s (and whom he embodied in a series of literary figures), combined a liberal's revulsion against doctrinaire narrowness with envy of those who had succeeded in "destroying" their egos through self-forgetful service to an ideal. He confesses that his feelings about the radical hero of *Fathers and Sons* "were confused (God knows whether I loved or hated him!)."[62] His fiction abounds in characters who through wholehearted commitment to some passion or ideal had achieved a harmony denied to him. Whether displayed in the performance of austere duty or the pursuit of selfish passion, unreflecting strength of purpose is presented as deeply desirable from the standpoint of those introspective personalities who occupy the foreground of his fiction.

There is a curious passage in his very ambivalent essay "Hamlet and Don Quixote" where, having castigated the "insane" enthusiasm of the Don Quixote type, he chooses their side against the reflective Hamlets: "Who will take it on himself to say that always and in every case he will distinguish and has distinguished a barber's copper bowl from a magic golden helmet? Hence it seems to us that the most important thing is the sincerity and force of the conviction itself—the result is in the hands of fate. The fates alone can tell us whether we have been fighting phantoms or real enemies, and with what armor we covered our heads. Our business is to take up arms and fight."[63] Here Turgenev seems to be asserting (as Schopenhauer's disciple Nietzsche and his existentialist followers would do) that with the demise of a religiously sanctioned morality, personal "authenticity"—the intensity of commitment to some inner imperative or ideal, whatever its nature—must be the supreme moral value and the criterion of good and evil. Herzen shared Turgenev's fascination with the quixotic type, devoting several pages of his memoirs to the more fanatical of the Italian revolutionaries, some of whom he knew intimately and who, he wrote, "overwhelm one with the grandeur of their somber poetry." But he was better able than Turgenev to separate his admiration for their commitment from a moral evaluation of their acts. Such personalities as

Orsini (the would-be assassin of Napoleon III) "astonish us by the strength of their passion, the strength of their will. . . . [They are] ready for any privation, any sacrifice. . . . Self-denial and devotion in them go hand in hand with vengefulness and intolerance. . . . They set no value on their own lives but equally none on the life of their neighbor." He admits to regarding them with the "nervous pleasure, mingled with trepidation with which we admire the graceful movements . . . of a panther," but observes that their cruel energies were no substitute for an understanding of the processes they sought to turn to their advantage. Italy's freedom was currently being determined by the diplomacy of self-interested powers, not by these bloodthirsty martyrs. "They are children, but wicked children."[64] Frozen at a primitive stage of moral awareness, they had reneged on the obligation of development that each owes to himself. Herzen was to apply similar stern criteria to personalities on the Russian Left.

Wickedness is not a category that figures in Turgenev's judgments of those who are driven by an all-consuming passion. Like Schopenhauer, he is sometimes ambiguous on the question of whether moral criteria are applicable at all to a world determined by irrational forces—a "killing field," he once despairingly observed, in which all living creatures are intent on devouring their fellows: "Destroy or be destroyed—there is no middle way! Let us then be the destroyers!"[65] Bakunin gleefully used similar reasoning to justify his glorification of the elemental force of popular revolt.[66] Turgenev hated violence and Bakunin's revolutionary cant, but unlike Herzen he could offer no coherent moral opposition to either. In his fearful fascination with unreflective spontaneity, his self-castigating Hamlet seems to anticipate liberals of the next century who were overly eager to acknowledge their moral inferiority before the "authenticity" of the Left.

A Lesson from the Life of the Mole

We have seen already that Herzen believed that the philosophical pessimism whose inner contradictions he exposed in *From the Other Shore* and in his polemics with Turgenev would be no more than a short-lived transitional stage in the movement away from teleological explanations of the phenomenal world. In this he was mistaken.

Schopenhauer's atheism, irrationalism, and mockery of "optimistic" theories of progress are a potent mix that has continued to exercise a significant influence on ethics, aesthetics, and cultural theory, not least by way of the man who claimed him as his "educator"—Nietzsche. Although Schopenhauer's ascetic denial of the will may appear to be the antithesis of the Nietzschean superman's "yea" to life, it is often argued that the latter may be seen as the affirmation of a despair that refuses to recognize itself as such. The superman asserts his will to be the meaning of the world, in defiance of a historical process dominated by the desire of the resentful for revenge and destined (according to Nietzsche's fatalistic theory of eternal recurrence) to repeat its absurdities, the future being a replica of the past. In a fundamentally irrational world his feat can have no aim other than itself; his own authenticity and the value of his actions derive from his readiness to undertake the most difficult moral and existential tasks, irrespective of their accepted moral worth. In this strange ethic, moral strenuousness is an end in itself. In Nietzsche's purposeless world there is "no better purpose . . . than to be destroyed by that which is great and impossible." This "penitential theology of a God-less universe" (as Joseph Stern describes it)[67] can be seen as an activist variation on the Schopenhauerian theme of self-renunciation of a will irrevocably at odds with a meaningless reality.

It has been debated whether, in its Nazi form, the doctrine that all is permitted to the self-sacrificing hero was a terrible abuse or a logical application of Nietzsche's ethic. But undoubtedly, for many self-designated Nietzscheans, the justification and the compelling attraction of Nietzsche's doctrine has lain in its claim to dare and bear a truth from which all but the strongest flinch away.

Herzen dismisses this kind of argument. The pessimists and the "optimists" whom they despised were brothers under the skin, equally driven by a secret fear of confronting the fact that we are not central to the cosmic scheme of things, and equally cavalier in their disregard for evidence that did not suit their purposes. Optimists conjured up something out of nothing; the "destructive creativeness" of pessimistic nihilism transformed something into nothing, ignoring the chances of improvisation offered by the lack of a historical script. In his appraisal of those chances, Herzen could not be accused of optimism in

Schopenhauer's sense of the word. As the realist tells the pessimist in *From the Other Shore*, "I prize every fleeting pleasure, every minute of joy, for there are fewer and fewer of them. . . . I should not say that my present point of view is a particularly consoling one, but I have grown calmer: I have stopped being angry with life because it does not give what it cannot give—that is all I have managed to achieve."[68] The individual human being seeks to affirm his existence "between two voids—the void before his birth and the void after his death"[69]—on this Herzen and Turgenev could agree. Nor would Herzen dispute that this brief existence is pervaded by suffering. Turgenev, meeting him at the end of a decade of personal and political tragedies, notes that he is only beginning to emerge from the gnawing sadness of those years.[70] He had a deep attachment to the poetry of Leopardi, whom he describes as an "apologist of death . . . who represents the world as a league of the wicked waging savage war against a few virtuous madmen." He recalls defending him against Mazzini, who was incapable of comprehending "these poisonous reflections, these shattering doubts."[71]

Schopenhauer, too, deeply admired Leopardi, considering him unsurpassed by any other poet in the nineteenth century in his treatment of life's "tragic farce."[72] But while Schopenhauer sees Leopardi's despair as expressing the eternal truth about mankind's predicament, Herzen draws attention to the historical circumstances that attended his "gloomy, satanic laughter": the reaction after 1848, which dashed hopes for Italian liberation. In Herzen's view it was no coincidence that Lermontov—the only other poet of the age who was his equal in touching "the somber chords of the human soul"—died before the first stirrings of political liberation in his country.[73] The despair of these two poets was for Herzen one of those signs of a painful deviation in the organism that, in the historical as in the natural world, is a challenge to battle.

The hope of the fighter is our compensation for surrendering the secret aspirations that fuel the pessimist's despair, along with the arrogant belief that we have somehow been cheated of the destiny we deserve. Only when we cease to measure our finite life by inappropriate criteria can we exploit our contingency and make it work for us. For Herzen, this was a matter of logical consistency: having observed correctly that human beings are subject to the same natural necessities and accidents as other living creatures, we go on to conclude that the same dispensation offers them similar possibilities of adaptation and development—however inadequate these may appear when judged by the criteria of idealism. Human reason is, nevertheless, a component of the historical process, which can therefore never be totally irrational and uncontrollable. In his novel *Smoke* Turgenev declares that nature has her own logic, which we only come to recognize after it has crushed us. Herzen, too, notes that nature's ways do not conform to rational categories, but advises Turgenev that recognition of the inevitable is a source of strength. Of course, *sub specie aeternitatis* our tiny area of creative maneuverability vanishes into nothingness—a point that Herzen makes with a nicely calculated irony in the seventh letter of *Ends and Beginnings*, where he presents modern disillusionment in the historical process in the form of a dialogue between two friends, one of whom refers to "a German book, in which the laborious existence of the mole is described—it is very funny. The little beast, with big paws and little chinks instead of eyes, digs in the dark, underground, in the damp, tunnels day and night, without weariness, without diversion, with passionate persistence. It barely stops to have a bite—some little grains and worms, and sets to work again; but in return for all this the hole is ready for the sons, and the mole dies in peace; and the sons begin boring holes in all directions for their own sons. What is the price paid for a lifetime of toil underground? What relation is there between effort and attainment? Ha, ha, ha!" The book in question is Schopenhauer's *Die Welt als Wille und Vorstellung*, in which the life of the mole is selected as an outstanding example of the "evident want of proportion between the effort and the reward" of all phenomenal existence. Herzen ends the seventh *Letter* with this reminder to Turgenev: "Within two days we shall have the New Year, and I wish you a happy one; we must gather up fresh strength for it, for our mole-like labor; my paws are itching to begin."[74]

Contrary to Turgenev's belief, Herzen did not hold reality to be other than prosaic. Where the two differed was on the creative possibilities to be found in humble prose.

* * *

Herzen perceived correctly that Turgenev's opposition to the idea of a separate path of development for Russia was motivated by cosmic pessimism rather than liberal pragmatism. In the 1870s Turgenev became increasingly sympathetic to the personalities of the young radicals, but not to their cause. Petr Lavrov, one of the leaders of the radical émi-grés at that time, records that his views on Russian affairs were char-acterized above all by "skepticism that anything of real benefit to Russia could come from anyone: government, liberals, or revolution-aries."[75] In Western commentaries on his polemic with Herzen, Tur-genev is commonly presented as a thoroughgoing liberal—even, in the words of one critic, "the moral authority for liberal Westernizers in Russia," opposing hard facts to his opponent's dreams.[76] As a tailpiece to Herzen's deconstruction of Turgenev's arguments, it is interesting to consider one such account of their debate by Leonard Schapiro, a liberal historian of Russia and biographer of Turgenev. Herzen, he as-serts, presented Russia as a repository of spiritual gifts that would eventually triumph over the forces of darkness that imprisoned them. In contrast, Turgenev's viewpoint was empirically self-evident: to ad-mire the West meant not to accept uncritically all the features of bourgeois life, but "to recognize that the Western countries have ad-vanced beyond Russia in the creation of certain institutions and a cer-tain social order, and that Russia must, in order to advance, travel the same path and cease—like Herzen and the Slavophiles—to glory in her backwardness."

Schapiro strives for evenhandedness in his treatment of the two protagonists, describing Herzen as "a noble and tragic man, striving to the end to serve his people in the way that seemed best to him." But Turgenev's position relied less on facts than on the following five as-sumptions: the progress of countries is a linear movement through time from a backward to an advanced state; this process travels a single path, exemplified by the development of what are currently the most "advanced" countries (western European constitutional democracies); those that do not conform to this model are by definition "backward"; they may "catch up" with more advanced ones only by accelerated development along the prescribed path; by so doing, Russia will de-velop her "true place" in civilization.

Schapiro is one of those historians for whom Herzen's dispute with Russian liberalism casts a long shadow, giving him a share of respon-sibility for the growth of that mood of utopian impatience that favored Lenin's catastrophic intransigence. This argument stands on histori-cist assumptions that support what may be called a liberal paradigm of history. Whereas Marxist historicism is predictive, that of liberal

historians tends to be retrospective—liberals deem the failure of socialist theory to confirm the historical realism of its liberal opponents
in the past. From the perspective of hindsight, emphases and nuances
may disappear and ideas come to mean something quite different from
what their progenitors intended. Just as the Marxists yoked Proudhon
to "utopian socialism," so Schapiro yokes Herzen to the Slavophiles.[77]
An essay on Herzen published in 2010 (over twenty years after Schapiro's study) takes a similarly negative view of Herzen's opposition
to the Russian liberals, and portrays him as "a socialist thinker who
occupied a permanent position in the Soviet pantheon," viewing the
Russian peasants through a haze of "Rousseauesque abstraction" and
commending their commune as a model for a "collectivist utopia."
According to its author, Herzen "persistently predicted that Western
civilization was about to die, and devoutly wished that it would." He
declined unequivocally to condemn revolutionary violence and to
advertise the benefits of political stability, thereby helping to weaken
Russian liberalism in its battle to promote the very freedoms he advocated.[78] (A curious view of the leading representatives of liberalism at that time; in this corner of Herzen studies nothing changes,
it seems.)

* * *

The collapse of communism at the end of the twentieth century has
been cited as proof that Russia was not exempt from universal laws determining the progress of all Western societies to forms of liberal democracy. In a book much discussed on its publication in 1999, Martin
Malia interpreted the Soviet period as a mere hiccup in a process that
was inevitably leading Russia to convergence with her more advanced
Western neighbors in an ineluctable movement from absolutism to
some form of liberalism.[79] Reactions to this view revealed the existence
of a lively skepticism about the existence of one right way. The historian David Joravsky argues that liberal proclamations of "the end of
ideology" are themselves the expression of a committed ideological
stance, "clinging to a totalistic vision while condemning the totalitarian kind." Are we not obsessed, he asks, with an historical norm,
or with "the myth of such a norm set by 'the West'?"[80]

Political and cultural theory have some way to go before they are
freed from what Stephen Jay Gould has called the straitjacket of linear

advance, with its superannuated view of history and culture. In his discussion of popular iconographies of evolution, Gould suggests that while most people may know that life is not a ladder of predictable progress, they know it as "a phrase to be uttered, but not as a concept brought into the deep interior of understanding." Our culture still has a deep-seated allegiance to the comforting idea of a single order underlying the diversity of life—"a universe of intrinsic meaning defined in our terms," its processes mirroring those of human thought and thereby reassuring us of our centrality in the scheme of being. The myths and prejudices that nurtured this belief survive in the metaphors commonly used to represent development in nature, history, and culture as movement through time from simple to complex, less to more, primitive to advanced. Gould draws our attention to the continued potency of these metaphors in intellectual discourse, where they masquerade as neutral descriptions of facts, leading us to equate the tentative with the unambiguously factual. It is to this phenomenon that Herzen is referring in *From the Other Shore* when he implores the reader: "Let us not be children. Let us not shrink either from reality or logic, or reject the consequences. They are beyond our power."

The saddest aspect of linear ranking, Gould observes, is "the acceptance of inferiority by bottom-dwellers and their persistent attempts to ape inappropriate methods that may work higher up the ladder."[81] It is no longer universally maintained by liberals that their preferred mode of government represents an ideal for all humanity, but Herzen's pioneering contribution to this development continues to be obscured by others' confusion of his thought with an outworn Romantic socialism. It should be remembered that he drew comfort from comparing his fate with that of another heretic whose originality was equally subject to misinterpretation: that "classical liberal," John Stuart Mill.

CHAPTER TWENTY

The Polish Uprising

The rarest of characters, a revolutionary without fanaticism.

ISAIAH BERLIN ON HERZEN

IN 1862 Herzen remarked on an odd feature of the war waged against him by his compatriots: while "old Russia" accused him of a thirst for violence, a new extremist group, "Young Russia," was reproaching him for having lost his taste for revolution.[1] Each side would find ample confirmation for its views in his response to the Polish uprising of 1863. Led by Katkov's press, the Russian Right accused him of almost singlehandedly inspiring and directing the uprising, while the Left concluded, in Bakunin's words, that he was "an incurable skeptic [who] lacked the stuff of which revolutionaries are made."[2]

Historians have tended to favor the latter verdict.[3] It has been argued that Herzen's deep-seated ideological commitment to the principle of peaceful reform prevented him from exploiting the options opened up by the revolutionary situation in Poland: by hesitating at this crucial time, he forfeited the respect of the Russian Left and lost his chance to influence the developing revolutionary movement in his country. But as Herzen would observe at the time, what the Left required of him was not leadership but adherence to their view that violent revolution was the only path to progress in Russia. His refusal to commit himself to this belief was not faintheartedness. His day-to day responses to events in his letters and proclamations during the Polish revolt—the subject of this chapter—show that his position on revolutionary violence was inspired by a considered and consistent inconsistency, based on his view of the openness of historical time.

By a historical irony, Poland, not Russia, was to be the arena where Herzen accomplished his descent into "life's marketplace," influencing the daily course of a revolutionary struggle. This role was a result of a relationship of trust between Polish radical emigrants and the editors of the *Bell*, which from its foundation had given unequivocal support to the cause of Polish independence. They would do all in their power to continue this support during the ten months of the uprising's duration. In January 1862 Herzen and Ogarev were joined by Bakunin, newly escaped from his Siberian exile and eager to resume agitation for the independence of all Slav peoples. Polish emigrants' considerable acquaintance with Herzen was soon extended through Bakunin's tireless propaganda and voluminous correspondence, and the Poles began to perceive the London offices of the Free Russian Press as an organizational center for the planned uprising. In the autumn of 1862 emissaries began to arrive there from the aristocratic *szlachta* (a class with some legally recognized privileges of nobility but containing both rich and impoverished aristocrats) and the "National Revolutionary Committee." The two groups had very different goals: the revolutionaries of the *szlachta*, many of whose estates included tracts of Lithuania, Belarus, and the Ukraine, were determined that these provinces should be included in a "free Poland," ruled by the landed gentry, whereas the National Revolutionary Committee sought liberation from both the Russian yoke and the Polish landowners. On the territorial question the members of this group were split: some shared the *szlachta*'s expansionist aims; others were prepared in varying degrees to take the wishes of the indigenous population into account.

The divisions within the Polish camp, the preponderance of material forces against it, and the delicate internal situation in Russia in the wake of the Emancipation, with a government wavering between reform and reaction and a society prone to hysteria before the prospect of peasant revolt—all these factors convinced Herzen that the Polish uprising could scarcely be more badly timed. If it failed, the resulting reaction in Russia would crush the emerging revolutionary movement. In a letter of October 1862 to a member of the Warsaw committee charged with planning the uprising, he stressed that the Poles were mistaken in their belief that the *Bell* represented a powerful revolutionary force in Russia, ready to spring to their aid. An organization existed, but only in an embryonic stage. Nor could the Poles hope for help from elsewhere in Europe. Given these circumstances, "it would be a shameful act for us to tell your officers . . . 'Go ahead, you will have our support!' "[4]

In a letter to Garibaldi published in the *Bell* after the Poles' defeat, he explains his predicament. Far from having incited them by assuring them that the Russian peasantry were on the verge of revolt (the version presented by the right-wing press), he had interpreted the uprising as a misfortune. "We knew well that nothing was prepared, that there were only embryos. . . . We would have given our blood to have deferred the uprising for one or two years." But what were they to do? The necessity and timing of the uprising were up to the Poles to decide: "We had to accept their decision and stand on the side of justice and freedom."[5] History did not produce ideal timetables, perfect conjunctures of circumstances; one had to seize on those that presented themselves and try to turn them to one's advantage. He insists that the policy on which he and Ogarev had embarked had been clear and consistent: publicly to express support for the rebels, while privately urging them to include in their program acceptance of the peasants' right to land and of the autonomy of the border provinces. In this way it would be clear that the Poles' battle was with the tsar and not with the Russian people.

This last point he had believed could be of great practical importance in leading to a positive outcome. There were increasing rumors from a number of sources in Russia that peasant discontent over the terms of the Emancipation Act would explode into an uprising in the spring or summer of 1863, when the two-year transitional period after the promulgation of the Act came to an end and it would become clear to the peasants that they would not be given all the land they saw as theirs.

The Polish National Committee included a league formed from among Russian officers garrisoned in Lithuania and Poland. In the summer of 1862 this group contacted the *Bell*, requesting advice on how to act in the event of insurrection in Poland. Herzen replied that, whatever the consequences, the officers were morally obliged to refuse to become the executioners of a people who were justly seeking their freedom; but they should work to ensure that their sacrifice was not futile by trying to persuade the Polish revolutionaries to adopt a common program, based on the self-determination of peoples. The other priority was to extend their league by propaganda within the army in Russia as well as Poland. He tells them not to discount the "colossal" success the officers' league had already achieved since its foundation in 1861. It had begun to alarm the authorities; a number of officers had been arrested in the spring of 1862. Three had been shot and a soldier connected with the group had died as a result of flogging. "In a few months you have thrown a bridge across the abyss that separates the nobleman in epaulettes from the peasant with a rifle in his hand, have inspired brotherly trust in the Poles and through four martyrs have shown to the world the invincible power of your convictions." It was now imperative to increase their organization's strength in preparation for a peasant uprising, which might not be far off:

> The Russian people, having preserved a grim silence for centuries over its ill fate, has raised its head twice in our century. In 1812, fearful for the integrity of the Russian land, it turned into a people's militia. Now it fears not for the Russian land but for its own land of meadows and pastures. . . . The government in its confusion is incapable of giving it its land honorably and directly. After the end of the transitional stage, that is, in the spring of next year, it will be impossible to equivocate any longer. The peasant will not give up his land; he will surely resist. If Poland rises then, if you and your colleagues and their soldiers throw yourselves into Lithuania and Little Russia in the name of the peasants' right to land, where will sufficient strength be found to resist you? The Volga, the Dniepr, the Don and the Urals will take up your call![6]

These were scarcely defeatist words. Herzen was doing what he had counseled to all idealists: to accept the force of circumstances when these seemed to close off their chosen options (in this case, peaceful reform), the better to exploit the potential of other paths opened up by the new situation. As he observed subsequently, there were grounds at the time for believing in the possibility of a combined uprising of peasants and army in Russia. The government shared this belief; hence a succession of repressive measures, officially inspired journalism, and punishments by special decree. It had raised expectations that it could not satisfy; all of society was in a ferment, "and no one foresaw at that time that this would turn into ferocious patriotism."[7]

Herzen was nevertheless much less sanguine in his hope of an uprising than was Bakunin, who, "not too much prone to weighing every circumstance, looked only toward the distant goal. . . . He *wished* to believe, and believed, that the Zhmud and the Volga, the Don and the Ukraine, would rise as one man when they heard of Warsaw."[8] It was difficult to assess the situation in Warsaw from the distance of the *Bell*'s offices, where a complex picture of events had to be constructed with the help of informants eager to present their cause in the most positive light. But Herzen doggedly pursued the course he had recommended so frequently to others, adapting his tactics on a day-to-day basis in response to the most reliable information at hand. A letter to Ogarev of February 1863 illustrates his openness to events. He writes that the insurrection is holding up well, but that it is impossible to make long-term plans or predictions with two crucial facts as yet unknown: whether there will be a peasant uprising in Russia, and whether there will be significant support for the Poles from elements in the Russian army; it might be time for a new proclamation to the army.

The precise content of propaganda to the army was a cause of great anxiety to Herzen at that time; he believed the need to encourage rebellion among the officers had to be set against the danger of misleading them as to the existing extent of dissidence among their ranks. His letters in the first months of the insurrection, their mood varying in response to the development of events, show none of the pessimism of which the Left would accuse him. In March he affirms that against the odds it is holding firm, having gained sufficient momentum to be a credible threat to the Russian throne: "The palace of ice on the Neva is beginning to melt."[9] His optimism grew with news that a number of Russian officers had joined the insurgents, and that a peasant uprising was being planned in Lithuania in the spring. On this latter development (to which Marx and Engels also attached much significance) Herzen placed great hopes: a Lithuanian revolt could spread to the Russian countryside. Even as government forces gained the upper hand in Poland in the summer, he saw fresh grounds for hope as public protest grew in England and France, with threats of an ultimatum and intervention in Poland by the European powers.

From all these distant events, threads stretched back to the *Bell*'s London offices. There propaganda was written and printed, addressed to students in Warsaw and Krakow, to the educated classes of the Russian cities, to soldiers, peasants, and sectarians. Arrangements were made for its transportation to Russia and its distribution, in close col-

laboration with representatives of Land and Liberty, the first revolutionary organization of significance, which had its own small printing
press in Berne and with which in February the *Bell*'s editors agreed to
coordinate all operations concerned with the revolt. The London office
served as a center for the collection and distribution of funds for its
activities, the setting up of channels into Russia for illegal literature
via Sweden, Norway, and Turkey, and the funding of couriers and of
volunteers and arms for the fighting in Poland. Information gleaned
from correspondence, the Russian press, and the daily influx of visitors from Russia and Poland was passed on to the Poles through their
committees abroad, and to the detachments of volunteers preparing to
join the fighting in Lithuania in the spring.

The driving forces behind the propaganda to the Russian people
were Ogarev and Bakunin; it was they who composed the appeals to
peasants, soldiers, and merchants. That Herzen gave his two collaborators virtually no help with these activities has been seen as proof of
his lack of enthusiasm for a cause that he saw as doomed—but it was
merely the result of a division of labor. His correspondence in the spring
of 1863 reflects the importance he attached to propaganda among the
sectarians, whom he described as standing in the foreground of the
Russian drama as a channel to the peasantry at large. He believed that
a paper, *Obscheye veche* [The Common Assembly], edited by Ogarev
and addressed to Russian merchants, was the most successful propaganda initiative since the Emancipation. But his own efforts were directed to a different audience. In the *Bell* of 1 February 1863 he greeted
the outbreak of the Polish revolt with an article entitled *"Resurrexit!,"*
and in each successive issue he sought to counter government disin-
formation with detailed reports of events in Poland, along with commentaries designed to force Russian educated society into recognition
of its complicity in a national crime.

This prodigious journalistic output is not the only evidence of Herzen's commitment to the Polish cause. His letters in March and early
April 1863 to V. Kasatkin, one of the operators of Land and Liberty's
Berne press, and to a member of the committee of Russian officers attached to the revolt, serve to illustrate his commitment to the prosaic
work of day-to-day organizational support for it. They detail the mi-
nutiae of the propaganda effort (250 copies of the *Bell* and seventy books

had been dispatched to Kasatkin in response to a request from Krakow),
touch on the problem of setting up communications and finding new
routes for the transport of material into Russia, pass on requests for
information from émigré communities in various European cities, arrange for the transfer of money between two such committees for the
funding of volunteers, and note that the *Bell* is subsidizing a certain
individual whose talents will be useful in Poland ("with his abilities
it is shameful to sit here doing nothing"). Discreet details are given of
other individuals who have successfully crossed the Russian border;
of a multinational "detachment of desperadoes" currently being formed
in London in preparation for the Lithuanian campaign in the spring,
and of groups of volunteers gathering in Austria. "After all, they can't
surround the entire border with palisades—the transport of weapons,
and above all, of propaganda, will continue." He comments favorably
on a new committee of Land and Liberty ("a model of intelligence and
logic") that had been set up in Kazan: "They are printing endless proclamations, which the youth are eagerly reading. . . . We have sent them
notes on how they should proceed." A member of the group is planning to return to Russia to recruit support for the Polish forces among
the youth. Herzen urges that he concentrate his efforts on the sons of
gentry and officials: "What will these soulless intriguers say when they
see their own offspring in the opposing camp?"[10]

There is no hint of flagging enthusiasm in these letters; on the contrary, Herzen seeks to stir up the young revolutionaries to more energetic activity, assuring Kasatkin that in London work is "in full
swing . . . the cause is advancing with giant's strides." He urges him
to do all he can to support the Polish cause, "so that in its turn it can
support you." The flow of propaganda must be kept up: "Do not lose
heart, develop our ideas." Much may be expected from the revolt
planned in Lithuania. If it succeeds, it will be "the dawn of our
freedom."[11]

Support for that revolt soon fizzled out. Herzen's increasing pessimism about its outcome was due, not, as the young radicals believed, to
an onset of faintheartedness, but to the same openness to the pressure
of contingent circumstances that had inspired his decision to give it his
full support. As the months passed, he noted the limitations of the
Bell's power to affect events: the absence of "businesslike people" to

"Farewell Europe": Poles sentenced to exile in Siberia after the failure of the Polish national uprising of 1863. Painting by A. Sochaczewski, one of the exiles, who includes himself as the figure to the right of the obelisk.

liaise between London, Russia and Poland, and the decline of its influence in Russia in the face of a nationalist backlash against the Poles. He cautioned the radicals that there were no signs of an incipient peasant uprising in Russia; to incite one prematurely would be to destroy promising beginnings before they could develop.

Herzen's emphasis on historical timing led to increasing friction with Bakunin and Ogarev. A central source of contention between them was their relationship with Land and Liberty, created after discussions between Nikolai Serno-Solovevich and the editors of the *Bell*. The first Russian revolutionary organization with wide significance, it consisted mainly of intellectuals and students opposed both to the autocracy and liberal ideas of reform. A. A. Sleptsov, Serno's self-appointed successor with regard to relations between his organization and the *Bell*, made a highly unfavorable impression on Herzen with an arrogant proposal that he should become an "agent" of Land and Liberty, an offer that Herzen refused, despite Sleptsov's assurance that the membership of his society numbered "some hundreds in Petersburg and three thousand in the provinces."

> "Do you believe it?" I asked Ogarev afterward. He did not answer.
> "Do you believe it?" I asked Bakunin.
> "Of course; but," he added, "well, if there are not as many now, there soon will be!" and he burst out laughing.
> "That is another matter."
> "The essence of it all is to give support to weak beginnings; if they were strong they would not need us," observed Ogarev, who was always dissatisfied with my skepticism on these occasions.[12]

This dissatisfaction is echoed by a biographer of Bakunin who sees Herzen's attitude as reflecting a deep-seated opposition to revolutionary action in any circumstances, a fainthearted pessimism comparing unfavorably with Bakunin's radical ardor.[13] But what separated the two was not the strength of their commitment to social change. Rather, it was the clash between two irreconcilable visions of historical development, each with its own moral and tactical consequences.

Bakunin's vision of the historical process had not changed since his famous "Appeal to the Slavs" of 1849, which had called for total destruction of the material and moral conditions of contemporary life, predicting that the star of revolution would rise in Russia "out of a sea of blood and flames" to become the guide of all mankind. Friedrich Engels (like Bakunin, a former Hegelian) sums up well the crude schema of oppositions on which Bakunin's faith in the imminent transformation of humanity was based: "There is not a word about the actually existing obstacles to such a universal liberation, or about the very diverse degrees of civilization and the consequently equally diverse political needs of all the individual peoples. The word 'freedom' replaces all that. There is not a word about actual reality or, insofar as that is treated at all, it is described as absolutely reprehensible, arbitrarily established by 'congresses of despots' and 'diplomats.' To this evil reality is counterposed the alleged will of the people with its categorical imperative, with the absolute demand simply for 'freedom.'"[14] From Bakunin's standpoint, the defeat of an uprising in Russia would be a mere local hitch in a process predestined to lead to "absolute liberty"—a risk well worth taking; whereas Herzen's fears arose from the long-term and possibly irreparable consequences of a mistiming in the present, given the complex and hazardous embryology of the historical process. He also had fears about the role of Land and Liberty in the uprising: the first threads of a vast web of resistance were being formed in Russia, but "every violent shock threatened to ruin the work for a whole generation."[15] His desire that the Poles should have no illusions about the strength of Russian support for them was based on the same view, as was his anxiety about the timing and justification of proclamations inciting the Russian forces to revolt before there was any clear indication of the number of officers willing to join the insurgents. Contrary to Bakunin's belief, he argued, Russia was nearer the second month of pregnancy than the ninth.

His premonitions were confirmed by the visit to London of the Russian peasant Petr Martyanov.

Russian Reaction

In the early 1860s the *Bell* had established a direct channel to the sect known as the Old Believers, whom Herzen considered the most resolute element of the common people. Through centuries of persecution they had maintained their faith and their hostility to the secular power.

About 20 million of them were scattered in communities in rural Russia and bordering territories and in many towns, where their literacy and entrepreneurial skills had led them to dominate the merchant class. Barely tolerated by the regime, they had sought to win guarantees of religious freedom. The possibility of reaching the people through the sects had been impressed on Herzen and Ogarev by a young émigré, Vasilii Kelsiev, who had made a close study of them, and in 1862 the Free Russian Press began to print a periodical whose propaganda was based on the slogan "Without the opportunity to live freely, there is no opportunity to believe freely." As Ogarev announced in the inaugural issue, it was the first paper to be addressed "to the so-called lower classes . . . Old Believers, businessmen and craftsmen, peasants and small bourgeoisie, domestic serfs, soldiers, in fact anyone not belonging to the privileged classes."[16]

The paper never achieved more than a very limited circulation, and nothing came of the London émigrés' hopes of reaching the people through the sects. On a secret journey into Russia, Kelsiev found that the merchants he met in Moscow were ignorant about politics and interested exclusively in religious freedom. An Old Believer bishop who came to London to discuss the question with the *Bell*'s editors was unresponsive to their attempts to introduce wider issues and scandalized by Bakunin's raucous rendering of a sacred hymn, a *faux pas* that may have prompted the circular letter subsequently sent out by the Metropolitan of the Old Believers, urging the faithful to obey the tsar and shun his enemies, in particular "the wily Godless ones who nest in London."[17]

Herzen and Ogarev were able to observe the outlook of the sectarians at first hand in the person of Martyanov, a peasant of extraordinary initiative. His former owner having defrauded him over the terms of the Emancipation, his thoughts had turned to the historical fate of the Russian people. He traveled to London, where Herzen printed in the *Bell* his petition to Alexander to crown his great reforms by a return to the pre-Petrine role of a "people's tsar." In a subsequent essay on Martyanov and his fate, Herzen recalls that this remarkable individual had retained all the mentality of a true Russian peasant. He describes the dogmatic fervor of Martyanov's religious beliefs and his faith in the historical myth of a tsar who was the father of his people.[18]

He discovered to his dismay that Martyanov's patriotism was coupled with a strident nationalism. He had hitherto dismissed the nationalism of the Slavophiles as an offshoot of European Romanticism, a literary and philosophical phenomenon without deep roots in the national psyche. Martyanov's was unpleasant evidence to the contrary. Greater shocks were to follow.

In his memoirs Herzen recalls that in the spring of 1863 Martyanov had told him gloomily that by meddling in Polish affairs, "You have sunk the *Bell*." Toward the end of 1863 the paper's circulation dropped from over 2,000 to 500 copies and never rose again above 1,000: "the Daniel from the peasants had been right."[19]

Herzen had attempted to dissuade the Poles from an uprising that he predicted would be catastrophic for both Polish independence and Russian reform; but once the insurrection had broken out, he believed that the *Bell* had no alternative but to declare its support for the rebels. He was instantly reviled as a traitor by many of his former admirers as the Russian gentry rallied en masse behind the government. Liberals who had believed that Poland should be granted a measure of autonomy had been transformed overnight into xenophobic nationalists by the rebels' demand for the restoration of Poland's historic borders, including the western provinces taken from her in the notorious partitions of the eighteenth century and now overwhelmingly populated by White Russians and Ukrainians. With the exception of the *Contemporary*, the nongovernmental press joined in the clamor for Polish blood. The pack was led by the Pan-Slav journal *The Day*, edited by Ivan Aksakov, and Katkov's two papers. According to the Pan-Slavists, Poland was a renegade from the Slav world, which she had betrayed through her adherence to the Roman Catholic Church and Western culture. They argued that the conflict between the two countries was not political but cultural and spiritual: an independent Poland would threaten Russia's mission as the protector of Slav religious and social values. Throughout the first half of 1863 Aksakov and Katkov headed a *galère* of journalists and historians who argued in tones of mounting hysteria that the Poles' rebellion was part of a crusade inspired by the West and aimed at reducing Russia to the confines of medieval Muscovy. To a society still traumatized by the Crimean defeat, this reversal of the roles of victim and oppressor was more plausible than it seems in retrospect: the concert of Europe's diplomatic backing for the Polish cause did much to fuel Russian paranoia.

Although the Pan-Slavists believed that the uprising should be mercilessly suppressed, Russia's domination over another Slav nation was an embarrassment to them, and they hoped that in the long run, persuasion would bring the Poles back to true Slavic principles. Their doctrines were attractive to many intellectuals (Dostoevsky among them), but they had less impact on broader sections of Russian society than the coarser jingoistic nationalism preached by the former liberal Katkov. Described by the London *Times* as the leader of Russian public opinion in the 1860s, Katkov was at the peak of his influence at the time of the Polish revolt. In 1863 his papers the *Moscow Gazette* and the *Russian Messenger* had 12,000 and 5,700 subscribers, respectively. (Their main rival, Chernyshevsky's *Contemporary*, had 7,000.)

Katkov's message was simple: the conflict between Russia and Poland was a struggle for the very existence of the Russian state. He sought to persuade the minister of the interior that the uprising had been engineered by a clique of Jesuitical Polish conspirators, agents of a wider European plot to destroy Russia, and that all the "evil elements" in Russian society, embodied in the revolutionary movement, had been spawned by the Polish revolt. He attacked those in the government who recommended a soft approach, and welcomed the regime of terror installed by General Mikhail Muravyev (known by his troops as "the hangman"), whom the tsar sent to quell the uprising in June 1863. The broad sympathy with Katkov's views among the gentry was reflected in the congratulatory telegrams showered on him and the numerous banquets organized in his honor.

The lowest strata of society added their voices to the call for savage retribution. The press printed a quantity of "loyal addresses" from groups of peasants and Old Believers expressing patriotic solidarity with Muravyev's forces, and huge crowds attended memorial services for soldiers killed during the suppression of the revolt. Such manifestations may not always have been spontaneous, but it is clear that jingoistic sentiments were widespread among the common people.

Herzen viewed this national vengefulness with horror and disgust. As a symptom of the "patriotic syphilis" that had infected Russian society, he cites the toast raised to Muravyev at a dinner of writers and journalists in Moscow's English Club. "Everything nasty in the Russian nature, everything that has been perverted by slavery and the landowner culture, by bureaucratic insolence and lawlessness, by the lash and the system of spies—all this has floated to the surface, decked out in a *liberal* cap and bells, has risen up in a hideous combination composed of Arakcheev and Pugachev, the serf-owner, the minor official, the district police officer, and the rabble of the drinking-houses."[20] The Slavophiles had cause to rejoice: "The national, pre-Petrine *fond* has remained unchanged—at least as regards its primitive intolerance, its hatred of everything foreign and its lack of fastidiousness in the choice of punishments." Herzen remarks that the attitude of the common people is unknown. The loyal addresses, composed by bureaucrats, are no indicator. But he was uneasy on this question: "Surely this mixture of mud and blood will not be the cement that binds our estates and castes *into a single people?* . . . Surely, when we make our exit from the Petrine period, we shall not take with us all the inhumanity of Peter together with all the clannish nationalism of the period that preceded him?"[21]

Might nationalism, rather than socialism, prove to be the bridge between educated society and the people? Herzen took this new threat seriously enough to sound warnings in the *Bell*. In January 1864 he asserts that there is nothing incongruous about the alliance between the "German emperor" and the Slavophiles: the latter are quite prepared to go hand in hand with a conservative power they can idealize as a reincarnation of the Muscovite state. If Russian popular culture follows their urging and turns its back on Western science and enlightenment, it will exchange the prospect of freedom for the product of their ravings. He returns to this point in his reflections on Martyanov, who had gone back to Russia against Herzen's advice after publishing his appeal to Alexander II and was immediately arrested on a charge of insolently criticizing the established order of government. His sentence (confirmed by the tsar in whose fatherly benevolence he had had such faith) was five years' hard labor followed by permanent exile in Siberia. Herzen writes that the naïveté of Martyanov's faith in the "people's tsar" had been his undoing: more calculating individuals were currently engaged in exploiting the same myth to advance their careers. The Polish revolt had seen the rise of new demagogues, "degenerate offshoots of Slavophilism" who had presented the actions of the Russian army as the crusade of a democratic "people's tsardom" to liberate the Polish peasants from their landlords.[22] Herzen cites Ivan Aksakov's paper *The Day* and the more lowbrow *Northern Bee*, which, in common with the rest of the reactionary press, had depicted the political conflict between the two countries as the battle of a Westernized oligarchy (the *szlachta*) with a state that drew its strength from the people and the land; Aksakov's editorials had been careful to distinguish between the Polish state and the Polish people, whom he represented as the salt of the earth.

Herzen accuses the new nationalists of manipulating the Russian peasantry's dreams in order to whip up a murderous hatred of the Poles, presenting hopes and distant ideals as present realities—as though the Russia of Arakcheev, Nicolas I, and Muravyev had already been transformed into "some sort of democratic empire," dedicated to the liberation of less fortunate peoples.[23] A crude deception; yet, as Herzen admits implicitly, its authors had proved more successful than he in finding a common language with Martyanov and his kind.

In one of his most austere reflections on 1848, Herzen observed, "The people have no need of what we have to say"—theirs was a different anger, a different struggle. The theory of Russian socialism was based on the belief that his country was an exception in this respect. He had insisted that he did not idealize the peasants, but claimed that their reverence for the tsar and their lack of respect for individual rights were symptoms of their stage of development and less intrinsic to their mentality than their socialist instinct; however long it might take to establish a common ground with the peasants, the radical intelligentsia were their natural allies. That the Russian people's anger might attract them to causes other than revolutionary socialism seems not to have figured seriously in his calculations, despite the fact that in his responses to 1848 he had cited the support of the French masses for Louis-Napoleon as evidence that nationalism, with its appeal to primitive minds, had an advantage over the more reasoned arguments of socialism. He returns to this theme in *Ends and Beginnings*. In the years of reaction after 1848 he had observed how the peoples of Europe had begun to embrace the "wretched ideal of patriotism," egged on by governments bent on distracting them from aspirations more threatening to the status quo. "*Political* parties have dissolved into *national* parties. . . . The universal aspirations of Catholicism and of revolution have given way to pagan patriotism, and the honor of the flag is the one honor that remains inviolate among the nations." But the Slavophiles' bellicosity put an end to his hopes that Russia would be immune to this development. In an essay on contemporary thought and literature published in the French edition of the *Bell* in 1864, he cites their paper *The Day* as proof that love of one's country was not the same as love of truth or love of justice. "Patriotism remains a virtue based on partiality: it leads sometimes to self-sacrifice, but always to a jealous concupiscence, a niggardly and egoistic conservatism, in which love of one's kin is not far removed from hatred of one's neighbor."[24]

The efforts of human societies to break out of the rule of unreason take blind and unpredictable turns: along with a little progress, new forms of bondage make their appearance. Reason is "the final endeavor, the summit to which development seldom attains." To the author of "Robert Owen" the nationalist frenzy that accompanied Russia's first great step toward freedom should not have been so unexpected as to induce despair. Yet Herzen admits to having been close to despair at that "unbearably hard time."[25] Only twice before in his life had he confessed to a similar mood: in 1842, when he had first sensed the futility of seeking a rational purpose in history, and ten years later, after the family tragedy that he had seen as the ultimate test of his acceptance that there was no way out, no universal framework in which the fortuitous and the irrational in human life made sense.

But humans tend to find ways of compensating for too much reality. The belief that he represented a rising historical force had been Herzen's way of restoring his shattered sense of personal worth, and he had shown no inclination at the time to scrutinize the ideological pedigree of the notion of his country's youthfulness. The year 1863, not 1852, was when he parted with his last illusions. The event was marked by the laconic admission in the preface added to *Ends and Beginnings* in August of that year: "My outlook changed." The inhuman butchery in Poland and the "still more inhuman applause" forced him to revise all his assumptions about Russia's youthful vigor and Europe's decline.[26]

Lessons of the Polish Uprising

In a long essay written three years later, after Karakozov's attempt on the life of the tsar had plunged Russia more deeply into reaction, Herzen took stock of the change in his outlook wrought by the disillusionment of 1863. The Emancipation had been followed by administrative and legal reforms that, truncated though they were, seemed to have the inevitability of a syllogism. He had hoped that the granting of land and village self-government would trigger a bloodless revolution in which the peasant would transform his obligatory bond with the commune into a voluntary one. The Emancipation, together with the mood of society as a whole, seemed to be pointing that way. Then, wholly unexpectedly, the *Bell* had lost its audience, as Russian society in its patriotic fervor forgot the inhumanity of the tsarist system. Landowners, newly liberated peasants, Old Believers, Jews, Cossacks, Volga Germans—all rushed, in word if not in deed, to uphold the altar and the throne. The government chose not to reward their devotion by extending their rights; instead, it began a savage persecution of a tiny minority of young radicals who had responded to terror with terror. Herzen reaffirmed his faith in a future socialist transformation of Russia (the commune still survived, and socialist ideas had spread among the young), but declared that he had lost his conviction that such a change could occur without a bloody upheaval. "It is irritating that history uses such dirty byways; but after all, only *consciousness* marches in a straight line."[27]

This was an idea of the kind that Herzen (following Proudhon's recommendation) had dinned into other people's heads "over and over again, in order that the mind may no longer be surprised by it, that it may ... obtain real rights of citizenship in the brain."[28] But it was clearly still capable of surprising Herzen himself in 1863.

* * *

"Life realizes only that aspect of an idea that falls on favorable soil, and the soil in this case doesn't remain a mere passive medium but adds its sap, contributes its own elements." So Herzen had alerted the dreamer in 1849. But while making a point of his own prosaic concern with the Russian soil, he had fixed his attention on its bridges rather more than its ruts. He had been engaged in concluding *Ends and*

Beginnings with yet another commentary on this theme when events forestalled him with "their own commentaries and their own conclusions."[29] As news flowed in of the brutality of the reprisals in Poland, he issued a warning in the *Bell:* by justifying the reprisals as a measure of national self-defense, Russia's new patriots were seeking to inculcate in the masses a tribal solidarity with a criminal state. If they succeeded, they would achieve the "ultimate denial" of the individual's moral dignity—the dissolution of the personality in the instinctive ebb and flow of the mass. "If indeed all Russians come to believe . . . that it now behooves them to embrace Muravyev and extend their hand to the Third Department, if they become so *patriotic* that they will not shudder at executions or at seeing them glorified in the press—then, when the Russian empire has crushed the uprising, it will turn into a vast Slavonic backwater, another China, martial, stagnant and tedious, condemned to frozen immobility by the hopeless slavery of its faceless people." This image reveals how total Herzen's disillusionment had been. Four years before, comparing Europe's "ends" with Russia's "beginnings," he had admired Mill's lonely stand against the herd morality of a "new China." Now he foresees the same fate for himself—if the noise of the patriotic orgy continues to drown more sober words, "if no ray of reason can penetrate that dark night . . . , *we will remain alone with our protest,* but will not give it up."[30] In October 1863 he writes of the pain of being repelled as before by developments in Europe, but unable any longer to derive comfort from events at home; such had been the fate of those individuals who had been estranged equally from the decadence of Rome and the barbarism of the new Germanic world. Once he had used that image to define the predicament of those who could identify neither with the European old order nor with the "new barbarians, marching to destroy" in 1848. Now it acquires added pathos, as he faces the possibility that the new Russian barbarism may be as alien to him as the old.

"We try to impose our wishes, our thoughts, on our surroundings, and these attempts, always unsuccessful, serve to educate us," the recalcitrant dreamer's interlocutor had told him in *From the Other Shore.* Herzen's despair was short-lived, but it cured him of the temptation to seek a special historical dispensation for his country. He would continue to insist on the advantages of the commune as the nucleus of a new social order, but would no longer hint that it might confer some kind of immunity from the tensions and diseases of contemporary Western societies. There were no "special paths" in history. Progress at all times and in all places was an ad hoc affair, a matter of more or less imperfect adjustments, drawing on contingent resources with the aim of achieving a provisional equilibrium between competing needs and demands. He had repeated these ideas for fifteen years, but it was only in 1863 that they attained full citizens' rights in his brain.

* * *

Herzen's final transition from visionary to prosaic worker was marked by a revision of his views on the historical function of the bourgeoisie. It took place, with dramatic symmetry, in Italy, where he had spent the most intoxicating early months of his life in Europe, and which had impressed him with the advantages of "backwardness"—in particular, of the absence of a centralized state and a bourgeoisie. Caught up in the euphoria of Italy's Risorgimento, he had been enchanted by the sense of municipal independence that had survived centuries of foreign domination. No people, he had concluded admiringly, was less capable of discipline, of submitting to a police system or monarchical order. His mood was very different in October 1863 when, following a visit to his wife's grave in Nice, he spent three weeks in Genoa and Naples to recover his forces after the horrors of that year. He was struck by the inertia of the country, newly united under the house of Savoy: the passive expectation of the city populations that the new order would bring new forms of patronage and protection. The only initiative was shown by the mob: robbery and banditry were rife in the decayed cities and the countryside. The texture of ordinary life was a blend of primitive violence and chaotic disorder, disturbing to the civilized mind and, he reflects, possible only in states lacking a substantial educated middle class. "Like a rubber cushion, a middle class softens all collisions, effaces all differences, averts revolutions, averts reactions, ruins the rich, swallows up the poor, introduces balance and order into everything, puts limits on theft and fraud, if only by scaling them according to privilege, . . . sweeps dirt from the street, and, together with the dirt, the petty tradesman and the pauper."[31] Is the rule of a mob under a corrupt aristocracy preferable to this kind of order? With Russian mob psychology fresh in his mind, Herzen admits that this is a difficult question. History showed that over the centuries the Neapolitan variety had changed as little as cats and monkeys; it would seem to have less chance of rising to a human existence than the conscious proletariat of bourgeois democracies. One could not refrain from speculating that perhaps, by some perverse law of natural selection, peoples are destined to reach a more developed existence only by way of the bourgeois state.

He muses that perhaps the bourgeoisie is the general limit of historical development, the limit to which all that has run too far ahead returns, and that is finally reached by all who lag behind. Perhaps it is the resting place of nations who have hurled themselves in all directions, calm after national growth, heroic feats, and youthful ideals; in the comfortable entresols of the bourgeoisie, people can live an untrammeled life. "Some inner voice, some human grief makes us protest against such an ultimate solution. . . . But we have experienced many such sorrows; alchemists were saddened by the prose of technology, and we ourselves mourn the passing of many ideals. Very recently I experienced the pain of standing at a graveside with the knowledge that *the next world does not exist!*"[32]

He was to draw similar sobering lessons four years later from a visit to Venice to meet Garibaldi, who had come in order to support the radical opposition in new elections. (Venice had passed from Austria to the Italian Crown in the previous year.) He notes that the Venetians, who gave the liberator of Italy a rapturous reception, had adapted with ease to the less than liberal regime of Victor Emmanuel and his minister Cavour. This pliability suggested that beyond the goal of independence, Italians had lacked any unifying moral or social vision—except the desire to present *una bella e grande figura* in the array of European states. Victor Emmanuel having performed this function to their satisfaction, they had few complaints. But the majority, weary and ill-prepared for heroism, were not to blame for deserting the ideals of Garibaldi and Mazzini; nor were the masses, subjected for so long to indoctrination by clerics. Not even the government could be blamed for its narrowness, ignorance, and lack of imagination. It was born in the palace of the Dukes of Savoy, "among rusty Gothic swords, old-fashioned powdered wigs, and the starched etiquette of little courts with vast pretensions." Herzen's attitude had not softened to the representative system toward which he saw Italy moving—a "fantastic world of lies and empty phrases," of unreal struggle. The "potato-dough of parliamentarism and the rhetoric of the Chambers" could offer only a pretense of nourishment; [33] but now he concedes that this pabulum may serve a positive purpose. "The representative system in its continental development really works best of all when there is nothing clear in mind or nothing possible in deed. It is a great 'meanwhile,' which grinds away the angles and extremes of both sides and gains time. Part of Europe has passed through this mill, the other part will pass through it, and we sinners along with it. What about Egypt? It, too, has ridden on camels into the representative mill, driven on by the hunting whip." [34] "And we sinners along with it": Herzen had come a long way since his proud boast to Michelet that his country would have nothing to do with the "semi-freedom" of the West. This was not his first suggestion that Russia's development might take a constitutional path. Following the pragmatic approach he had set out in the *Bell*, he had declared in 1860 that he was not opposed in principle to this means of exercising restraint over a government that did not seem to know its own mind. "There are circumstances when it is impossible to avoid these transitional forms." [35] His preferred solution (a homegrown Land Assembly) depended on a broad national consensus on goals and ideals that the events of 1863 had proved not to exist. Like the government, the Russian people had turned out to have contradictory aspirations, some of which seemed as greatly in need of social restraint as the instincts of the Neapolitan crowd.

In May 1865 Herzen takes stock after the two-year "orgy of bloodshed and servility." In Russia, as in western Europe, the bright dawn of socialist ideals is long past. It has been followed by "everyday labor, with its obstacles and errors, its rain and its buckets, its stony soil and its swamps, its deviations, concessions, compromises, and shortcuts." In the harsh noon light the view of the historical plain is less inspiring, but also less deceptive: one can now see more clearly in which directions it is possible to look for answers and where they cannot be found. The majority are dissatisfied with the economic conditions under which they live, but are not disposed to follow the utopians who would like to put them into communal barracks, abolishing private property and the family on the way. "[People] want renewal and rebirth, but at the same time they want to retain as much as possible of the life they are used to, harmonizing it with the new conditions. On what rational foundations can this be done, how can such complex and contradictory demands be reconciled? This is the whole problem, this is what the entire social question comes down to, once you remove all the thunder and lightning."[36] Herzen insists that his form of sobriety is not to be seen as pessimism. For the pessimist, truth has a single dimension; he has no interest in the steps between the general and the particular, the way in which ideals have to adapt to the contingencies of time and place. If socialism is to be true to its conception of freedom, it must perform a great moral feat, demanding the most intense inner discipline: it must accept the prosaic nature of history.

As a political activist, Herzen was undoubtedly a failure. But he had foreseen such an outcome, and his criteria of success were not those of his critics. He had praised Proudhon for not papering over his differences with the Left for the sake of popularity and political influence, choosing instead to defend his vision of historical truth at the cost of political isolation. Such behavior—who knows?—might eventually attract imitators; but even if not, no matter: it remained "a virtuous act."

This was the example he chose to follow in his last years.

CHAPTER TWENTY-ONE

True Nihilism

I should like to save the young from historical ingratitude, and even from historical error.

HERZEN

Precisely in the dissected frog lies the salvation and the revitalization of the Russian people.

DMITRII PISAREV

"Now we know how much Arakcheev there is in our blood, how much Nicolas I there is in our brains," Herzen wrote during the patriotic delirium of 1863. "Much that had lain buried in silence under the coffin lid of past oppression has come to the surface and revealed the utter rottenness of the organism. . . . Now our Minotaur has surfaced not in the palaces and torture chambers, but in society, in literature, in the university. We thought that our literature was so noble, that our professors were apostles; we were mistaken in them, and how painful that is!"[1]

It was to be more painful still to have to admit that the Minotaur's realm had encroached on the subterranean zone inhabited by the radical youth. In July 1864 Herzen boasts in the *Bell* that this "new Russia" is weighed down "neither by ancestral property nor by ancestral memory,"[2] but his memoirs reveal how little he believed that to be true after more than five years of contending with the condescending or openly hostile attitudes of their leaders. These clashes have been seen as a skirmish in the battle between gentry "fathers" and plebeian "sons," as depicted in Turgenev's novel, an indication that Herzen's socialism was less deep than his aristocratic loathing of uncouthness and youthful insolence, and that his true affinities lay with the liberal culture of his own generation.[3] But his principal opponents on the Left were neither all young nor all plebeian. Chernyshevsky, the leading radical figure of the 1860s, was thirty-five at the time of his arrest in 1863. (He and Dobrolyubov were both sons of provincial priests.) Aleksandr Serno-Solovevich and Nikolai Utin, Herzen's most poisonous enemies among the émigré Russian Left, issued from gentry families. His quarrel was not with their manners (repulsive though these sometimes were) but with their ideology—the dogmatic materialism, proclaimed with a religious fervor, that would lead Lenin (another son of the gentry) to acknowledge Chernyshevsky as one of the formative influences on his thought.[4]

There were a number of factors compelling Herzen to deal gently with the Left in the pages of the *Bell*. He was sensitive to the image he would present as a "father" in late middle age berating the radical youth. A more important consideration was the need to present the multiple facets of a complex truth: to relate the aims and actions of the Left to the rapidly changing situation in Russia. When the Slavophile Yurii Samarin, with whom he had had warm relations in the 1840s, complained to him of the intellectual shallowness and political impatience of the young generation, he recommends that Samarin develop a sense of context: "there are periods in the history of peoples when the pulse quickens." Surely no one with any knowledge of the human heart could expect that in the current circumstances young people would remain at their studies, "calmly and submissively, with the same artificially induced indifference to life and despairing devotion to learning with which we sat on our university benches?"[5]

Herzen was aware also that in commenting on events in the *Bell*, he was influencing their further development. Therefore, the least reticent of his remarks on the men of the 1860s were confined to the memoirs he continued to write but published only selectively throughout that decade. It is here that he describes his first encounter with the new type as a wave of émigrés, driven abroad by the repression after the defeat of the Polish uprising in 1863, arrived at his door in London:

> These men, while still very young, had finished with ideas, with culture; theoretical questions did not interest them . . . partly because they were concerned with their application. They had been physically defeated but had given proofs of their courage. They had furled their flag, and their task was to preserve its honor. Hence their dry tone, *cassant, raide,* abrupt and rather overwrought. Hence their martial,

impatient aversion for prolonged deliberations, for criticism, their somewhat elaborate contempt for all intellectual luxuries, among which they put art in the foreground. What had they to do with music? With poetry? "The fatherland is in danger, *aux armes, citoyens!*" In some cases they were theoretically correct, but they did not take into account the complex, intricate process of balancing the ideal with the real and, it goes without saying, they assumed that their views were the views and theories of the whole of Russia. To blame for this our young navigators of the coming storm would be unjust. It is the common characteristic of youth.[6]

The manuscript variations of this passage show how carefully Herzen chose his words in his desire to leave an objective record of the new radical type.[7] In his day-to-day journalism a more immediate consideration took precedence: the importance of not providing the government and its supporters with ammunition against the young generation. He refers repeatedly in the *Bell* to the viciousness of the sentence of six years' hard labor imposed in 1861 on the poet M. L. Mikhailov for his part in composing and disseminating a revolutionary proclamation entitled "To the Young Generation." In May 1864 in the aftermath of the Polish uprising Herzen completed a long survey of recent political and literary developments in Russia. Published in a French edition of the *Bell*, it was issued as a separate pamphlet in Russian. After two years of tsarist repression targeted principally at the radical youth, he intended to leave no doubt as to where his allegiance lay in the battle between fathers and sons. Through a relentless piling on of detail, he builds up two contrasting pictures: one of self-sacrificing heroism, the other of cowardice and collaboration with crime.

He recapitulates the successive stages in the conflict between unequal forces that began after the first news of killings in Warsaw. While liberal society engaged in patriotic agitation against the Poles, students and young army officers had requiem masses sung in the major Russian cities for the Polish victims. In Kazan students gathered in the university church to pray for the soul of the peasant Anton Petrov, shot during the protests in Kazan province over the terms of the Emancipation. The organizers of these events were arrested and political trials, suspended since Nicolas's death, were resumed. Some officers who had supported the Poles' cause were executed, others were given long sentences. Other radicals were tried in secret, among them the greatly respected Nikolai Serno-Solovevich, who as a junior official had dared to approach the tsar with a proposal for an emancipation on equitable terms, and when his project was ignored had published it abroad under his own name. Student demonstrations against new regulations depriving the universities of their last vestige of freedom were met with beatings and arrests. A spate of mysterious fires in Moscow and Saint Petersburg served as the pretext for a mass roundup of dissident students and writers. The *Contemporary* was suspended and Chernyshevsky sentenced to seven years' hard labor followed by permanent exile.

In all these measures the government was supported by prominent Russian liberals. From his chair of jurisprudence Chicherin preached the virtue of absolute obedience; the influential journalist Mikhail Katkov, admirer of the British political system, expressed vociferous approval of the government's methods of suppressing dissent, and most of liberal opinion, along with the Slavophiles, fell into line behind him. Addressing Samarin's criticism of the young, Herzen emphasized the heroism of the imprisoned radical leaders, none of whom had renounced his beliefs in the hope of clemency. Yet the Slavophile press denounced them as atheists and moral degenerates, providing the authorities with a useful justification for strong measures. "You express your anger in diatribes; the government expresses it through penal servitude and executions. Surely this unequal battle is not to your taste?"[8]

Herzen would defend his generation against the "new men," as they called themselves, but he did not share the view of most of his contemporaries that their successors had gone too far in their emancipation from beliefs and ideals unsupported by experience. On the contrary, he believed that they had not gone far enough along the path he and a few others had opened up for them. In a letter of June 1866 he reproaches a Russian correspondent who had used the word "nihilist" (put into currency by Turgenev as the self-description of the young radical scientist Bazarov in *Fathers and Sons*) as a term of abuse against the young generation in connection with Karakozov's attempt on the life of the tsar: "How is it that you have not noticed that I belong body and soul not only to the ranks of the nihilists, but also to those who brought them into the world?"[9]

He signaled his distance from most of the "fathers" by appropriating the detested term; yet the meaning he gave to it was very different from that which was dominant among the sons. In spelling out that difference he would be accused of joining forces with their persecutors; but the issues were too important to avoid.

His polemics with the new Left have one dominant theme: the attempt to define and defend true nihilism.

What is a Nihilist?

"We do not build, we destroy; we do not proclaim a new revelation, we eliminate the old lie." When Herzen wrote his introduction to *From the Other Shore*, a new breed of Russian radicals was beginning to emerge who would see this form of destruction as their life's work. "A nihilist," Bazarov's young friend explains, "is a man who bows down before no authorities, who accepts no principles whatsoever on faith, however great the respect in which that principle may be held."[10]

The term was taken up by the leaders of the new generation. Looking back on the 1860s, the revolutionary Serge (Stepniak) Kravchinsky defined Russian nihilism as "a passionate and powerful reaction . . . against the moral despotism that weighs upon the private and inner life of the individual."[11] As Herzen was to remind his readers during that decade, he, Belinsky, and Bakunin had been the first Russian nihilists in this sense of the word. Along with Belinsky's literary criticism, his attacks on moral absolutes had been the intellectual nourishment of the young men who came to socialism through contact with the Petrashevsky circle in the late 1840s. One of these was Chernyshevsky, who, even in exile, would remain the acknowledged leader of the "men of the sixties." Reading Herzen's Left Hegelian essays prepared him for what he would describe as the most important event in his life—his encounter with Feuerbach's *Essence of Christianity*. From Feuerbach's demystifying "new science," focused on the physical reality of human beings, the young generation proceeded to the full-blown "scientific" materialism that was the dominant intellectual fashion in the Germany of the 1850s. Its principal popularizers, the radical-minded natural scientists Ludwig Büchner, Jacob Moleschott, and Herzen's friend Karl Vogt, believed that the startling conceptual and experimental advances then being made in chemistry, physics, and physiology (particularly in the analysis of cellular processes) were the beginnings of an ontological revolution that would destroy the foundations of religious faith and political conservatism. But while Herzen had welcomed these advances as proof that nature and history were not determined by immutable laws with predictable outcomes, the new materialists were persuaded that the methods of experimental inquiry, with their grounding in facts and their rigorous logical systematization, could yield equally fruitful results in the human sciences.

With the "thaw" of 1855, the principal texts of the new faith began to appear in Russia, where they were seized on by the young generation, fueling expectations that the momentous social changes promised by the new regime would result in the appearance of a new kind of human: intellectually, socially, and morally free. At the end of the decade, as resolve gave way to vacillation on the part of government and society, the young radicals turned their iconoclasm against the liberals of the older generation, condemning their speculative idealism as a selfish indulgence that had shielded them from harsh realities. The targets (for the moment, at least) were irrational and harmful beliefs; the weapon of destruction—scientific materialism. In the *Contemporary* Dobrolyubov used his essays on Russian literature as the vehicle for a savage dissection of the personalities and ideals of the "men of the forties," and Chernyshevsky expounded his radical views in the guise of historical, philosophical, and economic analysis.

When Turgenev's novel appeared in 1862, Herzen was among those who saw the crude and narrow Bazarov as a caricature of the Russian radicals whom he had described in his letter to Michelet of 1851 as the most independent men in Europe: "We accept your doubts, but your faith does not move us. . . . We do not comprehend your attachment to the heritage of your ancestors; we are too oppressed, too wretched to be content with demi-freedom."[12] Herzen would accuse Turgenev of misrepresenting both this type and the methods of the natural sciences, which he himself had long recommended as the optimal means of training the intellect in the investigation and acceptance of truths, however unpalatable these might be. "It seems to me that in general you are unfair to the serious realistic, empirical standpoint, and mistake it for some kind of crude and swaggering materialism."[13] But

Turgenev had not caricatured the approach to science currently dominant among the new generation; it was Herzen who had confused it
with his own Baconian empiricism. As he would come reluctantly to
acknowledge, he and the new Left approached science with incompatible demands.

* * *

One of those radicals whose outlook was formed in the 1860s, N. K.
Mikhailovsky, subsequently wrote that his contemporaries' passionate
interest in science could be explained only partly by the fact that in
pre-reform Russia it had enjoyed the status of a forbidden fruit—for this
had been true of most areas of knowledge. There was a more important reason why the newly awakened urge for enlightenment was bound
to concentrate on the natural sciences: "They provided genuine knowledge, because their evidence was based not on mere speculation, but
on observation . . . and experiment, leaving little room for equivoca-
tion. We stood in need of something unambiguous in order to cope
with the mass of problems that were showering down on us. It is not
surprising that we sometimes expected science to do what is not on
its agenda."[14]

This expectation was shared by the new government of Alexander II,
the Crimean defeat of 1855 having been widely interpreted as being a
result of Russia's technological backwardness. There was a great increase in the number of students specializing in science during his
reign. The "superfluous men" of the 1830s and 1840s were progressively
edged out by a new generation of self-designated "realists" who believed
that the natural sciences were the key to a radiant future for their
country.[15]

Their hopes were fed by the books and articles on the latest developments in Western science, which were translated, reviewed in radical journals, and passed from hand to hand until they fell apart. The
most popular texts were by the German materialists Büchner, Moleschott, and Karl Vogt, who shared the metaphysical commitment of their
vitalist opponents, aspiring like them to explain the ultimate essence
of life. The vitalists found it in irreducible "vital forces," the materialists in the combination of "force and matter" (the title of the hugely
popular book by Büchner that one of Turgenev's "sons" thrusts into

his father's hands). They were optimistic that fundamental questions about the source of human thought and will would eventually be resolved through the same rigorous experimental methods that had proved so spectacularly successful in furnishing precise and dependable knowledge about questions of organic function. Serious physiological inquiry in the second half of the nineteenth century did not commonly commit itself to assertions about essences or purposes; but the German popularizers, with their own radical agenda, were less modest and self-critical. The laboratory acquired a fetishistic importance: a light dressing of experimental method magically transformed the metaphysical assumptions of eighteenth-century materialism into the authoritative pronouncements of sober men of science. Vogt asserted that thinking was a product of the brain in the same way that urine and bile were secreted by other bodily organs; Büchner, more cautious, contended that although we did not yet know precisely how matter produces consciousness, we did know that the behavior of humans, like that of all other organisms, was determined by the immutable laws of a mechanistic universe.

With all the optimism of their eighteenth-century predecessors, these new materialists believed that the laws of universal causal determinism were the expression of a harmonious universal order whose principles were reflected in the workings of human reason. With the progress of education and science, social conflict would be eradicated; enlightened individuals would come to perceive that their self-interest coincided with the common good.

The crude reductionism and moral utilitarianism of the German materialists was parroted faithfully by the *Contemporary*'s two editors. Chernyshevsky compared thought to the chemical processes of digestion, and in his chief philosophical work (a long and rambling essay of 1860) pronounced the human animal to be a complex of physical and chemical processes bound strictly by the laws of causality and motivated, like all other sentient creatures, by the desire to attain pleasure and avoid pain. The natural sciences, he wrote, "have attained such heights that they can now offer plenty of material for the solution of moral [i.e., social] questions. Among the scholars engaged in the moral sciences, all the progressive ones have begun to apply exact methods, similar to those that are used in the natural sciences."[16] Dobrolyubov ridiculed the "fathers" for their love of philosophical speculation: "Facts, facts, that's where we must begin!"[17] Contemptuous of the great metaphysical systems, these ideological leaders of the 1860s were shamelessly eclectic in their rummaging through European thought— adopting Comte's view that mathematical exactitude is the ideal of all the sciences but ignoring his belief that knowledge can extend only to relations and laws and not to things-in-themselves, approving Mill's moral utilitarianism while reviling his liberalism, and mixing the rationalist optimism of Feuerbach with the Rousseauian faith that mankind would regain its natural goodness by shedding the false ac- cretions of exploitative societies.

"Facts!" was the insistent refrain of the men of the 1860s. "Bien raisonner est bien faire": the "new men," as they styled themselves, shared the French Enlightenment's faith in the omnipotence of reason as the instrument of progress. A generation trained in the methods of the natural sciences would, they believed, command the precise knowl- edge based on empirically verified data that was the essential premise of efficient social action—a euphemism for revolutionary activity. Under the censor's eye the radical leaders were endeavoring to con- struct a model for emulation that would be free from the hesitations of the liberal fathers. Once such people existed in sufficient numbers, it was hoped, revolution would be an accomplished fact.

The values of the new enlighteners were disseminated through lit- erary criticism, which Belinsky had made the vehicle for radical pro- paganda in Russia. The campaign began with the publication in 1855 of Chernyshevsky's notorious dissertation: On the Aesthetic Rela- tions between Art and Reality. The target was carefully chosen. All that the new men most detested in their predecessors' approach to the world was, they believed, epitomized in the prevailing idealist aes- thetics, according to which art was a pathway to an understanding of the essence of the universe. Chernyshevsky's treatise was based on a materialist assumption of the primacy of reality over its artistic re- creation. Art, he argues, has two functions: to reproduce the beauty of the physical world for the benefit of those who lack the opportunity to enjoy it firsthand, and to provide a critical interpretation, from a moral standpoint, of the phenomena it portrays. He evades the question of how art can pass judgment on a reality for which it is a mere surrogate, sacrificing philosophical consistency to serve a moral and political argument—that art, like all other human activities, is justified only inasmuch as it contributes to social progress.

The "new men" were devoted not (as they believed) to science but to what Herzen had called "the religion of science, of universal, transcendental, hereditary reason." They welcomed Darwin's theories on evolution as grist to their ideological mill, confirming their faith in the inexorable movement of progress. One of their number, V. A. Zaitsev, put it: "Every one of us would have gone to the scaffold and laid down his life for Moleschott or Darwin."[18] This faith admitted no *Magnum Ignotum*. Chernyshevsky dismisses the proposition that things in themselves are unknowable as metaphysical nonsense. Evolutionary science had definitively explained how all that exists came to be what it is, by revealing the unvarying laws of cause and effect characterizing the phenomena of nature and human nature. Along with the avant-garde of Western socialists, Chernyshevsky defined the moving force of history as the struggle between property-owning and property-less classes, and declared categorically that it could be resolved only by revolution: "Peaceful development is impossible. . . . Not a single step forward in history has occurred without convulsions."[19]

This doctrinairism had clear affinities with that of Herzen's old enemies on the Hegelian Right. Herzen's indignant reaction to Turgenev's portrayal of Bazarov suggests that he was initially misled by the new generation's insistence that they had no a priori system and were enemies of "modern scholasticism" in all its forms. Partly to confuse the censors, they preferred to call themselves realists or empiricists rather than materialists. Their emphasis on the value of a training in experimental science must have seemed compelling evidence to him that they were not prey to the sterile rationalism that had paralyzed many of the revolutionaries of 1848. It was not until the mid-1860s that he would turn his critical scrutiny onto the teleological assumptions of the new materialism as professed by his son Sasha and Sasha's scientific mentor Vogt. By then his encounters with the Russian Left would have thoroughly disabused him of the belief that they were unencumbered by ideological baggage from the past. Like the experience of 1863, his disillusionment with them would serve to sharpen his perception of the ways in which human ideals and aspirations are shaped, deflected, and deformed by the accidents of time and place.

* * *

"They attacked him bitterly, they defended their traditions with the inflexibility of legitimists. . . . And when logic and eloquence failed them . . . they placed him under a revolutionary anathema, expelling him from their communion of true believers."[20] Herzen's description of the French Left's rejection of Proudhon in the aftermath of 1848 applies equally well to his own relations with the editors of the *Contemporary*, who were engaged in maneuvering within the boundaries set by censorship to convey their uncompromising opposition to the existing regime. Dobrolyubov's literary reviews were designed to expose the evils of the existing order through commentaries on contemporary Russian literature, while Chernyshevsky's political ideas, conveyed in the form of book reviews and essays on historical subjects, played a crucial part in propelling the revolutionary movement of the 1860s. Both were strongly opposed to Herzen's attempts to encourage a nonviolent transition to socialism.

In March 1860 the *Bell* printed a strident call to action entitled "Letter from the Provinces." Its authorship is unknown, but its ideas were close to the *Contemporary*'s platform. It was a response to the *Bell*'s position as expressed in Herzen's programmatic article of 1 January that year, imploring the tsar not to be swayed by his conservative advisors, to align himself with the forces of growth and initiate a bloodless revolution from above: *"Even now,* the friends of Russia can be *yours* as well." Herzen's correspondent accuses him of being out of touch with the desperate mood of the people, who rightly have no faith in Alexander's intentions. "Only the peasant's axe can save us . . . ; let your *Bell* sound not to prayer but to the charge. Summon Russia to take up the axe!!"

Herzen accompanies the letter with a defense of his position. Compared with the awakening national force of the commune, none of Russia's institutions was so deeply entrenched that it needed to be hacked out with an axe; the nobility, aware of their origins as the slavish satraps of despotism, lacked their Western counterparts' conviction in their rights as a caste.[21]

This view was at odds with the clamor with which groups of land-owners throughout Russia were attempting to rein back the Emancipation. Characteristically Herzen, as if in dialogue with himself, admits this fact—"the majority of the nobility holds onto its bones with the ruthlessness of a wolf from the steppes"—but he reminds the reader that the debate about whether or not the peasants should be freed with land was now moving toward a consensus that they should. Russian society was faced on all levels with fundamental institutional and economic questions on which it could expect no help from Europe, which was itself in turmoil. It was essential to have time to introduce some clarity into this mass of ideas, to allow one opinion to dominate. "What can you do with an axe, when one semi-choir says that the question of communal holding has been resolved by all in the Russian sense, another that it must be resolved in the English sense, in the belief that the commune's unviability has been demonstrated?" He cites the example of 1848: the socialists had believed that they were constructing a socialist republic, the democrats that they had proved socialism to be unviable. He had seen the results with his own eyes, and that physiological fact was perhaps the principal source of his differences with his critic. "The blood of June has entered my brain and nerves; I have since cultivated a revulsion against blood, if it flows without the utmost necessity." He assures his correspondent that they differ only on means: he sympathizes with the passion behind his youthful extremism. "We understand your one-sidedness; it is close to our hearts."

But there was nothing conciliatory in his attitude to the young generation's ideological mentors. He was stung into a public confrontation with the editors of the *Contemporary* by the journal's contemptuous treatment of his generation. He responded in June 1859 in the *Bell* with a counteraccusation: in ridiculing the "superfluous men" and their literary depiction, the new generation were playing into the hands of the Russian Right. He calls their attention to Belinsky's essays, Granovsky's lectures, and the role of writers such as Pushkin, Gogol, and Lermontov in exposing the devastating effect of Nicolas's reign on the personalities and talents of its victims. (Coincidentally, in the same year he republished in London his own contribution in that regard, *Who Is to Blame?*)

He objected equally strongly to a critique of Turgenev's novels in which Dobrolyubov maintained that the vague and puerile aspirations of colorless, passive people were deserving only of satire. His unhappy generation, Herzen protested, deserved protection from its equally scarred successors. The honorable few who merited the title of super-fluous men—pathological formations called into being by the conditions of life under Nicolas I—had passed on the poison in their blood to their embittered children. These, born under Nicolas's bureaucratic tyranny, had assimilated something of its style, bringing to the surface what Herzen defines in his memoirs as the "Arakcheevan element" in the national character, after the minister under Alexander I who was notorious for his bureaucratic rigidity, rages, and brutality:

> In the name of his ideal of a grenadier guardsman, Arakcheev flogged living peasants to death; we flog to death ideas, art, humanity, past leaders, anything we please. In dauntless ranks we advance step by step to the limit and beyond, never falling out of step with logic, but only *with truth*; unaware, we go further and further, forgetting that a true sense and understanding of life are manifested precisely in stopping short before extremes. . . . That is the *Halte* of moderation, of truth of beauty, the eternal balance of the organism.
>
> The oligarchic pretension of the have-nots to possess a monopoly on suffering in society is as unjust as all forms of exclusiveness and monopoly. Neither through evangelical mercy nor through demo-cratic envy will you get beyond charity or violent spoliation, re-distribution of property and general poverty. In the Church it has remained a theme for rhetoric and a sentimental exercise in compas-sion; in the ultrademocrats, as Proudhon has observed, it is confined to the feeling of envy and hatred; in neither case has it advanced toward any constructive idea, any practical result.[22]

Predictably, there was no meeting of minds in June 1859 when Cher-nyshevsky visited London in order to patch up relations with Herzen. He subsequently wrote to Dobrolyubov that he had wasted his time. Herzen was "Kavelin squared," that was all there was to it.[23]

The New Enlighteners

For all their differences, Russian radicals and liberals shared a common view of the intelligentsia as enlighteners, conveying the principles of rationalist universalism to the benighted masses. After the official promulgation of the Emancipation Edict in the spring of 1861, this belief became a central point of contention between Herzen and the Left. The edict burdened the peasants with heavy redemption payments designed to compensate the former serf owners, and its ambivalence allowed the latter to seize peasant land in the two-year transitional period. Nevertheless the *Bell* gave it a conditional welcome as a "first step," ending centuries of slavery.[24]

In an essay published in the *Contemporary* in May 1861, Chernyshevsky accused Herzen of perpetuating the Slavophiles' "absurd dreams" that the moribund culture of Europe would be regenerated by a tribe from the East. How could it possibly advance the cause of progress "if peoples who are to some extent educated are replaced by peoples scarcely out of the animal state?" Europe had its own brain, "far more developed than ours, and has nothing to learn from us." Russia's communal land tenure might at best provide a convenient way of easing the country's passage to a collectivist socialism on a Western model. He subsequently concedes that the patriotic enthusiasm with which the peasantry had repelled the enemy in 1812 gave grounds for hope that, directed by "the strong, skilled hand" of the educated minority, the people could achieve a better life.[25] Thus Chernyshevsky managed under the censor's nose to convey his expectation of a socialist revolution in which the masses would provide the physical momentum under the leadership of the Westernized intelligentsia.

Herzen responded angrily to what he described as a deliberate distortion of his thought. He was not one of those who claimed that Russia had a new revelation to impart to the West. History tended to advance through various combinations of two interacting forces—tradition and ideals: the richer a nation's past and the more entrenched its institutions, the more tradition infuses the ideal, pulling it back in its direction. The West appeared to have reached a boundary beyond which it could not pass without transforming the views of property, society, and human relations on which its civilization had been built and thus "ceasing to be itself." How this problem would be resolved could not be predicted, but it was not absurd to hypothesize that countries with a rich historical culture would prove less fertile soil for new social forms than a country lacking such a past. When, as recently transpired in Europe, ideals succumb to the forces of conservatism, it is not unnatural that attention should turn to less well-defended territories—the more so as the most valuable achievement of western European culture—modern science—was eminently exportable. Individuals stifled by tradition had migrated to Canada and Australia; Russia had the advantage of a homegrown way of life in which the gap between tradition and ideal was far narrower than in the West.[26]

He returned to the attack in February 1862 in an essay entitled "Liberation Fodder," noting that he had been reproached for his lack of a program by doctrinaires of all denominations, including some "very young people" looking for authorities to speed things up. Why, they ask, does he criticize the existing order without pointing out the way forward? The reason is that it is time to stop playing at being wise pastors of human flocks. "The method of *enlightenment* and *liberation* devised behind the people's backs and foisting on it its own inalienable rights and its own well-being by means of the axe and the whip has been exhausted by Peter I and the French Terror." The "perfecting of mankind" had been shown to be no more than the slow process of learning from past mistakes. In this, backward peoples arriving on the field of history after a bitter harvest had an advantage. New experiences would lead to new blunders; the most that one could ensure was that they would differ from the old. There were no magic formulas. The Social Contract and its like were no more than markers in the unceasing struggle to liberate thought from superstition. "Manna does not fall from the sky . . . it grows out of the soil. Coax it forth, learn to listen to the grass growing, and don't lecture each blade, but help it to develop, remove obstacles, that's all one can do, and that's quite sufficient in itself! It's time to be more modest; enough of educating entire peoples, preening oneself on one's enlightened intelligence and theoretical comprehension."

He reminds the reader of the turn of events after 1789, when those who had seen the light were eager that others should not be left in the dark. The people whose coming of age was celebrated in the Declaration of Human Rights became "liberation fodder, *chair au bonheur public*," like the cannon fodder of Napoleon. The French issued edicts on freedom and equality, the Germans developed the notion of constitutions into a science, while socialists created phalansteries without bothering beforehand to seek out the kind of people who might wish to live in them. Then came the June Days, in which the best and most wretched of the masses, driven by need and despair, went forth madly, without plan or goal, and said to their guardians, tutors, legislators, and educators: *"We do not recognize you!* We were hungry, you gave us parliamentary chatter; we were naked, you sent us abroad to kill other hungry and naked people; we asked to be taught how to escape from our predicament; you gave us rhetoric. We'll return to our damp cellars—some will perish in the unequal . . . battle but before that we'll say to the bookish revolutionaries loud and clear: *The people are not with you!"*[27]

In May 1862 great alarm was caused by the appearance in Moscow, Saint Petersburg, and the provinces of a bloodthirsty proclamation entitled *Young Russia,* purporting to issue from a "Central Revolutionary Committee."[28] Its authors were a small group headed by a nineteen-year-old student, P. G. Zaichnevsky, an ardent admirer of the French Jacobins. It called for the "bloody and pitiless" destruction of the existing order and all who supported it, followed by a revolutionary dictatorship presiding over a federation of communes. A memoirist of the time described it as bursting over the capital like a clap of thunder.[29] The government took advantage of the coincidence of its appearance with the Saint Petersburg fires to launch a succession of arrests and repressive measures, ranging from the closure of journals, Sunday schools, and public reading rooms to the suppression of grants to poor students. Public lectures could henceforth be given only with the joint permission of two ministers and the head of the Third Department: all this, Herzen remarks, in response to one pamphlet that clearly was written by very young people. In two successive essays in the *Bell* that summer he outlines his own simple objection to it: the irrelevance of its program to the current situation in Russia. Living in a world of comrades and books remote from the world of facts, its authors had constructed a variation on the metaphysics of the French Revolution. They accused him of losing faith in violent revolution—the fact was that he had simply lost any taste for it. It was sometimes inevitable, and that might yet be the case in Russia, but to resort to it when other options had not been exhausted was a form of self-indulgence. Terror was easy and quick, the guillotine a rapid method of persuasion. "Terror gives full rein to the passions, cleansing them through the notion of the common good and the absence of personal goals. Hence it is much more attractive than *self-restraint for the good of the cause.*"[30]

He recalls how he too had once been captivated by the French Terror of the 1790s. The authors of *Young Russia* represented a predicament with which he was closely familiar as a member of the Russian intelligentsia: "In return for the slavery under which we lived, the alienation from our countrymen, the break with the people, the inability to act, we had one . . . consolation: the nakedness of denial, merciless logic; and with a sort of joy we pronounced those . . . *extreme* words that our teachers scarcely whispered. . . . We had nothing to lose."[31] But with the emancipation of the peasants the situation had changed. In the complex process of embryogenesis in which it was engaged, Russia needed the experience of the West but not the revolutionary rhetoric of a bygone era.

Herzen remarks on the evidence that the Russian people, too, seemed to have little sympathy with their would-be liberators. In the atmosphere of public alarm following the fires in Moscow and the capital, V. A. Obruchev, the author of a radical manifesto, was subjected to the ritual of civil execution on a public square (the prelude to a sentence of hard labor followed by lifelong exile in Siberia). This had been greeted with vociferous approval by the common people, who clung to the traditional belief that the tsar was their protector against the depredations of the Westernized classes (the official press recorded that the crowd had demanded that he be put to death on the spot). The issues at stake were still deeply confused, and the authors of the proclamations were intensifying this muddle by calling on the people to rise against the tsar and the nobility—"against the hated caste *among which it numbers you,* and the power it sees as its defender." There was no shadow of possibility that the Russian peasant would take to the axe in the name of the republicanism of Louis Blanqui or the metaphysics of the French Revolution. The principal defect of "Young Russia" was that there was nothing Russian about it: its ideal revolutionary was an amalgam of Schiller's noble-hearted bandit with the eighteenth-century communist conspirator Babeuf. "Do not take offense if we say that your costume of Karl Moor and Gracchus Babeuf, when worn on Russia's public squares, is not only old-fashioned, but looks like fancy dress."[32]

Russian civilizers had traditionally combined faith in their own omniscience with contempt for the ignorance of the people, who had nevertheless developed the commune and its internal structures without their pedagogical help. Their response to those who saw them as clay to be sculpted into statues in the French manner or the English, or the German, would continue to be either obstinate nonparticipation or offensively passive obedience. What was currently happening in Russia should give these would-be liberators pause for thought. The people had long borne serfdom because of the superior force that imposed it, but they were now showing themselves capable of determined and violent resistance to efforts to free them that did not coincide with their own perception of their relation to the land. Without knowledge of the people, one could oppress them, shackle them, but not liberate them. Western theories should be applied, not as medicine from foreign dispensaries, but as instruments for understanding the nature and potential of the existing structures of popular life. The successful suitor of the Russian people would combine the fruits of a Western intellectual culture with a sympathetic comprehension of native institutions and a commitment to realizing popular aspirations. Such persons might issue from the ranks of the intelligentsia or from the masses. Even the tsar himself, by renouncing the Petrine tradition, might place himself at the head of a popular movement. The task of the "prosaic workers" of the present was to prepare the ground for such developments by making contact with the people, preaching to them "neither Feuerbach nor Babeuf, but the *religion of the land,* which they understand. . . . If the sun rises without bloody clouds, so much the better, no matter whether it is wearing the hat of Monomach or the Phrygian cap."[33] The French Revolution had shown all too clearly that it was not worth shedding blood or even ink over institutional forms.

* * *

It was in London that Herzen first established direct relations with the Russian revolutionary youth. The organization subsequently known as the first Land and Liberty was founded as a result of discussions at the beginning of 1860 among Herzen, Ogarev, and the former civil servant Nikolai Serno-Solovevich, who had been inspired by Herzen's and Chernyshevsky's ideas to resign his post and travel to London to discuss the future of the peasant commune with the *Bell*'s editors. They were both deeply impressed by the young man's intelligence and courage. It seems to have been Herzen who suggested the name of the new clandestine organization, as summing up what Russia most needed at that time. On his return to Russia, Serno established a committee in Saint Petersburg as the center of a network in a number of provincial centers, composed mainly of intellectuals and university students. Little is known about its overall size. In July 1862 Serno was arrested together with Chernyshevsky after incriminating letters from the *Bell*'s editors were intercepted at the Russian frontier. He died in Siberia four years later.

The closure of Russian universities in 1861 greatly increased the flow of young Russians to universities in the West. To these radical-minded but "legal" emigrants were added many who had fled abroad to avoid arrest. The most prominent were members of Land and Liberty. They formed colonies, in particular in the Swiss centers of Berne and Geneva, where they led an intense political life, copying and distributing radical literature and collecting money for the support of political émigrés and the "Russian cause."

Their attitude to Herzen and the *Bell* was condescending. Most of them had been acquainted with his writings before they emigrated, but the heroes of their own generation had taught them to mistrust his "reformist" tendencies. Many of those who met him found additional reasons for their disapproval. One of their number, N. V. Shelgunov, an enthusiastic follower of Chernyshevsky who met Herzen in London in 1859, attributed Herzen's disagreements with the young émigrés to the fact that, although he was a brilliant orator in the defense of freedom, he was "insufficiently democratic both in mode of life and intellectual temperament for the streets and the barricades."[34] In the early 1860s some of their leaders saw these defects as outweighed by his usefulness as a source of access to the "Bakhmetev fund," a substantial sum of money entrusted by a well-wisher to the *Bell*'s editors for purposes of propaganda. Herzen resisted their ever more peremptory demands to put this at their disposal for their own ends. Despite their hostility he could not afford to break off relations with them: they were his only channel to the radical youth in Russia, and through them to the peasantry. But faced with the unconcealed contempt of the most hostile of the young émigrés, and repelled by their style of argument (as epitomized in the subtitle of Land and Liberty's propaganda sheet: "À tout venant je crache"), he came increasingly to reflect in his memoirs on the difference between "true" nihilism and the version preached and practiced by their leaders. These prided themselves on their rejection of the regime into which they had been born, but how much of the manners of imperial Russia they retained was clear from the nature of their challenge to the older generation, as summed up by Herzen: "You are hypocrites, we shall be cynics; you have been moral in words, we shall be villainous in words. You have been polite to your superiors and rude to your inferiors; we shall be rude to everyone. You bow down to those whom you do not respect; we shall jostle people without apology. Your sense of personal dignity consisted solely in decorum and external honor; we shall make it a point of honor to flout all decorum and to scorn all *points d'honneur.*"[35] Herzen was to suffer firsthand from their bullying. But in laying the principal blame for it on the pseudoscientific dogmatism preached by their leaders in Russia, he failed to perceive the singular affinity between his conception of true nihilism and that of the young radical whom the tsarist authorities considered the greatest firebrand of them all: Dmitrii Pisarev.

Herzen and Pisarev

Born in 1840, Pisarev issued from the impoverished lower nobility. On graduating in philology at Moscow University, he devoted himself to his consuming interest: the effect of the Darwinian revolution on the natural sciences. He was the only Russian radical of his generation to attempt a serious study of Darwin's discoveries, which he approached from the materialist perspective of Büchner, Moleschott, and Vogt, with the intention of becoming, like them, a competent popularizer, pronouncing expertise in the natural sciences to be "the most urgent need of our society"—to distract the young from this study would be to impede Russia's progress.[36] Imprisoned for two years in the mid-1860s, he used his enforced leisure to produce a substantial study on *The Origin of Species*, which has been recognized as an outstanding example of *haute vulgarisation*— one of the first to acquaint the Russian public with Darwinism. But he made it clear enough that he saw no room for teleology around Darwin's theories. It has been observed that he shared Herzen's idea of a life force, irreducible to any normative or teleological principles. There is only one necessity, he declared: "the blessed necessity of being oneself."[37] His emphasis on individual autonomy led to increasing tension between the *Contemporary* and the journal of which he became editor, the *Russian Word*. In 1862 he protests its treatment of a recent reprint of Ivan Kireevsky's celebrated 1832 article, "The Nineteenth Century," accusing its editors of preferring a sterile polemic against Slavophile ideology to an analysis of its historical and psychological significance: "Slavophilism is not an epidemic that has come from nowhere: it is a psychological phenomenon springing from unsatisfied needs. Kireevsky wanted to live a rational existence, to enjoy everything to which the human soul aspires, to love, to believe. Reality did not provide the elements for this. But he animated it and colored it according to his taste. He has thus become a Knight of the Sorrowful Countenance, like the unforgettable Don Quixote."[38] Pisarev's defense of the right to be oneself had its limits: he was at one with the radical critics of his time in condemning the principle of art for art's sake, on the premise that genuine art must serve the function of presenting a moral commentary on society. The principal target of his campaign against aesthetics was Pushkin, whose novel in verse, *Eugene Onegin*, he dismissed as the apotheosis of a bored socialite. He reconciled his individualism with his commitment to social justice through the utilitarian principle of enlightened self-interest, maintaining that a developed personality would necessarily conceive of his personal self-fulfillment as inseparable from the common good. The gulf separating him from his radical contemporaries was manifest in his reaction to Turgenev's novel *Fathers and Sons*, which had introduced the word "nihilist" into common parlance as the self-description of the work's radical hero, Bazarov, a medical student who spent his afternoons dissecting frogs and believed a decent chemist to be "twenty times more useful than any poet."[39] Turgenev had foreseen that the novel would be regarded as a deliberate caricature of the Left, writing in his diary: "The *Contemporary* will probably shower me with contempt for Bazarov, and won't understand that throughout the time I was writing [the novel] I was feeling an involuntary attraction to him."[40] The Left performed as expected, and Herzen added his voice to the general outrage, accusing Turgenev of a travesty of "the serious, realist, empiricist standpoint."[41]

The sole dissenting voice in this chorus of condemnation was Pisarev's. In a commentary of some thirty pages on the novel, he praises Turgenev for his evenhanded approach to the merits and failings both of his own generation and its successor. Turgenev belonged to a generation of Romantic idealists; but their representatives in the novel were no match for Bazarov in force of intellect or character. Bazarov's rough manners and undiscriminating rejection of values that he did not understand were directly linked with his striving for the common good. But contrary to the view of some of his admirers, these were faults, not virtues. Turgenev could never become a Bazarov, but he had thought his way into the type and sympathized with him more deeply than any of the new "realists" who were now imitating the young scientist's contempt for the preceding generation. " 'Bazarovism' is the malady of our times." The men of the 1860s seemed unaware that one day they too would "look down at" their past "from the heights of the future." Turgenev had refrained from identifying either with the fathers or the sons: his criticism was thereby "more profound and more serious than the negation of those who, by destroying what has preceded them, imagine that they are the salt of the earth and the purest example of complete humanity." He had shown himself to be both a great artist and an honest critic of Russia.[42]

Pisarev was alone among radical critics in this view of the author's attitude to his subject. He was to pay dearly for his defense of the "fathers." In February 1862 there appeared in the bookshops of Moscow and Saint Petersburg an officially inspired pamphlet aimed at discrediting Herzen and thereby diminishing the prestige of the *Bell*. The presence of Herzen's name (its public use hitherto strictly proscribed) on the cover resulted in a rush to buy; four editions were exhausted in a few weeks. Pisarev composed a refutation and submitted it to the censor who controlled the *Russian Word*. When it was rejected for publication, he passed it to a friend who had access to an illegal printing press. Before it could be printed, his friend was arrested, and Pisarev's document was found among his papers. After a lengthy process of inquisition, he was declared guilty of composing a seditious text directed against the Russian government and the tsar in person: he was imprisoned until 1866.

His manuscript remained in the official archives until it was published in 1907. It accuses the government of seeking through its agent to tarnish the reputation of a man the publication of whose writings it had already forbidden. This man was the incarnation of liberty; he should be glorified for having chosen as the epigraph of his journal *The Polar Star* Pushkin's words: "Long live Reason!" Yes, long live reason, "and down with decrepit absolutism, decrepit religion, and the decrepit skeleton of official morality!"[43]

Pisarev's incarceration accounts for the fact that Herzen first came upon his writings only in January 1868, after enduring three years of humiliation at the hands of the group who dominated the Russian émigré community in Geneva, subjecting him to a campaign of slanderous allegations about his personal wealth and his lack of commitment to the cause to which he had devoted his life. Their implacable enmity and contempt would poison his last years. His response to Pisarev's writings shows that they also seriously skewed his judgment. He knew nothing of Pisarev's imprisonment or its cause, but was predisposed to respond with hostility to any works emanating from a self-professed nihilist of the 1860s. Informing Ogarev of their existence, he admits they had given him "a prickly kind of pleasure," and asks him to search out copies of the *Russian Word*. "How annoying that I took so long to acquaint myself with this Maccabeus of Petersburg nihilism: here's an example of independent perception and self-mastery, acquired not by an idiot nor a rogue, but by an intelligent man." He sums up his impressions: some interesting insights on Turgenev's Bazarov, a "boundless" hatred of Pushkin, a patronizing attitude to Belinsky, and contempt for himself and Ogarev as "restless old men who have lost their wits."[44]

The editors of the *Bell* could not be mentioned by name in anything published in Russia. This fact apart, the last remark is so grotesquely at variance with the truth that it can only be attributed to Herzen's tendency to paranoia toward the end of the 1860s. In May of the same year (his suspicions having been stoked up by what he perceived as veiled contempt for his generation in the preface to an edition of Chernyshevsky's collected works), he reads a similar hidden message into

Pisarev's study of Bazarov: "Note that like true scoundrels they don't mention us by name; they attack us with allusions which it is easy to disavow and hard for us to refute."[45]

Sadly, he remained unaware of the following allusion to himself in an essay by Pisarev in the *Russian Word* praising the literary embodiments of the ideals of the "men of the forties": "The age of the Beltovs, the Chatskys and the Rudins passed forever from the moment when the appearance of the Bazarovs, the Lopukhovs and the Rakhmetovs became possible. But we, modern realists, feel an intimate kinship with this outdated type; we recognize in it our predecessors, in it we respect and love our masters, we understand that without them we also would not have been able to exist."[46] The reference here to Herzen's alter ego Beltov in *Who Is to Blame?* was the only way in which Pisarev could express in print his admiration for the man whom he was to describe as the incarnation of liberty. Ignorant of Pisarev's heroically impetuous defense of him against his official slanderers, Herzen contrived to read into his evenhanded portrayal of Bazarov an idealization of "all nihilism's riff-raff. . . . I hate them and I want to ridicule them," he informs Ogarev.[47] The resulting long essay, "Bazarov Once More" (published in the *Polar Star* of 1869), considers the meaning of "true" nihilism. Herzen accuses his attackers of being unable to tolerate the fact that the protest of his contemporaries had been expressed differently from theirs. It was the circles of the 1840s who had sponsored the growth of nihilism in his sense of the word: "the summer lightning of that complete freedom from all ready-made concepts, from all the inherited obstructions and hindrances that prevent the Western mind from advancing with its historical cannonball chained to its leg." When they were silenced in Russia, their principles were propagated from London by the Free Russian Press, whose influence in opening minds is an undeniable fact of history. In the natural sciences it was normal to approach phases and degrees of development, declinations and deviations, even abortions, *sine ira et studio*, as objects of analysis. Why then in the approach to history should the "physiological method" be abandoned in favor of the methods of the police station and the criminal court? Instead of pitting Bazarov against the "superfluous men," it would be more productive to focus on their respective resemblances and differences and the reasons for their appearance. If Turgenev's character had not been condemned to death by typhus, he might have developed into a true scientist:

> He would have ceased to look down on people with profound and un-concealed contempt. Even more than the Gospels, science teaches us humility. It cannot look down on anything, it does not know what superiority means, it despises nothing, never lies for the sake of a pose, conceals nothing out of vanity. It stops short before the facts as an investigator, sometimes a physician, never an executioner, and still less with hostility and irony.
>
> Science . . . is love, as Spinoza said of thought and cognizance.

The essay concludes with Herzen's final definition of true nihilism:

> [It] is logic without strictures, science without dogmas; it is uncon-ditional obedience to experience and uncomplaining acceptance of all the consequences, whatever these might be, if they follow from observation and are required by reason. Nihilism does not turn *something* into nothing but reveals that *nothing* taken for *some-thing* is an optical illusion, and that every truth, however much it contradicts our fantastic imaginings, is healthier than them and in any case is binding.[48]

It is unsurprising that, isolated and systematically humiliated during most of his last decade, Herzen failed to maintain the dispassionate objectivity that he preached. But his view of Pisarev changed radically after the latter's death from drowning in July 1868. In his obituary in the *Bell* he writes: "Another disaster has struck our little phalanx. A brilliant star of great promise has died, taking with him talents that had scarcely matured and ending a literary career that had scarcely begun to take shape . . . a mordant critic, sometimes inclined to exag-geration but always full of wit, nobility and energy. . . . Despite his youth, he had undergone much suffering. He had only recently emerged from the fortress in which he had been imprisoned for some years."

Herzen cites from reports of the funeral in Saint Petersburg jour-nals: " 'An enormous crowd of people from all classes and all strata of society followed the cortege . . . to the cemetery. The tomb disappeared under flowers. A collection was made to fund a bursary that will bear the name of the young publicist.' . . . All this is fine, but is it really necessary that death must always separate a man of progress from the living in order to reconcile him with the multitude of the lazy and the inert?"[49]

Herzen's own belated reconciliation with Pisarev's version of nihilism clearly owed much to the reports emanating from Saint Petersburg after Pisarev's death, although he may never have known of the reason for his imprisonment. Had he had that knowledge, it would have alleviated to some extent the sense of isolation that obsessed him in his last years.

CHAPTER TWENTY-TWO

The Last Years

The individual is a powerful fermenting agent whose action is not always terminated even by death.

HERZEN

Lately I've been reading Herzen. . . . What a marvelous writer; and our Russian life for the last twenty years would have been different if this writer had not been hidden from the young generation. As it is, a very important organ was forcibly removed from the body of Russian society.

L. N. TOLSTOY TO THE ARTIST N. N. GÉ,
13 FEBRUARY 1888

INFORMING Pavel Annenkov of Herzen's death in January 1870, Turgenev wrote: "Probably everyone in Russia will say that he should have died sooner: that he outlived his fame."[1]

The common image of Herzen in the West owes much to his portrayal by E. H. Carr as a Romantic exile whose last years were blighted by domestic misery and a sense of futility, born of the realization that his voice was no longer heard. These years were indeed, in Herzen's own words, unbearably hard, but the fruit of his experiences would be his final and most compelling essays on the theme that had dominated his thought for four decades: the nature of history and the limits of human freedom.

Since 1851 I have never entered a new year with such a feeling of horror. I see no hope of any light either in my public or my personal life. . . .

Even lifelong ties are giving way. We are humiliating ourselves in each other's eyes. Is it old age? The laurels are fading; there remain only old faces trying to look young.

There is no harmony in my domestic life. The task is growing more difficult, the egoism more extreme. . . . And it all falls on the children.

Everywhere around me there is only darkness, horror, blood and contemptible people.[2]

Thus Herzen wrote in his diary as he entered 1864. He had good reasons for being close to despair. With its echoes of the slaughter of 1848, the Polish tragedy of the previous year had shattered the hopes that had inspired his writing over the previous decade, and deprived him of most of his audience at the same time. His personal life provided no refuge. Alternating between extremes of guilt and resentment over the ambivalence of her position, Natalie constantly threatened to go back to Russia with her children. Meanwhile Sasha, on whom he had placed high hopes as his intellectual and political heir, showed little interest in fulfilling the role set out before him.

* * *

The academic and political education of his elder children became a major concern for Herzen in his last years. When his daughters came from Paris to join him in 1853, he had engaged Malwida von Meysenbug, a German émigrée with considerable intellectual culture and radical views, to teach Tata, then aged eight. His most pressing anxiety was the future of Sasha, aged fourteen on his arrival in England. Herzen engaged a number of tutors for him, steering him from the start toward the natural sciences. Natalie Ogarev records in her memoirs that the custom was introduced for him to mark each of his father's birthdays by performing a scientific experiment, accompanied by a lecture.[3] At the age of eighteen Sasha enrolled at University College London; Herzen informed Michelet that he was studying comparative anatomy under a friend of Geoffroy Saint-Hilaire (Robert Grant, an early speculator on evolution). But he complained to Karl Vogt, professor of natural science in Würzburg and a close friend who had given him strong support during his successive family tragedies, that Sasha's fellow students consisted of rich and debauched bourgeois; in general, bourgeois depravity in London surpassed that of Paris in its "bestial vulgarity."[4] In the following year, therefore, Sasha was sent to Würzburg to continue his studies while living with the Vogt family. Describing his departure as "a revolution in my life," Herzen exhorted him to hasten to make acquaintances among "good Russians" and apply himself to the study of philosophy, "otherwise science becomes a mere façade: in accumulating facts one can lose sight of the whole."

He provided him with a list of historical works, emphasizing the writers of antiquity, and urged him to be guided by Vogt in his studies, while warning him against Vogt's materialism: "he talks nonsense on philosophy." Sasha did not respond to repeated paternal requests for details of his studies, and Herzen wrote to inform him of the pain inflicted by the infrequency of his letters. "For me you have taken the place of family, home, and, above all, your mother; I sought in you a kind of continuation of her and of our lives together. It's not much to ask."[5]

This plea did not have the desired effect: Sasha remained a sporadic correspondent. Three months later, Herzen complains: "You have not once sent me a serious résumé of the teaching in your department." When Sasha explained his silences by a lack of news, Herzen responded, "But I don't look for news from you, but only for that exchange and those confidences that keep relationships alive."[6] Shocked to hear from Vogt that his son was well intentioned but lazy, he accused Sasha of a lack of commitment to science, and was alarmed by his intention to specialize in medicine alone: "Do you think you can seriously progress without a knowledge of physics? . . . If you want to circumvent it like a mountain, it will end by . . . casting a huge shadow on you." He urges him to precede the study of medicine by the broadest possible education in the natural sciences. "Remember my eternal rule: science, serious science most of all and above all; and remember that behind all practical, applied studies, observations and experiments, it is reading, and reading alone, that can give form to thought."[7] Concerned that his son's intellectual interests seemed confined to the current state of human knowledge, he recommends that he immerse himself through history and literature in the triumphs and disasters of the past, as a fellow traveler on a common path, an experience without which no human was complete.

A summer vacation with Sasha on the Isle of Wight in 1859 did not improve their relationship, Sasha having made it clear that he did not envisage an eventual return to the land of his birth. "I see that you comprehend nothing about the Russian question and your relation to Russia," Herzen writes; everywhere else a foreigner, in Russia he would have the immense distinction of being the inheritor of the work of his father and Ogarev. Their struggle against despotism was now part of history; it was open to Sasha to emulate the renowned anatomist and pedagogue, Nikolai Pirogov, whose work, *Questions of Life,* was a devastating critique of the state of education in his native country. Instead, Sasha's ideal was to be a professor in Switzerland. "Surely you don't lack the curiosity . . . to learn about the country that is now becoming a riddle for all far-seeing minds?"[8]

In March 1860 Herzen views as "madness" Sasha's intention to marry one of Vogt's nieces. To embark on the responsibilities of marriage at the age of twenty while still a student would be to destroy "the whole edifice that I have built in dreams about your future life, . . . you will proceed along trivial paths." He implored him at least to postpone the marriage until he reached the age of twenty-five. An added blow was that the father of the proposed bride was the owner of a plantation worked by slaves in Trinidad. "Since 1852," he writes to Sasha, "I have had two missions: my work for Russia and the development of my children." He had failed with Sasha: "You have become a foreigner."[9] He now turned to his daughters. "Remember," he writes to Tata, "that you and Olga are the only consolation left to me in my private life . . . , *my respite from my labors.*" To Maria Reichel he writes of his desperate wish to preserve the two girls as "models of a different way of life."[10] Sasha had become a Swiss, and nothing would change that.

After Sasha gained his doctorate in the spring of 1861, Herzen suggested that he at least visit the country of his birth. "I'm not calling on you to assume a political role; you haven't enough links with Russia, nor any attraction to it."[11] But his son pleasantly surprised him at the end of that year by volunteering to act as an agent of Land and Liberty: during the Polish uprising he took on the responsibility of representing it in Paris, Stockholm, and Heidelberg.[12] Herzen expressed delight at this development. "As a father and a friend I want you to follow that path so that I may always and entirely rely on you, and bequeath to you a part of our cause." But he continued to doubt whether Sasha possessed the moral strength to persevere in an academic or political career: "You are *twenty-two;* time is going by."[13] In the autumn of 1863 he heard of a heated quarrel between his son and Bakunin about which of the two could claim to be the legal representative of Land and Liberty, which was on the verge of extinction after the failed uprising. In letters to the pair he describes this squabble as "comic to the highest degree," and expresses the hope that Sasha will recognize that his talent for politics is as nonexistent as Bakunin's expertise in natural science.[14] He thenceforth reverted to criticism of his son's approach to science. Sasha, who had obtained a post as a lecturer in Florence, asked his father to provide him with an expensive microscope. Herzen replied that such extravagances were in the category of thoroughbred horses and costly carriages. "Ten times more important are two things without which your science will fail, no matter what tools you have: without a knowledge of chemistry and physics one cannot be a natural scientist."[15]

Herzen's last years in England were blighted by Natalie Ogarev's hostility to his two elder daughters, which forced him at the end of 1862 to break up his family. When Malwida von Meysenbug, who had taken charge of Olga's education, declared her intention to move to Italy for reasons of health and proposed to take Olga (then aged twelve) with her, Herzen arranged for Tata, aged eighteen and eager to pursue studies in art, to accompany them in order to distance her from Natalie's poisonous tongue. In his letters to them he repeatedly requests—apparently without success—news about the progress of Olga's study of Russian, fearing that Olga (born in Nice) would soon wholly cease to be Russian. Faced with the prospect of the permanent dissolution of his family, he arranged to bring them together in 1864 for a summer in the resort of Bournemouth, but the experiment proved disastrous. Friction between Tata and Olga was intensified by Malwida's strong preference for Olga, which she expressed in a letter of seven pages demanding that the two of them return to Italy without Tata. Meanwhile, after a series of hysterical scenes, Natalie declared her intention to petition Alexander II for permission to return to Russia with her three children. Faced with the prospect of the permanent loss of contact with them, Herzen threatened to reveal their true paternity to her parents in Russia.

He described the summer to Ogarev as "a triple Bedlam." "I'm falling apart through grief, humiliation, and helplessness." Back in London the situation did not improve. He informs Sasha: "Malwida and Natalie go insane in turns."[16] In addition he was beset with anxiety about the effect of the civil war in the United States, where almost all his fortune was invested; the economic future of his dependents and of his Russian press was a constant concern of his letters in the early 1860s. His financial worries increased when he was forced to take on sole responsibility for the support of Ogarev's household. N. M. Satin,

Natalya Tuchkova-Ogareva.

a former member of their Moscow circle, had engaged to pay in yearly installments for the purchase of Ogarev's Russian estate. Due to Satin's gambling habits, the payments rarely materialized. Herzen wrote to Ogarev that he was prepared to believe Satin's professions of affection for them both, "but why can one not rely on a single Russian, and why do the words 'duty,' 'obligation' exist only when there's a stick in the vicinity?"[17]

An added cause of anxiety was Ogarev's declining health. His epileptic fits had increased, along with his consumption of alcohol. He had formed a relationship with a London prostitute, Mary Sutherland,

and established her and her young son in lodgings where he found refuge from Herzen's chaotic household. Herzen maintained a cool distance from the relationship, which he summed up as follows: "Mary cares for Ogarev excellently, feeds him marvelously, but is a totally vacuous woman, with a streak of cunning and an incessant laugh."[18]

It was decided in the same summer that the family should move to Geneva, together with Ogarev, who accepted on condition that Mary Sutherland and her son accompany them. The three were to form a separate household together with Charlotte Hudson, a working-class woman who had been seduced by Sasha in London, and their son Alexander, known as Toots. Herzen would be nearer to his three elder children, and by moving his press to Geneva, a center of émigré activity and a crossroads for those going to and from France and Italy, he might succeed in reviving the *Bell*. In the first stage of this complex move Herzen accompanied Natalie and their three children to Paris in November 1864. Their arrival coincided with a diphtheria epidemic; both twins succumbed to the disease. This tragedy almost drove Natalie insane. She declared that she could not live in Geneva and eventually settled with Lisa in Nice, where the twins had been buried in the family vault. Herzen would spend most of his last years dividing his time between the two cities.

* * *

That Geneva contained the largest and most active of the Russian émigré colonies was not necessarily an advantage. Some of its members had approached Herzen in London in the aftermath of 1863 in the hope of revitalizing the revolutionary movement with the financial support of the editors of the *Bell*, to whom they were prepared to concede a subordinate role. Led by Nikolai Utin, a former member of the finally defunct Land and Liberty, they were increasingly insistent in their demands that Herzen hand over to them control of the Bakhmetev fund, for projects that he did not regard as serious. He refused to give in to their bullying; but at the same time he was eager to distinguish himself from liberal critics of the young. In an essay of 1864 he reflects that Turgenev's *Fathers and Sons*, published at the height of the repression following the student disturbances of 1861, had been disastrously mistimed. His improbable nihilist had presented the government and its supporters with a type that they could ridicule and a word that perfectly expressed their fear and hatred of the young generation at a time when many of these were showing great heroism in their response to oppression.

The advantages of a move to Geneva seemed at first to outweigh Herzen's fear of intolerable interference from Utin's group. He formed warm relations with individuals in the colony, many of whom he helped to support financially with money from his own pocket. But the émigrés in Switzerland were a very disparate collection. Some had taken part in the radical disturbances of the early 1860s and escaped abroad to avoid arrest. Others had chosen to study or lead a bohemian existence in a freer atmosphere, and wore their radicalism as a fashionable dress. This mixture of tragic and trivial figures composed the community with which Herzen would do battle in the mid-1860s. His most unrestrained enemy, Aleksandr Serno-Solovevich (brother of Nikolai and a devout follower of Chernyshevsky) was mentally unstable and spent some time in the Geneva asylum; he eventually killed himself. Another implacable foe was a member of Utin's group, M. K. Elpidin, who had been prominent in student revolutionary circles in Kazan. With the Russian press that he set up in Geneva, he began a campaign of slander against Herzen. Although Herzen's generosity to émigrés in need was widely known, he was accused of leading a life of idle luxury while young revolutionaries starved. His ideological differences with the young émigrés deepened as a result of his response in the *Bell* to Karakozov's attempt on the tsar's life in 1866. Condemning the tactic of individual terrorism, he commented: "Only among primitive and senile peoples is history advanced by murder."[19]

At the beginning of 1867, on the initiative of two young émigrés, a last attempt was made to establish a communal enterprise in the form of a review to be published concurrently with the *Bell*. Although convinced that in the absence of the requisite talent and skills among the youth, the work involved would fall on him and Ogarev, Herzen reluctantly agreed to finance the enterprise from the Bakhmetev fund. The project fell through in April, with an increase in ill feeling on both sides. His final break with the leaders of the émigrés came when Elpidin's press printed an attack on him by Serno-Solovevich representing him as a vain poseur guilty of a litany of errors, including lack of faith in political violence and excess of faith in the government's reforming

intentions. Sending the pamphlet to Bakunin (who was in close relations with the Geneva group), he writes, "You and Ogarev fed those
scorpions with your milk." He reported to Natalie that with the exception of Elpidin's circle, the Geneva émigrés disapproved of the pamphlet's tone: but "no one dares to *protest*."[20] Like Proudhon, he had
been expelled from the community of true believers.

"As a Family Man I am Worthless"

Herzen's personal life gave him no comfort; his last years were overshadowed by the failure of his attempts to bring his family together
and reconcile his daughters with Natalie after the catastrophic summer
in Bournemouth. In April 1865 he rented a magnificent house, the Châ-
teau de la Boissière, on the outskirts of Geneva, for this purpose, but
was defeated by Natalie's state of mind. The violent quarrels continued.
He wrote to Tata that she was in a state of complete prostration, and
wallowing in her suffering. After moving around Switzerland in a fruitless search for the ideal school for her daughter, she returned to Nice,
declaring her wish to live separately from the rest of the family with
Lisa. Tata and Olga arrived from Italy at the end of May, but after the
failure of efforts to find a Swiss school for Olga, departed for Florence,
where Sasha had just taken up a post as a lecturer in physiology. Fear
of the consequences of Natalie's unchallenged influence on Lisa led
Herzen to make protracted stays in Nice, where he was subjected to
Natalie's regular fits of hysteria and threats to take Lisa back with her
to Russia; he confessed to Ogarev that on each journey to Nice he felt
as though he were traveling to his execution.[21] In his last years he experienced an increasingly pressing need to acknowledge publicly Lisa's true parentage. After much hesitation he informed his other
children, and suggested to Natalie that Lisa should carry the surname
Herzen-Ogareva as a living monument to the *Bell*'s founders. Her reaction to this proposal is not known.[22]

In Geneva, Ogarev's health was deteriorating through the combined
effects of epilepsy and alcohol. Herzen's letters to him from Nice in
the New Year of 1867 are permeated with self-flagellating despair:
"Everything is so sad, so sad, so hopelessly sad that I lose heart." He is
starting the year with the bitter awareness that life is draining away;

that instead of performing heroic actions on a grand stage, "one has fallen into a mousetrap and the door has slammed shut. . . . If I say that your mode of life jars on me, I also say that I detest my own. In one way mine is the poorer one: you, like an opium eater, have your world of dreams and art—I have only action and the real world. You have cut yourself off from most of the cares of this world—I have the responsibility not only for children, but for adults. . . . And I can decidedly not (my conscience won't permit it) reject the duty of being the *garde-fou* of you both."[23] Reflecting in this mood on their joint pursuit of the revolutionary cause, he sees it as a form of self-indulgence for which those closest to them had to suffer. *"We are unhappy in our private lives—and I hear the answer clearly and distinctly: 'that's what you deserve'—and I bear this thought like a chain on my legs."* But his deep affection for his friend had not diminished over the years. Some months after that admonition he assures him that he has no need to repent: alcohol had ruined his health and reduced his capacity to contribute to their common cause, but he had lost nothing of his youthful purity.[24]

Meanwhile the divisions within Russian society, combined with increased government vigilance in the wake of the Polish uprising, had deprived the *Bell* of nearly all its audience. Herzen informs Ogarev that according to reports from Saint Petersburg and Moscow, "absolutely no one reads the *Bell* and it is nowhere to be seen." The booksellers who had previously sold it "under the counter" now shrugged their shoulders, saying "there's no demand for it."[25] It was consequently suspended in July 1867. He attempted to revive it in a French edition, arguing the need to correct the image of Russia prevalent in the West after its barbaric suppression of the Poles. But the supply of contributions from Russia had dried up, and at the end of 1868 he confessed to Ogarev that the French *Bell* had been a mistake: "Our true vocation has been to call to the living among us and ring the knell for our dead, not to recount to our neighbors the story of our graves and our cradles. All the more so as they've no great interest in it."[26]

"If . . . there is something within you . . . that will stir others profoundly, it will not be lost. . . . Your strength like a pinch of yeast, will surely agitate, ferment all that comes under its influence." With the silencing of the *Bell*, Herzen was thrown back on the reassurance given to the pessimist in a dialogue in *From the Other Shore*. The effort to connect his elder children with their Russian heritage and with the radical tradition that inspired him and Ogarev became a major preoccupation of his last years. He had already acknowledged his failure with Sasha, complaining to Ogarev that if it were not for his pride in being his father's son he would have turned his back on everything Russian. "The living tradition is fading."[27] In the 1860s he transferred his hopes to his daughters, writing to Sasha: "I have set the education of Tata and Olga . . . as one of the fundamental tasks of my life."[28] When Tata's life was threatened by an attack of smallpox, he wrote to Ogarev that her loss would be terrible for him: after his deceased wife and Ogarev, she had come closest to understanding him.[29] A talented artist, Tata kept in close touch with her father while studying art in Florence. The peacemaker of the family, she was persuaded by him to spend the summer of 1867 in Nice tutoring Lisa, Natalie being "completely deranged on the subject of education."[30]

His greatest anxiety concerned Olga, whom he had told to regard Malwida as a second mother, a role she interpreted as entitling her to keep her protégée at a distance from the quarrels of her kin. His letters to the pair request repeatedly (and apparently without result) news about the progress of Olga's study of Russian, and he is reduced to corresponding with her in French. In the last year of his life, fearing Olga's complete estrangement from her family and culture, he implores Malwida to send her to stay with him alone for at least a month, and is distraught to find both equally opposed to the plan. Unknown to Herzen, Olga was already secretly betrothed to the French historian Gabriel Monod, whom she had met in Florence. Another blow in his last years was the news of Sasha's intended marriage to Teresina Felici, an Italian working-class girl who had sat as a model for Tata, to whom Herzen described the intended marriage as an "inescapable disaster." To Ogarev he describes Teresina as "plebeian through and through, cold and calculating. She . . . worships money out of regard for her former poverty." He urged Sasha at least to postpone the wedding and to work on her education, a parity of intellectual development being a more secure basis for a marriage than mere physical attraction. He suggests to Tata that a year in a Swiss finishing school might achieve the desired result. The marriage went ahead and Herzen was informed only after the event. "Another battle lost!" he commented to Ogarev.[31] Despite the dismal record of two past reunions, Herzen never wholly lost hope of this method of welding his family together, but in a letter to Ogarev in August 1867 he rejects the idea that the effect could be permanent. "Can one construct a family from such heterogeneous elements?" He acknowledged his guilt for the rifts in his family; in giving way to his attraction to Natalie, he had failed to learn lessons from Herwegh's seduction of his wife. "Only in the public arena do I have significance. As a family man I am worthless."[32]

The last years of his life were overshadowed by his efforts to repair the damage for which he held himself responsible. In the summer of 1868 he succeeded in bringing the family together for a month in a chateau on the shores of Lake Geneva. Natalie cast her habitual blanket of gloom over the gathering. Nevertheless, he wrote to Malwida of his intention to repeat the experiment in the following spring "in order to bring Olga back into our tradition . . . not an easy task, but a very necessary one."[33] Nothing came of this plan; undeterred, in the final months before his death he was engaged in a fruitless search for a suitable house in Paris to accommodate the family (in addition to Ogarev's ménage) for a longer-term exercise in communal living.

"When will fate allow me even a moment of peace?" Herzen's letters to Ogarev in his last years convey the image of a man broken by the disappointments of his public and private life and the absence of any clear prospect of the development of the revolutionary movement in Russia or the West. "My personal life has been destroyed. . . . Time is passing, our strength is ebbing, banal old age is knocking at the door. We can't even work productively; our labor is either irrelevant or aimed at the twentieth century." Less than two months before his death he writes, "I know myself to the extent of self-disgust. I've taken to drink and regret that I can't get as drunk as you only because it makes my head ache."[34]

Writing to Ogarev from the Herzen household in Nice in the spring of 1869, Tata remarks that his constantly irritable state of mind was extremely painful to observe, and that there seemed no way of relieving it. "He himself seems at a loss as to what corner of the globe he would like to inhabit and *how* he would like to live." She has left dramatizations of the interchanges during family meals that convey with grim humor the permanent state of tension between the irascible Herzen, the capricious and refractory Lisa, and the frequently hysterical Natalie.[35] In September 1868 Herzen was diagnosed with diabetes and advised to avoid emotional upheavals. In July of 1869 the rumor of an impending marriage between Tata and Hugo Schiff (the younger brother of Moritz Schiff, the distinguished and pioneering physiologist with whom Sasha was working in Florence) prompted him to write to Sasha of his bitterness at the fact that none of his children had followed along the path laid by him and Ogarev: "All my most well-grounded wishes and dreams have burst one by one, like soap bubbles." Malwida had turned Olga into a foreigner. Tata, with her sympathy for things Russian, was the repository of his last hope for a continuation of the work he and Ogarev had begun.[36]

The rumor of the marriage proved unfounded, but at the end of October 1869 there came news from Florence that Tata had suffered a severe mental breakdown as a result of threats of violence made to her by a blind Italian musician, a member of Malwida's circle, whose proposal of marriage she had rejected. Her recovery was very slow, and Herzen spent an agonizing month with her in Florence before she was well enough to return with him to Nice. To have come near to losing the member of his family who was closest to him had been a terrible experience. "I'm tired . . . very tired," he wrote to Turgenev from Florence. To his son he wrote, "I look forward to nothing, I have faith in no one. I don't even greatly desire a long continuation of my life."[37]

These declarations of disillusionment and despair were belied by his activities in his two last years.

Herzen's restlessness after the closure of the *Bell* was prompted to a large degree by the search for an appropriate city in which to pursue what became a major preoccupation in the last year of his life: the publication in French of his principal writings. Geneva and Italy were out of the question—he observed to Malwida that books published there did not sell well. He had begun to settle in Brussels when a visitation from the Belgian political police warned him not to proceed with his project there.

His next choice was Paris, where he conducted negotiations over several months with various publishers for the piecemeal publication of a selection of his essays and fragments of his memoirs, and he also explored the possibility of having a collection of his essays published in Russia. He wrote to Sasha that, unlike Ogarev, he needed stimulation from outside, and this he came to find in Florence, in the circle around Moritz Schiff. His interest in science remained undiminished to the end. Writing to Sasha a few months before his death, he describes a recent paper by Schiff as an extraordinary intellectual feat: *"Ecce homo!"* He had come increasingly to respect Sasha's true abilities and commitment to his work. "It may be that your real talent is in the popularization of science. I've nothing against that."[38] In March 1867 he and Tata attended a public lecture by his son on the physiology of the nervous system that was highly praised by a learned academic audience. He described it glowingly to Ogarev as a masterly performance, in both content and presentation. It was followed by a very convivial dinner with the Schiff family and a young French historian (Olga's future husband, Gabriel Monod), an event Tata related to Ogarev as an instance of how her father's mood could be transformed by his surroundings—he had only to be freed from squabbles with the Geneva émigrés and savage disputes with Natalie to lose his irascibility.[39]

He never reached that state. He died in Paris in the morning of 21 January 1870 from inflammation of the lungs, in the presence of his three daughters, Natalie, Malwida, and Gabriel Monod.

Herzen and Bakunin

Herzen did not leave the world quietly. In the last months of his life he composed *Letters to an Old Comrade*—a work that has been described as "perhaps the most instructive, prophetic, sober and moving essays on the prospects of human freedom written in the nineteenth century."[40] Their inspiration was the appearance in Geneva of Bakunin, who had arrived in Italy in January 1864 in search of revolutionary action. In Florence he gathered a few disaffected Italian intellectuals into a secret society, which he replaced, when he moved to Naples a year later, by an anarchist "International Brotherhood" that, he informed Herzen, had supporters in almost every European country. For this largely mythical group he composed a "revolutionary catechism" demanding the destruction of all existing institutions—religious, political, economic, and social—and their replacement by federations of "absolutely autonomous" communes. In August 1867 Bakunin left Italy for Geneva to attend a congress of European democrats, the preparatory stage of a duel with Marx for control of the International Working Men's Association (known to history as the International). The other motive for his move was the prospect of renewing his association with Herzen and Ogarev, whom he had kept informed of his activities in Italy (which he described as the founding of an "international revolutionary-socialist secret society"), admonishing them for failing to support the young radicals' call to revolution: "Stop being Erasmuses and become Luthers."[41]

Herzen was rarely in Geneva after the closure of the *Bell,* and Ogarev's powers were increasingly diminished by alcohol and infirmity. Bakunin's efforts to enroll the émigré colony in a nonexistent organization called the "Secret Alliance" came to nothing, but he found the conspirator of his dreams in Sergei Nechaev, a young fanatic who arrived in Geneva in March 1869, claiming, falsely, to have escaped from the impregnable Peter-and-Paul fortress in Saint Petersburg. His aim was to increase his influence by enlisting the support of Russia's three senior revolutionaries. Herzen had heard enough about him to refuse to meet him, but Nechaev convinced Bakunin and Ogarev that he represented an organization of tens of thousands of revolutionaries in Russia engaged in orchestrating a peasant revolution due to break out in the following year (there were rumors, at that time, of renewed unrest among the peasantry). Bakunin was enchanted by the ruthless consistency with which his new acquaintance held to the principle that the cause of revolution sanctified the use of any means. In the words of a "Revolutionary Catechism" composed by Nechaev at that time: "All the tender sentiments which make men effeminate, feelings of kinship, friendship or love, gratitude, even honor itself, must be stifled in [the revolutionary] by the single cold passion for the revolutionary cause. There exists for him only one voluptuous pleasure, only one consolation, reward and satisfaction—pitiless destruction. Day and night he should have only a single thought, a single aim: pitiless destruction. In the cold and indefatigable pursuit of this goal he must be ready both to perish himself and to destroy with his own hands everything that impedes its realization."[42] The first meeting of the two men had the character of high comedy. Not to be outdone by Nechaev's inventions, Bakunin presented him with a document enlisting him in the Russian section of a nonexistent World Revolutionary Alliance whose central committee he claimed to represent. The two conspirators set to work on proclamations addressed to the various social groups in Russia, exhorting them to join the coming revolution, which they described in bloodcurdling terms. In September 1869 Nechaev returned to Russia and on the strength of the authority of Bakunin's document founded a new secret society in Moscow, "The People's Revenge," based on cells of five members. It seems never to have consisted of more than a dozen initiates, although a much larger number had some connection with Nechaev. When a member of his cell became suspicious of his credentials, he induced the others to murder him, cementing their fidelity by complicity in crime and providing the inspiration for Dostoevsky's novel *The Possessed*. The discovery of the victim's body led to a mass roundup of all those found to have associated with Nechaev. He himself had managed to escape abroad, where he resumed his association with Bakunin, who refused to believe the rumors circulating in émigré circles about the murder and continued to defend him despite his increasingly contemptuous attitude to the old revolutionary. Nechaev's career ended in 1872 when a fellow émigré denounced him to the Swiss police, who deported him to Russia. He was imprisoned in the fortress from which he had once claimed to have escaped, and where he died a decade later.

* * *

Bakunin's unsuccessful efforts to raise support in Sweden for the Polish uprising had familiarized Herzen with his imaginative campaigning methods. In a speech at a banquet of Swedish bourgeois democrats sympathetic to the Polish cause, he had described Land and Liberty (then close to extinction) as "a vast patriotic association, at once conservative, liberal and democratic," composed of "generals and officers *en masse*, high and minor officials, landowners, priests and sons of priests, peasants and millions from the dissenting sects." A state within a state, it had its own finances, administration, police, and army. Its aim was both "humane" and "conservative"—to produce the inevitable great political and social revolution with no needless bloodshed.[43] Herzen had reacted to news of this "colossal invention" by sending Bakunin an extended analysis of his character: he had emerged in middle age from his long imprisonment still submerged in the phantom world of the German idealism of his youth, combined with "an itch for revolutionary activity that lacked a revolution." If turned loose on the Polish cause, this had the potential for great damage.[44]

Bakunin's role in Nechaev's bid for power qualifies him fully for inclusion in the category of "useful idiot," a label whose invention is usually credited to Lenin. Alarmed by Ogarev's association with the pair, Herzen traveled to Geneva in the spring of 1869 to observe at close quarters the effect of Nechaev's influence on Bakunin's itch. He reports to his son that Bakunin is behaving like a derailed train oversupplied with fuel, racing at full speed and sweeping along with it everything in its path. His arrival in Geneva coincided with the publication of Nechaev's latest proclamation, "How the Revolutionary Question Presents Itself," exhorting Russian youth to join the brigands' ranks. His comments on the old revolutionary's supporting role combine ironic amusement with increasing concern. To Maria Reichel, Herzen observes: "The mastodon Bakunin roars and thunders, calls on workers to destroy towns and public records . . . a real Attila, no less." To Tata he describes Bakunin's "amazing" activity: "He goes from one meeting to another, is borne like a social midwife now to Lausanne, now to Le Locle. Everywhere he preaches universal destruction, conservatives grow pale, pastors curse him, while he calmly sits down to three pounds of meat and, having devoured it, begins again to preach. Meanwhile the Russian youth take his program *au pied de la lettre.* Students are beginning to form bands of brigands. Bakunin is advising them to burn all documents, destroy property and not to spare people."[45] Herzen might have expected his alarm about Bakunin's bellicosity to be shared by Ogarev, who had censured Bakunin's efforts to advance the outbreak of the Polish uprising as the expression of a "self-regarding zeal" prompted by the fear that if it were delayed he might not be there to take part.[46] But prematurely aged, and isolated between Herzen's infrequent visits, Ogarev was now ready to seize on any hope that he would survive to see the revolution to which he had devoted his life. He found Herzen's attitude to the Geneva colony too rigorous, and was greatly impressed by Nechaev, informing Herzen that he had gradually adapted to the rough manners of this little peasant, and they had become very close.[47]

Meanwhile Nechaev and Bakunin were engaged in producing a succession of bloodthirsty pamphlets whose themes can be summed up in the famous conclusion of *Die Reaktion in Deutschland:* "There can be no revolution without passionate destruction." One of their most ferocious efforts, "Principles of Revolution," recommends the extermination of selected individuals as a preliminary to the social revolution: "Poison, the knife, the rope, etc.! In this struggle revolution sanctifies all means." The new order must be built on a *tabula rasa:* discussions in advance about its nature could only impede the process of destruction, which must proceed "crescendo" until there was nothing left to be destroyed. The work of creation that followed would be in the hands of those "pure forces" that would emerge in the course of the battle. They hailed brigandage as proof of the people's vitality and strength, and (as exemplified by its role in the great uprisings of Stenka Razin and Pugachev) the only genuine revolutionary force in Russia, urging the revolutionary youth to join their ranks en masse.

Bakunin's faith in the revolutionary potential of what was a marginal phenomenon in nineteenth-century Russia was pure fantasy, the expression of a yearning born in his Romantic youth to transcend the limitations of everyday existence. "Principles of Revolution" compares the Russian brigand to the comrades of Schiller's Karl Moor, with the additional virtue of "grim, cold, and pitiless consistency." Like the demonic rebel of the Romantics, Bakunin's brigand was infinitely more noble in his wickedness than the common run of humans with their petty virtues and vices. As with other products of his collaboration with Nechaev, that pamphlet was not signed, but the reference to Schiller gives his identity away.[48]

Herzen feared that this proclamation could cause terrible damage. Its aim was to induce such panic in the authorities that the universities and the printing presses would be closed down, thereby increasing the attraction of "Nechaevism" for the radical youth. In letters to Ogarev from Brussels in the autumn he attempts to dissuade him from his new alliance: "You and Bakunin are as far removed from *applicable truths* as were the first Christian monks." Not one iota of their program could be realized in the foreseeable future. "I foresee our cause advancing by a hundred different routes, in some places in drastic forms, in others more peacefully; but nowhere will it advance through 'the unleashing of evil passions' (a favorite image of Bakunin's), the cutting out of tongues, ambushes by brigands, drownings and executions. These are sinful dreams, too ancient and too infantile."[49]

In the same letter he cites a report in a radical paper of the proceedings in Basel of the third congress of the International Working Men's Association. Founded in 1864 at a workmen's meeting in St. Martin's Hall in London, its members included followers of Proudhon and Blanqui, English Owenites, Irish and Polish nationalists, republicans, and German socialists (the Marxists had not yet gained control over the organization). The congress had rejected all forms of terrorism and coercion as means to its goal. Herzen was wholly in agreement with its resolutions as reported: "a great step forward."[50]

Although Ogarev believed that Bakunin and Nechaev had gone too far in their latest proclamations, he was equally opposed to Herzen's rejection of an armed uprising as the first step toward a socialist transformation of Russia. Herzen began to compose an extended polemic against Bakunin's views. The resulting work, *Letters to an Old Comrade*, was completed a few months before his death.

The Final Testament

All Herzen's major political writings after *From the Other Shore* had echoed its insistence on the relevance of the natural sciences and evolutionary theory to an understanding of the historical process. On the eve of the Emancipation he had attempted to restrain the ideological doctrinairism of the next generation by insisting that progress in Russia, as elsewhere, would proceed not by the laws of abstract logic but by a complex process of embryology. To ignore aspects of a people's collective physiology that one might find unattractive—such as religious belief—was "to fall into the error of French revolutionary algebra, whose formulas did not apply to any one nation because they applied equally to Timbuktu and Greenland."[51] His *Letters* to Bakunin are his final printed words on the subject.[52]

The importance Herzen attached to this work is reflected in the lengthy and complex process of its composition, during which he submitted successive drafts to Ogarev for comment and discussion.[53] He begins with a quotation from Jeremy Bentham: "Motives alone, however sufficient they may be, cannot be effective without sufficiency of means."

The issue between him and his old comrade of 1848 was one not of ends but of means: evaluation of the "historical material" at hand. Upon witnessing the slaughter of 1848, he had shared Bakunin's thirst for bloody vengeance. But twenty years had since passed: "Neither you nor I have changed our beliefs, but we have come to approach the problem in different ways. You rush ahead as before with the passion for destruction, which you see as a creative passion . . . smashing down obstacles and respecting history only in the future. I have lost faith in the previous revolutionary paths and try to understand the people's pace in the past and present, so as to know how to keep pace with it, not falling behind and not rushing ahead into the distance where it will not, cannot, follow me." The slowness of the historical process with its aberrations and deviations was hard to bear, but the events of 1848 and 1863 had shown the folly of attempts to speed it up by the use of force alone. Mankind had been taught by Peter the Great and the French Convention to stride from the first month of pregnancy to the ninth by smashing indiscriminately all that lay in its path, a tradition continued in Bakunin's faith in the constructive nature of the urge for destruction. "Surely civilization through the whip, liberation through the guillotine are not the eternal necessity for every step forward?"

The bourgeois world could not be destroyed by gunpowder alone. When the smoke dispersed and the ruins were cleared, it would reappear in some form, for lack of an alternative sufficiently developed to take its place. The popular consciousness was the product of a long process of growth: to order people to surrender a belief was as futile as compelling them to believe.

In dealing with false beliefs, the criminological approach should cede to the methods of the physiologist. Property, the Church, and the State had had a positive effect on the past development of human societies—to call for their violent destruction was the equivalent of executing a marquis because he was not a Jacobin. In an allusion to the crude materialism of Chernyshevsky's followers, Herzen declares: "We betray the fundamental principles of our outlook when we condemn whole classes while simultaneously rejecting the responsibility of individuals." The new order should be not only an instrument of destruction but also a force for the preservation of all that was worth saving from the old. "Woe to the revolution, poor in spirit and meager in aesthetic substance, that will transform all that has been acquired in the past into a tedious workshop, whose sole advantage will consist in subsistence."

The transition to such an order would have to be gradual, a word that was anathema to Bakunin, but Herzen insists that, although debased by the dithering of some reformers, it is essential to any process of understanding. "Mathematics is imparted gradually; why should the latest conclusions of . . . sociology be injected like a vaccine, or poured into the brain as medicine is poured in one dose into the mouths of horses?" Between ultimate goals and the current state of society there existed practical compromises and diagonal paths: to grasp which of them was the shorter, the more feasible, or the more convenient, was the business of a revolutionary strategy whose beginnings Herzen perceives in the International.[54] He argues that structures that fetter individuals, albeit sometimes with their willing collusion, will not in the long run withstand the pressure of logic and the development of insight into the workings of society. Some of these might be dislodged with a simple kick, others had deep roots. To apply the same method to both would be to alienate the great majority, the strongest defenders of the oppressive traditions often being those who had most to lose from them: foolish perhaps, "but it's time we reckoned with stupidity as a formidable force." The strength of the existing order in Europe was entirely based on ignorance and irrationality. Thanks to the accession to power of Louis-Napoleon, they now knew what it was to misjudge the level of maturity of a nation. "When foisted on a people unprepared for it, universal suffrage served as a razor with which it nearly cut its own throat." Lack of development could not be overcome by force; great upheavals were not created through the unleashing of "evil passions." Terror did not destroy beliefs, it merely drove them underground: Christianity had emerged all the stronger from centuries of persecution.

He points in particular to the irony of Bakunin's calls to the young to quit the universities and turn their backs on science as the product of a privileged elite, in order to merge with the spontaneous force of the masses. Former students who like him continued to live in a world of abstractions were further removed from the people than the latter's sworn enemies: "The priest, the aristocrat, the policeman and the merchant, the landowner and the soldier, have more direct links with the masses than they do. This is why they regard it as possible to launch an economic revolution with a *tabula rasa*, reducing the whole field of history to ashes, not suspecting that this field, with its crops and its weeds, is the immediate ground of the people's existence, its entire moral life, all its customs and all its consolations. The people's conservatism is harder to combat than the conservatism of the throne and the pulpit." Herzen's sympathy extended also to things, "and to some things more than to some people":

> Along with the capital amassed by usurers, an uncontrolled revolutionary upheaval will destroy another form of capital, passed on from generation to generation and from nation to nation. Capital in which is accumulated the character and the creative work of various periods, in which there has been deposited the chronicle of human life and where history has crystallized. The raging force of destruction will obliterate, together with boundary marks, those *summits* of human endeavor people have striven to attain in all directions, from the beginning of civilization. It's sufficient that Christianity and Islam destroyed the ancient world, sufficient that the French Revolution punished statues, paintings, monuments: it's not for us to play at being iconoclasts.
>
> I felt this so acutely, standing with numb sadness and almost with shame in front of some custodian pointing at a bare wall, a shattered sculpture, and a sarcophagus cast to one side, repeating: "All this was destroyed during the Revolution."

The *Letters* were conceived as a final confession of faith, rather than the prelude to a fruitful exchange of views. Herzen quotes the response from Ogarev, a keen student of anatomy in the 1840s, to one of the drafts he had sent him for comment: "It's very hard to persuade a person of something on which that person has different views. There's a physiological process involved here. . . . The brain never processes anything arbitrarily, but always works out the result of the relationship between the impressions it has received. Hence, when the impressions of one individual differ from those of another to some degree, the further development of these impressions and the conclusion deduced from this . . . can differ from one person to the other to an extent that renders no agreement possible."

Sadly, Herzen reflects, Ogarev is right. One point, however, he holds to be self-evident: to counsel gradualness in the revolutionary milieu in which he and Bakunin moved required "if not more, then certainly not less courage and independence than to adopt the most extreme of extreme positions on all questions."

Herzen had foreseen his isolation in *From the Other Shore* and kept his resolve to be true to himself, neither surrendering his beliefs nor sinking into pessimism. In the wake of his family tragedies he had written to Maria Reichel, "I will remain to the end of my life the same revolutionary nature, *semper in motu*." This inner ferment, he predicts, will save him from despair in the midst of terrible events; in Goethe's words: "Ich hab' mein Sach auf nichts gestellt [in Herzen's meaning, "Nothing will make me lay down my task"]."[55]

Semper in motu was the motto engraved on Herzen's seal; he was true to it in the last months of his life when, in a determined effort to reinsert the *Bell*'s distinctive voice into the narrative of history, he made overtures to the men who had humiliated him. A publishing collaboration with Utin fell through when the latter again demanded that he surrender the Bakhmetev fund. According to V. F. Luginin, a young émigré who had formed a friendship with Herzen, he had begun further negotiations shortly before he died to resurrect the *Bell* there in collaboration with (among others) Alexander Serno-Solovevich.

He was to achieve a posthumous victory over Nechaev: shortly before his death he had expressed regret to Ogarev that the *Letters* had not been published. Ogarev considered that their publication would be untimely, and it might never have occurred at all if Tata had not received a threatening letter from the "Bureau of Foreign Agents of the Russian Revolutionary Society and the People's Revenge" (a.k.a. Nechaev) demanding that none of Herzen's last works be printed, as being detrimental to the revolutionary cause. Incensed by the letter's tone and content, Sasha Herzen declared it his sacred duty to print all his father's writings. *To an Old Comrade* appeared first in a collection published in the autumn of 1870.

* * *

Two days after his death, Herzen's coffin was carried to the Père Lachaise Cemetery in Paris, where it would stay until its transfer to Nice. There, he would join his wife and his two infant children in the family grave. Fearing that the journey to Père Lachaise could be used as a pretext for public unrest, the Paris police had misinformed the press as to its timing. Nonetheless, the coffin was followed by a mixed procession of about 500 people, including workers, women, and many of the French republicans of 1848. Pierre Malardier, a Montagnard in the Constituent Assembly of that year, threw the first bouquet onto the coffin, exclaiming loudly: "To the Voltaire of the nineteenth century!"

Jules Michelet was one of the first to pay tribute to Herzen. In a letter to the family on the day after their bereavement, he wrote that the oppressed populations of eastern Europe had lost their defender: "Yesterday there fell silent the voice of numerous millions of people."[56]

Epilogue

To deny false gods is necessary, but not sufficient: one must look beneath their masks for the reason for their existence.

HERZEN, *LETTER ON FREE WILL*

In his *Magna Instauratio* Francis Bacon spelled out clearly the dual difficulty faced by those who sought to change fundamental categories and modes of thought: "For that knowledge which is new and foreign from opinions received, is to be delivered in another form than that which is agreeable and familiar . . . for those whose conceits are seated in popular opinions, need only to prove or dispute: but those whose conceits are beyond popular opinions have a double labor; the one to make themselves conceived, and the other to prove and demonstrate." The second labor leads to something of a vicious circle: "This must be plainly avowed: no judgement can be rightly formed either of my method or of the discoveries to which it leads, by means of . . . the reasoning which is now in use; since I cannot be called on to abide by the sentence of a tribunal which is itself on its trial. Even to deliver and explain what I bring forward is no easy matter; for things in themselves new will yet be apprehended with reference to what is old."[1]

Two centuries after this complaint by the founder of modern science, Herzen was to be similarly frustrated in his efforts to convey the revolutionary significance of new discoveries in the natural sciences for the understanding of the nature and extent of human freedom. In his letters and essays he would often refer sardonically to the multiplicity of labels his contemporaries attached to his thought. All of these, he believed, bore witness to their profound incomprehension of his central message. His life had been devoted to the service of "two or three ideas," but these had proved too upsetting to received beliefs to be given sanctuary in the brains of the time. In his last years he reflected that he had been variously classified as a moderate, a socialist, a Jacobin, an anarchist, a bloodthirsty terrorist, and a timid gradualist. "What is most offensive of all is that people seem to understand you, to agree with you, and yet your thoughts remain foreign in their heads, without ever acquiring relevance to reality."[2] A single underlying cause was responsible: fear. There were two kinds of reason, he wrote: one the product of a dying world, the other of a world that was just emerging. But while many guessed at the truths revealed through the new reason, "none dares come straight out with them, so little have we yet succeeded in freeing our intellect and our tongues from the thrall of various paper dragons and outworn sacred relics."[3]

Herzen's two or three ideas have continued to elude commentators on his career. He is still commonly classified as a utopian socialist despite his prediction (well over a century before the fall of communism in Europe) that after developing "its own extremes and absurdities," socialism would in its turn have to give way to new needs and demands. His attack on teleological visions of history was aimed against the Left as much as the Right. A few months before his death he observed that socialism remained a religion, albeit one equipped with new icons— "but it may yet outgrow this stage."[4] His place in the history of ideas is not with the last of the socialist romantics but in the avant-garde of the very few thinkers who anticipated the significance of the Darwinian revolution for our understanding of history.

Evolutionary theory had already started to dismantle the boundaries between history and the natural world when Herzen began his studies at Moscow University, but it was only in 1871 that Darwin ventured to argue explicitly that man was not a wholly separate creation. Herzen's originality in singling out the role of chance in history thirty years before Darwin's explosive *Descent of Man* was itself the product of a concatenation of contingencies, beginning with the presence of his father's eccentric cousin in the family house. He was already committed to his studies in history and philosophy; without the interest in science aroused by the Chemist, he would doubtless have followed the intellectual elite of his generation to pursue those studies at Moscow University, where the natural sciences were then the habitual choice only of students destined for a career in government service. The professors of the Faculty of Physical and Mathematical Sciences, however, had come to be a remarkable and fully modern source of intellectual energy: echoing the debates of European anatomists over the relation of hypothesis to observation in the interpretation of data emerging from fossil beds, they kept abreast of the ideas that would develop into Darwin's theory of evolution, and which Herzen avidly absorbed from his principal mentors. When on his return from exile he embarked on the study of anatomy and physiology, he responded to his friends' incomprehension and derision by insisting that a background in the natural sciences was an essential precondition for the serious study of history: man was part of nature and subject to its laws.

Herzen's approach to history as a complex process of embryology was to make him particularly receptive to the discoveries that would culminate in the Darwinian revolution. Of the two sets of essays to which he attached particular importance, one was composed in the immediate wake of the publication of *On the Origin of Species,* and the other a full decade before it. *From the Other Shore* and the essay "Robert Owen" both focus on what continues to provoke opposition to Darwin's theories even now: destruction of the image of the self that had determined the forms of European civilization from the ancient Greeks through Christian theology to Enlightenment rationalism, a self grounded in a timeless reality, the source of universal ideals and norms. Herzen's views on the openness of time and the dominant role of chance in history and human life are all the more compelling because they were the products of a lifelong struggle against the attractions of an unquestioning faith in his country's future that could give a redeeming significance to his personal frustrations in the past and present. His insights into the psychology of radical messianism are rooted in his own continuing experience of the difficulty of coming to terms with the consequences of his acceptance of the transience of human lives and goals. In the European impasse of 1849, the proposition that in history "all is *ex tempore,* all is improvisation" had been a source of hope. But when Russia embarked on its hazardous course of reform, Herzen's writings took on an insistent note of urgency as he saw the fragile consensus in Russian society beginning to fall apart. "I see a chance at hand, I feel it, I touch it." If the fleeting opportunity were not grasped, it might never recur—hence his "passionate impatience": "'Time is money,' say the English. In reality, time is much, much more precious than money: *time is ourselves!*"[5]

* * *

The last of the polemics in which Herzen defended his view of freedom was with Sasha, whom he had groomed from adolescence as a natural scientist. During his university studies Sasha had been much influ-

Drawing from a research voyage toward North Cape, Jan Mayen, and Iceland organized by Karl Vogt, early 1860s. Vogt, in overcoat, is seated at the central table. Herzen's son Sasha stands behind him, holding an open book.

enced by Herzen's friend, the eminent physiologist Karl Vogt, whose unequivocally materialist approach to the human being had been a dominating influence on Chernyshevsky's generation. In the 1830s Herzen had described materialism as characterized in general by "a many-sided and precise knowledge of the parts, combined with total ignorance of the whole."[6] This view was reinforced in January 1867 when he began to attend a series of colloquia on the physiology of the nervous system organized by Moritz Schiff in Florence. Linked to Schiff's work in this area, the discussion flowed around the question of freedom of the will. Herzen reported to Ogarev that although Schiff's exceptional eloquence and logical powers had dispatched the notion of free will like a lamb to the slaughter, he was dissatisfied with the narrowness of the discussion on the subject. The question could not be resolved by remaining within the bounds of physiology.[7] Lacking the time to respond in print, he delegated the task to Ogarev, but was unimpressed with the result. "Neither you nor Schiff has addressed the entire complexity of the problem, especially in its historical incarnation." He was particularly irritated by the abstraction of Ogarev's language. Noting his fondness for the word "volition," he urges him to call it "practical reason, active reason, and explain its laws and relations in such a way that when, at this moment, I say that this action is wrong, I can know that I'm not talking nonsense."[8] In June of the following year his son sent him a paper on the subject he had published in Milan. He replied that its title "Sulla volontà" was inappropriate: it was a dissertation on the development of various physiological functions, among which Sasha Herzen had wrongly included the will, "interpersonal" phenomena and functions being primarily the province of history and sociology. In the last year of his life Herzen responded vigorously to another of Sasha's papers, in which, he maintained, Sasha had been insufficiently clear in his rejection of the role of Providence in the descent of man.[9]

Herzen's ideological opponents habitually misconstrued his demand that philosophy approach the problem of freedom as embodied in the particularity of historical events and personalities. The Slavophiles called him a materialist; but this, he had asserted in a polemic with Samarin, was a "scholastic label" that did not go to the heart of the matter.[10] What interested him, he explained to Ogarev in the course of his debate with Schiff, was not the antithesis between freedom and inevitability, but that margin "where each term of the antinomy passes over into the other: that is, where a conscious individual avails himself of his right to step forward with his left or right foot, although the action is performed according to the laws of physiological necessity."[11]

His last word on this subject became known only six years after his death, when it appeared in print under the heading "Lettre inédite de A. I. Herzen sur la volonté" in a French philosophical review, with a covering note from his son explaining that it had been written in response to his own paper of 1868 on the functioning of the nervous system.[12] In this "Lettre" Herzen observes that philosophy had alternately deified the will as Absolute Mind and denied its existence by reducing it to a conditioned reflex of matter, but had scarcely begun to approach freedom as human beings experience it: "a phenomenological necessity for the human intellect, a psychological reality."[13] He pays due tribute to the role of the biological sciences in dispelling the last illusions of primitive religious dualism, but argues that they went beyond their competence when they proceeded to declare the ego a hallucination and the notion of liberty a misconception. As a necessary premise of social existence, our sense of moral freedom is, at the very least, an anthropological reality. Human reason, passions, and memory are subject to the same laws of organic life as breathing and digestion, but they have an added dimension. Molded by historical and social existence into the faculty of choice, they have created a "moral milieu" with laws of its own, which are no less real for being unverifiable by scientific experiment. By methods of extreme generalization and simplification, consciousness may be reduced to a set of physiological first principles. But by so doing we lose the social dimension, in which individuals define themselves by the freedom to choose between particular options in particular sets of circumstances: "the phenomenalized differentiated, specific, detailed world——the one in which we live, and which is our sole reality."[14]

The fundamental problem of knowledge was not, as philosophers had commonly maintained, to break out of the vicious circle of freedom and necessity, but to comprehend it. The dualistic systems that had taught us to perceive the world as divided into subject and object, mind and matter, body and spirit, had ensured that we possessed neither the language nor the categories nor the words to discuss the nature of choice in the nexus of contingency and invariant laws. But that purpose could be served by aesthetic metaphor: Herzen expresses the relationship between physical determinism and moral freedom through the distinction between a sound in isolation—a physical phenomenon subject to the laws of acoustics—and a sound in a musical phrase, where "it acquires for us another value (or existence, if you like)." This aesthetic existence does not exempt it from the physical laws to which it is subject. The string may break, and the sound will disappear:

> But as long as the string remains unbroken, it belongs not just to the realm of vibrations, but also to the realm of *harmony* where it exists as an *aesthetic reality*, functioning in a symphony that allows it to resound, dominates it, absorbs it, to leave it behind in its wake.
>
> Human individuality in society is a conscious sound that resonates not only for others but also for itself. The product of physiological and historical necessity, the individual strives to affirm

himself between two voids: the void before birth and the void after death. Even as he develops according to the laws of the most fatal necessity, he constantly posits himself as free. This is a necessary condition for his activity, this is a psychological fact, a social fact. . . .

But what, you will ask, is the objective reality? . . . The thing in itself, the *an sich* of the Germans, is a *magnum ignotum*, like the Absolute, and final causes: What is the ultimate objective nature of time, the ultimate reality of space? I do not know, but I do know that these coordinates are essential to me, and that without them I shall sink into the darkness of a chaos without measure or end.[15]

Here is the abyss that can be glimpsed behind the notion of history's play with which Herzen teased the Russian liberals. The fleeting and precarious present is our sole domain and our only source of meaning. Herzen's philosophy of existence is built on what, half a century later, John Dewey would describe as the new logic epitomized by Darwin's scientific method. This logic "outlaws, flanks, dismisses—what you will—one type of problem and substitutes for it another type."[16] As at many other turning points in the history of ideas, the old problems were not solved; the new movements merely abandoned them, setting aside inquiries about remote causes and eventual goals as ultimately futile and not of urgent concern.

The shift in philosophical priorities to which Dewey refers is strikingly reflected in Darwin's responses to those who pressed him after the appearance of *On the Origin of Species* for an opinion on the origin and purpose of being. In the last two decades of his life, he remained "in the same sort of muddle . . . as all the world seems to be in with respect to free will"; but defining his position on such matters became increasingly unimportant to him. He conscientiously rehearses the arguments for and against the existence of an intelligent First Cause, but admits that his opinions on the subject are vague and denies that his theories have any relevance to it. "Science has nothing to do with Christ, except insofar as the habit of scientific research makes a man cautious about admitting evidence." Its methods were not conducive to belief in revelation and miracles. On questions such as that of life after death, "every man must judge for himself, between conflicting vague probabilities." Issues of this sort were "beyond the human intellect, like 'predestination and free will' or 'the origin of evil.'" Darwin asserts that he cannot pretend to throw the least light on such abstruse problems: "I for one must be content to remain an Agnostic." In what appears to have been his final word on the matter, he wrote, "The safest conclusion seems to me that the whole subject is beyond the scope of man's intellect, but man can do his duty."[17]

Such, too, was Herzen's position in the "Lettre." Unlike the materialists, he acknowledged the world to be ultimately unknowable by science; but unlike idealists (and anticipating Ludwig Wittgenstein), he concluded that on that of which we cannot speak we had best be silent: what we know of our moral nature derives solely from our experience of action and choice within the nexus of contingent circumstances that is "our sole reality."[18]

Darwin admitted that science did not yet understand the causes of each evolutionary change. He relegated such insoluble problems to a "black box"—his version of Bacon's *magnum ignotum*, the notion that had driven Herzen's approach to knowledge as a student and become his battle cry against the dominant ideologies of his time.[19] "Now there's an honest thinker," he wrote to Sasha in 1859, "whereas others, as soon as they come up against something they can't solve, invent a new force, such as a soul."[20]

The first of these great scientific revolutionaries had inspired Herzen with an approach to humans' place in nature that would be validated by the discoveries of the second. He stands alone among the thinkers of his century in his grasp of the consequences of evolutionary thought in transforming our understanding of history and freedom; but no less impressive was his determination to embody his conclusions in his own personal and political life. He rejected the utopias of the system builders of his century, without falling into the philosophical pessimism with which his thought is often confused: in a passage in his memoirs he presents the pessimism of his time as a muddled transitional stage in the process of shedding foundationalist notions of ultimate purpose. "It grieves us to realize that the Idea is impotent, that truth has no binding power over the real world. A new kind of Manichaeism takes hold of us, and we are ready, *par dépit,* to believe in rational (that is, purposive) evil, as we believed in rational good —the last tribute we pay to idealism."[21]

He had expressed deep regret to Ogarev that he had not sought to publish *To an Old Comrade* immediately after writing it. Only literature had the luxury of biding its time—"a new thought or point of view

Herzen lives! 1905 family group assembled around its patriarch Sasha Herzen.

should be published at once, or another will take its place tomorrow."[22] He was wrong in this case. The work can now be seen as a uniquely prescient indictment of the political messianism that attained its evil maturity only in the next century and marked that century for all time with its imprint. Writing in a period when the full horrors of Stalinism had become known in the West, Isaiah Berlin called attention to Herzen's remarkable early perception of the dangers to humanity from the pursuit and the pursuers of ideologies: an outstanding demonstration of "one of the elements of [Herzen's] political genius . . . a sensibility to characteristics and processes in society while they [were] still in embryo and invisible to the naked eye."[23] Half a century later, when the system that brought Stalin to power had vanished into the past, a Russian scholar pronounced *To an Old Comrade* to be part of the treasure house of the philosophical thought of humanity: "a kind of Historical Testament."[24]

No more fitting tribute can be paid to Herzen's life and work than Berlin's observation that in an age when thought was dominated by system builders of every political and religious persuasion, "Herzen retained his incorruptible sense of reality."[25]

You've got my philosophy of history wrong. It's not a systematic science but an indictment, a scourge to use on absurd theories and absurd liberal specialists in rhetoric; a fermenting agent, and nothing more. But it holds people's attention and draws them into life, it angers them and makes them think . . .

HERZEN TO HIS MOSCOW CIRCLE, JUNE 1851

Notes

ABBREVIATIONS

FOS   A. I. Herzen, *From the Other Shore*, trans. M. Budberg (London, 1956).

PSS-L   *A. I. Gertsen: Polnoe sobranie sochinenii i pisem*, ed. M. K. Lemke (Peterburg, 1915–Moscow, 1925). Early postrevolutionary-period edition of works of Herzen prepared by M. K. Lemke.

SS   A. I. Herzen, *Sobranie sochinenii v tridtsati tomakh* (Moscow, 1954–1966). Thirty-volume Soviet-period edition of the collected works of Herzen.

T-P   I. S. Turgenev, *Pis'ma* (Moscow, 1966–1968). Collected edition of letters.

DATES

The dates of letters from and to Herzen before his departure from Russia in 1847 follow the Julian calendar in use in Russia, twelve days behind the Gregorian calendar in use in the West. Otherwise the dates refer to the Gregorian calendar. Where there is any ambiguity or where the Soviet edition of the Herzen collected works shows both dates, both dates are given here.

I. WHO WAS HERZEN?

1. Nietzsche to Malwida von Meysenbug, in *Friedrich Nietzsche: Briefe der Basler Zeit, 1869–1873*, ed. W. Hoppe (Munich, 1940), 284; Tolstoy cited in Susanna Abramovna Rozanova, *Tolstoi i Gertsen* (Moscow, 1972), 63.

2. See *A. I. Gertsen: Polnoe sobranie sochinenii i pisem*, ed. M. K. Lemke (Moscow, 1923), 21:562. See also Michelet, *Oeuvres complètes*, ed. P. Viallaneix (Paris, 1987), 20:698: "Où reverrai-je jamais un coeur plus ardent qu'Herzen. . . . Quel brillant esprit, quelle lumière rayonnait autour de lui."

3. See W. Weidemaier, "Herzen and the Existential World View," *Slavic Review* 40 (1981): 557–569.

4. V. I. Lenin, *Collected Works*, 4th ed., trans. S. Apresyan, ed. C. Dutt (Moscow, 1963), 18:31.

5. *Voprosy filosofii*, no.12 (2010): 68–104.

6. A. A. Guseinov, "Slovo o Gertsene," in *Aleksandr Ivanovich Gertsen i istoricheskie sudby Rossii: Materialy mezhdunarodnoi nauchnoi konferentsii k 200-letiu A. I. Gertsena* (Moscow, 2013), 3.

7. A. V. Pavlov, "Zabvenie i aktualnost Aleksandra Gertsena segodnia," in *Aleksandr Ivanovich Gertsen*, 264–273; and M. N. Arkhipova, "Khudozhestvennii obraz A. I. Gertsena v piesy T. Stoppards 'Bereg Utopiia,'" in *Aleksandr Ivanovich Gertsen*, 296–299. See my essay on Berlin's affinities with Herzen: "A Revolutionary without Fanaticism," in M. Lilla, R. Dworkin, and R. Silvers, *The Legacy of Isaiah Berlin* (New York, 2001), 3–30.

8. A. I. Volodin, "Ob istoriosofii Gertsena: (Po stat'e Robert Owen)," *Voprosy filosofii*, no. 9 (1996): 82–89. On evidence such as this paper, Volodin has been the most interesting and original post-Soviet Russian scholar of Herzen. He signaled his awareness of the importance of science to Herzen even during the Soviet period—e.g., in "A. I. Gertsen o razvitii nauki," in *Uchenie o nauke i ee razvitii*, ed. N. I. Rodnyi, Yu. I. Slov'ev, and B. S. Griazov (Moscow, 1971), 159–193—but circumspectly enough to avert any suspicion that his picture of Herzen might differ in any significant respect from Lenin's. Regrettably, he made no contribution to the proceedings of the 2012 conference; apparently he died in 2004.

9. One exception is the contribution by I. N. Sizemskaya ("A. I. Gertsen o 'rastryopannoi improvizatsii istorii,'" in *Aleksandr Ivanovich Gertsen*, 147–154). An interesting sign of the post-Soviet development in Russian scholarship on Herzen, it discusses his view of the "tattered improvisation of history" as expressed in his major works. Subsequently published as "A. I. Gertsen: Istoriosofskie idei i predosterezheniia potomkam," *Filosofskie nauki* 2 (2013): 57–67.

10. See his two essays on Herzen in his book *Russian Thinkers* (London, 1978). The quotation is from L. N. Tolstoy, *Perepiska s russkimi pisateliami* (Moscow, 1978), 2:135.

11. Martin Malia, *Alexander Herzen and the Birth of Russian Socialism, 1812–1855* (Cambridge, MA, 1961), 382. Malia defines Herzen's morality as "absolute egoism. . . . In contemporary thought there was no individualism so extreme except the very similar egoism of Max Stirner" (277). Malia's study stops short of the last fifteen years of Herzen's life—his most productive as a writer and political activist.

12. See E. Acton, *Alexander Herzen and the Role of the Intellectual Revolutionary* (Cambridge, 1979), 27n5, on the distortion involved in Malia's picture of Herzen. Acton concludes his own study with an account of Herzen facing an impasse through his "failure to grasp the nettle of revolution" (177).

13. D. Offord, "Alexander Herzen," in *A History of Russian Philosophy, 1830–1930*, ed. G. M. Hamburg and R. A. Poole (Cambridge, 2010), 52–68; *A Herzen Reader*, ed. and trans. with an introduction by K. Parthé, with a critical essay by R. Harris (Evanston, 2012), 361. The latter book is essentially a collection of translations of passages from Herzen's journalism in *Kolokol (The Bell)* not otherwise available in English.

14. Malia devotes the first five chapters of his biography to this theme.

15. A. Vucinich, *Science in Russian Culture: A History to 1860* (London, 1963), vii. This work includes a brief account of Herzen's views on science.

16. I. Berlin, introduction to Herzen's *From the Other Shore*, trans. M. Budberg; and Herzen, *The Russian People and Socialism: An Open Letter to Jules Michelet*, trans. R. Wollheim (London, 1956), xxii.

2. RUSSIA AND THE ROMANTIC REVOLUTION

1. A. I. Herzen, *Sobranie sochinenii v tridtsati tomakh* (Moscow, 1954–1966) (hereafter cited as *SS*), 14:157.

2. See the chapter "The Expressivist Turn" in C. Taylor, *Sources of the Self: The Making of the Modern Identity* (Cambridge, 1989), 368–390.

3. H. Heine, *Deutschland: Ein Wintermärchen* (Hamburg,1844).

4. F. C. Beiser, *Enlightenment, Revolution, and Romanticism* (Cambridge, MA, 1992), 8.

5. Martin Malia, *Alexander Herzen and the Birth of Russian Socialism, 1812–1855* (Cambridge, MA, 1961), 84.

6. L. G. Leighton, *Russian Romanticism: Two Essays* (The Hague, 1975), 36.

7. Cited in A. Koyré, *La philosophie et le problème national en Russie au début du XIXe siècle* (Paris, 1928), 49.

8. Malia, *Alexander Herzen*, 71.

9. Koyré, *La philosophie*, 49.

10. N. Riasanovsky, *A Parting of Ways: Government and the Educated Public in Russia, 1801–1855* (Oxford, 1976), 150.

11. Cited in Leighton, *Russian Romanticism*, 89.

12. I. V. Kireevsky, "O kharaktere prosveshcheniia Evropy i o ego otnoshenii k prosvescheniiu Rossii," *Sochineniia*, vol. 1 (Moscow, 1911), 174–222.

13. I. Berlin, *Russian Thinkers* (London, 1978), 120.

14. Letter to Botkin, 13 June 1840, V. G. Belinsky, *Polnoe sobranie sochinenii*, vol. 11 (Moscow, 1956), 527.

3. A ROMANTIC YOUTH

1. Prior to Herzen's departure from Russia in 1847, dates of letters from there will be given according to the "old style" or Julian calendar, in the nineteenth century twelve days behind the Western calendar. After his move to Europe, they will be given according to the "new style," or Gregorian calendar.

2. This hypothesis is advanced widely and plausibly, by Martin Malia and several other authors. As far as can be discovered to date, Herzen himself offered no explanation for the choice of his surname.

3. Yegor was brought up in the Yakovlev household and shared Herzen's surname, but he was ignored by his father, who reserved all his affection for his younger son. Yegor entered government service, and after Ivan Yakovlev's death in 1846 took on the responsibility for dealing with his estate and the regular transfer of money abroad to Herzen and his mother. There is no mention of Yegor in the chapter of Herzen's memoirs dealing with his childhood. In a footnote he writes that although he felt great affection for his half brother, Yegor's withdrawn character and chronic ill health prevented any close relationship between them. Some extracts from Yegor's letters to Herzen, his wife, and their close friends are contained in *Literaturnoe nasledstvo*, vol. 63: *Gertsen i Ogarev III* (Moscow, 1956), 416–429.

4. *SS*, 8:21.

5. Ibid., 22.

6. Ibid., 86.

7. Ibid., 87.

8. T. P. Passek, *Iz dal'nikh let: Vospominaniia*, vol. 1 (Moscow, 1963), 147.

9. Ibid., 183.

10. *SS*, 21:234, 22:190.

11. Ibid., 8:61.

12. Letter of 22 February 1854 to the editor of *L'Homme*, *SS*, 30:502.

13. *SS*, 1:277.

14. Ibid., 278.

15. Passek, *Vospominania*, 261.

16. *SS*, 1:270.

17. "Moia ispoved," in *Literaturnoe nasledstvo*, vol. 61: *Gertsen i Ogarev I* (Moscow 1953), 686, 687.

18. *SS*, 8:78, 79.

19. "Moia ispoved," 696.

20. *SS*, 1:329.

21. "Moia ispoved," 692.

22. *SS*, 8:80.

23. Ibid., 84.

24. See note 14 of M. Nechkina to "Ispoved," *Gertsen i Ogarev I*, 672. She concludes that the most likely date would have been in February 1826.

25. *SS*, 8:81.

26. Martin Malia, *Alexander Herzen and the Birth of Russian Socialism, 1812–1855* (Cambridge, MA, 1961), 52.

27. *SS*, 8:112.

4. A REVOLUTION IN SCIENCE

1. L. Ginzburg, *O psikhologicheskoi proze* (Leningrad, 1971), 255.

2. *SS*, 8:117, 123.

3. Ibid., 9:16–17.

4. Martin Malia, *Alexander Herzen and the Birth of Russian Socialism, 1812–1855* (Cambridge, MA, 1961), 69, 91. In the preface to the first volume of his pioneering history of the formative years of Russian science, Alexander Vucinich observes: "Political history, social and religious thought, the arts, and most of the other dimensions of Russian thought have been dealt with rather extensively in Western historical literature, but science as a component of Russian culture has been almost completely ignored." Vucinich, *Science in Russian Culture: A History to 1860* (London, 1963), vii. The situation has not changed significantly in the half-century since the publication of Vucinich's book.

5. *SS*, 21:12.

6. E. Mayr, *The Growth of Biological Thought: Diversity, Evolution and Inheritance* (Cambridge, MA, 1982), 309–312.

7. According to the philosopher A. N. Whitehead, "the safest general characterisation of the Enlightenment philosophy is that it consisted of a series of footnotes to Plato." Whitehead, *Process and Reality, an Essay in Cosmology* (1929), pt. 2, chap. 1, sec. 1.

8. Mayr, *Growth of Biological Thought*, 99.

9. See Berlin's essay on Montesquieu in *Against the Current: Essays in the History of Ideas* (London, 1979), 130–161.

10. Cited in J. C. Greene, *The Death of Adam: Evolution and Its Impact on Western Thought* (Ames, IA, 1959), 132.

11. Buffon, "Initial Discourse: On the Manner of Studying and Expounding Natural History," in *From Natural History to the History of Nature: Readings from Buffon and His Critics*, ed. J. Lyon and P. R. Sloan, trans. J. Lyon (Notre Dame, IN, 1981),101.

12. See Mayr, *Growth of Biological Thought*, 39. Listing Buffon's contributions to natural science and evolutionism, Mayr concludes: "Except for Aristotle and Darwin, there has been no other student of organisms who has had as far-reaching an influence" (337). For the opinion due to Kant, see his *Gesammelte Schriften*, vol. 4 (Berlin, 1902), 470.

13. Buffon, "Initial Discourse," 126; Georges-Louis Leclerc, Comte de Buffon, *Natural History: General and Particular*, trans. W. Smellie, 3rd ed., vol. 7 (London, 1791), 98.

14. Mayr argues that there is no contradiction between these two statements (*Growth of Biological Thought*, 335). On Buffon's positive contributions to evolutionism, see Buffon, "Initial Discourse," 336–337.

15. S. Toulmin and J. Goodfield, *The Discovery of Time* (London, 1965).

16. Buffon, "Initial Discourse," 121, 123.

17. Buffon, *Natural History*, 1:34; Buffon, "Initial Discourse," 106; Montesquieu, *De l'esprit des lois*, ed. R. Derathé (Paris, 1973), 1:5, 2:429.

18. Buffon, "Initial Discourse," 121–122.

19. According to P. J. Bowler, "Certainly he was no Christian, nor even a very typical deist." Bowler, *Evolution: The History of an Idea* (Berkeley, CA, 1984), 68. Jacques Roger describes him as a "sceptical materialist," citing his comment in 1749 that "in physics one must avoid as far as possible having recourse to causes outside nature" to show that the role of the cosmogonic hypothesis, which he first proposed in that year, "avowedly is to replace the direct creation by God." G. S. Rousseau and R. Porter, eds., *The Ferment of Knowledge: Studies in the Historiography of Eighteenth-Century Science* (Cambridge, 1980), 279, 280. Ernst Mayr notes that "the wording of the first three volumes of the *Histoire naturelle* [1749] indicates that at that time he might have been an atheist. In 1764, he uses the language of a deist." Mayr speculates that in later life Buffon began to believe that the order in Nature needed a lawgiver responsible for the second causes. However, he also suggests: "It is probable that at least some of Buffon's observations were phrased in such a manner as to placate the theologians." Mayr, *Growth of Biological Thought*, 332, 331.

20. Vucinich, *Science in Russian Culture*, 174.

21. Ibid.,183.

22. The University of Dorpat, opened by Alexander I in 1802, had been founded by his predecessor, Paul. On its complex history after its initial foundation as a Swedish university in 1632, see *History of Tartu University, 1632–1982*, ed. K. Siilivask (Tallinn, 1985); see also Vucinich, *Science in Russian Culture*, 190n and chap. 5 on the development of science in Russian universities under Alexander.

23. Cited in *Science in Russian Culture*, 247, 248.
24. *SS*, 8:107.
25. Ibid.,120.
26. N. I. Pirogov, *Sochineniia*, vol. 3 (Kiev, 1910), 375. Cited by Vucinich, *Science in Russian Culture*, 238.
27. Vucinich, *Science in Russian Culture*, 208–210.
28. G. Himmelfarb, *Darwin and the Darwinian Revolution* (New York, 1968), 38, 40.

5. SCIENCE AND HISTORY

1. See the chapter on eighteenth-century science in D. Outram, *The Enlightenment* (Cambridge, MA, 1995); and J. Roger, "The Living World," in *The Ferment of Knowledge: Studies in the Historiography of Eighteenth-Century Science*, ed. G. S. Rousseau and R. Porter (Cambridge, 1980), 255–283.
2. Cuvier, *Leçons d'anatomie comparée*, vol. 1 (1800), iv. Cited in W. Burkhardt, *The Spirit of System: Lamarck and Evolutionary Biology* (Cambridge, MA, 1977), 46.
3. On Herder's pluralism, see I. Berlin, *Three Critics of the Enlightenment: Vico, Hamann, Herder* (Princeton, 2000), 231–239. On Buffon's influence on Herder, see Max Rouche, *La philosophie de l'histoire de Herder* (Paris, 1940), esp. 207.
4. See Ernst Mayr, *The Growth of Biological Thought: Diversity, Evolution and Inheritance* (Cambridge, MA, 1982), 338.
5. S. Toulmin and J. Goodfield, *The Discovery of Time* (London, 1965), 137.
6. On the influence of religion on Herder's scientific ideas, see H. B. Nisbet, *Herder and the Philosophy and History of Science* (Cambridge, 1970), 293–300. But see also Isaiah Berlin's contention that despite the tension between Herder's naturalism and his teleology, his view of history as a single progressive ascent "remains a vague conception; his skill and imagination, even in the *Ideen*, go into the evocation of the individual cultures and not of the alleged links between them. The whole thrust of the argument . . . is to show and celebrate the uniqueness, the individuality and, above all, the incommensurability with one another of each of the civilizations which he so lovingly describes and defends." *Three Critics*, 234.
7. Mayr, *Growth of Biological Thought*, 387.
8. The name was proposed independently by three scientists, including Lamarck. See Mayr, *Growth of Biological Thought*, 108.
9. Cited in T. A. Appel, *The Cuvier-Geoffroy Debate: French Biology in the Decades before Darwin* (Oxford, 1987), 152, and see chaps. 6 and 7 for a detailed account of the debate and its ramifications.
10. Cuvier, *Histoire naturelle des poissons*, vol. 1 (Paris, 1828), 406.
11. Mayr, *Growth of Biological Thought*, 310, 501. See also Mayr, "The Nature of the Darwinian Revolution," *Science* 176 (1972): 981–989.
12. Roger, "The Living World," 283.
13. A. O. Lovejoy, *The Great Chain of Being: A Study of the History of an Idea* (New York, 1965), 184.

14. Cuvier, "Preliminary Discourse," in *Georges Cuvier, Fossil Bones and Geological Catastrophes*, ed. and trans. M. J. S. Rudwick (Chicago, 1997), 183.

15. W. Coleman, *Georges Cuvier, Zoologist: A Study in the History of Evolution Theory* (Cambridge, MA, 1964), 171, 160–161. In his chapter on Cuvier's attitude to evolution, Coleman notes that Cuvier "seems to have been constitutionally unable to support or to appreciate the basic idea of change" (174).

16. Ibid., 154. Ernst Mayr remarks: "A concept of evolution was quite incompatible with Cuvier's concept of the harmonious construction of each organism. Each species had been created by divine will, and each was assigned from the beginning its special place in the economy of nature from which it could not depart. Fish, for example, were designed for an aqueous environment: 'This is their place in the creation. They will remain there until the destruction of the present order of things' ([Cuvier], *Histoire naturelle des poissons*, 1:543)." *Growth of Biological Thought*, 366–367.

17. Cuvier, "Nature," in *Dictionnaire des sciences naturelles*, vol. 34 (Strasbourg-Paris, 1825), 265. Cited in Coleman, *Georges Cuvier, Zoologist*, 154. Coleman sums up how Cuvier reconciled his deism with his emphasis on diversity: "Cuvier's physical world . . . was a machine, proceeding harmoniously under direction of the Creator's laws. Cuvier believed that the Creator, always immanent in nature and an omnipotent, wise, and good being, had promulgated these laws, probably at the moment of creation, and that since the origin of the world He had only rarely acted on, or through, the intermediation of physical events. Nevertheless, the laws of nature. however simple they were assumed to be, did not compel nature herself to be simple. Quite to the contrary, Cuvier held that complexity and profusion of form were equally a part of nature." Ibid., 29.

18. J. C. Greene, *The Death of Adam: Evolution and Its Impact on Western Thought* (Ames, IA, 1959), 173.

19. P. Bowler, *Evolution: The History of an Idea* (Berkeley, CA, 1984), 105.

20. Appel, *The Cuvier-Geoffroy Debate*, 67–68. He notes, "Authors of controversial theories found it difficult to obtain a hearing among serious scientists in nineteenth-century France. In England a Robert Chambers could pen a speculative theory of evolution and have it reviewed (albeit viciously) in the major journals by the best-known scientists of the day."

21. See L. J. Jordanova, *Lamarck* (Oxford, 1984), 45.

22. On the relation of Lamarck's and Darwin's theories, see Mayr, *Growth of Biological Thought*, 358–361. Mayr takes issue with the tendency of biological historians to mention Lamarck only for his erroneous ideas, ignoring his pioneering stress on behavior, the environment, and adaptation; although they differed fundamentally on the mechanism of evolution, Lamarck was clearly a forerunner of Darwin in being the first to adopt a consistent theory of genuine evolutionary change, as opposed to notions of the development of the immanent potentialities of essences. "It is time he receives credit for his major intellectual contributions: his genuine evolutionism which derived even the most complex organisms from infusorian or wormlike ancestors, his unflagging uniformitarianism, his

stress of the great age of the earth, his emphasis on the gradualness of evolution, his recognition of the importance of environment, and his courage to include man in the evolutionary stream" (359).

23. Describing as "startlingly modern" Lamarck's description in *Zoologie* of the pathway by which our anthropoid ancestor became humanized, Mayr comments: "Lamarck here presented his view on the origin of man with far more courage than Darwin fifty years later in the *Origin*" (*Growth of Biological Thought*, 352).

24. On the occasional confusing presence of teleological arguments in Lamarck's work, see Greene, *The Death of Adam*, 164–166.

6. AN EDUCATION IN METHOD

1. A. P. Shchapov, *Sochineniia*, vol. 3 (Saint Petersburg, 1906–1908), 187. Cited in Alexander Vucinich, *Science in Russian Culture: A History to 1860* (London, 1963), 249.

2. T. Passek, *Vospominaniia*, vol. 1, 328. Vucinich writes that from the 1830s, in biology "Russian scholars kept pace with the fast growing body of fact and theory, subsequently coordinated and codified by Darwin into the grand idea of evolution. . . . The universities had a whole array of professors who can justly be numbered among Darwin's forerunners; the best-known and most productive of these were Yu. E. Dyadkovsky, G. E. Shchurovskii, and K. F. Rouillier." *Science in Russian Culture*, 335.

3. Vucinich observes that "none of these philosophical orientations showed much consistency or elaboration." *Science in Russian Culture*, 210.

4. *SS*, 8:120. Vucinich lists him among those foreign scholars in Russian universities who were recognized names in the European learned literature: *Science in Russian Culture*, 208. Herzen's course in his first year encompassed botany, physics, chemistry, analytical geometry, and zoology. See V. N. Guryanov, "A. I. Gertsen—student fiziko-maticheskogo fakulteta Moskovskogo universiteta," *Trudy instituta istorii estestvennogo znaniia AN SSSr*, vol. 5 (Moscow, 1953), 380.

5. *SS*, 9:226.

6. E.g., "a Moscow University professor who during the first decades of the nineteenth century was one of the chief propagators of Schellingian philosophy in Russia" (G. M. Hamburg, *Boris Chicherin and Early Russian Liberalism, 1828–1866* [Stanford, CA, 1992], 23). A. Walicki gives him a passing mention along with D. M. Vellansky as "two Russian Schellingians" who acted as mentors of the secret society of the "Wisdom Lovers," representatives of philosophical Romanticism in the 1820s and 30s (Walicki, *A History of Russian Thought from the Enlightenment to Marxism*, trans. H. Andrews-Rusiecka [Stanford, CA, 1979], 76). In contrast, A. Koyré remarks on the curious fact that although it is held to be a universally accepted truth that Schelling's philosophy was the major— if not the only—influence on Russian thought of the 1820s, a close examination of the thought of any of the commonly recognized purveyors of this influence will reveal that none of them can be properly called a Schellingian (Koyré, *La philosophie et le problème national en Russie au*

début du XIXe siècle [Paris, 1976], 128–129). Vucinich contends that Pavlov's speculations on the relation of philosophy to science "drifted away from Schellingian metaphysics into the new regions of a philosophy of science" (*Science in Russian Culture*, 284).

7. Koyré cites the example of the medical scientist Vellansky as typical of those who called themselves disciples of Schelling, Oken, or the *Naturphilosophie* in general. "Vellanski avait repris quelques formules 'philosophiques,' telles que l'identité entre le sujet et l'objet, l'indifférence, etc. Mais, au fond, une philosophie de la nature n'avait pour eux tous qu'un seul sens: c'était l'affirmation de l'unité de la nature, de la vie universelle, d'un Univers-Organisme. . . . C'etait une métaphysique très vaste et très vague, . . . un organicisme dans lequel se confondaient en une demi-obscurité des idées venant de Schelling avec celles qui provenaient de Paracelse, de Bruno ou de Herder. Le vague, voilà le trait le plus caractéristique . . . de cette philosophie qui se plaisait aux 'correspondances' et abusait des analogies." *La philosophie*, 138–139.

8. V. Odoevsky, "Vospominaniia," *Russkii arkhiv*, no. 1 (1874): 316–318. Cited in Koyré, *La philosophie*, 49–50.

9. V. Rozanov, "Vospominaniia o D. Vellanskom," *Russkii vestnik* 11 (1867): 126. Cited in Koyré, *La philosophie*, 178.

10. "O vzaimnom otnoshenii svedenii umozritelnikh a opytnikh," *Atenei*, no. 1 (1828): 3–15, and no. 2 (1828): 1–19: see G. S. Vasetsky and S. R. Mikulinsky, eds., *Izbrannye proizvedeniia russkikh estestvoispytatelei pervoi poloviny XIX veka* (Moscow, 1959), 89.

11. "Otvet na vozrazheniia 'Moskovskogo Telegrafa,'" *Atenei*, no. 11 (1828): 333–356, and Vasetsky and Mikulinsky, *Izbrannye*, 595.

12. "O vzaimnom otnoshenii," 97.

13. Ibid.

14. Victor Cousin, *Cours de l'histoire de la philosophie moderne* (Paris, 1847), 289.

15. *SS*, 8:122–123. He mentions only one other professor by name in this connection: the historian M. T. Kachenovsky, who was censured by the guardians of official nationalism for questioning the authenticity of some of the ancient Russian chronicles.

16. As Koyré points out, in one aspect of his thought he can be seen as a true disciple of the *Naturphilosophie:* he approached physics as a study of the dynamic forces of Nature as being the source of phenomena, hence his opposition to the use of mathematical methods in physics, which he saw as an attempt to introduce a mechanistic and materialist approach. *La philosophie*, 179.

17. Herzen writes that Pavlov's great value lay in the "unusual clarity" of his philosophical exposition. "The young philosophers, on the contrary, adopted some kind of conventional language; they did not translate philosophical terms into Russian, but transferred them whole, even, to make things easier, leaving all the Latin words *in crudo*, giving them orthodox endings and the seven Russian cases . . . carried away by the spirit of the time, I myself wrote in exactly the same way, and was actually surprised

NOTES TO PAGES 74–80

when Perevoshchikov, the well-known astronomer, described this language as the 'twittering of birds.' No one in those days would have disavowed a phrase like this: 'The concretion of abstract ideas in the sphere of plastics represents that phase of the self-seeking spirit in which, defining itself for itself, it actualizes its potential in passing from natural immanence into the harmonious sphere of figurative consciousness in beauty." *SS*, 9:19.

18. Cited in Vasetsky and Mikulinsky, *Izbrannye*, 593. On Rouillier, see Chapter 10.

19. Letter to Ogarev, 5 July 1833, *SS*, 21:18.

20. See Raoul Labry, *Alexandre Ivanovich Herzen, 1812–1870: Essai sur la formation et le développement de ses idées* (Paris, 1928), 100; Martin Malia, *Alexander Herzen and the Birth of Russian Socialism, 1812–1855* (Cambridge, MA, 1961), 71, 72. The misreading of Maximovich's position, due presumably to use of secondary sources rather than Maximovich's own extensive publications, appears also in some unexpected places—e.g., G. Luckyj, *Panteleimon Kulish* (Boulder, CO, 1983), 11, and (perhaps less unexpectedly) the *Great Soviet Encyclopedia*.

21. Review in *Moscow Telegraph*, no. 8 (1826), cited in S. R. Mikulinsky, "M. A. Maksimovich kak estestvoispytatel'," *Trudy instituta istorii estestvoznaniya*, vol. 5 (Moscow, 1953), 198.

22. Cited in Mikulinsky, "M. A. Maksimovich," 198.

23. Ibid., 199.

24. See ibid., 199–200.

25. Review in *Telescope*, no. 5 (1831); see Mikulinsky, "M. A. Maksimovich," 199.

26. Cited in Mikulinsky, "M. A. Maksimovich," 207.

27. Ibid., 206.

28. "O sisteme rastitelnogo tsarstva," published in Dvigubsky's journal. Mikulinsky, "M. A. Maksimovich," 205.

29. Mikulinsky, "M. A. Maksimovich," 209. On Shchurovsky, a geologist with a background in zoology and paleontology who established the subject at Moscow University and was an opponent of Oken's vitalistic biology, see Vucinich, *Science in Russian Culture*, 335, 346.

30. "M. A. Maksimovich," in Vasetsky and Mikulinsky, *Izbrannye*, 597.

31. "O russkom prosveshchenii," cited in Mikulinsky, "M. A. Maksimovich," 210.

32. "M. A. Maksimovich," in Vasetsky and Mikulinsky, *Izbrannye*, 596.

33. Letter of 11 February 1832 to N. I. Astrakov, *SS*, 21:7–8.

34. *SS*, 8:113.

35. Malia, *Alexander Herzen*, 88–89. Malia presents Herzen as having subsequently fallen "completely under the influence of the *Naturphilosophie*" in his years at Moscow University: "Everything he wrote at university is thoroughly in the spirit of Schelling" (90).

36. *SS*, 8:112.

37. Ibid.

38. Cuvier, "Preliminary Discourse," in *Georges Cuvier, Fossil Bones and Geological Catastrophes*, ed. and trans. M. J. S. Rudwick (Chicago, 1997), 183.

39. *SS*, 1:525.

40. Ibid., 1:19–20. See the variant at 461.

41. Ibid., 20, 24, 22, 24.

42. Ibid., 24, 20–21.

43. Ibid., 38, 51.

44. Letter of 1–2 August 1833, *SS*, 21:21.

45. Ibid., 1:462.

46. Ibid., 21.

47. See the editors' commentary to the essay (ibid., 480), and the vigorous refutation by I. Novich in *Molodoi Gertsen* (Moscow, 1986), 37. Novich points out that the "new school" on which Herzen places high hopes is an explicit description of the École Normale under Cousin, and not, as the editors assert, an Aesopian reference to the Saint-Simonians.

7. SCIENCE AND SAINT-SIMONISM

1. Letter of 21 November 1837, *SS*, 21:234.

2. *SS*, 8:116–117, 117.

3. Ibid., 117.

4. On the birth of the Russian intelligentsia, see Isaiah Berlin's essay "A Remarkable Decade," in *Russian Thinkers* (London, 1978), 114–209.

5. I. S. Turgenev, *Polnoe sobranie sochinenii i pisem. Sochineniia*, vol. 14 (Moscow, 1960–1968), 50. See Belinsky's letter to Botkin of 13 June 1840: Belinsky, *Polnoe sobranie sochinenii*, vol. 11 (Moscow, 1956), 527.

6. To N. A. Zakharina, 24–26 February 1838, *SS*, 21:302. On Vadim Passek, see *SS*, 8:136–138, 144.

7. *SS*, 9:223–254.

8. Ibid., 10:317.

9. To N. A. Zakharina, 24–26 February 1838, *SS*, 21:302; to N. Ketcher, 1–4 March 1841, *SS*, 22:101.

10. *SS*, 9:39, 10:318.

11. See L. I. Nasonkina, "K voprosu o revoliutsionnom dvizhenii studentov Moskovskogo Universiteta," *Vestnik Moskovskogo universiteta*, no. 4 (1954): 153–164.

12. See Herzen's account of Polezhaev's fate in *SS*, 8:165–168.

13. On the "Sungurov affair," see ibid., 144–148.

14. See *SS*, 8:460, note referring to page 145 in the same volume.

15. See Herzen's account of the Malov affair in ibid., 118–122, and the editors' note, ibid., 456.

16. P. V. Annenkov, *Literaturnie vospominaniia* (Leningrad, 1928), 317, 325.

17. Letter to Ogarev, 5 July 1833, *SS*, 21:17.

18. Ogarev to Herzen, 7 June 1833. N. P. Ogarev, *Izbrannye sotsialno-politicheskie i filosofskie proizvedeniia*, vol. 2 (Moscow, 1956), 202; "Den' byl dushny," *SS*, 1:52–55.

19. *SS*, 8:134.

20. E. J. Brown, *Stankevich and His Moscow Circle, 1830–1840* (Stanford, CA, 1966), 13.

21. D. G. Charlton, *Secular Religions in France, 1815–1870* (Oxford, 1969), 161.

22. D. Johnson, "Historians," in *The French Romantics*, vol. 2, ed. D. G. Charlton (Cambridge, 1984), 279.

23. Cited in L. G. Leighton, *Russian Romanticism: Two Essays* (The Hague, 1975), 89.

24. Essay of 1829, cited in Koyré, *La philosophie*, 244. "Deviatnadtsaty vek," *Evropeets: zhurnal I. V. Kireevskogo, 1832*, ed. L. G. Frizman (Moscow, 1989), 303; Kireevskii, *Sochineniia*, vol. 1 (Moscow, 1911), 85.

25. Letter of 29 July 1833, Ogarev, *Izbrannye*, 2:265.

26. Lakhtin to Ogarev, 28 June 1833, *Literaturnoe nasledstvo*, vol. 63: *Gertsen i Ogarev* (Moscow, 1956), 294–295; for the record of Herzen's and Ogarev's interrogation in July of the following year, see 273–286.

27. On the changing perspectives on Peter's reforms in Russian cultural circles, see N. V. Riasanovsky, *The Image of Peter the Great in Russian History and Thought* (Oxford, 1985).

28. "Deviatnadtsaty vek," 303–304.

29. "Dvadtsat osmoe ianvaria," *SS*, 1:29–35; for the Investigating Committee's annotations, see ibid., 482.

30. Letter of 5 July 1833, *SS*, 21:17.

31. Reply to the Investigating Commission, *SS*, 21:482.

32. "Neskolko slov o lektsii g-na Moroshkina," *SS*, 1:319–320.

33. Letter of 5 July 1833, *SS*, 21:17. The work in question was *Obozrenie istoricheskikh svedenii o svode zakonov* [Survey of the Historical Data on the Code of Laws] (Saint Petersburg, 1833).

34. Letter of 5 July 1833, *SS*, 21:17.

35. Letter of 1–2 August 1833, *SS*, 21:21.

36. Letter of 19 July 1833, *SS*, 21:20.

37. Letter of 7–8 August 1833, *SS*, 21:23.

38. "Program and Plan for the Publication of a Journal," *SS*, 1:59–61. Confiscated with Herzen's other papers, this plan made its way from the police archives into an antiquarian shop, and thence into the hands of M. K. Lemke. See editors' note, *SS*, 21:479.

39. Letters of 26 August and 29 July 1833, Ogarev, *Izbrannye*, 1:269, 264–265.

40. Letters of 7–8 August 1833 and 19 July 1833, *SS*, 21:23, 19.

41. Undated letter and letter of 10 July 1833, *Izbrannye*, 2:267, 263.

42. Letter of 19 July 1833, *SS*, 21:20.

43. Letter of 3 September 1832, *Izbrannye*, 2:253, 254.

44. Pierre-Simon Ballanche, *Esquisse d'une philosophie*, vol. 3 (Paris, 1840–1846), 273.

45. "Deviatnadtsaty vek," 94.

46. Letter of 5 July 1833, *SS*, 21:20. (The letter to which he refers has not been preserved.)

47. See Martin Malia, *Alexander Herzen and the Birth of Russian Socialism, 1812–1855* (Cambridge, MA, 1961), chap. 6.

48. *SS*, 8:161–162.

49. Raoul Labry gives strong significance to Herzen's letter of 5 July 1833, asserting that as a result the pair "devoted themselves" to the study of Saint-Simonism (*Alexandre Ivanovich Herzen: 1812–1870* [Paris, 1928], 143).

There is no documentary evidence to support this view. Arguing that Herzen's essay of December 1832, "On Man's Place in Nature," already clearly reflected Saint-Simon's influence, Labry cites Herzen's reference to "palingenetic" centuries, a term the Saint-Simonians had borrowed from Ballanche, but there were many other sources from which Herzen could have borrowed this term. As conclusive evidence of the influence of the Saint-Simonian sect, Labry singles out the epigraph Herzen chose for his essay: a quotation from the Saint-Simonian Olinde-Eugène Rodrigues: "Like physiologists, critical philosophers have made of the universe what the former have made of living man, a corpse." The same essay is cited by the editors of the Soviet edition of Herzen's works as evidence of the "profound impression" made on Herzen by Saint-Simonism. They interpret his comments on Cousin's "new school [the École Normale] . . . in harmony with the spirit of the times" as referring to the Saint-Simonians (mainly alumni of the École Polytechnique, in whom Herzen first expressed interest in the following year; see SS, 1:480). The mistake is repeated in L. I. Matiushenko, A. I. Gertsen: Khudozhnik i publitsist (Moscow, 1977), 20, and in V. Prokofiev, Gertsen (Moscow 1979), 48. Suggesting as the source of this error the significance given by critics to the Rodrigues quotation that heads Herzen's essay, I. Novich points out that nothing in the argument that follows links it to the Saint-Simonian school. See Novich's strongly argued refutation of the above views in his excellent study Molodoi Gertsen: Stranitsy zhizni i tvorchestva (Moscow, 1980), 35–37, 56–66.

50. SS, 21:20.
51. Response to interrogators, SS, 21:414 (Herzen refers to the title as Science du développement humain). On Buchez, see F. A. Isambert, Politique, religion, et science de l'humanité chez Philippe Buchez (Paris, 1967); and A. Cuvillier, P. J. B. Buchez et les origines du socialisme chrétien (Paris, 1948).
52. Letter of 19 July 1833, SS, 21:22.
53. Letter of 29 July 1833, Izbrannye, 2:265.
54. Letter of 7/8 August 1833, SS, 21:23.
55. Response to interrogators, SS, 21:422.
56. Ibid.
57. See Labry, Herzen, 1812–1870, 136.
58. Malia's chapter "Saint-Simon and Socialism" is especially confusing in this regard. Only at the end of his discussion of the pair's "Saint-Simonism" are we told that it derived "not from Saint-Simon himself but from the Saint-Simonian 'church.' . . . At no time do Herzen or Ogarev seem to have read Saint-Simon himself . . . with his technocratic rationalism and emphasis on economics" (Alexander Herzen, 127). Labry argues that Herzen was less interested in Saint-Simonian theories of social reorganization than in its "general philosophy," whose parallels with Schelling's theory of polarities allowed him to integrate it into his "Schellingian concept of the universe" (Herzen, 1812–1870, 142, 141).

59. Henri Saint-Simon, "Survey of the Scientific Studies of the Seventeenth Century," *Selected Writings on Science, Industry, and Social Organization*, ed. and trans. K. Taylor (New York, 1975), 88 (extract from *Introduction aux travaux scientifiques du XIXe siècle*, 2 vols. [Paris, 1807–1808]).

60. Francis Bacon, *Works*, ed. J. Spedding et al. (London, 1857–1874), 4:79.

61. Saint-Simon, *Selected Writings*, 15.

62. Ibid., 168.

63. To cite two examples: G. D. H. Cole, *Socialist Thought: The Forerunners 1789–1850* (London: 1962), 46–47, regards this claim as open to question; but K. Steven Vincent, *Pierre-Joseph Proudhon and the Rise of French Republican Socialism* (Oxford, 1984), 75, describes Saint-Simon and Fourier as "the first generation of French socialists."

64. *Lettre sur les Bourbons: Du système industriel, Oeuvres de Claude-Henri de Saint-Simon*, 6 vols. (Paris, 1966), vol. 3, pt. 2, p. 81.

65. Saint-Simon, "De l'organisation sociale: Fragments d'un ouvrage inédit," in *Opinions littéraires, philosophiques et industrielles* (Paris, 1825), third fragment; Saint-Simon, *Selected Writings*, 265–266.

66. Saint-Simon, "Les interêts politiques de l'industrie," in *Selected Writings*, 181. The same thinking lay behind his eccentric proposal in a work of 1803 to endow scientists and artists with the spiritual power previously exercised by the Catholic Church through the creation of a "Religion of Newton" in keeping with the level of enlightenment attained by modern man. The idea was stillborn. See ibid., 20–21.

67. Cited in F. E. Manuel, *The New World of Saint-Simon* (Cambridge, MA, 1956), 365.

68. *SS*, 1:422.

69. M. E. Prior has suggested that if the history of the changing conception of the scientist is ever written, "the chief irony in it may be that Bacon, . . . who has been condemned for having destroyed the connection between science and religion and thus deprived science of its ethical foundations, should have created in the first clearly realized image of the scientist a figure more impressive in some respects than its successors and possibly too flattering to human nature." B. Vickers, ed., *Essential Articles for the Study of Francis Bacon* (Hamden, CT, 1968), 161. On Herzen's interest in Bacon, see Kelly, *Views from the Other Shore* (New Haven, CT, 1999), 17–46.

70. Both Malia and Labry contend that Schelling's idealism was the key influence on Herzen's thought during this period, determining his approach to Saint-Simonism. According to Malia, "Once at the university, Herzen fell completely under the influence of *Naturphilosophie*"; all that he and Ogarev took from the Saint-Simonians "could be, and was, fitted into the biography of the Absolute as written by Schelling" (*Alexander Herzen*, 90, 127). Labry asserts that "Herzen est nettement allé de la Naturphilosophie à la philosophie de l'histoire, en passant par la métaphysique de l'identité" (*Herzen, 1812–1870*, 126). Elsewhere Labry writes of "la fusion vivante qui s'opère dans son esprit entre l'enseignement de la philosophie de la nature et celui du Saint-Simonisme" (*Herzen, 1812–1870*, 149). The source of these views might be Herzen's memoirs, where

Pavlov is identified as the chief exponent of Schelling's philosophy, without reference to his reservations regarding idealism—another indication of the dangers of treating the memoirs as objective truth.

71. Letter of 4 September 1832, *Izbrannye*, 2:255.
72. Letter of 31 August 1833; *SS*, 21:26.
73. On this subject, see M. Mervaud, "Herzen et la pensée allemande," *Cahiers du monde russe et soviétique*, no. 1 (January–March 1964): 32–73.
74. *SS*, 1:65. In the introduction to his memoirs, Herzen recalls reading Heine's *Travel Pictures* (the collective title for his early work) with "passion" during the period of provincial exile following his imprisonment. His depiction of the philistinism, stupidity, greed, and "monstrous, grotesque, ennui" of petit-bourgeois provincial society (in this case, the town of Göttingen) closely resembled Herzen's own experience in his first period of exile, in the town he later portrayed in fictional form under the name of Malinov.
75. See editors' note, *SS*, 21:454–455.
76. Letter of 31 August 1833, *SS*, 21:26.

8. PRISON AND EXILE

1. *SS*, 8:331.
2. Ibid., 21:25.
3. Document cited in A. I. Herzen, *Polnoe sobranie sochinenii i pisem*, ed. M. K. Lemke (Peterburg, 1919), 12:333.
4. *SS*, 21:414 (record of investigation).
5. Ibid., 8:206.
6. Record of investigation, *SS*, 21:416.
7. Ibid., 417, 421–422.
8. Ibid., 422.
9. Ibid., 422, 425, 426.
10. Ibid., 593–594, 597.
11. *SS*, 8:181.
12. Ibid., 192.
13. Martin Malia, *Alexander Herzen and the Birth of Russian Socialism, 1812–1855* (Cambridge, MA, 1961), 138.
14. *SS*, 8:208–209.
15. Ibid., 197.
16. Ibid., 21:28.
17. Ibid., 33.
18. Ibid., 8:223–225.
19. Ibid., 21:42.
20. Ibid., 55, 85.
21. Ibid., 88.
22. Ibid., 123, 60, 90.
23. Ibid., 8:245.
24. Ibid., 21:150.
25. Ibid., 44.
26. Ibid., 59.
27. Ibid., 61.

28. Ibid., 54, 55.
29. Ibid., 112.
30. Ibid., 118.
31. See *SS*, 1:381–452. On Herzen's relations with Witberg, see the editors' commentary, ibid., 531–534.
32. Malia, *Alexander Herzen*,151.
33. *SS*, 21:127, 78, 106.
34. Ibid., 118, 106.
35. Malia, *Alexander Herzen*, 160–161. Malia observes that repentance over his treatment of Medvedeva occupied Herzen unceasingly from 1835 until his marriage in 1838.
36. *SS*, 21:106.
37. Ibid., 143.
38. On this aspect of Herzen's exile, see I. Novich, *Molodoi Gertsen: Stranitsy zhizni i tvorchestva* (Moscow, 1980), 116–120.
39. *SS*, 21:206.
40. Ibid., 45.
41. Ibid., 1:132.
42. Ibid., 374.
43. Ibid., 79.
44. Ibid., 22:12.
45. Ibid., 1:367–368.

9. AWAKENING

1. *Sochineniia i pis'ma P. Ya. Chaadaeva*, ed. M. Gershenzon, vol. 1 (Moscow, 1913), 79, 84. (Chaadaev would later admit that he had overstated his case: the Orthodox tradition had produced in its saints figures of great moral beauty. "Apologie d'un fou," ibid., 233.)
2. Ibid., 77, 78.
3. Ibid., 78, 80, 79, 82.
4. *SS*, 9:139.
5. Letter of 20 August 1838, *SS*, 21:386.
6. To N. I. and T. A. Astrakov, 15–18 March 1839, *SS*, 22:16. To Ogarev, 21 March 1839, *SS*, 22:20.
7. *SS*, 9:12.
8. Ibid., 8:288.
9. The first volume of *Histoire parlementaire de la révolution française*, containing a preface by Buchez interpreting the revolution's continued significance for France, would not appear until 1843.
10. *SS*, 21:297–298.
11. The erudition of the articles Leroux furnished for this popular journal, *L'Encylopédie pittoresque à deux sous ou Encyclopédie nouvelle*, was highly praised by the critic Sainte-Beuve. See D. O. Evans, *Le socialisme romantique: Pierre Leroux et ses contemporains* (Paris, 1948), 38–39.
12. Pierre Leroux, "Aux Philosophes," *Revue Encyclopédique* (September 1831); Leroux, "De l'individualisme et du socialisme," *Revue Encyclopédique* (October 1833). These essays are reproduced as appendixes in Evans, *Le socialisme romantique*, 212–222.

13. Ibid., 213.
14. Ibid., 232, 233, 234.
15. "Système des contradictions économiques ou philosophie de la misère," *Oeuvres complètes de P. J. Proudhon* (Paris, 1923–1959), 1:368.
16. Letter of 20 August 1838, *SS*, 21:386.
17. *SS*, 1:183.
18. Ibid., 10:238.
19. Letters of 28 February and 1 March 1838, *SS*, 21:306, 309.
20. To N. I. Astrakov, 5 June 1838, *SS*, 21:381. George Sand, *Mauprat* (Paris, 1981), 178–179.
21. Cited in Evans, *Le socialisme romantique*, 110.
22. Letter of 18 April 1839, *SS*, 22:25–26.
23. "Litsinii i Vil'iam Pen," *SS*, 1:340; letter of 20 August 1838, *SS*, 21:386.
24. *SS*, 21:337–342.
25. *SS*, 22:25.
26. Ibid., 13.
27. Letters of 25 June and 28 July 1839, *SS*, 22:38.
28. G. W. F. Hegel, *Elements of the Philosophy of Right*, ed. A. W. Wood, trans. H. B. Nisbet (Cambridge, 1991), 228.
29. Ibid., 22.
30. N. V. Stankevich, *Perepiska ego i biografiia* (Moscow, 1914), 471.
31. Cited in A. Koyré, *Études sur l'histoire de la pensée philosophique en Russie* (Paris, 1950), 117.
32. B. N. Chicherin, *Vospominaniia*, pt. 2 (Moscow, 1991), 32.
33. Cited in D. McLellan, *The Young Hegelians and Karl Marx* (London, 1968), 11. See McLellan also on Saint-Simon's influence.
34. Belinsky to Bakunin, 16 August 1837, in V. G. Belinsky, *Polnoe sobranie sochinenii*, vol. 11 (Moscow: 1956), 175. On Bakunin's role in Stankevich's circle, see A. Kelly, *Mikhail Bakunin: A Study in the Psychology and Politics of Utopianism* (New Haven, CT, 1987), chap. 1.
35. Belinsky, *Polnoe sobranie sochinenii*, 191.
36. Cited in Kelly, *Mikhail Bakunin*, 46–49.
37. Letters of 10 September 1838 and 29 September–8 October 1839, in Belinsky, *Polnoe sobranie sochinenii*, 11:282, 387.
38. Ibid., 3:436.
39. Letter of 4 October 1840, ibid., 11:556.
40. Letter of 10–11 December 1840, ibid., 576–577.
41. Letter of 8 September 1841, ibid., 12:66.
42. *SS*, 9:28.
43. Letter of 7 February 1839, *SS*, 22:11.
44. *SS*, 9:18–20.
45. Letter of 14 November–4 December 1839, *SS*, 22:53.
46. Ibid., 54.

10. THE DISCOVERY OF CHANCE

1. *SS*, 9:80.
2. Ibid., 2:213.
3. Ibid., 201.

4. Letter of 11 February 1841, *SS*, 22:98.

5. Letters of 1 March and 2 March 1841, *SS*, 22:101, 104.

6. *SS*, 2:204-205.

7. Ibid., 219.

8. Ibid., 216, 277, 260, 347.

9. Ibid., 409-410.

10. Ibid., 2:348-349; letter of 22 November 1845, *SS*, 22:246.

11. *SS*, 2:241.

12. M. K. Lemke, *Nikolaevskie zhandarmy i literatura, 1826-55* (Saint Petersburg, 1909), 305.

13. *SS*, 2:268.

14. Ibid., 226, 276, 388.

15. Ibid., 226-227.

16. Ibid., 384, 383, 268.

17. Ibid., 4:92, 120-121.

18. Ibid., 122.

19. Ibid., 153.

20. Ibid., 20:109-118; 4:239-268, 106, 154.

21. Ibid., 4:121-122.

22. "Po povodu odnoi dramy," *SS*, 2:50.

23. *SS*, 2:257.

24. Letter to Natalya Zakharina, 9 January 1837, *SS*, 21:134; letter of 30 January 1837, *SS*, 21:140.

25. Letter to Ogarev, 11 February 1841, *SS*, 22:100.

26. *SS*, 2:370.

27. Nicolas Ogarev, *Letopis zhizni i tvorchestva A. I. Gertsena,1812-1850* (Moscow, 1974), 330.

28. *SS*, 2:251.

29. Letter of 2 March 1841, *SS*, 22:104.

30. *SS*, 3:93. For evidence of the Pavlovian origins of Herzen's assertion, see "O vznaimnom otnoshenii," *Atenei*, no. 11 (1828): 97, and the epigraph for chapter 6.

31. Ibid., 2:386, 387. The works by de Candolle that Herzen is most likely to have read are *Organographie* (1827) and *Physiologie végétale* (1832).

32. Letter to Ketcher, 4-11 October 1844, *SS*, 22:201.The works Herzen was consulting were probably Carus's *Grundzüge der vergleichenden Anatomie und Physiologie* (1827), Boch's *Handbuch der Anatomie des Menschen* (1838), which enjoyed great popularity at the time, and Burdach's six-volume work *Die Physiologie als Erfahrungswissenschaft* (1835-1840).

33. Letter from Ketcher, February 1845, *Letopis zhizni i tvorchestva A. I. Gertsena, 1812-1850* (Moscow, 1974), 332.

34. *SS*, 22:233; N. P. Ogarev, *Izbrannye sotsialno-politicheskie i filosofskie proizvedeniia*, 2 vols. (Moscow, 1956), 2:376.

35. Letter of 2 March 1845, *SS*, 22:233. *Qu'est-ce que la propriété?* (1840) and *De la création de l'ordre dans l'humanité* (1843) are two of Proudhon's earliest expositions of his ideal of a social order based on mutual associations that would resolve the contradictions of existing society.

36. *SS*, 2:404.

37. On Rouillier, see G. S. Vasetsky and S. R. Mikulinsky, eds., *Izbrannye proizvedeniia russkikh estestvoispytatelei pervoi poloviny XIX veka* (Moscow, 1959), 31–33, 40–42, 585.

38. Letter to A. A. Kraevsky, 23 December 1845, *SS*, 22:249.

39. *SS*, 2:390.

40. "Publichnye chteniya g-na Professora Roulie," *SS*, 2:140, 141.

41. *SS*, 2:141, 142, 144.

42. Ibid., 145.

43. See Ernst Mayr, *The Growth of Biological Thought: Diversity, Evolution and Inheritance* (Cambridge, MA, 1982), 438.

44. *SS*, 2:206. Still on the subject of the great thinkers of the eighteenth century, he couples Buffon's name with Montesquieu's (208).

45. "Po povodu odnoi dramy," *SS*, 2:62–63.

46. Ibid., 67, 346.

47. Ibid., 345–346, 49.

48. Ibid., 371.

49. *SS*, 4:130; letter to Ogarev and Satin, 1 January 1845, *SS*, 22:218; *SS*, 2:275.

50. *SS*, 2:217–218.

51. Ibid., 369.

52. Ibid., 394–395.

53. Letters of 15 December 1844 and 1 January 1845, *SS*, 22:210, 217–218.

54. S. J. Gould, *Wonderful Life: The Burgess Shale and the Nature of History* (London, 1990), 282.

55. Letter of 18 April 1843, *SS*, 22:142.

56. Mayr, *Growth*, 520.

57. Gould, *Wonderful Life*, 283, 284, 289–290.

58. Cited in ibid., 290.

11. FROM BACON TO FEUERBACH: NATURE AND TIME

1. Kireevsky's unpublished essay, "A Reply to Khomyakov," was subsequently expanded in a long study, "On the Character of European Civilization and its Relationship to Russian Civilization," *Sobranie sochinenii Ivana Vasilievicha Kireevskogo*, 2 vols. (Moscow, 1861), 2:229–280.

2. P. V. Annenkov, *Literaturnye vospominaniia* (Leningrad, 1928), 309–310.

3. *SS*, 9:127.

4. Ibid., 121–132.

5. Letter of 3 February 1842, *SS*, 22:127.

6. *SS*, 9:23.

7. Hegel, *The Philosophy of History*, trans J. Sibree (New York, 1956), 447.

8. Hegel, *The Philosophy of Right*, vol. 7 (Frankfurt, 1970), 26. See F. E. Beiser, "Hegel's Historicism," in *The Cambridge Companion to Hegel*, ed. F. Beiser (Cambridge, 1993), 270–300.

9. Beiser, "Hegel and the Problem of Metaphysics," in *Cambridge Companion to Hegel*, 2.

10. Charles Taylor, however, argues that this category, "far from being another incomprehensible, 'mystical' Hegelian idea, is indispensable for any theory of history which wants to give a role to unconscious motivation." *Hegel* (Cambridge, 1975), 393.

11. See R. Plant's discussion of Hegel's treatment of the absolute in politics and history in *Hegel: An Introduction* (Oxford, 1983), chap. 10. Plant observes that to represent freedom as a continuous process of self-transformation would be inconsistent with Hegel's major philosophical premises. If its achievement remained an "ought," consciousness would remain "unhappy" and the process of history would be what he called a "bad infinity" (238).

12. See R. B. Pippin, "You Can't Get There from Here: Transition Problems in Hegel's Phenomenology of Spirit," in *Cambridge Companion to Hegel*, 52–85. Pippin cites the summing-up of one of the best-known scholarly deconstructions of the work, Rudolph Haym's 1857 *Hegel und seine Zeit*: "The Phenomenology is a psychology brought into confusion and disorder through a history, and a history brought to ruin through a psychology" (Pippin, "You Can't Get There," 55).

13. W. Kaufmann, trans. and ed., *Hegel: Texts and Commentary* (Notre Dame, IN, 1977), 5.

14. Ibid., 20.

15. Ibid., 18, 24, 26, 88, 80.

16. Ibid., 77.

17. Ibid., 88, 8.

18. Ibid., 78, 10, 70, 80.

19. Ibid., 22.

20. Ibid., 52, 46, 84.

21. Ibid., 74.

22. See M. Inwood, *A Hegel Dictionary* (Oxford, 1992), 197–199.

23. Kaufmann, *Hegel: Texts and Commentary*, 66, 62.

24. Kaufmann footnotes a clause he has translated as "to be their Concept in their being" with the comment: "This clause sounds even far worse in German: 'in seinem Sein sein Begriff zu sein'" (ibid., 85).

25. Ibid., 78, 42, 48.

26. Arguing that Hegel was neither an orthodox theist, nor a pantheist, nor an atheist, Peter Singer (citing an earlier scholar) suggests the term "panentheist." Singer, *Hegel* (Oxford, 1983), 81–83.

27. On the political background to the development of the Left Hegelian movement, see J. E. Toews, *Hegelianism: The Path toward Dialectical Humanism, 1805–1841* (New York, 1980), 207–216.

28. See ibid., 203.

29. Ludwig Feuerbach, *The Essence of Christianity*, trans. G. Eliot (New York, 1957), 230–231, 270, 271.

30. Ibid., 163.

31. Ibid.,157, 63, 93, 161, 110, 15.

32. Ibid., 91.

33. *SS*, 9:27.

34. Feuerbach, *The Essence of Christianity*, xxxiv.

35. Ibid.

36. Ibid., 83, 152–153.

37. Ibid., 103, 105, 110.

38. Ibid., 140.

39. *SS*, 2:206.

40. Ibid., 317.

41. Ibid., 324.

42. Ibid., 229.

43. Ibid., 223–224.

44. Ibid., 265.

45. M. A. Bakunin, *Sobranie sochinenii i pisem, 1828–76*, 4 vols., ed. Yu. M. Steklov (Moscow, 1934–1935), 3:126–147.

46. *SS*, 2:409.

47. Ibid., 313–314.

48. Ibid., 352–353.

49. Ibid., 254, 230.

50. Ibid., 206.

51. Ibid., 3:46.

52. Ibid., 2:221, 321.

53. Ibid., 3:11.

54. Ibid., 2:242, 240.

55. Ibid., 3:79, 81.

56. Ibid., 2:265.

57. Ibid., 3:66.

58. Ibid., 68.

59. Ibid.

60. Ibid., 62, 83, 74. The quotation is from the preface to *The Philosophy of Right*.

61. Ibid., 74–75.

62. Ibid., 71, 76.

63. Ibid., 85.

64. Ibid., 86–87.

65. Ibid., 6:34–35.

66. Ibid., 3:75–76, 87.

67. Ibid., 2:404.

68. Ibid., 405.

69. Ibid., 9:204.

70. The *Letters* were destined for a new journal to be founded by Herzen's Moscow friends. In December they were told that Nicolas I had vetoed the venture. Hence the delay in publication of the *Letters*, which found a new home in *National Notes*. See the editors' commentary in *SS*, 3:331.

71. Diary entry, 15 September 1844, *SS*, 2:382.

72. *SS*, 3:121.

73. Ibid., 93–94.

74. Ibid., 118.

75. Ibid.

76. Ibid., 2:349. Hegel's *Philosophy of Nature* was combined with his *Logic* and his *Philosophy of Spirit* in *Enzyklopädie der philosophischen Wissenschaften im Grundrisse* (the first complete presentation of his system) in 1817.

77. *SS*, 3:120, 119, 127.

78. In a footnote damning Hegel with faint praise, Herzen contrasts the "artistic perfection" of his treatment of ancient philosophy with his chapters on the modern period, which he described as "saturated" with idealism: "In these cases he was untrue to himself and rendered tribute to his time." Ibid., 146–147.

79. See, for example, the passage on the identity of man and nature: *SS*, 3:126–127.

80. G. W. F. Hegel, *Lectures on the History of Philosophy*, vol. 3 (London,1896), 172–173, 172.

81. *SS*, 2:303–304. On Herzen and Bacon, see Kelly, *Views from the Other Shore* (New Haven, CT, 1999), 7–46.

82. *SS*, 2:412.

83. Ibid., 22:240. "Descartes and Bacon" and "Bacon and His School in England," *SS*, 3:242–254, 255–273.

84. Letter to A. A. Kraevsky, 23 June 1845, *SS*, 22:240.

85. *SS*, 3:251, 264, 261.

86. Ibid., 280.

87. Ibid., 114.

88. Ludwig Feuerbach, *Kleine philosophische Schriften* (Leipzig, 1950), 36.

89. *SS*, 3:251.

90. Letter to Kraevsky, 27 November 1845, *SS*, 22:247.

91. *SS*, 8:48.

92. Ibid., 3:138; 2:388.

93. Goethe, "Bedeutende Fördernis durch ein einziges geistreiches Wort," in *Werke*, vol. 13 (Munich, 1981), 37–41.

94. *SS*, 1:120.

95. Ibid., 3:53.

96. Herzen, "Zapiski odnogo molodogo cheloveka," *SS*, 1:278.

97. Letter to Ogarev, 14 November 1839, *SS*, 22:55.

98. *SS*, 3:38.

99. Schiller, "Ueber Anmuth und Würde," *Schiller's Werke, Zwanzigster Band: Philosophische Schriften*, pt. 1 (Weimar, 1962), 286. For an extended comparison of Herzen's and Schiller's notions of an aesthetic education, see Kelly, *Views from the Other Shore*, chap. 2.

100. "Concerning a Certain Drama," *SS*, 2:62.

101. Ibid., 60–61.

102. *SS*, 3:195. The source is Schiller's poem "Die Philosophen."

103. Ibid., 2:298, 114. On Herzen and Schiller, see Kelly, *Views from the Other Shore*, chap. 2.

104. Schiller, *On the Aesthetic Education of Man, in a Series of Letters*, ed. and trans. E. M. Wilkinson and L. A. Willoughby (Oxford, 1967), 189, 141, 153.

105. Letter from Schiller to C. Garve, quoted in *Aesthetic Education*, xviii; ibid., 7.

106. Schiller, *Aesthetic Education*, 19n85.

107. Ibid., 47.

108. T. J. Reed, *Schiller* (London, 1991), 104.

109. "Novie variatsii na starye temy," *SS*, 2:93.

110. Ibid., 97, 98.

111. Labry's and Malia's biographies restrict their discussion of the influence of Schiller's works on Herzen to Schiller's early Romantic period. Neither mentions the *Aesthetic Education*. See also Malia, "Schiller and the Early Russian Left," *Harvard Slavic Studies* 4 (The Hague, 1957): 169–200.

112. For a survey of the reactions in Germany, France, and England to Schiller's treatise over the last two centuries, see Wilkinson and Willoughby's introduction to the *Aesthetic Education*. They maintain that in England it was not realized that the work had any political content until this was pointed out in articles by the philosopher Stuart Hampshire in the early 1960s.

12. MAN IN THE MIDDLE

1. *SS*, 2:354.

2. Ibid., 293.

3. Ibid., 291, 242, 291, 242.

4. Ibid., 10:320.

5. Letter of 26 November 1841, *SS*, 22:116.

6. Letter of 3 December 1842, *SS*, 22:161.

7. *SS*, 2:273, 245.

8. Ibid., 397.

9. Ibid., 356.

10. Ibid., 310.

11. Ibid., 289, 292.

12. Ibid., 291, 289, 340, 381.

13. Letter to Ketcher, 15–16 November 1844, *SS*, 22:206; *SS*, 2:390.

14. *SS*, 2:403.

15. *La destinée sociale*, vol. 1 (Paris, 1834), 32.

16. *SS*, 2:289, 359.

17. Proudhon, "Qu'est-ce que la propriété?," in *Oeuvres complètes de Proudhon* (Paris, 1926), 317.

18. Letter of 2 March 1845, *SS*, 22:233.

19. See Proudhon, *De la création de l'ordre dans l'humanité*, chap. 3.

20. *SS*, 2:408.

21. Ibid.

22. Ibid., 266.

23. Ibid., 361, 346.

24. Ibid., 283.

25. Martin Malia, *Alexander Herzen and the Birth of Russian Socialism, 1812–1855* (Cambridge, MA, 1961), 330–331.

26. *SS*, 2:266.

27. Ibid., 294.

28. Ibid., 288.

29. Ibid., 289.

30. Ibid., 314–315, 328.
31. Ibid., 311, 333, 334, 335.
32. Ibid., 337, 336.
33. Ibid., 342, 300.
34. Ibid., 338; see also 363.
35. Ibid., 334.
36. Letter of 1–4 March 1841, *SS*, 22:103.
37. *SS*, 2:354, 339.
38. Ibid., 388.
39. Ibid., 363.
40. Ibid., 9:134.
41. *PSS-L*, 1:25.
42. *SS*, 1:329.
43. Ibid., 2:303.
44. Ibid., 1:320.
45. Letter of 6–7 September 1835, *SS*, 21:50.
46. *SS*, 2:214.
47. Ibid., 287–288.
48. Ibid., 379.
49. Ibid., 281–282.
50. Ibid., 359.
51. Ibid., 4:232.
52. Ibid., 49.
53. Ibid., 2:305, 214.
54. Ibid., 217.
55. Ibid., 214.
56. Ibid., 327.
57. Ibid., 125.
58. Ibid., 278.
59. Letter of 5–8 October 1846, *SS*, 22:259. Dostoevsky's opinion of Herzen was more favorable. He wrote to his brother in April of that year, "A multitude of new writers have appeared. Some are my rivals. The most remarkable are Herzen (Iskander) and Goncharov" (*Sochineniia*, vol. 28, book 1 [Leningrad, 1985], 120); Herzen, *Letopis, 1812–1850* (Moscow, 1974), 358.
60. Letter of 1 March 1844, *SS*, 22:176.
61. *SS*, 2:381.
62. Ibid., 282.
63. Ibid., 314, 315.
64. Malia, *Alexander Herzen*, 310.
65. *SS*, 2:412–413.
66. Ibid., 10:25–26.
67. Malia, *Alexander Herzen*, 6.
68. To Ketcher and his Moscow friends, Ogarev, *Izbrannye*, 2:283–285.
69. On Ogarev's Aksheno experiment, see *Literaturnoe nasledstvo*, vol. 61, *Gertsen i Ogarev I* (Moscow, 1953), 719–726.
70. Letter to Herzen, Ogarev, *Izbrannye*, 2:342, 349; 1:36.

71. Letter to Granovsky, Ogarev, *Izbrannye*, 2:398.
72. Letter to Herzen, Ogarev, *Izbrannye*, 2:370.
73. "École Polytechnique Populaire," Ogarev, *Izbrannye*, 1:14.
74. Ogarev, *Izbrannye*, 2:392.
75. Ibid., 392, 414, 413, 411. See also his letter to Herzen complaining of the difficulties in dealing with factions among the peasants, which were increasing his skepticism about the virtues of the traditional commune. Ibid., 727–728.
76. Ibid., 1:9.
77. Ibid., 2:367, 345.
78. Malia, *Alexander Herzen*, 48.
79. Letter to Ketcher, 15 February 1845, Ogarev, *Izbrannye*, 2:374; letter to Herzen, 29/17 December 1844, Ogarev, *Izbrannye*, 2:349.
80. Ogarev, *Izbrannye*, 2:388–389.
81. Letter to G. I. Klyucharev, 4 December/22 November 1847, SS, 23:48.
82. Letter of 8 July/26 June 1847, SS, 2:410; Herzen to Ogarev, 3 August/22 July 1847, SS, 23:34.
83. Letter of 17/5 October 1848, SS, 23:107.
84. Letter of 16/4 December 1848, Ogarev, *Izbrannye*, 2:417–418.
85. Letter of 3 March 1847, Ogarev, *Izbrannye*, 2:403.
86. Letter of 8 July/26 June 1847, Ogarev, *Izbrannye*, 2:408.
87. To E. Korsh, 28 June 1847, Ogarev, *Izbrannye*, 2:415.

13. A CONSERVATIVE REVOLUTION

1. Martin Malia maintains that the Romantic nationalism Herzen brought with him to the West made it inevitable that nothing would please him in European life and culture. "From the beginning, Europe was for Herzen a slogan in the battle of Russian political ideologies much more than a society to be understood in itself." Malia, *Alexander Herzen and the Birth of Russian Socialism, 1812–1855* (Cambridge, MA, 1961), 349–350. Edward Acton asserts on the contrary that Herzen had seen the Provisional Government as "blessed with a brilliant chance to realize his ideals"; hence the traumatic effect on him of the failure of 1848 (Acton, *Alexander Herzen and the Role of the Intellectual Revolutionary* [Cambridge, 1979], 44–50). On the respective positions of Acton and Malia on Herzen's response to 1848, see my "Respublika pod sudom: Gertsen i 1848," *Novoe literaturnoe obozrenie*, no. 53 (2002): 49–50.
2. V. I. Lenin, *Polnoe sobraniie sochinenii*, vol. 21 (Moscow, 1961), 255–262.
3. See K. Steven Vincent, *Pierre-Joseph Proudhon and the Rise of French Republican Socialism* (Oxford, 1984), 11–12, 123–126. Vincent observes that because the early French socialists coined the term "socialism," "it will simply not do to lecture them on the meaning of the term."
4. Herzen's *Letters from France and Italy* were revised for publication in German in 1850 and in Russian in 1858. The latter edition is used in this chapter with the exception of cases where it differs significantly from the original text. On the various editions, see the editors' comments in SS, 5:452–453.

5. Ibid., 5:21, 25, 26.

6. P. V. Annenkov, *Literaturnye vospominaniia*, ed. B. M. Eikhenbaum (Leningrad, 1928), 490–491.

7. *SS*, 23:14.

8. Ibid., 5:141.

9. Annenkov, *Literaturnye vospominaniia*, 400–401.

10. Ibid., 489.

11. *SS*, 5:232.

12. Ibid., 23:8.

13. Ibid., 10:36.

14. Ibid., 5:141.

15. Ibid., 23:20.

16. Ibid., 5:43.

17. Ibid., 34.

18. Cited in Malia, *Alexander Herzen*, 360.

19. *SS*, 5:232. Taken from the original version of Herzen's fourth "Letter from the Avenue Marigny," which differs significantly from the version reworked after 1848. On the different forms and titles Herzen gave these Letters, see Malia, *Alexander* Herzen, 469n78 and 571n7.

20. Ibid., 238. From the original version of Herzen's fourth "Letter from the Avenue Marigny." The phrase in brackets was added in the 1858 edition of the *Letters*.

21. See A. Koyré, *Études sur l'histoire de la pensée philosophique en Russie* (Paris, 1950), 213. Malia presents Herzen as arriving in Paris "prepared to be appalled" and in search of ammunition to hurl against his Westernizing friends (*Alexander Herzen*, 341).

22. *SS*, 5:233. From the original version of Herzen's fourth "Letter from the Avenue Marigny."

23. *SS*, 5:68. Begun for publication in the *Contemporary*, they first appeared in German in a revised form (after Herzen had realized that they would not be passed by the Russian censor), and in Russian in 1854 as part of a cycle of *Letters from France and Italy*. For Herzen's revisions of the texts and the titles of these letters, see Malia, *Alexander Herzen*, 469n78 and 470n7.

24. *SS*, 5:74.

25. Ibid., 10:26, 28.

26. Ibid., 5:292.

27. Ibid., 376; *SS*, 23:86.

28. Ibid., 5:132, 137–138, 132.

29. See Herzen's account of this episode in *SS*, 10:28–35.

30. *SS*, 5:139.

31. Ibid., 150.

32. Ibid., 161.

33. Ibid., 23:95.

34. Ibid., 5:162.

35. Ibid., 30:502. *Du contrat social: Oeuvres complètes de Jean-Jacques Rousseau*, ed. B. Gagnebin and M. Raymond, 4 vols. (Paris, 1959–1970), 3:364; *SS*, 5:160.

36. Ibid., 169.
37. *SS*, 6:42, 43.
38. Ibid., 112, 113, 112.
39. Ibid., 6:322.
40. Ibid., 321.
41. Ibid., 23:79, 136, 137, 138.
42. Ibid., 10:46.
43. See *Letopis zhizni i tvorchestva A. I. Gertsena, 1812–1850* (Moscow, 1974), 493–494.
44. *SS*, 23:188. See his sardonic descriptions of the émigrés in Geneva in chap. 37 of *My Past and Thoughts*. The original is in *SS*, 10:58–64 and 86–87.
45. *SS*, 23:190–191.
46. Ibid., 169–170, 186.

14. A GLOWING FOOTPRINT: HERZEN AND PROUDHON

1. See Raoul Labry, *Herzen et Proudhon* (Paris, 1928), 81. Labry questions the importance Herzen gave to Proudhon's influence as compared to that of Feuerbach, arguing that Herzen "molded Proudhon in his own image" (30). Michel Mervaud focuses on the ideological and tactical differences between the two thinkers: see Mervaud, "Herzen et Proudhon," *Cahiers du monde russe et soviétique* 12, nos. 1–2: (1971): 110–145. J. Zimmerman, *Midpassage: Alexander Herzen and European Revolution, 1847–1852* (Pittsburgh, 1989), a study of Herzen's thought in the years of his closest association with Proudhon, foregoes any analysis of their relationship, as do Malia and Acton. In contrast with the above, and for further details of the relationship, see my presentation of Herzen and Proudhon as "two radical ironists," in Kelly, *Views from the Other Shore* (New Haven, CT, 1999), 82–113.
2. *SS*, 18:314.
3. Letters to Proudhon of 26 December 1851 (draft) and 24–31 July 1855, *SS*, 24:217, 25: 283.
4. *SS*, 7:111.
5. Proudhon, *De la justice dans la révolution et dans l'église* (1858) (Paris, 1930), 2:56–57.
6. See P. Haubtmann, *Proudhon, Marx et la pensée allemande* (Grenoble, 1981), 20–21.
7. Letter to A. M. Ackermann, 27 May 1842, *Correspondance de P.-J. Proudhon*, vol. 2, ed. J.-A. Langlois (Paris, 1875), 47.
8. Proudhon, *De la justice*, 1:423; Proudhon, *Solution du problème social* (Paris, 1868), 93.
9. Proudhon, *Qu'est-ce que la propriété?* (Paris, 1923), 324–325.
10. Marginal comments on a manuscript by the German Young Hegelian A. H. Ewerbeck, translated by the author from German into French for Proudhon's benefit. Cited in Haubtmann, *Proudhon, Marx*, 90.
11. Proudhon, *Système des contradictions économiques, ou philosophie de la misère*, vol. 1 (Paris, 1923), 368; Proudhon, *Qu'est-ce que la propriété?*, 326, 325.

12. Proudhon, *Système des contradictions*, 2:396.
13. Ibid., 410; Proudhon, *De la célébration du dimanche* (Paris, 1923), 61.
14. Proudhon, *Philosophie du progrès* (Paris, 1946), 50–51.
15. See Vincent, *Pierre-Joseph Proudhon and the Rise of French Republican Socialism* (Oxford, 1984), 123.
16. Letter to Marx, 17 May 1846, *Correspondance de P.-J. Proudhon*, 2:47.
17. Proudhon, "Aux Citoyens Rédacteurs du Populaire," 20 March 1849, cited in K. S. Vincent, *Proudhon*, 288.
18. Proudhon, *Idée générale de la révolution au XIXe siècle* (Paris, 1923), 159.
19. See Vincent, *Proudhon*, 91.
20. Proudhon, *Système des contradictions*, 2:175.
21. Ibid., 1:391–392, 394.
22. Ewerbeck manuscript, cited in P. Haubtmann, *Proudhon, Marx*, 95.
23. Proudhon, *Système des contradictions*, 1:395.
24. Ibid., 2:174, 175.
25. Ibid., 412.
26. Comment on the margin of Ewerbeck's "Christianity, German Philosophy, and Socialism," cited in Vincent, *Proudhon*, 99.
27. Proudhon, *Système des contradictions*, 1:56, 44, 398.
28. Letter to A. Maurice, 4 August 1843, *Correspondance de P.-J. Proudhon*, 2:89.
29. Proudhon, *Système des contradictions*, 1:397.
30. See the chapter "Herzen and Proudhon: Two Radical Ironists" in Kelly, *Views from the Other Shore*, esp. 100.
31. See Haubtmann, *Proudhon, Marx*, chap. 7; and Vincent, *Proudhon*, chap. 3.
32. Proudhon, *Système des contradictions*, 1:394.
33. Ibid., 33, 2:409.
34. Ibid., 1:85.
35. Ibid., 396.
36. Ibid., 394; Proudhon, *Qu'est-ce la propriété?*, 325.
37. Proudhon, *Qu'est-ce que la propriété?*, 327.
38. Ibid., 311.
39. On Schiller's distinction, see Kelly, *Views from the Other Shore*, 49–56.
40. Proudhon, "Toast à la révolution," in *Oeuvres: Confessions d'un révolutionnaire* (Paris, 1929), 399.
41. Proudhon, *Idée générale de la révolution*, 93.
42. Proudhon, *De la justice*, 3:470.
43. Letter to Marx, 17 May 1846, *Correspondance de P.-J. Proudhon*, 2:200.
44. Proudhon, *Confessions d'un révolutionnaire*, 399.
45. Proudhon, *Système des contradictions*, 1:244.
46. Cited in Vincent, *Proudhon*, 212.
47. Proudhon, *Système des contradictions*, 1:384; Proudhon, *Qu'est-ce la propriété?*, 1: 132.
48. Proudhon, *Confessions d'un révolutionnaire*, 202, 180.
49. Letter cited in Mervaud, "Herzen et Proudhon," 141.
50. Proudhon, *Qu'est-ce que la propriété?*, 1:317.

51. Proudhon, *Système des contradictions*, 2:397.

52. *SS*, 5:314.

53. Ibid., 148.

54. *Carnets de J-P. Proudhon*, vol. 2 (Paris, 1961), 154.

55. Cited in Vincent, *Proudhon*, 169–170.

56. Ibid., 176.

57. Official report of the session, cited in Vincent, *Proudhon*, 183.

58. Obituary in *Der Sozialdemokrat*, February 1865.

59. Motion of censure; see Vincent, *Proudhon*, 185.

60. Letters of 2–8 August and 27–28 September 1848, *SS*, 23:80, 189.

61. Letter of 19 August 1849, cited in Mervaud, "Six lettres de Herzen à Proudhon," *Cahiers du monde russe et soviétique* 12, no. 3: (1971): 309–310.

62. *SS*, 10:191.

63. Cited in Mervaud, "Correspondance de Herzen et de Proudhon," *Cahiers du monde russe et soviétique* 12, nos. 1–2: (1971):149.

64. Letter to Proudhon, 27 August 1849, *SS*, 23:175.

65. Cited in Mervaud, "Herzen et Proudhon," 118.

66. Proudhon, *Système des contradictions*, 1:219.

67. Vincent, *Proudhon*, 101.

68. Letter of 15 September 1849, cited in Mervaud, "Correspondance de Herzen et de Proudhon," 152–153.

69. *SS*, 5:179.

70. Ibid., 20:586.

71. Letter to Herwegh, 10 July 1850, *SS*, 24:107. The text appears in a slightly altered form in *From the Other Shore* in the essay entitled "Epilogue 1849."

72. *SS*, 2:388.

73. Draft letter of 26 December 1851. *SS*, 24:217.

74. See letters to Emma Herwegh, 10 October 1849 and end of March 1850, *SS*, 23:197, 322.

75. *SS*, 18:314. In November 1851 Proudhon sent Herzen a message of condolence from prison on the drowning of his mother and son: "I can't get over this terrible calamity. I love you and bear your image deep in my heart, which many think is made of stone." Cited in Mervaud, "Correspondance de Herzen et de Proudhon," 153–154. Herzen responded: "Such sympathy from those whom we love, whom we esteem without bounds, makes suffering more human, less overwhelming." *SS*, 24:216 (draft).

76. Proudhon to Herzen, 23 August 1849, cited in Mervaud, "Correspondance de Herzen et de Proudhon," 149.

77. A. Darimon, *À travers une révolution* (Paris, 1884), 180. Cited in Raoul Labry, *Alexandre Ivanovich Herzen: 1812–1870* (Paris, 1928), 85.

78. *SS*, 10:197.

79. Ibid., 185.

80. Ibid., 185, 186.

81. To A. A. Chumikov, 9 August 1851, *SS*, 24:201.

82. Letter of 27–28 September 1849, *SS*, 23:186; *SS*, 10:188.

83. *SS*, 5:175–176.

84. Proudhon, *Confessions d'un révolutionnaire* (Paris, 1929), 341–342.
85. Richard Rorty, *Contingency, Irony, and Solidarity* (Cambridge, 1989), xv. See my chapter "Herzen and Proudhon: Two Radical Ironists," in *Views from the Other Shore*, 82–113.
86. Letter of 7 November 1849, *SS*, 23:207.
87. *SS*, 10:189.
88. Bernard Williams, "Liberalism and Loss," in *The Legacy of Isaiah Berlin*, ed. Mark Lilla et al. (New York, 2001), 95.
89. Proudhon, *Qu'est-ce que la propriété?*, 311; Schiller, *Aesthetic Education*, 23.
90. *SS*, 9:23.

15. TOWARD ANOTHER SHORE

1. Alexander Herzen, "Du développement des idées révolutionnaires en Russie," *SS*, 7:9.
2. Ibid., 31.
3. "'La Russie,' à G. H.," *SS*, 6:183.
4. *SS*, 7:115.
5. Ibid., 112.
6. Ibid.,114, 113.
7. Ibid., 185.
8. Ibid., 162, 169.
9. "Le peuple russe et le socialisme," *SS*, 7:284.
10. "La Russie," *SS*, 6:172, 167.
11. "Le peuple russe," *SS*, 7:291.
12. Ibid., 296, 295.
13. "Du développement," *SS*, 7:117, 108.
14. Ibid., 121.
15. "Le peuple russe," *SS*, 7:298–299.
16. Ibid., 112.
17. To Moses Hess, March 1850, *SS*, 23:289–290. On Herzen's correspondence with Hess, see *Literaturnoe nasledstvo*, vols. 7–8 (Moscow, 1933), 72–89.
18. To Herwegh, 10 July 1850, *SS*, 24:107.
19. To V. Linton, 1 April 1850, *SS*, 24:7.
20. To A. A. Chumikov, 9 August 1851, *SS*, 24:199.
21. *SS*, 5:211.
22. To Proudhon, 26 December 1851, *SS*, 24:216–217.
23. To J. Jacoby, 24 April 1850, *SS*, 24:35.
24. To E. Haag, circa 16 March1852, *SS*, 24:244.
25. Letters to Herwegh, 31 December 1849, 7 February 1850, and 18 February 1850, *SS*, 23:227, 259, 271.
26. Postscript of Herzen to Herwegh, 17 February 1850, *SS*, 23:269.
27. Herzen devotes eight chapters of his memoirs to his family drama. For a rather more objective account, see E. H. Carr, *The Romantic Exiles: A Nineteenth-Century Portrait Gallery* (London, 1968).
28. *SS*, 10:254.
29. Ibid., 267.

30. Ibid., 24:184.
31. Ibid., 10:274.
32. To M. Reichel, 8 December 1851, *SS*, 24:213–214.
33. *SS*, 24:306; 25:110, 110.
34. Herzen reproduces the letter in *SS*, 10:290–291.
35. Letter of 17 January 1850, *SS*, 23:234.
36. *SS*, 5:209. To M. K. Reichel, 5 April 1852, *SS*, 24:265.
37. *SS*, 5:202.
38. Ibid., 207–209.
39. Ibid., 216–217.
40. To Proudhon, 26 December 1851, *SS*, 24:217.
41. *SS*, 27:456, 34.
42. For a full list of their successive addresses, see Carr, *Romantic Exiles*, 328.
43. *SS*, 25:128, 158.
44. Ibid., 241.
45. Ibid., 24:375.
46. Letter to Herzen, cited in Carr, *Romantic Exiles*, 326.
47. *Literaturnoe nasledstvo*, vol. 61 (Moscow, 1953), 231.
48. *SS*, 11:53.
49. C. Schurz, *The Reminiscences of Carl Schurz*, vol. 2 (London, 1909), 53–56. Herzen continued to keep in regular touch with Schurz after the latter emigrated to the United States, where he was eventually a U.S. senator and secretary of the interior. After the 1849 defeat of the Baden uprising, Schurz had evaded capture, and a potential death sentence in the Prussian military occupation of Rastatt, by escaping from the town through a sewer. In the following year he organized the jailbreak of his university teacher and fellow revolutionary Gottfried Kinkel from the Berlin fortress of Spandau and smuggled him to safety in Britain. Once reassured through official channels that he would not be arrested if he set foot on Prussian territory again, Schurz accepted Bismarck's personal invitation to a grand dinner in Berlin in 1868; after all the notable guests had left, Schurz amused the chancellor with his account of the Kinkel affair. As Herzen commented, "How times are changing!" *SS*, 29:273.

16. VIEW FROM THE OTHER SHORE

1. *SS*, 11:9, 11.
2. The volume was first published anonymously in German in Hamburg in 1850. The first Russian edition, containing two additional essays, was published in London in 1855. An edition with minor revisions (the source of the citations in the present chapter) followed in 1858. Some of the essays were also published independently in German, French, and Italian journals. On the variations between editions, see the editors' notes in *SS*, 6:486–488.
3. E. Lampert, *Studies in Rebellion* (London, 1957), 244.
4. Herzen, *From the Other Shore*, trans. M. Budberg (London, 1956) (hereafter cited as *FOS*), 3; all further references to the work are to this translation, with whose stylistic qualities I cannot compete.

5. See *SS*, 6:490; Martin Malia, *Alexander Herzen and the Birth of Russian Socialism, 1812–1855* (Cambridge, MA, 1961), 381–382. Malia contends that by 1848 Herzen had moved to "an almost unique existential egoism."

6. R. M. Davison argues that Herzen shared "a profound similarity of outlook" with Kierkegaard: "Herzen and Kierkegaard," *Slavic Review* 25, no. 2 (June 1966): 191–209.

7. See W. Weidemaier, "Herzen and Nietzsche: A Link in the Rise of Modern Pessimism," *Russian Review* 36 (1977): 477–488. Weidemaier describes Herzen's thought as bearing a clear resemblance to Nietzsche's in its "pervasive pessimism," due to the erosion of teleological faith (480, 478). The Russian philosopher Nikolai Berdyaev, in *The Realm of Spirit and the Realm of Caesar*, trans. D. Lowrie (New York, 1952), 28, draws comparisons between Herzen's "tragic humanism" and Stirner, Sartre, and Camus.

8. E. Lampert has remarked on the "bewildering" variety of critical views on Herzen's religious position, which "contradict each other so wildly that no complete reliance can be placed on any one of them." He has been described variously as a mystic, a herald of religious revival, or an atheist on the threshold of materialism (Plekhanov's interpretation): *Studies in Rebellion* (London, 1956), 216, 284 n.49. In contrast with all the above, V. Zenkovsky defines Herzen's thought as "a philosophy of *despair, hopelessness, and disbelief*": "a revolt against tarnished reality . . . dictated by the last remnants of a religious consciousness which could have found peace . . . only in God" (Zenkovsky, *A History of Russian Philosophy*, trans. G. Kline [London, 1953], 296).

9. See *FOS*, xiv. See also the essay "Herzen and Bakunin on Individual Liberty" in Isaiah Berlin, *Russian Thinkers* (London, 2013), 93–129.

10. John Dewey, *The Influence of Darwin on Philosophy and Other Essays on Contemporary Thought* (New York, 1951), 2, 1, 13.

11. G. Himmelfarb, *Darwin and the Darwinian Revolution* (New York, 1968), 400.

12. Charles Darwin to A. R. Wallace, 22 December 1857, in *Life and Letters of Charles Darwin*, ed. Francis Darwin, 3 vols. (London, 1887), 2:109.

13. Himmelfarb, *Darwin*, 287.

14. Ibid., 283.

15. Ibid., 309.

16. Darwin, *On the Origin of Species* (Cambridge, MA, 1964), 488, 489.

17. Darwin to C. Lyell, 11 October 1859, in *Life and Letters*, 2:210; letter to Asa Gray, 8 May 1868, in *Life and Letters*, 3:85.

18. "The Variation of Animals and Plants," cited in *Life and Letters*, 1:309.

19. Darwin, *Origin of Species*, 322; see also *Life and Letters*, 3:84–85.

20. Darwin, *Origin of Species*, 314, 73.

21. Darwin, *On the Origin of Species by Means of Natural Selection, or the Preservation of Favoured Races in the Struggle for Life*, 6th ed. (London, 1872), 163 (one of the passages added to this expanded edition of *On the Origin of Species*).

22. Darwin, *Notebooks on the Transmutation of Species, Bulletin of the British Museum (Natural History), Historical Series* 2, no. 2 (London, 1960): 50.

23. Darwin, *The Descent of Man and Selection in Relation to Sex*, 2 vols. (London, 1871), 1:186.

24. Darwin to F. Muller, 2 August 1871, in *Life and Letters*, 3:150.

25. Darwin, *Descent of Man*, 1:92.

26. Darwin, *Notebooks*, 4:136.

27. R. M. Young, *Darwin's Metaphor: Nature's Place in Victorian Culture* (Cambridge, 1985), 97.

28. Darwin, *Descent of Man*, 1:152–153.

29. *Life and Letters*, 3:237.

30. Young, *Darwin's Metaphor*, 122.

31. *FOS*, 69.

32. Darwin, *Descent of Man*, 152–153. For Herzen's confession, see the introduction to Chapter 17.

33. *FOS*, 49–51.

34. *SS*, 10:233.

35. F. M. Dostoevsky, *Polnoe sobranie sochinenii*, 30 vols. (Leningrad, 1972–1988), 21:8. On affinities between Herzen's and Dostoevsky's thought, see my essay "Irony and Utopia in Herzen and Dostoevsky," in Aileen M. Kelly, *Toward Another Shore: Russian Thinkers between Necessity and Chance* (New Haven, CT, 1998), 307–325.

36. *FOS*, 2; *SS*, 24:84.

37. *FOS*, 31, 28, 40–41.This dialogue was inspired by conversations in Nice with A. P. Galakhov, a member of Herzen's Moscow circle.

38. Ibid., 32.

39. Darwin to Asa Gray, 22 May 1860, in *Life and Letters*, 2:311–312. See the commentary on this exchange by Stephen Jay Gould, *Wonderful Life* (London, 1990), 290.

40. *FOS*, 38, 35–36.

41. Ibid., 37, 38–39.

42. Ibid., 67.

43. Ibid., 76.

44. Ibid., 114–115.

45. Ibid., 106, 108, 110.

46. Ibid., 68.

47. Ibid., 93.

48. Ibid., 66–67.

49. Ibid., 89–90.

50. Ibid., 33–34.

51. Ibid., 147.

52. Karl Marx, *Early Writings*, trans. and ed. T. B. Bottomore (London, 1963), 155.

53. *FOS*, 141.

54. See Weidemaier, "Herzen and Nietzsche," 480; Malia, *Alexander Herzen*, 381. Also from Malia, *Alexander Herzen*: "Essentially, *From the Other Shore* takes up the conclusions of *Dilettantism in Science* and the *Letters on the Study of Nature* and pushes them to the *nec plus ultra* of philosophical anarchism" (376). "The universe was a meaningless anarchy . . . and nature was a hostile force arbitrarily granting life or death to the

individual . . . this was the bitter wisdom he found on 'the other shore.' "
Malia argues that Herzen salvaged one value—an existentialist view of
freedom. "Although rationally the world may be meaningless, the individual is existentially aware of the force of his will, of the reality of
his choices, and of his capacity to act; and therefore he is free" (380–381).
Morality for him "had become an affair of absolute self-determination
without reference to anything outside the individual. . . . In contemporary
thought there was no individualism so extreme except the very similar
individualism of Max Stirner" (277).

55. See, for example, the letter from Nietzsche to Malwida von Meysenbug, in
Friedrich Nietzsche: Briefe der Basler Zeit, 1869–1873, ed. W. Hoppe
(Munich, 1940), 284.

56. *FOS*, 103, 140, 128.

57. This central plank of the argument of *From the Other Shore* has been
overlooked by the critics cited above.

58. *FOS*, 34, 39, 34.

59. Ibid., 37.

60. Ibid., 142.

61. See Friedrich Nietzsche, "Schopenhauer als Erzieher," *Werke in Drei
Bänden* (Munich, 1956), 1:287–365.

62. Arthur Schopenhauer, *Essays and Aphorisms*, trans. R. J. Hollingdale
(London, 1970), 51.

63. *FOS*, 35.

64. Schopenhauer, *The World as Will and Representation*, 2 vols., trans. E. F. J.
Payne (New York, 1966), 2:353.

65. The first explicit reference in Herzen's works to Schopenhauer's doctrines
is in the cycle of essays *Ends and Beginnings*, published in 1862–1863,
where he takes issue with Turgenev's pessimistic nihilism, shared with
"his favorite philosopher, Schopenhauer." *SS*, 20:349. See the comparison
of Herzen and Schopenhauer in Kelly, *Toward Another Shore*, chap. 16.

66. *FOS*, 34; Schopenhauer, *Will and Representation*, 2:572.

67. *FOS*, 78, 74, 33.

68. Ibid., 134–135.

69. Ibid., 136–137.

70. Ibid., 138–140.

71. Ibid., 24, 25.

72. *SS*, 10:120.

73. Gould, *Wonderful Life*, 31.

74. *FOS*, 19, 20.

75. Ibid., 119.

76. Ibid., 133.

77. See ibid., 113: "I have no system, no interest except the truth."

78. See Chapter 7 for Herzen's use of the metaphors of the stone wall, the
flesh of history, and the Bacchanalian whirl of the temporal in his two
cycles of essays.

79. *SS*, 10:185.

80. *FOS*, 3, 120.

81. Ibid., 151.

17. THE LIVING TRUTH

1. *SS*, 10:122–123.
2. In the conclusion to his study of Herzen's "Russian Socialism," Malia observes that "the utopian form in which Herzen's ideals . . . were expressed is alien and even disturbing to the empirical, pragmatic Anglo-Saxon mind." Martin Malia, *Alexander Herzen and the Birth of Russian Socialism, 1812–1855* (Cambridge, MA, 1961), 419.
3. *SS*, 24:375.
4. Ibid., 12:235.
5. Ibid., 63. On the subsequent productions of the London Press, see *Alexandre Ivanovich Herzen, 1812–1870: Essai sur la formation et le développement de ses idées* (Paris, 1928), 366–367 nn. 1 and 2.
6. *SS*, 10:361.
7. Ibid., 12:296.
8. *The Athenaeum*, no. 1419 (1855): 7–9. The article is unsigned.
9. *SS*, 13:195.
10. Ibid., 14:33.
11. On the documentary evidence testifying to this, see editors' notes, *SS*, 12:511–512; and I. S. Smolin, "Tsarizm v borbe s volnoi pechati Gertsena," *Uchenye zapiski Leningradskogo pedinstituta* 61 (Leningrad): 57–58.
12. *SS*, 14:21.
13. Ibid., 11:297.
14. See Edward Acton, *Alexander Herzen and the Role of the Intellectual Revolutionary* (Cambridge, 1979), chap. 8.
15. The letter was subsequently printed in the *Bell* in January 1864. *SS*, 18:26, 23.
16. *SS*, 19:193. See John Stuart Mill, *Autobiography*, ed. J. M. Robson (London, 1989), 136, 133.
17. *SS*, 18:8.
18. Ibid., 14:15, 275, 189.
19. "Mortuos plango," *SS*, 16:10.
20. "1864," *SS*, 18:9.
21. See Franco Venturi, *Roots of Revolution*, trans. F. Haskell (Chicago, 1983), chap. 7.
22. Ibid., 218.
23. *SS*, 14:10, 18: 24.
24. Its content appeared in the *Bell* of 2 March 1862. See editors' commentary in *SS*, 18:536–537.
25. *SS*, 18:25.
26. Ibid., 19:189.
27. Ibid., 20:78–79.
28. Ibid., 19:286.
29. Acton, *Alexander Herzen*, 177.
30. "May God preserve us from the sight of a Russian peasant uprising, senseless and merciless": epigraph to the manuscript of Pushkin's novella *The Captain's Daughter* (not included in the printed version).
31. E. Lampert has remarked on "a curious, almost jarring discrepancy between the quality of Herzen's search and that of his discovery, between

the importance of his question and the apparent triviality of his answer." *Studies in Rebellion* (London, 1957), 244.

32. *SS*, 14:11, 10, 11, 33.
33. Ibid., 41, 46.
34. Ibid., 10:185.

18. IN DEFENSE OF INCONSISTENCY

1. R. Pipes, *Russia under the Old Regime* (London, 1974), 270. See also the studies by L. Schapiro referred to in note 4 below.

2. Other prominent members of these groups were the critic and memoirist P. V. Annenkov, the writer M. E. Saltykov-Shchedrin, the classical historian P. N. Kudriavtsev, and the economist I. K. Babst.

3. See P. R. Roosevelt, "Granovskii at the lectern: a conservative liberal's vision of history," *Forschungen zur osteuropäischen Geschichte* 29 (1981), 63.

4. For example, L. Schapiro contrasts Chicherin's "pragmatic" approach to politics with Herzen's "almost lighthearted" calls to revolution: *Rationalism and Nationalism in Russian Nineteenth-Century Political Thought* (New Haven, 1967), 94, 100. See also A. Walicki, *Legal Philosophies of Russian Liberalism* (Oxford, 1987), 51–55. For a different view of Herzen's polemics with the Russian liberals see Kelly, "Byl li Gertsen liberalom?" *Novoe literaturnoe obozrenie*, nr. 58 (2002), 87–99.

5. J. Plamenatz, *Readings from Liberal Writers* (Oxford, 1965), 37. Plamenatz observes that in spite of Hegel's influence on that strand of liberal thought which emphasizes man's social essence and lays less stress than classical liberalism on "negative" liberty, the claim that he or his more orthodox followers were liberals is "not often" made (ibid., 25). See also J. G. Merquior's description of the Philosophy of Right as "a grand endeavor to insert modern 'civil society,' with its vigorous bourgeois individualism, into the framework of a holist state accommodating the traditional hierarchies of the *ancien regime*." *Liberalism Old and New* (Boston, 1991), 49.

6. C. Taylor, *Hegel and Modern Society* (Cambridge, 1979).

7. Schiller, *On the Aesthetic Education of Man*, ed. and trans. E. M. Wilkinson and L. A. Willoughby (Oxford, 1982), 47; I. Berlin, *Four Essays on Liberty* (Oxford, 1969), 134.

8. Merquior, *Liberalism*, 4.

9. See G. M. Hamburg, *Boris Chicherin and Early Russian Liberalism, 1828–1866* (Stanford, CA, 1992), 57–66.

10. K. D. Kavelin, "A brief survey of the juridical way of life of Ancient Russia," *Sobranie sochinenii*, 4 vols. (Saint Petersburg, 1897–1900), 1:6–66.

11. A. Yanov, *The Origins of Autocracy. Ivan the Terrible in Russian History*, trans. S. Dunn (Berkeley, CA, 1981), chapters 8 and 9.

12. *P. V. Annenkov i ego druz'ia. Literaturnie vospominaniia i perepiska 1835–85 godov* (Saint Petersburg, 1892), 1:530.

13. See Schapiro, *Rationalism*, 99–102. On Chicherin as liberal see also Walicki, *Legal Philosophies of Russian Liberalism*, 105–164.

14. See Kelly: "What is real is rational: the political philosophy of B. N. Chicherin," *Cahiers du monde russe et soviétique*, XVIII (1977), 195–222. Against this interpretation Walicki argues that even though Chicherin

was "too tolerant of absolute monarchy, too Hegelian in his glorification of the modern centralized state and . . . too authoritarian in his emphasis on the need for a strong government," he was nonetheless a liberal, his thought being close to the ideal model of the liberal conception of law as the indispensable safeguard of freedom; the only discernible difference being his Hegelian view that the state was endowed with unlimited authority: an unimportant difference, inasmuch as he had in mind the Hegelian state which presupposed freedom of conscience and the autonomy of civil society. Walicki does indeed note that at the end of his life Chicherin "came to recognize that . . . no form of the rule of law was compatible with arbitrary personal rule. In this conviction he proclaimed the necessity of transforming Russian absolutism into a constitutional monarchy." (*Legal Philosophies*, 116.) This belated development in Chicherin's views is not relevant to the present chapter, which focuses on his ideas at the period when he sought to define and direct the Russian liberal tradition during the period of the Great Reforms. By the time he proclaimed his change of heart (in an obscure and anonymous pamphlet printed in Berlin in 1900) he had long ceased to have any influence on Russian liberalism or on public life.

My differences with Walicki turn on the vexed question of the definition of liberalism. For classical liberalism as he defines it, "it is obvious that socialism must be enemy number one" (a definition that fits Chicherin but has the unfortunate effect of excluding Mill, who once laid claim in print to the title of socialist [see note 53 below]). He concludes that "the only discernible difference" between Chicherin and more conventional liberals (his Hegelian theory of the state) was of negligible importance. While acknowledging Chicherin's failure to "carefully" distinguish between the existing Russian state and an ideal *Rechtsstaat*, G. M. Hamburg describes him as a *juste milieu* liberal (*Boris Chicherin*, 337, 228). But Kavelin's letter of protest (see below, n.26) is strong evidence to the contrary.

15. Chicherin, *Vospominaniia: Moskva sorokovykh godov* (Moscow, 1929), 74, 77, 89.
16. A. D. Gradovsky, "Russkaia uchenaia literatura," *Russkii vestnik* 70 (1867): 730. Quoted in Hamburg, *Boris Chicherin*, 297.
17. Chicherin, *Neskolko sovremennikh voprosov* (Moscow, 1862), 34, 197.
18. On the contemporary reaction to Chicherin's lecture, see Hamburg, *Boris Chicherin*, 226–233.
19. N. G. Chernyshevsky, *Polnoe sobranie sochinenii* (Moscow, 1950), 10:62.
20. From an unpublished letter of 1857, in D. Hammer, *Two Russian Liberals: The Political Thought of B. N. Chicherin and D. V. Kavelin* (Ph.D. diss., Columbia University, 1962), 114.
21. *Golosa iz Rossii: Sborniki A. I. Gertsena i N. P. Ogareva:* 3 vols. (Moscow, 1974), 1:9–36.
22. A. V. Stankevich, *T. N. Granovsky i ego perepiska*, vol. 2: *Perepiska* (Moscow, 1897), 455–456.
23. *Pis'ma K. D. Kavelina k Al. I. Gertsenu i N. Pl. Ogarevu, 1857–63*, ed. M. Dragomanov (Geneva, 1892), 6–7; *Literaturnoe nasledstvo*, vol. 62 (Moscow, 1955), 386.

24. "Nas uprekayut," *SS*, 13:361–363.

25. B. N. Chicherin, letter to the *Bell*, in Herzen, *Polnoe sobranie sochinenii i pisem*, ed. M. K. Lemke (Peterburg, 1919), 9:409–415.

26. Chicherin includes this protest in its entirety in his *Vospominania: Puteshestvie za granitsu* (Moscow, 1932), 57–62.

27. A. V. Nikitenko, *Dnevnik*, 3 vols. (Leningrad, 1955–1956), 2:54. Only two prominent "men of the forties," Korsh and Ketcher, took Chicherin's side in the dispute.

28. *SS*, 9:248.

29. Ibid., 250–252.

30. Unpublished letters cited in Hamburg, *Boris Chicherin*. Commenting on these "astonishing" letters, Hamburg suggests that the sentiments in the second were "unworthy even of Metternich. They belong to the brutish politics of our own [twentieth] century." *Boris Chicherin*, 262.

31. *SS*, 9:248.

32. "Russkie nemtsy i nemetskie russkie," *SS*, 14:148–189.

33. *SS*, 16:306.

34. D. Offord, *Portraits of Early Russian Liberals: A Study of the Thought of T. N. Granovsky, V. P. Botkin, P. V. Annenkov, A. V. Druzhinin, and K. D. Kavelin* (Cambridge, 1985), 209–212.

35. *SS*, 10:187.

36. Ibid., 11:480.

37. E. Lampert, *Studies in Rebellion* (London, 1957), 244.

38. *SS*, 4:130.

39. John Stuart Mill, *Autobiography*, ed. J. M. Robson (London, 1989), 96.

40. *Collected Works of John Stuart Mill*, ed. J. M. Robson, 33 vols. (Toronto, 1963), 1: 207–208.

41. Mill, *Autobiography*, 118.

42. *Essential Works of John Stuart Mill*, ed. M. Lerner (New York, 1971), 205.

43. Ibid., 219.

44. J. S. Mill, *On Liberty and Other Writings*, ed. S. Collini (Cambridge, 1989).

45. See Mill, *Autobiography*, 191. For his summary of Humboldt's thesis, see Mill, *On Liberty*, 58.

46. Wilhelm von Humboldt, *The Limits of State Action*, ed. J. W. Burrow (Cambridge, 1969), xlii.

47. I. Berlin, "John Stuart Mill and the Ends of Life," in *Four Essays on Liberty* (London, 1969), 192.

48. Mill, *Autobiography*, 139.

49. Schiller, *Aesthetic Education*, 19.

50. John Stuart Mill, *August Comte and Positivism* (London, 1882), 14–15. See his comments on Comte's *Système de politique positive*: "the completest system of spiritual and temporal despotism which ever yet emanated from a human brain, unless possibly that of Ignatius Loyola" (Mill, *Autobiography*, 162–164). In the words of J. M. Robson, "Comte is a scientific humanist; Mill, a *humanist* using science" (*The Improvement of Mankind: the Social and Political Thought of John Stuart Mill* [Toronto, 1968], 103).

51. Mill, *Autobiography*, 141.

52. Ibid., 133, 175.

53. Mill, *Collected Works*, 3:804.

54. Mill, *On Liberty*, 64.

55. *SS*, 11:66–77.

56. Mill, *Autobiography*, 174.

57. *SS*, 13:95.

58. Ibid., 24:216.

59. Ibid., 18:96.

19. WHAT IS HISTORY?

1. I. S. Turgenev, *Polnoe sobranie sochineniia i pisem* (Moscow / Leningrad, 1960–1968), in Turgenev, *Pis'ma* (Moscow, 1966–1968), (hereafter cited as *T-P*), 2:316.

2. Ivan Turgenev, *Sochineniia* (Moscow, 1960), 1:244.

3. *T-P*, 5:65.

4. *SS*, 27:264–265.

5. Ibid., 217.

6. Response to the Senate Investigating Commission, Turgenev, *Sochineniia*, 5:394.

7. *SS*, 28:35; 27:454–455; 29:102, 105.

8. Ibid., 12:423–436.

9. On the controversy over Chicherin's article, see A. Walicki, *Legal Philosophies of Russian Liberalism* (Oxford, 1987), 125–127.

10. *SS*, 17:38.

11. C. Lyell, *Principles of Geology*, 2 vols. (London, 1867–1868), 1:492.

12. Letters to Turgenev, 19 December 1860, *SS*, 27:122; to Sasha Herzen, 17–19 April 1869, *SS*, 30:87; "Robert Owen," *SS*, 11:205–253. See A. I. Volodin's very perceptive analysis of "Robert Owen" as a graphic demonstration of Herzen's "methodological skepticism" in *Voprosy filosofii*, no. 9 (1996): 82–89.

13. G. Himmelfarb, *Darwin and the Darwinian Revolution* (New York, 1968), 356.

14. Ibid., 388.

15. *SS*, 19:131.

16. *Life and Letters of Charles Darwin*, ed. Francis Darwin, 3 vols. (London, 1887), 1:313–314, 2:353, 1:309.

17. Letter of 30 April 1861, *SS*, 27:150.

18. To V. F. Luginin, *T-P*, 5:49.

19. *SS*, 16:136.

20. Ibid., 137, 136, 178, 179.

21. Ibid., 147–148.

22. Ibid., 139.

23. See Martin Malia, *Alexander Herzen and the Birth of Russian Socialism, 1812–1855* (Cambridge, MA, 1961), 358.

24. See A. Walicki, *A History of Russian Thought from the Enlightenment to Marxism* (Oxford, 1980), 170.

25. *SS*, 16:148.

26. Ibid., 132.
27. Ibid., 183–184.
28. Ibid., 156.
29. Ibid., 173, 174.
30. Ibid., 133.
31. Ibid., 167.
32. *T-P*, 5:67–68.
33. *SS*, 16:195–196.
34. Ibid., 196.
35. Ibid., 197.
36. Ibid., 198.
37. Ibid., 146.
38. Ibid., 147, 161.
39. Ibid., 162, 164.
40. Ibid., 172.
41. Ibid., 130, 129, 131.
42. Ibid., 151.
43. *T-P*, 5:65.
44. *SS*, 27:264–266. On Herzen's assault on Schopenhauerian pessimism, see Aileen M. Kelly, *Toward Another Shore: Russian Thinkers between Necessity and Chance* (New Haven, CT, 1998), 326–344.
45. *SS*, 20:349.
46. *T-P*, 5:73.
47. Ibid., 276.
48. Ibid., 7:14.
49. Schopenhauer, *The World as Will and Representation*, 2 vols., trans. E. F. J. Payne (New York, 1966), 2:443.
50. *T-P*, 5:74.
51. "Dovol'no!," *SS*, 9:117–118.
52. *SS*, 6:93.
53. Schopenhauer, *Will and Representation*, 1:311.
54. *SS*, 8:166.
55. Schopenhauer, *Will and Representation*, 2:574.
56. *T-P*, 3:354. See letter to Herzen of March 1869, *T-P*, 7:310. Compare Schopenhauer, *Will and Representation*, 1:322: "The life of every individual, viewed as a whole . . . is really a tragedy."
57. *SS*: 14:103.
58. Schopenhauer, *Will and Representation*, 1:312.
59. *T-P*, 12:199.
60. Ibid., 3:306.
61. Ibid., 4:306.
62. Ibid., 8:152.
63. Turgenev, *Sochineniia*, 8:178.
64. *SS*, 10:74–75.
65. *T-P*, 7:172.
66. See Aileen Kelly, *Mikhail Bakunin: A Study in the Psychology and Politics of Utopianism* (Oxford, 1979), chaps. 2, 3, 5, and 6.
67. J. P. Stern, *A Study of Nietzsche* (Cambridge, 1971), 141.

68. Herzen, *From the Other Shore*, 20.

69. *SS*, 20:437.

70. *T-P*, 3:303.

71. *SS*, 7:296.

72. Schopenhauer, *Will and Representation*, 2:588.

73. *SS*, 7:295–296.

74. Ibid., 16:191–192.

75. Reminiscences of P. Lavrov, *Turgenev v russkoi kritike: Sbornik statei*, ed. K. I. Bonetsky (Moscow, 1953), 414.

76. A. Walicki, *History of Russian Thought*, 170.

77. L. Schapiro, "Turgenev and Herzen: Two Modes of Russian Political Thought," in *Russian Studies* (New York, 1987), 321–337. See A. M. Kelly, "Leonard Schapiro's Russia," in Kelly, *Toward Another Shore*, 25–33.

78. D. Offord, "Alexander Herzen," in *A History of Russian Philosophy, 1830–1930*, ed. G. M. Hamburg and R. A. Poole (Cambridge, 2010), 52–68. Offord describes as a "limitation" of Herzen's defense of personhood the fact that "he did not hold up for emulation any contemporary western institutions which might have helped protect it"—such as parliamentary democracy (65). The reason, of course, was Herzen's view of the negative record of European parliamentary democracy in his time.

79. Martin Malia, *Russia under Western Eyes: From the Bronze Horseman to the Lenin Mausoleum* (Cambridge, MA, 1999). Malia's claim that Russia has no choice but to become a "normal" European power seems to rest less on empirical evidence than on teleological assumptions rooted (like Marx's historical determinism) in the European Enlightenment's faith that humanity is progressing toward a single form of society in which rationality and justice will be optimally combined.

80. D. Joravsky, "Communism in Historical Perspective," *American Historical Review* 99 (1994): 845. The historian Stephen Cohen remarks on the missionary faith that led U.S. policymakers into "a virtual crusade to transform post-Communist Russia into some facsimile of the American democratic and capitalist system." From the beginning of the 1990s, "advisors" spread across Russia and, supported by influential opinion-makers back at home, worked to prevent the country from wandering off (in the words of one media supporter of the crusade) on "a strange, ambivalent path of its own confused devising"; they backed Yeltsin's corrupt appointees and ignored less-destructive, less-costly alternatives to his policies, such as a mixed economy. S. F. Cohen, *Failed Crusade: America and the Tragedy of Post-Communist Russia* (New York, 2000), 5, 7.

81. S. J. Gould, *Wonderful Life* (London, 1991), 235, 239; Herzen, *From the Other Shore*, 117.

20. THE POLISH UPRISING

1. *SS*, 16: 220.

2. Herzen, *Polnoe sobranie sochinenii i pisem*, ed. M. K. Lemke (Peterburg, 1920), 14:230–231.

3. Edward Acton portrays him as an intellectual revolutionary whose goals ultimately evoked no political response. Malia describes him as a "gentry

revolutionary," characterized by a preference for a "middle gentry" revolution. Edward Acton, *Alexander Herzen and the Role of the Intellectual
Revolutionary* (Cambridge, 1979), 42.

4. *SS*, 27:258.
5. Ibid., 18:27–28.
6. Ibid., 16:251–257.
7. Ibid., 11:368.
8. Ibid.
9. Ibid., 27:296.
10. Ibid., 301–303.
11. Ibid., 301.
12. Ibid., 11:372–373.
13. E. H. Carr credits Bakunin with a fine appreciation of Herzen's defects;
    on Bakunin's own defects he is somewhat restrained. Carr, *Michael Ba-
    kunin* (New York, 1975), 298.
14. "Der demokratische Panslawismus," in Karl Marx and Friedrich Engels,
    Werke (Berlin, 1964–1968), 6:271–272.
15. *SS*, 11:371.
16. The paper's title, *Obshchee veche* [The Common Assembly], recalled the
    assemblies of all the citizens in medieval communes.
17. Kelsiev has left an amusing account of this visit. See V. I. Kelsiev, *Ispoved',
    Literaturnoe nasledstvo*, vols. 41–43. On the relations between the Old
    Believers and the London émigrés, see Yu. Steklov, *Mikhail Aleksan-
    drovich Bakunin: Ego zhizn' i deiatelnost, 1814–1876* (Moscow, 1926–
    1927), 2:56–64.
18. *SS*, 18:11–15.
19. Ibid., 11:374.
20. Ibid., 17:215.
21. Ibid., 236, 215.
22. Ibid., 18:13.
23. Ibid., 14.
24. Ibid., 16:179, 18: 164.
25. Ibid., 11:547.
26. Ibid., 16:129, 130.
27. Ibid., 19:199.
28. Ibid., 16:160.
29. Ibid., 129.
30. Ibid., 17:217.
31. Ibid., 285–286.
32. Ibid., 286.
33. Ibid., 11:477, 479.
34. Ibid., 477.
35. Ibid., 14:263.
36. Ibid., 18:363, 364.

21. TRUE NIHILISM

1. *SS*, 16:130.
2. Ibid., 18:243.

3. R. W. Mathewson, *The Positive Hero in Russian Literature* (Stanford, CA, 1975), 99. Russian historians writing in the Soviet period classified him as a "gentry revolutionary." Martin Malia sees his "utopia of the socialist commune" as "a projection into the world of peasant Russia of his own aristocratic and idealist education, its extension from the Moscow salons and lecture halls into the humble huts of the village" (*Alexander Herzen and the Birth of Russian Socialism, 1812–1855* [Cambridge, MA, 1961], 423).

4. See N. Valentinov (N. V. Volsky), *Encounters with Lenin*, trans. P. Rosta and B. Pearce (London, 1968), 63–68.

5. *SS*, 18: 284,285.

6. Ibid., 11:341–342.

7. See ibid., 620–622.

8. Ibid., 18:288.

9. Ibid., 28:215.

10. Turgenev, *Sochineniia* (Moscow, 1964), 8: 216.

11. Sergei Stepniak-Kravchinsky, *Underground Russia* (London, 1883), 4.

12. *SS*, 7:298.

13. Letter of 21 April 1862, *SS*, 27:217.

14. N. K. Mikhailovsky, *Literaturnye vospominaniia i sovremennaia smuta*, 2 vols. (Saint Petersburg, 1900), 1:307.

15. See Vucinich, *Science in Russian Culture: A History to 1860* (London, 1973), 378–390.

16. N. G. Chernyshevsky, "The Anthropological Principle in Philosophy," *Izbrannye filosofskie sochineniia*, vol. 3 (Moscow, 1951), 208.

17. Nikolai Dobrolyubov, *Polnoe sobranie sochinenii* (Leningrad, 1934–1939), 4:308.

18. Cited in Stepniak-Kravchinsky, *Underground Russia*, 6.

19. Nikolai Chernyshevsky, *Polnoe sobranie sochinenii*, 16 vols. (Moscow, 1939–1953), 1:357.

20. Herzen, *From the Other Shore*, trans. M. Budberg (London, 1956), 132–133.

21. *SS*, 14:538–541, 238–244.

22. Ibid., 10:320–321.

23. Dobrolyubov, *Polnoe sobranie sochinenii*, 14:379. Chernyshevsky's contempt nevertheless did not prevent Herzen from making an objective assessment of his didactic novel of 1867, *What Is to Be Done?*, a portrayal of the "new men" of the 1860s that became a cult model for that generation. On its appearance he commented in letters to Ogarev that, although repelled by its style, an apparent reflection of a seminary education, he would concede that "there's an enormous amount that's good in it" and that it contained a multitude of perceptions of "both the good and the bad sides of the 'ultra-nihilists.'" *SS*, 29:159, 167; see also 157.

24. *SS*, 15:52.

25. Nikolai Chernyshevsky, "O prichinakh padeniia Rima," *Izbrannye ekonomicheskie proizvedeniia* (Moscow, 1948), 572–605.

26. "Repetitio est mater studiorum," *SS*, 15:143–149.

27. *SS*, 16:25–29.

28. See B. N. Kozmin, *P. G. Zaichnevsky i 'Molodiia Rossiia'* (Moscow, 1932); and *SS*, 16:411–412.

29. N. Ya. Nikoladze, *Katorga i ssylka* (1927), no. 5, 37.

30. *SS*, 16:221.

31. Ibid., 204.

32. Ibid., 224, 204.

33. Ibid., 225. The Monomach hat was one of the insignia of royal power said to have been inherited by Vladimir Monomach, ancestor of the princes of Moscow, from his grandfather, the Byzantine emperor Constantine Monomakh, and used to crown all tsars up to Peter the Great.

34. N. V. Shelgunov, *Vospominaniia* (Moscow, 1967), 125.

35. *SS*, 11:351.

36. Cited in A. Coquart, *Dmitri Pisarev et l'idéologie du nihilisme Russe* (Paris, 1946), 321.

37. See E. Lampert, *Sons against Fathers: Studies in Russian Radicalism and Revolution* (Oxford: 1965), 300, 298–299.

38. Cited in Coquart, *Pisarev*, 131.

39. Turgenev, *Sochineniia*, 8, 219.

40. Ibid., 14, 99.

41. Letter of 21 April 1862, *SS*, 27:217.

42. *Polnoe sobranie sochinenii D. I. Pisareva* (Saint Petersburg, 1900), 2:379–426.

43. Cited in Coquart, *Pisarev*, 184.

44. Letter of 8–9 January 1868, *SS*, 29:256. Pisarev distinguished between Belinsky the "realist" critic and Belinsky the admirer of Pushkin, whom he dismissed (with *Eugene Onegin* in mind) as a frivolous versifier. See Coquart, *Pisarev*, chap. 9, for Pisarev's crusade against aestheticism. *SS*, 29:339.

45. Letter of 15 May 1868 to Ogarev, *SS*, 29:339.

46. Coquart, *Pisarev*, 266. (Pisarev adds: "But to the Onegin type, we have absolutely no attachment whatsoever.")

47. Letter of May 1868, *SS*, 29:352.

48. "Bazarov once more," *SS*, 20:335–350.

49. Ibid., 376.

22. THE LAST YEARS

1. Turgenev, *Pis'ma* (Moscow, 1964), 8, 168.

2. *SS*, 20:605–606.

3. N. A. Tuchkova-Ogareva, *Vospominaniia* (Leningrad, 1929), 216.

4. *SS*, 26:143. On Herzen's friendship with Vogt, see their correspondence between 1852 and 1864 with accompanying commentary in *Literaturnoe nasledstvo*, 96:92–174.

5. *SS*, 26:203, 212, 215, 228.

6. Ibid., 243, 273.

7. Ibid., 269, 253.

8. Ibid., 27:9, 16.

9. Ibid., 24–25, 60.

10. Ibid., 66, 71.

11. Ibid., 141.

12. On Sasha's activities as an agent of Land and Liberty, see B. N. Kozmin, "Gertsen i Ogarev – redaktoru «The Morning Star»," *Literaturnoe nasledstvo* (Moscow, 1956), 63:128–129.

13. *SS*, 27:203, 236.

14. Ibid, 370, 387.

15. Ibid., 426.

16. Ibid., 509, 514.

17. See the editors' notes in *SS*, 27:825; writing to Malwida in 1864 he describes himself as having been tormented by uncertainty over the previous three years: "We don't even know how much we still have and how much we've lost." *SS*, 27:453. See letter to Ogarev, 29 December 1867, *SS*, 29:251.

18. *SS*, 29:368.

19. Ibid., 19:58.

20. Ibid., 29:110, 89.

21. Ibid., 37.

22. Ibid., 30:112.

23. Ibid., 28:260; 29:8.

24. Ibid., 29:25, 161.

25. Ibid., 49.

26. Ibid., 20:9–10, 402.

27. Ibid., 26:288.

28. Letter of 12 January 1866, Herzen, *Polnoe sobranie sochinenii i pisem*, ed. M. K. Lemke (Peterberg, 1922), 18:312.

29. *SS*, 29:503.

30. Ibid., 171.

31. Ibid., 328; 30:265; 29:311. The unfortunate Teresina did not measure up even to the standards Herzen had demanded of a governess for his two daughters some years before: as transmitted to his son, who was to carry out the search, the paramount requirement was an ability to conduct herself in society. "Of course a French / Swiss education is preferable to a German one." *SS* 26:235.

32. *SS*, 29:169, 170.

33. Ibid., 453.

34. *SS*, 30:34, 265.

35. *Literaturnoe nasledstvo*, 63:470, 473–477.

36. *SS*, 30:155.

37. Ibid., 255, 274.

38. Ibid., 30:94; 29:116.

39. *Literaturnoe nasledstvo*, 63:460.

40. Isaiah Berlin, *Russian Thinkers* (London, 2013), 113. The importance Herzen attached to these *Letters* is reflected in the complex process of their composition, during which he submitted successive drafts to Ogarev for comment. See *Literaturnoe nasledstvo*, 61:151–204.

41. *Pis'ma M. A. Bakunina k A. I. Gertsenu i N. P. Ogarevu*, ed. M. G. Dragomanov (Saint Petersburg, 1896), 186.

42. Cited in Aileen Kelly, *Mikhail Bakunin: A Study in the Psychology and Politics of Utopianism* (Oxford, 1979), 266.
43. Ibid., 166.
44. *SS*, 27:370–372.
45. Ibid., 30:110, 137, 134.
46. Ogarev to Bakunin, 31 August 1862, in Dragomanov, *Pis'ma*, 87–89.
47. N. P. Ogarev, *Izbrannye sotsialno-politicheskie proizvedeniia*, vol. 2 (Moscow, 1956), 543, 186.
48. On the products of this collaboration, see Kelly, *Mikhail Bakunin*, 212–217.
49. *SS*, 30:191, 198–199.
50. Ibid., 198.
51. Ibid., 14:40.
52. "K staromu tovarishchu," *SS*, 20:575–593.
53. See *Literaturnoe nasledstvo*, 61:151–204.
54. In his tribute to Herzen on the centenary of his birth, Lenin cites this passage as proof that at the end of his life he had turned his gaze "to *the International:* the International which was led by Marx" ("Pamiati Gertsena," *Polnoe sobranie sochinenii*, 5th. ed. [Moscow, 1961], 21:257). But as noted in the present chapter, Marx gained control of the International only after Herzen's death.
55. Letter of 23 December 1852, *SS*, 24:374–375.
56. Herzen, *Polnoe sobranie sochinenii*, 21:560, 562.

EPILOGUE

1. *The Works of Francis Bacon*, 3:406, 4:52.
2. *SS*, 16:160. As cited in Chapter 1, the latest Herzen scholarship, particularly (but not only) in Russia, gives some reason to hope that Herzen's pessimism in the quotation will at last lose its force during this century. Realism, however, demands that researchers take account of the three strands of past activity that may hinder such a development, if they wish to avoid them. One of those strands is post-Soviet: the inclination to be "modern." Perhaps the most adventurous such book (R. Khestanov, *Aleksandr Gertsen: Improvizatsiia protiv doktriny* [Moscow, 2001]) has at least the virtue of showing that the author is up to date with postmodernism; but as noted in one review (I. Kaspe, "Gertsen kak metod i ob'ekt" ["Herzen as Method and Object"], *Novoe literaturnoe obozrenie*, no. 49 [2001]: 191–196), Herzen becomes there a vehicle or target for a mixture of methods (or methodologies) extracted from fashionable Western figures—such as Derrida, Adorno, Todorov, and Horkheimer—while he himself and his writings, actions, and historical context risk being somewhat lost in the process. A second strand is now venerable, having first appeared more than a hundred years ago: it is driven by the desire to represent Herzen as some kind of closet religious thinker, usually with an Orthodox flavor. A literally weighty message of this kind is sent by the choice of articles from all of that period collected together in the large volume *Alexandr Gertsen: Pro et contra*, ed. D. K. Burlaka and K. G.

Isupov (Moscow, 2012). The final strand has had a braking effect in both Russia and the West, for different reasons in the two cases: strongly national sentiment in the first, resistance to thinking "outside the box" of familiar specialized Russian scholarship in the second. The Western variety is best illustrated by a short dialogue I experienced at first hand several years ago and to which I made the contribution in the middle. "What are you working on now?" "Herzen." "Herzen? Why don't you do some work on a real *Russian* thinker instead, like Chernyshevsky?"

3. *SS*, 14:107.

4. Ibid., 20:554.

5. Ibid., 14:275.

6. Ibid., 1:22.

7. Ibid., 29:23, 26. Here, too, Herzen was ahead of his time. In the 1850s and 1860s, the leading figures in physiology were vigorous materialists. They were also forceful advocates for that standpoint; working in close association with them as a junior researcher, Herzen's son would have found it difficult to form an independent view (e.g., see his statement in n.12 below). But in the history of physiology, antimaterialism had effectively replaced materialism as a philosophical position by the early twentieth century. The individual scientist who probably had most to do with this change of perspective, not necessarily intentionally, was Wilhelm Wundt.

8. Ibid., 42.

9. Ibid., 362; 30:77.

10. Ibid., 18:281.

11. Ibid., 29:26.

12. The letter was published in the *Revue philosophique de France et de l'étranger*, 1876. Sasha Herzen accompanies it with a summary of the paper (originally a public lecture) to which his father had objected: "I had maintained that all human and animal activity is merely an involuntary development of the reflexes and can be reduced to the latter as its prototype, and that consequently free will is impossible and must be seen as an illusion. My father's comments gave me much thought; but I continually returned to the idea that the problem of freedom is purely and exclusively a problem of physiological competence." See the editors' notes: *SS*, 20:818.

13. Ibid., 438.

14. Ibid., 436.

15. Ibid., 437–438.

16. John Dewey, *The Influence of Darwin on Philosophy and Other Essays on Contemporary Thought* (New York, 1951), 13.

17. *Life and Letters of Charles Darwin*, ed. Francis Darwin (London, 1887), 2:378; 1:308, 307; 2:304; 1:13.

18. *SS*, 20:436.

19. See Ernst Mayr, *The Growth of Biological Thought: Diversity, Evolution and Inheritance* (Cambridge, MA, 1982), 682.

20. *SS*, 26:314. Bacon's view of the relation of theology to the investigation of nature rested on an absolute distinction between the ultimate causes of

things—*deus absconditus*—inaccessible to the human mind, and the investigation of nature for which the mind had been designed. See S. Matthews, *Theology and Science in the Thought of Francis Bacon* (Aldershot, 2008), 68.

21. *SS*, 10:120.
22. Ibid., 30:197.
23. Isaiah Berlin, *Russian Thinkers* (London, 1978), 209.
24. V. K. Kantor, "Tragediia Gertsena ili iskushenie radikalizma," *Voprosy filosofii*, 12 (2012): 84.
25. Berlin, *Russian Thinkers*, 111 (the essay itself was first published in 1955).

Illustration Credits

It is a pleasure to put on record my gratitude to Sarah Chapalay, Olga Fokina, Ricci de Freitas, Sylvie Jenoud Jungo, Anna Lapidus, Benoît Mahuet, Agnieszka Rozciecha, Shakko Kitsune, Zbigniew Stanczyk, and Irina Zhelvakova for various permissions and help during my search for suitable illustrations for this book. Tracking some of those illustrations to where they could be found was not a simple exercise; I am grateful for all the friendly cooperation I received during the search.

The relevant institutions and people associated with each of the illustrations are:

Herzen's mother Luise Haag (p. 25); Herzen's father I. A. Yakovlev (p. 26); Sparrow Hills (p. 33); Herzen's wife N. A. Zakharina (p. 143); Herzen with his children Sasha, Tata, and Olga (p. 375); 1905 Herzen family group (p. 532): A. I. Herzen House Museum (Dom-muzei A. I. Gertsena), State Literary Museum, Moscow

Herzen as painted by A. A. Zbruev (p. 34): State Historical Museum, Moscow/ Shakko Kitsune

M. A. Maximovich (p. 78): *Světozor*, issue 12, 17 March 1882, digitization by the Czech Academy of Sciences

Sketch of Vyatka in the 1830s (p. 129): Institute of Russian Literature (Pushkinsky Dom) of the Russian Academy of Sciences, Saint Petersburg

Paris barricade, 1848 (p. 276): *Illustrated London News*, 1 July 1848/Cambridge University Library

P.-J. Proudhon cartoon (p. 305): Musées de Mâcon

Free Russian Press, London (p. 361): Marchmont Association/Ricci de Freitas

Kolokol front page (p. 370): Cambridge University Library

1860 London studio photograph of Herzen and Ogarev (p. 376): Russian State Library/Mayer Brothers

Russian peasant disturbance, as visualized by S. V. Gerasimov (p. 399): *Literaturnoe nasledstvo*/Institute of Russian Literature (Pushkinsky Dom) of the Russian Academy of Sciences, Saint Petersburg

"Farewell Europe," painting by Alexander Sochaczewski (p. 459): Museum of Warsaw, MHW 1735. Displayed in the Tenth Pavilion of the Warsaw Citadel Museum of Independence

Natalya Tuchkova-Ogareva (p. 505): *Literaturnoe nasledstvo*/State Literary Museum, Moscow

Karl Vogt Arctic research voyage (p. 527): *Pro Fribourg* no. 113, December 1996, page 98

Index